Myanmar (Burma) Handbook

Joshua Eliot and Jane Bickersteth

Footprint Handbooks

"The old leaders made the country free. Now it is our duty to make the people free."

Aung San Suu Kyi at the alternative National Day celebration, November 1995

6 Riverside Court, Lower Bristol Road
Bath BA2 3DZ England
T 01225 469141 F 01225 469461
E mail handbooks@footprint.cix.co.uk
www.fooprint-handbooks.co.uk

ISBN 0 900751 87 8 ISSN 1363-7436
CIP DATA: A catalogue record for this book is available from the British Library

In North America, published by

4255 West Touhy Avenue, Lincolnwood
(Chicago), Illinois 60646-1975, USA
T 847 679 5500 F 847 679 24941
E mail NTCPUB2@AOL.COM

ISBN 0-8442-4919-X
Library of Congress Catalog Card
Number: 96-72527
Passport Books and colophon are registered trademarks of NTC Publishing group

First published in 1992 as part of *Thailand, Indochina & Burma Handbook* by Trade & Travel Publications Ltd

Every effort has been made to ensure that the facts in this Handbook are accurate. However travellers should still obtain advice from consulates, airlines etc about current travel and visa requirements and conditions before travelling. The authors and publishers cannot accept responsibility for any loss, injury or inconvenience, however caused.

The maps are not intended to have any political significance.

Cover design by Newell and Sorrell; cover photography by Life File/Richard Powers; Life File/Stuart Norgrove; and TRIP

Production: Design by Mytton Williams; Typesetting by Jo Morgan, Ann Griffiths and Melanie Mason-Fayon; Maps by Sebastian Ballard, Kevin Feeney and Aldous George; Charts by Ann Griffiths; Original line drawings by Andrew Newton; Proofread by Rod Gray and David Cotterell.

Printed and bound in Great Britain by Clays Ltd., Bungay, Suffolk

Contents

The Editors

Joshua Eliot

Joshua has a long-standing interest in Asia. He was born in India, brought up in Hong Kong and has spent the last two decades studying and working in the countries of Southeast Asia. He has undertaken research in Thailand, Laos and Sumatra (Indonesia) and as well as editing Footprint Handbooks' guides to Southeast Asia, has also written or edited six other books on the region. He speaks Thai, and some Indonesian and Lao.

Jane Bickersteth

Jane has worked on the guidebooks since the first edition in 1992. She has been visiting the region for over 10 years, spending a year there whilst she researched the first edition. Jane is an artist by training and is particularly inspired by the Khmer ruins of Thailand and the candis of Java and Bali.

Acknowledgements

Much help has been received from friends, colleagues, researchers and fellow travellers during the preparation of this edition. All contributions have been tremendously helpful and are acknowledged on page 371. However there are a number of people we would particularly like to thank for their assistance: Kevin Mills for providing the Burmese script; David Steinke for his meticulous notes; Patrick and Nicole Millischer for their helpful letters; and Pilou Grenié for his notes and maps.

Introduction and hints

THERE ARE two stories that can be told of Myanmar – or Burma as it is still better known in the West. One narrative is Myanmar as the 'Golden Land'. A country of glittering pagodas, irridescent rice fields and peaceful monks. A country where the curse of modernization has barely made an imprint, where village life has been preserved, and where the serenity of the past can be quietly savoured in the present. A place where the ruins of ancient and glorious kingdoms stand stark and unrenovated, where cities and towns retain their ambience and charm, and where people are courteous and mindful of others.

The other narrative is Myanmar as the 'brutalized nation'. A country where decades of incompetent economic management have destroyed a once flourishing economy, where real incomes are lower today than they were at independence, and where malnutrition is endemic and fewer than one in four children complete their primary schooling. A country where the government represses and tortures its people, where the generals suck any wealth that remains for their own use, and where slave labour is used for public works. A country where the democractic wish of the people is flagrantly ignored, where multiple rebel groups fight for independence in the hills, and where exports of opium are reported to equal the value of all official exports.

Both these narratives are true. Both are there to be discovered in the streets, hills, markets and paddy fields of a still beautiful country. And as this book went to press,

Myanmar's government – the unattractively acronymed Slorc – was heralding the start of its Visit Myanmar Year, laying out the metaphorical red carpet for the rich of the East and West. Given the country's quite appalling record on human rights the key question, perhaps, is whether anyone should go to Myanmar. We clearly have an interest in you going; or at least an interest in you buying this book. There are persuasive arguments on both sides of the 'go'/'don't go' coin and these are rehearsed on the pages that follow this introductory sketch.

Perhaps the last words on Myanmar's split personality should be left to a monk in Mawlamyine (Moulmein) who explained to James Strachan of London's *Financial Times*: "You see, we live in a lion's cage. He must never know that we are even frightened, let alone that we might be plotting to kill him. He would eat us just in case. So we always smile broadly."

Whether to go

1996-1997 is Visit Myanmar Year and the Slorc government is one of the most reviled in the world. The question, therefore, is: should tourists be visiting the country? Like South Africa under Apartheid this is an area of heated debate. Discussions on radio and television frequently descend into dialogues of the deaf as each side sticks to a hard line. There seems to be no middle ground when it comes to Myanmar. Although this is a travel guide, and although we are not in the business of telling people what to do, the self-serving hypocrisy of some people in the travel industry does need to be challenged. The government in Myanmar has one of the most appalling human rights records in the world. Below, the arguments for and against visiting Myanmar are rehearsed. What they add up to is far from obvious.

RECENT DEVELOPMENTS

1992: Levi Strauss withdraws from Myanmar on human rights grounds claiming that most factories are owned by the Slorc and its associates.

1994: Liz Claiborne, a clothing manufacturer, withdraws from Myanmar on human rights grounds.

1995: Macy's (Federated Department Stores) withdraw from Myanmar citing corruption and Slorc ownership of factories.

1995: The Swiss Federation of Travel Agents (SFTA) recommends to its members not to promote tours to Myanmar. They state: "Human rights violations...are directly related to tourism."

February 1996: The American Chamber of Commerce supports US investment in Myanmar, arguing that it will help improve standards of living and help towards building a freer and more democratic society.

February 1996: A sanctions bill is introduced to the US Senate by Mitch McConnell.

March 1996: Aung San Suu Kyi asks British tourists to stay away from the country.

March 1996: Aung San Suu Kyi states that: "It is not right for the British government to do all it can to support human rights here and then to promote trade with Burma against democracy."

April 1996: Aung San Suu Kyi accuses Japanese firms of ignoring the use of slave labour on infrastructure projects. She calls for a halt to foreign investment until more progress has been made towards democracy.

April 1996: PepsiCo decides to sell its 40% share in Pepsi Cola Products Myanmar after Harvard University bans Pepsi's products from the campus. (Student slogan: 'Pepsi can take the red off its cans, but Pepsi can't wash the blood from its hands'.)

July 1996: Carlsberg shelves plans to build a brewery after the arrest and death in custody of James Nichols, the honorary consul for several European countries.

July 1996: Heineken pulls out of preliminary talks on building a brewery in Myanmar citing the adverse effects that political conditions in Myanmar would have on its brand and corporate image. (Carlsberg and Heineken products are later banned by the government.)

November 1996: Storehouse, the British retailing group, stops buying products from Myanmar in response to campaigning by the Burma Action Group.

By the end of 1996: Around 30 international companies had pulled out or stopped trading with Myanmar, from Disney Co to

Apple Computers and Oshkash B'Gosh Inc. For a listing of companies still operating or trading, contact Investor Responsibility Research Centre, 1350 Connecticut Ave NW, Suite 700, Washington DC 20036-1701, USA.

REHEARSING THE ARGUMENTS

ARGUMENTS AGAINST VISITING MYANMAR

- It lends credence to the Slorc government and provides much needed foreign exchange to bolster the armed forces.
- The Slorc has used slave labour to upgrade and repair tourist infrastructure. It is not possible for a tourist to claim that it is 'no business of mine'.
- Uninformed tourists can visit the country unaware of the appalling human rights record and leave claiming that conditions are exaggerated.
- Because tourism remains controlled, it is hard for tourists to see beyond the government-created facade of normality.
- Visit Myanmar Year is being used by the regime to reinforce its credibility.
- Tourists and tourism is seen as a lead sector in Myanmar's international rehabilitation. Tourists are on the front line.
- Because so much of the economy is controlled by the army and the Slorc it is impossible not to support companies under their ownership.

ARGUMENTS IN FAVOUR OF VISITING MYANMAR

- 'Constructive engagement' can help to stimulate democratic reforms. South Korea and Taiwan, two former Asian dictatorships, embraced the democratic road while being supported – 'engaged' – by the West and especially the US.
- Isolating the government by awarding them pariah status will mean there is no incentive for the Slorc to change its ways. Only through engaging and cajoling will things change. Look at the success that sanctions on other governments have had in changing their ways: neither Cuba, Vietnam nor Iraq were pressured by economic sanctions. In the case of Cuba they have been in place for decades.
- Tourists can be just as effective a force for change as faceless economic sanctions
- Tourists can also be agents of change by reassuring the Burmese that the international community does care.
- The presence of so many foreigners has been a headache for the Slorc who are in danger of losing control.
- Tourists can use non-Slorc facilities and make sure that their money does not go to the government.
- Economic liberalisation, of which the tourist 'boom' is a part, will inevitably bring political liberalisation.
- Although some Western-based pressure groups and some individuals in Myanmar support a tourist boycott of the country, there are also democracy activists in Myanmar who welcome visitors. Like Tibet, another repressed country, tourists can make a difference.
- The presence of foreigners will make it much more difficult for the Slorc to mount another human rights tragedy like the 1988 massacre. It was the absence of foreign people and the foreign media which meant that such appalling carnage occurred with comparatively little international outcry.

WHAT CAN TOURISTS DO AND NOT DO TO HELP?

- Stay in private hotels and guesthouses.
- Use private tour companies and tour guides.
- Talk to people (but don't put them in danger) and reassure them that the outside world is aware of what is going on in their country and that the international community does care.
- Visit the country informed of its recent political history and be sensitive to the conditions there.
- Don't be fobbed off with the cry that things aren't as bad as the press in the West makes out. Find out for yourself.

Where to go

Until recently, foreign visitors to Myanmar were tightly constrained in where they could go, how long they could stay, and how they could travel. Visas were restricted to just seven days, all visitors had to book a tour through government-run or approved agencies, travel was only permitted on certain modes of transport, much of the country remained closed to visitors, and only a handful of hotels were permitted to accept foreigners as guests.

This tight control of tourism is now at an end and the trend over the last few years has been towards ever greater loosening. Visas are now granted for four week stays, the bulk of the country is open to foreigners, there has been a mushrooming of private guesthouses, hotels and tour companies, and independent travel is permitted. This is not to say that the loosening of controls on tourists reflects any relaxation in the government's tight grip on society and politics. It merely reflects the driving need to generate more foreign exchange.

TRANSPORT AND TRAVELLING

After decades of under-investment, Myanmar's physical infrastructure is in a woeful state. Roads beyond the main highways are in a poor state of repair, the rail network uses ancient rolling stock and the national airline is not held high as an example of excellent service and high technology. Nonetheless, the influx of visitors weighed down with dollars and the arrival of private companies in the transport sector has already revolutionised travel.

Myanmar's **bus network** is fast expanding and also improving. With greater numbers of tourists visiting the country and the loosening of controls on independent travel, entrepreneurs have set up new companies and invested in new vehicles. This extends from large coaches down to smaller converted pick-ups. However these improvements are largely restricted to the main routes and especially those used by tourists. Anyone venturing off piste will quickly find the bus network of old with decrepit vehicles, pot-holed roads, slow speeds and long and uncertain journey times. There is a certain charm and frisson in travelling in this way, but it also requires a deal of patience.

The British left Myanmar with a reasonable **rail network** but this has been allowed to fall into decreptitude – along with some of the rolling stock that runs on it. Most visitors' only experience of Myanmar Railways is the Yangon-Mandalay line, although the branch lines from Thazi to Shwe Nyang (for Inle Lake) and from Pyinmana to Kyauk Padaung (for Bagan) are also well used. The Yangon-Mandalay line is reasonably well maintained and special tourist trains ply the route giving a somewhat false impression of the state of the rail network overall. Other lines less frequently used by foreigners are alloted the most uncomfortable carriages and the least reliable locomotives: journey times are best described as movable feasts.

Almost as important as road and rail transport in a country which lays claim to some of Southeast Asia's largest rivers, and in particular the Ayeyarwady (Irrawaddy), is **river transport**. Again though, tourists tend to confine themselves to just one stretch of river – between Mandalay and Bagan. Because of the numbers of tourists who opt to travel by river from Mandalay to Bagan (around a 12 hour journey), the choice (and comfort) of boats is greatest on this stretch and there is even a dedicated 'tourist' boat.

There are also some **coastal ferries and passenger-carrying ships**. Those run by the state-owned Myanmar Five Star Line (MFSL) call at ports from Dawei (Tavoy) in the far south to Sittwe (Akyab) in the north. The difficulty is finding a vessel that meets your travel needs. They leave at varying times through the year and booking a ticket tends to be a time consuming business. As a result it is rare to find tourists using MFSL vessels.

Myanmar's principal **domestic airline**, and the national flag carrier, is *Myanmar Airways*. The airline operates old aircraft in a rather desultory manner (though the service has improved in recent years) and there is no guarantee that a booked seat will not disappear at the first sight of a VIP. Two new and much better-run airlines operating modern aircraft (French-built ATR 72s) have also entered the domestic aviation fray. However *Air Mandalay* and *Yangon Airways* only serve the more popular routes and ticket prices are around 25% higher than on *Myanmar Airways*. Anyone intending to visit more out of the way spots will have to calmly suck boiled sweets on *Myanmar Airways*.

TIMETABLING A VISIT

Now that tourist visas are issued for four weeks, the frantic 7-day scramble across the country that used to be all visitors were allowed has ended. Nonetheless, the size of the country – it is just under 2,000km from north to south – and the ambling pace of most overland transport means that visitors still need to think carefully about how they timetable their visit. Even air travel does not necessarily get around these problems: *Myanmar Airways* which operates by far the largest network of routes is renowned for its inefficiency and the annoying habit of bumping passengers off the manifest whenever it chooses. It is also not possible to book a sequence of flights – at each intermediate stop the next leg has to be reconfirmed Those on organised tours have some distinct advantages when it comes to dealing with *Myanmar Airways*: which is that they don't have to deal with the company. Instead they will have the services of a local tour guide to apply pressure and perhaps supply gifts to free seats on overbooked planes. Local guides are also much more aware when problems are likely to arise. A lone traveller, with no Burmese, will find it hard to do the same deals and may find themselves floundering on the tarmac. The arrival of two new domestic operators – *Air Mandalay* and *Yangon Airways* – which respect a booked seat and allow tickets to be booked ahead has eased this problem somewhat but only on the main routes.

Nonetheless, a two to three week visit to Myanmar is sufficient to allow a visitor to see many of the key sights, even if it might not allow enough time to savour the country. It is quite possible to visit Yangon, Mandalay, Bagan, and Inle Lake in two weeks, and a three week stay allows time to explore the country beyond these key tourist destinations.

Myanmar
INDIA
BANGLADESH
CHINA
LAOS
THAILAND
KACHIN
SAGAING
CHIN
RAKHINE
MAGWE
SHAN
KAYAH
BAGO
AYEYARWADY
KAREN
MON
TENASSERIM
Putao
Hukawng Valley
Myitkyina
Indawgyi Lake
Chindwin River
Mingun Range
Bhamo
Katha
Wuntho
Museh
Kalemyo
Tagaung
Namhran
Mogok
Lashio
Falam
Shwebo
Hsipaw
Kyaukme
Monywa
Mingun
Sagaing
Pyin U Lwin
Ava Amarapura
Mandalay
Kehsi
Paletwa
Pakokku
Bagan
Kengtung
Mrauk-U
Meiktila
Heho
Kalaw
Taunggyi
Thanlwin River
Shwesetdaw
Minbu
Sittwe
Yamethin
Inle Lake
Magwe
Ann
Taungdwingyi
Loikaw
Aunglan
Thayetmyo
Taunggok
Pyay
Toungoo
Thandwe
Chiang Mai
Myanaung
Papun
Bay of Bengal
Henzada
Bago
Kyaiktiyo
Pathein
Thaton
Yangon
Thanlyin
Myawadi
Mae Sot
Pyapon
Mottama
Mawlamyine
Kyaikkami
Andaman Sea
Three Pagodas Pass
Dawei
Bangkok
0
100
km
Gulf of Thailand
Myeik

HIGHLIGHTS

River trips and hiking

Ayeyarwady: Myanmar's life-giving Ayeyarwady or Irrawaddy River can be navigated from its mouth all the way north to Bhamo and, in the wet season, as far as Myitkyina – some 1,500 km. Though river transport is not very comfortable, those who have endured it say it offers a unique insight into the Burmese landscape, both human and natural.

Natural (and unnatural) features

Yangon: the Maha Pasan Guha is an extraordinary artificial cave erected for the Sixth Buddhist Synod.

Central Myanmar: the Botanic Gardens at Pyin U Lwin (Maymyo) were established by the British and feature some interesting flora.

The Eastern and Northern Hills: Inle Lake is firmly on the tourist trail because of its beauty, serenity and rich human mosaic. There are also the lake's unique leg-rowing fishermen at which to marvel.

Historical and religious sites and ancient cities

Yangon: Shwedagon Pagoda, Myanmar's most important stupa, attracting tens of thousands of pilgrims each year. Other important pagodas in Yangon include the Sule Pagoda and the Botataung Pagoda. The *Strand Hotel* has become a tourist site of sorts and in fact the whole city is interesting for its colonial architecture which unlike capital cities in neighbouring countries has not (yet) been torn down to be replaced by generic and characterless modern buildings.

Lower Myanmar: Bago is on the map because of its huge reclining Buddha, the Shwethalyaung Buddha. There is also a cluster of interesting pagodas nearby to make the trip to Bago even more worthwhile. The Shwesandaw Pagoda at Pyay is one of Myanmar's holiest sites, set impressively on a hill above town.

Mandalay: this city is on virtually every visitor's itinerary. Its focal point is the palace and moat. There is a cluster of fascinating pagodas to the north of town at the foot of Mandalay Hill and the Mahamuni Pagoda in the south of the city is Mandalay's holiest shrine, containing a 3.8m-tall Buddha encrusted in gold leaf.

Around Mandalay: a number of towns clustered on or near the Ayeyarwady are within easy reach from Mandalay and all have sites of interest. At Amarapura, the Mahagandayon Monastery is the largest in Myanmar, with 700 resident monks and several hundred more during Lent. Sagaing, on the west bank of the Ayeyarwady is regarded as the religious hub of Myanmar, with almost 100 meditation centres, 600 pagodas and monateries and more than 3,000 monks. Mingun, upriver from Mandalay, is an attractive settlement, now in ruins, containing a 90 tonne bell and some earthquake damaged pagodas, one of which would have been the largest in Myanmar – had it ever been completed. Pyin U Lwin, formally known as Maymyo, is an example of an old colonial hill station, with a temperate climate, horse and carriage transport, a golf course and attractive colonial hotels.

Bagan: this is undoubtedly the finest historical site in Myanmar, and one of the most spectacular in Southeast Asia. Situated on the banks of the Ayeyarwady, thousands of 12th and 13th century pagodas lie scattered acorss the plain as far as the eye can see.

Central Myanmar: Shwesetdaw Pagoda features two revered Buddha footprints.

The Eastern and Northern Hills: Hsipaw, though it has no sights as such, is well worth a visit for its serene atmosphere

The West Coast: Mrauk U, the last royal capital of Rakhine (Arakan), is an important archaeological site, centred on a palace and surrounded by pagodas.

The South: the Golden Rock Pagoda or Kyaiktiyo Pagoda at Kyaiktiyo is one of the most photographed sights in Myanmar, perched spectacularly on an outcrop of rock.

Museums

Yangon: the National Museum is Myanmar's largest and finest but is not famed for its imaginative layout and interactive displays and would not feature as a 'highlight' in many countries. The Buddhist Art Museum really speaks for itself.

Festivals

The Nat Festival is the most important in Myanmar and can best be seen in Mandalay (in August) or at Mount Popa, where there are two full moon celebrations, one in May/June and one in November/December. Thousands of pilgrims climb the mountain to honour the nats.

Beach resorts

Myanmar is not the place to come for a beach holiday. Most of the beaches are disappointing, the hotels are pretty uniformly dismal, and there is little to do but sit and read. The best of the bunch is probably Ngapali, although Chaung Tha and Letkhokkon also sometimes get a mention.

Shopping and handicrafts

Mandalay: the city is one of the better places to seek out local handicrafts, being a centre for artisan's guilds. Woodcarving, stone working and bronze casting all take place here. There are also several silk weaving factories.

Bagan: this is the best place to buy lacquerware as there are quite a few places making good quality (and plenty of bad quality) pieces.

NB The above is only a selection of places of interest and is not exhaustive. It is designed to assist in planning a trip to the region. Any 'highlight' list is inevitably subjective.

How to go

BEST TIME TO VISIT

The best time to visit Myanmar is during the dry and comparatively cool months between November and the end of February. Because the 'best time to visit' (from a climatic point of view) is comparatively tight, this is also the period when hotel room rates are highest and when flights get booked up. So there are advantages of travelling out of the main tourist season. Although the months of March and April remain dry (meaning that road transport is still relatively easy), they can be extremely hot. As the wet season gets under way in May, so unsurfaced roads begin to suffer and overland transport becomes more difficult in some areas. For more information on climate see the section in the introduction on page 33, and the monthly climate graphs for the following towns: Yangon (page 106), Mandalay (page 145), Lashio (page 240), and Sittwe (page 254).

HEALTH

Health care in Myanmar is poor and most foreign residents go to Bangkok (Thailand) or Singapore for treatment beyond simple illnesses and injuries. For a comprehensive roundup of health related issues, see page 383.

WHAT TO TAKE

Travellers usually tend to take too much, even to a place like Myanmar which is not noted as a shopping Mecca. In Myanmar's main towns it is possible to buy basic toiletries and most simple consumer items like batteries and photographic film. However anything of a specialist nature is either expensive or unavailable.

Suitcases are not appropriate if you are intending to travel overland by bus. A backpack, or even better a travelpack (where the straps can be zipped out of sight), is recommended. Travelpacks have the advantage of being hybrid backpacks-suitcases; they can be carried on the back for easy porterage, but they can also be taken into hotels without the owner being labelled a 'hippy'.

In terms of clothing, dress in Myanmar is relatively casual – even at formal functions. Suits are not necessary. However, though formal attire may be the exception, dressing tidily is the norm. There is a tendency, rather than to take inappropriate articles of clothing, to take too many of the same article. Laundry services are cheap, and the turnaround rapid. If travelling during the cool season, and especially if intending to visit one of the hill stations, then a warm sweater is needed. During the rainy season a waterproof is useful.

Checklist

Earplugs
First aid kit
Insect repellent and/or electric mosquito mats, coils
International driving licence
Passports (valid for at least 6 months)
Photocopies of essential documents
Short wave radio

Spare passport photographs
Sun protection
Sunglasses
Swiss Army knife
Torch
Umbrella
Wet wipes
Zip-lock bags

Those intending to stay in budget accommodation might also include:
Cotton sheet sleeping bag
Money belt
Padlock (for hotel room and pack)
Soap
Student card
Toilet paper
Towel
Travel wash

MONEY

Money in Myanmar is not a simple business because the government insists on maintaining a ludicrous official exchange rate which overvalues the kyat (pronounced 'chat') by a factor of about 27. In addition, the authorities stipulate that on arrival visitors should change US$ into FECs or Foreign Exchange Certificates. The various controls are all intended to make sure that tourists part with as many dollars as possible and that they accrue to the state and not private individuals. It is all an attempt to boost Myanmar's foreign exchange earnings. For more detail on the intricacies of money, see page 354.

On arrival, visitors are required to change US$300 into FECs which are officially valued at US$1 = 1 FEC. Only US$ and pounds sterling (cash or TCs) are accepted. In the past visitors tried to avoid changing FECs as they were grossly over-valued. Now, however, they can be converted into kyat at the free market rate. FECs can be used in lieu of dollars and as many services have to be paid for in dollars/FECs (some hotels, rail and air tickets etc) it is not such a handicap.

There is no doubt, however, that the US$ is king. They can be converted into kyat at the free market rate and can be used as cash to pay for many services. Understandably given the government's past record with the kyat, traders and businesspeople would rather have dollars tucked under their matresses. Note, however, that only those few businesses with a license to take US$ are legally permitted to do so – everyone else (and it seems to be most people) does it illegally. Changing US$ into kyat is best done in shops or hotels rather than out on the street where the chance of being short changed is much higher.

Major credit cards – Visa, MasterCard, Amex, and Diners Club – are accepted but only in a handful of places. MTT, however, does accept credit cards.

In February 1997, US$1 was officially worth 6.2 kyat. On the free market, however, kyat were changing hands at upto 160 to the US$, though more usually at about 120.

ISIC

Anyone in full-time education is entitled to an International Student Identity Card (ISIC). These are issued by student travel offices and travel agencies across the world and offer special rates on all forms of transport and other concessions and services. The ISIC head office is: ISIC Association, Box 9048, 1000 Copenhagen, Denmark, T (45) 33 93 93 03.

GETTING THERE

AIR

Most people arrive in Myanmar via Bangkok which has become a transport hub for the whole mainland Southeast Asian region. There is at least one and sometimes more flights a day between Bangkok and Yangon. Many airlines offer non-stop or direct flights to Bangkok from Europe, North American and other cities within the Asian region. In addition to Bangkok, there are direct air connections with Yangon from the following cities: Hong Kong, Singapore, Kuala Lumpur (Malaysia), Kunming and Beijing (China), Dhaka (Bangladesh), and Hanoi (Vietnam). The national flag carrier is *Myanmar Airways International* which operates Boeing 757s and is a joint venture with a Singapore company. It is also possible to fly from Chiang Mai in northern Thailand to Mandalay on *Air Mandalay* and they are considering flying from Chiang Rai (also in northern Thailand) too.

Discounts

It is possible to obtain significant discounts on flights to Bangkok, especially outside European holiday times, most notably in London. Shop around and book early. It is also possible to get discounts from Australasia, South Asia and Japan. Note that 'peak season' varies from airline to airline – many using 8-10 bands. This means one airline's high season may not be another's.

OVERLAND

It is not possible to enter Myanmar 'proper' overland from Thailand. However short trips are permitted from Mae Sai in northern Thailand and Ranong in the south. The border crossing near Mae Sot may also open soon. But currently entry is only permitted to the immediate local area and often only for the day.

THAILAND SECTIONS IN THIS GUIDE

Because so many people enter Myanmar through Thailand we have included information on Bangkok (the main gateway) and also Chiang Mai. The information is arranged towards the end of the book.

SAFETY

Myanmar is more dangerous for locals than it is for visitors. Though there are all the usual risks of thieves and pick pockets this is much less serious than in, say, neighbouring Thailand. There are still border areas which are pretty lawless, although less so today than even two or three years ago. The government remains highly sensitive to what it regards as potential threats to national security and soldiers may question tourists who visit more out of the way spots. It is not unusual to be followed by MI (Military Intelligence – see the box on page 81). The main danger, however, is not to tourists but to the people with whom they come into contact. Remember that anyone speaking with a foreigner is suspect and visitors should be aware of the potential danger that they pose to ordinary Burmese (see the box on page 352, 'Visiting rural Myanmar').

WOMEN TRAVELLING ALONE

Women travelling alone face greater difficulties than men or couples although in Myanmar these problems are less pronounced than in many other countries. Women are nonetheless advised to dress modestly.

WHERE TO STAY

It was only really in the mid-1990s that private enterprise began to transform Myanmar's hotel industry. Hotels which might be classified as 'international' are few and far between and are restricted, essentially, to Yangon and Mandalay. However private entrepreneurs have invested in smaller hotels which are quite comfortable and usually well-run. Competition from the private sector has also had a knock-on effect on the government-run establishments which were a by-word for surly service and incompetent management. However because visitors tend to visit just a handful of places, even being mildly adventurous means staying in guesthouses that are largely geared to Burmese. Though the service may be charming, do not expect much in the way of creature comforts and cleanliness. Note that more expensive hotels (roughly, US$15 up) expect bills to be paid for in US$ or FECs.

FOOD AND DRINK

Food

Like the hotel industry, the restaurant sector has also undergone something of a revolution as privatization and a growing influx of visitors has created the conditions in which good restaurants can flourish. This is not to say that Myanmar is a gastronomic heaven: in general, food is average and the range of dishes is limited. The main cuisines available in just about every town of any size are Indian, Chinese and, of course, Burmese. European food is available in the main tourist centres, but it is pretty mediocre. Many people find that the best food available is from roadside stalls.

Water

Bottled water (Myanmar Mineral Water) is easily obtainable. It is not advisable to drink water straight from the tap. Imported soft drinks are also widely sold (though comparatively expensive), and there are cheap locally produced – but rather sickly – equivalents. Imported and locally brewed beers are available.

GETTING AROUND

AIR

Myanmar Airways flies Fokker F27s and F28s and has the most extensive network of routes. *Air Mandalay* and *Yangon Airways* operate new ATR 72s but only on the main tourist routes.

ROAD

On the main routes there are reasonably comfortable a/c buses, many operated by private firms recently established to serve the tourist market. Road conditions are adequate. Routes between minor towns or away from the main tourist destinations are served by rather more ramshackle vehicles and roads tend to be poor. There are more likely to be delays and disruptions during the wet season, especially off the main surfaced routes. Converted pick-up trucks tend to service the shorter routes; these are faster than travelling by bus.

CAR AND MOTORCYCLE HIRE

Cars for self-drive hire are not available; only resident foreigners are permitted to drive themselves. But it is common and easy to hire a car and driver. As roads in Myanmar are so poor and road sense is merely nascent it makes good sense to pay a local to negotiate the human and physical obstacles.

Motorcycles, however, can be hired for self-drive. That said, there is not exactly a booming motorcycle-hire business and you will need to search one out and probably enter into some sort of informal agreement. It is likely that you will be required to provide a large deposit.

HITCHHIKING AND CYCLING

Hitchhiking is not common in Myanmar but does seem to be comparatively easy. Long-distance bicycle touring is also not (yet) a popular way to see the country. However it is common to hire bicycles in many towns and because traffic is comparatively light and speeds slow, exploring local areas by bicycle is an attractive option.

BOAT

Rivers remain important arteries of communication and the Ayeyarwady (Irrawaddy) carries large quantities of both cargo and passengers. There is also a coastal shipping line which takes passengers but it is rarely used by visitors.

LANGUAGE

English is quaintly spoken by a reasonably large proportion of the older generation although because it was withdrawn from the curriculum soon after independence (but is now back), younger Burmese tend not to speak English.

Tourism: counting the costs

"Tourism is like fire. It can either cook your food or burn your house down". This sums up the ambivalent attitude that many people have regarding the effects of tourism. It is potentially one of Myanmar's largest foreign exchange earners, and the world's largest single industry; yet many people in receiving countries would rather tourists go home. Tourism is seen to be the cause of rising prices, loose morals, consumerism, and much else besides. In Myanmar this general view of tourism needs to be qualified because of the nature of the government in the country. Some people would argue that tourists and tourism in Myanmar can help to promote change. Others, of course – and they include Aung San Suu Kyi – say that tourist dollars are helping to sustain the government (see the section entitled 'Whether to go' on page 9, above).

The word 'tourist' is derived from 'travail', meaning work or torment. Travail, in turn, has its roots in the Latin word *tripalium*, which was a three-pronged instrument of torture. For many people struggling through the back roads of Myanmar this etymology should strike a chord. And yet, as *The Economist* pointed out in a survey of the industry in 1991:

> "The curse of the tourist industry is that it peddles dreams: dreams of holidays where the sun always shines, the children are always occupied, and where every evening ends in the best sex you have ever had. For most of its modern life, this has been matched by a concomitant dreaminess on the part of its customers. When asked, most tourists tell whopping lies about what they want on holiday..." (Economist, 1991).

Most international tourists come from a handful of wealthy countries. Half from just five countries (the USA, Germany, the UK, Japan and France) and 80% from 20 countries. This is why many see tourism as the new 'imperialism', imposing alien cultures and ideals on sensitive and unmodernized peoples. The problem, however, is that discussions of the effects of tourism tend to degenerate into simplifications – culminating in the drawing up of a checklist of 'positive' and 'negative' effects, much like the one on page 9. Although such tables may be useful in highlighting problem areas, they also do a disservice by reducing a complex issue to a simple set of rather one dimensional 'costs' and 'benefits'. Different destinations will be affected in different ways; these effects are likely to vary over time; and different groups living in a particular destination will feel the effects of tourism in different ways and to varying degrees. At no time or place can tourism (or any other influence) be categorized as uniformly 'good' or 'bad'.

SEARCHING FOR CULTURE

Myanmar has a rich cultural heritage and many tourists are attracted to the country because of its 'exotic' peoples – whether they be hill peoples or lowland Buddhists – and traditional (ie un-modernised) culture. When cultural erosion is identified, the tendency is to blame this on tourists and tourism. Turner and Ash have written that tourists are the "sun-tanned destroyers of culture", while Bugnicourt argues that tourism:

> "...encourages the imitation of foreigners and the downgrading of local inhabitants in relation to foreign tourists; it incites the pillage of art work and other historical artefacts; it leads to the degeneration of classical and popular dancing, the profanation and vulgarization of places of worship, and the perversion of religious ceremonies; it creates a sense of inferiority and a cultural demoralization which 'fans the flames of anti-development' through the acquisition of undesirable cultural traits" (1977).

The problem with views like this is that they assume that change is bad, and that indigenous cultures are unchanging. It makes local peoples victims of change, rather than masters of their own destinies. It also assumes that tourism is an external influence, when in fact it quickly becomes part of the local landscape. Cultural change is inevitable and on-going, and 'new' and 'traditional' are only judgements, not absolutes. Thus new cultural forms can quickly become key markers of tradition. Tourists searching for an 'authentic' experience are assuming that tradition is tangible, easily identifiable and unchanging. It is none of these.

'Tribal' people wearing American baseball caps or Burmans giving up their *longyis* for jeans are assumed to have succumbed to western culture. But such changes really say next to nothing about an individual's strength of identity. There are also problems with identifying cultural erosion, let alone linking it specifically with tourism, rather than with the wider processes of

Tourism Development Guidelines

- Tourism should capitalise on local features (cultural and natural) so as to promote the use of local resources.
- Attention should be given to the type of tourist attracted. A mix of mass and individual will lead to greater local participation and better balance.
- Tourist development should be integrated with other sectors. Coordination between agencies is crucial.
- Facilities created should be made available to locals, at subsidised rates if necessary.
- Resources such as beaches and parks must remain in the public domain.
- Different tourists and tourist markets should be exploited so as to minimize seasonal variations in arrivals and employment.
- A tourist threshold should be identified and adhered to.
- Environmental impact assessments and other surveys must be carried out.
- Provision of services to tourists must be allied with improvements in facilities for locals.
- Development should be focused in areas where land use conflicts will be kept to a minimum.
- Supplies, where possible, should be sourced locally.
- Assistance and support should be given to small-scale, local entrepreneurs.

'modernisation'. This is exemplified in the case of Bali in Indonesia where tourism is paraded by some as the saviour of Balinese culture, and by others as its destroyer. Michel Picard in his paper "'Cultural tourism' in Bali" (1992) writes:

> "No sooner had culture become the emblematic image of Bali [in the 1920s] than foreign visitors and residents started fearing for its oncoming disappearance. ...the mere evocation of Bali suggested the imminent and dramatic fall from the 'Garden of Eden': sooner of later, the 'Last Paradise' was doomed to become a 'Paradise Lost'" (Picard,1992:77).

Yet the authorities on Bali are clearly at a loss as to how to balance their conflicting views:

> "...the view of tourism held by the Balinese authorities is blatantly ambivalent, the driving force of a modernisation process which they welcome as ardently as they fear. Tourism in their eyes appears at once the most promising source of economic development and as the most subversive agent for the spread of foreign cultural influences in Bali" (Picard,1992:85).

TOURIST ART: FINE ART, DEGRADED ART

Tourist art, both material (for instance, sculpture) and non-material (like dances) is another issue where views sharply diverge. The mass of inferior 'airport' art on sale to tourists demonstrates, to some, the corrosive effects of tourism. It leads craftsmen and women to mass-produce second rate pieces for a market that appreciates neither their cultural or symbolic worth, nor their aesthetic value. Yet tourism can also give value to craft industries that would otherwise be undermined by cheap industrial goods. Some people argue that the craft traditions of Myanmar should be allied with tourism to create vibrant new rural industries. The corrosive effects of tourism on arts and crafts also assumes that artists and craftsmen are unable to distinguish between fine pieces and pot-boilers. Many produce inferior pieces for the tourist market while continuing to produce for local demand, the former effectively subsidising the latter.

Some researchers have also shown how there is a tendency for culture to be 'invented' for tourists, and for this to then become part of 'tradition'. The anthropologist Lewis Hill of the Centre for South-East Asian Studies at the University of Hull has demonstrated how objects made for the tourist market in one period are later enthusiastically embraced by the host community.

ENVIRONMENT AND TOURISM

The environmental deterioration that is linked to tourism is due to a destination area exceeding its 'carrying capacity' as a result of overcrowding. But carrying capacity, though an attractive concept, is notoriously difficult to pin down in any exact manner. A second dilemma facing those trying to encourage greater environmental consciousness is the so-called 'tragedy of the commons', better described in terms of Chinese restaurants. When a group of people go to a Chinese restaurant with the intention of sharing the bill, each customer will tend to order a more expensive dish than he or she would normally do – on the logic that everyone will be doing the same, and the bill will be split. In tourism terms, it means that hotel owners will always build those few more bungalows or that extra wing, to maximize their profits, reassured in the knowledge that the environmental costs will be shared among all hotel owners. So, despite most operators appreciating that over-development may 'kill the goose that lays the golden eggs', they do so anyway. In short, tourism contains the seeds of its own destruction.

But many developing countries have few other development opportunities. Those in Southeast Asia are blessed with beautiful landscapes and exotic cultures, and tourism is a cheap development option. Other possibilities cost more to develop and take longer to take-off. It is also true that 'development', however it is achieved, has cultural and environmental implications. For many, tourism is the least environmentally corrosive of the various options open to poor countries struggling to achieve rapid economic growth.

THE 'POST-TOURIST' AND THE TRAVELLER

In the last few years a new tourist has appeared; or at least a new type of tourist has been identified – the 'post-tourist'. The post-tourist is part of the post-modern world. He or she is aware that nothing is authentic; that every tourist experience is new and different; that tourism begins at home, in front of the television. The whole globe is a stage on and in which the post-tourist can revel; the crass and crude is just as interesting and delightful as the traditional and authentic to the post-tourist. He – or she – is abundantly aware that he is a tourist, not a brave and inquisitive searcher for culture and

A Tourism Checklist

Costs	Benefits
vulnerable to external developments - e.g. oil price rises, 1991 Gulf War	diversifies an economy and is usually immune to protectionism
	requires few technical and human resources and is a 'cheap' development option
	requires little infrastructure
erodes culture by debasing it; strong cultures overwhelm sensitive ones (often tribal)	gives value to cultures and helps in their preservation
leads to moral pollution with rising crime and prostitution	changing social norms are not due solely, or even mostly to tourism
often concentrated in culturally and environmentally sensitive areas, so effects are accentuated	helps to develop marginal areas that would otherwise 'miss out' on development
lack of planning and management causes environmental problems	poor planning and management is not peculiar to tourism and can be rectified
foreigners tend to dominate; costs of involvement are high so local people fail to become involved and benefit	costs of involvement can be very low, tourism is not so scale-dependent as other industries
tourism increases local inequalities	
jobs are usually seasonal and low-skilled	
economic leakages mean revenue generated tends to accrue to foreign multi-nationals	leakage is less than with many other industries; local involvement generally greater and value added is significant
tourism is not sustainable; tourism ultimately destroys tourism because it destroys those attributes that attracted tourists in the first place	tourism is not monolithic; destination areas evolve and do not have to suffer decay

truth; just another sunburnt, probably over-weight, almost certainly ignorant foreigner spending money to have a holiday (not a travel 'experience') in a foreign country. Paradoxically this lack of apparent discernment is what is seen to identify the post-tourist as truly discerning. Feifer, in 1985, stated that the post-tourist is well aware he is "not a time-traveller when he goes somewhere historic; not an instant noble savage when he stays on a tropical beach; not an invisible observer when he visits a native compound. Resolutely 'realistic', he cannot evade his condition of outsider". Of course, all this could be discounted as the meaningless meanderings of a group of academics with little better to do than play with words and ideas. But, there is something akin to the post-tourist of the academic world beginning to inhabit the real world of tourism. These people might have once been described as just cynics, marvelling in the shear ironies of life. They are tourists for whom tourism is a game to be taken lightly; people who recognize that they are just another 'guest', another consumer of the tourist experience. No-one, and nothing, special.

The 'traveller' in contrast to the post-tourist finds it hard even to think of him or herself as a tourist at all. This, of course, is hubris built upon the notion that the traveller is an 'independent' explorer somehow beyond the bounds of the industry. Anna Borzello in an article entitled 'The myth of the traveller' in the journal *Tourism in Focus* (no. 19, 1994) writes that "Independent travellers cannot acknowledge – without shattering their self-image – that to many local people they are simply a good source of income. ...[not] inheritors of Livingstone, [but] bearers of urgently needed money". Although she does, in writing this, grossly underestimate the ability of travellers to see beyond their thongs and friendship bracelets, she does have a more pertinent point when she argues that it is important for travellers realistically to appraise their role as tourists, because: "Not only are independent travellers often frustrated by the gap between the way they see themselves and the way they are treated, but unless they acknowledge that they are part of the tourist industry they will not take responsibility for the damaging effects of their tourism."

GUIDE BOOKS AND TOURISM

Guide books themselves have been identified by some analysts as being part of the problem. They are selective in two senses. First, they tend to selectively pick destination areas, towns and regions. This is understandable: one book cannot cover all the possibilities in a country. Then, and second, they selectively pick sights, hotels and restaurants within those places. Given that many travellers use guide books to map out their journey, this creates a situation where books determine the spatial pattern of tourist flows. As John McCarthy writes in *Are sweet dreams made of this? Tourism in Bali and Eastern Indonesia* (1994, IRIP: Victoria, Australia):

> "Such is the power of guide books that, unless they are carefully written, one writer's point of view can determine the commercial success or failure of a hotel or restaurant for years after. Even when the enterprise changes, the loathing or love of a travel writer who passed through a village 3 years ago remains too potent a testimony" (page 93).

There are no easy answers to this. If guide books were more diverse; if travellers really were more independent; and if guide books were not so opinionated and subjective, then this would all help in spreading the tourism phenomenon. But none of these is likely: guide books exist to 'guide'; humans are by nature subjective; and the notion of the free spirit 'traveller' has always, in the most part, been a mirage brought on by a romantic collective sense of what tourism *should* be. One answer is for books to become more specialist, and certainly one identifiable trend is towards guide books covering sub-national regions. It seems that people are now more willing to spend an extended period of time exploring one area, rather than notching up a large number of 'must do's'. Although even such specialist books also tend to suffer from the dangers of selectivity noted above, those people who do spend a longer period of time in an area are in a position to be more selective themselves, and to rely more on their own experiences rather than those of a guide book writer who may have visited a town in a bad mood 3 years previously.

In the opening page to his *Illustrated guide to the Federated Malay States*, Cuthbert Woodville Harrison wrote:

> "It has become nowadays so easy and so common a venture to cross the world that the simple circum-navigation of the globe 'merely for wantonness' is very rapidly ceasing to be in fashion. But as the rough places of the earth become smooth to the travellers, and they no longer fear 'that the gulfs will wash us down', there is growing amongst them a disposition to dwell awhile in those lands whose climate and inhabitants most differ from ours. The more completely such places are strange to us the more do they attract us, and the more isolated they have lived hitherto, the more do we feel called upon to visit them now."

Cuthbert Woodville Harrison's book was published in 1923.

SUGGESTED READING AND TOURISM PRESSURE GROUPS

In the UK, **Tourism Concern** aims to "promote greater understanding of the impacts of tourism on host communities and environments", "to raise awareness of the forms of tourism that respect the rights and interests of [local] people", and to "work for change in current tourism practice". Annual membership is £15.00 which includes subscription to their magazine *In Focus*. Tourism Concern, Froebel College, Rochampton Lane, London SW15 5PU, T (0181) 878-9053.

The most up-to-date book examining tourism in Southeast Asia is: Hitchcock, Mike *et al*. (edits) (1993) *Tourism in South-East Asia*, Routledge: London.

Horizons

In 1989 the military government changed Burma's name to Myanmar. This meant little in practical and political terms: the Burmese have always referred to their country as Myanmar, as well as 'Bama'. It was just as if Germany, through sheer caprice, had suddenly decided it wanted all foreigners to refer to it as Deutschland. In tourist brochures, Myanmar sells itself as *Shwe Pyidaw* – 'The Golden Land' – another old Burmese name for the country. Apart from its thousands of glittering pagodas, the name reflects Myanmar's wealth of natural resources, from teak and oil to jade and rubies, huge fish stocks in the Andaman Sea and some of the richest farmland in Asia, in the Ayeyarwady (Irrawaddy) delta area. But despite its potential, and the fact that more than three quarters of the population is literate, Myanmar has been reduced – today – to a state of abject poverty.

Myanmar was one of Britain's most profitable colonies. Kyaw Nyein, deputy prime minister in the late 1950s, described Myanmar under colonial rule: "The country presented a picture of a social pyramid which had the millions of poor, ignorant, exploited Burmese at its base, and a few outsiders, British, Indians and Chinese, at its apex." Hopes that this situation could be reversed were vested in national hero Aung San (see page 48). But tragically, Aung San was assassinated less than 6 months before independence in 1947. Since then Myanmar's social fabric and economy have disintegrated. Today, instead of a few outsiders at the apex, a corrupt, incompetent and repressive military élite sits at the top, maintaining opulent lifestyles at the expense of the majority. In the way people associate the name Cambodia more with the Khmers Rouges Killing Fields than with the glories of Angkor Wat, Myanmar has become known more for its tyrannical government and its suppression of dissent than for its historical, artistic and cultural heritage.

Following Ne Win's military coup d'état in 1962, Myanmar turned its back on the outside world. Inside the country, the government became deeply unpopular and economic stagnation and

Name Games: Burma or Myanmar?

The Economist writes of Myanmar. The *Far Eastern Economic Review* talks of Burma. Politically aware students avoid any reference to Myanmar except when it is safely coralled within inverted commas. The postal service in Myanmar – or is that Burma? – sends back any letter addressed 'Burma': 'Country Unknown'.

So what's the fuss? Well, for lexicographers, it's all a storm in a teacup as Myanmar is not a name that the SLORC have conjured out of thin air. It has always been in use as the more formal name for the country. While 'Burma' is taken from the more popularly used name, *Bama*. The father of independence, Aung San, seems to have preferred Burma because he believed it was more inclusive, embracing both the lowland Burmans and the minority highland groups. But looking back through historical documents it is clear that the Burmese (or Myanmaris) were generally happy to use both.

It is because of Aung San's wish to create a country for all the people of Burma/Myanmar that opposition groups and human rights activists continue to insist on referring to Burma. No doubt it is also because it was the SLORC who decided on the name change. Yet the realities of the nation state mean that in the UN, on letters, in the World Bank, and elsewhere the country is called Myanmar. There is a third option for those who want one – and most people in Myanmar really don't give a jot – Shwe Pyidaw, the 'Golden Land'.

deterioration led to years of sporadic protests, culminating in the mass-demonstrations of 1988. The military junta – the State Law and Order Restoration Council, or the Slorc – tried to rectify the situation by adopting an 'open door' policy. It has courted foreign investors in a desperate bid to earn hard currency and plundered the country's natural resources in the process. The Slorc also held a general election in 1990 in which they were overwhelmingly voted out of power – a vote which they have studiously chosen to ignore. More than US$1bn a year is spent on defence; the army rules by fear and continues to wage war on minorities.

But tyranny is not new to Myanmar: since the 9th century, its enthralling history has been a blood-curdling tale of warring kingdoms and violent dynastic infighting. In contrast, the gentility and warmth of the Burmese people has always left a lasting impression on visitors. In the mid-19th century, the colonial Chief Commissioner to Myanmar, Lieutenant General Albert Fytche, said: "No European has ever been into free and kindly intercourse with [the Burmese] without being struck with their virtues". For the time being, however, they remain under a government which, in many people's eyes, is almost virtueless. A foreign diplomat in Yangon says: "The only way things will change will be on the Slorc's terms. They can't afford to give up too much, but there are people within the Slorc who would like to see the back of brutal military dictatorship."

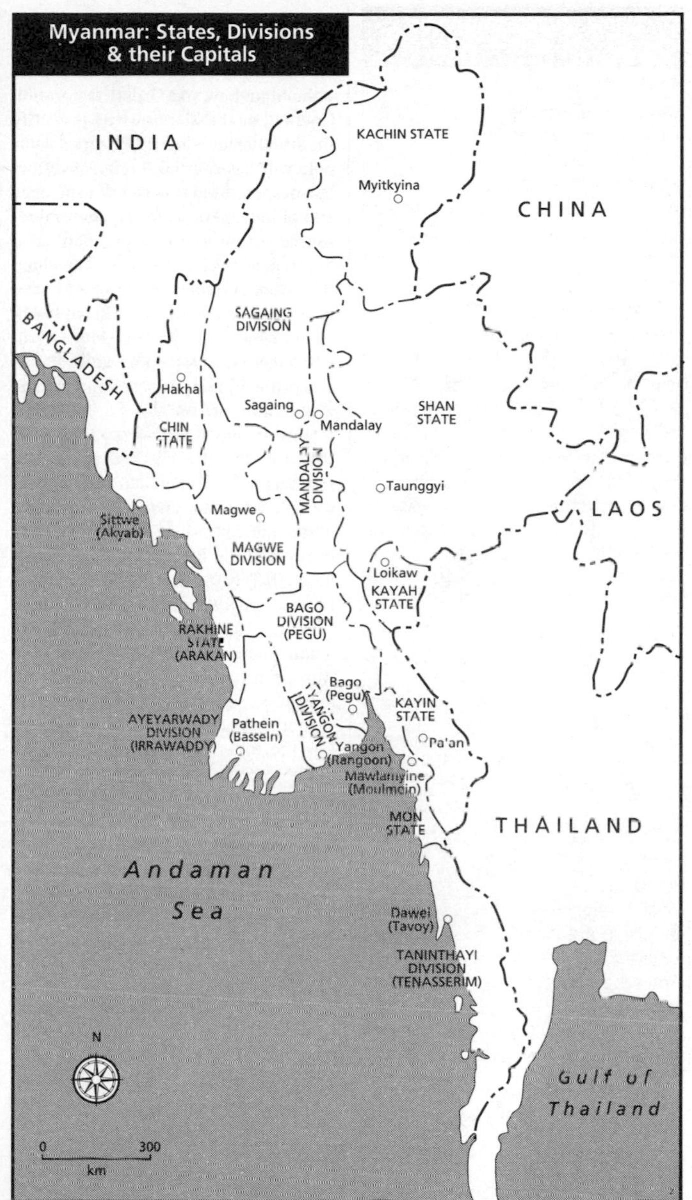
Myanmar: States, Divisions & their Capitals
INDIA
CHINA
BANGLADESH
LAOS
THAILAND
KACHIN STATE
Myitkyina
SAGAING DIVISION
Hakha
Sagaing
Mandalay
SHAN STATE
CHIN STATE
MANDALAY DIVISION
Taunggyi
Magwe
Sittwe (Akyab)
MAGWE DIVISION
Loikaw
KAYAH STATE
BAGO DIVISION (PEGU)
RAKHINE STATE (ARAKAN)
Bago (Pegu)
YANGON DIVISION
KAYIN STATE
AYEYARWADY DIVISION (IRRAWADDY)
Pathein (Basseln)
Pa'an
Yangon (Rangoon)
Mawlamyine (Moulmein)
MON STATE
Andaman Sea
Dawei (Tavoy)
TANINTHAYI DIVISION (TENASSERIM)
N
Gulf of Thailand
0
300
km

Land and life

GEOGRAPHY

Myanmar covers a land area of 676,552 sq km and stretches for over 1,930 km from the inaccessible N Himalayan region to the S tip of the Tenasserim region, which extends down the Kra Isthmus and faces the Andaman Sea. It is about the size of the United Kingdom and France combined and twice the size of Vietnam. Myanmar borders India and Bangladesh to the NW and W, China and Laos to the NE and Thailand to the E and SE. It is shaped like a rhomboid – vaguely like a kite, with the long, narrow Tenasserim region as its jungled and mountainous tail. Its borders do not correspond to ethnic boundaries – they are mainly defined by mountain ranges which surround Myanmar on three sides and form a great horseshoe enclosing the Ayeyarwady, Chindwin and Sittang (Sittoung) River systems. Myanmar's mountains pose great obstacles to commerce and transportation, impeding E-W communication. Even during British colonial times, when Myanmar was part of the Indian Empire, the links between Myanmar and India were exclusively by sea. The mountains also prevent the SW monsoon from blowing into central Myanmar: the annual rainfall on the W Rakhine coast usually exceeds 5,000 mm, whereas in central Myanmar – the Dry Zone – the annual rainfall in places can be as low as 640 mm.

Burmese names – changing places

The Burmese government has reverted to calling the country and the main cities by their original Burmese names, which can cause confusion. The decision to change Burma to Myanmar, which followed consultations between General Ne Win and his astrologers, was announced on 27 May 1989. The old dictator's lucky number is nine – hence the 27th (2+7=9). The change befuddled Myanmar-watchers, but Bangkok-based journalist Bertil Lintner believes it was done "in order to protect Burma's indigenous character... when foreign capital and outside influences were entering the country..." Ne Win has always tried to keep one step ahead of fate. The "Burmanization" is inconsequential – in Burmese, Burma has always been Myanmar as well as 'Bama'. The decision to change town names was announced on 18 Jun (1+8=9). The former names and the new names are listed below:

Former	New
Akyab	*Sittwe*
Amherst	*Kyaikkami*
Arakan	*Rakhine*
Bassein	*Pathein*
Burma	*Myanmar*
Chindwin	*Chindwin*
Irrawaddy	*Ayeyarwady*
Mandalay	*Mandalay*
Martaban	*Mottama*
Maymyo	*Pyin U Lwin*
Mergui	*Myeik (or Beik)*
Moulmein	*Mawlamyine*
Myohaung	*Mrauk U*
Pagan	*Bagan*
Pegu	*Bago*
Prome	*Pyay or (Pyi)*
Rangoon	*Yangon*
Salween	*Thaniwan* or *Thanlwin*
Sandoway	*Thandwe*
Sittang	*Sittoung* or *Sittaung*
Sri Ksetra	*Thiri Kettaya*
Syriam	*Thanlyin*
Taunggyi	*Taunggyi*
Tavoy	*Dawei*
Yaunghwe	*Nyaung Shwe*

The cycle of wet rice cultivation

There are an estimated 120,000 rice varieties. Rice seed – either selected from the previous harvest or, more commonly, purchased from a dealer or agricultural extension office – is soaked overnight before being sown into a carefully prepared nursery bed. Today farmers are likely to plant one of the Modern Varieties or MVs bred for their high yields.

The nursery bed into which the seeds are broadcast (scattered) is often a farmer's best land, with the most stable water supply. After a month the seedlings are up-rooted and taken out to the paddy fields. These will also have been ploughed, puddled and harrowed, turning the heavy clay soil into a saturated slime. Traditionally buffalo and cattle would have performed the task; today rotavators, and even tractors are becoming more common. The seedlings are transplanted into the mud in clumps. Before transplanting the tops of the seedlings are twisted off (this helps to increase yield) and then they are pushed in to the soil in neat rows. The work is back-breaking and it is not unusual to find labourers – both men and women – receiving a premium – either a bonus on top of the usual daily wage or a free meal at midday, to which marijuana is sometimes added to ease the pain.

After transplanting, it is essential that the water supply is carefully controlled. The key to high yields is a constant flow of water, regulated to take account of the growth of the rice plant. In 'rain-fed' systems where the farmer relies on rainfall to water the crop, he has to hope that it will be neither too much nor too little. Elaborate ceremonies are performed to appease the rice goddess and to ensure bountiful rainfall.

In areas where rice is grown in irrigated conditions, farmers need not concern themselves with the day-to-day pattern of rainfall, and in such areas 2 or even 3 crops can be grown each year. But such systems need to be carefully managed, and it is usual for one man to be in charge of irrigation. He decides when water should be released, organizes labour to repair dykes and dams and to clear channels, and decides which fields should receive the water first.

Traditionally, while waiting for the rice to mature, a farmer would do little except weed the crop from time to time. He and his family might move out of the village and live in a field hut to keep a close eye on the maturing rice. Today, farmers also apply chemical fertilisers and pesticides to protect the crop and ensure maximum yield. After 90-130 days, the crop should be ready for harvesting.

Harvesting also demands intensive labour. Traditionally, farmers in a village would secure their harvesters through systems of reciprocal labour exchange; now it is more likely for a harvester to be paid in cash. After harvesting, the rice is threshed, sometimes out in the field, and then brought back to the village to be stored in a rice barn or sold. It is only at the end of the harvest, with the rice safely stored in the barn, that the festivals begin.

The huge and rugged Shan Plateau borders Thailand and runs the length of the states of Karen and Tenasserim. The N borders are high in the remote Himalayan region, which is partly a continuation of China's Yunnan plateau. The Burmese, Chinese and Indian frontiers meet next to Myanmar's highest peak, Hkakobo Razi (5,881m), which overlooks E Tibet and is the highest mountain in Southeast Asia (not Mount Kinabalu in Sabah, as many people state). The N border with China runs for 2,185 km and the Kachin Hills has long been a disputed area. The Bangladesh and Indian borders follow the natural barrier formed by the Chin, Patkai, Manipur and Naga hills. These are actually substantial mountains, rather than hills, and the frontier line runs from mountaintop to mountaintop.

The universal stimulant – the betel nut

In Myanmar it is not uncommon to meet men and women whose teeth are stained black, and gums red, by continuous chewing of the 'betel nut'. This, though, is a misnomer. The betel 'nut' is not chewed at all: the three crucial ingredients that make up a betel 'wad' are the nut of the areca palm (*Areca catechu*), the leaf or catkin of the betel vine (*Piper betle*), and lime. When these three ingredients are combined with saliva they act as a mild stimulant. Other ingredients (people have their own recipes) are tobacco, gambier, various spices and the gum of *Acacia catechu*. The habit, though also common in South Asia and parts of China, seems to have evolved in Southeast Asia and it is mentioned in the very earliest chronicles. The lacquer betel boxes of Myanmar illustrate the importance of chewing betel in social intercourse. Galvao in his journal of 1544 noted: "They use it so continuously that they never take it from their mouths; therefore these people can be said to go around always ruminating". Among Westernized Southeast Asians the habit is frowned upon: the disfigurement and ageing that it causes, and the stained walls and floors that result from the constant spitting, are regarded as distasteful products of an earlier age.

There are several crossing points from Thailand into Myanmar – the best known being the Three Pagodas Pass – SE of Kyaikkami (in Karen State, better known as Amherst) and NW of Kanchanaburi in Thailand. Further W, on the W side of the Sittang (Sittoung) River, is the volcanic Bago Yoma (Bago Range) which stretches to the N and culminates – just to the SE of Bagan – at Mount Popa (see page 200). The Bago Yoma's southernmost hill is crowned with the magnificent Shwedagon Pagoda. This range runs lengthwise down the centre of Myanmar, between the E and W ranges.

Two river valleys dominate the central plain of Myanmar both running N-S: the Ayeyarwady to the W, and the smaller Sittang to the E. The Ayeyarwady is Myanmar's main communications artery and was known as the 'Road to Mandalay' by British colonialists – giving rise to Rudyard Kipling's famous lines:

On the road to Mandalay,
Where the flyin'-fishes play,
An' the dawn comes up like thunder
outer China 'crost the Bay!

The Ayeyarwady flows over 2,000 km from the Kachin Hills in the N to the Andaman Sea. The river effectively divides Myanmar in two. It is navigable for 1,450 km – even in the dry season. The Ayeyarwady originates in E Tibet and flows S through the state of Kachin. It is joined by the river Chindwin SW of Mandalay. Before it reaches the sea it divides into the sprawling delta region, one of the richest farming areas in the world. The central plain is divided into Upper Burma – the area surrounding Mandalay, Pyay (Prome) and Taungoo (Toungoo) – and Lower Burma, focusing on Yangon. Central Myanmar is seismologically unstable; a severe earthquake in Jul 1975 caused serious damage to the ancient capital of Bagan. The Bago Yoma, running between the two rivers, is heavily forested and until recently there were no roads running E-W linking the two river-valleys. The Sittang River, to the E of the Ayeyarwady basin, has a tidal bore which is a notorious hazard to shipping. Further E, the Salween (Thaniwan) River is only navigable close to its mouth.

CLIMATE

The Tropic of Cancer crosses the country 160 km N of Mandalay. Myanmar is usually classified as having a tropical monsoon climate, although roughly half the country lies outside the tropical zone. Its climate is similar to India's – 'cool' from Oct to the end of Feb (21-28°C), hot from the beginning of Mar to the beginning of Jun (temperatures can reach 45°C in central Myanmar) and rainy from Jun to the end of Sep. The NE monsoon, from the dry uplands of the Yunnan Plateau, blows from Nov to Mar bringing a long, dry season. From May to Oct the prevailing wind shifts and the SW monsoon dominates, bringing rain from the Bay of Bengal.

Regions facing the prevailing winds – particularly Rakhine and Tenasserim, which are both backed by steep mountain ranges – receive some of the heaviest rainfall in the world. Sittwe (Akyab) in Rakhine receives an average of 5,180 mm of rain a year, of which 4,980 mm falls during the 6 months of the SW monsoon. The mountain areas – particularly the Shan Plateau – are cool and comparatively dry. One traveller during the British colonial era described them as a 'tropical Scotland'. There is an arid belt in the heart of the country around Bagan. This Dry Zone is in the rainshadow of the SW monsoon and some parts of the central lowlands receive as little as 640 mm of rain a year.

For monthly rainfall and temperature graphs see pages 106 (Yangon), 145 (Mandalay), 240 (Lashio) and 254 (Sittwe).

FLORA AND FAUNA

Myanmar's natural vegetation varies according to regional rainfall patterns. But on the whole Myanmar is densely forested with conifers, teak, and tropical forest. The Ayeyarwady delta area used to be thickly forested but has been cleared over the past century for agriculture. The

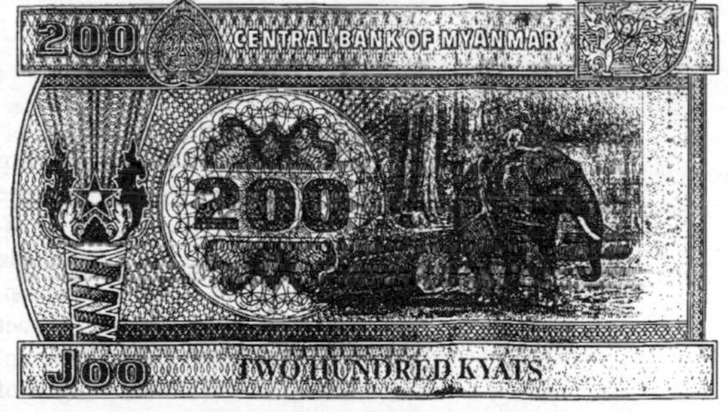

* An elephant pulling teak illustrated on a 200 kyat note

forests have also been destroyed by shifting cultivation and, increasingly, by logging – mainly by Thai timber companies. But Myanmar's forests still account for about three quarters of the world's teak reserves. In the Dry Zone of central Myanmar (around Bagan), cacti and acacia trees are a common sight. Myanmar's flora has not been as thoroughly studied as other areas of Southeast Asia but is known for its diversity; there are thought to be over a thousand varieties of orchid, for example.

Myanmar still has a large population of wildlife, including elephants, tigers, leopards, the mithan (a type of wild buffalo), the endangered Sumatran rhinoceros, wild boar, monkeys, flying squirrels, porcupines, civet cats, red and black deer, black bears and the Malayan sun bear. Myanmar is home to some 1000 species of birds, 40 of which are under worldwide threat of extinction. There are also 52 varieties of poisonous snake – Myanmar has the highest death rate from snakebites in the world. The most highly infested areas are the Dry Zone (snakes live in many of Bagan's ruined temples) and the Ayeyarwady delta. The deadliest snakes are Russel's viper and the Asiatic king cobra. The animal most westerners associate with Myanmar is the Burmese cat. It is actually from Thailand and was the result of a lengthy period of experimental crossbreeding with Siamese cats.

History

Myanmar's early history is practically uncharted but by the 8th century the Mon – who probably originated in Central Asia – occupied the lower portions of the Ayeyarwady basin, while the Burmans had established themselves on the upper reaches of the Ayeyarwady. Myanmar's subsequent violent history largely concerns the struggle between these two predominant racial groups. Kings fought wars in order to carry off slaves from the kingdoms they conquered; it was important to have a large labour force to build temples and pagodas, and to grow rice. In this way, a king's power was measured not in terms of the size of his kingdom, but the number of people that came under his sway.

The Glass Palace Chronicle of the Kings of Burma (a 19th century historical mythology) claims that the Burmese kings were descendants of the Buddha's family but historians have found no evidence of any ruler before the 11th century King Anawrahta of Bagan. From the 10th century, the Burmans were the largest group; they were also the most important in terms of their historical, cultural and political contribution to Myanmar's heritage. Between the 11th and 19th centuries, the Burmans succeeded in uniting the country under one monarch on three separate occasions. When each of these empires fragmented, Myanmar became a muddle of quarrelling races. In the 19th century, the Burmese frequently clashed with the British and were defeated in 1885, resulting in the capture and exile of the last king.

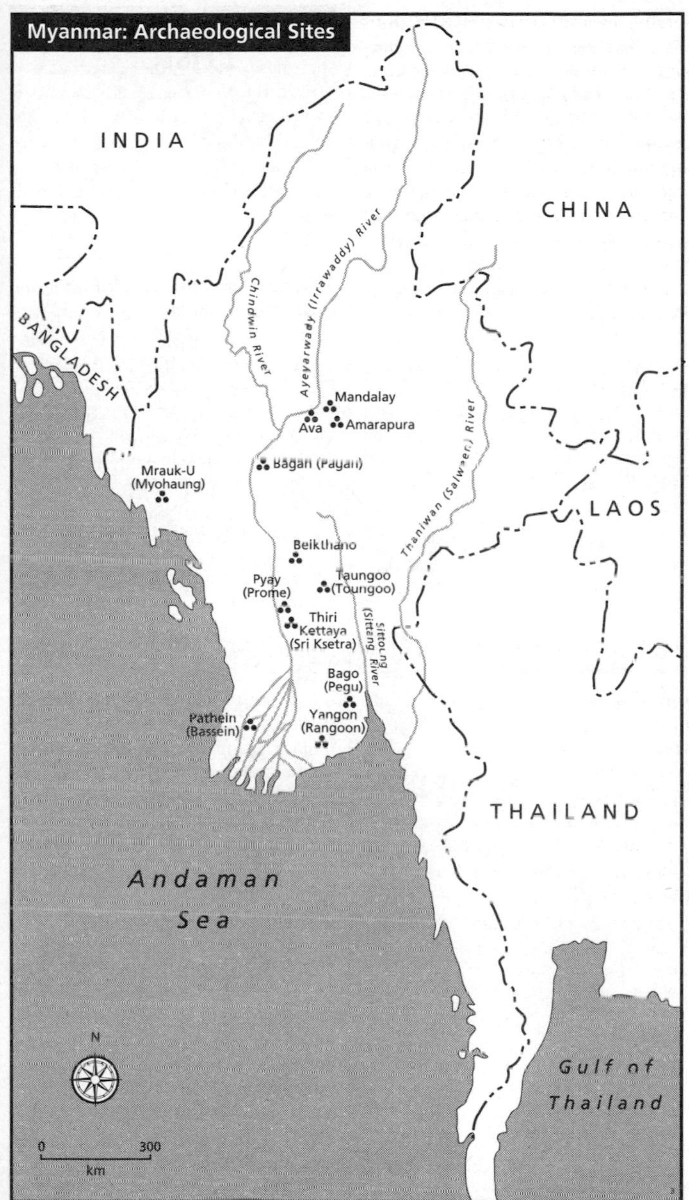
Myanmar: Archaeological Sites
INDIA
CHINA
BANGLADESH
LAOS
THAILAND
Chindwin River
Ayeyarwady (Irrawaddy) River
Thanlwan (Salween) River
Sittoung (Sittang) River
Mandalay
Ava
Amarapura
Bagan (Pagan)
Mrauk-U (Myohaung)
Beikthano
Pyay (Prome)
Taungoo (Toungoo)
Thiri Kettaya (Sri Ksetra)
Bago (Pegu)
Pathein (Bassein)
Yangon (Rangoon)
Andaman Sea
Gulf of Thailand
N
0
300
km

EARLY HISTORY

There are traces of some form of settlement in Myanmar as far back as 2,500-2,000 BC. The Pyu were the first settlers and occupied the upper Ayeyarwady River. The early Pyu city of Sri Ksetra, near present day Pyay (see page 135), was enclosed in a massive wall and was possibly even bigger than the later Burmese cities of Bagan and Mandalay. When the Pyu capital was captured and the people enslaved by the neighbouring power in Yunnan, the Burmese moved into the power vacuum in the Ayeyarwady area. The Burmese came to dominate both the Pyu and the Mon.

The Mon settled in the lower Ayeyarwady delta region around Thaton and were the first people to establish Buddhism in Myanmar. Little is known about the earliest phases of Mon art – although their artistic and architectural skills were obviously coveted and their works have been unearthed not just in Myanmar, but also in Thailand and Cambodia. The great King Anawrahta brought Mon craftsmen to Bagan where their temple and stupa designs characterized the first recognizable architectural 'period' – the Mon Period. The last group to migrate from China were the Tai, who fled the Mongul invasions from the 9th-11th centuries and settled in the hills on the present Thai-Myanmar border.

THE FIRST BURMESE EMPIRE

Bagan was founded in 849 at a strategic location on the banks of the Ayeyarwady. The site was also imbued with considerable mystical significance – it was close to Mount Popa, the most important centre of *nat* (spirit) worship in Myanmar, which pre-dated the arrival of Buddhism (see page 67). In 1044 **King Anawrahta** seized the throne at Bagan. 12 years later, he was converted to Theravada Buddhism by Shin Arahan, a missionary-monk from the Mon court at Thaton. With his conversion, King Anawrahta

Penis balls and sexual roles in historical Southeast Asia

One notable feature of Southeast Asian society is the relative autonomy of women. This is most clearly illustrated in sexual relations. As the historian Anthony Reid writes in his book *Southeast Asia in the age of commerce 1450-1680*: "Southeast Asian literature of the period leaves us in little doubt that women took a very active part in courtship and lovemaking, and demanded as much as they gave by way of sexual and emotional gratification". He then goes on to describe the various ways – often involving painful surgery – that men would try to satisfy their partners. Metal pins, for example, were inserted into the penis, and wheels, studs and spurs attached as accessories to increase the female's pleasure. Alternatively, metal balls or bells, sometimes made of gold or ivory, would be inserted beneath the skin of the penis. Numerous early European visitors expressed their astonishment at the practice. Tome Pires, the 16th century Portuguese apothecary observed that Pegu lords in Burma "wear as many as nine gold ones [penis bells], with beautiful treble, contralto and tenor tones, the size of the Alvares plums in our country; and those who are too poor...have them in lead...Malay women rejoice greatly when the Pegu men come to their country... [because of] their sweet harmony". Whereas in Africa, genital surgery was, and is, often intended to suppress pleasure for women or increase it for men, in Southeast Asia the reverse was the case. The surgery described above was also widely practiced – in Burma, Siam, Makassar, among the Torajans of Sulawesi, and Java.

Philip de Brito – King of thieves

In 1603 the Portuguese adventurer Philip de Brito y Nicote, a former ship's cabin-boy, declared himself King of Lower Burma, with his capital at Syriam. He had the backing of the Portuguese Viceroy of Goa (having married his daughter), the friendship of the Mon, the acceptance of the Arakanese, and was tolerated by the Burmans. However, he quickly undid his feats of diplomacy by compelling about 100,000 Mon to convert to Christianity, plundering relic chambers throughout Lower Burma and stealing the 32-tonne bell which the Mon King Dhammazedi had donated to Yangon's Shwedagon in the 15th century. Having overstepped the mark once too often, De Brito was damned by Myanmar's monks and then attacked by the Burman King Anaukhpetlun, Bayinnaung's grandson, whose troops besieged Syriam for a month. De Brito was captured by the Burmans and impaled on a stake. He was allowed to choose where, but ignored advice to have it run through his vital organs. As a result, it took him 3 days to die. All the leading Portuguese were executed and the remainder were employed as palace servants at Ava.

immediately set about showing his devotion by ordering the construction of the Shwezigon temple (see page 191). In 1057 Anawrahta declared war on the Mon to capture the Tripituka, the Buddhist scriptures, which the Mon King Manuha refused to give up. Anawrahta beseiged the Mon capital of Bago (Pegu) for months until Manuha surrendered and the city was destroyed. Anawrahta returned to Bagan with the Mon royal family, 32 white elephants (each of which was laden with the sacred books of the Tripitaka) and Thaton's remaining 30,000 inhabitants – including craftsmen and builders. The Mon king was dedicated to the Shwezigon as a pagoda slave. But despite their inglorious defeat, the sophisticated Mon proceeded to dominate Bagan's cultural life for the next century – many of the thousands of pagodas at Bagan are Mon in style and the Burmans adapted their script from Mon.

Anawrahta also succeeded in breaking the power of the Shan states – the S ones came under Burmese suzerainty – and he brought Rakhine into his dominion. Despite his war-like tendencies, Anawrahta is said to have been a very religious man. He is believed to have dispatched a ship laden with treasure to Bodhgaya in India, where the Buddha gained enlightenment, to pay for the restoration of the Mahabodhi temple. Anawrahta was killed by a wild buffalo in 1077, but by then he had already put in place the foundation of the First Burmese Empire.

During his son, **King Sawlu's, reign** (1077-1084), the kingdom continued to expand. It grew even bigger under **King Kyanzittha's reign** (1084-1113), when parts of the S Tenasserim region came under the control of Bagan. Kyanzittha began the construction of the Ananda pagoda – the most famous temple on the Bagan Plain. The 12th century was Bagan's Golden Age, when it was known – rather optimistically – as 'the city of 4 million pagodas'. The Bagan civilization is believed to have been supported by rice

Selected kings of the First Burmese Empire at Bagan, 849-1287 AD

Bagan established	849
Anawrahta	1044 1077
Sawlu	1077-1084
Kyanzittha	1084-1113
Narathihapati	1248-1287
Kublai Khan takes Bagan	1287

NB: for further details see page 181.

Burmese Kings: rules of succession

As there was no rule of ascendancy in Myanmar, it was fairly usual for a new Burmese king to execute all his rivals to secure his claim to the throne. The only rule seems to have been that no royal blood could be spilt on Burmese soil; over the years, a number of innovative techniques were masterminded by which kings disposed of their relatives. Burning them alive and drowning were quite popular – Bodawpaya, when he came to the throne, got rid of all his relations, including their children and servants, by setting them alight. One of the more blood-thirsty royal purges was carried out by King Thibaw, Myanmar's last king, who outraged British Victorian society with his 'savagery' when it was discovered how he had dispensed with rival heirs. He had them all tied up in blood-red velvet sacks and beaten to death during a *pwe* (festival) which lasted 3 days and conveniently drowned the cries of his victims. The British had no idea that this barbaric behaviour was standard practice and the London press told the world about the horrors of the Burmese court and the inhumanity of King Thibaw.

cultivation, made possible by a highly developed system of irrigation canals.

In 1248 **King Narathihapati** ascended to the throne of Bagan. Historical records portray him as a hedonist enjoying a luxurious lifestyle. He completed the lavish Mingalazedi pagoda at Bagan in 1274 – but appears to have gone bankrupt in the process. Bagan's economy fell apart and no more pagodas were built. In 1287 **Kublai Khan** led a Mongul invasion which captured the city and brought the First Burmese Empire to an undignified end. The king fled to Pathein (Bassein) earning the title *Tayokpye-min* (meaning the 'king who fled from the Chinese'), leaving the Monguls in his beautiful royal capital. The Mongul military campaign against the Burman Kingdom of Bagan was recorded in the diary of Venetian merchant Marco Polo when he visited the Imperial Court of China 5 years later. After 5 months' exile in Pathein, the Burmese king tried to return to Bagan but made it only as far as Pyay, where his eldest son was a governor. He murdered his father by forcing poison down his throat and then battled with his two brothers for the throne. He succeeded – but was deposed in 1298, marking the end of the Anawrahta Dynasty.

Burma in disarray and the rise of the Mon

With the end of the Anawrahta Dynasty, the kingdom broke into a number of smaller states. From 1298-1364 the Shan established power in Upper Burma, with their capital at Ava (founded 1364/5), near modern Mandalay. From 1364-1554, the Shan dominated the Ayeyarwady rice growing area and expanded into what is now Kachin state and along the Chindwin River. The Shan did not manage to amalgamate into a single powerful empire – but remained split into small kingdoms, frequently feuding against one another. Only the W kingdom of Rakhine remained completely independent and spread N into Chittagong (in present-day Bangladesh). The Rakhine capital was at Wethali (Vessali) until 1433 when they moved it to Mrauk U (Myohaung, meaning 'Ancient City').

Meanwhile, the Mon, who had been under Burman subjugation for

Selected kings of the Mon kingdom, 1287-1492

Wareru	1287-1296
Binnya U	1353-1385
Razadarit	1385-
Shinsawbu	1453-1472
Dhammazedi	1472-1492

2½ centuries, formed their own kingdom in Lower Burma. King Wareru – son-in-law of King Ramkhamhaeng, ruler of the Thai kingdom of Sukhothai – re-established Mon dominance, based first at Mottama (Martaban). In 1385, Razadarit succeeded to the Mon throne and ruled Lower Burma from Bago. The Mon Kingdom prospered as a trading centre, exporting rice to India and Malaysia, and became a centre of artistic excellence. Queen Shinsawbu (1453-1472) raised the height of the Shwedagon pagoda in Yangon. The queen went so far as to donate her own weight in gold to gild the outside.

THE SECOND BURMESE EMPIRE

Many Burmans fled S from Shan domination and established a centre around Taungoo and the Burmese and the Shan kingdoms remained in a permanent state of war. The kingdom survived, sandwiched between the Shan to the N and the Mon to the S. When **King Minkyino** came to the throne in 1486 there was a revival of the Burman national spirit and the Taungoo Dynasty was founded. In 1530, the 16-year-old Tabengshweti succeeded his father and decided to re-unite Burma. He captured the Mon port of Pathein in 1535 and then went on to attack Bago. He stormed the city three times, finally finally succeeding in 1539. With Pathein and Bago under his belt, he then captured Pyay and was recognized as the undisputed king of Lower Burma.

Meanwhile, to the N, the Shan King of Ava was gaining notoriety for persecuting monks and plundering pagodas. Kings who engaged in such activities never lasted long in Myanmar, and, sure enough, his actions prompted a conspiracy to overthrow him. When he was successfully ousted, the Shan united and took Pyay and then beseiged the strongly fortified capital of Rakhine, Mrauk-U. While besieging the city the Shan heard word of a Siamese invasion from the E. The Shan had expanded their empire too quickly and were unable to control such a vast swathe of territory. As the Shan kingdom began to disintegrate, **Bayinnaung** (King Tabengshweti's brother-in-law) inherited the throne in 1551 after a year of civil strife when the kingdom was effectively leaderless – and re-established Burman control over Lower Burma. He attacked Bago 3 years later and the Mon population fled to Pyay; Bayinnaung then targeted Pyay and the city was starved into surrender in 1552. Bayinnaung crowned his successes with the capture of Ava in 1555. In doing so, he destroyed the power of the Shan states and laid the foundations of the Second Burmese Empire. But Bayinnaung was not content to stop there and turned his attention to neighbouring Siam. First, he captured Chiang Mai, then set his sights on Ayutthaya. The King of Ayutthaya was known to have four white elephants which Bayinnaung coveted – white elephants had great religious significance as they were (and are) believed to symbolize an earlier incarnation of the Buddha. On the pretext of a manufactured border dispute, King Bayinnaung launched a successful attack on the Siamese capital in 1564.

The Siamese king, queen and youngest son were taken prisoner and the heir to the throne was left to govern as a tributary king. In Burma, the deposed king of Ayutthaya became a monk and his younger son died. King Bayinnaung, in a compassionate moment, then allowed his widow and children to return home to Ayutthaya – a move which proved to be a tactical error as their

Selected kings of the Taungoo Dynasty (1486-1752)	
Minkyino	1486-1530
Tabengshweti	1530-1550
Bayinnaung	1551-1581
Nandanaung	1581-1599
Thalun	1629-1648

return prompted the tributary king to re-assert his independence. Bayinnaung was furious and launched a fresh Burmese invasion of Siam. He left with 200,000 troops, many of whom died during the subsequent 7-month siege of Ayutthaya. The Burmese finally captured the city however and the belligerent King Bayinnaung went on to attack Vientiane in Laos. But King Razagyri of Rakhine took advantage of the depleted Burman army remaining at home and attacked Taungoo, taking the white elephants as booty. From then on the King of Rakhine had the title 'Lord of the White Elephant'.

For all his warmongering, Bayinnaung seems to have been a model Buddhist: he forbade the sacrificing of slaves, horses and elephants and sent brooms of his own hair (and that of his wives) to sweep the Temple of the Sacred Tooth in Kandy, Ceylon. He eventually died in 1581, apparently leaving 97 children, and was succeeded by the eldest, **Nandanaung**, who ruled from 1581-1599. King Nandanaung did not have his father's force of character, military skills or administrative ability. In 18 years, he lost nearly everything his father had fought for and the empire broke up again due to internal feuding. In 1636 the capital was moved to Ava, but by then the empire was in decline. The Mon were once again becoming increasingly assertive; they re-established their kingdom in the S, with Bago as the capital. Ava was recaptured by the Mon in 1752, with the help of French arms. Nandanaung was taken captive back to Bago and the Second Burmese Empire floundered and the Taungoo Dynasty dissolved. The Mon then shifted their capital to Ava.

THE THIRD BURMESE EMPIRE

The Mon conquest of Ava was short-lived. The southerners were unpopular and when they tried to force **Alaungpaya**, a minor lord based at the nearby city of Shwebo, to swear allegiance, he refused. The Mon attacked Alaungpaya on three occasions, each time with a larger army, and each time their efforts were repulsed. His success in thwarting the Mon spread by word of mouth and thousands joined his revolt. Soon he was strong enough to turn the tables on the Mon and attack Ava which fell within a month, in 1753.

Alaungpaya was a charismatic man and a brilliant general who appreciated the importance of propoganda. He used chain letters and ballads to reinforce his reputation, and promised to free slaves and give minority groups their autonomy. In addition to using propoganda to devastating effect – apparently enemies would simply capitulate in the face of his fearsome reputation – he also created a superb army to complement his PR. Within 4 years of his recapture of Ava, Bago had also fallen to Alaungpaya's forces; the Mon fled to the small town of Dagon, to the SW. Three years later, Alaungpaya sacked the town, renaming it *Yangon* – 'the end of war'. Although the name might have been appropriate so far as the Mon were concerned, it did not extend to the Siamese as Alaunpaya turned his attention to lands beyond Myanmar. In 1760 Alaungpaya attacked Ayutthaya, the capital of Siam. He was fatally wounded in the process. But in his few short years as King of Burma, he had founded the Konbaung Dynasty, and with it, the Third (and final) Burmese Empire. The dynasty lasted for

Kings of the Third Burmese Empire (Konbaung) 1752-1885

Alaungpaya	1752-1760
Naungdawgyi	1760-1763
Hsinbyushin	1763-1776
Bodawpaya	1782-1819
Bagyidaw	1819-1838
Tharrawaddy	1838-1846
Pagan Min	1846-1853
Mindon May	1853-1878
Thibaw Min	1878-1885

over a century (1752-1865), during which time the capital – which was first at Shwebo – shifted between Ava (1765-1783, 1823-1837) and Amarapura (1783-1823, 1837-1857) before moving to Mandalay in 1857. In many respects the Kingdom of Ava was heir to Bagan.

Alaungpaya's second son, **Hsinbyushin**, came to the throne after a short reign by his elder brother, **Naungdawgyi** (1760-1763). He continued his father's expansionist policy and finally took Ayutthaya in 1767, after 7 years of fighting. He returned to Ava with Siamese artists, dancers, musicians and craftsmen who gave fresh cultural impetus to Burma. The Mon had been crushed and the Shan *sawbwas* (feudal lords) were made to pay tribute to the Burmese. The kingdom's NE borders came under threat from the Chinese – they invaded four times between 1765 and 1769 but were repulsed on each occasion. In 1769 King Hsinbyushin forced them to make peace and the two sides signed a treaty. At about this time, Europeans began to set up trading posts in the Ayeyarwady delta region; the French struck deals with the Mon while the English made agreements with the Burmese.

Bodawpaya, Alaungpaya's fifth son, came to the throne in 1782. He founded Amarapura, moving his capital from Ava. Bodawpaya conquered Rakhine in 1784 and recovered all the Burman treasures taken by the Arakanese (Rakhine) 2 centuries before, including the Mahamuni image (see page 155). Burmese control over Rakhine resulted in protracted wrangles with the British, who by then were firmly ensconsed in Bengal. Relations with the British deteriorated further when Bodawpaya pursued Arakanese (Rakhine) rebels seeking refuge across the border – this was not to be the last time refugees flooded over the border (see page 65). Conflict ensued; the British wanted a demarcated border while the Burmese were content to have a zone of overlapping influence. To add to their annoyance, British merchants complained about being badly treated by the king's officials in Rangoon. The British decided enough was enough and diplomatic relations were severed in 1811.

Bodawpaya turned his attention to the administration of his empire. He investigated the existing tax systems and revoked exemptions for religious establishments which incurred the wrath of the monkhood – as did his claim to be a Bodhisattva (a future Buddha). Bodawpaya died in 1819 at the age of 75, one of Burma's greatest kings. He had re-established the stability which Alaungpaya had brought to the Kingdom, re-gained many of the lands which had been lost, and importantly also restored the kingdom's economic base.

Bodawpaya was succeeded by King **Bagyidaw**. The Maharajah of Manipur (a princely state in the W hills to the S of Nagaland) who previously paid tribute to the Burmese crown, did not attend Bagyidaw's coronation. This resulted in the subsequent punitative expedition that took the Burmese into British India.

THE EXPANSION OF THE BRITISH INTO BURMA

This intrusion was used by the British as a pretext for launching the First Anglo-Burmese War. The British took Rangoon in 1824 and then advanced on Ava. In 1826, the Burmese agreed to the British peace terms and the **Treaty of Yandabo** was signed. This ceded the Rakhine and Tenasserim regions to the British – which were ruled from Calcutta, headquarters of the British East India Company. Manipur also became part of British India.

Most accounts of this treaty take a British perspective: they were either written by Britons, or by people sympathetic to the British cause. When historians have quoted from Burmese sources they have tended to use the translation of the Burmese chronicle *Kon-baung-zet* in John Crawfurd's (1829) *Journal of an embassy from the Governor-General of India to the court of Ava in the year 1827.* Crawfurd quotes from the chronicle:

"In the years 1186 and 87, the kula-pyu, or white strangers of the West, fastened a quarrel upon the Lord of the Golden Palace. They landed at Rangoon, took that place and Prome, and were permitted to advance as far as Yandabo; for the King, for motives of piety and regard to life, made no effort whatever to oppose them. The strangers had spent vast sums of money in their enterprise; and by the time they reached Yandabo, their resources were exhausted, and they were in great distress. They petitioned the King, who, in his clemency and generosity, sent them large sums of money to pay their expenses back, and ordered them out of the country."

This quote has traditionally been used to illustrate the arrogance of the Burmese kings in the face of superior military and economic might.

But the peace treaty did little to ease relations between the British and Burmese. The Burmese kings felt insulted at having to deal with the viceroy of India instead of British royalty. In 1837 King Bagyidaw's brother, **Tharrawaddy**, seized the throne and had the queen, her brother, Bagyidaw's only son,

Snodgrass, JJ (Major) (1827)
Narrative of the Burmese War detailing the operations of Major-General Sir Archibald Campbell's army, from its landing in Rangoon in May 1824, to the conclusion of the peace at Yandaboo in February 1826.

White elephants and theatre at the royal court

The British were amazed at life in the Burmese court: the strict rules of protocol prompted much debate, particularly 'the shoe question'. They were indignant at having to remove their shoes on entering pagodas and while having an audience with the king. In contrast, the British were amused by the ritual quandary surrounding the decision of which umbrella the king should use, and were more bemused by the status accorded the white elephant. The 'Lord White Elephant' – or *Sinbyudaw* – commanded social status second only to the king in the hierarchy of the royal court. Sinbyudaw were treated with reverence and had white parasols held over them wherever they went. Young white elephants were even suckled by women in the royal court who considered it a great honour to feed the elephant with their own milk. The elephants were ritually washed, perfumed and entertained by court performers. In reality albino elephants are a pinky pale grey. The Sinbyudaw gave rise to the English term – 'a white elephant' – which originally meant a rare or very valuable possession, the upkeep of which was very expensive. In time, it came to mean an elaborate venture which proves useless and unwanted.

his family and ministers all executed. He made no attempt to improve relations with Britain, and neither did his successor to the Lion Throne, **Pagan Min**, who became king in 1846. He executed thousands – some history books say as many as 6,000 – of his wealthier and more influential subjects on trumped-up charges. During his reign, relations with the British became increasingly strained. In 1852, the Second Anglo-Burmese War broke out after two British shipmasters complained about unfair treatment. They had been imprisoned having been charged with murder and were forced to pay a large 'ransom' for their release. British military action was short and sharp and within a year they announced their annexation of Lower Burma. Early in 1853, hostilities ceased, leaving the British in full control of trade on the Ayeyarwady.

The same year – to the great relief of both the Burmese and the British – Pagan Min was succeeded by his younger brother, the progressive **Mindon Min**, who ruled from 1853-1878. The new king moved the capital to Amarapura and then to his new city of Mandalay. The move was designed to fulfil a prophesy of the Buddha that a great city would one day be built on the site. Court astrologers also calculated that Mandalay was the centre of the universe – not Amarapura. King Mindon attempted to bring Burma into greater contact with the outside world: he improved the administrative structure of the state, introducing a new income tax; he built new roads and commissioned a telegraph system; he set up modern factories using European machinery and European managers. He also sent some of his sons to study with an Anglican missionary and did all he could to repair relations with Britain. A commercial treaty was signed with the British, who sent a Resident to Mandalay. King Mindon hosted the Fifth Great Buddhist Synod in 1872 at Mandalay. In these ways he gained the respect of the British and the admiration of his own people.

The Burmese found the foreign presence in Mandalay hard to tolerate and with the death of Mindon, the atmosphere thickened. King Mindon died before he could name a successor, and Thibaw, a lesser prince, was manoeuvred onto the throne by one of King Mindon's queens and her daughter, Supayalat. (In his poem *The Road to Mandalay*, Rudyard Kipling remarks that the British soldiers referred to her as 'Soup-plate'.) In true Burmese style, the new **King Thibaw Min** proceeded, under Supayalat's direction, to massacre all likely contenders to the throne. His perceived inhumanity outraged British public opinion. London was becoming increasingly worried by French intentions to build a railway between Mandalay and the French colonial port of Haiphong in Annam (N Vietnam). When Thibaw provoked a dispute with a British timber company, the British had the pretext they needed to invade Upper Burma. In 1886 they took Mandalay and imposed colonial rule throughout Myanmar; Thibaw and Supayalat were deposed and exiled to Madras in S India. Supayalat was eventually buried at the foot of the Shwedagon pagoda in Yangon (the stupa can be seen today on Shwedagon Rd), as the British feared nationalist rebellion if the funeral took place in Mandalay.

BRITISH COLONIAL RULE

Myanmar was known as 'Further India' and was run on the principle of 'divide and rule'. The colonial administration relied heavily on Indian bureaucrats and by 1930 – to the resentment of the Burmese – Indian immigrants comprised half the population of Yangon. The British permitted the country's many racial minorities to exercise limited autonomy. Myanmar was divided into two regions: Burma proper, where Burmans were in a majority – which included Rakhine and Tenasserim – and the hill areas, inhabited by other minorities. The Burmese heartland was administered by direct rule. The hill areas – which included the Shan states, the Karen states, and the minority groups in the Kachin, Chin and Naga hills – retained their traditional leadership, although they were under British supervision. Karenni State (now Kayah State) remained nominally independent. These policies gave rise to tensions that continue to plague today's government.

The colonial government built roads and railways, and river steamers, belonging to the Ayeyarwady Flotilla Company, operated between Rangoon and Mandalay. The British brought electricity to Yangon, improved urban sanitation, built hospitals and redesigned the capital on a grid system.

While the British set about building and modernizing, they benefited greatly from an economic boom in the Ayeyarwady delta region. When they first arrived in Myanmar, much of the delta was swampland. But under the British, Burmese farmers began to settle in the delta and clear land for rice cultivation. In 1855, paddy fields covered 400,000 ha; by 1873 the forests had been cleared sufficiently to double the productive area. Land under rice cultivation increased by another 400,000 ha roughly every 7 years, reaching 4 million ha in 1930. Population in the area – which was about 1.5 million in the mid-19th century – increased more than 5-fold.

Initially the rice paddys were farmed by Burmese smallholders but as rice prices rose, larger holdings were bought up and large tracts of land cleared by pioneers from central Myanmar. The agricultural economy in the delta region was dependent on complex credit facilities, run by Indian Chettiars – S Indian money-lenders – who extended credit to farmers at much lower rates than Burmese money-lenders. The Chettiars grew into a very prosperous community. Land rents had risen dramatically during the boom years and when the world economic depression set in in the 1930s, rice prices slumped and small-holders went bust. Between 1930 and 1935, the amount of land owned by the Chettiars trebled in size due to foreclosures, leaving them with well over a quarter of the delta's prime land. The agrarian crisis triggered anti-Indian riots, which

The Burma Road

Mandalay was the gateway to the Burma Road, a strategic highway built between 1937 and 1939 to link the W interior of China with the sea. It ran for 1,200 km from Lashio (NE of Mandalay) to Kunming in China's Yunnan Province and was the chief supply route for Chiang Kai-shek's Chinese nationalist forces (the Kuomintang – or KMT) in the run-up to and during WW2. The Burma Road carried munitions from India to KMT forces, who spearheaded the resistance to the Japanese occupation of China. Having occupied Yangon in Mar 1942, the Japanese 15th Army pushed N in three columns, smashing through Allied defences and driving N, through the Shan states to the Yunnan border. The Japanese troops were supported by Thai forces: Bangkok forged an alliance with Tokyo in the hope that it could lay claim to the Shan states. The E column of the 15th Army finally cut the Burma Road on 30 April 1942. (Chiang Kai-shek entered into an alliance with the Chinese Communists against the Japanese.) The Burma Rd was recaptured in 1945 and is now a principal overland drugs trail from the Golden Triangle (see page 86). Traffickers take consignments of raw opium on mule-trains up to the heroin refineries that in recent years have been mushrooming along the Yunnan border. The road has been improved to carry the greatly increased border trade between China and Myanmar. Teak, jade, heroin, cigarettes, gems and food goes out to China; pots, pans, beer, car parts, mechanical goods, carpets and clothes come back in.

started in Yangon in May 1930 and then spread to the countryside.

From the beginning of the colonial period, the British stressed the benefits of education, and formal western-style schooling replaced the traditional monastic education system. Rangoon University was founded in 1920 and a new urban élite evolved. They attempted to bridge the gap between old and new Myanmar by calling for the reform of traditional Buddhist beliefs and practices. In 1906, the Young Men's Buddhist Association (YMBA) was established in an effort to assert Burmese cultural identity. In 1916, the YMBA objected to the fact that Europeans persisted in wearing shoes inside religious buildings, an practice considered disdainful. After demonstrations in over 50 towns, the government ruled that abbots should have the right to determine how visitors should dress in their monasteries – a ruling hailed as a victory for the YMBA.

Following the introduction of greater self-government in India and the spread of Marxism, the YMBA renamed itself the General Council of Burmese Associations and demanded more autonomy for Myanmar. A strike was organized at Rangoon University, and this spread across the country as schools were boycotted. The most serious uprising was initiated by a monk called Saya San; it represented the first concerted effort to expel the British by force. From 1930-1932, during what became known as the Saya San Rebellion, 3,000 of his men were massacred and 9,000 taken prisoner, while the government suffered casualties of only 138. Saya San was hanged in 1937. The underground nationalist movement also gained momentum in the 1930s and at the University of Rangoon the All-Burma Student Movement emerged. The colonial regime was clearly shaken by the extent of the unrest and the level of violence and in 1935 the Government of Burma Act finally granted Myanmar autonomy. In 1936, the groups' leaders – Thakin Aung San and Thakin Nu – led another strike at the University. They called themselves Thakin, meaning 'master' as this was the honorific term the British insisted on when Burmese referred to them. In 1937 Myanmar was formally separated from British India. It received its own constitution, an elected legislature and four popular governments served before the Japanese occupation.

WW2 AND INDEPENDENCE

Japan invaded Myanmar in 1942, assisted by the new Burmese Independence Army (BIA) – a band of men secretly trained by the Japanese before the war and led by Aung San, who had emerged as one of the outstanding leaders during the student riots in Yangon. The BIA grew in number from 30 to 23,000 as Japan advanced through Lower Burma. The Burmese saw the Japanese occupation as a way to expel the British colonialists and to gain independence. The British were quickly overwhelmed by the rapid advance of the Japanese 15th Army and retreated, still fighting, to India. Their 'scorched earth' policy – which involved torching everything of value and sabotaging the infrastructure they had built up over decades – left devastation in its wake. Fierce warfare erupted between the British and the Japanese and BIA, in which casualties were high – as many as 27,000 may have died. Many of the British and Allied troops who died – some in hand-to-hand combat – are buried at the Htaukkyan Cemetery near Yangon (see page 128).

The war in Myanmar, though limited when compared with other conflicts of the Second World War, produced more than its fair share of heroes. Stilwell, an American, having retreated through the jungle into India with 114 men, retraced his steps through Assam, across the Chindwin River to Myitkyina, and helped recapture Yangon in May 1945. Wingate, a British war-hero, successfully penetrated the Japanese lines. His men were known as the Chindits – after the mythological Chinthes, the undefeatable temple lions. In the air, Chennault led the highly successful 'Flying Tigers' airborne division. US ground forces in Myanmar were known as 'Merrill's Marauders' and consisted of about 3,000 men, of which many were killed. But perhaps the outstanding hero of the Myanmar campaign was General William Slim, head of the 14th Army, which killed all but a few thousand of the 200,000 Japanese in Myanmar.

The 800 km-long Ledo Rd – from Assam to Mong Yo, where it joins the Burma Road – was built during the war by 35,000 Burmese and several thousand engineers, as a supply route to China. Many died during the construction process; the Ledo Road ran through jungle and mountainous terrain and became known as 'the man-a-mile road'. Until it was completed, supplies were flown in over the 'hump' – the high Himalayan peaks – one of the most hazardous air routes of the war. Scores of planes were shot down and more than 1,000 airmen killed.

Under Japanese occupation, Myanmar was declared independent, with Aung San as Minister of Defence and General Ne Win as Chief-of-Staff of the newly formed Burma National Army (BNA). The BNA initially fought with the Japanese, but began to realize that the occupiers did not have their best interests at heart. The Japanese alienated the local population and throughout the country there were stories of Japanese cruelty. Aung San eventually dispatched an envoy to India to negotiate with the British – although his critics claim he was really only prompted to do this because the Japanese were losing the war elsewhere in Asia and he did not want to end up on the wrong side. In Mar 1945, under the leadership of Aung San, Burmese troops switched their allegiance to the Allies and participated in the final stages of the Allied victory, helping British General Slim and the

14th Army recapture Yangon. The Japanese surrendered in Aug 1945 but as they departed they too left a trail of destruction.

By the end of the war the Burmese economy, which before the conflict had been one of the most productive in Asia, was devastated. Oil production had slumped as wells fell into disrepair, and about a third of all cultivated land lay idle. After the war the British tried to re-establish colonial rule, but the nationalist movement, led by Aung San, proved too strong. In Sep 1946, a general strike forced the colonial government to the negotiating table and Aung San demanded independence. The wartime leadership of British Prime Minister, Sir Winston Churchill, came to an end and Clement Atlee's new Labour government in London was far more sympathetic to the cause of Burmese self-determination. A conference was held in London in Jan 1947 – at which minority groups were not represented – and the British dropped all opposition to Burmese independence. The support of the hill peoples was crucial to Aung San's plan to form a union and he signed the Panglong Agreement with minority leaders. Under the terms of this treaty, some ethnic minority groups would be allowed to secede from the union after 10 years. Each state was to have an elected council charged with the management of education and local taxation.

National elections were held in Apr 1947. Aung San and his Anti-Fascist People's Freedom League (AFPFL) won a landslide majority – capturing 248 of the 255 seats. But on 19 Jul, a few months before Myanmar was to be granted full independence, Aung San and five of his ministers were assassinated while attending a meeting in the Secretariat in Yangon. U-Saw, a overly ambitious right-wing prime minister in the pre-war colonial government was convicted of hatching the plot, and executed. It was a tragedy for Myanmar as Aung San seemed the only person with sufficient prestige and political skill to unite the many different factions and minorities. Had he lived, post-war Burmese history may have taken a very different course.

INDEPENDENCE

On 4 January 1948 at 0420 – an auspicious hour determined by Burmese astrologers – the Union Jack was lowered to the strains of *Auld Lang Syne* and U Nu, one of the early leaders of the student movement, became the first Prime Minister of independent Burma. It fell to U Nu to attempt to forge a national identity, build political institutions and rebuild the war-shattered economy. But Myanmar plunged immediately into chaos. Within 3 months, the Communists were in open revolt. The People's Volunteer Organization, a key component of the AFPFL split in two, with the majority siding with the Communists. Muslim separatists rebelled in Rakhine and the Karen National Union (KNU), upset at the prospect of Burman domination, refused to be a part of independent Myanmar and unilaterally declared their own independence on 5 May 1948. A large number of Karen had converted to Christianity during the 19th century and sided with the British before and during the war. Other ethnic groups also revolted: within the first year U Nu's government faced nine separatist insurrections.

BUILDING SOCIALISM AND THE RISE OF NE WIN

Gradually the government regained military control – aided by the fact that the rebels were busy fighting each other as well as the government. By 1951, U Nu was finally in charge of the situation. He set about building a socialist state, nationalizing former British companies and expanding the health service and education. Elections were held in 1951 and 1956; both were won by U Nu's faction of the AFPFL. But in 1958 the party

Bogyoke Aung San – young blood

Myanmar's national hero and most famous martyr, whose portrait was held aloft in the pro-democracy demonstrations of 1988, was born in Natmauk, central Myanmar in 1915. At Rangoon University he read English, modern history and political science and became involved in politics. He emerged as a leader of the Burmese student movement and at one stage was suspended from the university for provocative articles which were published in the university magazine. He was a leading light of the All-Burma Student Movement and as an organizer of the 1936 student strike, he gained notoriety with the British colonial regime. He was arrested in 1939, the year he became secretary of the Communist Party of Burma. The following year he fled to Japan and received military training from the Japanese. His group of 'Thirty Comrades' founded the Burma National Army (BNA) which fought alongside the Japanese 15th Army for much of WW2.

The BNA gained prestige in Myanmar by taking over day-to-day administration of the country – particularly in rural areas – during the Japanese occupation. Bogyoke (General) Aung San became defence minister of the Japanese-backed 'puppet' administration. In 1943 Myanmar was granted nominal independence by the Japanese, but by then, Aung San and his colleagues had turned against their erstwhile supporters, and had formed the Anti-Facist People's Freedom League, which established contacts with the British army in India. In the dying months of the war, Aung San switched allegiance to the Allies and his forces joined British troops in recapturing Yangon and driving the Japanese out.

The British wanted to treat Aung San as a collaborator but Admiral Lord Louis Mountbatten – the Supreme Commander of Allied Forces in Southeast Asia – stepped in, believing the 30-year-old Aung San to be the one man who could bridge the warring political and ethnic factions in Myanmar. The following year, Aung San negotiated a deal with British Prime Minister Clement Atlee by which Myanmar would be granted independence. In 1947, 3 months before his party swept the polls, he signed an agreement with ethnic minority leaders. All seemed set for Aung San to emerge as the leader of an independent, united Myanmar. These hopes were shattered on 19 July 1947.

The fateful event is described by Myanmar-specialist Bertil Lintner: "...two military jeeps sped down the streets of Yangon. They stopped outside what was then the Secretariat in Dalhousie Street [now Maha Bandoola Street]. Some young men in uniform, armed with sub-machine guns, jumped out and rushed into the old, colonial red-brick building. On reaching the room where Aung San was holding a cabinet meeting... they pointed their guns at the assembled ministers, shouting: "Remain seated! Don't move!" Aung San rose to his feet – and the men opened fire. The shooting continued for about 30 secs, and then the uniformed men left the building, jumped into their jeeps outside and sped off... It was 10.37 am." Later the same day, U Saw, a right-wing politician who had been a rival for the premiership, was arrested and charged; the following May, he was convicted and hanged. Aung San left a widow and three children; two boys (one of whom drowned) and a daughter, Suu Kyi. 41 years later, Suu Kyi brought the Aung San name back to the forefront of Burmese politics by stepping into her father's activist shoes (see page 82).

formally split and to avoid open revolt, U Nu invited his defence minister and army chief-of-staff, General Ne Win, to form a military caretaker government until elections could be held. Some analysts have argued that this so-called 'constitutional coup' provided Ne Win with the confidence to attempt the second permanent, and this time unconstitutional, coup 4 years later. But on this occasion the general relinquished power gracefully and when elections were finally held in 1960, U Nu won an overwhelming victory – despite the split in the AFPFL. But rebel insurrections confounded his plans for a second time: by 1961 minority revolts by the Shan and Kachins were in full swing. Tensions were exacerbated when U Nu pushed a constitutional amendment through parliament making Buddhism the state religion, which alienated the Christian minorities, like the Karen, still further.

On 2 March 1962 the military engineered a surgically efficient – and almost bloodless – coup d'état, under the leadership of Ne Win. Government ministers and ethnic minority leaders were arrested: they had all been in Yangon attending a conference aimed at resolving the secessionist insurrections. The constitution was swept aside and a 17-man Revolutionary Council (hand-picked by Ne Win) began to rule by decree, ending Myanmar's 14-year parliamentary democracy. The ideology of the military government – called the 'new order' – was set out in a communiqué entitled *The Burmese way to socialism*, published the month after the coup. The other seminal document of the regime was published in 1964: *The correlation of man and his environment*, which was an eccentric mix of Marxism-Leninism and Theravada Buddhism.

State control was gradually extended over most aspects of Burmese life: industries were nationalized and the economy began its long journey from stagnation into effective collapse. The country entered a state of self-imposed isolation and the military government – which maintained rigid internal control – faced insurrection after insurrection from ethnic minorities and Communists. To mobilize popular support the Revolutionary Council formed the military Burma Socialist Programme Party (BSPP or *Lanzin*).

Five months after the government was installed, students protested against the military dictatorship. The next day the student union building was blown up by the army. Ne Win imprisoned all opposition politicians. U Nu was released in 1968 and demanded a return to democracy; he then travelled around the world, denouncing the Ne Win government before accepting asylum in Thailand where he formed the National United Liberation Front (NULF). The NULF rebels launched a series of raids across the Thai border into Burmese territory, but these failed to pose a threat to the government in Yangon. In 1972 U Nu resigned from politics altogether. This came as a great relief to the government as the former Prime Minister had provided a focus for countless opposition groups.

In 1971 the Revolutionary Council announced plans to draw up a new constitution aimed at transferring power to civilian politicians. The following year Ne Win and 20 of his senior commanders in the military élite resigned their army posts and declared themselves the civilian Government of the Union of Burma.

The Socialist Republic of the Union of Burma came into existence on 3 January 1974, following the promulgation of a new constitution. Myanmar became a unitary state with effective power in the hands of the Burman majority at the centre. Lip service was paid to minority rights. Political power was vested in the BSPP which was the only recognized party in the country; as its chairman, Ne Win became the head of the Council of

General Ne Win – the man who would be king

Myanmar's old military dictator, Ne Win, has been at the helm of Myanmar's military regime since his coup d'état in 1962. Burmese do not mention him by name – they simply call him 'Number One'. He is believed to have amassed a sizeable personal fortune which is held in foreign banks. It was Ne Win who created Military Intelligence (MI) which over the years has built up a network of spies throughout Myanmar (see page 81). Unsurprisingly, however, he is said to be paranoid about his personal security – he reportedly keeps a revolver on his desk and on the rare occasions he ventures out in public, he is surrounded by bodyguards.

Ironically, Ne Win is not a Burman. The man who expelled foreign nationals from Burma is himself half-Chinese and was called Shu Maung before he settled on what he thought was an appropriate Burmese name: Ne Win means 'Brilliant as the Sun'. In the early 1940s he became one of nationalist leader Aung San's 'Thirty Comrades' who led the Burma National Army during WW2 and who all took their own *nom de guerre* like Ne Win. They received their military training from the Japanese Imperial Army before the war, and in the days running up to the Japanese invasion of Myanmar, gathered in Bangkok where they pledged undying allegiance, drinking each other's blood from a communal cup.

Before the war Shu Maung studied medicine at Judson College, Yangon, but failed to complete the course and became involved in politics through his uncle, who was a member of the pre-war Thakin Party. Following Aung San's assassination in 1947, Bogyoke (General) Ne Win headed the army and 10 years after independence, when Prime Minister U Nu's elected government was threatening to fall apart, he was invited to form a caretaker government – the so-called 'constitutional coup'. This evidently gave the general a taste for power, for on 2 March 1962 he led a successful coup, after which he headed the Revolutionary Council and presided over the disintegration of the economy. In 1974, he suddenly announced that he had become a civilian and was to be known as U Ne Win. He now led a one-party 'socialist' state. In 1981 he retired as head of state but maintained political control as chairman of the Burma Socialist Programme Party, the country's only legal party. Regular purges of the military leadership, in which those exhibiting leadership qualities were eliminated, allowed Ne Win to retain power.

Ne Win's superstitious convictions are legendary. He believes in *yedaya chay*, the old Burmese theory that fate can be outwitted by prompt action. On one

State and the new President of Myanmar. Discontent with the state of the economy triggered a coup attempt in Jul 1976, led by junior military officers. Everyone who did not turn state's evidence was shot and General Tun U, the chief-of-staff was sentenced to 7 years' hard labour for failing to forewarn Ne Win. Because of growing political unrest, the BSPP was reorganized and tens of thousands of party members were expelled for 'being out of touch'; more than half the central committee was forced to resign. Over the course of the next year, the vacant places were gradually filled again by retired military officers.

Despite continued dissatisfaction and ongoing insurgencies (about 40% of the country was outside government control), Ne Win managed to bring the Buddhist *sangha* (order of monks) under his wing, giving Ne Win the confidence occasion, he ordered the introduction of bank notes in denominations of 45 and 90 kyat on the grounds that they were divisible by nine – his lucky number. Many people lost their life-savings as a result. When his chief astrologer pronounced that the left side was unlucky and that he should "move the country more to the right", he directed that traffic should immediately change to driving on the right. According to some reports he ordered the demolition of the village at Pagan because he was embarrassed to be seen consulting Pagan's astrologers on such a regular basis (see page 183). During the 1993 National Convention Ne Win's hand was obvious in the choice of astrologically-sound numbers. It was convened on 9 Jan – a very auspicious date. A total of 702 delegates were invited (7+0+2=9). That only 699 attended was regarded as an astrological catastrophe.

Ne Win is said to have married seven times. He has four children from Daw Khin May – better known as Kitty – who he married just before the coup in 1962. His eldest daughter, Sanda, is supposed to be his favourite. He is thought to live in the same house – a magnificent villa – as Sanda on Ady Road, on the shores of Inya Lake in Yangon. She is known to be close to Major-General Khin Nyunt, Ne Win's protegé and the head of MI. When Kitty died in 1974, he married an academic, Daw Ni Ni Myint, then divorced her and married June Rose Bellamy (Yadana Nat Mai). She is an Australian great-granddaughter of King Mindon, penultimate monarch of Myanmar's Konbaung Dynasty (see page 43). There was much speculation in the 1980s that Ne Win was interested in declaring himself King and his marriage to June Rose was probably calculated to legitimize his claim. On one occasion he went to great trouble to retrieve a statue of King Alaungpaya, founder of the last dynasty of Konbaung, from London's Victoria & Albert Museum.

His marriage to June Rose did not last long and he remarried Daw Ni Ni Myint. In 1988 astrologers recommended he should take another wife and he is believed to have married an Arakanese girl in her mid-20s. Ne Win is now an octogenarian and rumours surface every so often that he is dead; other rumours suggest he is suffering from senile dementia. Calculating that his days were numbered, and having headed a brutal regime since 1962, Ne Win spent the 1980s making merit. He did this in the traditional manner employed by Burmese kings – he built a pagoda. His Maha Wizaya (Great Conquerer) Pagoda (see page 112) stands on the site of Signal Pagoda near the Shwedagon in Yangon. Although he no longer holds a title, Ne Win remains the most influential man in the country.

to declare an amnesty which allowed dissidents like U Nu to return to Myanmar in 1980. Ne Win resigned as president in 1981 but remained chairman of the BSPP and retained his grip on the leadership. By the mid-1980s his once self-sufficient country was on the verge of bankruptcy and in 1987 was conferred 'least-developed nation' (LLDC) status by the UN and international aid agencies. Economic mismanagement, poverty and the demonetization of the kyat helped spark the pro-democracy demonstrations of 1988 (see page 79).

Art and architecture

A result of Myanmar's international isolation has been the preservation of its varied cultural traditions. Unlike most other countries in the region, it has not been invaded by Coca-Cola culture. In the late 1940s, former Prime Minister U Nu remarked: "We gained our independence without losing our self respect; we cling to our culture and our traditions and these we now hold to cherish and to develop in accordance with the genius of our people". Since Burmese independence, many minority groups have clung a little too tenaciously to their tribal cultures for the government's liking.

Myanmar was at the confluence of Indian and Chinese cultural traditions; ethnically, most Burmese are more closely linked to the Chinese than the Indians – other than the Arakanese (Rakhines). However, Chinese influence in Myanmar is far less pronounced than it is in Indochina as Myanmar was so distant from Peking. (The four Chinese invasions from 1765 to 1769 under the Ch'ing Dynasty failed.) Culturally, Indian influence has predominated. Myanmar adopted Pali, the Indian language of the Theravada Buddhist scriptures, and Buddhism was brought to Myanmar from India. Indian architecture provided the inspiration for most early Burmese monumental art and the Indian concept of kingship – rather than the Chinese Confucian bureaucracies – was a model for the Burmese dynasties. Burmese food is based on the Indian curry, and the most visually obvious of all Indian influences is the *longyi*, the Burmese sarong.

The diffuse cultural traditions of Myanmar's various ethnic groups have influenced mainstream Burmese art; they in turn have been influenced by Burmese art. One of the earliest cultures was the Pyu. Early Chinese accounts talk of the wealth of the Pyu civilization and of the opulence of court life at Sri Ksetra. The king was carried on a golden litter, women wore silk and men and women were adorned with jewels. Inscriptions suggest that the Pyu were influenced by Indian culture. The Pyu left behind bronze and stone sculptures which indicate a high level of craftsmanship. Many pieces are similar in style to the late Gupta or post-Gupta style in India – Buddha statues are seated with their legs crossed and wearing tight clinging robes. Hindu statues dating from the same period show similarities with the Pallava period in S India.

The Mon created the next great Burmese civilization and developed a sophisticated culture, which was also deeply Indianized. For most of their history the Mon were Theravada Buddhists, but Hinduism later became more popular – little material evidence of the earlier Buddhist culture remains. The Mon were eventually absorbed into other states but continued to exert a strong cultural influence on other kingdoms – particularly Bagan. The Burmans founded Bagan in the 9th century and a large amount of high-quality sculpture and painting has survived. This period is usually regarded as the Golden Age of Burmese art. The art of Bagan was mainly connected with Theravada Buddhism: most remains are sculpted images of the Buddha. Crowned Buddha-figures appear for the first time during the Bagan period.

After Bagan fell to Kublai Khan in 1287, the stylistic variety of the Buddha images increased; most art historians speculate that this was due to the increased influence of the Siamese, or the Shan, or possibly because of the re-emergence of the Mon in the S. Traits of typical Burmese Buddhist figures became firmly established after the 13th century – fingers and toes are of equal length, tall projections (representing flames or lotus buds) crown the Buddha's head and the earlobes touch the shoulders. Towards the end of the 18th century a more naturalistic style arose in which the Buddha's robes were depicted in loose folds, fingers and toes were of unequal length and a wide band often decorated the forehead.

Some of the best relief work found in Myanmar is on the large gilded *sutra* chests, which are used to store the manuscripts of the sacred Buddhist texts. They often carry scenes from the Buddha's life. Another kind of temple furniture in which the Burmese excelled was red lacquerware (see page 77), usually with black figures and intricate ornamentation. The most common items were alms bowls to receive food offerings; many of these are also of beautiful design, with tiered and spired lids, like pagodas.

The Burmese arts fell into disarray during the British colonial period mainly because, with the demise of the monarchy in 1886, there was no longer any royal patronage. Burmese artists tended to adapt to English Victorian and Edwardian ideas of decoration. The magnificent wall paintings and frescoes at Bagan contrast sharply with the stagnation of contemporary Burmese painting, which, for the most part, still caters for 19th century English watercolour tastes. Woodcarving has also declined, and like lacquerware and embroidery, it has been imitated in Thailand; just S of Chiang Mai, for example, there are factories turning out 'Burmese handicrafts' for the tourist industry and for export to the West. Silversmiths in Yangon and Mandalay are not in much demand these days either.

Most of the monumental remains in Myanmar are religious buildings. Buddhists lavish much of their surplus wealth on the construction and upkeep of stupas and temples – the surest way of attaining merit (see page 66). Because most secular structures – even palaces – were built of timber, bamboo and thatch, they have since rotted away.

The normal stupa is a tall structure incorporating a solid dome, surmounted by a *harmika* with a relic chamber set into the dome. Above the harmika is a pointed spire with *hti*, or honorific umbrellas of decreasing size set one above the other. Burmese architecture, which reached great and soaring beauty in the temples at Bagan, is now a lost art. A detailed account of the evolution of architectural styles at Bagan and the component parts of Burmese religious architecture starts on page 179. Only one or two Burmese architects have had a hand in any of the major buildings erected since WW2; most designs were submitted by foreign – particularly British – architects.

Mudras and the Buddha image

An artist producing an image of the Buddha does not try to create an original piece of art; he is trying to be faithful to a tradition which can be traced back over centuries. It is important to appreciate that the Buddha image is not merely a work of art but an object of, and for worship. Sanskrit poetry even sets down the characteristics of the Buddha – albeit in rather unlikely terms: legs like a deer, arms like an elephant's trunk, a chin like a mango stone and hair like the stings of scorpions. The Pali texts of Theravada Buddhism add the 108 auspicious signs, long toes and fingers of equal length, body like a banyan tree and eyelashes like a cow's. The Buddha can be represented either sitting, lying (indicating *paranirvana*), or standing, and (in Thailand) occasionally walking. He is often represented standing on an open lotus flower: the Buddha was born into an impure world, and likewise the lotus germinates in mud but rises above the filth to flower. Each image will be represented in a particular *mudra* or 'attitude', of which there are 40. The most common are:

Abhayamudra – dispelling fear or giving protection; right hand (sometimes both hands) raised, palm outwards, usually with the Buddha in a standing position.

Varamudra – giving blessing or charity; the right hand pointing downwards, the palm facing outwards, with the Buddha either seated or standing.

Vitarkamudra – preaching mudra; the ends of the thumb and index finger of the right hand touch to form a circle, symbolizing the Wheel of Law. The Buddha can either be seated or standing.

Dharmacakramudra – 'spinning the Wheel of Law'; a preaching mudra symbolizing the teaching of the first sermon. The hands are held in front of the chest, thumbs and index fingers of both joined, one facing inwards and one outwards.

Bhumisparcamudra – 'calling the earth goddess to witness' or 'touching the earth'; the right hand rests on the right knee with the tips of the fingers 'touching ground', thus calling the earth goddess Dharani/Thoranee to witness his enlightenment and victory over Mara, the king of demons. The Buddha is always seated.

Dhyanamudra – meditation; both hands resting open, palms upwards, in the lap, right over left.

Other points of note:

Vajrasana – yogic posture of meditation; cross-legged, both soles of the feet visible.

Virasana – yogic posture of meditation; cross-legged, but with the right leg on top of the left, covering the left foot (also known as *paryankasana*).

Buddha under Naga – a common image in Khmer art; the Buddha is shown seated in an attitude of meditation with a cobra rearing up over his head. This refers to an episode in the Buddha's life when he was meditating; a rain storm broke and Nagaraja, the king of the nagas (snakes), curled up under the Buddha (seven coils) and then used his 7-headed hood to protect the Holy One from the falling rain.

Buddha calling for rain – a common image in Laos; the Buddha is depicted standing, both arms held stiffly at the side of the body, fingers pointing downwards.

Bhumisparcamudra – calling the earth goddess to witness

Dhyanamudra – meditation

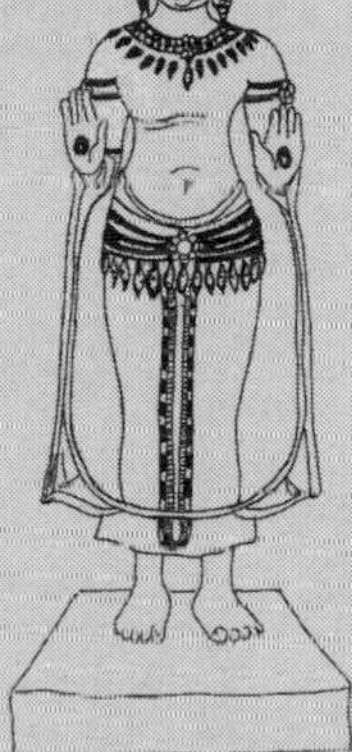

Abhayamudra – dispelling fear or giving protection

Vitarkamudra – preaching, "spinning the Wheel of Law"

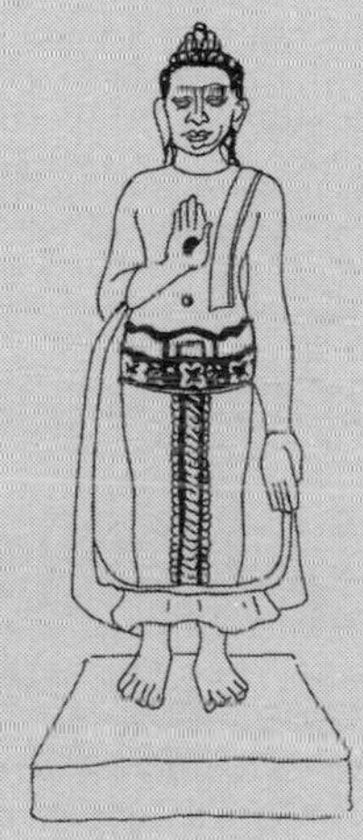

Abhayamudra – dispelling fear or giving protection; subduing Mara position

ZTB 201

Culture

PEOPLE

Myanmar's population was estimated at about 46 million in 1995. The greatest concentration is in the Ayeyarwady delta region, where – along with Rakhine and Tenasserim – the Burmans form the majority. The term 'Burman' refers to the largest and culturally dominant ethnic group in Myanmar, while 'Burmese' includes all ethnic groups within the Union of Burma – the ruling State Law and Order Restoration Council recognizes 135 nationalities. The upland areas are inhabited by minorities of which the Karen are the most numerous.

There were three main migrations from the N into Myanmar:

1) The Mon-Khmer entered Myanmar mainly from the E and are now represented by a number of small tribes – the Wa, La, Tai, Loi, Palaung, Pale, Miao, Yao, Riang, En, Padaung and the Mon, who gained a foothold in the S of Myanmar.

2) The Tibeto-Burmans occupied the upper reaches of the Ayeyarwady River and founded Bagan. They were then associated with a number of succeeding capitals at Taungoo, Ava, Amarapura, Sagaing and Mandalay. This group subdivides into:

i) the proto-Burmese such as the Taungoo, Yau, Kadu, Hpon, Lashi, Atsi, Danu, Intha and Arakanese (Rakhines)

ii) the Chin-Kachin including the Chin, Kachin, Gauri, Sing-po and Duleng

iii) the Lolo including the Lolo, Lisu, Lahu, Muhso, Kwi, Moso, Kaw and Ako.

3) The Tai-Chinese migrated from Yunnan to the Shan states. It was this movement which broke up the Burmese civilization at Bagan and turned most of Upper Burma over to Shan control during the 13th and 15th centuries.

Today roughly two-thirds of the population is Burman while the remaining population is divided into five main minority groups, each with its own history, language and culture. The most sizeable ethnic minorities are Shan 11%, Karen 7%, Kachin 6%, Arakanese (Rakhines) 4% and Chin 2%. These figures, though, are only rough estimates. The proportion of Burmans in the total population is a politically charged issue and the last census which recorded ethnicity was conducted in 1931.

The Burmese flag: minority stars

The old Burmese national flag symbolized the country's minorities in an interesting way. The flag was red, to symbolize courage. In the top left-hand corner was a blue field, in the middle of which was a large white star. The star represented the whole country. Around this star were five smaller stars: one represented the Kachin, another the Shan, a 3rd the Karen and a 4th the Chin. The 5th star represented the largest group, the Burmans, who shared the star with the Mon and Arakanese.

THE BURMANS

The central plains are the traditional home of the Burmans, the largest ethnic group in the country. They comprise about two thirds of the population and are of Tibeto-Burman descent, having migrated from SW China. The Burmans gradually replaced or absorbed another Tibeto-Burman group, the Pyu, who occupied the central Ayeyarwady valley and left important monuments at Sri

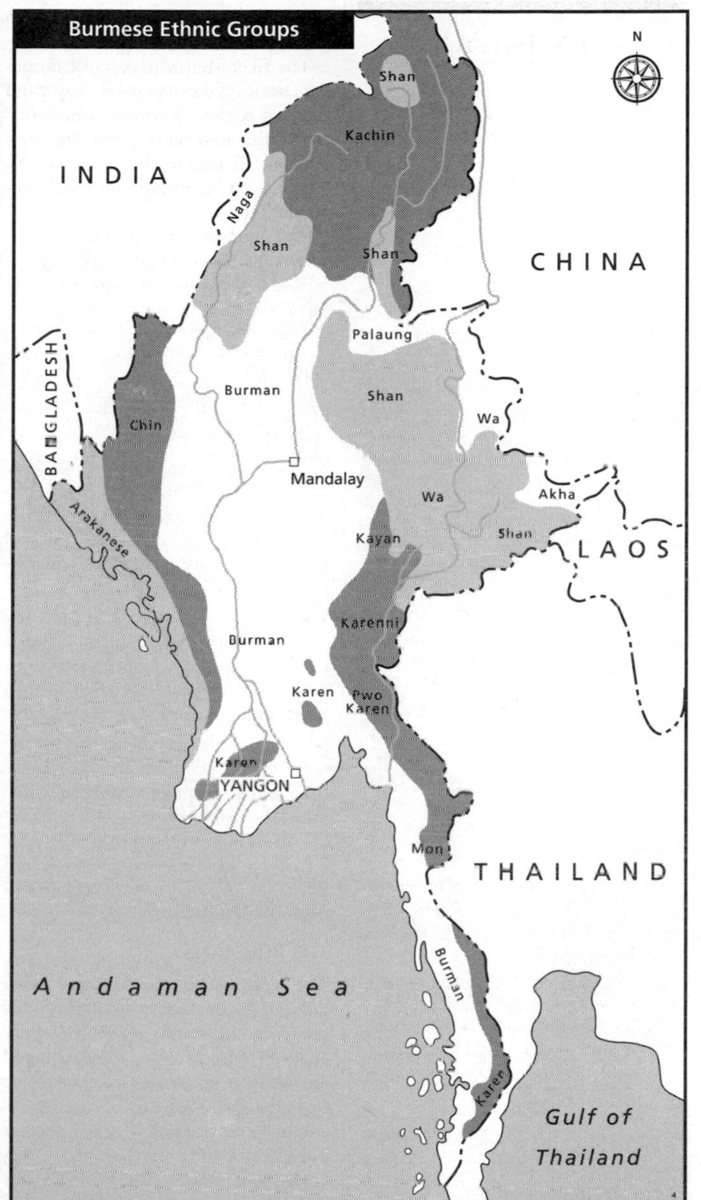
Burmese Ethnic Groups
N
INDIA
CHINA
BANGLADESH
LAOS
THAILAND
Andaman Sea
Gulf of Thailand
Shan
Kachin
Naga
Shan
Shan
Palaung
Burman
Shan
Chin
Wa
Mandalay
Wa
Akha
Arakanese
Kayan
Shan
Karenni
Burman
Karen
Pwo Karen
Karen
YANGON
Mon
Burman
Karen

Ksetra near Pyay. The Burmans built their first and greatest capital at Bagan (849-1287) on the banks of the Ayeyarwady – now one of the world's archaeological treasures (see page 178). Successive Burman capitals were built at Taungoo, Ava, Sagaing, Amarapura and Mandalay. While the Burmans are all Burmese, the converse is not true; the language Burmans speak is, however, called Burmese.

THE MON

Although the Mon were a powerful group in Burmese history they have largely been assimilated into Burman culture. There is an historical irony in this however, because many of the most important elements of Burman culture were originally derived from the Mon. It was also the Mon who introduced Theravada Buddhism to Myanmar along with the Indian alphabet. The Mon are of Mon-Khmer descent and were linguistically closer to the Khmers of Cambodia than to Burmans. They had major cultural centres first at Pyay and Thaton. Thaton, to the E of Yangon, across the Gulf of Mottama, was a busy port through which the Mon developed strong ties with India. The Mon were later centred at Bago which became an important trading centre.

THE SHAN

The Shan migrated from Nanchao in present-day Yunnan Province, SW China. They are of Tai descent – they are ethnic kinsfolk of the Tai and Lao – and speak a Tai dialect. Politically, the Shan enjoy greater autonomy than other minority groups and occupy the Shan plateau. The Shan State forms a large part of the Golden Triangle (see page 86) and opium poppy cultivation helps finance Shan military activity. Originally the plateau area was comprised of sub-states ruled by feudal princes or *sawbwas*. Whenever these sawbwas could bury their differences, they posed a serious threat to the rival Burman dynasties. Following the sacking of Bagan in 1287, the Shan nearly succeeded in creating their own empire, but internal rivalries prevented them from uniting into a cohesive political force. They did, however, expand to control central Myanmar for about 2 centuries. In 1959 the sawbwas signed an agreement with the Ne Win caretaker government, renouncing all their hereditary rights. Today the Shan area is called Shan State encompassing all the old Shan states. The Shan are historically the most autonomous and politically sophisticated group. The main party is the Shan State Progress Party (SSPP) which came second in the 1990 elections after the National League for Democracy (NLD).

The 4 million people who live in Shan State belong to 32 different groups; these can be divided into six main ones – the Shan, Pa-O, Intha, Taungyoe, Danu and Palaung. Many ethnic minorities from all the different groups congregate at the regional periodic markets which rotate around the area over a 5-day period (see page 224).

The **Shan** are the most numerous and were the first immigrants to the region. As they are descended from Tai-Chinese stock they have a paler complexion than some other minority groups. The Shan are traditionally traders but are also very artistic and are well known for their silverware and lacquerware. The traditional Shan dress is usually worn only on formal occasions now – most wear Burmese costume, although men still wear traditional baggy trousers. Their traditional dress includes a Chinese-style jacket with a turban, which is usually pink, blue or yellow. Shan women also wear turbans embroidered with gold or bright primary colours as well as a colourful striped lungyi and a tight-fitting jacket.

The **Pa-O** are the second most numerous minority group in the region and mainly live around Taunggyi. They are descended from Tibeto-Burman stock. The Pa-O are very religious, and although previously animist, most are now Buddhist. They are farmers and their main cash crop is leaves from the *cordia* trees, which are used for rolling cheroots (see page 234). The men wear similar trousers, jackets and turbans to the Shan but they are always black. The women wear lungyis, long sleeveless shirts and cropped long-sleeved jackets, which are also jet black, but with a brightly coloured turban.

The **Intha** people live around Inle Lake; *Intha* means 'sons of the lake'. Like the Pa-O, they are Tibeto-Burman, but they are thought to be descendants of the S Burmans, who migrated N during the reign of King Narapatisithu (1173-1210). The Intha are well known for their one-legged rowing technique, which the fishermen developed to enable them to keep two hands free for fishing. Because they do not have much fertile land, the Intha also developed a system of floating gardens which now provide most of the vegetables for the surrounding area (see page 229). The majority of the Intha are Buddhist. Most of the Intha wear Burmese costume – lungyis and open-necked shirts.

The **Taungyoe** tend to live in the hill regions above Inle lake and are also farmers of Tibeto-Burmese stock. There is a large group of Taungyoe in the Heho area. The Taungyoe wear a similar costume to the Pa-O but the women can be distinguished by the heavy rings below the knee. If they are married the bronze rings are just under the knee but if they are single they wear silver rings at the ankles.

The **Danu** – who are also of Tibeto-Burmese descent – live in the Pindaya Cave area (see page 227). The name *Danu* comes from *donake*, meaning 'brave archers'. In the 16th century the Danu were King Alaungpaya's archers and on returning from wars in Thailand settled in the Pindaya area. They are a farming people and speak Burmese, with a slightly different accent, and wear Burmese costume.

The **Palaung** are descended from Mon-Khmer stock and inhabit the Kalaw area; they were amongst the earliest inhabitants of Myanmar. They are famous for growing tea – unlike other minorities they have never grown opium. Their traditional dress is very colourful. The women wear white, green, pink, red and blue jackets and a red striped lungyi. They also wear cane rings around the waist when they are married and heavy strings of beads around their necks. The older women shave their heads and wear white hoods. Unlike other tribes the Palaung live in small longhouses – several families share a longhouse on stilts.

THE KAREN

If Karen legends are to be believed, this group originated somewhere around the Gobi Desert, but practically nothing is known of their early history. Half the Karen live in NW Thailand, half in E Myanmar. They are the largest single minority in Myanmar. About 20% of the Karen are now Christian – most were converted by American missionaries at the beginning of this century. Karen mythology tells of a Great Book and a Teacher, which missionaries were quick to exploit. Their strong Christian background exacerbates the cultural rift between them and the Buddhist Burmans. The Karen group incorporates 11 smaller groups, including the Paku (White Karen), Pwo Karen and the Padaung (who live in the vicinity of Loikaw, Kayah State).

The Karen National Union or KNU have been in armed opposition to the government since 1948, representing one of the world's longest-running armed conflicts. Until it was taken in early 1995, the KNU's headquarters was the town of Manerplaw, near the Thai border and about 300 km NE of Yangon. The town was the capital of the self-declared independent state of 'Kawthoolei' or 'The Land of the Flower that Grows out of the Ashes'. The Karen fought for the British during the Second World War and hoped that their allegiance to the crown would be repaid with their being granted independent status. As it turned out, the British ignored their pleas, and the Karen found themselves unwilling included in a 'Greater' Myanmar. Until 1995 they managed to mount a highly effective armed struggle from their Manerplaw headquarters (see the Modern Myanmar section for more detail on the taking of the town).

Padaung womenfolk traditionally wear an uncomfortable stack of rings around their necks, which pushed their shoulders down and therefore gives the impression of lengthening their necks – this has resulted in their being dubbed the 'giraffe women' or 'long-necked Karen'. Every year a Padaung girl would traditionally add new rings to her collection, until she got married. The practice is dying out, although some younger women still wear the rings. Traditionally, however, their necks and legs were literally encased in brass wire. The brass collar apparently leads the head to shrink in size. The rings affect the shoulders which are compressed by their weight. Some say the custom began because Padaung men wanted to prevent invading tribes from kidnapping their women. (For more background on the Padaung see page 220.)

In the West, the Karen are one of the better known Burmese minorities as they were widely recruited by the British Army and fought against the Japanese during WW2. Because Burmese nationalists sided with the Japanese for most of the war (see page 46), the Karen were ostracized by other groups. The Karen National Liberation Army has been one of the best organized of Myanmar's ethnic insurgencies, and is mainly financed by tax revenue from the thriving smuggling business across the Thai border as well as from teak.

THE KACHIN

The Kachin are also a Tibeto-Burman people and originally migrated from W China, although more recently than the Burmans. They now occupy N Myanmar. They practice slash-and-burn agriculture and are skilled hunters. Most Kachin are animist but a significant number have converted to Christianity. The Kachin Independence Army (KIA) is the main party and has about 5000 regular fighters.

Burmese names

Family names are not used in Myanmar and it is impossible to determine a person's sex or marital status from their name. Boys and girls may have the same name, and women do not adopt their husband's name on marriage. Names reflect the day of the week a child is born – certain letters and consonants are divided up between the eight planets (see page 108). The day of the week on which a Burmese is born also determines which corner of a pagoda platform the person should pray on. There is a complex system of titles which denote social standing: as an adult a man will be called *U* (pronounced *Oo*) – which literally translates as 'uncle', but is a respectful 'Mr'. A woman is called *Daw* or 'aunt'; *Ko* means 'elder brother', *Maung*, 'younger brother' and *Ma* 'sister'. Many Burmese have now adopted first names. Other common titles are connected with the military: *Bogyoke* means General – but is only used for the very top generals. *Bo* and *Bohmu* are also titles for army officers.

THE CHIN AND THE NAGA

The Chin occupy the W mountains and are related to the Naga to the N – both are of Tibeto-Burmese stock. Both groups spread over the border into India. The Naga have gained a certain notoriety because of their hard-fought guerrilla war for independence in India. Both groups lead a more settled agricultural life than the Kachin. Many are still animist, although a number of Christian converts have begun to migrate away from the hills and into the valleys. Some Chin, like the neighbouring Naga, practised headhunting until quite recently. The Chin have 44 related languages.

THE ARAKANESE (RAKHINES)

The Arakanese have long been influenced by their proximity to India; they had independent kingdoms at Vesali until 1018 and then at Mrauk-U(1433-1784). Many are devout Buddhists (Rakhine). The main party is the National United Front of Arakan (NUFA). About one fifth of the Arakanese population is Muslim of Bengali descent; they are known as **Rohingyas** and have been persecuted over the past 200 years. The present government does not recognize the Rohingyas as one of Myanmar's 135 nationalities and has made a concerted effort to chase them out of the country (see page 65).

SMALLER ETHNIC GROUPS

The darker-complexioned, stocky **Wa** practiced headhunting as a part of their fertility rites until fairly recently; they are one of the better known of the smaller ethnic groups. About 30,000 Wa live along the border with China. The Beijing-supported Burma Communist Party recruited them to fight in their ranks against the Yangon government.

There are also **Indian** and **Chinese** minorities in Myanmar – the former comprises both Hindus and Muslims. Large numbers of Indians settled in Myanmar when it became part of British India. In 1939 it was estimated that 58% of the population of Yangon was Indian. Most of the Indian migrants were Chettiar moneylenders, who gained control of large areas of paddy land in the Ayeyarwady Delta region during the Great Depression in the 1930s (see page 44). Some fled when growing resentment triggered riots against them. But until 1960, Myanmar still had a large Indian minority of over a million. The bulk subsequently left the country due to the military government's economic mismanagement. The present Indian population is now greatly reduced (about 2% of the total population) and is probably exceeded by the Chinese. The Chinese have mainly settled on the NE trade routes and along the great rivers. A large number of Chinese left in 1967 when there were anti-Chinese riots in Yangon.

INSURGENCY

About a quarter of Myanmar's land area lies under the control of insurgent groups: it is a very divided Union. Many of the minorities feel subjugated politically, economically and culturally by the Burman majority. The resentment, which built up over centuries, has been aggravated by the events during WW2. The Karen remember massacres during the war; the Shan *sawbwa* (princes), the loss of their rights; the Kachin the loss of many of their villages to China under the border settlement of 1960; and the Rohingya Muslims, mainly in Rakhine state, have been persecuted and repeatedly driven out of the country by a government which claims they do not exist. Some groups want independence, others, just more autonomy. The main rebel offensives against the government began with the Karen in 1949, followed by the Shan in 1958 and the Kachin in 1961.

The concept of national loyalty is alien to many of these groups as so many straddle Myanmar's international frontiers.

Some Shan live in China, Thailand and Laos for example, Kachin live in both Myanmar and China and Karen live on both sides of the Thai-Burmese border. Since independence in 1948, several groups have been engaged in protracted armed struggles against the government. The existence of the insurgencies is partly due to the British colonial policy of divide and rule, which gave the groups some measure of autonomy. Today, minority groups wield no political power – national policies are determined by the predominantly Burman government in Yangon.

The government has tried to court some minorities, while it has remained in a constant state of war against others. While national unity is, for the most part, in the government's interests, some analysts speculate that the military junta relishes ethnic conflicts as they provide a rallying call for ethnic Burmans. The civil wars also serve to divert attention away from the military's heavy-handedness within the Burmese heartland. Commentators believe that today there are too many historical and emotional impediments to be overcome for the government to ever hope of unifying the country.

In the past few years, however, some insurgent groups have been 'bought over' by the government. This started with the Communist Party of Burma (CPB) which, until Apr 1989, had posed constant security problems. A sudden mutiny sent its leaders fleeing into China and ended the CPB's 41-year insurgency; the government promptly signed a peace treaty with the CPB mutineers, many of whom were heroin addicts. Similar peace deals were negotiated with smaller insurgent groups which had relied on the CPB for arms and ammunition. These included a brigade of the Kachin Independence Army (KIA) and the Shan State Army. The rebels were awarded lucrative logging concessions and development aid in return for peace. Such policies have typified the government's way of dealing with insurrections: it has attempted to befriend smaller groups, while trying to obliterate the most powerful ones. The remaining three brigades of the KIA have come under mounting Chinese pressure to sit around the negotiating table with the Slorc. Talks between them were held in Jan and Mar 1993. The KIA wants the Slorc to talk to all the remaining rebel groups, which are loosely affiliated under the Democratic Alliance of Burma, along with elected members of the National League for Democracy (NLD) (see page 84), who fled following the 1990 election, and groups of students, who fled during and after the 1988 uprising. Yangon is thought unlikely to want to do this, preferring to do deals with individual groups. But both the regime and the rebels are being urged by countries as diverse as the US, China, Australia and Thailand to start talking. Myanmar specialists point out that peace deals with insurgent groups would negate the need for Myanmar's quarter-of-a-million strong army. The junta in Yangon would not feel secure without its huge military back-up.

The rebel coalition is headed by Bo Mya, President of the Karen National Union (KNU). The 'parallel government' of the NLD, which dates from Dec 1990 has said that if it ever gets to form a government in Yangon, the rights of minorities will be respected. The NLD has suggested that it may try to reinstate Aung San's 1947 constitution, which guarantees eventual autonomy to ethnic minority groups within a federal framework, based on his 1947 Panglong Agreement with minority leaders. In 1991 the Burmese government sent an ultimatum to villages in frontline areas; it read: "if we hear of any guerrillas in the village, we will totally wipe it out".

Some analysts say political independence does not make much practical economic sense for minorities as they would have few means of support. But much of Myanmar's oil, mineral and timber wealth – let alone opium – lies in minority territories. The Shan states and some of the Karen territories along the Thai border, for example, are rich in teak. This is another very good reason why the Burmese government has no wish to let them go. There are large jade deposits in N Myanmar and the Kachin Independence Army is partly funded through jade exports to China. The smuggling trade between Myanmar and Thailand has given Karen and Shan insurgents – who operate in the border regions – a secure economic base. By taxing shipments transiting their areas and by logging teak and mining precious stones for export, the rebel groups have developed sophisticated administrations. Lately, smuggling revenues have been undermined by Thai companies who have chosen to deal directly with Yangon in the hope of securing more logging concessions and facilitating commercial joint-ventures.

Thai logging companies – most connected to the Thai military – have the official approval of the Burmese government to negotiate with rebel groups to work in their territories. This strange triangular agreement between the rebels, Thai logging concerns and the junta in Yangon exists because the Burmese government is so in need of foreign exchange. In addition, the logging roads have allowed the Burmese military better access to rebel-held areas, enabling it to remain on the offensive year-round. The army has struck deals with Thai logging firms by which the timber companies build roads in exchange for lucrative logging concessions. Road construction teams were declared legitimate military targets by KNU leader Bo Mya in 1991.

MYANMAR'S DRUG BARONS AND THE OPIUM TRADE

The opium trade in the Shan and Kachin states provides funds for their armies as it did for the Burma Communist Party who were, until recently, operating in the remote N region. About half the heroin on America's streets comes from the Golden Triangle and Myanmar is by far the biggest producer (see page 86). To put

Khun Sa and Homong (Ho Mong)

In Jan 1996 the drug warlord Khun Sa surrendered to the military in Myanmar. He was airlifted to Yangon and Burmese soldiers took control of his former headquarters at Homong in Shan State, N of Mae Hong Son in Thailand and close to the border between the two countries. From being one of the wealthiest corners of Myanmar, it became just another destitute town in a destitute country. Within a few months the population dropped from 18,000 to 4,000 as people abandoned a place whose economic raison d'être had vanished in a puff of (opium) smoke. Khun Sa's army vanished, and with the men gone so the prostitutes and others who supported their various needs also left. The prostitutes went back to Thailand; and the soldiers melted into the jungle. The SLORC's men now dominate the town and there are plans to turn the textile mill into a chopstick factory, and the military hospital into a communication centre. The great hope, though, is that Homong can cash in on the tourist dollar. The town is just 40 mins from the Thai border, and then another 90 mins by 4WD vehicle from the border to the tourist centre of Mae Hong Son. Local businessmen are rubbing their hands at the thought of making Khun Sa's hill top 'White House' into a Golden Triangle Museum the size of Myanmar's drug trade into perspective, the US embassy in Yangon believes that the value of narcotics exports "appear to be worth as much as all legal exports" or close to US$1,000 million.

Much of the area where opium is grown was, until recently, controlled by independent opium warlords. The best known and the most powerful was **Chang Chi Fu**, better known by his alias **Khun Sa** – meaning 'Prince Prosperous', although he is more appropriately regarded as the 'Prince of Darkness'. Khun Sa in his heyday during the 1980s and through to 1995 was regarded by America's Drug Enforcement Agency as the 'most important mafia druglord in the entire globe'. He had his own private Mong Tai Army with 15,000 men under arms that controlled much of highland Shan state. His headquarters at Homong, near the Thai border, boasted its own factories, brothels, street lighting, telephones and power station. Although he may have sometimes claimed that he was a freedom fighter – Mong Tai means Shan State – few people believed that he was anything more than a drug baron. Other private armies that have been operating in the Golden Triangle – which are also mostly drugs-related – include the Kokang Army and the United Wa State Army.

Although he is the best known of these drug war lords, Khun Sa began to lose influence in the drug trade during 1995 and at the end of the year surrendered to the Slorc. It seems that the Thai government was anxious to cut off links with Khun Sa (all his supplies were trucked or carried by mule from Thailand) as Bangkok cultivated better relations with Yangon's generals, while Khun Sa's position in Shan state was being eroded by the Slorc's increasingly well-armed men. Being squeezed by Bangkok and Yangon, he decided to strike a deal with Yangon and surrender while he was still ahead. He was later airlifted to the capital where he claimed he just wanted to enjoy a quiet retirement. His HQ is now in the hands of the Slorc (see box page 63). The American authorities are anxious that he be extradited and stand trial in the US. This is unlikely: over the years he has allegedly gathered sufficient evidence to severely embarrass many of the Slorc generals and this is his guarantee of safety. He is apparently living in a plush villa on one of Yangon's lakes and has adopted the Burmese name U Htet Aung. It is assumed he enjoys the support and protection of the authorities.

With Khun Sa gone, attention has instead turned to the Wa. The United Wa State Army is said to be able to field a force of 20,000 to 30,000 people, headed by former Communist Chao Nyi Lai. It is the Wa who have replaced Khun Sa as the major player in the drug trade. This presents something of a dilemma for the US Drug Enforcement Agency who would like to work with Yangon to stamp out opium production, but who are barred from doing so because of the US government's policy of isolation towards Yangon. The other militia operating in the Golden Triangle is the Chinese nationalist Kuomintang-linked United Revolutionary Army.

With Khun Sa apparently out of the drug equation, most analysts took this to be good news for the enforcement agencies and bad news for drug traffickers. As if to reinforce this belief, by the middle of 1996 the price of heroin in Chiang Mai has quadrupled to nearly US$20,000 per kilo while on the streets of Bangkok it had increased 10-fold as supplies began to dry up. However, this optimism proved to be short-lived. By the end of the year, prices had begun to fall back to their level before Khun Sa's arrest and in Chiang Mai stood at around US$10,000 per kilo. The US State Department estimated that the 1996 harvest was around 250 tonnes, almost 10% up on the previous year.

Analysts have suggested that this could be interpreted in one, or both, of two ways. Either the authorities in Yangon were permitting Khun Sa to continue operating; or smaller producers had quickly expanded production to fill the void left by Khun Sa's exit. US Assistant Secretary of State for International Narcotics and Law-enforcement Affairs Robert Gelbard (and it has to be admitted that the US is hardly the junta's best friend) suggested that the Slorc was protecting "narco traffickers and harnessing their drug money for projects that do little to improve the lives of the Burmese people". Though Khun Sa may have withdrawn from hands-on management of opium production in the Golden Triangle, it has been suggested this has made control more difficult. Refining is now scattered among numerous small centres rather than being concentrated in a handful of large operations.

REFUGEES

The net effect of the continued Burmese army offensive against ethnic minority groups has been a growing refugee problem. There are an estimated half-a-million displaced persons within Myanmar itself, but it was refugees pouring into neighbouring Bangladesh, India, Thailand and even China that has caused mounting international concern. Numbers are hard to estimate and they also fluctuate from month to month. In the middle of 1996 there were 90,000 refugees from Myanmar in neighbouring Thailand, and 50,000 in Bangladesh. All refugee groups tell similar stories of human rights abuses by the army. The most serious refugee problem in recent years arose from the Yangon regime's refusal to recognize the Muslims of Rakhine state – who are known as Rohingya – as one of Myanmar's national minorities.

There is said to be a Burman proverb which goes: "If you see a snake and an Arakanese, kill the Arakanese first". There is a deep-seated loathing between the two. In the late 18th century, relations between Myanmar and British India became strained when King Bodawpaya chased tens of thousands of Rohingya over the border into what is now Bangladesh. That was the first recorded mass-exodus of Rohingya refugees; more recently, about 200,000 flooded across Myanmar's 237 km-long border with Bangladesh in 1978. The Burmese government claimed it had been trying to stamp out illegal immigration from Bangladesh. The problem was resolved quickly and the refugees repatriated. But the same thing happened in 1991/1992 when another 260,000 escaped from well-documented persecution by the Burmese Army. An Amnesty International report said: "Muslim men have been rounded up in large numbers and pressed into forced labour for the military, often as porters. They are ill-fed and abused, many are reported to have been beaten to death when they became too weak to carry their loads. Muslim women have been gang-raped in their homes, others have been held in army barracks and repeatedly raped." The men have also been forced to work as human mine-detectors.

The army has long exploited divisions between Rakhine's Buddhist population (known as the Mogh) and the Rohingya. Intervention by the UN eventually helped (but far from solved) the refugee problem and the government promised to curb the excesses of the armed forces. In May 1993, the UN High Commissioner for Refugees, Mrs Sadako Ogata, signed an agreement with the Bangladesh government providing for the repatriation of the refugees from camps around Cox's Bazaar. By Feb 1995, 135,000 had been repatriated, and at the end of the year it was thought that around 30-40,000 Rohinhyas remained in Bangladesh. Howev some commentators have question whether they have gone returned voluntarily, and wonder what has happened to them since their arrival 'home'. The Arakan Rohingya Islamic Front, under the command of Nurul Islam, stepped up its attacks on the Burmese military in the wake of the 1991/92 refugee crisis. It is reportedly receiving arms and military training from former Afghan *mujahiddin* guerrillas and Muslim Filipino Moro rebels – both of whom rallied to the Islamic cause. There is also a second, more militant group, the Rohingya Solidarity Organisation (RSO) who claim to have a small army.

RELIGION

Buddhism is Myanmar's state religion and about 85% of the population is Buddhist – almost every hill-top in the country has a pagoda on it. Buddhism came to Myanmar in several stages; first to arrive were Indian merchants and missionaries who travelled to Myanmar and taught the scriptures. The Moghul emperor Asoka is said to have visited the Shwedagon Pagoda in around 260 BC. But Theravada Buddhism was only fully established in Myanmar after King Anawrahta came to the throne at Bagan in 1044 (see page 36). He was converted by a famous Mon monk called Shin Arahan.

The monastery is the focal point in a Burmese village. Monks are not only respected community leaders – they are also often healers, councillors, and teachers. Pagodas are beautifully maintained and families spend much of their hard-earned incomes on donations. They also offer food to the monks every morning, spend considerable sums on pilgrimages, and save up to cover the cost of their sons' initiation and ordination ceremonies. Traditionally the monastery was also the centre for education – *kyaung* is the Burmese word for a monastic school – which were commonplace until the British introduced a formal education system.

In Myanmar every boy should spend some time as a monk; initiation day (*shinbyu*) is considered one of the most important days in his life. The time and date of the shinbyu is set by the family astrologers, and the young boy is dressed in the finest silks and richest jewels his family can borrow or buy. His hair is allowed to grow long and tied into a topknot. The boy's family often goes deep into debt to provide a level of grandeur fit for a prince – for on initiation day the son is dressed to resemble Siddhartha, the prince of the Sakya clan who later renounced his wealth and his birthright to become, eventually the Gautama Buddha. The boy is paraded around the village and visits all his relatives; at the induction ceremony, prayers are chanted, family snapshots are taken, and sometimes even video cameras are used to record the event. The ceremony is followed by as lavish a feast as the family can afford, for monks and guests (including any visitors who happen to stumble across the proceedings).

At the height of the festivities the boy's jewels come off, as do his locks and he puts on the orange or crimson robes of a monk, which symbolize his renunciation of worldly pleasures, following the example of the Buddha. As a monk he must beg for his food and he remains in the monastery for as long as his family can do without him. The period spent at the monastery provides religious education and merit for both the novice and his family. Novice ceremonies mostly take place during religious festivals – such as Thingyan – the New Year water festival – and Buddhist 'lent' – during the month of Waso (Jun/Jul) (see page 369). Novices and monks follow the 227 rules of the monastic code. After ordination they can return to the monastery at any time. Monks have three robes: the *ultarasanga*, which is wound round the upper body leaving the right shoulder bare; the *antaravasaka*, wound round the loins and reaching to the ankles and, over these two garments, a large rectangle of cloth called the *gaghati*, worn like a cloak.

Burmese nuns are not ordained and few women choose to follow a religious life. Monks are regularly fed as donors gain merit in offering food, but nuns have to beg for money. Although Burmese women have a respected place in Burmese society they are considered spiritually inferior and are often barred from entering the upper terraces of temples; nor are they permitted to put gold-leaf on the Mahamuni Image in Mandalay (see page 155). Women are believed to occupy a lowlier position in the cycle of birth and rebirth.

In Myanmar, merit making counts for a great deal – the best thing a Buddhist can possibly do is to build a pagoda – as this is thought to exemplify one's consideration for fellow men and is also evidence of detachment from worldly luxuries. Most of the kings of Bagan are thought to have achieved nirvana quite comfortably, thanks to their obsession with pagoda-building; by building stupas and temples, a king is also believed to make merit on behalf of his subjects. No special merit is to be gained from rebuilding someone else's pagoda, however. For ordinary people, who cannot afford to build pagodas, the easiest way to make merit is by gilding stupas and Buddha images. This happens throughout Myanmar, but the most remarkable example is the Mahamuni Image in Mandalay (see page 155) where so much gold-leaf has been applied to the statue that its features have been lost. A little square of gold-leaf costs about 20 kyat. In Mandalay, gold-leaf-making is a major industry.

Buddhism also occupies an important role at the national level. When political organizations were banned in the early period of colonial rule, Buddhist organizations became the focus of nascent nationalism (see page 45). Monks played a major role in the pre-independence period; one monk called Saya San led the first serious rebellion against the colonial regime in the early 1930s – although his uprising was brutally put down by the British and he was disrobed. There are more than 200,000 monks in Myanmar and they remain at the forefront of political resistance to the military government. Because of their reverential status in Burmese society, the army has been more reluctant to crack down on their political agitation. But the degree of monastic defiance in recent years has prompted less timidity from the ruling junta. On 8 August 1990, at a demonstration in Mandalay to commemorate the 8-8-88 uprising, two monks and two students were killed when the army opened fire. The monks continued to demonstrate in open defiance; they also excommunicated the government. The army countered by surrounding 133 temples and monasteries in Mandalay, cutting off water and electricity supplies until the disturbances subsided. About 150 monks were arrested. During their excommunication of the military, monks turned their begging bowls upside down and refused food from soldiers; they also mockingly knelt before them. *Thapeik hmauk* is the term used for a strike in Myanmar and literally translates as 'turning the alms bowl upside down'.

NAT WORSHIP

The Burmese brand of Buddhism is unique as it incorporates **nat** – or spirit – worship. In the way the early Anglican Church adopted pagan vitality symbols such as holly, ivy and mistletoe, King Anawrahta tolerated spirit-worship in pagoda precincts in an attempt to fuse Buddhism and pre-Buddhist animism. He also decreed that Thagyamin, the king of gods and guardian-spirit of Buddhism, was to be added to the original 36 nats as their leader. After Thagyamin, the celestial lady, Thurthati, guardian of the

In Siddhartha's footsteps: a short history of Buddhism

Buddhism was founded by Siddhartha Gautama, a prince of the Sakya tribe of Nepal, who probably lived between 563 and 483 BC. He achieved enlightenment and the word *buddha* means 'fully enlightened one', or 'one who has woken up'. Siddhartha Gautama is known by a number of titles. In the W, he is usually referred to as *The Buddha*, ie the historic Buddha (but not just Buddha); more common in Southeast Asia is the title *Sakyamuni*, or Sage of the Sakyas (referring to his tribal origins).

Over the centuries, the life of the Buddha has become part legend, and the Jataka tales which recount his various lives are colourful and convoluted. But, central to any Buddhist's belief is that he was born under a *sal* tree (*Shorea robusta*), that he achieved enlightenment under a bodhi tree (*Ficus religiosa*) in the Bodh Gaya Gardens, that he preached the First Sermon at Sarnath, and that he died at Kusinagara (all in India or Nepal).

The Buddda was born at Lumbini (in present-day Nepal), as Queen Maya was on her way to her parents' home. She had had a very auspicious dream before the child's birth of being impregnated by an elephant, whereupon a sage prophesied that Siddhartha would become either a great king or a great spiritual leader. His father, being keen that the first option of the prophesy be fulfilled, brought him up in all the princely skills (at which Siddhartha excelled) and ensured that he only saw beautiful things, not the harsher elements of life.

Despite his father's efforts Siddhartha saw four things while travelling between palaces – a helpless old man, a very sick man, a corpse being carried by lamenting relatives, and an ascetic, calm and serene as he begged for food. These episodes made an enormous impact on the young prince, and he renounced his princely origins and left home to study under a series of spiritual teachers. He finally discovered the path to enlightenment at the Bodh Gaya Gardens in India. He then proclaimed his thoughts to a small group of disciples at Sarnath, near Benares, and continued to preach and attract followers until he died at the age of 81 at Kusinagara.

In the First Sermon at the deer park in Sarnath, the Buddha preached the Four Truths, which are still considered the root of Buddhist belief and practical experience. These are the 'Noble Truth' that suffering exists, the 'Noble Truth' that there is a cause of suffering, the 'Noble Truth' that suffering can be ended, and the 'Noble Truth' that to end suffering it is necessary to follow the 'Noble Eightfold Path' – namely, right speech, livelihood, action, effort, mindfulness, concentration, opinion and intention.

Soon after the Buddha began preaching, a monastic order – the *Sangha* – was established. As the monkhood evolved in India, it also began to fragment as different sects developed different interpretations of the life of the Buddha. An important change was the belief that the Buddha was transcendent: he had never been born, nor had he died; he had always existed and his life on earth had been mere illusion. The emergence of these new concepts helped to turn what up until then was an ethical code of conduct, into a religion. It eventually led to the appearance of a new Buddhist movement, Mahayana Buddhism which split from the more traditional Theravada 'sect'.

Despite the division of Buddhism into two sects, the central tenets of the religion are common to both. Specifically, the principles pertaining to the Four Noble Truths, the Noble Eightfold Path, the Dependent Origination, the Law of

Karma and nirvana. In addition, the principles of non-violence and tolerance are also embraced by both sects. In essence, the differences between the two are of emphasis and interpretation. Theravada Buddhism is strictly based on the original Pali Canon, while the Mahayana tradition stems from later Sanskrit texts. Mahayana Buddhism also allows a broader and more varied interpretation of the doctrine. Other important differences are that while the Thervada tradition is more 'intellectual' and self-obsessed, with an emphasis upon the attaining of wisdom and insight for oneself, Mahayana Buddhism stresses devotion and compassion towards others.

Punishments in the eight Buddhist hells, commonly found on murals behind the principal Buddha image in the bot.
Adapted from Hallet, Holt (1980) *A thousand miles on an elephant in the Shan States*, William Blackwood: Edinburgh

Buddhist scriptures is the most popular nat. She is believed to be a Burmanization of Surasati, the Hindu goddess. Statues of her riding on the mythical hintha bird can often be found in temple stalls. The nats are the spirits of trees, rivers, stones, the ghosts of ancestors or Burmese versions of Hindu gods. The pantheon of Burmese nats is a mixed crew: there are deities as well as rogues and alcoholics. There is even one nat who is an opium smoker. He is a local nat from central Myanmar by the name of U Min Kyaw.

The 37 nats are capable of all kinds of mischief and have to be placated regularly. They are also capable, when appeased, of doing favours. Even devout Buddhists will go to nat seances where the spirits are believed to enter the bodies of trance-dancing mediums. Seance ceremonies – which can be quite spectacular – can often be seen at temple festivals. The nats have kept alive Burmese music, drama, dance and song. Natchins, songs in honour of the nats, are beautiful pieces of literature, comparable to the ballads of medieval Europe. Apart from temple festivals, nats may be offered special ceremonies, or kadaw-pwe, by private people who want to attract good fortune. These festivals are a release from daily life; alcohol flows abundantly and the Burmese lose their inhibitions and self-restraint and these ceremonies are often pandemonium. Offerings are made to the nats at every occasion: the first pillar of a house is never erected without an offering made to the nats; a road is made safe by tying an offered bunch of flowers to the yoke of an ox cart or the mirror of a car. There is now a strong 'fundamentalist' movement in Myanmar which disregards nat worship as superstitious.

Nonetheless, few people would be foolish enough to ignore the nats or reudiate their power. In his book *The Burman* (1882), Sir George Scott who wrote under the pen name Shway Yeo, translated a well-known Burmese lullaby:

> But to make black darkness vanish,
> Sweet sleep from my babe's eyes banish.
> Fairies wiled him,
> Dreams beguiled him,
> In his cradle wrapped so snugly,
> Cradle carved with *nyás* [four legged dragon] ugly,
> Craved with Nats and Kings and Princes,
> Every splendour that evinces
> Royal state and princely usance,
> There he slepyt, when what a nuisance!
> Come the light
> To affright
> And scare him back to home from elfin land.
>
> Nasty, naughty, noisy baby,
> If the cat won't, the Nats will maybe
> Come and pinch and punch and rend you!

In his book *The thirty-seven nats: a phase of spirit worship prevailing in Burma* (1906), Sir RC Temple opens the first chapter by writing: "No one can be long in Burma without hearing of the Nats, and every book on the Burmese – from the writings of the most learned scholars and most competent observers to those of the butterflies of literature, who flutter through the country and write about it – contains more or less elaborate and more or less accurate notices of them..." In other words, just as most Burmese are unwilling and unable to escape the power of the Nats, so most visitors will be unable to miss the presence of the Nats – whether real or in the popular imagination!

The thirty-seven nats

With the exception of one of the 37 nats – namely Thagya Nat – all are the ghosts or spirits of deceased heroes, and in most cases they also have royal blood, or are linked to royalty. Most are associated with historical figures who lived between the 13th and 17th centuries. The 37 nats are:

* Thagya Nat*
(nat No 1)

* Mahagiri Nat*
(nat No 2)

1. **Thagya Nat**: the chief nat
2. **Mahagiri Nat**: Nga Tinde in the Duttabaung cycle
3. **Hnamadawgyi Nat** ('Golden cheeks'): Ma Sawme in the Duttabaung cycle
4. **Shwe Nabe Nat**: The naga daughter in the Duttabaung cycle
5. **Thonban Hla Nat**: Duttabaung's neglected wife Queen Okkalaba in the Duttabaung cycle
6. **Taung-ngu Mingaung Nat**: King Mingaung of Taungoo in the Tabengshweti cycle
7. **Mintara Nat**: King Sinbyushin Mintaragyi of Ava in the Ava Mingaung and

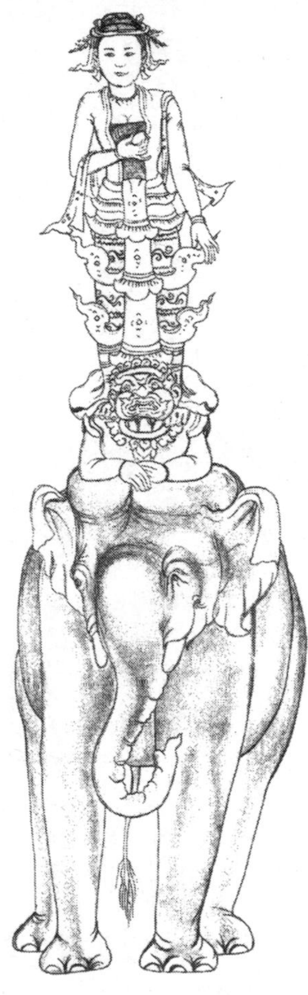

* Hnamadawgyi Nat*
(nat No 3)

Bagan Alaungsithu mixed cycle

8. **Thandawgan Nat**: King Mingaung of Taungoo's secretary in the Tabengshweti cycle
9. **Shwe Nawratha Nat**: the nephew of King Shwe Nangyaw of Ava in the Ava Mingaung and Bagan Alaungsithu mixed cycle

* Nyaung-gyin Nat*
(nat No 16)

10. **Aungzwamagyi Nat**: Nga Aungzwamagyi, who married the widow of King Narathenga of Bagan in the Ava Mingaung and Bagan Alaungsithu mixed cycle
11. **Ngazishin Nat**: Ngazishin Kyawzwa of Pinya in the Ava Mingaung and Bagan Alaungsithu mixed cycle
12. **Aungbinle Sinbyushin Nat**: King Thihathu Sinbyushin of Ava in the Ava Mingaung and Bagan Alaungsithu mixed cycle
13. **Taungmagyi Nat**: Shin Byo in the Duttabaung cycle
14. **Maung Minshin Nat**: Shin Nyo in the Duttabaung cycle
15. **Shindaw Nat**: the son of King Nyaung-yan Min of Ava who died while residing in a monastery in the

* Maung Po Tu Nat*
(nat No 21)
* Source: Temple, RC (1906) *The thirty-seven nats: a phase of spirit worship prevailing in Burma*, W Griggs: London

Bayinnnaung cycle
16. **Nyaung-gyin Nat**: the leper relative of King Manuha of Thaton in the Anawrahta Cycle
17. **Tabengshweti Nat**: King Tabengshweti in the Tabengshweti
18. **Minye Aungdin Nat**: the son of King Anaukpyetlon Mintara of Ava who died of drink in the Bayinnnaung cycle
19. **Shwe Sippin Nat**: King Sawkin-hnit of Bagan's son in the Ava Mingaung and Bagan Alaungsithu mixed cycle
20. **Medaw Shwesaga Nat**: one of King Sawkin-hnit of Bagan's wives in the Ava Mingaung and Bagan Alaungsithu mixed cycle
21. **Maung Po Tu Nat**: a trader from Pinya who was killed by a tiger
22. **Yun Bayin Nat**: Yun Shan chief of Zimme in the Bayinnnaung cycle
23. **Maung Minbyu Nat**: the son of King Bayinnnaung of Ava in the Bayinnnaung cycle
24. **Mandale Bodaw Nat**: Mandale Bodaw in the Anawrahta cycle
25. **Shwebyin Naungdaw Nat**: the Elder Shwebyin in the Anawrahta cycle
26. **Shwebyin Nyidaw Nat**: the Younger Shwebyin in the Anawrahta cycle
27. **Mintha Manung Shin Nat**: Anawrahta in the Anawrahta cycle
28. **Tibyusaung Nat**: Sukade in the Anawrahta cycle
29. **Tibusaung Medaw Nat**: Sukade and Kyizo's mother in the Anawrahta cycle
30. **Bayinmashin Mingaung Nat**: Kyizo in the Anawrahta cycle
31. **Min Sithu Nat**: one of the two sons of the northern queen in the Ava Mingaung and Bagan Alaungsithu mixed cycle
32. **Min Kyawzwa Nat**: on the other

two sons of the northern queen in the Ava Mingaung and Bagan Alaungsithu mixed cycle

33. **Myaukpet Shinma Nat**: King Mingaung of Taungoo's mother in the Tabengshweti

34. **Anauk Mibaya Nat**: the northern queen of King Mingaung-gyi of Ava (1480-1501) in the Ava Mingaung and Bagan Alaungsithu mixed cycle

35. **Shingon Nat**: the concubine of King Thihathu Sinbyushin in the Ava Mingaung and Bagan Alaungsithu mixed cycle

36. **Shingwa Nat**: Mandale Bodaw's sister in the Anawrahta Cycle

37. **Shin-nemi Nat**: Queen Okkalaba's daughter in the Duttabaung cycle

The Duttabaung cycle

Seven of the 37 nats are linked with the story of King Duttabaung of Pyay. Nga Tinde, an immensely strong Burmese hero was burnt alive by the evil King of Tagaung who was married to Ma Sawme, Nga Tinde's sister. She threw herself on to the pyre and died with her brother. Nga Tinde then married the daughter of a naga (sea serpent) and she gave birth to two sons – Shin Byo and Shin Nyo – who were killed in a boxing match arranged by the King Duttabaung of Pyay. King Duttabaung's wife, Queen Okkalaba was a legendary beauty who he neglected and condemned to weaving. Nonetheless she had a daughter who died with her mother.

The Anawrahta cycle

Nine of the 37 nats can be linked to King Anawrahta of Bagan (1044-1077) and his story. King Kyaungbyu Min of Bagan had three sons by two wives: Kyizo and Sukade by one wife, and Anawrahta by a second. Kyizo and Sukade plotted against and deposed their father and Kyizo acceded to the throne. After his accidental death Sukade became king but in time he was killed in combat by Anawrahta. Anawrahta, as the new king of Bagan, sent two Indian brother in his service, the elder and younger Shwebyin, to fetch a tooth relic of the Buddha from China. On their return Anawrahta had them both executed for insolence. At the same time he also executed a Brahmin minister – Mandale Bodaw – who was a close friend to the brothers, and his sister. Another subplot concerns Manuha, the King of Thaton who was defeated by Anawrahta and he and his family taken to Bagan to become pagoda slaves. One of his sons subsequently died of leprosy.

The Ava Mingaung and Bagan Alaungsithu mixed cycle

Eleven nats are associated with this cycle, which revolves around two kings of Ava, confusingly both named Mingaung. They reigned at the end of the 15th century but there is some confusion over the identity of some of the personages and the story is so convoluted as to be almost labyrinthine.

The Tabengshweti cycle

There are four nats in this cycle and they are associated with the rein of King Tabengshweti of Taungoo (1530-1550). King Tabengshweti built his kingdom until it encompassed Taungoo and Bago, and was then killed by his chief minister, Thamin Sawdok. The wife of the keeper of the royal umbrella, Minye Thengathu, gave birth to a son but died in the process. This man subsequently became King Mingaung of Tougoo on the murder of Tabengshweti. King Mingaung had an assistant who died to snake bite who also features in this cycle.

The Bayinnaung cycle

These four nats are linked to the rather later story of the great King Bayinnnaung of Bago (1551-1581), but only very loosely.

Other nats

The two remaining nats are Nos 1 and 21. No 1, Thagya Nat is not a historical figure; he is the chief of the nats and is derived from Indian Buddhism. Nat No 21 is said to have been a trader form Pinya who was killed by a tiger while travelling home.

Note: the information above is collated from Sir RC Temple's (1906) *The thirty-seven nats: a phase of spirit worship prevailing in Burma*, W Griggs: London (reprinted by Kiscadale).

LANGUAGE AND LITERATURE

Several hundred languages and dialects are spoken in Myanmar by the various ethnic groups. Besides the indigenous languages, various Chinese and South Asian languages are also spoken. Burmese is the national language and has been influenced by Pali and English. It is a tonal language – like Thai and Chinese – and has 32 consonants, eight vowels and four diphthongs. The language is comprised of one-syllable words which are strung together to make longer or more complex constructions. As in Thai, slight variations in the tonal pronunciation of syllables can completely alter the sense of the word. An elaborate court language also evolved in Myanmar: addressing the king required the use of a special, flowery language – the king was known, for example, as 'Lord of the Sunrise'. The court language has mostly died out, although it is still spoken by a few people in Mandalay.

In an attempt to unify the country, the languages of the minority ethnic groups have been banned from the schools of the country since 1947. As a result, so it is said, in parts of Lower Burma where the Karen are in a majority, very few are actually able to speak their own language. This attempt at nation-building is not unusual to Myanmar, and indeed made some sense at independence when forging a sense of Burmese identity amongst the assorted ethnic, linguistic, cultural and religious groups that comprised the country was a pressing concern. Much the same policy has been adopted in Indonesia, another country marked by its linguistic and cultural diversity.

The earliest examples of written Burmese date from the early 12th century, mostly from Bagan. It was a Mon script, written from left to right without any spaces between the words. Prose writing was influenced by the Pali scriptures and retained this formal, religious association until the end of the 19th century, when the arrival of the printing press and contact with European literature altered its function. The first widely-read Burmese novel was published in 1904. The end of WW2 and the attainment of independence in 1948 gave impetus to the novel as an art form and short story-writing became popular. Although a new bookstore (Inwa, Sule Pagoda Rd, Yangon) opened in 1993, foreign books are still censored and hard to get hold of. Burmese best sellers are also limited, and prices rise as copies become scarce. Paper quality of Burmese books is poor and so is the binding. There is a flourishing book binding business (31st and 32nd sts, Yangon), as it is customary to have your book re-bound before reading it. Foreign books are photocopied and bound, as are most university and medical text books. There are no copyright laws in Myanmar. Books are so expensive that they are often rented out and most streets in Yangon have a shop/rental store.

Myanmar's bestselling author is a 35 year old woman, 'Fu', and many of her books are made into films. Her novels are mostly love stories, but she has been criticized for the topics of some of her books and the depraved ideas that she might encourage in her readers: living together without being married, for example. Burmese cartoonists seem to have been granted a freedom of expression which other artists do not have; cartoons in magazines and newspapers are often witty and daring in the way they portray Burmese society.

DANCE, DRAMA AND MUSIC

The most popular form of entertainment in Myanmar is the *pwe* – an all-night extravaganza which combines song, dance and theatre. Slapstick comedy and satirical skits are interlaced with religious and historical plays (*zats* – see below). At temple *pwe* it is quite usual to see dancers in trance, possessed by the spirits of local nats. Nat dancers can be men or women, and are often transvestites. Nat *pwe* are mainly held by rich villagers who can afford to hire the orchestra and dancers. The nats often make outrageous demands for gifts and different nats have different predilections – some go around asking for money, while others seem to prefer rum and whisky. Although *pwe* are intensely spiritual, they can also be extremely entertaining; they are highly charged frenetic occasions with the continuous background din of the orchestra. The popularity of the *pwe* has kept alive traditional music, dance and theatre.

The classical *zat* dramas are usually based on the Jataka tales or the Ramayana. Theatre is perhaps Myanmar's liveliest art. A national dance performance is organized every year at the national theatre (built by the Chinese). Each ethnic group is represented (to show that Myanmar is united). Traditional dancing can be seen at local festivals. Contemporary comedies – called *pyazat* – are most common in Yangon. Pyazat have become unusual since 1888, when the government banned large gatherings of people; yet there are still theatre groups travelling the country.

The *yokthe pwe*, or marionette theatre, was well established by the Bagan Period (11th century). Aimed more at adults than children, the *yokthe pwe* was once Myanmar's major form of entertainment; master puppeteers used to enjoy an even higher social status than that accorded actors. Puppetry blossomed under royal patronage. Puppet shows were often part of the court reception for visiting embassies. There was an official post, Thabin wun, at the Burmese court for organizing entertainment. Because of their popularity, Ah-yoke Kyoka, the dance of the stringed ones, was even executed by court dancers. Shows were mainly reinacted Buddhist stories or scenes from the Ramayana (which took 45 nights to perform). Puppet faces were painted to conform to contemporary ideas of beauty, and characters which were natural enemies were never stored together. After the British annexation of Myanmar in 1886, marionette theatre declined, as did many of the other arts which relied on royal patronage. It is, in many ways, a dying art form although the Mandalay Marionette Theatre has recently been established and it can still be seen at some temple fairs, local festivals and street pwe.

Traditional music is alive and well in Myanmar. Pwe are staged whenever there is something to celebrate – from weddings to funerals – and *zat* are usually performed during religious festivals. Both types of theatre involve song, dance and music and the cast is often supported by an 8-10 man *saing orchestra* (similar to Indonesian *gamelan*), dominated by percussion instruments. There are no written scores, so all the music is learnt by heart. Typical instruments include the *pattala* (xylophone), *kyee waing* (gongs), *yagwin* (cymbals), *palwe* (bamboo flute) and the *hne*, a wind instrument. An apprenticeship system ensures the music is passed down from generation to generation. The most interesting of the instruments is the circle of small horizontal metal gongs or *kyee waing*. To the western ear, Burmese music is overly percussive and can sound tinny and unmelodious.

There are many professional dance troops in the country and several state schools teaching music and drama. Dancers are usually dressed in costumes which originated at the royal courts. The skirt is not the usual lungyi but a long split skirt with a train and dancing involves the rhythmic kicking away of the train. Most of the dances imitate the movements of the Burmese marionettes, popular in the royal courts during the 18th century; others are derived from classical Siamese dances. Ayutthaya's dancers were captured by the Burmese in 1767 when they sacked the Siamese capital, and brought back to Ava. Thai classical *khon* and *lakhon* dance forms were used to form the basis of modern Burmese dance. The Konbaung Dynasty (1783-1885) patronized masked dance dramas, which still survive today. Short dances are usually interspersed with routines by clowns who satirize contemporary politics – although these days they have to be careful.

SPORT

Everywhere in Myanmar there are circles of young men playing *chinlon* – the national game and all-consuming male pastime. Chinlon – or 'basketball' is played throughout the region, and is known in Thailand as *takraw*, and in Malaysia as *sepak raga*. A phenomenal demonstration of *chinlon* skills can be seen at the Karaweik Cultural Centre on Royal Lake, near the *Kandawgyi Hotel* in Yangon (see page 122), where a girl with a long pigtail, in a brown nylon tracksuit (reputed to be the best chinlon-maestro in the land), performs acrobatics with the wicker balls to the beat of drums and traditional music. Rowing is a traditional Burmese sport. Rowers can sometimes be seen training on Kandawgyi and Inya lakes in Yangon.

CRAFTS

Embroidery

Centuries of migration led Myanmar's hill peoples to develop portable art forms, and embroidery is one of their specialities. From early childhood a girl learns to sew and her needle-skills play an important role in helping her win a husband. Designs often reflect tribal legends, passed down the generations and geometric designs are stylized images of flowers, trees, rivers and mountains. *Kalaga* – or appliqué-work – in gold and sequins is common in Myanmar. These embroideries, often depicting figures from Buddhist mythology, are hung in temples or on bullock carts at festivals. Originally this type of appliqué-work was used for coffin covers for royalty and monks. Today, Mandalay's embroidery factories (see page 360) do a roaring trade in embroidered baseball hats, wall hangings, cushion covers, hats, bags and waistcoats for sale to tourists, or export to the West and Thailand. The Mandalay factories also make traditional clothes for dancers.

Weaving

Mandalay and Amarapura are the most important weaving centres and produce the *acheik*, the horizontal-weave patterned silk, once popular with royalty. This silk is still highly prized.

Lacquerware

Lacquered receptacles – mainly begging bowls – are used daily by monks in Myanmar and lacquerware was formerly in daily use by royalty too. It is the Burmese answer to everything from porcelain to plastic. Bagan is famous for its lacquerware, although the technique was probably imported from China, where it has a 3,000 year old history. The Burmese adopted the craft early in their history – Bagan is where the earliest-known surviving piece was unearthed; it is believed to date from 1274.

Traditionally the frame of a lacquerware item is made of woven bamboo which is then interwoven with horse hair – this makes it very flexible. Today many of the bases are wooden or just bamboo; high quality horse hair pieces are still made, but they are very expensive. But all in all, there are few shortcuts when it comes to making lacquerware. The base of the frame is coated with lacquer, which comes from the *thitsi* tree – found in N Myanmar – and is then coated with a second mixture of clay and lacquer together. The next layer is called *thayo* – ground bone ash – which is also mixed with lacquer; this is followed by a final layer of ground paddy husk mixed with lacquer. Between each layer, the item has to be dried for a week and then smoothed with a lathe before the next layer can be applied. The inside and the outside have to be painted separately. The piece is finally rubbed down with sesame oil and put on a hand-lathe and polished before being decorated.

On cheaper pieces the decorations are painted on; for more expensive pieces the patterns are engraved with a *kauk* blade and then the colour applied in separate stages. Red, green, yellow and gold are the traditional colours for lacquerware. Blue and pink-painted pieces are modern. Many of the traditional designs are inspired by paintings on Bagan's temple walls. The best lacquerware is black, the next grade down is brown and yellow is inferior quality. Although Bagan is the main centre for lacquerware and has many lacquerware shops (see page 203), handicraft and antique shops throughout Myanmar sell it too. Good examples of traditional and antique lacquerware can be found at the Bagan Lacquerware Museum (see page 190), the Buddhist Art Museum in Yangon (see page 115), the National Museum in Yangon (see page 114), the Mandalay Museum (see page 154) and the Taunggyi Museum (see page 234).

Silverware

Silver objects were often put in relic chambers of pagodas and were a measure of wealth. Many early inscriptions list the cost of materials to construct pagodas and monasteries in tical of silver. Silver was also important in royal ceremonies: elephants wore silver bells round their necks and silver rings on their tusks. King Thirithuhamma, King of Mrauk-U, Rakhine, had a silver howdah at his coronation in 1634. Silversmiths were often part of the booty of war. The Burmese and the hill peoples coveted silver and much of the silverware sold today is from minority areas. Typical Burmese pieces are lime boxes, part of a betel set, with scenes from the jataka tales inscribed round the sides.

Modern Myanmar

POLITICS

Poverty and political repression were the underlying factors which sparked the anti-government riots of 1988 that catapulted the otherwise dreamy capital of Yangon (Rangoon) into the international headlines. Initially, however, they were largely ignored in the West despite the fact there had been sporadic disturbances throughout 1987. But in Mar 1988, students from the Yangon Institute of Technology became involved in a fight in a tea house and the army shot several students dead. Rallies and demonstrations continued through the following months as protests spread from Yangon to other major towns. The flashpoint occurred on 8 Aug, when huge street demonstrations accompanied a general strike. The **'8-8-88' protest** culminated with the army firing into the crowds and led to similar demonstrations and massacres throughout the country in the days that followed. Universities, colleges and schools were shut down. The demonstrations were brutally crushed by the army; most estimates put the number of casualties as high as 12,000 and 3,000-4,000 shot dead.

In late Jul, Ne Win had tactically resigned as party chairman amid mounting opposition against the one-party rule of the BSPP. Sein Lwin, nicknamed the 'Butcher of Rangoon' for ordering riot police to fire into demonstrators, was appointed President, but resigned after just 18 days in office in the face of huge protests. He was succeeded by Dr Maung Maung, a long time associate of Ne Win. He lasted just 1 month and his tenure as President was marked by daily demonstrations and strikes which by then had spread to over 50 towns and cities. Finally, on 18 Sep, General Saw Maung announced that the military had assumed power and had formed the **State Law and Order Restoration Council (the Slorc)**. About 10,000 students fled from the cities following the demonstrations to seek refuge in jungle camps along the Thai border. From here the students, along with more experienced rebels, have mounted a military campaign against the authorities in Yangon.

Swedish journalist Bertil Lintner's book *Outrage* provides a blow-by-blow account of the events of 1988. Lintner is one of the regime's best-informed critics. The most telling review of *Outrage* appeared in *The Working People's Daily* in Yangon. It described the book as "...a pot-pourri of maliciously selected misrepresentations, misinterpretations, fabrications and rumour-sourced disinformation about the Myanmar Naing-Ngan [Union of Myanmar] put together into book-form by past master of sensationalism, foreign journalist Bertil Lintner". A translation of his book became widely available in Yangon, disguised behind a plain brown paper cover.

THE SLORC

Since the coup d'état on 18 September 1988, Myanmar has been ruled by the State Law and Order Restoration Council, or the Slorc – many would say an appropriately ugly acronym. The 19-man military junta, which ordered the streets to be cleared with bullets while promising free and fair elections, has been nationally and internationally condemned. In Myanmar the Slorc is known as *Nyain Wut Pi-pya* – which literally translates as "quiet, kneeling, lying flat" – which describes how the generals expect Burmese

The search for 'balance' in Myanmar

In presenting contemporary political and economic developments we try to be 'balanced', recognizing that there are many views. This is always difficult, but in the case of Myanmar it is almost impossible. There are startling few governments or commentators who find anything for which to praise the Slorc. Charles Humana who has produced probably the most widely accepted index of human rights (itself, admittedly, a slippery concept) based on 40 'freedoms' and 'rights' placed Myanmar not near the bottom, but at the bottom. Myanmar achieved, if that is the right word, the lowest human rights index of any country in the world – lower even than Iraq. This illustrates the difficulty of not appearing to be gratuitously critical of the government in Yangon. There is no 'balance' to be found. The Slorc, and previous administrations, have devastated a previously rich economy, subjected the Burmese people to manifold abuses, controlled the press, persecuted opposition politicians and degraded the environment. As a piece in London's *Sunday Telegraph* put it in July 1995, "The Burmese regime has some claim to be the most cruel, incompetent and paranoid in the world."

to behave. According to Bertil Lintner, "the country is ruled by corporals and sergeants who have become generals". But the man with the real influence in the Slorc was the dreaded intelligence chief, Major-General Khin Nyunt (see page 81).

For months after the Slorc takeover, *The Working People's Daily* carried prominent notices that the military junta was just a temporary administration which would hand the country over to a civilian administration just as soon as everything was in order. A typical notice read (under the headline Noble Desire):

> "Although the State Law and Order Restoration Council has had to take over, due to unavoidable circumstances, the sovereign power of the State to prevent the Union from disintegration and for ensuring the safety and security of the lives, homes and property of the people, it wishes to retransfer State power to the people, in whom it was initially vested, through democratic means within the shortest time possible. Therefore, the entire people are urged to give all their co-operation to ensure the rule of law and for prevalence of peace and tranquility."

THE TATMADAW – THE PROTECTOR OF THE PEOPLE

Among the first things a visitor notices on entering Myanmar are the huge red billboards emblazoned with white block capitals. American diplomats used to enjoy posing for snapshots beneath the one which faced their Yangon embassy; it read: "DOWN WITH THE MINIONS OF COLONIALISM". Most of these billboards, however, are advertising hoardings for the Tatmadaw or the army. Near Bagan there is one which reads: "NEVER HESITATING, ALWAYS READY TO SACRIFICE BLOOD AND SWEAT IS THE TATMADAW"; outside Mandalay another says: "THE TATMADAW AND PEOPLE CO-OPERATE AND CRUSH ALL THOSE HARMING THE UNION". In 1992, many of the English translations on these sign-boards were painted out. The Tatmadaw have come to be known sarcastically throughout Myanmar as 'Piyithu chin bat' a type of pickled vegetable, somewhat sour and stinks to high heaven.

The Burmese Army has grown dramatically in recent years. Shortly after independence the army numbered around 12,000 men. By 1955 it had more than tripled to 40,000 and in the late

1980s this number had swollen to 200,000. A few years on, and after the demonstrations of 1988, the army had an estimated 350,000 troops. Not content with this massive military presence – which exists to contend with internal insurrestion, not external agression – the army's goal is to have a well equipped military machine of around 500,000. The army is divided into nine infantry divisions under 10 regional commands. It is supplied with weapons from China. The army has not found it difficult to recruit; living standards are so poor in many rural areas that men are pleased to earn a stable income of about 700 kyat a month. In 1990 there were reports that the army had recruited orphaned children from the countryside – even from the hillpeoples – who are taught to regard the army as their family.

Army officers – most of whom are

Military intelligence – spy v spy

Yangon's paranoid intelligentsia jokes that while George Orwell's novel *Burmese Days* is popular, the sequel is even better – *1984*. The recruitment drive by Military Intelligence (MI) since the 1988 demonstrations has given this black humour a ring of Orwellian truth, for in Myanmar, Big Brother really does watch you. MI chief Major-General Khin Nyunt's thought police have now infiltrated every section of a society which is seeped in fear. In the wake of the 1988 disturbances, an estimated 20,000 people disappeared. MI agents keep close tabs on the remaining elected 'politicians' from the National League for Democracy.

Colleges and universities – the hotbeds of unrest – have remained closed for much of the time since 1988; when they did reopen in 1991, there was reckoned to be a spy from the Division of Defence Services Intelligence for every 20 students.

Teachers and lecturers receive regular visits from MI. To avoid the fate of scores of their dissident colleagues, they are required to sign an undertaking to 'behave in a way befitting their status', a privilege which costs them 5 kyat. Students and their parents have had to give similar guarantees and assurances that they will pursue their education peacefully. Most students were so desperate to return to classes that they did not wish to further jeopardize their education.

In Myanmar's 350,000-strong army there is thought to be an agent for every 10 soldiers. Intelligence operatives – who are not blackmailed into spying – earn less than 1,000 kyat a month (under US$10 at the black market exchange rate) and a pension after 10 years. Khin Nyunt also has files on all his senior military colleagues detailing their black market business links with the gemstone and opium trade – information which can easily be used against them, should the need arise. Even in the top echelons of the military hierarchy there is mutual distrust.

Spies keep an eye on the *hnakaung shay* community too – the foreign 'long-noses' – to make sure they "do not instigate further disturbances" – as they were alleged to have done in 1988. When lottery ticket sellers set up opposite their front gates, foreign residents know they are under surveillance. The giant red and white sign boards at strategic locations in most towns and cities complement intelligence operations by extolling patriotic virtues and constantly reminding Burmese to "LOVE AND CHERISH THE MOTHERLAND" and to "SAFEGUARD NATIONAL INDEPENDENCE". Perhaps more telling is the prominently placed board in Yangon which reads: "ONLY WHERE THERE IS DISCIPLINE WILL THERE BE PROGRESS".

Aung San Suu Kyi

In Oct 1991, Aung San Suu Kyi (whose last name is pronounced *Chi*) was awarded the Nobel Peace Prize. Her prize citation said she had provided "one of the most extraordinary examples of civil courage in Asia in recent decades". She is also the recipient of the Sakharov Prize for Freedom of Thought. Suu Kyi was born in 1945, the daughter of Aung San, the Burmese national hero who had negotiated independence from the British (see page 47). She never really knew her father – she was just two when he was assassinated. Aung San is to Myanmar what Mahatma Gandhi is to India – except for the fact that Aung San was a soldier, and founder of the Burmese Army. In contrast, Suu Kyi is committed to Gandhi's philosophy of non-violent protest; in every other way she is very much her father's daughter. In 1991, her husband, Michael Aris wrote: "There is a certain inevitability in the way she, like him, has now become an icon of popular hope and longing."

Suu Kyi left Myanmar in 1960 to join her mother in New Delhi where she was ambassador. She went on to read philosophy, politics and economics at Oxford before joining the United Nations in New York. On New Year's Day 1972, she married Michael Aris, an English academic and Tibetan specialist. There were conditions attached to the marriage: it was agreed that if destiny ever called her back to Myanmar, she would go. She joined her husband in Bhutan where she learned Tibetan, then learned Japanese in Kyoto; after that they returned to live in London where she became a post-graduate student at the School of Oriental and African Studies (SOAS). In Apr 1988 she left her husband and their two children and returned to Yangon to nurse her mother who had suffered a stroke.

When the demonstrations began to mount in the summer of 1988, Suu Kyi decided to enter politics, becoming the co-founder of Myanmar's main opposition party, the National League for Democracy (NLD). She made her first speech on the steps of the Shwedagon Pagoda to a crowd of at least 500,000; overnight she became the most popular person in Myanmar. She said: "I could not, as my

Burman – have come to expect a taste of the good life. This might include a house, a car, cheap petrol and access to special shops. They enjoy enormous privileges: army wives go on shopping trips to Singapore and Bangkok and their children can afford to eat out in restaurants and travel abroad. Senior officers often retire from military service to manage state-owned enterprises. The Slorc has been able to buy the continued loyalty of the armed forces thanks to its skill at plundering the country's natural resources. Nobel laureate and opposition leader Aung San Suu Kyi wrote that "fear of losing power corrupts those who wield it and fear of the scourge of power corrupts those subject to it".

The Tatmadaw sees enemies everywhere and is motivated by its determination to stamp out all existing political threats, whether from ethnic minorities, urban politicians, students or monks. According to human rights groups like Amnesty International, Asia Watch, the UN, the US State Department and the Burma Action Group, the army regularly commits atrocities in ethnic minority areas, levying illegal taxes, stealing food and supplies and forcing villagers to work as ammunition porters. It has also been accused of using punitive 'scorched earth' tactics against villagers in contested areas.

Yet although there can be little doubt that the army in Myanmar is firmly in father's daughter, remain indifferent to what was going on". Tens of thousands of people attended her mother's funeral in Jan 1989; by then Suu Kyi had the appeal of a film star, and had already become the focus of a personality cult. During early 1989 she campaigned throughout Myanmar. At one point during the campaign, soldiers threatened to shoot her if she continued to lead a peaceful demonstration down a street in Danubyu, a provincial town not far from Yangon. She refused to stop and the troops levelled their sights. Seconds later, an army major ordered his men to hold fire. The Burmese marvelled at her fierce courage in the face of military might – particularly in view of her delicate physique. Such incidents simply added to her popular appeal. Michael Aris later noted that: "The more she was attacked, the more people flocked to her banner. She brought overwhelming unity to a spontaneous, hitherto leaderless revolt."

On Martyr's Day (19 Jul) 1989, when Aung San and his cabinet are traditionally remembered, Suu Kyi decided to launch an unprecedented personal attack on General Ne Win, accusing him of ruining the country, and casting doubt on the junta's promise to transfer power to a civilian administration. This was more than the old dictator could stomach. The following day she was placed under house arrest. When the NLD won a landslide at the polls on 27 May 1990, it was as much a personal vote for the charismatic Suu Kyi as it was for the NLD, despite the fact that she had, at that time, not been seen or heard of for 10 months.

Suu Kyi was to remain under house arrest for just under 6 years – until her release in early Jul 1995. During her long term of imprisonment, outside her big white colonial bungalow on University Avenue, the military presence was almost invisible. Inside the compound Military Intelligence officers were frequently rotated as, in the words of one British journalist, they "were becoming too friendly with their brave, beautiful, bewitching captive." She endured at least one hunger strike and in one vindictive act her piano was taken away – apparently because people had taken to gathering at the gates to hear her play.

control of events – at the moment – there is a sense that the military are searching for a more stable, and more acceptable, role for themselves. Forever being portrayed as the black hats eventually gets through to generals even with the thickness of skin of those in Myanmar. In searching for a new raison d'être the army have looked to the example of Indonesia where the military fulfils what is known as *dwifungsi*, or a 'dual function'. Like Myanmar, the Indonesian military played a leading part in the independence movement. Partly as a result, today, Abri – as the Indonesian armed forces are known – fulfil critical roles in both military affairs and in civil politics. This is the position that the Tatmadaw would like to emulate and the discussions over a new constitution which were still underway in early 1997 would seem to be marking out the ground with Indonesia's *dwifungsi* in mind (see page 85)

THE 1990 ELECTION AND ITS AFTERMATH

"The past 26 years of brutal totalitarian rule, incompetence, corruption and the withering of the economy have not stamped out the memory of the struggle for independence and the first 14 years of democratic rule in which diversity and choice were recognized and, in the main, respected." Joseph Silverstein, historian.

Perhaps the most remarkable thing

about recent political events in Myanmar is that the Slorc allowed the 1990 election to be held at all. What was even more bizarre was that it was generally acknowledged to have been clean – there was little intimidation or vote tampering – although the junta did try to make conditions difficult for the opposition by declaring martial law, banning gathering of more than 5 people, and censoring the opposition parties' publications. Thai journalists covering the election joked that it was much cleaner than any Thai election. The trademark of the **National League for Democracy** candidates had become the straw *topi*-style peasants' hat, the *kha-mut*, and it was reported that even on polling day, NLD supporters were openly wearing these hats to indicate voting intentions.

The Slorc seriously miscalculated. The government was humiliated and the NLD won 392 out of 485 seats – 82% of the seats or around 60% of the 13 million votes cast – and despite the fact that its two leaders, Aung San Suu Kyi and U Tin U had been detained since Jul 1989. The only areas the NLD failed to sweep were states where ethnic minority parties fielded candidates of their own. Many of these smaller political groups had reached an understanding with the NLD and formed the United Nationalities League for Democracy (UNLD).

But, as many had expected, the Slorc failed to honour its pledge and did not hand over power to the newly elected MPs. (It justifies its actions by claiming they are the saviours of the nation preventing it falling into Imperialist, or alternatively Communist, hands – only Slorc can avoid a disintegration of the Union of Myanmar. There may be a shred of truth in the latter point – the one thing that Ne Win and his successors have achieved since 1962 is the maintenance of the Union, even if there are areas which are not under Yangon's control.) Instead, Slorc imprisoned at least 80 of them, including Aung San Suu Kyi and U Tin U – as well as hundreds of their supporters – which caused the remainder to flee to Manerplaw, on the Thai border, where they set up a 'parallel' government-in-exile, called the National Coalition Government of the Union of Burma in Dec 1990. It was led by Sein Win, cousin of Aung San Suu Kyi. This parallel government gained little international recognition or credibility and has since virtually melted away.

In the wake of the election, the Slorc cracked down on the Democratic Party for a New Society (DPNS), successor to the banned All Burma Students' Federation Union (ABSFU), which had been a key force in the uprising in 1988. The Slorc also banned many other, lesser, parties. Their leaders and members were arrested and others fled into the hills to Manerplaw and the squalid jungle camps along the Thai border. There are also several thousand students and activists in Bangkok.

MUSICAL CHAIRS AND THE SEARCH FOR LEGITIMACY

In Apr 1992, when the Slorc suddenly announced that Aung San Suu Kyi's family could visit her in Yangon, several other dissidents and NLD 'MPs' were released from detention – including the indomitable former Prime Minister U Nu (who died, aged 87, at the beginning of 1995). The previous week Prime Minister General Saw Maung had been replaced by army commander-in-chief and the Slorc vice-chairman, General Than Shwe. He joined the army after primary school and is not known for his leadership qualities. Saw Maung's replacement followed reports that he had suffered a nervous breakdown and had become increasingly unable to lead the country. He had begun to cause serious embarrassment to the government, due to his obsession with the kings of Bagan and their tyrannical ways. Real power is thought to be concentrated in the hands of intelligence chief Major-General Khin Nyunt, Ne Win's 'golden boy'. He is deeply resented by many high-ranking army officers due to his detailed intelligence files on all of them (see page 81). Commentators played down the changes as 'old wine in a new bottle'.

In early 1993, 700 hand-picked delegates were invited by the generals to come to Yangon for a long-promised **national convention**, whose purpose was to **draft a new constitution** to give the Slorc some semblance of legitimacy. The 700 delegate convention – which was still in progress at the beginning of 1997 – is widely regarded as a sham, intended to rubber stamp a constitution already written by the Slorc. Only a small minority of the delegates have been elected; the rest are representatives of social and economic groups largely appointed by the Slorc. It is likely that the new constitution will not only give the military a role in the executive, the legislative and the judiciary, and in all levels of government from the national to the local, but will also hand over to the armed forces complete autonomy in all military matters (including the defence budget). The army will be able to appoint 110 of the 440 seats in the proposed lower House of Representatives, and 56 of the 224 seats in the upper House of Nationalities. This would enshrine the army's role as not just the defender of the people, but also as important players in civilian politics. The military will have the right to declare an emergency and to assume power should they decide that conditions warrant such a step. It is also likely that the constitution will bar any Burmese married to a foreigner from assuming high office, anyone who has not been continuously resident in Myanmar for 20 years, and will also stipulate that the prime minister have military experience. These three clauses are seemingly aimed squarely at Aung San Suu Kyi who is married to British Oxford academic Michael Aris, who has spent most of the last 20 years abroad, and who has no working experience of the military.

The junta's latest political creation, a successor to failed pro-military political parties of the past, is the 'non-political' Union Solidarity and Development Association (USDA). With civilian leaders, USDA has been designed to mobilize the population in support of the Slorc by, for example, convening pro-government mass rallies in support of the new convention. Most of those attending these rallies are civil servants and school children given the day off to attend – if they refuse to attend the households are fined upto 500 kyat.

In Feb 1993 the Slorc refused to allow a Nobel laureate's peace mission into Myanmar. The group included the Dalai Lama and Bishop Desmond Tutu. Their primary goal was to call for the release of Aung San Suu Kyi. However, they also called for the withdrawal of Myanmar's membership of the UN, the imposition of a strict arms embargo, and an end to the 'constructive engagement' policy of Myanmar's neighbours. The government has been making small moves to improve its image abroad. 1,700 political prisoners were released in 1993, according to Amnesty International. However, this still left over 1000 behind bars.

The Slorc's strengthening position

One development which the Slorc must view with some pleasure is the progress that has been made in improving relations with the **rebel armies of ethnic groups** based along the country's borders, after years of guerilla warfare. The Wa, Pa-O National Organization, Palaung, Kachin Independence Organization, the Karenni Nationalities People's Liberation Front, and the Shan State Army all signed a ceasefire with the Slorc on the condition that they be allowed to retain their arms and territory. By the beginning of 1996, the government had managed to negotiate

The Golden Triangle and the smack of official complicity

In Mar 1992, government ministers from Myanmar, Laos and Thailand met in Bangkok to sign an agreement on the eradication of narcotics production and trafficking in the area where their borders meet, the notorious Golden Triangle. It was the first such meeting and was designed to boost the image of the three countries, which account for most of the world's heroin supply. Southeast Asian heroin now comprises about 80% of the drugs on America's streets, despite being overshadowed during the late-1980s by crack cocaine. Enforcement agents predict heroin will be the drug of the 1990s and even South and Central American producers are starting to cultivate opium poppies.

Myanmar, along with Laos and Afghanistan, is the biggest raw opium producer in the world. In 1996 the US State Department estimated that the year's harvest would amount to 256 tonnes. Output has tripled since 1987, mainly in the N Shan and Kachin states. Opium production in the Lao sector of the Golden Triangle was stepped up during America's secret war in Laos in the 1960s and 1970s and it too is now a significant producer, yielding 10 times as much heroin as Thailand. US and UN drug enforcement agencies believe that 70% of the heroin seized in the US is thought to come from the Golden Triangle.

The 1992 Bangkok agreement focused on plans for joint operations to eradicate poppy fields, heroin laboratories and opium caravans. But foreign anti-narcotics agents are sceptical about the level of commitment that can be expected – particularly from the Burmese government, which is known to launder profits from drugs money to help prop up the economy and line the pockets of military generals. Periodically the Burmese junta publicizes the supervised destruction of opium refineries and puts sacks of heroin on bonfires as part of a public relations drive to satisfy the demands of the foreign drug enforcement agencies. Thai officials – many of them connected with the military – are also involved in the alleged drugs trade. Between 1992 and 1994, it was revealed that a number of serving and former Thai MPs had had their visa requests turned down by the US State Department due to suspected drugs links while the surrender of Khun Sa to the authorities in Yangon in 1995 was widely regarded to have included a deal guaranteeing his safety – for his silence. (See the section headed 'Myanmar's drug barons and the opium trade'.)

Much of Myanmar's opium traffic passes along the old Burma Road (see page 45) into China's Yunnan province. In 1992, the Chinese authorities began cracking down much more effectively on both the refining and trafficking of heroin on its side of the border. On both sides of the frontier, heroin-addiction rates have reached alarming levels: a heroin fix is much cheaper than a bottle of beer. There has been an associated increase in infection by the HIV virus which causes AIDS. High-grade ('No 4') heroin from the border region mostly finds its way to drugs syndicates in Hong Kong and from there goes to Europe, America and Australia. Opium also transits to Chiang Mai and Fang in N Thailand (Bangkok is a major international trafficking centre) and through Mawlamyine (Moulmein) in the S of Myanmar, where it supplies the S Thai, Malaysian and Singapore markets. Singapore – where drug traffickers receive a mandatory death sentence – is still an international trans-shipment centre.

Following the Burmese Army's suppression of the pro-democracy demonstrations in 1988, the US government suspended its US$18mn-a-year drug enforcement project in Myanmar, in which it cooperated with the government in spraying defoliants on opium crops. Since then opium production has increased markedly, and former members of the now-disbanded Communist Party of Burma have emerged as the new drugs warlords, all with private armies and operating with the blessing of Yangon. The most famous of the warlords was Khun Sa, 'the self-proclaimed king of opium'. However, since 1990, Khun Sa was gradually eclipsed by the new warlords who have been groomed by Myanmar's military government. These new opium *sawbwas*, like Chao Nyi Lai who heads the United Wa State Army, are former commanders of rebel insurgencies who have been bought off by Yangon.

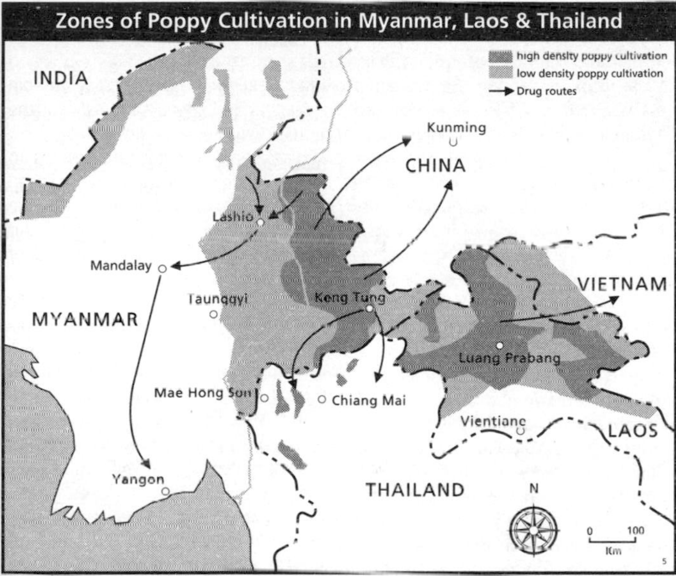

ceasefires with no fewer than 15 of the country's 16 major insurgent groups.

But these ceasefires do not necessarily stop government forces from pursuing their military aims should the opportunity arise. Indeed, in the case of the Karen, the Slorc agreed on a ceasefire, it seems, primarily to give its troops the opportunity to scout out the territory in the notoriously rugged and inhospitable mountains along the border with Thailand. (In 1992 an assault on Karen positions failed partly due to inadequate knowledge of the area.) Having become familiar with the territory, and taking advantage of a split between Buddhist and Christian factions within the Karen rebel army, the Burmese army mounted a series of raids throughout 1994 and into early 1995 – despite the fact that this violated a ceasefire negotiated in 1992. Rebel student forces based along the Salween (Thaniwan) River were also under heavy military pressure in early

1995, and their HQ at Dagwin was repeatedly shelled. While the army was mounting these raids Myanmar's ambassador at the UN, and apparently with no hint of irony, was calling for 'national reconciliation'. At the end of Jan 1995, the Karen rebel headquarters of Manerplaw (meaning, accurately, but unintentionally in this case, Field of Victory) finally fell to a Burmese army assault numbering 15,000 men. This was a serious blow to the Karen National Union who, in the process, lost their most important base to the junta. The fall of Manerplaw was, at the same time, a considerable morale-boosting victory for the junta in Yangon. An estimated 8,000 Karen fled across the border into Thailand. In Feb 1995, another major Karen stronghold in Myanmar, Kawmoora, also fell. As this book went to press at the beginning of 1997, the KNU's 4,000-odd armed rebels once more found themselves facing a government onslaught and thousands more Karen had crossed into Thailand to join the 80,000 Karen refugees already in the country.

Later in 1995, the Burmese army shifted its attentions to Shan guerillas around Tachilek – not far from the Thai border town of Mae Sai. An estimated 3,000 people fled into Thailand to escape the battle. At the end of the year the infamous opium warlord Khun Sa also capitulated to the Slorc's men, and was airlifted to Yangon (see page 64).

There has been speculation that the defeat of the Karen is merely symptomatic of a far more serious challenge to the opposition. Until the recent release of Aung San Suu Kyi (see below), the pro-democracy movement was in danger of faltering. Almost all overt opposition to the government in Yangon is based outside the country, and despite the government's lack of democratic credentials, it is in a stronger position, militarily, economically and politically, than at any point since the late 1980s. As a western diplomat remarked to Myanmar-watcher Bertil Lintner at the beginning of 1995, "The pro-democracy movement has been marginalized. It's been overtaken by events inside the country".

Despite ceasefire agreements, NGOs, which assist refugee camps along the Thai border, reported the refugee total in May 1993 to be 75,281 – a 10% increase on the previous year. And there is no evidence that the status of the Rohinga Muslims being repatriated across the Bangladesh border – some 135,000 between Sep 1992 and Feb 1995 – has changed. Perhaps this explains why, at the end of 1994, there were still reportedly over 150,000 in refugee camps in Bangladesh. The junta's appalling human rights record prevents the resumption of aid from international development agencies, although Japan has begun to fund small-scale aid projects focussing on health and other humanitarian areas.

Aung San Suu Kyi's release

Towards the end of 1994 some cracks appeared in the stand-off between the most famous political prisoner in the world, Aung San Suu Kyi (see box on page 82) and the junta – or at least so it seemed. She was shown on state television and in the newspapers – for the first time in more than 5 years – smiling as she met two generals. There was much talk that she was about to be released; that she had 'done a deal' with the military. As it turned out she was not immediately released, and her husband stated that no secret deal had been negotiated. As Bertil Lintner explained in the *Far Eastern Economic Review* the meeting "amounted to recognition by the military junta that Suu Kyi is a problem that won't go away". Her imprisonment effectively blocked western support for the economic reforms being introduced, cutting off millions in investment. In a strange twist of logic, as a Yangon-based diplomat put it, the Slorc were as much a prisoner of Suu Kyi as she was of them.

However, with the victories over the Karen rebels in early 1995 (see above), some analysts identified a hardening in tone on the part of the Slorc. A diplomat in Yangon was quoted by Lintner as saying that since the visit of Chinese premier Li Peng in Dec 1994 "the Slorc has resumed the old hardline rhetoric. There is no more talk of Suu Kyi being 'our dear sister'. Now she is once again 'a foreigner who should go back to Britain'." The Slorc's new-found confidence was reflected in their reaction to the death of former prime minister U Nu on 14 February 1995: they simply ignored it; the state-controlled media did not even report his demise. U Nu, the last democratically elected prime minister, was overthrown by Ne Win in 1962. With his overthrow, Myanmar began its quick decline from being one of the richest countries in Southeast Asia, to one of the poorest. Now that he is dead, one of the few links with the past has been snuffed out. But a second link in the eyes of most Burmese is very much alive: pictures of Aung San Suu Kyi sitting on the knee of her father, Aung San, the father of independence, are hugely popular in the country.

As the 6th anniversary of her house arrest approached, few commentators held much hope that Daw [Aunt] Aung San Suu Kyi would be released from her residence on University Ave. Most believed that come 20 July – when her term would have been completed – the authorities would simply extend her sentence on some flimsy pretext. So her release on 10 July 1995 caught most commentators and diplomats by surprise. Indeed, just a few days before, Lt Gen Khin Nyunt had retorted to western human rights critics that the "rights of 45 million...are more important than the rights of the individual". Her picture was shown on television screens and in newspapers across the globe and most reporters initially interpreted the release as a great victory for the democracy movement. However it has since become clear that the Slorc were releasing her from a position of strength – not weakness – and it has not presaged a softening of line.

In mid-1995, the junta was in a comparatively secure position: most of the numerous insurgent groups had cast their lot with the Slorc, foreign investment was up, the democracy movement fragmented, and Myanmar's neighbours in Southeast Asia were following a policy of 'constructive engagement' or, alternatively, 'appeasement'. Yet, for as long as Suu Kyi remained under house arrest, western support and investment was frozen. Like Nelson Mandela in South Africa, she had become the symbol of repression and her release became an effective precondition for normalization. The Slorc no doubt reasoned that the country was now sufficiently stable to give Suu Kyi her freedom. With her release, Myanmar might then throw off it's label of 'pariah' state, opening it to flows of investment and multilateral and bilateral aid, and hastening the resumption of normal diplomatic relations with the international community. It is significant that Tokyo – Myanmar's largest aid donor – almost immediately announced it's resumption of official lending, while members of ASEAN saw the release as a vindication of their policy of constructive engagement.

The role of Japan in the release seems to have been considerable: it was the Japanese Foreign Ministry which first released news of Suu Kyi's release, before even Suu Kyi herself had been told. The Slorc may also have been prompted by the prospect of a debate in the American Congress banning all economic contacts with Myanmar which was due to begin on 11 July. If the motion had been passed, Myanmar's largest single foreign investment project – a gas pipeline being constructed by Unocal and Total

– would have been severely affected (see below). Nonetheless, it is likely that Yangon would have been willing even to have allowed this project to suffer if it felt that national stability might have been compromised.

Political developments since Suu Kyi's release

Although Suu Kyi claimed she was released without condition, laws are in place which make it difficult for her actively to campaign: there is a ban, for example, on gatherings of more than 5 people "walking, marching in procession, chanting slogans, delivering speeches...". Initially the media in Myanmar stayed silent on Daw Suu Kyi's release. *The New Light of Myanmar* ran stories on nation-building; the local television station, the usual fare of ministers' meetings and production targets. A government spokesman was reported in the London *Sunday Telegraph* as explaining: "The junta views her as an ordinary individual who does not merit a special mention in the media", adding, "Here we do not have censorship, we have selective presentation". However, later, the local television station did show pictures of her house and even an unprecedented interview with one supporter who said to the camera that he trusted "no other politicians in this country but the [late] Gen Aung San and Daw Aung San Suu Kyi". Suu Kyi's first public announcements were notably conciliatory, even referring to the Slorc's leaders as 'charming'. However, she also observed that Myanmar now had a stark choice between "dialogue and utter devastation".

To begin with the outside world, in the finely honed vernacular of diplomacy, was 'cautiously pessimistic' about the chances that Suu Kyi's release might presage a significant softening in the junta's line. But this was not to be. As this book went to press some 20 months on from Suu Kyi's release from house arrest, little seemed to have changed. The Slorc was just as cruel and cack-handed as ever. In July 1996 James Nichols, a Myanmar national and honorary consul for a number of European countries – as well as a friend of Suu Kyi – was arrested and sentenced to three years in prison for owning an unlicensed fax machine. He died in custody shortly after he began his sentence and the *New Light of Myanmar* contemptuously dismissed him as an 'unimportant crook'. The National League for Democracy, Suu Kyi's party, appeared no closer to influence, let alone power, and the convention drawing up the new constitution was carrying on without any input from the NLD. (The convention must be one of the longest running in history: it began its deliberations in Jan 1993 and was still up and running at the beginning of 1997.) Senior Minister Lee Kuan Yew of Singapore, was quoted in 1996 as saying: "At the end of the day, the opposition in Myanmar has to face the realities of life. The one instrument of effective government there is the army."

During 1996 the Slorc and Suu Kyi's positions hardened. Suu Kyi explicitly called on foreign companies not to invest in the country and asked foreign tourists to stay away from the Golden Land. After initially being conciliatory, later she wondered how peace and stability could be achieved "on a foundation of vindictiveness and violation of trust". For their part, the Slorc gave no ground and each week found new and friendly names for the opposition leader like 'snake' and 'sorceress'. In May 1996 the NLD held a congress for all its parliamentary members elected in 1990. The Slorc responded by arresting just as many of the MPs-elect as it could, managing to track down 238. (Most were released within a relatively short period, although Suu Kyi's assistant Win Htien was sentenced to 14 years in jail for allegedly attempting to smuggle a video tape recording the failure of Myanmar's rice harvest out of the country.) But 17 evaded the sweep and attended the congress. The government allowed the congress to go ahead and around 10,000 supporters attended the first day.

Through early and mid-1996, Asean continued to follow its policy of 'constructive engagement' while the West toyed with imposing sanctions. In August 1996 Asean invited Myanmar to its annual summit with observer status. Nonetheless even Lee Kuan Yew was circumspect as to the ability of Asean to sort out the mess that is Myanmar: "Asean cannot rescue Myanmar, even if it wants to, and I have the awful feeling rescuing Myanmar is beyond the capacity of even the United States." When Slorc's chairman General Than Shwe visited Malaysia in August 1996 almost 30 KL-based NGOs protested against his arrival. Prime Minister Mahathir, perhaps the most vocal advocate of the constructive engagement line, responded to journalists' questions by stating: "We believe that the way to bring people round to our way of thinking is to talk to them. Not to squeeze them or twist their arms behind their backs." Mahathir's view appeared to prevail when, at the end of 1996, Asean agreed that Myanmar would be admitted 'simultaneously' to the Association along with Laos and Cambodia – probably in mid-1997.

In the middle of 1996 the Slorc hit upon the novel idea of giving press briefings to present its side of events and allowing ministers travelling abroad to field questions from journalists. But this attempt at PR – however laughable it may have seemed to international observers – did not help to ease tensions in the country. Indeed, the situation became more tense as the year wore on. In late September riot police sealed off Aung San Suu Kyi's house on University Avenue and tried to prevent the public from listening to her weekly speeches. In October they began to arrest NLD supporters and democracy activists – something like 600 in total. Finally, in November, they seemed to orchestrate an attack on Suu Kyi herself. Her car was attacked by thugs and one seemed to have attempted to kill her, although whether it was an assasination attempt remains unclear. The junta denied involvement, but nobody believed them. The police and army stood by as the attack went ahead, and it seemed that the attackers came from the United Solidarity Development Association, effectively an arm of government. (A series of student demonstrations during December 1996, though they caused the military some loss of sleep, did not seem to be linked to opposition leader Suu Kyi.)

The Slorc's actions seemed, to most outsiders, to be untimely in the extreme. Myanmar has been angling for membership of Asean and seemed to be making good progress with vocal support from Malaysia's Prime Minister Mahathir Mohamad. The Philippines (particularly) and Thailand have always been more circumspect than Malaysia and openly expressed their doubts about awarding the generals with Asean membership when conditions in Myanmar are so fraught. Indeed, this was one of the few occasions when open disagreement has surfaced between the members of Asean, which tries hard to present a united front. The events in Yangon also brought the US closer to activating a new law which allows the government to impose economic sanctions if political repression becomes 'large scale' or if Suu Kyi is rearrested for 'political acts'. Even the EU seemed to be inching towards some political response. Josef Silverstein, a Myanmar specialist working in Rutgers University in the US, hazarded an explanation which called into question whether the Slorc had any idea about norms of international behaviour. "The Burmese generals", he suggested, "are living in a mythical world that they have created for themselves". Having been out of international circulation for so long, rather like someone new to courting, they have become incompetent, fumbling their way through relations.

Another explanation may be that the generals are feeling increasingly insecure. There have been rumours of splits in the army, of the *sangha* (monkhood) reasserting its influence, and of some of the rebel groups with which the Slorc has negotiated peace deals reneging on their agreements. Add to this mix of fears and insecurities, the US and Europe's hardening position, the failure of the rice crop, and an effective international sanctions movement using methods as diverse as cyber-campaigning and good old fashioned streetprotest, and it is not hard to see why Myanmar's generals are tightening their grip on debate at home. The key question, and one that is none too clear to even the most seasoned observer, is where it will go and, more to the point, where it will end.

Double-speak in Myanmar

- Foreign Minister Ohn Gyaw explained that Leo Nichols died in police custody because he was unused to the 'rich food' served to prisoners (press briefing to journalists, Jakarta, mid-1996)
- Planning Minister General David Abel stated that Myanmar's economic statistics – which even the World Bank and the International Monetary Fund find impossible to interpret – were 'totally transparent' (press briefing to journalists, Jakarta, mid-1996)
- Myanmar is "on the road to democracy suited to our history and unique to our conditions" (*New Light of Myanmar*, September 1996)
- Aung San Suu Kyi is "free to go where she wants" (junta spokesman, October 1996 while army barricades blocked access to Suu Kyi's house)
- The Slorc "is working hard to establish multi-party democracy" (junta spokesman, October 1996, paraphrased in *The Economist*)

ECONOMY

The path to poverty

In the 19th and early 20th centuries, Myanmar was a wealthy British colony, thanks to its fertile rice lands and other natural resources. Because of the fractious political climate in the **wake of independence** in 1948, there was no concerted effort to reconstruct the war-damaged economy. In the late 1950s private enterprise was encouraged, but following General Ne Win's 1962 coup d'état more than 15,000 private enterprises were nationalized. Ne Win tried to build an industrialized socialist state, free from foreign exploitation and influence. The policies excluded all foreigners – including Europeans, Indians and Chinese – from the commanding heights of the economy. Thousands of Myanmar's prosperous Indian merchants and Chinese shopkeepers fled the country and the economy stagnated. Economic control was placed firmly in the hands of the central government which was almost exclusively Burman. The approach to economic development adopted by the government at this time was based on the junta's seminal document, ***The Burmese way to Socialism***.

Only agriculture remained in private hands, although all surplus production had to be sold to the government for internal distribution and export. The economy was managed by soldiers who had no experience of business. Half the state budget was pumped into public sector industries; the value of goods produced represented a fraction of what was invested in their production. Agricultural production slumped, distribution

Myanmar's AIDS crisis

Myanmar is thought to be on the verge of an AIDS epidemic on a scale equivalent to Thailand's. It is also believed that the progress of the epidemic will mirror Thailand's experience, and after being confined mainly to intravenous drug users will rapidly spread among the heterosexual population. As of the end of Jun 1994 there were only 261 reported AIDS cases in Myanmar. However, over three-quarters of intravenous drug users are thought to be HIV-infected, and 11% of sex workers. It is this latter figure which suggests that AIDS will become a serious problem within the heterosexual population. Already, 1% of pregnant mothers are HIV-infected.

networks collapsed, black markets emerged and smuggling increased; unemployment became a serious problem. Ethnic insurgencies emptied state coffers as defence expenditure soared. By the early 1970s the government was conceding that its economic policies had failed and some reforms were introduced, although they failed to revitalize the economy.

Eventually, in Jun 1974, riots broke out which were sparked by food shortages. Further riots erupted 6 months later when the body of U Thant – the Burmese Secretary-General of the United Nations, who died in the US – was returned to Myanmar and students hijacked the funeral cortège and carried the coffin to Rangoon University, where he was buried. Though the assembled masses were brought together by grief, the cause of the riots was probably the declining economic conditions, soaring corruption and resentment over the ostentatious lifestyle of the members of the junta. After four days of student-led demonstrations focused on the University campus, the army moved in and crushed the movement. U Thant's coffin was disinterred and he was buried elsewhere in the city. Student demonstrations broke out again in 1976 and dissatisfaction even penetrated the ranks of the military élite, sparking a coup attempt by junior officers in Jul 1976.

By the late 1980s Myanmar was in **economic crisis**. Malnutrition was widespread, the few factories still working were operating at a fraction of their capacity, and the former world's greatest rice exporter was on the verge of becoming a rice importer. Hyper-inflation loomed and the value of the kyat – the national currency – on the black market had plummeted to one twentieth of its official value. Over the space of 40 years, Myanmar had gone from being one of the richest of the developing world's newly-independent states to being ranked the globe's 9th poorest country, with an estimated average per capita income of about US$280 a year and a foreign debt of nearly US$5bn. In 1987 the government was forced to go to the UN requesting **'Least Developed Country'** (LLDC) status.

What little foreign exchange the economy did generate was pumped into defence expenditure. The Slorc steadily obtained modern weapons and military technology from around the world. Primarily from China, but also from France, Germany, Sweden and the former Yugoslavia. China has helped to remodel Myanmar's navy – still largely based on WW2-era patrol boats. Six first class attack craft were supplied in 1991 accompanied by 70 Chinese naval personnel to assist in training local crews and maintainence workers. Intelligence sources report Chinese technicians have also helped build new bases at Hainggyi in the Ayeyarwady Delta near Pathein and in the Coco Islands, S of the Burmese mainland, installing new Chinese-made radar equipment. In the 5 years to 1993, the army had expanded to 350,000 men and military expenditure was absorbing at least 5% of GDP, probably considerably more, and 40-50% of government expenditure. A popular saying in Yangon is 'join the army if you want to get rich and have a privileged life'. Recruiting is easy: Myanmar has thousands of poor eager to take the generals' shilling.

The Slorc embraces the market

Following the 1988 uprising, the regime did a U-turn, reversing its isolationist stance and embracing an ostensibly market-based **'open-door policy'**. Foreign investment-friendly laws were put on the statute books and the government began searching for likely partners. But after nearly ten years of economic reform, the results – bar one or two areas of growth – have been disappointing. Corruption, poor planning, political instability, and the drain on resources due to the need to support a massive military machine, have retarded growth. The military still controls many businesses and few people can remember how a capitalist system operates. Some factories are working at about 10% of their capacity. Initially, in order to pay for new construction projects the government simply ordered that more money be printed, fuelling inflation, and this Micky Mouse approach to economics still, apparently, holds attractions for many generals.

In mid-May 1993 the Ministry of Planning issued a 300-page report in which it claimed the economy had expanded by 11% the previous year. In 1996 the government claimed growth of 8.2% in the four years from 1992. There is no doubt that trade and investment have picked up in recent years. The border with China only officially opened to trade in 1988 following an agreement with Beijing. Two-way trade quickly rose to at least US$1.5bn a year – not including opium trafficking – and cheap Chinese goods have flooded into the country. Under the Slorc's market reforms, entrepreneurs have flourished, especially in the Mandalay area (while the rest of Myanmar sinks into recession). Border trade with China is helping Myanmar's economy to grow by as much as 6% per year. The army, collaborating closely with officials in China's neighbouring Yunnan province, encouraged Chinese businessmen to settle in Myanmar. In Mandalay, the newly built luxury villas that can be seen on many streets are, it is said, almost all owned by Chinese. According to one local source, corrupt immigration officials began selling the papers of dead Myanmaris to business immigrants from China, Thailand and even Singapore. Arrivals with dubious connections soon set up shop. Lo Hsing Han, a former drug warlord whose death sentence for trafficking and high treason was suspended by Ne Win, has substantial investments in Mandalay. The two proprietors of the *Lucky Hotel* in Mandalay are related to the notorious Khun Sa, a Sino-Shan outlaw who commanded a 6,500 man opium army in the NE until he surrendered to the government in 1995. Along the China-Myanmar border, Chinese army sources report that the crack 99th Brigade has formed its own business arm – aptly named the 99th Co. Many of the large infrastructure projects currently underway in the country – including the highway being built from Yangon to Mandalay, and the railway line from Mandalay to near the Chinese border at Myitkyina – are being undertaken by

Myanmar: tabulating destitution

Life expectancy at birth	58 years
% of population with access to safe water	33%
Infant mortality per 1,000 live births	80
% of under-5 year olds malnourished	31%
per capita income	US$300

Chinese firms. The visit of Chinese Premier Li Peng to Yangon in Jan 1995 illustrated the growing ties between Beijing and Yangon.

Foreign investment has also risen following new foreign investment legislation in 1989 which permits 100% foreign ownership. Britain, the US and France have the largest single investments in the country, but more important in terms of number of projects are Malaysia, Singapore, Hong Kong and China. Many of these Asian-based firms are not accountable to share holders and eager for quick profits. Myanmar may still be unable to obtain funding from the World Bank, the International Monetary Fund and the Asian Development Bank (because of the pro-democracy crackdown of 1988), but gradually Myanmar seems to be losing its status as a pariah state. In 1994 Singapore's Prime Minister Goh Chok Tong visited Yangon and in 1996 ministers attended the Asean summit as 'observers'. Foreign investors are sneaking back as the Slorc tries to present the acceptable side of government.

The big S Korean manufacturer, Daewoo, now has three factories, making electronics and clothing, around Yangon. The attraction of the country to foreign investors lies in very low wage rates – even by Southeast Asian standards. In 1994, workers were being paid less than US$0.50 a day. In neighbouring Thailand the minimum wage in Bangkok is 10 times this figure. Pepsi have recently signed a joint venture with the government. The people of Yangon have been drinking Pepsi at the rate of 11,000 cases per week, a pittance compared to other Asian capitals but astounding in Myanmar's context. At the beginning of 1995 French oil company Total and the US firm Unocal signed a US$1bn deal to build a gas pipeline to Thailand.

Sorely in need of foreign exchange, foreign companies are being given access to Myanmar's wealth of natural resources by the Slorc. Lucrative fishing, logging and oil concessions are all up for grabs. This, according to some analysts, has turned Myanmar into a free-for-all jamboree. Although stringent environmental controls may exist on paper, the government has been unable to control and police the logging and fishing industries and foreign companies have little incentive to adopt sustainable practices. Another major source of foreign exchange is the annual Gems, Jade and Pearl Emporium which is held in Yangon every Mar (see page 216). This raises about US$11mn a year for the government. Historical animosities between Myanmar and Thailand, for example, have been swept aside in the rush to get rich quick. The Slorc government is trying to revive the mining sector and has begun approving foreign participation in exploiting the country's mineral resources. Until recently the development of Myanmar's mineral resources was severely hampered by the fact the rebel ethnic groups controlled large areas of the mineral-rich highlands. Now that many of these groups have laid down their arms the prospects are rather brighter.

A miracle in the making or developmental sleight of hand?

So: is Myanmar an economic miracle in the making, a tiger cub crawling out of its den? Government ministers would certainly wish potential investors to think so, and there is undoubtedly a great deal of visible activity, in Yangon particularly where ugly new skyscrapers are disfiguring the elegant city's colonial fabric and where colour televisions and CD players are piled high in boxes by the streetside. In this respect at least, Yangon feels much like Saigon (Ho Chi Minh City) did in the early 1990s as that country embarked on the market road. But there are alot of reasons to suspect that Myanmar's development experience is qualitatively different from that of the other Asian tigers.

The government of Myanmar claims that economic growth averaged 8.2% in the four years between 1992 and 1995 and that in 1996 it grew by 7.8%. However it should be remembered that that is growth from a very low base and after years of economic contraction. For example, in the early 1990s Myanmar's economic output was 10% lower than in the mid-1980s. In addition, it seems that the benefits of recent foreign investment-driven growth (see below) are accruing to only a very small minority of the population – the already rich and powerful. The rest of Myanmar's inhabitants are seeing little real improvement in their standards of living. In 1996, the official inflation rate was running at 23%; the real rate was at least 35%, and for certain essential products, like rice and cooking oil, prices rising even faster. At government stores, government workers can buy rice at 6 kyat per kilogram while it sells for anything up to 52 kyat in the markets. Similar policies favour the sale of petrol to civil servants. The official price is 4 kyat per litre but the black market rate is twice that. Car owners are rationed to 15 litres per week. Salaries in the public sector have not risen since 1989 while the prices of most daily necessities have roughly tripled in the same period. (In 1996, a civil servant earned between 600 and 2,000 kyat a month; while a chicken cost 300 kyat in the market.) The inefficiency of the state marketing system has prompted the rise of a nationwide black market, with huge disparities between official and unofficial prices. Only the military elite, their supporters and a handful of businessmen can afford to live well. Giant military enterprises grouped under a Defence Services holding company, whose capital amounts to 10% of the GDP, now reap wealth and distribute privileges for a minority. For instance, when military officers retire, they are transferred to positions of privilege in the civil administration, government-owned factories and embassies. As long as they remain loyal, their future is certain. And if lower order military men and businessmen remain loyal to those above them, then they too will be rewarded. Recently it was reported that businessmen presented 30 cars as wedding gifts to the child of a senior Slorc general.

The low salaries paid to civil servants and soldiers means two things. First, that many have to top up their meagre wages by moonlighting in other jobs or by taking bribes. It also means, however, that the government is almost obliged to top up their salaries by providing them with subsidized goods. This provides the government with a dilemma. To build a vibrant economy Myanmar needs to have a convertible currency. (At the end of 1996 the kyat was officially pegged at a rate of 5.9 to the US$. On the free market, kyat were changing hands at 160 to the US$.) Though the special stores for government workers have closed, those in positions of influence can still take advantage of the overvalued exchange rate by changing kyat into dollars at the official rate when they go abroad. In 1996 the World Bank highlighted currency reform as a key step that the government had to take if the economy was really to take off. Yet, as the Bank baldly explained, the Slorc was hamstrung by 'the fear that influential groups in the population would lose as a result'. Whether the generals will grasp the nettle of currency reform is to be seen, but most economists see it as critical.

On paper it seems that **foreign investment** is also picking up – the government likes to quote a figure of US$3, sometimes US$4 billion. But only around a third of this has been 'realised' – the remainder is hanging around waiting for something to do. There are many impediments to investment beyond Myanmar's unstable political climate. The official exchange rate, 30 times higher than the black market rate, is a major disincentive to foreign investors in Myanmar. It is notable how narrowly based foreign investment is in the country. Almost all is concentrated in natural resource exploitation (oil and gas, other minerals, timber and fisheries) or in the tourist industry. At the end of 1996 oil and gas alone accounted for US$1.4 billion of the cumulative foreign investment. Few foreign companies are building factories in Myanmar. The World Bank is understandably dubious that economic growth based on a such a narrow base is sustainable and they note that little money is going into improving the country's abysmal physical (roads, power) and human (education, health) infrastructures. It is thought that over recent years spending on health and education has actually declined. Instead almost half of government investment – 45% in 1995 – is pumped into the military. Yangon's port must be one of the most perhistoric in the world, with just two cranes able to service container vessels. Rather than braving Yangon and its interminable delays, many importers prefer to truck their goods from Thailand's capital Bangkok to the port of Ranong on the Andaman Sea, where they are transshipped to Victoria Point by little more than wooden fishing boats. The World Bank's July 1996 report on Myanmar's economy cannot have made for pleasant bed time reading for the leadership. It stated:

> "...the long term sustainability of Myanmar's economic growth is still questionable, due to the persistance of both macroeconomic instability and the potential for political instability as well as grossly inadequate human infrastructure development, especially in the field of basic education."

It is also true that not only is foreign investment perhaps not as great as the government would like the outside world to believe, but there has also been a degree of **disinvestment**, and some analysts wonder whether Myanmar will become the South Africa of the 90s. Levi Strauss, the American clothing giant, started the trend when it pulled out of Myanmar in 1992 on the grounds that the country's human rights record did not shape up with the company's ethical investment code. Reebok, the Massachusettes-based sports shoe manufacturer, took the same step in 1994 and in 1995 America's Federated Department Stores – which owns Macy's in New York – declared that it would stop buying clothes made in Myanmar. In 1996 these companies were followed by PepsiCo, Carlsburg and Heineken who all said they would either pull out of the country or shelve plans to set up shop there (see page 9). There can be little doubt that the Coalition for Corporate Withdrawal from Myanmar, a US-based pressure group, played a role in forcing the decision. Campaigners are picketing Unocal petrol stations in California, and share holders have filed resolutions against the company's investments in Myanmar. This is all part of an effort to, as activists say, 'take the battle out of the jungle and into the boardroom'. Companies like Pepsi, which try so hard to massage their youth appeal, must squirm when they see student slogans

Sources of foreign investment in Myanmar, 1988-1996 (cumulative)

Singapore	US$895mn
Britain	US$808mn
France	US$465mn
Malaysia	US$420mn
Thailand	US$420mn
US	US$241mn
Japan	US$106mn
Others	US$445mn
Total foreign investment	US$3,800mn

Note: a liberal foreign investment law was promulgated in 1989

like 'Pepsi can take the red off its cans, but Pepsi can't wash the blood from its hands'. Even Suu Kyi has come out against foreign investment in Myanmar. In mid-1996 she said that Japanese investors, among the country's largest, had ignored the human rights abuses and were directly and indirectly supporting industries which kept workers in slave-like conditions. She asked foreign companies to halt their investment in the country until political and human rights conditions had improved.

The claim that Myanmar is a market economy is also dubious, despite the impressively reformist policies that have been introduced. The government, often informally, still exerts a heavy hand and many of the key sectors – rice and teak for example – remain state monopolies. Those foreign investors hoping to discover a Golden Land of Market Opportunity often leave frustrated and disillusioned. The key player in the economy remains the army – under the auspices of the military's sprawling holding company, the Union of Myanmar Economic Holdings – which controls all the major industries and coordinates much of the foreign investment. Expatriate businessmen in Yangon say that it is virtually impossible for a foreign investor to get a project off the ground without close links with high-ranking army officers. One Western ambassador explained to Bertil Lintner in 1996: "Before the 1988 coup, there was sham socialism. Now the Burmese have to put up with sham capitalism."

Part of the problem with examining the tea leaves of Myanmar's economy is that even the best informed economists have only a very hazy idea of what is going on. Statistics are thin on the ground, and accurate statistics are virtually non-existant. It was for this reason that at the end of 1995 the Washington-based International Monetary Fund sent a group of economists to the country with the task of setting up a statistical database. Only when they know what is going on, the logic seemed to be, would the IMF been in a position to pronounce on what should be done.

Those who argue the case for constructive engagement sometimes suggest that there is a link between economic and political reform. Certainly, a UN report released in 1993 stated that if things did not change soon on the economic front, then further social and political instability could follow. The report concluded that fundamental reforms were needed and that the first step in bringing the economy back into line was political stability and the introduction of a civilian government. The economic reforms which date back over almost a decade have been a disappointment to the government. As U Set Maung, a former minister and now an economic advisor to the government explained – not entirely accurately – to the *Far Eastern Economic Review* at the beginning of 1995, "It was very easy to move from the capitalist economy to a socialist one – you just nationalize everything. But trying to do the reverse – we're in uncharted waters."

To some extent the state of Myanmar's economy is reflected in the number of workers who are willing to leave their homes and travel to Thailand to work – often illegally – in the dirtiest and poorest paid of jobs. In 1994 it was estimated that there were 283,500 Burmese working in Thailand, mostly as domestic servants, washerwomen, on trawlers, as construction workers and prostitutes. The greatest concentration are to be found in the provinces sharing their borders with Myanmar – Kanachanaburi, Rayong, Chiang Rai and Tak. In Mae Sot for example, Burmese workers are trucked across the border every morning, returning home to Myanmar in the evening. Because the majority of these economic migrants are illegally working in Thailand they are not protected in any way by Thai labour laws. Employers often take advantage of their status, treating them almost as slaves.

To try and ease Myanmar's chronic power deficit, and to supply electricity to Thailand, the two countries have agreed on plans to build several hyrdo-electric dams. This includes a US$5bn string of dams along the rivers on the Thai-Burmese border including a colossal 4,540 megawatt dam on the Salween (Thaniwan) River. A further seven dams are planned in the S (in Karen state), including one across the Kra River in the southernmost tip of Myanmar, three on the Moei Than Lwin River, and one on the Nam Hkok River. There are also plans to build the Golden Square highway from Chaing Rai in Thailand to Ta Lua via Kentung, and a second highway from Chiang Khong, also in Thailand, to Huai Xai in Laos, and eventually to Jinghong in China.

Agriculture

Although many people have migrated to towns and cities in search of work over the past decade, nearly three quarters of Myanmar's 45 million population is rural, and agriculture directly supports about two thirds of the population. In 1994, agriculture accounted for almost 63% of GDP.

Half a century ago Myanmar was the world's largest rice exporter. Since then the rice sector has recovered from near collapse – at one point Myanmar was a near rice importer – to being a significant exporter once more. There has been considerable public investment in new irrigation facilities in the Ayeyarwady Delta, and farmers are now more able to obtain subsidized inputs. In 1995 the country shipped just over 1 million tonnes and rice represented the country's single largest export, generating 22% of export revenue. The government sees agriculture as the lead sector in the country's transformation from Least Developed Country, to Tiger. Given the reluctance of foreign companies to invest to any great extent, and the government's own lack of funds, agriculture and other natural resources are the only areas of economic activity that show much potential. Unfortunately for many rice farmers, 1996 looks like being a poor year. The Summer (main) rice harvest is said to have failed.

During the British colonial period, the Ayeyarwady Delta region became one of the most productive rice-bowls in Asia. Following General Ne Win's 1962 coup, tenant farmers rejoiced as landlords had their land confiscated and debts were cancelled. But they had to sell their rice to the government at a third of the price on the international market. Within 10 years, the volume of rice exported had suffered a 12-fold decline from the heady days before WW2.

Today, population pressure on farmland is growing – both among the indigenous groups, which practice slash-and-burn agriculture, and in the traditional rice-growing areas. The Slorc's decision to give farmers greater freedom in choosing crops and partial deregulation of agricultural prices have boosted output. But for Myanmar to truly experience a Green Revolution the reforms will have to go much further. In 1995 the government set a rice quota of around 15% to 20% of production from each hectare, and then paid less than half the market price for that share. In some areas farmers simply do not see the point of producing a surplus if it is just going to be bought by the government at a take-away price. But where irrigation and inputs are available some farmers have responded to government exhortations. Win Oo a farmer in the Ayeyarwady Delta, for example, told Gordon Fairclough of the *Far Eastern Economic Review* that "Life has never been so good". He told the reporter that he was waiting for the day when he would be able to buy a car. "Then", he said, "I'll drive myself there. That is my dream."

Timber

About a third of Myanmar's land area is covered in forest, much of which is comprised of teak and other hardwoods. Myanmar has about 75% of the world's teak reserves – although it is disappearing fast. Many of the best known books written by British colonial residents were about the tough life of the teak-wallahs. In the days before World War II, there were said to be more than 5,000 elephants working Myanmar's teak forests. The elephants allowed selective logging to be practised and left minimal environmental impact compared with the bulldozers and trucks used today. Overlogging in neighbouring Thailand and then the imposition of a logging ban in the kingdom in 1989 led Thai companies to transfer their activities to Myanmar. They used to deal exclusively with the ethnic minority insurgent groups along the border – most notably the Karen – but more recently, they have begun to work directly with the Yangon government, which is keen to award logging concessions as a means of earning sorely needed foreign exchange.

At least 20 Thai timber companies raced to exploit the highly lucrative contracts awarded by the Slorc. (They realize these concessions will not last and so are mining the forests for short term gains. A report in the *Financial Times* in 1990 estimated that all Myanmar's teak forests will have disappeared within 15 years.) More than 160,000 tonnes of teak logs and a further 500,000 tonnes of other hardwood logs were being extracted annually by Thai logging firms in the early 1990s. In 1991/92, Myanmar earned US$112mn from the exports of logs, processed wood and wood products to Thailand. Thai timber firms are closely associated with the Thai military which has long fostered links with the junta in Yangon. The Thai logging companies are building logging roads into the jungle giving the Burmese army all weather routes to previously inaccessible insurgent areas. At the end of 1993, however, the Slorc announced the termination of all logging concessions in Myanmar, to the chagrin of Thai firms who had invested heavily in equipment. Several theories have been put forward to explain this move. One is that the Slorc was perturbed by the fact that Thai logging companies were paying a logging tax to ethnic rebel forces along the border. The second explanation is that the Slorc simply wants to increase their income from the sale of the country's natural resources. Significantly, in 1994 Burmese companies were awarded logging concessions and given permission to sell timber to Thai companies via Yangon.

Surprisingly, on paper at least, the Burmese government adopts a very enlightened environmental position. All the right words – sustainable development, social forestry, sustainable yield, reafforestation – are used, and government reports and documents might lead one to believe that the administration in Yangon is 'green'. The problem, and this applies almost as much to the other countries of Southeast Asia as it does to Myanmar, is that words are not sufficient. It seems that Yangon is playing a canny game of climbing on the green bandwagon hoping, in the process, to improve its international image.

Oil

International oil companies from America, Britain, the Netherlands, France, Australia, Japan, S Korea, Thailand and Malaysia have been awarded onshore and offshore exploration and production licences, mainly in the Tenasserim Peninsula. Before World War II, Myanmar was an important oil exporter – and was the birthplace of the Burmah Oil Company. Installations were sabotaged and destroyed during the war, but the surviving wells have been in use ever since – although production levels have declined. There are thought to be large untapped oil and gas reserves both on and offshore.

The single largest investment in Myanmar is a US$1bn joint venture between French and US oil companies Total and Unocal who are building a pipeline to carry gas from the off-shore gas fields in the Andaman Sea to Thailand. When it is completed – probably in mid-1988 – it should earn Myanmar US$200mn a year in exports. But because the pipeline will run through territory partially controlled by Mon and Karen rebels, Burmese soldiers have been needed to protect the pipeline from sabotage. In 1995, a Mon spokesperson stated that "Violence to destroy the pipeline would be our last option, but in the end we would have no choice". Unocal, in a letter to shareholders, in a fine example of business babble, claimed that "We would never allow our activities anywhere to be the cause of human suffering." How determined the insurgents are to prevent the pipeline being laid is uncertain. By late 1996 about 10 workers had been killed in armed attacks on the project and pressure from activists in the US was growing. Unocal even seemed to be contemplating selling out to an Asian oil company.

Tourism

In 1992 the military junta decided that the tourist industry was to be the panacea for Myanmar's economic ailments. Grand plans have been laid, and the target of attracting 500,000 tourists by 1996 was set (some officials state a figure of 1 million). Private tour operators are blossoming, while old hotels are being renovated and new ones built in joint ventures with private companies. Much of the finance comes from Japan, Singapore, S Korea and Hong Kong, and many of the projects are BOT (Build, Operate, Transfer) agreements. In these schemes, the foreign partner runs the business for 30 years, and then transfers it to the state, free of charge. China is also helping to build an international airport at Mandalay and is involved in numerous other infrastructural projects. More ambitious and outlandish plans still include a ski resort on Hkakobo Razi, resorts and golf courses on the Andaman Islands, and casinos in the Gold Triangle.

To further boost the tourist industry, 1996-1997 has been declared **'Visit Myanmar Year'** (the year began on 18 November 1996). Whether these targets will be met appears unlikely. In 1995, the country attracted around 100,000 visitors, up from a mere 5,000 in 1989, and 63,000 in 1994. To increase the number of visitors 5-fold in a year seems a tall order. Even with a frenetic building programme, it is likely that the tourist infrastructure will be woefully limited compared with other Southeast Asian countries. In 1996 the country could offer tourists just 6,000 hotel rooms – around 3,000 in Yangon – and there weren't even enough airline seats to carry half a million bums. At the end of 1995, international flights into Yangon could manage just 4,100 seats a week. With a domestic airline renowned for its poor safety record, a poorly maintained road system, still tight government controls on the movement of tourists, and hotels and restaurants in the government sector which are grossly overpriced, this is not a country that is likely to attract tourists looking for the good life. The *Strand Hotel* in Yangon, the finest hotel in the country, charges US$300 a night for a room when there is no swimming pool and no 24 hrs room service.

There is also the question of whether, in Myanmar's case, tourism is a 'good thing'. This is always a difficult question (see page 20 for a discussion of tourism), but in this instance there is also the issue of whether foreign visitors are helping to shore-up the Slorc by providing foreign exchange to assist in, for example, the army's war against minority ethnic rebels. It might also be argued that visiting the country is tantamount to supporting the government. On the other hand, visitors can, by their presence, also be sources of information in a country where news is tightly controlled. Ultimately, of course, every visitor makes their own decision; it is not a simple, nor an easy one. Visitors might consider staying in privately-owned hotels, eating in locally-owned restaurants, using local tour companies and generally avoiding state-owned and managed enterprises. They are also usually more professional, friendlier, and better value for money (see page 350).

In 1996 democracy leader Aung San Suu Kyi explicitly requested that tourists stay away from the country until political conditions had improved. "We would like people to keep away precisely during these months [of Visit Myanmar Year] as a demonstration of solidarity". In the past she has been rather more circumspect in her comments on tourism and tourists, seeing sensitive tourism by well-informed groups and individuals as potentially beneficial. Her view seems to have changed, and on being asked by James Pringle of the London *Times* whether this would not hurt many small businesses that have no links with the Slorc, she replied: "It is true that some will be hurt, but I am afraid it cannot be helped. We all have to put up with some hardship. We have to make sacrifices in order to get where we want to." For more information on the arguments that are deployed to argue for or against tourism see page 9.

Myanmar: fact file

Geographic

Land area	677,000 sq km	Hkakobo Razi	5,881 m
Arable land as % of total	14.5%	Average rainfall in Yangon	2,500 mm
Average annual rate of deforestation	0.3%	Average temperature in Yangon	27°C
Highest mountain			

Economic

Income/person (1988)	US$200	Total debt (% GNP)	8.8%
GDP/person (PPP*, 1992)	US$751	Debt service ratio (% exports)	15.4%
GNP growth (/capita, 1965-1980)	1.6%	Military expenditure (% total expenditure)	39%
GDP growth, 1994-95	6.8%	Total value of exports 1995	US$922mn
GDP growth, 1995-96	7.8%	1995 (including drugs)	US$1,800mn
% labour force in agriculture	73%		

Social

Population	45.6 million	Population in absolute poverty	15.3%
Population growth rate		Rural population as % of total	74%
1960-91	2.2%	Growth of urban population	
1990-94	2.2%	1960-92	3%/year
Adult literacy rate	83%	1990-94	3.3%/year
Mean years of schooling	2.5 years	Urban population in largest city (%)	32%
Tertiary graduate as % of age group	n.a.	Televisions per 1,000 people	2

Health

Life expectancy at birth	58 years	Calorie intake as % of requirements	116%
Infant mortality rate (/1,000 live births)	80	Malnourished children under 5 years old	31%
Population with access to clean water	33%	Contraceptive prevalence rate†	5%

* PPP = Purchasing Power Parity (based on what it costs to buy a similar basket of goods and services in different countries).

† % of women of childbearing age using contraception.

Source UNDP (1994-5) *Human development report 1995*, OUP: New York, World Bank (1996) *World development report 1996*, OUP: New York; and other sources.

Yangon (Rangoon)

ရန်ကုန်

WHEN King Alaungpaya captured the riverside village of Dagon from the Mons in 1755, he rechristened it *Yangon* – 'the end of war'. It was a gloriously optimistic name for the little trading settlement that was to become the capital of Burma: less than a century later, Yangon was destroyed during the Second Anglo-Burmese War. In more recent times its streets ran with blood during the army's brutal crackdown on anti-government demonstrators in 1988. Over the years, the city has also been rocked by violent earthquakes and devastated by fires – in 1841 it burned to the ground and was rebuilt by King Tharrawaddy.

Modern downtown Yangon suffers from decades of neglect – but therein lies its appeal. Its buildings are crumbling, their paintwork chipped and weather-beaten. Over-crowded teak-bodied Chevrolet buses, dating from the 1940s, still ply the pot-holed streets which are lined by fractured pavements. In recent years, migrants have flooded into the city from all over Myanmar and its population has more than trebled since the 1970s (to around 4 million). Yangon's markets and streets are thronging with longyi-clad traders and hawkers and the fact that the city is a disintegrating relic of the colonial age makes it one of the most fascinating capitals in Southeast Asia. One of the city's most famous landmarks, the *Strand Hotel*, has been restored at great expense. Its opulent trappings seem out of place in a city that has barely changed for half a century, and where tens of thousands of people live in squalor.

Yangon was never a royal capital like Mandalay or a religious city like Bagan, although the original settlement of Dagon grew up around the magnificent Shwedagon Pagoda, which was – and remains – the focus of Myanmar's Buddhist faith. When the British captured Yangon in 1852, it was still a jumble of thatched huts and when they united Upper and Lower Burma in 1885, after the Second Anglo-Burmese War, Yangon became the capital. It was rebuilt from scratch, on a grid system, with wide boulevards and tree-lined streets. The British transformed Yangon into the administrative centre for Further India; the river port was expanded and commerce became its raison d'être. Rangoon quickly grew into a booming entrepôt – trading in rice, oil and teak – and assumed a cosmopolitan air, attracting Indians, Chinese, Malays, Thais and Europeans. One traveller who visited it in 1912 wrote: "It was difficult immediately to grasp the paradox that the -capital of Burma was not a Burmese city, but a trade emporium." Its cosmopolitan air evaporated after Burmese independence in 1948 and in 1962, following General Ne Win's seizure of power, Myanmar closed its doors to the outside world. There was an exodus of foreign traders from Yangon – other than a few groups which hung on in the markets of Chinatown and 'Little India'. Yangon became an urban fossil, and for 3 decades has remained virtually untouched.

Yangon's British-designed grid system was devised with the monsoons in mind. Shorter streets act as ventilators: they run roughly NE to SW – in the direction of the two prevailing winds. Yangon is built on a spit and is surrounded by water on three sides: the Yangon (or Hlaing) River to the S and W, and Pazundaung Creek, a tributary of the Yangon River, to the E. The Yangon River is navigable up to the capital and beyond, and most of Myanmar's imports and exports go through the city's docks. The main wharves and warehouses are opposite the *Strand Hotel*.

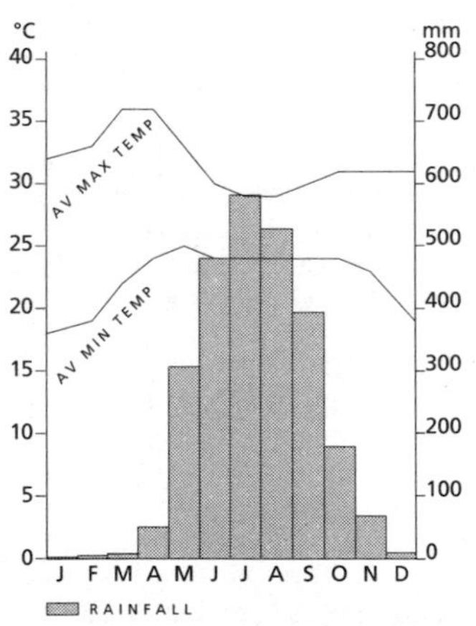

Climate: Yangon

Aung San Suu Kyi is making speeches from her house on Sat and Sun at about 1500. Some locals worry about attending for fear of being filmed and hounded by the authorities, but it is safe for foreigners.

PLACES OF INTEREST

The **Shwedagon Pagoda** sits about 3 km NW of the centre on Singuttura Hill. The physical presence of the Shwedagon's golden stupa dominates Yangon and its spiritual magnetism in turn dominates Myanmar, attracting tens of thousands of pilgrims each year. It is a visually impressive monument. The British writer, Somerset Maugham, when he visited Yangon early this century, was moved to write that the Shwedagon was "like a sudden hope in the dark night of the soul". The pagoda dates back about 2,500 years and was built to house eight sacred hairs of the Buddha. Its original shape has changed beyond all recognition over the centuries – it has remained in continuous use and has been periodically enlarged, restored and rebuilt.

Its bell-shaped superstructure, resting on a terraced base, is covered in about 60 tonnes of gold-leaf, which is constantly being replaced (100 sheets cost about 900 kyat). The gilded *hti*, on top, is hung with gold and silver bells and studded with rubies, sapphires and topaz. Even the gold and silver weather vane is decorated with 1,100 diamonds as well as precious and semi-precious stones; on it sits the diamond orb, encrusted with 4,350 diamonds and crowned with a 76 carat diamond, Kipling called it a 'winking wonder'. The priceless treasures of Burma's holiest shrine can only be marvelled at by visiting pilgrims, who donate around 10,000 kyat a day to pay for its upkeep. Walls, doors and stucco-work are continuously being torn down and replaced – although major renovations and architectural additions must now be approved by the Department of Archaeology.

The legend surrounding the pagoda's construction concerns two Burman merchants who travelled to India and met the Buddha under the sacred bodhi tree. They offered him cakes and honey and as a measure of his appreciation, the Buddha gave them eight sacred hairs, plucked from his head. On the way home to Burma, four of the hairs were given away to kings en route, but the remaining four were presented to the local ruler in Dagon, King Okkalapa, who enshrined them on the holy Singuttara Hill. The story goes that when the site was later excavated, the golden casket containing the sacred relics was miraculously found to contain all eight hairs.

The original pagoda was only 9m high. The Moghul emperor Asoka was its first notable pilgrim; he set the precedent by ordering its first restoration. Successive monarchs enlarged it over the years: King Byinnya-U of Pegu raised it to 22m in 1362 and Queen Shinsawbu of Pegu (1453-1472) built an even bigger Mon-style pagoda on top of it, which she gilded with her own weight in gold. Her son-in-law, King Dhammazedi later offered four times his, and his wife's, weight in gold, which was beaten into gold leaf and layered on the stupa. The Shwedagon expanded; every time an earthquake struck – and there were several during the 16th century – it was restored and rebuilt. In 1774 it attained its present height of 107m. The

Yangon place names

Botataung Pagoda
ဗိုလ်တထောင်ဘုရား

Buddhist Art Museum
ဗုဒ္ဓအနုပညာပြတိုက်

Kaba Aye Pagoda
ကမ္ဘာအေးဘုရား

Kandawgye
ကန်တော်ကြီး

Kyaukhtatgyi Pagoda
ခြောက်ထပ်ကြီးဘုရား

Maha Bandoola Park
မဟာဗန္ဓုလပန်းခြံ

Maha Pasan Guha
မဟာပါသာဏလိုဏ်ဂူ

Maha Wizaya Pagoda
မဟာဝိဇယစေတီ

Martyrs' Mausoleum
အာဇာနည်ကုန်း

National Museum
အမျိုးသားပြတိုက်

Ngahtatgyi Pagoda
ငါးထပ်ကြီးဘုရား

Shwedagon Pagoda
ရွှေတိဂုံဘုရား

Strand Hotel
စထရင်းဟိုတယ်

Sule Pagoda
ဆူးလေဘုရား

main gilding of the stupa was undertaken during the reign of King Hsinbyushin (of Ava) in the late 18th century and the present 7-tiered, gold-plated *hti* was donated by King Mindon in 1871. Above the plinth there are three terraces, and above them rises the dome, shaped like an inverted begging-bowl. Higher still there are multiple mouldings, two bands of ornamental lotus designs and a gold-plated spire, shaped like a banana bud, on which sit the jewel-encrusted *hti* and weather vane.

There are four entrances to the Shwedagon. The main entrances are on the S and the E side, where there are bazaars with stallholders licensed to sell goods for pilgrims. The W stairway was closed for almost 80 years during the British colonial period. It was originally built by Ma May Gale, King Tharrawaddy's wife, but was destroyed by fire in 1931. The N stairway was built in 1460 by Queen Shinsawbu. The walkways lead out onto the 5.7 ha pagoda terrace, which is a forest of 64 mini-pagodas, temples and shrines with four larger pagodas in the centre of each side. British writer Aldous Huxley described the Shwedagon as having a "merry-go-round style of architecture," a sort of "sacred fun fair," where pilgrims now pose for family photographs in front of the extravagant golden backdrop.

Around the terrace, at the eight compass points, are the eight planetary or birth posts; the Burmese leave offerings at their birth post, to appease the guardian spirit of their fate, which is represented by a planet and an animal. The Buddhist 8-day week is squeezed into the Gregorian 7-day week by dividing Wed in two – Rahu, Wed afternoon, is believed to be the planet which causes solar eclipses.

On the main terrace are several pavilions (*tazaungs*) and resting places (*zayats*) with traditional tiered roofs. Visitors, like the pilgrims, should walk around the pagoda in a clockwise direction. Starting from the top of the S stairway, the most notable features are:

- The *Arakanese Prayer Pavilion*, with intricate woodcarvings, is in the SW corner of the platform (to the left of the reclining Buddha prayer hall). It was donated by pilgrims from Rakhine (Arakan). Virtually opposite are the figures of Mani Lamu and the King of the Nats (see page 67).
- The *Kassapa Adoration Hall*, on the W side of the stupa, was gutted by fire in 1931 and rebuilt 4 years later. The main image is Kassapa, the Third Buddha.
- Opposite the Kassapa is the *Two-Pice Tazaung* (pavilion), which was also gutted by fire in 1931; its construction was funded by the merchants of Yangon market. The escalator here provides great entertainment for visiting pilgrims.
- The small pagoda in the NW corner is the *Eight-Day Pagoda*. It has eight niches, each containing a Buddha, in between which are the figures of the eight plane-

Day	Planet	Birth sign	Compass point
Monday	Moon	tiger	east
Tuesday	Mars	lion	south-east
Wednesday am	Mercury	elephant (tusked)	south
Wednesday pm	Rahu	elephant (tuskless)	north-west
Thursday	Jupiter	rat	west
Friday	Venus	guinea pig	north
Saturday	Saturn	dragon	south-west
Sunday	Sun	galon bird	north-east

The Shwedagon's diving bells

In 1612, Felipe de Brito, a Portuguese adventurer (see page 37), stole the 32-tonne bronze and brass bell which had been donated by King Dhammazedi in the 15th century. De Brito wanted to recast it into cannon and the bell was hauled down to the riverbank. But the boat ferrying it across the Yangon River to the port at Syriam sank and the bell was lost. When the British seized Yangon in 1825, during the First Anglo-Burmese war, they tried to take the 23-tonne *Maha Ganda* bell, which had been donated to the temple by King Hsinbyushin's son, Singu, 50 years earlier. It suffered the same fate. The bell tumbled off the boat and settled on the riverbed. The Burmese requested that should they be able to salvage it, the bell would be allowed to remain in the Shwedagon. To the amazement of colonial observers, the bell was retrieved and raised to the surface using bamboo floats. It was then returned to its rightful place in the NW corner of the pagoda platform. The British apparently learned from their mistake: the biggest of the Shwedagon's bells, the 42-tonne 3-toned bell donated by King Tharawaddy in 1841, still sits in its original resting place, in the NW corner of the terrace.

tary birds and animals (see above).

- The *Maha Ganda Bell Pavilion*, which houses the 32-tonne Maha Ganda bell (see page 109), is behind the Eight-Day Pagoda, to the left of the pavilion containing a 9m-high Buddha image.
- The *Northern Adoration Hall*, on the N side of the stupa, is dedicated to Gautama, the historic Buddha, and contains his image. (The Bogyoke Aung San Martyr's Mausoleum (see page 112) can be reached from the N stairway).
- The *Hair Relics Well* – which is said to be fed by the Ayeyarwady (Irrawaddy) River so that its water level rises and falls with the tide – is in the *Sandawdwin Tazaung*, opposite the N adoration hall. The Buddha's hairs were washed in it before their enshrinement.
- Next to the Sandawdwin Tazaung is the *Maha Bodhi Pagoda* modelled on the Maha Bodhi Temple in Varanasi, India.
- The large *Elder* or *Naungdawgyi Pagoda*, in the NE corner, is where the sacred hair relics were first placed before being enshrined in the stupa's relic chamber.
- Right in the NW corner of the platform is the 1485 *Dhammazedi inscription* which relates the history of the Shwedagon in Pali, Mon and Burmese.
- King Tharawaddy's 42-tonne bell, cast in 1841, is in a prominent pavilion in the NW corner of the Shwedagon (see page 109).
- The elegant *Eastern Adoration Hall* was destroyed by fire in 1931 but has been rebuilt and contains a statue of the first Buddha, Kakusandha.
- The *Eastern Stairway* is lined with stalls selling religious paraphernalia.
- In the SE corner is a sacred bodhi tree, supposedly a cutting from the original tree under which the Gautama Buddha attained enlightenment.
- The museum is next to the S entrance and exhibits a rich collection of artefacts given to the pagoda by devotees. Also notable is a 19th century minister's gold coat.

The most interesting times to visit the Shwedagon are early morning and evening when the pagoda terrace is thronged with pilgrims. Tourists should enter from the S end. Admission US$5 goes to the trustees of the pagoda and is the main source of foreign exchange for buying the gold needed to keep it shining. Open 0400-2100 Mon-Sun. **NB** Visitors returning close to closing time to the building where shoes are left before en-

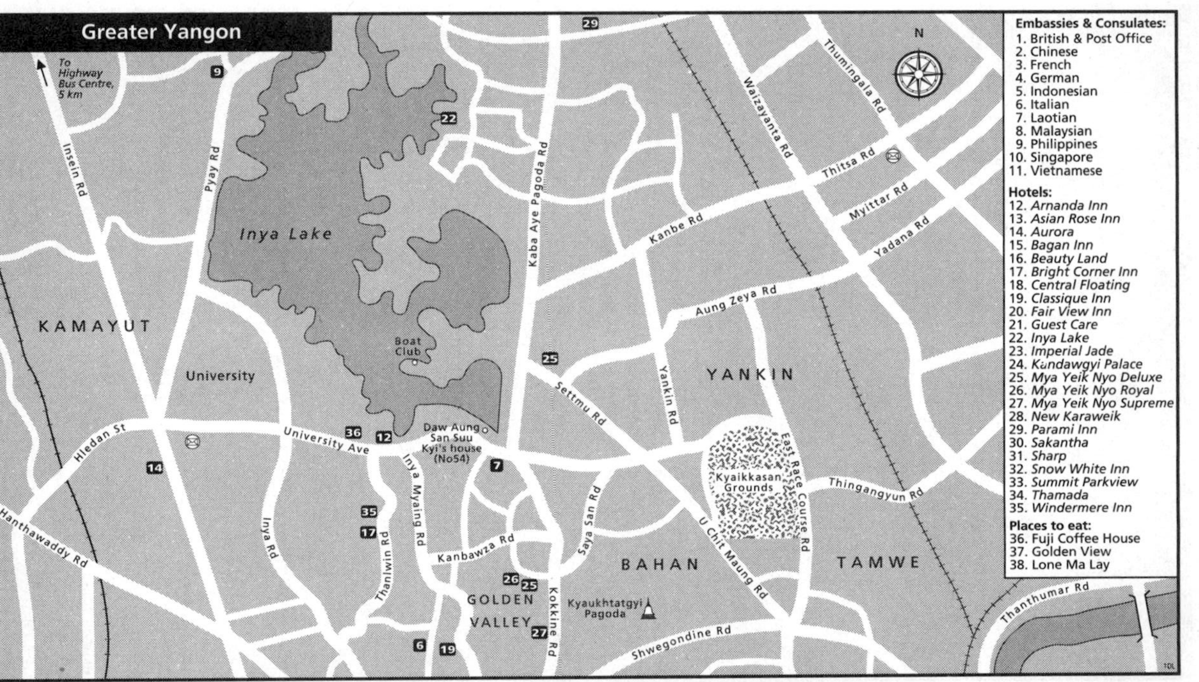
Greater Yangon
To Highway Bus Centre, 5 km
Insein Rd
Pyay Rd
Inya Lake
Boat Club
KAMAYUT
University
Hledan St
University Ave
Daw Aung San Suu Kyi's house (No54)
Inya Myaing Rd
Inya Rd
Thanlwin Rd
Hanthawaddy Rd
Kanbawza Rd
GOLDEN VALLEY
Kokkine Rd
Kyaukhtatgyi Pagoda
Saya San Rd
BAHAN
U Chit Maung Rd
Shwegondine Rd
Kaba Aye Pagoda Rd
Settmu Rd
Kanbe Rd
Aung Zeya Rd
Yankin Rd
YANKIN
Kyaikkasan Grounds
East Race Course Rd
Thingangyun Rd
TAMWE
Thanthumar Rd
Waizayanta Rd
Thumingala Rd
Thitsa Rd
Myittar Rd
Yadana Rd
N
Embassies & Consulates:
1. British & Post Office
2. Chinese
3. French
4. German
5. Indonesian
6. Italian
7. Laotian
8. Malaysian
9. Philippines
10. Singapore
11. Vietnamese
Hotels:
12. Arnanda Inn
13. Asian Rose Inn
14. Aurora
15. Bagan Inn
16. Beauty Land
17. Bright Corner Inn
18. Central Floating
19. Classique Inn
20. Fair View Inn
21. Guest Care
22. Inya Lake
23. Imperial Jade
24. Kandawgyi Palace
25. Mya Yeik Nyo Deluxe
26. Mya Yeik Nyo Royal
27. Mya Yeik Nyo Supreme
28. New Karaweik
29. Parami Inn
30. Sakantha
31. Sharp
32. Snow White Inn
33. Summit Parkview
34. Thamada
35. Windermere Inn
Places to eat:
36. Fuji Coffee House
37. Golden View
38. Lone Ma Lay

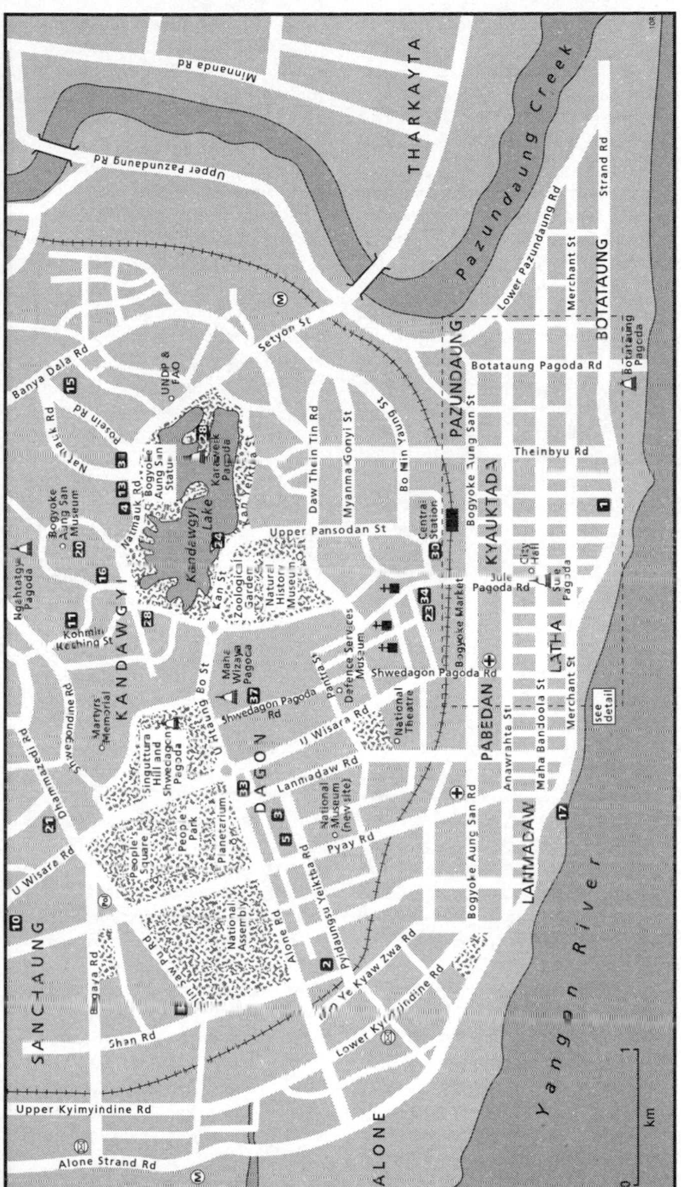
THARKAYTA
Minnanda Rd
Upper Pazundaung Rd
Pazundaung Creek
Strand Rd
Lower Pazundaung Rd
Merchant St
BOTATAUNG
Botataung Pagoda
Botataung Pagoda Rd
PAZUNDAUNG
Setyon St
Banya Dala Rd
UNDP & FAO
Posein Rd
Natmauk Rd
Bogyoke Aung San Statue
Kandawgyi Lake
Karaweik Pagoda
Kan Yeiktha St
Daw Thein Tin Rd
Myanma Gonyi St
Bo Min Yaung St
Theinbyu Rd
Bogyoke Aung San St
KYAUKTADA
Central Station
Upper Pansodan St
Bogyoke Aung San Museum
Ngahtatgyi Pagoda
KANDAWGYI
Kan St
Zoological Garden
Natural History Museum
City Hall
Sule Pagoda
Sule Pagoda Rd
Bogyoke Market
Shwedagon Pagoda Rd
LATHA
Merchant St
see detail
Maha Bandoola St
Anawrahta St
PABEDAN
Defence Services Museum
Pantra St
Maha Wizaya Pagoda
U Htaung Bo St
Shwedagon Pagoda Rd
U Wisara Rd
National Theatre
Martyrs Memorial
Shwegondine Rd
Dhammazedi Rd
Singuttura Hill and Shwedagon Pagoda
People's Park
People's Square
Planetarium
DAGON
Lanmadaw Rd
National Museum (new site)
Pyay Rd
Bogyoke Aung San Rd
LANMADAW
Yangon River
SANCHAUNG
U Wisara Rd
National Assembly
Alone Rd
Pyidaungsu Yeiktha Rd
Ye Kyaw Zwa Rd
Lower Kyimyindine Rd
Shan Rd
Upper Kyimyindine Rd
Alone Strand Rd
ALONE
0
1
km

tering the pagoda precincts may find the building locked – and their shoes incarcerated! *Getting there*: Bus 10 from Theinbyu Rd.

To the right of the S entrance to the Shwedagon is the new **Maha Wizaya Pagoda** (meaning 'great conqueror') built by General Ne Win in the 1980s. In a bid to make some much-needed merit, Myanmar's old military strongman began his 350 million kyat construction project with relish more befitting the kings of Bagan, which raised eyebrows over his supposed monarchic aspirations. The pagoda is hollow with a ceiling depicting Burmese constellations and a permanent display of pagoda styles through the ages. This pagoda is boycotted by many Burmese.

There are several important sights to the N of the Shwedagon. **Martyrs' Mausoleum** is on the hill N of the pagoda, just off Shwegondine Rd. It is the tomb of Bogyoke (General) Aung San, the father of the Burmese independence movement, and the five ministers assassinated with him on 19 July 1947 (see page 48). The **Aung San Bogyoke Museum** is also here. Admission US$3.

Kyaukhtatgyi Pagoda ('six-storeyed') is NE of Shwedagon, on Shwegondine Rd. The temple contains a gaudy, modern, 70m-long reclining Buddha, built in 1966, housed in a metal and corrugated iron pavilion. The image cost 5 million kyats – paid for entirely by public donation. The temple doubles as a monastery (there are over 600 monks) and a centre for the study of Buddhist manuscripts.

Ngahtatgyi (or Ngadatkyi) Pagoda ('five-storeyed') is S of Kyaukhtatgyi just off Shwegondine Rd, in the Ashay Tawya Monastery. It houses a huge seated Buddha, known as the 5-storey Buddha. The abbot's house beside the pagoda is a brightly painted Chinese-style building. *Getting there*: Bus 3 from city centre, 47 from Shwedagon.

Further S are the **Royal Lakes**. On the E side of **Kandawgye Lake** is the **Karaweik** stone boat, a concrete copy of a royal barge which is used as a restaurant and venue for cultural shows, see page 122. The lake is a good place to go to unwind. It is quiet and the admission charges are all in kyat and pitched the same for foreigners as for locals. There are several sections, each with its own entrance fee, and an array of stalls selling snacks and drinks as well as several larger restaurants including the *Karaweik*. On the N shore is the **Bogyoke Aung San Park**, with a statue of Aung San. **Yangon Zoo** is on the SW side of the lake; a miniature train runs round the grounds. It is a big zoo and animals on show can be fed by visitors; their living conditions are cramped. Admission US$5. Open 0600-1800 Mon-Sun.

The 48m-high golden dome of **Sule Pagoda**, on Sule Pagoda Rd is the main landmark in central Yangon. It stands in the middle of Yangon's equivalent of London's Piccadilly Circus: the British used the temple as the nucleus of their grid pattern for the city, when it was rebuilt in the 1880s. The pagoda's peculiarity is its octagonal-shaped stupa, which retains its shape as it tapers to the spire. This relates to the division of the week into 8 days, each of which are represented by a planet and an animal or bird (see page 108). Sule Pagoda is believed to date back over 2,000 years, although its historical significance has been undermined by the haphazard construction of shrines and brash temple art. Like the Shwedagon, it was founded to house sacred hair relics. Two Buddhist missionaries from India, Sona and Uttara, are said to have presented one of the Buddha's hairs to Maha Sura, a minister in Dagon, who built the temple. It was originally known as *Kyaik Athok*, Mon for "the pagoda of the sacred hair relic". Its more recent name, Sule, refers to the Sule nat, guardian spirit of Singuttara Hill. The entrances are unimpressive but the temple platform is

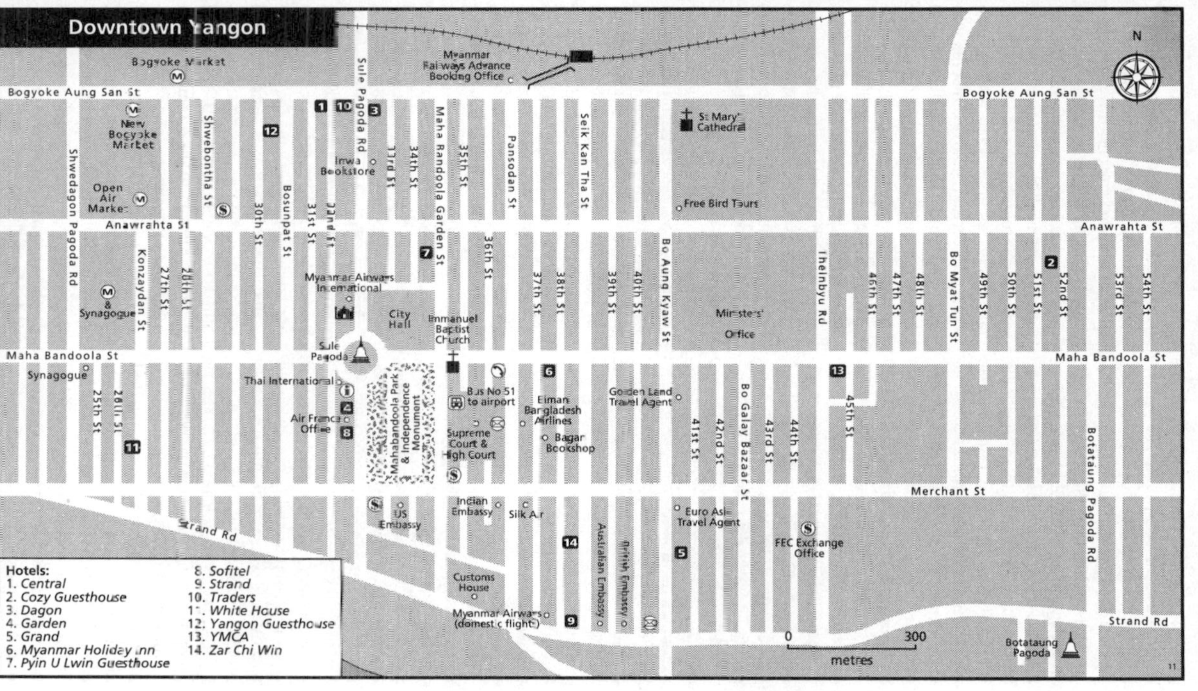
Downtown Yangon
N
metres
0
300
Bogyoke Market
Myanmar Railways Advance Booking Office
Bogyoke Aung San St
New Bogyoke Market
Open Air Market
St Mary's Cathedral
Free Bird Tours
Shwedagon Pagoda Rd
Shwebontha St
30th St
Bosunpat St
31st St
32nd St
Sule Pagoda Rd
Irrwa Bookstore
33rd St
34th St
Maha Bandoola Garden St
35th St
Pansodan St
Seik Kan Tha St
Anawrahta St
Konzaydan St
27th St
28th St
36th St
37th St
38th St
39th St
40th St
Bo Aung Kyaw St
Theinbyu Rd
46th St
47th St
48th St
Bo Myat Tun St
49th St
50th St
51st St
52nd St
53rd St
54th St
Synagogue
Myanmar Airways International
City Hall
Emmanuel Baptist Church
Ministers' Office
Sule Pagoda
Maha Bandoola St
Thai International
Mahabandoola Park & Independence Monument
Bus No 51 to airport
Eiman Bangladesh Airlines
Golden Land Travel Agent
Air France Office
Supreme Court & High Court
Bagar Bookshop
25th St
26th St
41st St
42nd St
Bo Galay Bazaar St
43rd St
44th St
45th St
Botataung Pagoda Rd
Merchant St
US Embassy
Indian Embassy
Silk Air
Euro Asia Travel Agent
Strand Rd
Australian Embassy
British Embassy
FEC Exchange Office
Customs House
Myanmar Airways (domestic flights)
Botataung Pagoda
Hotels:
1. Central
2. Cozy Guesthouse
3. Dagon
4. Garden
5. Grand
6. Myanmar Holiday Inn
7. Pyin U Lwin Guesthouse
8. Sofitel
9. Strand
10. Traders
11. White House
12. Yangon Guesthouse
13. YMCA
14. Zar Chi Win

always busy. Sule Pagoda is notable for its profusion of fortune tellers – and currency exchangers.

Nearby is **City Hall** (on the corner of Sule Pagoda Rd and Maha Bandoola St), a fine piece of British colonial architecture. Just to the SE is **Maha Bandoola Park**, named after a Burmese general from the First Anglo-Burmese war. The **Independence Monument** is at the centre of the park and represents Myanmar's five former semi-autonomous states, Shan, Kachin, Karen, Kayah and Chin. Admission 1 kyat. Facing the square on the E side are the old colonial **Supreme Court** and **High Court**.

Southeast of the park on Strand Rd is the **Strand Hotel** originally one of the leading hotels in the East and regarded as 'the finest hostelry E of Suez'. It belonged to the Sarkie Brothers' hotel empire, which included Singapore's *Raffles* and Penang's *Eastern & Oriental*. The hotel, built in 1901 by John Dawood – a leading British entrepreneur in the late 19th century – has witnessed wars, revolutions and riots before its decaying grandeur came to the attention of a consortium of Hong Kong hoteliers. They struck a US$12.5mn deal with the state tourism corporation to do for the *Strand* what had been done to *Raffles* in Singapore. Developers have, at the expense of Myanmar's teak forests, managed to retain the charm of this national institution even though its ancient lifts and quaint original fittings, such as GEC fans and Victorian bathtubs, have been ripped out. Australian diplomats, whose embassy occupies another former annex of the *Strand*, say they have more bathrooms than any other embassy in the world: the offices occupy former hotel suites. The British-built **General Post Office** on the W side of the hotel now houses Myanmar Airways (internal flights only). The main dock area is almost opposite the *Strand*, you can cross the river here on rowing boats, or the regular passenger boats.

To the E of Strand Rd on the waterfront is the **Botataung Pagoda**. 'Botataung' means 'one thousand officers' – a thousand soldiers were said to have constituted the guard of honour which received the Buddha relics donated by the king of Syriam. It is unusual in that visitors can enter the stupa, which is hollow. An Allied bomb completely destroyed the original pagoda in 1943, revealing a miniature golden stupa which contained Buddha relics and a hoard of treasure. An exact replica was rebuilt after the war. The central shrine contains the relics of the Buddha – they are actually kept in a safe below. The courtyard is not as busy as that of the Sule or Shwedagon pagodas but on the N side there is a large hall containing a Buddha image retrieved from Mandalay by the British, in front of which is one of the Buddha's hairs, rescued from the original Botataung stupa. The rotating model, depicting a scene from the life of the Buddha, is the latest ploy for attracting donations. There is a small market opposite the main E entrance.

North of the city centre on Shwedagon Pagoda St, just before the intersection with Pantra St, is the new **Defence Services Museum**. The immediate reaction on reading about this museum is to avoid it at all costs, for it is the Slorc's very own stab at immortality. It is a massive, and presumably expensive, example of the government's attempts to justify itself and its policies. Not only are there sections showing hardware (tanks, planes, artillery pieces etc) but also exhibits demonstrating how the military is involved in every facet of the nation's life from weaving and textiles to industrial production and health. The various ministries have their corners, as do the different states and divisions. It may be a hideous example of self-justification but it is also a telling insight into the power and insidiousness of the Slorc and into its thinking. Admission US$3.

The **National Museum** moved to

new premises on Pyay Rd NW of the city centre in 1996 from its old site in a bank building on Pansodan St. At the time of going to press it had not yet opened. Note that the description below is for the old museum – although the exhibits should be much the same. The first display just inside the entrance is an impressive array of gold ornaments labelled: "Replicas of some royal regalia not returned by the British." Some Burmese booty was returned to Myanmar in 1964 as a gesture of goodwill during Ne Win's official visit to London, but many other royal treasures continue to gather dust in British museums. The museum's ground floor, however, brims with the belongings of the last two kings of Myanmar. King Thibaw's intricately carved ivory chair, white umbrellas, swords and royal robes, jewelled baskets, betelnut boxes and silver spitoons. Many pieces – such as the gold betel cup, betel box and arak goblet – are studded with rubies, diamonds and other precious stones. Letters from King Thibaw to Queen Victoria before the last Anglo-Burmese war in 1885 are also on display. The room is dominated by the 8m-tall, gilded **Lion Throne** (Sihasana Throne), which was originally in the Royal Palace at Mandalay and was used by King Thibaw, the last Burmese monarch. It was returned from the palace by the British in 1945, before everything else in it was destroyed, and returned by Lord Louis Mountbatten in 1948 following Burmese independence. On the same floor is a scale model of the Mandalay Royal Palace.

The 2nd floor contains a room of prehistoric artefacts (which are not labelled in English) as well as reproductions of cave paintings and some Neanderthal busts. There is also an array of 4th-1st century BC weaponry. On the same floor, there are two rooms with pieces from Bagan and Thiri Kettaya (Sri Ksetra). There is also a good display of statues and carvings from old monasteries as well as tapestry coffin covers, pipes, musical instruments, silverware and lacquerware. There is an informative display of sandstone and bronze Buddha images, showing their Indian and Indo-European influence, with Gupta features. The top floor has an exhibition of Burmese watercolours and modern oil paintings. Admission US$4. Open 1000-1530 Mon-Fri.

On the N side of the city, between Inya Lake and the airport, is the **Kaba Aye Pagoda**, off Kaba Aye Pagoda Rd. This 'World Peace Pagoda' was built in 1952 by U Nu, the first Prime Minister of independent Myanmar, for the Sixth Buddhist Synod in 1954-56. As the name suggests, it was dedicated to world peace. The pagoda is not particularly beautiful but is famous for the silver Buddha in the inner relic chamber weighing 500 kg. There are five entrances to the pagoda each with a 3m-tall Buddha image – representing the four past Buddhas and one future.

The other building erected for the Sixth Buddhist Synod is the extraordinary **Maha Pasan Guha**, an artificial cave, surrounded by 28 bodhi trees, and able to seat 10,000 people. Inside are 2,500 seats for members of the Sangha (the Buddhist monkhood) and a separate 7,500 for members of the audience. It is meant to resemble India's Satta Panni Cave, where the First Buddhist Synod was held shortly after the Buddha's death but looks more like a gym. The nearby Institute of Advanced Buddhist Studies is translating the entire Buddhist canon into English.

Not far from the Maha Pasan Guha is the **Buddhist Art Museum**, housed in a 1952 Art Deco-style building in the grounds. The dominant lotus window depicts all the attitudes of the Buddha. The museum's contents were collected by the archaeology department: begging bowls, palm leaf scriptures and 18th-20th century wooden Buddha images and a palm leaf Pali manuscript. There are also models showing the evolution of stupa shapes and examples of the eight requisites of a Buddhist monk: an upper garment, underwear, girdle, robe, alms bowl, razor, needle and thread, a water strainer and a collection of rosary beads (*seitpadi*) used by celebrated monks. Open 0900-1630 Mon-Sun. The Ministry of Fine Arts is housed in the Chinese pagoda at the top of Kaba Aye Pagoda Rd; the house was built by a Chinese business tycoon at the beginning of the century.

TOURS

Tour agencies offer various city tours and excursions. Prices quoted are for a single tourist – it is much cheaper in larger groups. Tours must usually be paid for in US dollars. *Introducing Yangon*: 4 hrs, US$19; *Yangon city tour* (morning, afternoon or evening): 3½ hrs, US$14-18; *Highlights of Yangon*: 8 hrs, US$32; *Outside Yangon*: 4 hrs, US$17; *Shwedagon* (evening): 2½ hrs, US$12; *Bago*: 7 hrs, US$73; *Thanlyin*: 4½ hrs, US$32; *Twante*: 7 hrs, US$73. See page 124 for addresses of agents.

LOCAL FESTIVALS

Mar: *Gems and Pearls Emporium* (movable) held at the *Inya Lake Hotel*; *Full Moon of Tabaung Festival* (movable), 1 week long. Visitors come from all over Myanmar to visit the Shwedagon Pagoda. There are many stalls and sideshows.

Apr: *Thingyan* or *Burmese New Year* (movable: public holiday) lasting 4-5 days, the streets of Yangon are thronged with thousands of residents and visitors dousing each other with water and enjoying dance and music performances staged on roadside *mandats*.

May: *Kason Festival* (movable) takes place at the Shwedagon Pagoda to commemorate Buddha's enlightenment.

Oct: *Thadingyut* (movable), pagodas and houses throughout Yangon are illuminated with candles to celebrate the end of lent.

LOCAL INFORMATION

Orientation

Downtown Yangon along the river front is the main hub of the city with most of the shops and restaurants. There are not many guesthouses in this area. Most of the places to stay are around the two lakes, where there is a lack of places to eat.

Accommodation

Price guide

A+	over US$200	C	US$25-50
A	US$100-200	D	US$10-25
B	US$50-100	E	under US$10

Aware that its tourism industry cannot expand until more hotel rooms are built in Yangon, the government has undertaken some major refurbishment projects with the help of foreign private-sector developers and private guesthouses are opening up all over the city. A number of new luxury hotels are either under construction (like the *Traders Yangon Hotel*), or slated for construction (like one to be managed by Thailand's *Oriental Hotel*). The price of rooms in guesthouses can be bargained down, especially in the low season. Prices here incl breakfast, unless otherwise stated.

Downtown Yangon

A+ *Central Floating Hotel*, 1-2 Wah Dan Jetty, T 227288, F 227577, a/c, ensuite bathrooms, fridge, satellite TV, several restaurants, 2 pools, fitness centre, this is truly a wandering hotel, it started out life on the Great Barrier Reef in Australia, had a sojourn in Saigon (Vietnam) and has now floated its way to Yangon, it is comfortable with good business services, but the rooms are small and the walls thin, when Yangon's hotels have improved it will doubtless be floating its way to a new home – any offers?; **A+** *Sofitel*, Sule Pagoda Rd, corner of Merchant St, under construction; **A+** *Strand*, 92 Strand Rd, T 281533, a/c, coffee shop, restaurant, the *Strand* has been completely restored (see page 114 for a full description of the hotel); **A+** *Traders*, Sule Pagoda St, corner of Bogyoke Aung San St, very large 5-star hotel under construction.

B *Central*, 335-357 Bogyoke Aung San St, T 241007, F 248003, bright, sterile and Chinese with 'Top Club' disco on top floor; **B** *Imperial Jade*, 33 Yaw Min Gyi Rd, T 272299, F 283348, a/c, hot water shower attached, TV, minibar, restaurant, well located nr the railway station, a good middle range hotel with friendly and attentive service; **B *Strand annexe***, Strand Rd, T 281530, a/c, restaurant, the annexe of the old *Strand Hotel* is run as a separate entity with none of the charm of the original, don't get this and the restored *Strand* confused; **B *Thamada***, 5 Sule Pagoda Rd, T 271499, some a/c, restaurant, 1960s-style hotel nr the railway station, undergoing refurbishment; **B *Yuzana Garden***, 44 Signal Pagoda Rd, Mingalartaungnyunt, T 248944, F 240074, bright and a bit tacky, small fitness centre, beauty salon, popular nightclub.

C *Cozy Guesthouse*, 126 52nd St, Pazundaung, T 291623, F 292239, a/c, h/w, 5 small clean rm with separate bathroom, friendly, owner speaks English, 30% discount for longer stay, best budget place downtown, rec; **C-D *The Grand***, 108 Bo Aung Kyaw St, T 297493, F 283360, a/c, h/w, small rooms with no windows but clean and efficiently run, right in the centre of town; **C-D *White House***, 67/71 Konzaydan St, T 271522, clean, small breakfast incl, fan rooms are the best bet, very popular with backpackers who congregate here for a beer in the evening so good source of information, good location too but expansion underway and can be noisy at night, rec by travellers; **C-E *YMCA***, Maha Bandoola/25 St, T 294128, some a/c, fan, restaurant, place is a little run down, but the beds are clean and comfortable, some rooms with attached bathrooms, fridge and a/c, rooms at the front are noisy, breakfast incl, an interesting place to stay with lots of comings and goings of an entirely innocent sort, also benefits from very central location.

D *Dagon*, 256/260 Sule Pagoda Rd, T 241800, some a/c, some fans, shared bathrooms, clean rooms, baths are old but clean, friendly restaurant on ground floor, satellite TV in lobby, rooms at the front are noisy; **D *Garden Guesthouse***, 73 Sule Pagoda Rd, T 271516, fans only, restaurant, rooms are partitioned and have communal bathrooms, cheap but grubby; **D *Myanmar Holiday Inn***, 379 Maha Bandoola St, between 37th and 38th sts, T 240016, some a/c, some rooms with private bathroom, clean and friendly, most central of the cheap guesthouses, some rooms noisy because of the road; **D *Pyin U Lwin Guesthouse***, 183 Maha Bandoola Garden St (nr Sule Pagoda), T 240022, F 240058, fan, shared bathrooms, clean, well-run and friendly, rec by travellers; **D *Sakantha***, Yangon Station, T 282975, some a/c, restaurant, many of the rooms are right next to the railway line; **D *Sunflower***, U Pho Kya Rd/Bo Min Yaung Rd, nr station, T 276503, fan, communal bathroom, partition rooms, breakfast, rec by travellers; **D *Yangon Guesthouse***, 317/323 Bosunpat St, between Bogyoke Aung San and Anawrahta sts, convenient for the railway station, good, clean rooms with shared bathrooms (hot water), fan, breakfast incl, friendly place and good value and in many respects one of the best of the cheaper guesthouses, although it does lack the backpacking atmosphere as it is not (yet) popular; **D *Zar Chi Win***, 1st Flr, 59 37th St (Lower Block), T 275407, fan only, some rooms with bathroom, rather grotty building but rooms are clean, no sound proofing but central location and in a quiet area, friendly management, the cheapest place to stay downtown, car for hire for trips round Myanmar, breakfast incl, friendly place.

Golden Valley and Kandawgyi

A+-A *Mya Yeik Nyo Royal*, 20 Pa-Le Rd, Bahan, T 548310, F 548318, suites only; **A+ *Kandawgyi Palace***, Kan Yeiktha Rd, T 249255, F 280412, a/c, restaurant (both indoor and outside), pool, part of the old Kandawgyi Hotel was restored and a completely new wing has been built, some rooms with pleasant views overlooking the Royal Lake, occasional classical piano recitals, 'cave' disco and giant stone dinosaur in the grounds, some consider this the best hotel in town.

B *Asian Rose Inn*, 9A Natmauk Ave, Tamwe, T 550942, F 549451, a/c, h/w, restaurant on the balcony, only 7 rm all spacious and clean, well-run in a quiet area with a garden, slightly more expensive than other family hotels in the area but worth the price, rec; **B *Bagan Inn***, 29 Pusein Rd, Tamwe, T 550489, a/c, h/w, restaurant set up for businessmen, clean but featureless; **B *Best Inn***, 96/98 Pansodan St, T 272835, F 240084, new and central, IDD dialing; **B *Bright Corner Inn***, 38 Bawdi Yeiktha (Windermere), Bahan, T 531958, a/c, h/w, only 4 rm in a private house, family atmosphere although it is ideal for business men with a private meeting room, patio; **B *Classique Inn***, 53B Golden Valley, Bahan, T 30954, a/c, hot water, rooms are nothing special but run by a friendly family who will cook guests meals, quiet area, rec; **B *Guest Care***, 107a Dhammazedi Rd, Kamayut, T 283171, F 273573, a/c, h/w, clean but sterile rooms with all facilities (incl satellite TV), on the main road but has a small garden; **B** ***Sharp***, 3 Po Sein Rd, Bahan, T 551865, a/c, h/w, restaurant, rooms nothing special and expensive but it does have a small swimming pool; **B** ***Snow White Inn***, 12(B)1 Kokine Ave, Bahan, T 553156, F 289960, a/c, h/w, friendly (the owner's brother is a Burmese film star), but average rooms; **B** ***Windermere Inn***, Aungmingaung Ave, Thanlwin Rd, Kamayut, T 533846, F 289960, a/c, h/w, restaurant, friendly and well-run with free cars to the airport, they will also organize taxis downtown and tours round Myanmar, nice rooms and pretty garden make this one of the best value hotels in Yangon, despite being a bit out of town, rec; **B-C** ***Diamond Inn***, 182 Shwegondine Rd, Bahan, T 553865/550840, situated within walking distance of the Shwedagon Pagoda, this small and friendly hotel with just 10 rooms is highly rec by those who have stayed here, rooms and bathrooms are spotlessly clean and the staff are very accommodating, room rate incl a good breakfast, rec; **B-C** ***Fair View***, 16 Sawmaha St, Kandawgyi, Bahan, T 553526, F 283360, a/c, h/w, family house with attractive garden, clean rooms at the back, good option if you don't want to stay in town but book ahead, minibus shuttle downtown am and pm, breakfast incl in price; **B-C** ***Green Hill Inn***, 12 Posein Rd, Tamwe, T 550330/38618, F 549388, a/c, simple restaurant, small hotel with 15 rooms in an old, 2-storeyed building (formerly a private house), rooms are wood panelled giving the place a quaintly dated feel, attached bathrooms, TV and minibar, good restaurant, rec; **B-D** ***Beauty Land***, 9 Bo Cho Rd, nr Shwedagon, Bahan, T 551525, F 549797, some a/c, hot water, rooms with and without attached bathrooms in this quiet converted private house, rooms are clean and the place is well-run with personal attention to service and a large garden, it is, though, outside the centre of town, IDD dialling and satellite TV available.

C ***New Karaweik***, Kandawgyi Lake, T 551313, friendly owner; **C** ***Princess Inn***, 129A Thanlwin Rd, T 530965, F 289708, small, cozy, similar to *Windermere Inn* but no garden; **C** ***Winner Inn***, 42 Thanlwin Rd, T 531205, F 524196, small hotel, average rooms and decor – but refurbishment may see some improvements.

D ***Mother Land Inn***, 99 Thanlwin Rd, Kamayut, T 530289, F 525536, free shuttle from airport, popular with travellers, **E** for dorm beds.

E ***Holiday***, 51 Posein Rd, nr *Green Hill Inn*, frequented by Burmese, good service and good food.

Inya Lake

A+-A ***Inya Lake***, Kaba Aye Pagoda Rd (9 km from centre), T 628579, F 655537, a/c, restaurant, nice pool, built with Soviet aid in the 1960s and described as 'the Russian bunker', the hotel is being completely refurbished by *New World Hotels International* of Hong Kong, at a cost of US$9mn; **A+-A** ***Sedona Hotel Yangon***, Kaba Aye Pagoda Rd, massive new hotel with 437 rm on 11 floors and set in 8 acres facing the SE end of Inya Lake, swimming pool, tennis courts, health centre et al, rooms with satellite TV and minibar, financed from Singapore and scheduled to have opened in 1996, this looks like the sort of hotel that elegant Yangon could do without.

B ***Arnanda Inn***, 21 University Ave, Aungzeya Lane, Bahan, T 531251, a/c, h/w, 4 large rm in a well cared for family house, free laundry, snacks through the day, reasonably priced; **B** ***Mya Yeik Nyo Deluxe***, 16B Thukhawaddy Rd, Yankin, T 556529, F 665052; **B** ***Mya Yeik Nyo Supreme***, 23/25 Kaba Aye Pagoda Rd, Bahan, T 553818, F 665052; **B** ***Parami Inn***, 34 Parami Rd, Yankin, T 661002, F 289862, a/c, h/w, clean standard rooms, meals cooked on request, convenient for the airport and buses at Highway Gate but otherwise too far out of town; **B** ***Summer Palace***, 160 University Ave, a/c, h/w, restaurant, run by the owners of *The Grand* and *Fair View*, and top of their 'chain', Colonial-style house with pretty garden and lake, large rooms; **B-C** ***Aurora***, 477 Pyay Rd, Kamayut, T 524080, F 532139, a/c, hot water shower, 5 rm in old house, all but one with character, tastefully furnished and decorated with antiques, often full, will pick up from airport, excellent restaurant attached, run by a French woman and popular with Francophone residents in Yangon who come to use the bar, avoid bedrooms nr the bar if you want an early night, hard beds, out of the centre, but in a green area, pleasant verandah on 2nd floor, rec.

C ***Highland Lodge***, No 1 Konemyint Yeiktha, 7 miles, Pyay Rd, T 660695, F 666152, a/c, hot water, international dialling, bit far from downtown, but set in peaceful countryside and a large tree-filled garden, own generator.

D ***Win Guesthouse***, 10 Zay St, Kamayut, across Hledan St from the Bathein bus station, a/c, cheapest private room in Yangon.

Other areas of the city

A *Summit Park View*, 350 Ahlone Rod, T 227966, F 227993, a/c, restaurant, pool, gym, caters for businessmen, also known for its pastries and cakes; **A-B** *Best Executive Suites*, 69 Pyay Rd, 6½ miles N of downtown, T 525795, F 664772, in garden, caters to business clientele.

C *Asia Villa*, 55 Inya Myaing Rd, T 533536, F 526325, out of town, some rooms a/c and private bathrooms, hot water, clean, quiet, good place but awkward location, food available; **C** *Ruby Inn*, nr airport, a/c.

● Places to eat

Price guide

♦♦♦♦	over US$15+	(over 180 kyat)
♦♦♦	US$5-15	(120-180 kyat)
♦♦	US$2-5	(60-120 kyat)
♦	under US$2	(under 60 kyat)

Burmese

♦♦♦*Lone Ma Lay*, Bogyoke Aung San Park, Natmauk Rd, T 550357, restaurant in Bogyoke Park, popular tour restaurant, as it has a Burmese cultural show with singing and dancing in the evening (1700-2030), the famous *chinlon* woman also does a great performance with hoops of fire. Open at lunch, surprisingly good food; ♦♦*Danubyu*, Upper Block 29th St, there are also several other small Burmese restaurants in this street; ♦♦*Khin Khin Gyi Restaurant*, Pyay Rd, Myenigon, well prepared Burmese food in a friendly atmosphere, the owner is an artist and his works are displayed in the restaurant, there is a menu in English, but it is always possible to have a look at the food at the back, the restaurant is not easy to spot, it is next to *Moe Nat Hai* bar and restaurant; ♦♦*999 Shan Khauk Swe*, 130b 34th St (enter the street from behind the Town Hall or from Anawratha), clean and cool, serves good quality Shan food: *mishé* (thick rice noodles), *shan kouq-swèh* (sticky rice noodles), *shan tâmìn, tohu nwèh* (shan noodles with a warm tofu sauce) and *sichè kouq-swèh* (soft wheat noodles), all with a choice of pork or chicken, or vegetarian (*theq-thaq-luq*), closes at 1900; ♦♦*Shweba*, Aung Thu Ka, Shwegondine Rd, nr Shwedagon Pagoda (opp Resistance Park, take the small road down the side of a football pitch), good assortment of curries; ♦♦Burmese restaurant in 37th St (no name), good choice of food early evening but runs out quickly, popular; ♦*Kone Min Tua*, 7½ miles Pyay Rd, serves *mohinga* until noon.

Chinese

♦♦♦♦*Golden View*, Shwedagon Pagoda Rd (right next to Ne Win's Pagoda), open air restaurant with stunning views of Shwedagon, good Chinese fare with traditional Burmese country dance; ♦♦♦♦*Mandarin*, 124 Maha Bandoola Garden Rd (behind the Sule Pagoda), good Chinese food in clean restaurant; ♦♦♦♦*Mya Kan Tha*, 70 Natmauk Rd, in a big house, to N of the royal lake, lobster is a speciality; ♦♦♦♦*The Man Restaurant*, Theinbyu St, rec by locals; ♦♦♦♦*The Panda*, 205 Wardan St, on corner of Keighley Rd and St, John's Rd, expensive, rec; ♦♦♦♦*Shan Kun*, Kandawmin Park, beautiful setting with view of Shwedagon, good quality Chinese. ♦♦♦♦*Yadana Gardens*, S entrance, Shwedagon pagoda; ♦♦♦♦-♦♦♦*The Great Wall*, Pan Soe Dan St, large menu; ♦♦♦*7-Up Hot Pot*, Kokine Swimming Pool Rd, Mongolian cuisine; ♦♦♦*Furusato*, Shwegondine Rd, opp Chinese temple, Japanese and Chinese food, not highly rated by foreign residents; ♦♦♦*Fu Sun*, 160 Kokkine, Kaba Aye Pagoda Rd, pavilion dining; ♦♦♦*Khun Loke*, 22nd St (between Maha Bandoola and Strand Rd); ♦♦♦*Lu Lu Chung*, 21 St; ♦♦♦*Oriental House*, 126A Myoma Kyaung Rd, Dagon, T 284068, good Chinese; ♦♦♦*Palace*, 37th St (between Merchant St and Mahabandoola St), excellent crab claws and crispy duck, rec; ♦♦♦*Pann Wut Yi*, 110 Bo Aung Kyaw St; ♦♦♦*Royal Garden*, Kandawgyi Kan Pat Lan, next to the *Karaweik Bird* restaurant and overlooks the lake, T 297716, superb Singapore/Chinese restaurant, always full, cheap dim sum lunch (US$5), sometimes a cultural show in the evenings; ♦♦♦*Ruby*, 50 Bo Aung Kyaw St, seafood particularly good, rec; ♦♦♦*Yin Swe*, 137 University Ave, garden; ♦♦♦-♦*Nan Yu*, Pansodan St; ♦♦*69*, 21st St, Chinese and Burmese dishes, speciality is 100 year-old eggs; ♦♦*Fame*, 113 University Ave Rd, large terrace; ♦♦*Haikhin*, Sule Pagoda Rd, (next to *Dagon Hotel*); *Dolphin*, next to boat club, good Chinese grub and live music.

Indian

♦♦♦*Ashoka*, 77 Pyidaungsu Yeiktha Rd, Dagon, small portions but excellent service and ambience; ♦♦♦*Nizam Durbar*, 62B Yaw Min Gyi Rd, Dagon, T 242291, live classical Indian music; ♦♦*Golden City*, 170 Sule Pagoda Rd, excellent Thali and Ohosa; ♦♦*New Delhi*, 262 Anawarahta Rd, highly rec by travellers; ♦♦*Sule*, Sule Pagoda Rd, thali; ♦♦*Simla*, 222 Anawratha Rd, good selection of curries; ♦*The Indian restaurant* on 32nd St (it doesn't have a name) serves first class thali; ♦*Kyet Shar Soon Biriani Shop*, 526 Mahabandoola St, between 27th and 28th sts, serves 'the best yellow rice in Myanmar', one dish only – saffron rice cooked with onions, served with a big hunk of chicken and a tiny plate of cucumbers and onions, a bargain at 80 kyat.

International

The bigger hotels all have restaurants serving international dishes. ♦♦♦♦*Aurora Hotel*, 477 Pyay Rd, T 524080, excellent French food; ♦♦♦♦*Italian* restaurant and ♦♦♦*Coffee Shop*, *Inya Lake Hotel*; ♦♦♦♦*Strand Restaurant*, *Strand Hotel*, a 5-star international-style menu which changes daily, the most expensive food in Myanmar; ♦♦♦*Chez Sylvie*, *Hotel Aurora*, 477 Pyay Rd, T 524080, a quirkily decorated, 1-room restaurant giving a strange faded European atmosphere, good set French menu for US$6 (3 courses); ♦♦♦*Mr Guitar*, 158-168 Mahabandoola Garden St, snacks, western dishes, live music every evening, open late, pretentious and overpriced; ♦♦♦*Tino's Best Executive Suites*, 69 Pyay Rd, 6½ miles, T 665105, tasteful Italian restaurant with superb food (pastas, pizzas, salads), helpful and attentive French manager; ♦♦♦-♦♦*Strand Cafe*, *Strand Hotel*, serves a range of international snacks if you fancy a treat, but expensive; ♦*Green*, 205 Pansodan Rd, a/c snack bar with a good line in milk shakes.

Other Asian cuisines

♦♦♦*Central Floating Hotel*, has an excellent restaurant with Asian and western dishes; ♦♦♦*Korean*, 38A Bawdi Yeiktha Rd, off Thanlwin Rd, Kamayut, T 531208, all seats outside, huge portions, delicious barbecue cooked in front of you; ♦♦♦*Malai*, 75 Thanlwin Rd, Kamayut, T 223500, average Thai food in an uninteresting atmosphere, often with TV blaring in Thai; ♦♦♦*Salathai*, 56 Saya San Rd, T 548661, very average food; ♦♦♦*Seoul House*, 232 Dhammazedi Rd, Bahan, T 552897, great Korean barbecue either cooked for you or you cook it yourself; ♦♦♦*Vietnam House*, 62B Thanlwin Rd, Kamayut, T 530109, excellent Vietnamese food, friendly and helpful proprioter (Burmese man with Vietnamese wife).

Bakeries: *Myaing Hay Wun*, Pyay Rd-Kaba Aye Pagoda Rd junction, recently opened supermarket with a bakery section (incl croissants); *Shwe Myin Bakery*, opp *Tourist Department Stores*, pizzas and pastries; *Strand Hotel*, excellent breads.

Coffee shops

Fuji Coffeehouse, 116 University Ave, Kamayut, T 531371, new, rather cold coffee house, serving coffees, teas, breakfast and some snacks.

Foodstalls

A selection of teashops and foodstalls can be found throughout the downtown area and in the main markets selling snacks such as samosas, *ko-pyan-kyaw* (spring rolls) and for breakfast, *mohinga* (noodles with fish sauce). Locals rec the noodle stall on the corner of 21st St and Mahabandoola.

Yoghurt shop

♦*Nilar Win's*, 377 Maha Bandoola St (between 37 and 38 sts), delicious assortment of yoghurt shakes and fruit shakes, Nilar Win was a well known Burmese boxer – his pictures decorate the shop walls; ♦*No Name Yoghurt Shop*, Basunpat and Mahabandoola, good lassis.

Ice-cream

Hawaii Tropical Ice Cream, 401-407 Maha Bandoola St, a/c ice cream parlour (no alcohol).

● Bars

Kandawgyi Hotel, Kanyoikhta Rd, bar overlooks Royal Lake; *Inya Lake Bar*, live music; *Narawat Hotel*, 257 Insein Rd, Hlaing (opened by Sanda Win), live Philipino band every night; *Strand Hotel*, Strand Rd, formerly a very popular old bar, now refurbished with refurbished prices to match but good value during Happy Hour, Fri 1700-1900; *Harbour Point Recreation Club*, Myanandar Park, Pansodan Seikan, nice to have drinks on an outdoor verandah upstairs, small disco downstairs with a heavy metal band; *The Sailing Club*, Inya Rd, happy hour for non-members between 1700 and 2000 on Fri, outdoor terrace over Inya Lake (bad mosquitoes); *Savoy Hotel*, small bar with a good ambience.

● Airline offices

Domestic flights must be paid for in dollars. Flights are always full and difficult to book. International tickets are 10-15% cheaper at travel agencies and can be paid for in kyat. **Aeroflot**, 501-3 Pyay Rd, 7th Mile, T 661066; **Air China**, 112-B Pyay Rd, T 665187; **Air France**, 69 Sule Pagoda Rd, T 274199; **Air Indian**, 533 Merchant St, T 272410; **Air Mandalay**, 209c, Shwegondine Rd, T 552629 or 146 Damazedi Rd, T 282561, F 525937; **Biman Bangladesh**, 106 Pansodan Rd, T 275882; **CAAC** (Air China), 67A Pyay Rd, T 275714; **Eva Air**, 345 Pyay Rd, T 287121;

Indian Airlines, 127 Sule Pagoda Rd, T 248174; **KLM**, 104 Strand Rd, T 274180; **Myanmar Airways**, 123 Sule Pagoda Rd, T 289772; **Silk Air** (Singapore), 537 Merchant St, T 284600, F 283872; **Thai Airways**, 441 Tavoy House, Maha Bandoola St, next to Sule Pagoda, T 275988/274922.

● Banks & money changers

The main hotels will change money at the official rate (and will stamp exchange papers) as well as the banks listed below. Visitors are advised to refer to the section **Money and the black market** (see page 354). The **Myanmar Foreign Trade Bank (MFTB)**, 80/86 Mahabandoola Garden St, Kyauktada, T 284911, is the main bank dealing in foreign currency in Yangon, it is possible to get cash advances on Visa or Mastercard (4% commission) and TCs can be converted to FEC. The **Myanmar Investment & Commercial Bank (MICB)** also gives cash advances on some credit cards (4% commission) and transfers to and from overseas banks (US$2 fee).

Most informal ('black market') currency changers operate around the Sule Pagoda (see page 112). FECs and US$ can be changed here, although the latter is illegal and expatriat residents advise against it in the open. Travel around for the best rate and count the bills carefully and calmly.

● Embassies & consulates

Yangon is a cheap and quick place to get visas for Laos, Vietnam, China, India and Thailand. **Australia** (also looks after Canadian interests), 88 Kan-nar Rd, T 280965, F 271434; **Austria**, 63 157th St, Tamwe, T 548863; **Bangladesh**, 56 Kaba Aye Pagoda Rd, Bahan, T 551174 (Mon-Fri 0830-1530) (also has consulate in Sittwe: Main Rd 043-21126, Mon-Thur 0800-1400, Fri 0800-1200, T 549556, F 548745); **Belgium**, 15 Myayagon St, Kandawgalay, T 276505; **Canada**, see Australia; **China**, 1 Pyidaungsu Yeiktha Rd, T 221280, F 227019, Mon-Fri 0900-1200, 1430-1630; **Denmark**, 65-A Kaba Aye Pagoda Rd, T 660883; **France**, 102 Pyidaungsu Yeiktha Rd, T 282122, F 287759, Mon-Fri 0800-1300, 1400-1800; **Germany**, 32 Natmauk Rd, T 548951, 548952, F 548899, Mon-Fri 0730-1400; **India**, 545-547 Merchant St, T 282551, F 289562, Mon-Fri 0830-1300, 1400-1700; **Indonesia**, 100 Pyidaungsu Yeiktha Rd, T 281714, F 282675, Mon-Thur 0800-1200, 1330-1600, Fri 0900-1200; **Israel**, 49 Pyay Rd, Dagon, T 222290, Mon-Fri 0800-1600; **Italy**, 3 Inya Myaing Rd, Golden Valley, T 527100, F 533670, Mon-Fri 0830-1630; **Japan**, 100 Natmauk Rd, Bahan, T 549644, F 549643, Mon, Tues, Thur, Fri 0830-1700, Wed 0830-1230; **Republic of Korea**, 97 University Ave, Bahan, T 527142, F 532630, Mon, Tues, Thur, Fri 0830-1230, 1400-1700, Wed, 0830-1230; **Laos**, A-1 Diplomatic Quarters, Taw Win Rd, T 222482, F 532630 (this is a good place to pick up a Lao visa – it is cheap (US$25) and quick, just 24 hrs), Mon-Fri 0800-1500; **Malaysia**, 82 Pyidaungsu Yeiktha Rd, T 220248, F 227446, Mon-Fri 0800-1500; **Nepal**, 16 Natmauk Yeiktha Rd, T 550633, F 549803, Mon-Fri 0800-1500; **Netherlands**, 53/55 Maha Bandoola Garden St, T 272810, F 286744, Mon-Fri 0930-1630; **Norway**, 65-A Kaba Aye Pagoda Rd, T 660883; **Pakistan**, A4 Diplomatic Quarters, Pyay Rd, T 222881; **Philippines**, 56 Pyay Rd, 6th Mile, T 664020; **Russian Federation**, 38 Sagawa Rd, Dagon, T 272427, F 273891, Mon-Fri 0745-1400; **Singapore**, 287 Pyay Rd, T 525688, Mon-Fri 0830-1300, 1400-1700; **Spain**, 563 Merchant St, T 280608; **Sri Lanka**, 34 Taw Pyay Win Rd, T 222812; **Sweden** (see UK); **Thailand**, 45 Pyay Rd, 6½ miles, Hlaing, T 525670, F 222784, Mon-Fri 0900-1200, 1400-1700; **Vietnam**, 36 Wingaba Rd, Bahan, T 548905, F 548329, Mon-Fri 0800-1130, 1300-1600, **UK**, 80 Strand Rd, T 281700, F 289566 (also looks after New Zealand and Swedish interests), Mon, Tues, Thur, Fri 0800-1300, 1400-1630, Wed 0800-1300; **USA**, 581 Merchant St, T 282181, F 280409, Mon-Fri 0800-1100; **Vietnam**, 36 Wingaba Rd, Bahan, T 548905, F 548329, Mon-Fri 0800-1130, 1300-1600.

● Emergency telephone numbers

Ambulance: T 192.
Fire: T 191.
Police: T 199.

● Entertainment

See *New Light of Myanmar* to find out what's on in Yangon. Traditional Burmese entertainment has been stifled by censorship. *A-nyeint* performances (burlesque) and *nat-pwes* are few and far between. There are occasional pop concerts in the sports stadium or National Theatre by local groups.

Cinema: The **Alliance Française** at 340 Pyay Rd, T 532900, F 287759, the **US Information Services** at 14 Taw Win Rd, Dagon, T 223106, F 221262 and the **British Council** at 80 Strand Rd, T 281700, F 289566, offer regular films and videos open to anyone. Schedules may be picked up at the institutions. There are more than 50 cinemas in Yangon, the following show English-language films: ***Bayint***, 321 Bogyoke Aung San St; ***Gon***, 223/229 Sule Pagoda Rd; ***Pa Pa Win***, Sule Pagoda Rd; ***Thamada***, 5 Signal Pagoda Rd; ***Waziya***, 327 Bogyoke Aung San St; ***Wizaya***, 224 U Wisara Rd.

Cultural Shows: *Karaweik Cultural Centre* on Royal Lake, not far from the *Kandawgyi Palace Hotel*. The Karaweik (a mythical bird with a beautiful song) is a copy of a royal barge and is decorated with designs in glass mosaic, marble and mother-of-pearl. (Traditionally rowers weren't allowed on board the royal barge and was towed by smaller boats called *hlaw sar*.) Traditional Burmese music and dance: the show incl folk dance, puppet dances, religious rituals, traditional court dances and an acrobatic *chinlon* (caneball) display. Performances usually only take place when requested by large tour groups; check with MTT. (Buffet supper available beforehand). Admission 40 kyat. Tickets available at the door, or from MTT. A number of restaurants also mount cultural shows in the evening for the edification of diners eg ***Lone Ma Lay***, Bogyoke Aung San Park (see **Places to eat**). Locals recommend the dance show at the National Theatre; tickets available on the door.

Football: matches at the stadium behind the railway station. Check the *New Light of Myanmar* for match details.

Nightclubs/discos: *Club Pioneer*, *Yuzana Garden Hotel*, 44 Sule Pagoda Rd, one of the most popular discos in Yangon, catering to foreigners, businessmen and the young and wealthy, government owned, US$10 admission; ***The Cave***, *Kandawgyi Palace Hotel*, Kan Yeiktha Rd, US$10 admission; ***Top Club***, *Central Hotel*, 335-357 Bogyoke Aung San St, small posh disco, with average band, US$10 admission; ***Mister Guitar***, Rm 1, Bldg 158-168 Mahabandoola Garden St, T 255462 (*Mister Guitar 2* at 93 A Shwe Gon Daing St, West Shwe Gon Daing, T 551949), small, smoky bar with snacks, teas, coffees, great atmosphere, cheap food, live country and classics music with guitar accompaniment and no microphones.

Theatre: the open-air theatre was replaced by the National Theatre which stages occasional performances by visiting cultural troupes and fund-raising pop concerts. ***State School of Music and Drama*** (associated with the State School of Fine Art, Music and Dancing in Mandalay). Traditional Burmese arts are taught and demonstrated. Open to visitors but mainly supplies cultural performers for diplomatic events. Closed in Apr.

● Hospitals & medical services

Clinics: two local health clinics have good reputations and a variety of specialists (many trained abroad) and equipment. These are the *Bahosi Medical Centre*, No B-31-36 Bahosi Housing Complex, Bogyoke Aung San St, T 224667 (enrolment 3 FEC, Consultation from 25 FEC) and the *University Avenue Health Clinic*, 439 New University Avenue, Bahan, T 540661, 548012 (consultation US$20). The latter also has a well stocked pharmacy and both have gynaecological services. *Australian Clinic*, 62 U Wisara Rd, T 276009, F 281346.

Dentist: an excellent dentist (with western prices) is *Aung Dental Surgery*, 32A Pyipaung Su Lane, Kokine Swimming Pool Rd, T 552434.

Hospitals: *Diplomatic Hospital*, Kyaikkasan Rd, T 550149. *Yangon General Hospital*, Bogyoke Aung San St, T 281722 (ask for medical superintendent). *Infectious Disease Hospital*, Upper Pansodan St, T 272497. *University Hospital*, University Ave, T 531541. (Some embassies also have nurses; see **Health**, page 354.)

Pharmacy: the *May Shopping Centre* on Merchant St has a well stocked and stored (in a/c) 24-hr pharmacy.

● Immigration offices

In the Government Office on Strand Rd, T 285505.

● International organizations

FAO, Insein Rd, T 641672, F 641561; **UNDCP**, 40 Thanlwin Rd, T 531582, F 531019; **UNDP**, 6 Natmauk Rd, T 292910, F 292739; **UNHCR**, 287 Pyay Rd, T 524022, F 524031; **UNICEF**, 132 University Ave Rd, T 531107, F 531515; **WHO**, 39 Shwetaungyar Rd, T 531135, F 530429.

● Meditation centres

The best known meditation centres for foreigners in Rangoon are: ***Mingun Meditation Centre***, ***Mahasi Meditation Centre***, Hermitage Rd and the ***International Meditation Centre*** and ***Chan Mye Yeiktha*** (about 100m N of *Inya Lake Hotel* on Kaba Aye Pagoda Rd) the Sayadaw (abbot) U Janaka, speaks good English.

● Post & telecommunications

Area code: 01. In 1996 phone numbers changed to 6 digits.

General Post Office: Strand Rd/80 Bo Aung Kyaw St (Poste Restante on the first flr).

Telephone and telegraph office: Pansodan/Maha Bandoola St, fax and telex facilities.

● Private guides

U Mya Win Maung, Me Da Wi Rd, Salain, T 699546, German and English; ***U Soe Myint***, 137 38th St, T 285116, French; ***Htay Htay Tin***, 92 Thunanda, T 281391, French and English; ***Rose Martha***, 38 Eiksathaya St, Kauikmyaung, T 553109, English and Japanese.

● Religious services

Catholic: *St Mary Cathedral*, 372 Bo Aung Kyaw St, T 272662, service at 0900 every Sun; *St Augustine Church*, No 64 Inya Rd, services at 0715 and 0900 every Sun.

Hindu: *Sree Sree Siva Krishna*, 141 Pansodan St, service hours 1000-1100 and 1500-2000 daily.

Islamic: *Surti Sunny Jama Mosque*, Shwe Bontha St; *Narsapuri (Moja) Mosque*, 227 Shwe Bontha St; *Cholia Jama Mosque*, Bo Soon Pat St; service hours: noon prayer – 1230-1330 daily; evening prayer – 1645-1700 daily; Fri prayer – 1230-1330 (congregation).

Jewish: there is a synagogue in 26th St where services are held when Jewish Communities gather.

Protestant: *Holy Trinity Cathedral*, 446 Bogyoke Aung San St, T 72326, service at 0830 every Sun; *Immanuel Baptist Church*, Maha Bandoola Garden St, T 75908, service at 0830 every Sun; *St John the Baptist American Church*, 113 Bo Aung Kyaw St, service at 0900 every Sun; *Judson Church*, Yangon University Estate, T 531509, service at 1600.

Sikh: 256 Theinbyu St.

● Shopping

Antiques: ***Augustines***, off Pyay Rd, nr the Pyay/University/Insein junction, one of the most popular antique dealers because of his good prices, lacquerware, silver, furniture, woodcarvings. ***Mme Thair***, 220 Edwards St, antiques, lacquerware, beads, carvings. There is also a row of 4 small grey-painted shops selling lacquerware, brassware, gemstones, antique ships' clocks and gramophones (many of which are replicas) close to the *Inya Lake Hotel* on Kaba Aye Pagoda Rd. Series of small antique stalls on Dhammazedi Rd, nr Inya Rd. There is another group of similar shops a little further into town opposite the mosque and the *Singapore Girl* cake shop. The pieces are magnificent but incredibly expensive.

Books: the Burmese are voracious readers and there are bookstalls all over Yangon. Few Western books find their way into Myanmar as government censors are strict and any book traded on the black market is a potentially 'dangerous' item; most literature branded 'subversive' by the government is, however, widely available. Burmese bookshops and the Burmese literary scene flourishes along 33rd St between Anawrahta and Bogyoke Aung San sts and along the middle blocks of Pansodan St. The ***Sa-pe Beikman*** at 529 Merchant St sells official government books, propaganda, laws, translations etc. ***Pagan Bookshop***, 100 37th St, has a good selection of books on Burma in English. ***Innwa Bookstore***, 232 Sule Pagoda Rd, Kyauktada, T 272761, limited selection of Penguin Classics (in English) and some textbooks. ***The Lantern House Book Centre***, 18 Sabeyon Lane, Mingyi Road, for maps and books on Burmese culture and life as well as directories and other handbooks on doing business in Myanmar.

Handicrafts: ***Bogyoke Market*** (or Scotts Market), NW of Sule Pagoda, entrance on Bogyoke Aung San St. Wide range of merchandise, incl lacquerware, ivory, teak, Shan bags, lungyis, mother-of-pearl and crushed shell boxes, monks' umbrellas, silver, watercolour cards, baskets. Visitors are advised to bargain hard. Closes 1700 but many stalls start closing at 1500-1600. At the S and E entrances to the Shwedagon Pagoda there are many stalls selling religious paraphernalia and puppets. ***Pearl***, Shwegondine/Link St, good selection of wood carvings; ***Rangoon Glass Factory***, Yogi Kyaung St, just off Insein Rd, NW of Inya Lake. Private enterprise; possible to watch glassblowers at work; stall selling finished products. Open 1000-1500 Mon-Fri. ***Shwe Myo Thu***, 16/3 Inya Rd, T 533145, diverse selection of handicrafts – lacquerware, paintings, longyis, wood carvings; ***Win Mar***, 150 Kaba Aye Pagoda Rd, some items on the tacky side.

Markets: ***Bogyoke Market*** (see above); ***New Bogyoke Market***, opp, on the S side of the road, sells local produce, longyis, clothes, shoes – mainly Chinese imports – and hardware. ***Indian market***, on the S side of Anawrahta St; spices, fruit and vegetables. ***Chinese market***, few blocks W of Indian market, opp General Hospital (Lan Ma Daw Rd). ***Nyaung Pin Lay*** is close to the main port area and mainly trades basic commodities from the delta and coastal regions, eg rice, salt, beans, pulses. The ***Lanmadaw Market*** (or *Iron Market*) is Yangon's main fish market and is only a short walk from *Nyaung Pin Lay*.

Precious stones: the ***Tourist Department Store*** (Diplomatic Store), just N of the Sule Pagoda on Sule Pagoda Rd, offers the best selection of gems. Purchases at the Tourist Department Store can only be made in foreign currency. (The store also has a small selection of handicrafts and sells imported brands of alcohol and cigarettes.) Open 0930-1630 Tues-Sat. The government has a monopoly on gem stones and tourists are encouraged to shop here – stones bought without a certificate have been confiscated on departure (see **Customs**, page 356). There is also ***Myanmar Gems Emporium***, a government-run shop, nr the Kataye Pagoda. ***Diamond Inn***, 182 Shwegondine Rd, sells precious stones and changes money. It is however possible to find some reasonably good quality stones in ***Bogyoke Market*** although, unlike the Tourist Department Store, authenticity is not guaranteed. The goldsmiths and jewellers in Chinatown (the area around Latha St) also sell unset stones. Foreign residents say Bangkok is a better bet.

● Sports

Golf: a whole series of golf clubs have sprung up around Myanmar to entertain the nouveau riche and Japanese tourists. Most of the clubs are within easy reach of Yangon. ***City Golf Club***, Thiri Mingalar St, 10th Mile Insein, T 40086, even has its own resort hotel; ***Yangon Golf Club***, Danyingone, Mingaladon, T 635563; ***Myanmar Golf Club***, 9th Mile, Pyay Rd, T 661702.

Rowing: *Rowing Club*, on Inya Rd, has 1 and 2-seater kayaks for rent at US$1 pp for 30 mins. Rowing on Inya Lake is pleasant but beware of water snakes.

Running: *Hash House Harriers (HHH)*, meet every Sat at 1600 at the *Sailing Club* (Inya Rd), everyone welcome. There is a running and a walking hash, usually 6-7 km.

Swimming: *Inya Lake Hotel*, *Kokine Swimming Club*, 23 Saya San Rd, *Summit Parkview Hotel*.

● Tour companies & travel agents

Columbus, 107 Seikhantha St, Kyauktada, F 274806, worldwide air tickets (Bangkok prices); ***Diethelm Travel Myanmar Ltd***, 1 Inya Rd, Kamayut, T 527110, F 527135, joint venture with local partner, ***Myanmar Express Travel Ltd***, expensive; ***Euro-Asie***, 116 Bo Aung Kyaw St, Botataung (close to *Grand Hotel*), T 274640, F 284981, clued up on off the beaten track places, extending visas etc, good guides (French speaking), but one of the more expensive set-ups, rec; ***Flying Dragon Tourism Business***, 337 Pyay Rd, Sanchaung, F 289960; ***Free Bird Tours***, 357 Bo Aung Gyaw St (upper block), T 294941, F 289960, one of the larger private operators in Myanmar, efficient; ***Golden Express***, 56 Wadan St, T 221479, also operate a small chain of good hotels in the main sightseeing areas; ***Golden Land***, 214 (2A) Bo Aung Kyaw St, T 296074, F 661900, well organized, connected to MTT; ***Insight Myanmar***, 85/87 Theinbyu Rd, Botataung Township, T 295499, F 295599; ***Journeys***, Room 38, 2nd Flr Suite, Building 4, 8th Mile Junction, Pyay Rd, T 664275, F 289960; ***Myanmar Typical Explorations Tours***, 49, 1st Flr, Mya St, Kyaikkasan, T 543574, F 524526; ***Nay Chi Oo Travel & Tours***, 497 Pyay Rd, Kamayut, T 530087, F 226552; ***Open Sesame***, Thirimingalar Rd, Kamayut, T 532890, F 289862; ***Rubyland Tourism Services***, 90 Upper Pansodan St, Mingalartaungnyunt, T 281219, rec; ***Skyline***, 284 Seikhantha St, a/c bus tickets to Taunggyi; ***Sunfar Travel Co***, 122 38th St, T 240205, F 287887 (Myanmar Airways agents for Bangkok at 48/5 Pun Rd, Silom, T 662-266-5155, F 662-266-8860); ***TMS Tours***, No 138-8, Yenantha St, T 5579470; ***Tour Mandalay***, 194/196 Mahabandoola Rd, Pazundaung, F 97917, English and French speaking guides, very reasonable prices, rec; ***Windermere Inn***, 15(A) Aungmingaung Ave, Thanlwin Rd, F 533846.

● Tourist offices

Myanmar Travels & Tours (MTT), 77-91 Sule Pagoda Rd, T 278376/275328/280321. Excursions, country and city tours, hotel room reservations, car hire, rail and air tickets and official currency exchange (maximum US$300 at any one time) but not as efficient as private operators. Open 0800-1730 Mon-Sun. At least half the information provided is inaccurate.

● Transport

Local Boat: ferries and riverboats from various piers (1-3 kyat). **Bus**: frequent bus services round town, can be very crowded, but cheap. Most rides cost 2 kyat. Many local buses leave from nr Maha Bandoola Park. (All are numbered in Burmese numerals.) Pick-up linecars run the same routes, 5 kyat.

Bus 3: leaves from Latha Rd in China-Town, between Mahabandoola and Anawratha. It also stops on Shwedagon Pagoda Rd by the new Bo Gyaw Market, just pass the crossing with Anawratha, and goes on the Shwedagon (stops at the S, W and N doors) and the Myenigon crossing.

Bus 7: goes from Shwedagon Pagoda Rd, between Mahabandoola and the Strand to South Okalappa. Stops at Kokaing, and goes up along Inya Lake (eastern side).

Bus 8: goes either from bo ta taung jetty (where boats leave to Syriam) or Mahabandoola Park eastern side (Barr St), to Insein along the Prome Rd, stops at Myenigon, Hle Dan. On its way back from Insein, goes up Mahabandoola all the way to Sule Pagoda.

Bus 9: leaves from Sule Pagoda Rd, western side of Mahabandoola park, and goes to Mingaladon (along Pyay Rd), stops at Myenigon and Hle Dan, Inya Lake western side (just after Hle Dan), If you want to get to the airport, you will still have to take a taxi or a linecar (50 kyat) from the last stop.

Bus 12: One of the longest bus rides, from Htin Pon Ze, to Yankin, along University Ave and through Kokaing (eastern side of Inya Lake), it will take you through some typically Burmese parts of town. If you ride from the stop in front of Bo Gyaw Market on Bo Gyaw Aung San Rd, under the bridge, you will be going towards Htin Pon Ze. From the corner of Maha Bandoola Garden St and Anawratha or from the stop called Latha, on Anawratha (after crossing with Shwedagon Pagoda Rd), you will go towards Kokaing and Yankin.

Buses 14 and 5: go to the Peace Pagoda.

Bus 37: goes to the Shwedagon (from Sule Pagoda, 1 kyat).

Bus 38: goes to Thida Jetty for Thanlyin.

Bus 46: goes around the Royal Lakes (down Signal Pagoda Rd).

Bus 48: leaves from Thein Phyu St between 44th and 45th sts, goes to Insein along the Pyay Rd.

Buses 51 and 9: go nr the airport.

Numerous **pick-ups** also operate as alternative buses on many routes. Their numbers are written using Burmese numerals, so it is worth mugging-up beforehand.

Taxi: fares should be negotiated before setting off. Blue Mazda taxis are cheaper than large cars. Large cars to out-of-town destinations cost about US$27/day. There are many private cars and pick-ups operating as unofficial taxis. **Train**: circular rail route around the city, 2 hrs. Can hop on and off – a good way of seeing the suburbs. **Trishaw**: Yangon's back-to-back trishaws take 2 passengers; the fare should be settled before setting off. Price is usually worked out per head. Trishaws are not allowed in the city centre.

Air Mingaladon airport, 19 km NW of Yangon. International connections with Bangkok, Dhaka, Hong Kong, Kunming, Jakarta, Moscow and Singapore but the most reliable are those to Bangkok and Singapore. Regular connections with Nyaung-U, Bagan; Heho, for Inle Lake/Taunggyi; Mandalay; Thandwe. See page 357 for details on transport to town.

Train Station lies between Sule Rd and Pansodan St at the N edge of the city centre. Regular connections with Mandalay, Pyay, Thazi, Bago. There is a special counter at the W end of the station where foreigners must buy tickets. Passport and hard currency required.

Road Bus: main bus station is at Highway Gate, 18 km out, just N of the airport. Regular connections to all main cities and towns, a/c buses are varied in quality, all have video and food provided. Mandalay 15-18 hrs (1,000 kyat or 10 FEC). Buses leave from in front of the railway station and the bus terminal between 1530 and 1800. There are several bus companies situated in front of the railway station: **Leo Express**, 21 Aung San Stadium, T 276547. **Myanmar Arrow Express**, Room 19/25 Aung San Stadium, T 240102. **New Orient Express**, A-2, 2nd floor, 216-222 Maha Bandoola St, T 297432, F 98086. **Car hire**: always look at the vehicle before making an agreement and ask for a driver who has some knowledge of your language before accepting the deal. Pay half on departure, half on return. Expect to pay about US$600 for 10 days.

Lower Myanmar

YANGON DIVISION

TWANTE တွံတေး

Twante is best known for its pottery. Visitors can watch artists at work and then buy from a good, reasonably priced selection.

• **Transport Ferry and bus** Cross the Yangon River by pedestrian ferry from the Pansodan St Jetty to Dalah. From Dalah there are regular pick ups through the day to Twante. **Boat** It is also possible to travel all the way to Twante by boat – a worthwhile experience in itself. Take a Hpayapon ferry which leaves from the Hledan and Kaingdan jetties every hour from around noon to 1600. The journey takes around 2 hrs.

THANLYIN (SYRIAM) သံလျင်

The Arakanese seized Thanlyin (still better known by most foreigners as Syriam) in 1596 but realized that their only way of retaining the town was to gain the support of the Portuguese, who were busy establishing trading posts along the coast. The opportunistic Portuguese adventurer Felipe de Brito was dispatched to take charge of the customs house at Thanlyin; he quickly consolidated his position, building a brick customs house and a fort to protect it (you can still see Portuguese buildings in Thanlyin today). He then persuaded a Portuguese officer to expel the Arakanese governor. This done, he appointed himself governor and then left his officer, Ribeyro, in charge while he set sail for Goa, in an effort to secure the Portuguese Viceroy of India's support. While he was away, the Mons beseiged the town for 8 months. Ribeyro put up a good defence and when de Brito returned with six ships, the Mons accepted him as King of Lower Burma in 1603 (see page 37).

Thanlyin place names

Kyaik Khauk Pagoda
ကျိုက်ခေါက်ဘုရား
Kyauktan Pagoda (Ye Le Paya)
ကျောက်တန်းဘုရား
(ရေလယ်ဘုရား)

The town thrived as a port until it was sacked in 1756 by King Alaungpaya, founder of the Third Burmese Empire, which promptly ended its days of glory. He laid out a new city at Yangon which took the place of Thanlyin as the country's chief port. Today, Thanlyin's local economy depends on the Peoples' Brewery, the largest oil refinery in Myanmar, and rice production. Like many villages in the Ayeyarwady Delta, the town has a large Indian population, descendants of labourers brought over from India by the British, during the Delta's rice-growing boom in the late 19th century. Many Indians were deported in the years following Burmese independence but the country's biggest concentration of ethnic Indians remains in Thanlyin.

Places of interest The main sight is the **Kyaik Khauk Pagoda**, on a hill 3 km out of town to the S, on the way to Kuaktan.

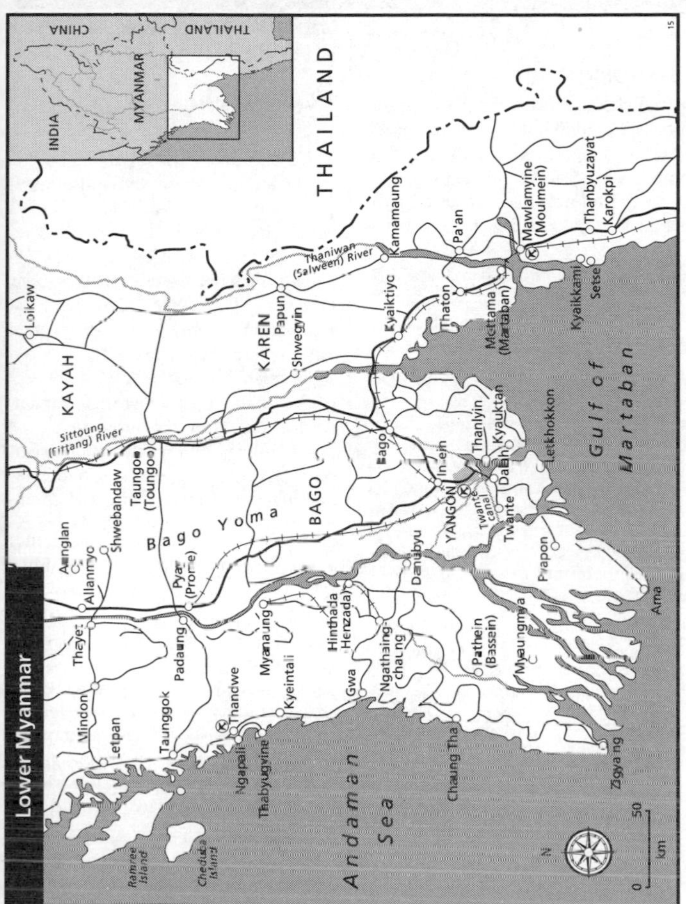

It has an imposing golden stupa, similar to the Shwedagon. The two tombs in front of the pagoda are of Burmese writers, Natshinnaung and Padethayaza, who wrote about ordinary people in the Ava period and were captured by the Mons.

The **Kyauktan Pagoda** or the **Ye Le Paya**, meaning 'the pagoda in the middle of the river' is 12 km S of Thanlyin, on a mid-river island on a tributary of the Yangon River. Inside there are paintings of all the most important pagodas in Myanmar. *Getting there*: Ye Le Paya is too far for a pony and trap. Taxis cost about 150-200 kyat/hr to charter, trishaws and ponycarts 40-60 kyat/hr. Prices should be negotiated in advance. From the river bank there are boats to carry pilgrims and visitors across to the islands and pagoda.

• **Transport Local Pony traps, trishaws, buses** and **linecars** mill around the ferry terminal. **Road Bus**: regular pickups from Sule Pagoda Rd, opp the City Hall in Yangon.

LETKHOKKON

Myanmar is not really the place to come for a beach holiday. However, the closest beach to Yangon with anything resembling sand and swaying palm trees is this place – **Letkhokkon Village** and the nearby **Letkhokkon Beach**. Because it is situated on an estuary the water is turgid and the 'sand', especially at low tide, muddy. The village is entertaining enough in a low-key and friendly sort of way, with fishing boats and a monastery.

• **Accommodation** **C** *Letkhokkon Beach Hotel*, T 01-223409, this is really a pretty sophisticated little hotel, with large a/c bungalows on the beach, attached bathrooms and a reasonable restaurant that serves decent seafood dishes; **E** *No Name Guesthouse*, the down market alternative to the *Letkhokkon Beach*, a gaggle of simple thatched chalets on the edge of the village, in early 1996 foreigners were still not officially permitted to stay here, although many have.

• **Transport Local Bus and ferry**: catch a ferry across the Yangon River to Dalah from the Sin Oh Dan St Jetty (vehicle ferry) or the Pansodan St Jetty (pedestrian). From there, there are sometimes buses and pickups to Letkhokkon (3 hrs). An alternative is to charter a vehicle in Dalah.

BAGO DIVISION

BAGO (PEGU) ပဲခူး

The 2 hrs' drive from Yangon to Bago is rather disappointing as the road was widened in 1991 and all the beautiful trees which lined it were chopped down reportedly to make it easier to get tanks into Yangon). There are a few sights *en route*, however. The **War Cemetery**, at Htaukkyan (30 km N of the Mingaladon airport) is a memorial to the 27,000 Allied servicemen who died in WW2; it is beautifully maintained by the Commonwealth War Graves Commission. The **Naga-Yone**, past the cemetery, has eight planetary posts (see page 108) with their guardian birds and animals and an unusual Buddha image, which is enwrapped by a cobra. The **Shwenyaungbin** (Golden Banyan Tree), is an ancient tree on the road to Bago, reputed, in local lore, to be home of nats, the guardian spirits of the highway. Passers-by often stop to make offerings, while owners take their new cars to the spot to be blessed. About an hour out of Yangon you will pass Yebo on your left. This highly fortified town was built by the Chinese in case the Burmese military have to make a swift exit. According to locals, inside are helicopters ready and waiting to fly to the Chinese border.

In 573 AD, Thamala and Wimala, two Mon brothers of noble birth – who were excluded from the succession order – founded Bago as an outpost of the Mon Thaton Kingdom. The site, which was then on the Gulf of Martaban, had already been earmarked as the location of a great city by Gautama, the historic Buddha. According to legend, the Buddha rested on a small hillock and two hintha birds came before him in obeisance. He prophesied that 1,660 years after his death, a city would be established on that spot which would be a capital. Sure enough, Bago developed into a prosperous port, while Thaton declined in importance.

In the 12th century, Bago came under the rule of the Burmese kings of Bagan and remained under their sway until 1323 when it became the Mon capital. Its golden age was from 1385-1635, when it was the capital of the Mon Kingdom of Lower Myanmar. In 1542, the King of Taungoo (which had become a prominent kingdom in the Sittoung valley), who built up a huge, rich and powerful kingdom based at Bago, almost the size of present-day Myanmar. His son and successor, Nandanaung, who came to the throne in 1581, was a feeble and paranoid ruler; suspecting some of his officers of complicity with the King of Ava, he had them burned to death, along with their wives and children. Nandanaung then waged war with Ava and then Siam, but sickened by the bloodshed, the people revolted and neighbouring kingdoms besieged the city.

Portuguese adventurer Felipe de Brito stepped into the breach in 1603; he occupied the desolated city for a decade, and declared himself King of Bago (see page 37). Another Portuguese official, Fernand Mendez Pinto, who visited Bago around this time wrote that the kingdom was "...the most abundant, and richest in gold, silver, and precious stones that may be found in any part of the world." After that, the King of Ava ruled his empire from Bago but he grew tired of living in the decaying city; when the port began to silt up, he transferred his capital to Ava in 1635. Bago was briefly re-established as the Mon capital in 1740 but was again destroyed in 1757 by King Alaungpaya, the founder of Myanmar's Konbaung Dynasty and the Third Burmese Empire (see page 40). By 1795, Bago had a population of less than 6,000. Alaungpaya's son, King Bodawpaya, undertook some restoration work in Bago at the end of the 18th century. But by then the city was already losing

Bago place names

Hinthagone Hill
ဟင်္သာကုန်းတောင်

Kyaikpun
ကျိုက်ပွန်

Mahazedi Pagoda
မဟာစေတီဘုရား

Shwegugale Pagoda
ရွှေဂူကလေးဘုရား

Shwemawdaw Pagoda
ရွှေမော်ဓောဘုရား

Shwenyaungbin
ရွှေညောင်ပင်

Shwethalyaung Pagoda
ရွှေသာလျောင်းဘုရား

its commercial raison d'être: in the early 1800s, the Bago River had changed its course, cutting the city off from the sea, finally sealing its fate.

Places of interest

There is little of secular interest left standing in Bago, apart from the remains of the old moated walls. The Mon-style **Shwemawdaw Pagoda** or 'Pagoda of the Great Golden God', on the N side of town, is one of the most venerated pagodas in Myanmar. It stands 114m high and is taller but similar in style to the Shwedagon Pagoda in Yangon. The temple has a 1,000 year history: it was originally built by two merchants, Taphussa and Bhalita, to house some hair relics of the Buddha. A sacred tooth was added by King Anurama in 982 AD and another by King Rajadarit in 1385. Successive kings have added to the stupa's height: in 1385 it was raised to 86m by King Dhammazedi; in 1796 King Bodawpaya built a new *hti* (using jewels from his crown) and raised

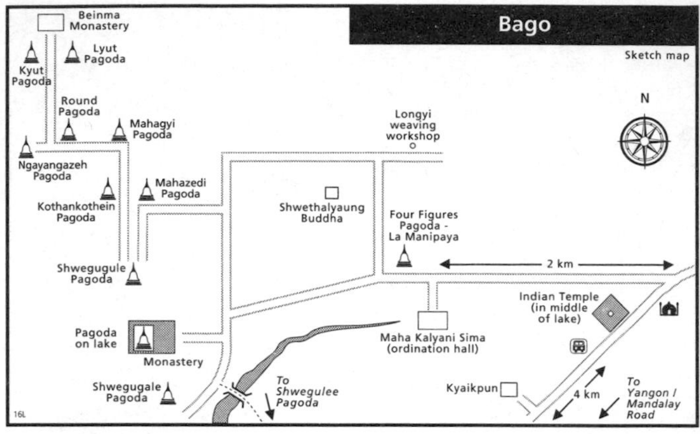

the height of the stupa to 90m.

Its architectural interest lies in its octagonal base and elaborate projections in the lower portion. The Shwemawdaw was severely damaged by earthquakes in 1912 and 1917 and completely destroyed by another earthquake in 1930. It was finally rebuilt between 1952 and 1954 in a slightly different style to the original and has a new diamond-studded hti, the stupa is covered with 1½ tonnes of gold. Over US$100 per day is collected from pilgrims to maintain the building. The stairways leading to the pagoda are guarded by huge white chinthes (temple lions), each containing a sitting Buddha in its mouth. There are eight planetary prayer posts (see page 108) and a small museum of Buddha images of stone and bronze, varying ages and styles, rescued from the original pagoda after the 1930 quake. The 'bananabud' from the original stupa has been left on the platform in memory of the earthquake. Admission US$3 (includes entrance to other pagodas in Bago). Camera fee 25 kyat. There is a small market at the bottom of the W entrance selling pagoda paraphernalia, as well as a few tea shops. There is a busy shopping area, a few guesthouses (not open to tourists at the moment) and the post office on the S side of the pagoda.

To the E of the Shwemawdaw is **Hinthagone Hill**, with a small pagoda on top. The hill is originally said to have been an island. According to legend, the original pair of mythological hintha birds (see page 128) perched on this hill. There are models of them in front of the main shrine – the male bird is carrying the female. The pagoda is down at heel but there are interesting paintings of Buddha's life on the ceiling. The popular shrine, to the right as you go up, is to a local nat (or spirit).

Most of the other sights are the other side of town, on the road to Yangon. The **Kalyani Sima**, or Ordination Hall, 1 km W of the station, was built in 1476 by King Dhammazedi, who was a fervent promoter of the Buddhist faith. The hall was the first of its kind in Myanmar and seems to have been built and rebuilt many times. The previous hall – dating from 1902 – was badly damaged by the 1930 earthquake; the present one was erected in 1954 and dedicated to its original purpose in a ceremony attended by former Prime Minister U Nu. To the W there are 10 huge stone pillars covered with inscriptions. These were set up by King Dhammazedi in 1476 to record the ceremony

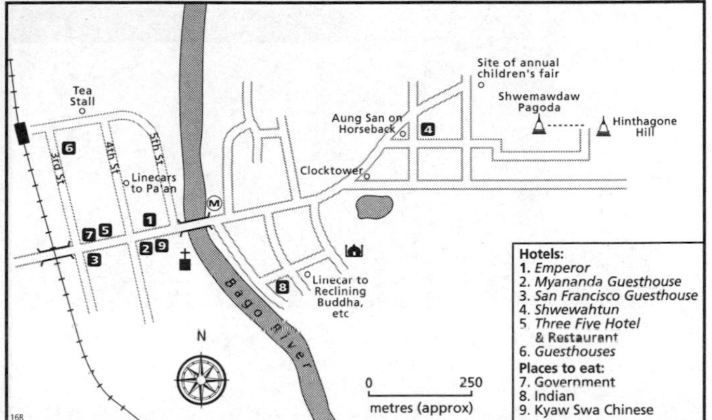

consecrating the sima. Their value lies in the detailed information on the early history of Buddhism in Myanmar that can be gleaned from the inscriptions. The language of the first three stones is Pali and the rest, Mon.

Bago is probably most famous for its huge reclining Buddha image, the **Shwethalyaung Buddha**, 55m long and 16m high, which is a short walk NW of Kalyani Sima. A helpful board gives his vital statistics: ear 4.57m, sole of foot 7.77m, great toe 1.83m, and eyelid 2.29m. It was built by King Migadippa I in 994 AD, but fell into a state of disrepair. Five centuries later King Dhammazedi restored the image and King Bayinnaung maintained it until it lapsed into obscurity once again following the destruction of Bago in 1757. The statue lay undisturbed for 125 years before being rediscovered in 1881 when the British were constructing the Yangon-Bago railway. It was restored to its former glory, and an open pavilion, rather like a railway station, was built over it in 1906. It is said to depict the Gautama Buddha on the eve of his attaining nirvana. It is a busy picnic site at the weekends and there are several tea shops round the entrance.

Mahazedi Pagoda, close to the Shwethalyaung, was built by King Bayinnaung in 1560 to enshrine a tooth-relic brought from Ceylon – a duplicate of the sacred tooth at Kandy. 10 years after Bago was conquered in 1599, the relics were moved to King Anaukhpetlun's capital in Taungoo. They were then transferred to Ava, and finally housed by King Thalun in the Kaunghmidaw Pagoda in Sagaing, near Ava. The building was destroyed by the 1930 earthquake and has been repaired – it is blindingly white. Only men can climb the stupa – ladies can walk around the platform. To the W lie some less famous pagodas. One of the most important is the **Shwegugale Pagoda** with its 64 seated Buddhas. It is a working monastery – visitors are requested not to wander round the monks' living quarters. There is a pretty pagoda in the middle of the lake beyond the monastery – Lamance paya. The small, and not very impressive, pagoda over the bridge is called Shwesugyi.

Next comes the **Kothankothein (9,900,000) Pagoda**. The number represents the number of incarnations the Buddha went through before reaching nirvana. The many smaller pagodas on the backs of animals represent some of his incarnations. (The stories of how he perfected the Buddhist virtues during

A white chinthe guarding the stairway of the Shwemawdaw Pagoda illustrated on a 200 kyat note

animal and human incarnations are told in the jataka tales.)

After leaving the Kothankothein pagoda one crosses the compound of the pretty but unexceptional **Mahagyi paya**. Follow the lane to the left and pass the locked round pagoda to see the photogenic **Ngayangazeh (550) Pagoda**. The large central stupa with a terrace is surrounded by 550 carefully lined-up little stupas.

Backtrack to the round pagoda and continue uphill to visit the **Kyut** and **Lyuk** pair of pagodas in different styles. The Lyuk stands clear of the trees, and has a small covered terrace on top, making it the best place to get sweeping views of the countryside. The Shwemawdaw can be seen in the distance.

The **Beinma Monastery** at the end of the lane has some edifying sculptured scenes, but is unexceptional.

The **Kyaikpun** is 5 km from Bago on the Yangon road and sits on a tributary of the Bago River. The entrance is just by the Kaikton ze Tawon meditation centre. It is a giant, 30m-high, version of the four seated Buddhas opposite the Hall of Ordination in Bago; they sit back-to-back, facing the four points of the compass. It was also built by the religious King Dhammazedi in 1476. The Buddha on the W side was damaged by the 1930 earthquake. Local legend says this was because each image represented one of four sisters who had a pact with each other that they would not marry. The youngest sister, however, did get married, and the image representing her cracked. Although it was repaired again and again, the cracks always reappeared. Note the interesting, but rather ramshackle, Indian temple – Sripalyandar Temple – on the road out to Kyaikpun.

Local festivals

The annual *Shwemawdaw Festival* is in Mar/Apr.

Local information

● Orientation

The main road from the S takes you over the bridge and directly N to the Shwemawdaw. The town is along this main axis. The railway station, a few restaurants and the main indoor market are below the bridge. The main hotel, smaller guesthouses, and a local market are centred around the Shwemawdaw.

● Accommodation

B *Shwewahtun*, not very central, T 21263, a/c, no h/w, restaurant (limited menu), government-run, poorly maintained, the new block is in slightly better condition, and the rooms have h/w, rather frosty management, quiet with a tatty garden.

D *Emperor*, T 21349, some a/c, some attached bathrooms, h/w, English-speaking management; **D** *Htun*, beside clocktower, T 21973, some a/c, some rooms with attached bathrooms and hot water; **D-E** *Myananda*,

10 Main Rd, T 22275, newest guesthouse in town, clinically clean, friendly, unobtrusive staff, English spoken, fans, hot water, map of area, advice about how to get to sights for free.

E *San Francisco Guesthouse*, nr railway station, noisy (ask for rooms at the back), friendly, the main travellers' rest.

● Places to eat

Kyawswa Restaurant, 6 Main Rd (W of Bago River), Chinese, cheap and clean; and the *Kyaiktiyo Hotel*.

● Post & telecommunications

Area code: 052.

● Shopping

Bago market, whose thatched roofs extend between the main road and the river, is full of local produce plus some handicrafts. The modern covered market next to it contains textiles and Chinese imports. There is a busy local market on the S side of the Shwemawdaw.

● Transport

80 km NE of Yangon.

Local Taxis, **ponycarts** and **trishaws** wait outside the train station. Driver may give you a guided tour. **Linecars** run from the market to sights.

Train The 0500 departure from Yangon allows plenty of time to visit most sights of interest in Bago; the last train to Yangon leaves at 2000 (2-3 hrs). Also connections to Mandalay, via Thazi (8 hrs).

Road Bus: buses leave from Highway Gate in Yangon every half hour, 1½-2 hrs from 0430 onwards (3 hrs). It is advisable to book tickets 1 day in advance as buses can be very crowded; the return bus journey should be booked on arrival in Bago. There are also frequent linecars, no need to book. The bus station in Bago is ½ km S of town on the Yangon road. Continuing S of Kyaiktiyo, the road is very poor, with huge potholes. **Taxi**: expensive, but many visitors prefer to take a taxi from Yangon for the day as it allows much greater flexibility. A full-day return trip from Yangon should cost about 1,500 kyats.

TOUNGOO (TAUNGOO)

A third of the way N between Yangon and Mandalay, the city of Toungoo – also spelt Taungoo – shelters in the shade of countless areca palm trees. Busy without being hectic, prosperous without being ostentatious, Toungoo deserves more than the quick overnight visit that most tourists afford it. Although it is hard to tell today, this was once the centre of one of Myanmar's most powerful kingdoms and was at its apogee during the 15th and 16th centuries. The population of 280,000 is roughly equally split between Karen and Burmese communities, with a small number of Indians remaining from a formerly much larger population. The many old mosques in the city indicate that the Indian Muslim population was once much larger, although the presence of several new mosques indicate that Islam still thrives in this important trading centre.

Teak comes into Toungoo from the eastern hills and is then transported by river S; fruit and areca nuts are grown on the plains. The areca nut is the critical ingredient in the erroneously named betel 'nut' wadge, the stimulant that keeps upcountry Myanmar buzzing. Toddy palms provide a juice which is the basis for an array of drinks from the Burmese equivalent of fizzy-pop, to strong alcohol. Fermented only slightly it makes a bubbly non-alcoholic drink; a bit more produces Karen beer; more still to make a strong spirit.

Places of interest

The N-S Yangon to Mandalay highway bisects Toungoo and the western and eastern sections of the city have markedly different characters. Both, though, are rewarding to roam around. To the W is the old town, with a moat and portions of the city wall enclosing many fine houses, pagodas, mosques and the main market. To the E is the village-like newer growth, with tall trees, wooden houses and the Thaniwan (Salween) River. For more ordered sightseeing there are unusual pagodas, Hindu temple ruins and a lively market.

Near to one another in the old town are the Shwesandaw and Myasigaw pagodas. The **Shwesandaw Stupa** is Toungoo's senior pagoda, and the main stupa was erected in 1597 – although it was probably built on top of a much older structure. The most important image here is the 3m-high seated Mandalay-style bronze Buddha which was cast in 1912. The image contains the ashes of the man who paid for and presented the image to the monastery. The pagoda is being renovated (as it has been since the early 1950s when it was identified by the government of Myanmar as a monument deserving of national funds) and for 300 kyat visitors can become part of this extended renovation effort. In return for the gift, the donor has a gold plate specially inscribed with his or her name and address. The temple is strong on mechanical scenes which move and play music at the donation of coins. Around the terrace are sculptures showing the demise of non-believers, the Buddha on his deathbed with over 100 devotees in attendance, regional patron spirits and local kings.

Close by to the SE is the **Myasigaw Pagoda** or **Myasigon Paya**. In the mirror-mosaic hall to the E is a large and beautiful Buddha image with an elaborate head-dress and paintings of the Toungoo kings. Also here is a pagoda trustee who can unlock the small museum where there are some important ancient ceramic work, two cannon cast in 1797, an image of Erawan the three-headed elephant god which was sacked during one of King Bayinnaung's forays into neighbouring Siam, fine old *parabeik* scriptures and lacquerware, among other exhibits.

About 1½ km W of the old town, down Bo Hmu Pho Kun Rd is **Kaunghmyudaw Pagoda**, founded in the 16th century. Walk three times clockwise around the mirrored obelisk for good luck. Frangipani trees scent the temple grounds, and a large bo tree – *Ficus religiosa*, the tree under which the historic Buddha attained enlightenment – throws shade over the compound.

The **market** area is along the E side of the old city, S of the Catholic Cathedral. Karen textiles, pottery, glassware and hats are good buys. South of the market, inside a ring of shops is a ruined **Hindu temple**. Some of the carvings are well preserved and the shrines still draw offerings. The temple's poor condition is explained by the fact that it is said to have been bombed by the Japanese towards the end of WW2.

Excursions

Pathichaung Park lies 21 km E of Toungoo, in Karen state, just beyond Thandaung village. A pretty creek (dry season) or river (rainy season) runs beneath large trees. In the dry season, islets and big smooth boulders midstream are the coolest picnic spots around. Take-away food is available in the village; soft drinks, beer and fruit are sold from a stand in the small parking lot. *Getting there*: the most enchanting way is to hire a pony trap – and visit some shady graveyards and a hill covered with pagodas en route. Much of the road is through replanted teak forest; shade is appreciated by those who choose to travel by linecar – these tend to be even more crowded than usual along this route. When the roof is full, passengers sit on the bonnet.

Okedwin is a pleasant town 13 km S of Toungoo. From here it is possible to arrange an elephant ride into a teak forest.

Local festivals

Feb: halfway between Toungoo and Yangon, the Catholic Festival of Nyaunglebin is held from 16-18 Feb annually. Up to 100,000 people attend, many of whom are dressed in traditional costume (in particular, Palaung).

Local information

● Accommodation

Four places in town accept foreigners.

B *Myanma Thiri Hotel*, T 21764, 1½ km S of *Beauty Guesthouse*, SE of the commons, a/c and private bathrooms with hot water, satellite TV and fridge, restaurant with Burmese food

(♦♦♦), Government run hotel with little character – despite the fact that it is an old colonial building, the staff speak good English, garden setting.

D *Min Kyee Nyo Guesthouse*, further S, with a sign in English on the highway, T 21338, new guesthouse, with very helpful staff, but little English, free ride into town, breakfast in bed, clean and quiet; **D** *Myanmar A Hla/Myanmar Beauty Guesthouse*, 7/134 Bo Hmu Pho Kun Rd (old town), T 21270, some a/c, in the old house there are wooden, fan-cooled rooms upstairs (without bathrooms), downstairs, concrete rooms have a/c and bath, an extension is under construction, with a/c and bathrooms, a good breakfast with plenty of fruit is included in the room rate, the owners speak English well; **D** *Nansanda Guesthouse*, Nansanda Rd, T 21089, some a/c, good central location nr the cathedral, rooms are acceptably clean with shared bathroom.

● Places to eat

♦♦♦-♦♦*Panyoma*, at the NE corner of the commons, serves excellent Burmese and Chinese food, the balcony upstairs is usually cooled by a breeze.

♦♦-♦*Pangabar*, E side of highway, opp the old town, Karen food.

Foodstalls: from the night market adjoining the central market for simple Indian dishes and snacks.

● Post & telecommunications

Area code: 054.

Post Office: opp the market's clock tower, N of the commons.

● Shopping

Some good buys incl Karen textiles, pottery, glassware and hats can be had in the market which runs along the E side of the old city, S of the Catholic Cathedral.

● Transport

Local Pony traps, linecars, sidecars.

Train Toungoo is on the Yangon-Mandalay route, which is plied by 8 trains/day (7-9 hrs each way, payment in FEC). The three express down trains leave Toungoo for Yangon at 0300, 0700 and 2300. Up trains for Mandalay depart Toungoo at 0200, 0300 and 2300.

Road Bus: regular bus and linecar connection with Yangon and Mandalay (7-10 hrs) from the main bus station at the N edge of the city. Connections to Pyinmana, Meiktila and Pyay (only in dry season – the road is rough) also operate from here. It is usually possible to flag vehicles down as they pass through town. Buses to Loikaw (6 hrs) leave from a second station across the Thaniwan (Salween) River. Various tour bus companies running services between Yangon and Mandalay also stop on the main road opp the *Tinechit Restaurant*, usually around midday.

PYAY (PROME or PYI)
ပြည်

Pyay lies on the E bank of the Ayeyarwady, near to some of Myanmar's newly developed oil fields. It is probably best known for the nearby archaeological site of Sri Ksetra – known as Thiri Kettaya in Burmese. It is an important trading centre between Lower and Upper Myanmar and crossing point to the Rakhine Yoma and Thandwe (Sandoway).

The **Shwesandaw Pagoda**, on the S side of town, is one of Myanmar's most holy sites – the Gautama Buddha is said to have preached a sermon here. The pagoda contains four hair relics. It was built when the area was ruled by Mons, hence the double hti; the lower one is the original Mon hti, and when the Burman's took control of Prome, they topped it with their own hti. The pagoda, a copy of the Shwedagon in Yangon, dominates the top of the hill and views from here are impressive. The ancient Payagyi can be seen on the horizon toward Thiri Kettaya. There are several traditional wooden pavilions on the platform with impressive metalwork. The eastern entrance is dominated by an enormous Buddha statue. Halfway up the hill to the S is the **Bo Bo Aung Pagoda**, a shrine to a mystic of the Konbaung Dynasty and a leader of a Tantric sect. One block E of the large market is **Shwepounpwint Pagoda**. The 'library' on the southeastern corner of the block has a better museum than the archaeological site of Sri Ksetra. Admission free.

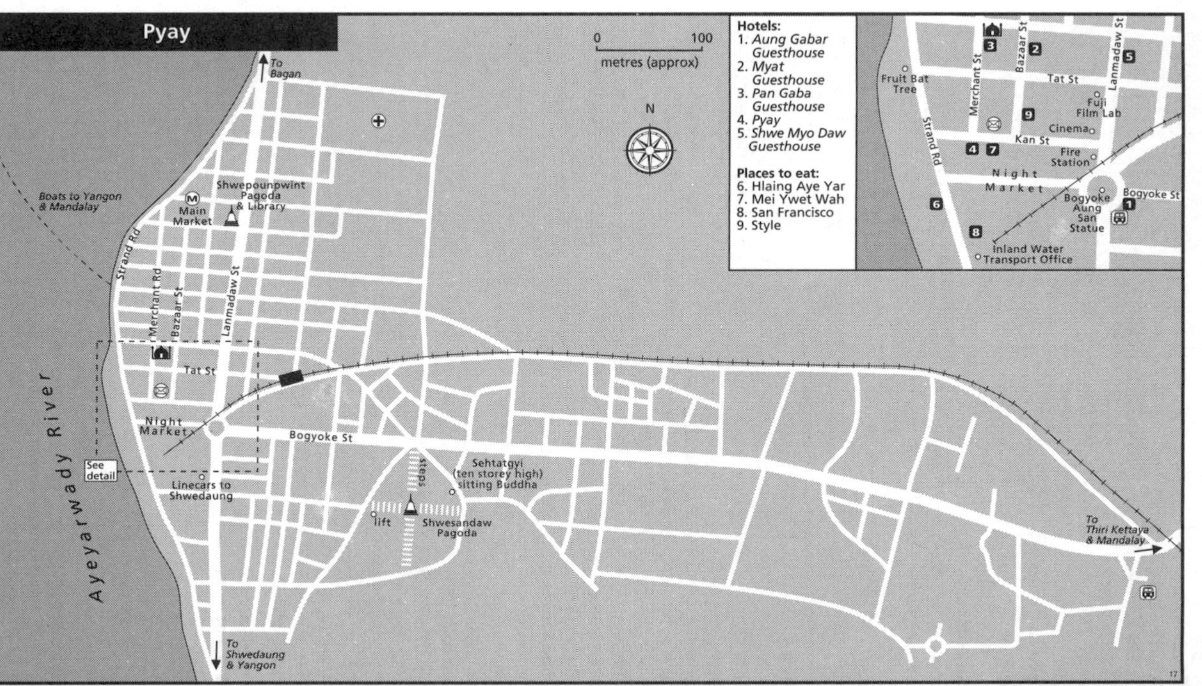
Pyay
To Bagan
0
100
metres (approx)
N
Hotels:
1. Aung Gabar Guesthouse
2. Myat Guesthouse
3. Pan Gaba Guesthouse
4. Pyay
5. Shwe Myo Daw Guesthouse
Places to eat:
6. Hlaing Aye Yar
7. Mei Ywet Wah
8. San Francisco
9. Style
Fruit Bat Tree
Strand Rd
Merchant St
Bazaar St
Tat St
Lanmadaw St
Fuji Film Lab
Cinema
Kan St
Fire Station
Night Market
Bogyoke St
Bogyoke Aung San Statue
Inland Water Transport Office
Boats to Yangon & Mandalay
Shwepounpwint Pagoda & Library
Main Market
Strand Rd
Merchant Rd
Bazaar St
Lanmadaw St
Tat St
Ayeyarwady River
Night Market
Bogyoke St
See detail
Linecars to Shwedaung
steps
Sehtatgyi (ten storey high) sitting Buddha
lift
Shwesandaw Pagoda
To Thiri Kettaya & Mandalay
To Shwedaung & Yangon

Excursions

Thiri Kettaya, better known in the West as **Sri Ksetra**, is an important archaeological site 8 km SE of Pyay. See the next entry (for details on the site). *Getting there*: the remains are spread over a large area, so it is best to charter a taxi or pony trap, or hire a bicycle, in Pyay.

Approximately 15 km S of Pyay, in **Shwedaung**, a pleasant riverside settlement, is the **Shwemyethman** (Golden Eyeglasses) **Pagoda**. This pagoda is said to have been founded over 2,000 years ago by King Dotabaung, who went with the queen to build a stupa in Shwedaung. As they rested there, the queen had a vision of a Buddha image. They searched for the image, but when they found it, it disappeared before their eyes. They constructed this image on the site, and the king went blind by the time it was finished. Someone suggested he have glasses made for it – he did, and his vision was restored. The glasses were stolen during the conflict with the British, but were replaced by a local mayor. However, to prevent theft, these were put inside the image. Another mayor, an Englishman with a Burmese wife, donated the glasses you now see, to cure his wife's blindness. They proved an effective remedy. The glasses are about 2m long and weigh over 10 kg. They make the Buddha look unusually attentive. *Getting there*: linecars leave from the street S of the Aung San statue. Shwedaung can also easily be reached by bicycle.

Local information

● Orientation

The centre of town is N of the Shwesandaw Pagoda along the river, where you will find the *Pyay (Prome) Hotel*, a few restaurants and the market. Electricity in Pyay is variable: expect lights to dim and fans to slow as you attempt to read in the sticky gloom.

● Accommodation

C *Pyay (Prome) Hotel*, nr the river, T 21890, privatized government hotel, a/c, attached bathrooms but no hot water, under repair but still grotty with thin partition walls and very ordinary restaurant, mainly used by locals; **C-D** *Myat Guesthouse*, 222 Bazaar St, T 21361, downstairs are simple, fan rooms while upstairs are spotless, well-furnished a/c rooms with attached bathrooms, 1 rm with hot water, good central location, close to restaurants, quiet.

D *Shwe Myo Daw*, 353 Lanmadaw St, T 21990, a/c, shared bathrooms, bath not clean, no breakfast; **D-E** *Aung Gabar Guesthouse*, T 21332, run by a friendly family, guests eat upstairs in the family's own living room (breakfast incl in rate), atmosphere rather spoiled by a noisy road out front, rather dirty rooms.

E *Pan Gaba*, 342 Merchant Rd, T 21277, plain but clean, free bicycle loan, good breakfast upon request (mohinga, fried rice) – rec, cold water, bath down the hall, quiet; **E** *Phyu Sin*, 1456A Bogyoke St, some a/c, shared bathrooms, basic, small rooms, not too clean, breakfast incl, quite friendly. The filthy guesthouse at the bus station will take you in for $1.

● Places to eat

♦♦♦*San Francisco Restaurant*, Strand Rd, inside a/c and tables outside. Near the *Pyay (Prome) Hotel* (see map), is a good Chinese restaurant – the ♦♦♦*Hlaing Aye Yar* on Strand Rd – with truly monumental dishes (a small dish will feed 3), and with stupendous views to the W of the river, distant hills and (at appropriate time) sunset, a good place to watch the evening flight of the bats, many bugs after dark. For Burmese food *Style* and *Mei Ywet Wah*, nr *Pyay Hotel* on Kan St, serve the usual fare. The ♦*Night Market* operates from 1700-2100.

● Post & telecommunications

Area code: 053.

Pyay place names

Bo Bo Aung Pagoda
ဘိုးဘိုးအောင်ဘုရား

Shwesandaw Pagoda
ရွှေဆံတော်ဘုရား

Thiri Kettaya
သရေခေတ္တရာ

● **Transport**
285 km N of Yangon.

Local Most of the cheaper guesthouses have **bicycles** for hire – they are a convenient way to explore Thiri Kettaya.

Train There are morning and evening rail connections with Yangon. From Pyay, trains depart at 0800 and 2200 (approx 10 hrs) – one train goes only to/from Kyimindine station in Yangon.

Road Bus: daily connections with Yangon (see below) and Mandalay (Express overnight air-con, leaving 1700, 800 kyat) and points en route. If the bus from Yangon is continuing to Mandalay, passengers may have to pay the full Yangon-Mandalay fare. Bus companies to Yangon are **Tie Da Ghoon Express**, **Sky Line Express**, and **Hot Line Express**. Some are a/c, most take 5 hrs and cost 200 kyat. The road has been recently upgraded and is very good by Myanmar standards. For Pathein, **Pyay Heina Express** leaves daily at 1000, 10 hrs, 150 kyat, or **Sanhtey Hlaing** leaves at 0430 and 1300, takes 3½-5 hrs, depending on the river crossing. Connections with Ngapali means changes at Taunggok and Thandwe – buses leave daily at 1200 and 1400, the road is poor and the buses are old and cramped. Daily connections with Bagan (Nyaung U) at 0530 on the buses coming from Yangon (1,000 kyat). Other connections with Hinthada (via Kyangin and rail, see page 144) and towns along the Ayeyarwady. Although Taungoo is not far, the road over the Bago Yomas is not used by buses. Private cars can cross this way, or you may be able to arrange a ride with a truck. The road is in a bad condition and may be impassable in the rainy season. For connections to Rakhine, see page 241. **Private car**: by private hire car/share taxi, the Yangon-Pyay journey is about 4½ hrs on a good road. **River** Connections with Mandalay (Mon, Tues, Thur, Fri, Sun) departs 0530, 4 days ($20-40), boat stops at Bagan and other Ayeyarwady towns – to Yangon on every day except Tues, departs 0600, 3 days (US$18-36). The boat stops at Myanaung for those wishing to catch the train to Pathein (Bassein).

THIRI KETTAYA (SRI KSETRA) သရေခေတ္တရာ

The archaeological site of **Thiri Kettaya**, better known to many as **Sri Ksetra**, is 8 km SE of Pyay. The site has not been maintained and most of the remains are overgrown and hidden among the village buildings and farms. The temples are spread out over a large area (there is a map in the museum), although the local villagers are friendly and will help budding Indiana Jones' find the pagodas. In fact, that life should go on in such a mundane manner amidst the remnants of grandeur is one of the more enchanting aspects of Thiri Kettaya.

Thiri Kettaya was the Pyu capital until the 8th century and was finally destroyed by King Anawrahta in 1057, and all the booty moved to his new capital at Bagan (Pagan). A Chinese chronicle of the Tang Dynasty paints a vivid picture of life at the Pyu capital around 800 AD: "The city wall, faced with green-glazed brick is 600 li in circumference and has 12 gates and pagodas at each of the four corners. Within there are more than 100 monasteries, all resplendent with gold, silver and cinnabar. Likewise the palace of the sovereign. The women wear their hair in a top-knot ornamented with flowers, pearls and precious stones and are trained in music and the dance. Having no oil, they use candles of perfumed beeswax. The people have a knowledge of astronomy and delight in the Law of the Buddha. At the age of seven, both boys and girls shave their heads and go to live at a monastery as novices until they are 20. If at this age they have not awakened to the religious life, they once again allow their hair to grow and return to town. The people deplore the taking of life. Their clothing is of cotton, for they maintain that silk should not be worn as it involves injury to the silkworm."

This large site has been excavated on and off for nearly 100 years. An impressive city wall (the road goes along part of it) and moat, which enclose three sides of Thiri Kettaya, have been unearthed. There are also remains of several pagodas: Payamna, Payagyi and Bawbawgyi, the most complete are outside the city wall. The cylindrical-shaped Baw-

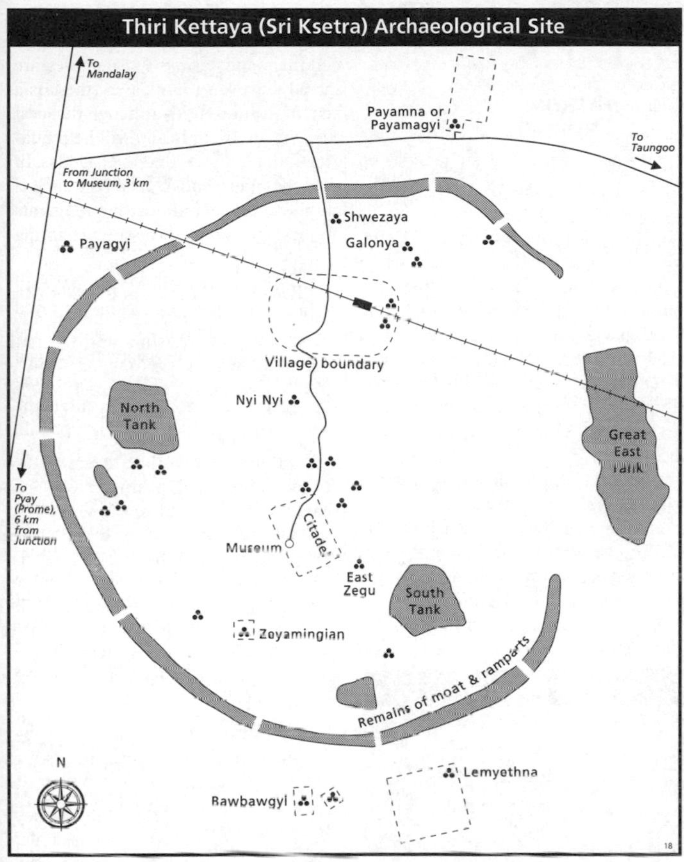

bawgyi and conical-shaped Payagyi and Payamna stupas with their commanding position over the plains were also used as lookout posts. The hollow-square Lemyethna and East Zegu temples, within the city walls, were prototypes for the temples at Bagan. At the centre of the archaeological zone is a small museum with a few, rather badly displayed and disappointing, exhibits including stone reliefs and covers of relic chambers excavated from the Pyu Dynasty palace. There are out of focus photographs of the more important finds, which are in the National Museum in Yangon and the Victoria and Albert Museum in London. Open 0900-1600 Mon-Sat. (In front of the museum is a cattle market.) *Getting there*: as the sites are spread over a wide area, it is best to hire a taxi, bicycle or pony trap in Prome.

AYEYARWADY DIVISION

PATHEIN (BASSEIN) ပုသိမ်

The history of Pathein, a port city 190 km from Yangon, dates back to when the Mons and the Burmese were fighting to gain control of the Ayeyarwady Delta. The British East India Company set up a trading post at Pathein in the 17th century but it was raided by King Alaungpaya during the 18th century. In 1852, after the annexation of Lower Myanmar, the British established a garrison in the town and began to vigorously promote the cultivation of rice in the delta.

Pathein's importance diminished with the growth of Yangon, but it remains the main town of the delta region and the principal market for the surrounding rice-growing area. Today the population includes Karen, Arakanese and many Indians, descended from Indian immigrant traders and farmers who migrated here during the British colonial era.

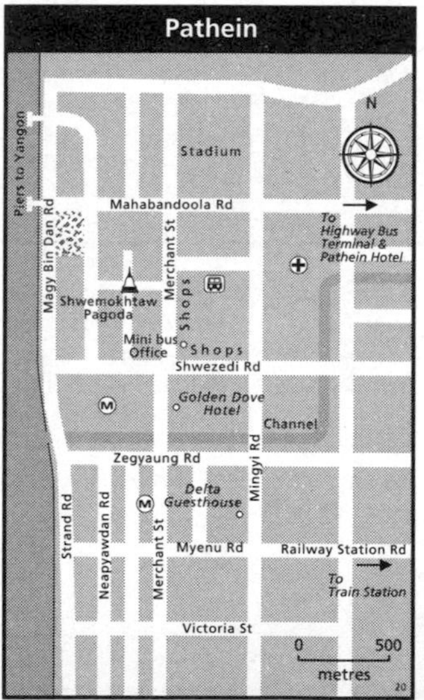

Pathein place names

Ne Win's Pagoda

နေဝင်းဘုရား

Shwemokhtaw Pagoda

ရွှေမုဋ္ဌောဘုရား

'Bassein' is the European pronunciation of Pathein, derived from the Burmese word for 'Muslim' and it is still better known by its 'old' name. The town's specialities are its red monks' umbrellas, fish paste and *halawa*, a sticky cake of rice, sugar and sesame.

The main sight is the **Shwemokhtaw Pagoda**, the 'golden stupa', which is banded with concentric rings and has a soaring spire. It was built by a Muslim princess, Onmadandi – the Tazaung and Thayaounga Yaung pagodas are also attributed to her. The most recent addition to the city is **Ne Win's Pagoda**, modelled on Htilominlo Pagoda (see page 191). At dusk thousands of large fruit bats fly down the river.

Local festivals Mar: *Tabaung* (movable: full moon) is the main regional festival; boats leave Pathein for Mawdinsun Pagoda, on a beach on the far SW tip of the Irrawaddy Delta.

- **Accommodation B-C** *Pathein*, Mahabandula Rd, 2½ km from centre and 500m from highway bus terminal, T 22599, some a/c, all with own bathroom, rooms are big but are in bad condition and are not too clean, breakfast incl, overpriced; **D-E** *Golden Dove*, Merchant St, some a/c, some own bathrooms, shared bathrooms are dirty, best of the three; **E** *Delta*, Mingyi Rd, very basic rooms with thin partition walls, fans need to be begged for, shared bathroom, not clean, not rec.

- **Places to eat** Chinese and local food available at the *Golden Dove Hotel*. There is a government-run restaurant right on the river front; the good views make up for the average food.

• **Shopping** There is a daily market.

• **Transport** 190 km from Yangon. **Train** The station is 15 mins' walk down Buda Lan Rd (Station Rd); at the end of the road, turn right. Connections with Henzada and Kyangin. At Kyangin there are bus connections with Prome, 3 hrs. **Road Bus**: minibus connections with Yangon at 0500 and 1230, 5 hrs (250 kyat) and to Pyay, daily at 0500, 11 hrs (200 kyat). Daily connections with Chaung Tha Beach at 0700 and 0900, 3 hrs (100 kyat) or a truck/bus at 1100 and 1300, 3 hrs (80 kyat). **Boat** Overnight boats leave Mawtin St jetty (about 2 km W of *Strand Hotel*), Yangon between 1500 and 1700 (depending on the tide) and arrive at 0800 the next morning. More expensive tickets give access to the saloon at the top of the boat. Boats leave Pathein for Yangon from the jetty at the end of Lanmadaw Rd. Book tickets (paid for in kyat) from the office near the pier, and go to the desk to the right of the ticket windows. If intending to book a 'cabin', tickets should be purchased about a week in advance, but for a strip of deck, the morning before departure is usually OK. (From Pathein, 0930 for the 1500 boat or 1100 for the 1700 boat.) Bring passports and FEC exchange document. Boats arrive in Pathein at highly variable times, but usually dock by midday so to make the 1500 and 1700 departure times for Yangon (fare: 50-120 kyat).

CHAUNG THA BEACH ချောင်းသာ

This 2 km long beach is sometimes paraded as a yet-to-be-discovered tropical paradise of the golden sands and crystal clear water variety. Prepare to be somewhat disappointed if this is the vision you are expecting to behold. The sand is grey, the water is cloudy (especially during the rainy season, although it is better offshore), and the beach is littered with rubbish. Locals depend on the high tide to do their rubbish collecting, while at low tide cars are driven up and down the beach by the local yuppies.

Having lowered visitors' expectations somewhat, the beach may prove to be a pleasant surprise. There is a small stretch of coral off-shore which provides for reasonable snorkelling during the dry season when the water clarity is best, and Chaung Tha village provides some human interest. There is a small market here and as most of the inhabitants are small farmers and fishermen the food, and especially the seafood, is reasonable. *Best time to visit*: the climate at Chaung Tha is highly seasonal and the

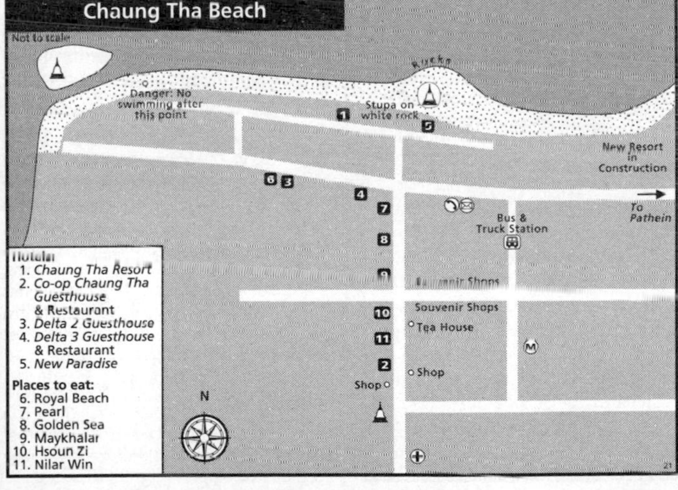

resort effectively closes down between mid-May and mid-Sep.

• **Accommodation** **NB** Most guesthouses have their own generators as the local town's power source is not strong enough to deliver the goods. In general, generators stop at 2200. **C-D** ***New Paradise*** (aka *Chaungtha Beach Hotel*), T 22587 or Yangon 87589, cheapest rooms are small with own bathroom and mosquito net but no fan, basic and not very clean, the more expensive rooms have a/c, fridge and satellite TV and are clean but the rates charged are excessive, breakfast incl; **D** ***Chaung Tha Resort***, this is next door to the *New Paradise* which, confusingly is also sometimes known as the *Chaungtha Beach Hotel*, cheaper rooms have 3 beds and you may have to share, basic but clean, with mosquito nets and some attached bathrooms, breakfast incl; **E** ***Co-op Chaung Tha***, very small and basic rooms with mosquito nets and shared bathrooms, not clean, restaurant downstairs; **E** ***Delta 2***, some twin rooms, some with 3 beds – you may have to share a room, every room has an attached bathroom, new and clean with a verandah, friendly; **E** ***Delta 3***, new establishment with shared bathrooms and mosquito nets, restaurant downstairs.

• **Places to eat** Quite a few Burmese restaurants, all with similar menus in English, strategically placed along Chaung Tha village's main street.

• **Post and telecommunications** **Area code**: 042.

• **Transport** 38 km from Bassein. **Road** Daily trucks leave Pathein at 0700 and 1100 daily (80 kyat), and minibuses at 1230 (100 kyat) and 1500 (150 kyat). It is worth reserving a ticket.

DANUBYU ဓနုဖြူ

This Ayeyarwady town's original name was *Daungphyu*, 'White Peacock'. According to local legend, when the Buddha was incarnated as a white peacock on his long quest for enlightenment, he often came to this place. If local legend is to be believed, human settlement commenced here around 2,000 years ago, when King Asoka's missionaries came to the site of Danubyu and recognized it as so extraordinary that they founded the Kyaikhan-Lonbon Pagoda. It remained a Mon and Karen village

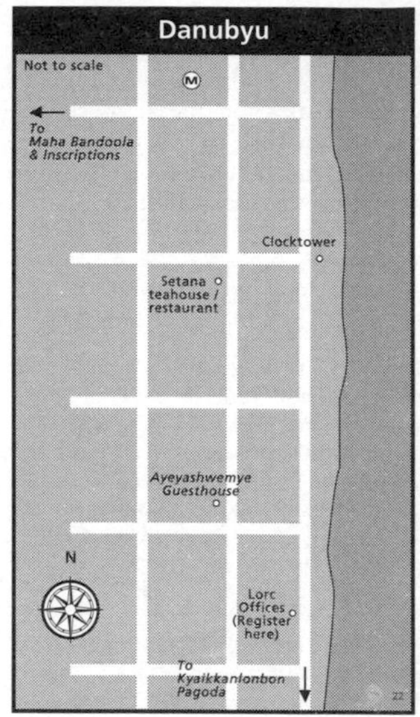

until taken by the Burmans in 1758, only to be lost to the British in the First Anglo Burmese War (see page 41).

Maha Bandoola, the great Burmese general, was killed here in 1826. British warships had come up the river and Maha Bandoola, shaded by a gold umbrella, was directing the battle from a hill. The British set their sights on the flashy umbrella and easily destroyed the frail command post. They were then able to advance to the Prome area, where the Treaty of Yandabo was signed, ceding the Arakan and Tenasserim regions to the British.

Like Maha Bandoola, Daw Aung San Suu Kyi also faced death here, but fortunately in her case, survived. During the election campaign of 1990, soldiers were ordered to shoot her, but before the countdown to the 'fire!' command was completed, a superior officer countermanded the order. 'Security' is very tight here still. You must register with Immigration if you stay the night and you will be followed by several police officers.

Places of interest The main entrance to **Kyaikhan-Lonbon Pagoda** used to be the E gate – leading to the river. Now pilgrims enter from the N. The original pagoda was built by the Mon Princess Onmandandi, but the present structure is much newer. One of the halls contains a large model of Asia in a pond, with figures marking important events in the history of Buddhism.

1 mile W of the market is a set of alabaster tablets inscribed with the **Buddhist scriptures**. The tablets, carved half a century ago, are housed in a quiet compound that is a cool retreat for local people. Next to the dike, a little to the N, is the spot where **Maha Bandoola** was killed. It is now within the grounds of a monastery. Follow the road along the W side of the dike just past the bronze statue of Maha Bandoola on horseback. Go up the monastery steps and along the raised walkway to the rather fanciful statue of the general by his former grave site. He was buried here only temporarily; his remains have since been moved to his native village.

Orientation We would like to apologise for what can only be described as a thin map of Danubyu; our researcher was followed that day by military intelligence. If anyone can fill in the gaps, we would like to hear from them.

• **Accommodation** The only guesthouse in the centre of town is the **E** *Aye ya shwe mye* (sign in Burmese only), not too dirty, although the rooms are small, management speaks a little English.

• **Places to eat** The best tea house in Danubyu is *Setana* (blue building, sign in Burmese only), which has good snacks and nan bread. There are 'liquor houses' by the riverside.

• **Transport River** From Henzada there are several departures a week to Danubyu (3 hrs). **Road** Linecars travel to Danubyu (6 hrs, 60 kyat); rough road, hard benches. Buses may drop you off at various spots in Danubyu. Linecars also come from Pathein. Better buses operate along the road to Yangon (3 hrs, 100 kyat). In Yangon they leave from (and arrive at) the West Park Bus Terminal off Maha Bandoola St. There is also a direct connection to Taunggok in Rakhine State, from where there are transport connections to Ngapali and Sittwe.

HINTHADA ဟသ်ာတ

During the rainy season, Hinthada is a riverfront town. The rest of the year, the Ayeyarwady runs along the far side of its course, and the riverbed is farmed. For a

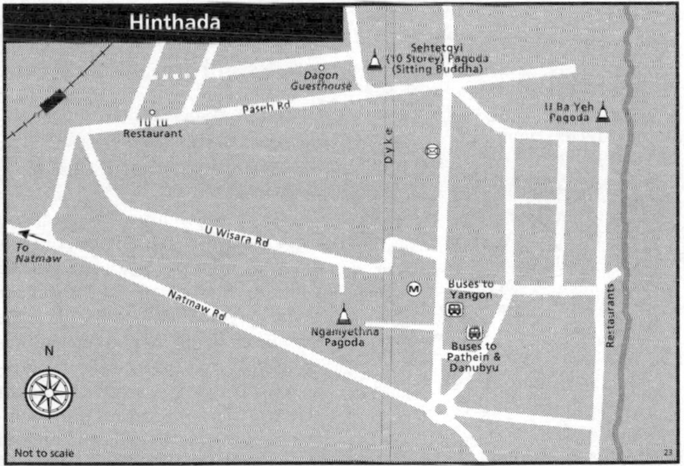

large, fairly prosperous town, it is not very lively. There are two mildly interesting pagodas in the centre, but the trophy is in a nearby village: a reclining Buddha which claims to be the largest in the world.

Places of interest The senior pagoda in town is **U Ba Yeh Pagoda**, on the river embankment. It was founded two centuries ago by a local minister, Myothugyi U Pay. An inscribed tablet to the right of the entrance as you go in gives its history from its founding up until recently, and includes a justification for the Slorc's seizing of power in 1988. When the river is high, the pagoda is a cool place to spend the evening. Frequent ceremonies are held in the hall of the compound.

Ngamyethna Pagoda (Five Faces) is across the dike from the market in the centre of town and was erected in 1815 but subsequently moved to this site in 1887 as the Irrawaddy shifted its course. The pagoda has a wonderful carnival atmosphere, with revolving bowls to entice donations, coloured tiles, painted nats, coin tosses and many Buddha images of various materials.

Excursions Approximately 10 km outside of Hinthada, in the village of **Natmaw**, is the *Tulawka Ohshaung Shin Thalyaung Payagyi* (Payagyi for short), a Buddha reclining in relative obscurity, that claims to be 76.8m, a few metres longer than the more famous one in Dawei (Tavoy), reputedly making this the largest reclining Buddha in the land. The small museum in the garden has photographs of its construction in the mid-19th century. It was built without the help of architects or engineers, so the proportions are not quite standard but the overall effect is very good and the soles of the feet are quite beautiful. *Getting there*: 3-wheeled yellow taxis leave from the market in Hinthada, 5 kyat per person. The pagoda is on the right, shortly after a small river.

• **Accommodation** None of the guesthouses has a license to take foreigners but all seem willing to take in a foreigner for a few hundred kyat and some paperwork. By far the best choice is **E *Dagon Guesthouse***, not far from the train station. Clean largish rooms, mosquito nets, large balcony for cooling off in the evening, owner is kind and speaks English, but is deaf, no house number, medium sized yellow sign in Burmese only.

• **Places to eat** The restaurants in Hinthada have mostly standard fare, but ***Tu Tu*** has masterful *a-thout*, blue sign in Burmese only, of the two restaurants on the block, *Tu Tu* is the left-hand one. There is another collection of restaurants S of U Ba Yeh Pagoda, by the embankment. The liveliest tea shops are in this area as well.

• **Transport Train** The train is recommended over the road which tends to be very bad on this side of the Irrawaddy. There are two trains per day from Pathein (5 hrs) and Kyangin (4 hrs) at the end ot the train line. So far, no-one is asking for FECs. A bus in Kyangin links with the train to take passengers to or from Prome (4 hrs). It is also possible to get off the Yangon-Prome line at Letpadan, and take a spur down to Tharrawaddy, and then a ferry to Hinthada. **Road** Hinthada also has bus connections to Yangon, Pathein, Danubyu and Thandwe, but the state of the road is horrendous. **Boat** There are scheduled boats to Pyay, Pathein and other river towns. They can be very slow, especially when the water is low, except the Danubyu boat, which is faster than the road connection.

MYANAUNG မြန်အောင်

A small and pleasant town on the Ayeyarwady, with a fairly big market, but not much else of interest – it could be a stopping off point on the way to Chaung Tha and Pathein.

• **Accommodation** There are two guesthouses in town but they do not have licenses for tourists. However, they will probably take in travellers who find themselves stuck here. ***Hlaing Htate Tin*** and ***Aye***.

• **Transport Train** The station is 1½ km from town. Daily connections with Bassein at 1330, 8 hrs (55-140 kyat). On arrival in town, it is wise to book a seat immediately on this train, as there are limited upper class seats.

Central Myanmar

MANDALAY
မန္တလေး

Mandalay is not an old city: it was founded by King Mindon in 1857 and was previously called Yadanatin. He decided to fulfil a prophesy that a sacred centre would be built at the foot of Mandalay Hill on the 2,400th anniversary of the founding of the Buddhist faith. The Irrawaddy lies to the W of the former royal capital and the hazy Shan hills stand to the E. In 1861, Mindon moved his court, government and about 150,000 of his subjects to Mandalay from the previous capital at Amarapura. The elaborate carved teak buildings of the Golden Palace at Amarapura were all transported to Mindon's chosen location. The town was centred on the extravagant moated royal palace with its parapets, distinctive tiered guard towers and palaces of teak, lacquer, gilt and glass.

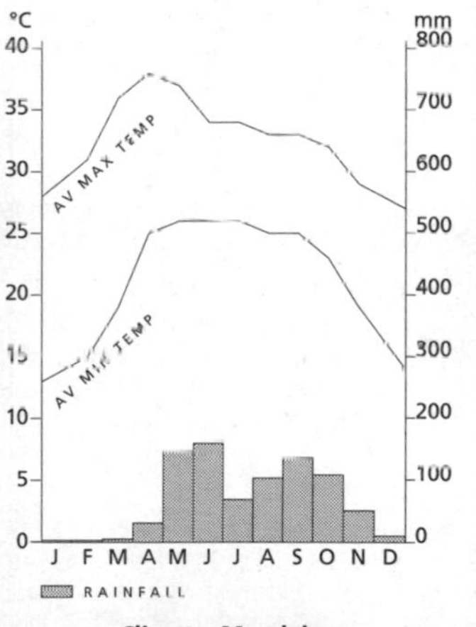

Climate: Mandalay

"Mandalay presented a series of violent contrasts: jewel-studded temples and gilded monasteries standing side by side with wattled hovels penetrated by every wind that blew; the haughty prince preceded by the respited murderer, his victor; the busy Chinaman next door to the gambling scum of the low country; the astrologer, learned in his mantras, overpersuaded by the glib talk of the Western adventurer..." (Shway Yoe, *The Burman: His Life and Notions*, 1882).

King Mindon was determined to ensure that his new city became the capital of the Buddhist world and the Fifth Buddhist Synod was held in Mandalay in 1879. It had long been the custom to bury people alive under the foundations of a new city or royal palace; the unfortunate victims were believed to become guardian spirits. King Mindon is said to have had 52 people buried beneath the four corners of the city. This approach to creating good fortune did not prove effective: 25 years after Mindon moved Mandalay, the British annexed Upper Burma following the Third Anglo-Burmese War, sending Mindon's son, King Thibaw and his wife, Queen Supayalat into exile in South India (there's a tomb to Queen Supayalat not far from the Shwedagon Pagoda in Yangon). The palace became a barracks for the British colonial administration, and renamed

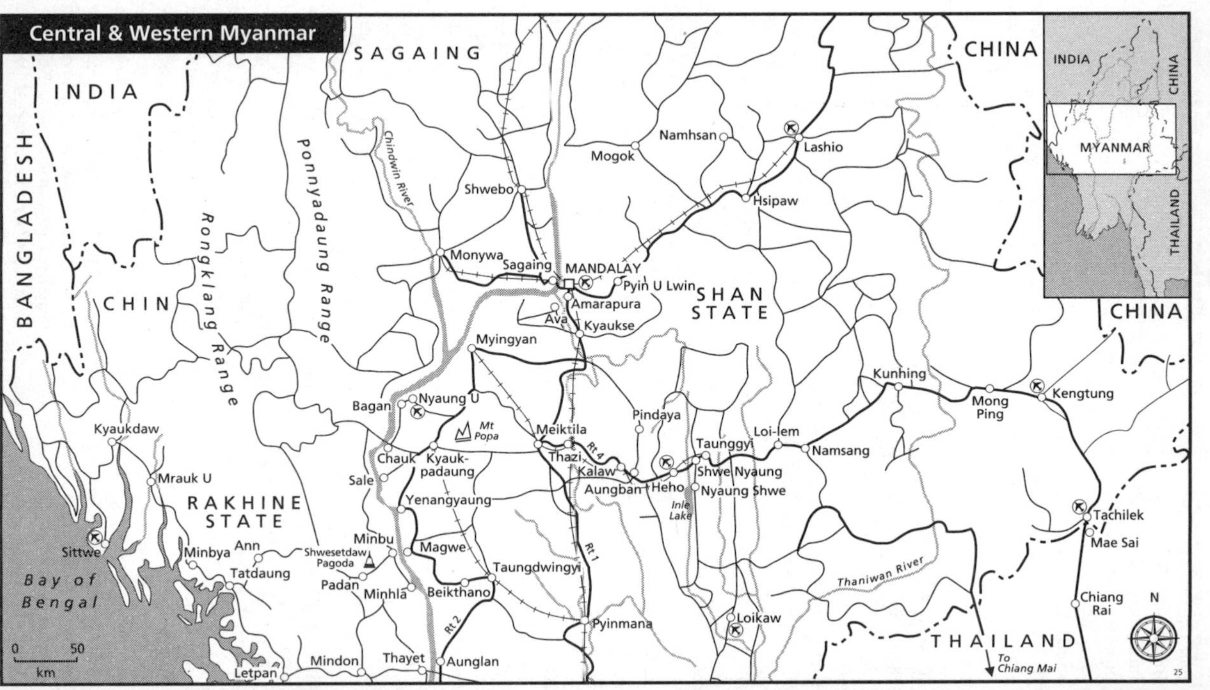
Central & Western Myanmar
SAGAING
INDIA
BANGLADESH
CHIN
CHINA
MYANMAR
THAILAND
SHAN STATE
RAKHINE STATE
Bay of Bengal
Ponnyadaung Range
Rongklang Range
Chindwin River
Thaniwan River
Shwebo
Mogok
Namhsan
Lashio
Hsipaw
Monywa
Sagaing
MANDALAY
Pyin U Lwin
Amarapura
Ava
Kyaukse
Myingyan
Bagan
Nyaung U
Mt Popa
Meiktila
Thazi
Rt 4
Kalaw
Aungban
Heho
Pindaya
Taunggyi
Shwe Nyaung
Nyaung Shwe
Inle Lake
Loi-lem
Namsang
Kunhing
Mong Ping
Kengtung
Tachilek
Mae Sai
Chiang Rai
N
To Chiang Mai
Loikaw
Pyinmana
Rt 1
Taungdwingyi
Beikthano
Rt 2
Aunglan
Thayet
Mindon
Letpan
Chauk
Kyauk-padaung
Sale
Yenangyaung
Minbu
Magwe
Shwesetdaw Pagoda
Padan
Minhla
Kyaukdaw
Mrauk U
Sittwe
Minbya
Ann
Tatdaung
0 50
km
25

Fort Dufferin. During WW2, after the British had fled back to neighbouring India, the Japanese 15th Army used the precincts of the magnificent royal palace as its high command centre for N Myanmar. In Allied bombing raids, it was the prime target, and was totally destroyed, along with a third of the city.

Today, despite the absence of the monarchy, Mandalay retains a few regal pretensions: some inhabitants still use the formal language of royal court and their manners are said to be the most polished in all of Myanmar. Because of its royal past, the city is also a centre for crafts, dance and music. But for a town whose name has romantic connotations – Mandalay has featured in the verse of Rudyard Kipling – its dusty streets can be a disappointment. All that remains of its royal heritage is to be found in Yangon's National Museum. Fast growth and easy transport have attracted people from all over Myanmar to Mandalay. This is resented by many of Mandalay's older residents. Slorc policies on urban renewal – eg decreeing that all houses on certain streets must have at least 2 storeys – have forced many old families to move to squalid 'new towns' a few miles away. Those who have remained in Mandalay proper typically complain of a rapid decline in the traditional courtesy of the old capital.

Mandalay is now Myanmar's second largest city, with a population of over half a million. The city is an important river port, the start of the overland route to China and a big market centre for the surrounding area.

The recent freedom of trade over the Burmese/Chinese border has turned Mandalay into a boom town: the Chinese have moved in. Some are wealthy traders whose families have long lived in Myanmar; others have been able to buy Burmese citizenship – reputedly the recycled identities of deceased Burmese. People, in Mandalay at least, say this is now Myanmar's premier city. Much of the money fuelling the boom is thought to be drug-related. Those in the trade sell houses to each other at highly inflated prices to launder their money. Mandalay is setting the pace for change – karaoke bars popped up all over the city a good 18 months before they took off in Yangon. It is also an important religious centre: one quarter of the city is covered in monasteries and there are over 20,000 monks in Mandalay.

More than any other city in Myanmar, the inhabitants of Mandalay have found their lives forcibly altered as the authorities make the place more amenable to tourists and tourism. In early 1995 the city's military commander decided to solve Mandalay's traffic congestion by widening the road running around the walls of the old city to 7m – causing those with houses facing onto the street to literally chop off any offending protuberances. Some guides reportedly now include a visit to the 'sliced' houses in their itinerary. Slave labour has been used to clean out the moat surrounding the Royal Palace and every family in the city has been ordered to 'donate' 3 days a month free labour to various public works projects – most of which have some tourist and tourism rationale.

Places of interest

Although Mandalay is Myanmar's cultural centre, most of its buildings are post-war. All that now remains of Mandalay's (admittedly short) history was built by the last two kings of the Alaungpaya Dynasty – Mindon and Thibaw – and date from the middle of the 19th century – with one or two unspectacular exceptions. The sights are dotted around the city; the best way to get around is by trishaw.

Most of the N section of the city is dominated by the moated grounds of the **Royal Palace** – which is called Nanmyo (for the whole area) or Mya Nan San Kyaw (for the reconstructed part) in Burmese. The palace was built in the

Mandalay place names

Atumashi Kyaung
အတုမရှိကျောင်း

Eindawya Pagoda
အိမ်တော်ရာဘုရား

Kuthodaw Pagoda
ကုသိုလ်တော်ဘုရား

Kyaukdawgyi Pagoda
ကျောက်တော်ကြီးဘုရား

Mahamuni Pagoda
မဟာမုနိဘုရား

Mandalay Hill
မန္တလေးတောင်

Mandalay Museum
မန္တလေးပြတိက်

Mandalay Royal Palace
မန္တလေးနန်းတော်

Sandamuni Pagoda
စန္ဒမုနိဘုရား

Set Kyathiha Pagoda
စကြာသီဟဘုရား

Shwekyimyin Pagoda
ရွှေကြီးမြင့်ဘုရား

Shwe In Bin
ရွှေအင်ပင်

Shwe Nandaw Monastery
ရွှေနန်းတော် ကျောင်း

Shwe Nandaw Museum
ရွှေနန်းတော်ပြတိုက်

Shweyattaw
ရွှေရပ်တော်

early 1860s by King Mindon and was decorated with elaborate woodcarvings. The original buildings were very ornate and made of teak, which was carved, lacquered, gilded or covered with glass mosaics. The artist R Talbot Kelley, visiting Mandalay in 1905, saw "a collection of twenty or more separate buildings, all built of specially selected teak, brightly painted and gilded, and having the same upturned eaves and carved ornamentation common to all royal religious buildings in Myanmar. It has many audience chambers, in each of which is a carved and gilded throne. Above the principal one towers the lofty and elegant *pyathat* called by Burmans 'The centre of the universe!'..."

All Burmese royal palaces were built according to the same formula and when the capital was moved, the royal buildings were transported, in their entirety, to the new site. According to ancient custom, the palace roofs were meant to be made of silver or lead; in the end this proved too expensive: they were made of corrugated tin. The palace area was home to 5,000 people in Mindon's time.

After annexing Upper Burma, the British set up a provincial government in the old palace, renaming it Fort Dufferin. But the new colonial administration quickly undermined its own credibility when it established its headquarters in the palace's 7-roofed court house – only buildings with nine roofs were considered suitable for rulers. The British also converted the Queen's royal reception room, the Lily Throne Room, into a clubhouse – known as the Upper Burma Club – and a picture of Queen Victoria was hung on the wall. This caused such resentment locally that the club was finally moved. Mandalay's Royal Palace was the last surviving example of royal Burmese wooden buildings; they were almost totally destroyed by fire following Allied bombing raids in WW2. Ironically, Japanese forces and Burmese collaborators had already

Reconstruction of Royal Palace, Mandalay

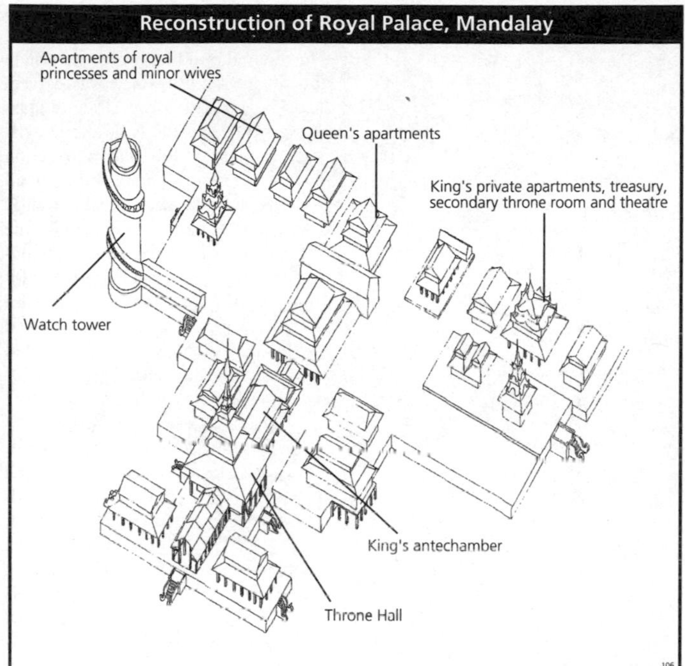

crept out of the palace complex, escaping along a drain which led into the S moat. No trace is left of the splendour and pomp witnessed by foreign envoys to the royal court of Myanmar.

During 1994, 1995 and 1996, apparently in preparation for Visit Myanmar Year in 1996-97, thousands of conscripted labourers were being used to dredge the moat – all 10 km of it. It is now filled with stagnant water and choked with waterweed. Local people were, reportedly, forced to donate their labour to the project and when local resentment grew too great, prisoners in leg irons were used to complete the task. It is medieval scenes like this which leads some people to argue that Burma, like South Africa formerly, should be boycotted by tourists and businessmen alike. In 1995, Tourism and Hotels Minister Lt. Gen Kyaw Ba justified this, and other similar labour policies by explaining: "They are happy. They have good rest, good food and we don't torture them."

The palace has been partially reconstructed in concrete (at no small expense) by the present government, which gives some idea of what the original structures must have looked like. The reconstruction programme, which has taken several years, is not without its critics. They charge that the undisclosed billions of kyats that have been spent would have been better invested in social welfare projects in what is one of the poorest countries in the world. A copy of the **Glass Palace** contains a display of the few remains salvaged from the old buildings. Open 0930-1630 Tues-Sun. The **Shwe Nandaw Cultural Museum** sounds as if it should be

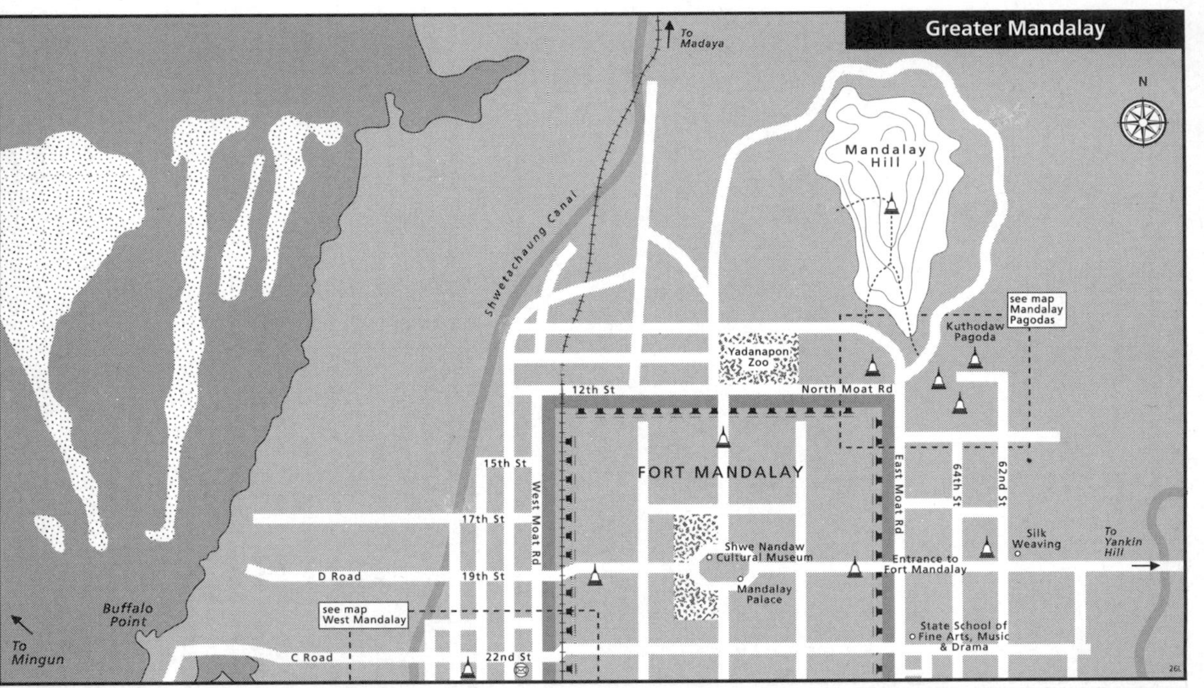
Greater Mandalay
N
To Madaya
Mandalay Hill
see map Mandalay Pagodas
Kuthodaw Pagoda
Shwetachaung Canal
Yadanapon Zoo
12th St
North Moat Rd
FORT MANDALAY
East Moat Rd
64th St
62nd St
15th St
West Moat Rd
17th St
Silk Weaving
To Yankin Hill
Shwe Nandaw Cultural Museum
Entrance to Fort Mandalay
D Road
19th St
Mandalay Palace
Buffalo Point
see map West Mandalay
State School of Fine Arts, Music & Drama
To Mingun
C Road
22nd St

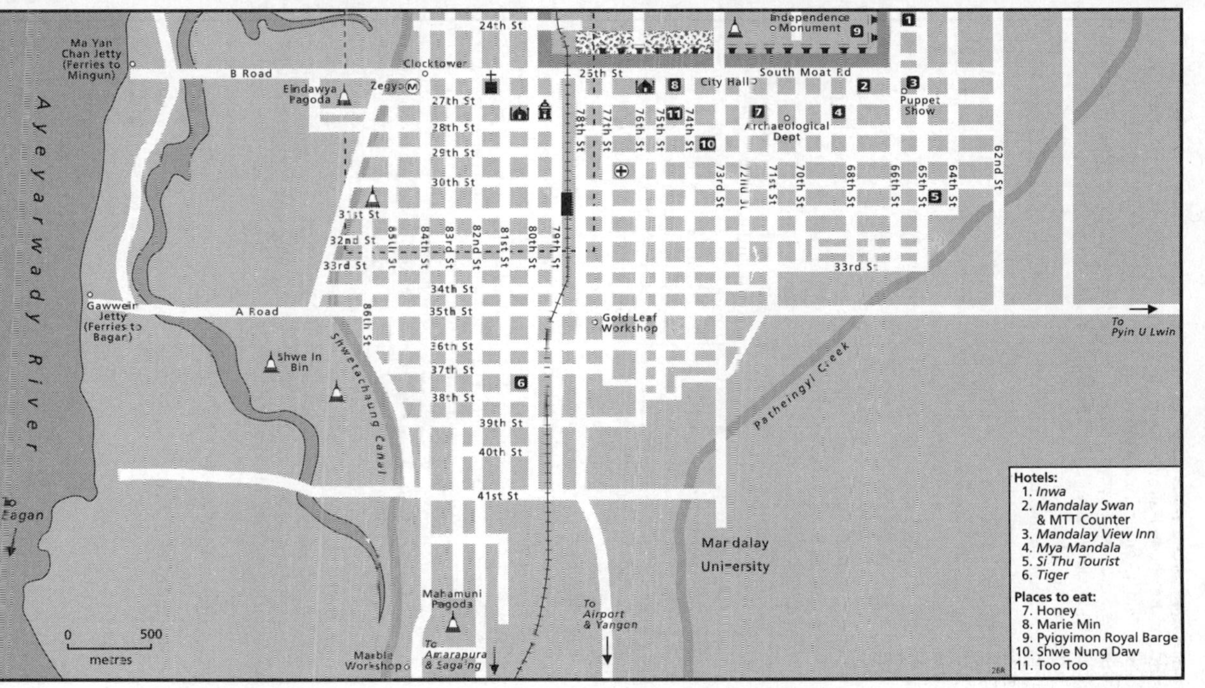
Hotels:
1. Inwa
2. Mandalay Swan & MTT Counter
3. Mandalay View Inn
4. Mya Mandala
5. Si Thu Tourist
6. Tiger
Places to eat:
7. Honey
8. Marie Min
9. Pyigyimon Royal Barge
10. Shwe Nung Daw
11. Too Too
Independence Monument
24th St
25th St
South Moat Rd
City Hall
Puppet Show
Archaeological Dept
27th St
28th St
29th St
30th St
31st St
32nd St
33rd St
34th St
35th St
36th St
37th St
38th St
39th St
40th St
41st St
62nd St
64th St
65th St
66th St
68th St
70th St
71st St
73rd St
74th St
75th St
76th St
77th St
78th St
79th St
80th St
81st St
82nd St
83rd St
84th St
86th St
Ma Yan Chan Jetty (Ferries to Mingun)
B Road
Clocktower
Eindawya Pagoda
Zegyo
Gawwein Jetty (Ferries to Bagar)
A Road
Gold Leaf Workshop
To Pyin U Lwin
Shwe In Bin
Shwetachaung Canal
Patheingyi Creek
Ayeyarwady River
Bagan
Mandalay University
Mahamuni Pagoda
To Airport & Yangon
Marble Workshop
To Amarapura & Sagaing
0
500
metres

interesting but only has statues of important Burmese figures. Admission US$3. The reconstructed watchtower, with its spiral stairway corkscrewing up the outside, can be climbed for 1 kyat. It is the symbol of Mandalay.

There is a scale model of the original palace buildings within the grounds, W of the old palace. It was made in 1952 from the original plans and is kept in an iron cage. The **Great Audience Hall**, with its seven tiered golden spire, stood at the 'centre of the universe' – on the model of Brahmin-Buddhist cosmology – and was surrounded by other throne halls containing the Duck, Elephant, Deer and Lily thrones. The great hall has been reconstructed by local craftsmen who have assembled a reasonable replica of the intricately carved roof ornamentation. It has been repainted in vermilion lacquer-colour. In the original there were 133 apartments and dormitories, mainly to accommodate the king's 53 wives and his concubines.

The **Lion Throne**, several tonnes of regal regalia – including the royal ruby – had been stolen in an 1885 raid on the palace by British Colonel Sladdon. The booty was then 'lost' in transit. The throne finally turned up in London and was returned to the National Museum in Yangon by Lord Louis Mountbatten at independence. It is still displayed there along with photographs of the palace (see page 115).

Within the palace grounds are the tombs of some members of the royal family, including King Mindon and his chief queen, Setkyadevi; these are in the NE corner. There is also a stone marking the spot where King Thibaw surrendered to the British. On the S side of the old palace grounds there is a monument to Myanmar's independence. The fort area is now used by the headquarters of the NW command – the *Tatmadaw* – and up to 10,000 troops are stationed within its walls. The palace area is not particularly exciting; it's a Sun afternoon playground for locals. Open 0800-1800 Mon-Fri, sometimes closed Sat and Sun. Admission US$5, tickets from the MTT desk at *Mandalay Hotel*. Entrance at the E gate of the fort.

At the NE corner of the palace grounds around **Mandalay Hill** is a group of important sights. One of the most spectacular buildings in Mandalay – which gives some insight into the original grandeur of the erstwhile palace – is the **Shwe Nandaw Kyaung**, or 'Golden Palace Monastery' (to the right near the top of the E moat road). It is all that remains of King Mindon's palace. The Nathanon or Scented Palace was moved to the site in 1880 by King Thibaw after his father King Mindon had inauspiciously died in it. The building was thus spared the bombing which destroyed the main palace. It is made of carved teak with glass mosaic and is heavily gilded inside. Each pillar is a single trunk of teak, and the remains of the original lacquering and gilding can still be seen on them. Hanging from the pillars are photographs of King Thibaw and his wife (the chief queen) and King Mindon – albeit a photograph of a painting – who had 49 wives. The Golden Palace is still in use as a monastery, and is now under its 4th abbot.

Around the ceiling are nats worshipping the Buddha. Inside are two halls: the main hall contains a copy of the Lion Throne, a Buddha image commissioned by King Thibaw (with the features of his father) and a golden couch used for meditation by the king. The second hall is partitioned off and used as a storeroom (it is not open to the public). The carvings of the 10 great jataka scenes on the outer walls are well preserved and still have some of their original gold leaf. They were only introduced when the palace became a monastery in 1880. Admission US$3. Opposite the Shwe Nandaw, there is a new religious university for 500 monks.

Atumashi Kyaung, or 'Incomparable

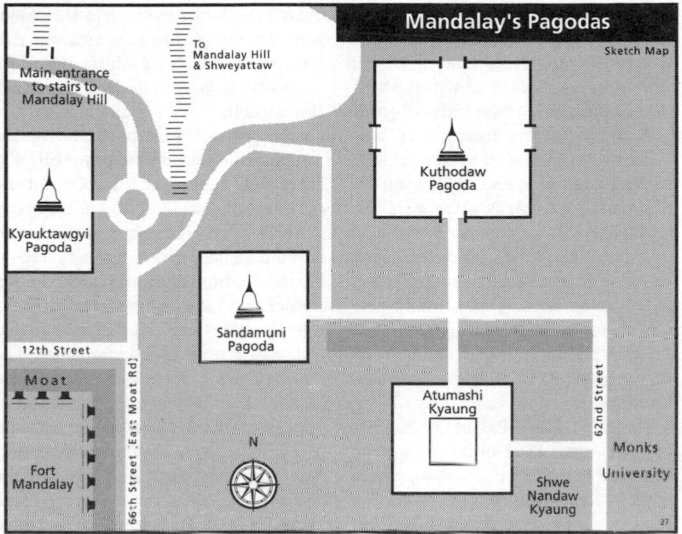

Monastery', next to the Shwe Nandaw Kyaung, is now a ruin. It was built by King Mindon in 1857, at vast expense, to house a valuable Buddha image – with a huge diamond on its head – as well as four sets of the Tripitaka scriptures. The building was of wood and covered with stucco. In 1885, the night after King Thibaw's surrender to British General Prendergast, the diamond was stolen. 5 years later, a fire gutted the building. Only the masonry balustrade and staircases with elaborate stucco carvings remain. Westerners who saw the monastery before its demise were captivated by its beauty.

North of the Atumashi, near the S stairway to Mandalay Hill, is the **Kuthodaw Pagoda**. It was built in 1857 by King Mindon, and is a model of the Shwezigon Pagoda at Bagan (see page 191). Large teak carved doors, painted a rich vermilion (the S entrance still has the original doors) open onto an arcade and a small gold-topped stupa. On the S and W sides are faded paintings of the palace gardens by a royal artist in 1892. This pagoda would not really figure on the Mandalay itinerary if it were not for its one claim to fame: row upon row of white miniature pagodas cover 5.3 ha in the temple's shaded grounds. These house 729 marble slabs inscribed (on both sides) with the entire Tripitaka. In the early 1870s, King Mindon commissioned 5,000 masons to carve the slabs, copying them from palm-leaf manuscripts, which took 8 years to complete. Originally the letters were inlaid with gold. This exercise was central to Mindon's plan to turn Mandalay into the centre of the Buddhist world – and as a show of prowess in the face of British expansionism which was threatening to erode his power. The project was also undertaken to fulfil the Buddha's prophesy that the faith would last 5,000 years. Mindon calculated that if the Tripitaka was recorded on stone – the first time in history that this had been accomplished – Buddhism would last at least that long. The inscribed stelae cover all the canons of Buddhism – the three pitakas: rules, philosophy and prayers.

In fitting with his vision for Mandalay, King Mindon convened the Fifth Buddhist Synod at his new capital in 1879. The whole work was read aloud without a pause – a task which occupied 2,400 monks for 6 months. It is the ambition of all monks to memorize the scriptures, but of the 300,000 monks in Myanmar today – 20,000 of whom reside in Mandalay – only five have managed it. The full scriptures take one monk around 2 years to recite. The oldest living monk to have memorized it all is now an octogenarian and resides in Mingun, and none of the others are younger than 50. Admission 3 FEC or US$2. Note that the monastery closes at 1700.

The **Sandamuni Pagoda**, W of the Kuthodaw and closer to the S stairway of Mandalay Hill, marks the spot where Prince Kanaung, King Mindon's younger brother and chosen successor, was assassinated in 1866. He was killed by two of Mindon's other sons who were aggrieved at being excluded from the succession. The pagoda contains an iron Buddha image, cast by King Bodawpaya of Amarapura in 1802 and moved by Mindon to his new capital in 1874. The Sandamuni houses marble slabs in the mini-stupas which are commentaries on the Tripitaka. Admission US$2. Note that the monastery closes at 1700.

On the other side of the S stairway to Mandalay Hill is the **Kyaukdawgyi Pagoda**. It was completed in 1878 by King Mindon and was originally styled on the Ananda Pagoda in Bagan. But the plan was interrupted by a palace rebellion in 1866, following the assassination of Prince Kanaung, and the Ananda design was dropped. The temple is well known for its Buddha image, carved out of a single block of pale green marble from the quarries of Sagyin, a few miles N of Mandalay. It was roughly hewn in the quarry and a canal was dug specially to bring the 800-tonne figure to Mandalay. It took 10,000 men 2 weeks to drag it to the pagoda. The Buddha's dress and shawl are inlaid with jewels, all of which are fake except the central diamond. Disappointing; the Buddha image is very dirty from pigeon excrement and the decoration – save gaudy. The entrance is lined with tourist stalls. A week-long festival is held at the pagoda every Oct. Admission US$2. Note that the gates close at 1700.

In 1945, it took a British Gurkha battalion a whole night to fight its way to the top of **Mandalay Hill** (236m), in the face of stiff Japanese resistance. Today, the hill's 1,729 steps take about 30 mins to climb (it is necessary to remove your shoes). The main stairway winds its way through a series of rather kitsch pagodas – there are three covered approaches to the hill. From a design perspective, Mandalay Hill ranks with Singapore's Tiger Balm Gardens as among the least tasteful pieces of landscape architecture in the region. The hill is scattered with shrines, many of which were the work of a pious hermit, U Khanti. Near the top of the hill stands the **Shweyattaw**, a huge image depicting the Buddha pointing towards the royal palace compound as the future centre of the capital. On this spot, the Buddha, accompanied by his disciple Ananda, is said to have prophesied the construction of a great religious city at the foot of the hill. It is an unusual image as the Gautama Buddha is normally portrayed in a mudra posture. From the top there is a good view over the town, the vast royal palace, and between the golf course and the river, to the W, the People's Brewery and Distillery, the national beer monopoly. On fine days the Shan Plateau can be seen to the NE, on the horizon beyond the military camp. It is possible to take a taxi to the top of the hill (500 kyats) or a linecar for only 5 kyat. Admission 4 FEC.

The main city of Mandalay is to the W and S of the palace grounds. Just off the W moat road on 24th St is the **Mandalay Museum** which houses an uninteresting collection of bits and pieces, including some royal garments which were probably those left behind by King Thibaw and Queen Supayalat when they were exiled by the British in 1885. Admission US$3. Open Wed-Sun, 1000-1600. **NB** Recent visitors have said that the museum closed sometime in 1996 and has not reopened at another site. Nearby, also on 24th St (between 82nd and 83rd sts), is the **Shwekyimyin Pagoda**. It was built in 1167 during the Pagan era by Prince Minshinzaw, an exiled son of King Alaungsithu. The temple still has the original Buddha image, which was consecrated in 1167, as well as a collection of gold, silver and crystal Buddha images – salvaged from the royal palace prior to the British occupation of Mandalay. Also on and around C Rd is the Zegyo Market, with a clocktower at its centre.

For those who want to explore the river a little more, it is possible to charter one of the small passenger boats which take people across the Ayeyarwady. Arrange a price beforehand – around 120 kyat for 1½ hrs. It is worth venturing out to the midstream islands – and there is also an interesting, highly primitive, brick works.

To the S of C Rd is the interestingly named B Rd, which also runs E-W; to the W it becomes 26th St, which runs along the S moat. At its E end is the **Eindawya Pagoda**, built by King Pagan Min of Amarapura in 1847 on the site of his home before he became king. It is well proportioned and is gilded from top to bottom. The Buddha image is made from chalcedony, a combination of quartz and opal. The Eindawya Pagoda was the home of the 'Eindawya Column', a group of monks who briefly took over the running of the city in Aug 1988 when the country was in chaos. The Column was later broken up by the Slorc and its leaders arrested. Just E of the pagoda is the distinctive Zegyo Market (see page 160), which serves as a useful landmark.

Set Kyathiha Pagoda is S of Zegyo Market on 31st/85th sts. It contains a 5m-high bronze Buddha cast at Ava in 1814 by King Bagyidaw. It was moved to Amarapura by King Pagan in 1849 and brought to Mandalay in 1884. The pagoda had to be rebuilt after WW2, when it was badly damaged. The Bodhi tree at the entrance was planted by U Nu, the first Prime Minister of independent Burma.

Shwe In Bin, Pe Boke Ian St (S of 35th St) is one of the most interesting monasteries in Mandalay. A Chinese merchant, U Set Shwin, married a local Burmese lady and with his newly acquired fortune built a monastery for his religious wife. It is built of teak, has Burmese carved doors and paintings depicting General Prendergast negotiating with court ministers prior to King Thibaw's exile.

The **Mahamuni (or Arakan) Pagoda**, on 82nd St is in the S quarter of town on the road to Amarapura. The Arakanese – from Myanmar's W state, on the Bay of Bengal – discovered the Mahamuni Image in the jungle and restored it, keeping it in Rakhine (Arakan) until 1784, where it acquired a magical aura and was revered as the guardian of the kingdom. Archaeologists date it to around 146 AD during the reign of Chandra Suriya, when Buddhism spread to Arakan. Others believe it is an actual image of the Buddha himself. In the 11th century, Bagan's King Anawrahta had raided Arakan with the intent of removing the Buddha to his capital, but failed to capture it. It was not until the late 18th century that 30,000 of King Bodawpaya's troops finally snatched it and brought it back to Amarapura where the king built a temple specially for it. The Arakanese say that it is only a copy of the original Mahamuni. The real one is said to have become invisible as the local people lost their religious virtue, and so it remains in its place. In the late 19th century 100 years later, a fire destroyed the temple in which it was

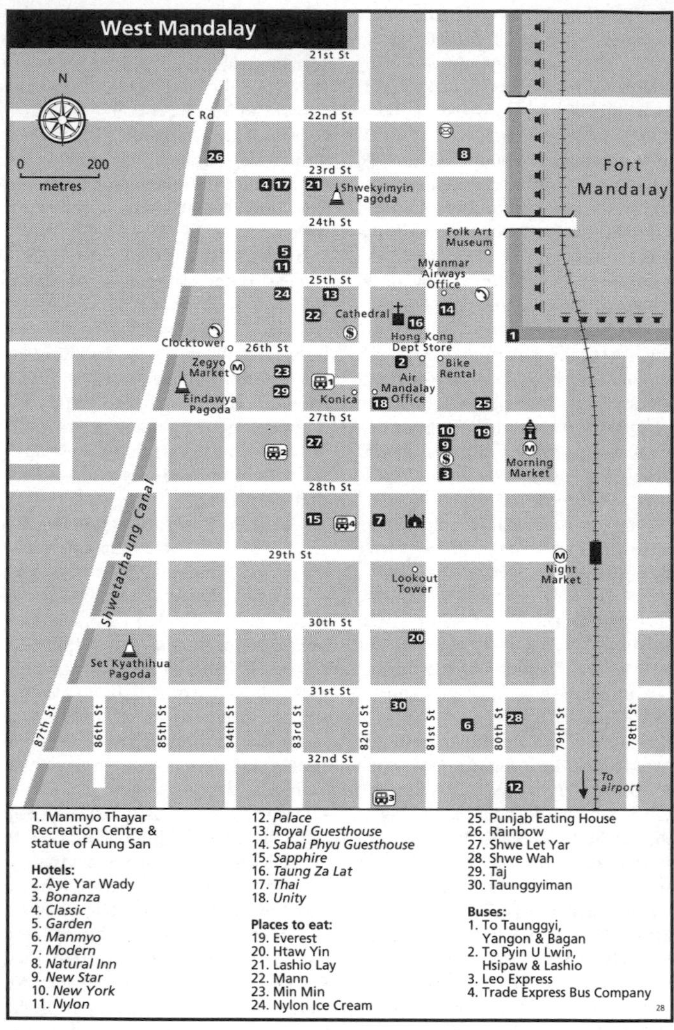

housed and it was then moved to the present site. The entrance arcade is packed with astrologers and palmists.

The 3.8m tall Mahamuni, or 'Great Sage', sits on a 2m-high podium covered in gold leaf in a posture symbolizing his calling the earth as witness in the face of temptation. The image is cast in bronze, but the original features have been blurred by millions of sheets of gold leaf which now form a layer more than 15 cm thick. The gilding covers the whole image other than the face itself – it even covers the chunks of ruby, sapphire and jade that originally adorned the chest and crown. There is a constant procession of pilgrims queueing up to cake the Buddha with tiny sheets of gold leaf which they buy for 10 kyat each. Women are not allowed into the inner sanctum and have to give their sheets of gold leaf to the men in charge of the Buddha's welfare. The image is believed to be alive – the face is said to have grown proportionally as the body has expanded under the layers of gold leaf. Photographs near the main shrine show the statue as it was 90 years ago, when the features were more precisely defined. The image's face is ceremonially washed every morning at 0500.

The Mahamuni Buddha image is the holiest shrine in Mandalay and greatly revered as it is believed to be a true likeness of the Gautama Buddha himself. The inner sanctum is very atmospheric, packed with worshippers and pilgrims praying, toying with their beads and chanting. The women's area is partitioned off, set back about 6m from the area where monks and laymen swarm around the image.

In the inner courtyard there are hundreds of stone slabs inscribed with copies of inscriptions recording religious endowments. Also within the precinct, N of the main pagoda, are six bronze figures: two warriors, three lions and a 3-headed elephant, all central to an extraordinary slice of history. They were brought from Rakhine (Arakan) by King Bodawpaya at the same time as he captured the Mahamuni Image. The Arakanese King Razagyi had removed the statues from the Burmese Kingdom of Bago (Pegu), 120 years earlier. The Burmese had originally taken them from the Siamese capital of Ayutthaya and the Siamese in their turn had looted them from Angkor Wat, Cambodia in 1431. The statues, which date from the 12th century, are said to possess healing powers – pilgrims can be seen touching the part of the statue that corresponds to the area of their affliction. The sheen on the metal suggests that the most common complaint in Mandalay is stomach ache.

The 1960s gallery on the far side of the courtyard has a series of paintings showing how Bodawpaya's army returned with the image. On the edge of the compound, steps lead up to a viewing balcony overlooking a gigantic neon-lit, technicolour, 3-dimensional map of the Buddhist world. Also in the complex is a small museum with a display of statues and Buddha images. The main entrance to the pagoda is busy with shops selling religious paraphernalia as well as lacquerware and embroidery. Admission US$4 from the ticket office deep within the monastery's precincts, just before the Mahamuni Buddha's face comes into view.

The **artisan guilds** in the S of the city, not far from the Mahamuni Pagoda, are the backbone of Myanmar's craft industry. The guilds were set up by King Mindon when Mandalay was under construction. They are still going today and include alabaster, marble and wood-carving guilds, and others for bronze casting and the production of gold leaf.

A **silk weaving factory** can be visited on the corner of 62nd and 19th sts. Young girls sit in dimly lit rooms, making up rather gaudy designs in silk (all the dyes are synthetic now). There are 30 or so set designs and the girls memorize four or five of them. In the days when the Royal Family was 500-strong, silk was much in demand. Today, however, almost all work is done to order and the client chooses the colours laid down by an astrological adviser.

Excursions

Amarapura, see page 162; **Ava**, see page 165; **Sagaing**, see page 167; river trip to **Mingun**, see page 169; **Myingyan**, see page 177; and **Pakokku**, see page 177.

Local festivals

Aug: *Taungboyone Nat Festival*, a 5-day

festival to placate the nats (spirits), a flamboyant event, with music, dance and much offering of food.
Oct: *Elephant Dancing Festival* in Kyaukse (S of Mandalay).

Local information

● Orientation

The city is built on a grid, with numbered streets running N-S and E-W as well as 4 alphabetically named roads running from the centre of the city down to the left bank of the Irrawaddy. In 1981 a fire gutted the NW quarter of town, and this area is still being rebuilt. The town 'centre' is SW of the moat – centred around Zegyo market; most of the guesthouses and restaurants are in this area. The larger, more expensive, hotels are in the area to the S of the fort. The W is known as the 'town side' and the E the 'country side'. The railway station is on the main road S, which also goes to the airport. The main centre for the 'express' bus companies is on 83rd, in the low 30s. **NB** Don't let sidecar drivers take you to their recommended shops or restaurants; they will receive up to 50% 'commission'.

● Accommodation

New hotels and guesthouses are opening every month in Mandalay. The US$30m *Novotel Mandalay* is due to open in 1997 and will become the city's top establishment.

A+-A *Sedona Hotel Mandalay*, junction of 26th Rd and 66th St, new hotel scheduled to have opened in 1996, over 200 rm with in-house movies and mini-bar, swimming pool and health centre, the publicity blurb does not create the impression that this place is being built with restraint but will probably have the best facilities; **A** *Mandalay Swan*, 26th St, T 22499, F 35677, a/c, restaurant, bar, pool, money-changing facilities, recently renovated, making it the best in town (for now); **A-B** *Tiger*, 628 82nd St (between 36th and 37th sts), T 23134, a/c, h/w, no charm but slightly better than government-run places elsewhere; **A-B** *Hotel Venus*, 22 28th St (between 80th and 81st sts), T 25612.

B *Emerald Land*, 14th St (between 57 and 88 sts), T 26990, a/c, pool, restaurant, garden, a relatively new hotel, tastefully furnished; **B** *Mandalay View Inn*, 66th St (between 26 and 27 sts), h/w, clean, terrace (but no view!); **B** *Inwa*, nr *Karaweik Restaurant*, 1 block from the SE corner of the moat, T 27028, a/c, restaurant, with teak floors and verandahs, rather run-down; **B** *Myit Phyar Ayer*, close to the station, a/c, bathroom, fridge, satellite TV, standard rooms small and handbasin only, more expensive rooms are good, small pool on the roof, good restaurant, no garden and 6 floors without a lift; **B-C** *The Dream Hotel*, 152 27th St (80/81st), T 26054, F 35656, a/c, hot water, minibar, satellite TV, IDD fax.

C *Golden Express*, 43 9th St, T 28767, same owners as the *Golden Express* in Pagan – one of the better bets in Mandalay; **C** *Mya Mandala*, 26B Rd, T 21283, a/c, restaurant, pool, better value than the Mandalay with its own – deserted – swimming pool, the outside sitting area, between the rooms and the dining area is a pleasant place for an evening drink; **C** *Sapphire*, 223 83rd St (between 28th and 29th sts), T 27327, a/c attached bathroom, breakfast incl, satellite TV, noisy, rather small rooms but rec; **C-D** *Garden*, 174 83rd St, between 24th and 25th St, T 27657, 25184, F 31047, some a/c, some bathrooms attached with hot water, in general not very clean, rooms at the back are quieter, friendly place; **C-D** *Unity*, corner of 27th and 83rd St, T 28860, F 32479, a/c, restaurant, all rooms with own bathroom and hot water, fridge, mini-bar, satellite TV, clean and quiet, laundry service, breakfast incl, friendly; **C-E** *Royal Guesthouse*, 41 25th St (between 82nd and 83rd sts), T 22905, some a/c, rooms with and without attached bathrooms, some with small living rooms, room rate incl breakfast, some rooms rather noisy, laundry service available, bikes for rent, money changer always available, competitively priced, clean and well managed, rec; **C-E** *Sabai Phyu*, 58 81st St (between 25th and 26th sts), T 25377, some a/c, cheaper rooms have shared (very dirty) bathrooms, more expensive have hot water in private bathrooms, breakfast incl, noisy as in the centre of town (quieter rooms on top flr) or at the back, geared up for travellers with cars for hire, pet money changers, etc, plans to open restaurant on the roof.

D *Aurora Pearl*, 29/30 San Pya St, Ahniektaw Quarter, T 34412, fan only, hot water shower attached, no restaurant (at the moment), new hotel owned by *Aurora Hotel* in Yangon, 8 rm in a charming Chinese building, decorated with taste, numerous Burmese antiques, located in a green and quiet quarter but a little far from centre, friendly service but chaotic management; **D** *Bonanza*, corner of 82nd and 28th sts, T 31031, F 35662, own bathroom, a/c, hot water, satellite TV, fridge, clean, rooms at back are quieter; **D** ***Mandalay Royal Guesthouse*** (moving location), clean, popular with travellers; **D** ***Natural Inn***, 4 23rd St, between 80th and 81st sts, T 26613, some a/c, some with bathroom and fridge, satellite TV, clean and roomy, has some character, although new, garden with exercise equipment, breakfast incl; **D** ***New Star***, 82nd St between 27th and 28th sts, T 28666, a/c, some bathrooms with hot water, satellite TV, clean and friendly; **D** ***New Waves***, 79th 26/27, some a/c, small and ugly, IDD available; **D** ***New York***, 82nd St, between 27th and 28th sts, T 28917, a/c, some bathrooms with hot water, clean; **D** ***Nylon Guesthouse***, corner of 25th and 84th sts, T 33460, a/c, some bathrooms attached (not too clean), unduly inquisitive and not always very friendly staff, breakfast incl, good value; **D** ***Royal City***, 27th St, between 76th and 77th sts, all rooms with a/c and bathroom with hot water, big rooms, breakfast incl, same owner as *Royal Guesthouse*, just opened; **D** ***Si Thu***, 29 65th St (between 30th and 31st sts), T 26201, fan only, family house in a small compound with only a few rooms, well kept and friendly, will cook meals on request, best value in Mandalay; **D-E** ***Aye Yar Wady***, 211 26th St, between 81st and 82nd sts, T 22848, cheap rooms, fan only, shared bathrooms, dirty, more expensive rooms have a/c, bathroom with hot water and big rooms (and are cleaner), friendly, but noisy; **D-E** ***Classic Hotel***, 59 23rd St, between 83rd and 84th sts, T 25635, some a/c, some private bathrooms with hot water, TV, fridge, helpful staff, clean rooms, quiet and quite good, price incl breakfast; **D-E** ***Taung Za Lat***, 61 81st St, corner of 26th St, T 23210, some a/c, opp *Sabai Phyu* and much the same set up, clean rooms, some with attached shower rooms, the ones away from the main street are much quieter, friendly, bicycles for hire, breakfast incl; **D-E** ***Thai***, 120 83rd St, between 23rd and 24th sts, T 21790, some a/c, shared bathrooms, not too clean, rather noisy and basic but friendly, breakfast incl for more expensive rooms.

● Places to eat

Restaurants in the main hotels serve standard European and Burmese food. Most restaurants close by 2100.

Burmese: ♦♦♦***Aung San***, 82nd St, between 33rd and 34th sts, well known for its fried pork; ♦♦♦***Sa Khan Thar***, 24 72nd St (between 27th and 28th sts), slightly more expensive than average but has a pleasant dining room opening onto a garden under a wooden roof, good Burmese food, rec; ♦♦♦***Too Too***, 27th St, between 74th and 75th sts, considered best Burmese food in town, very popular with locals, delicious fish and prawn curries, but meat is not so good, arrive early, before food runs out, closing down 2000, rec; ♦♦***Aye Myit Tar***, 530 81st St, good Burmese food; ♦♦***Taung Gyi Mar***, 193 31st St (between 81st and 82nd sts), don't be put off by surroundings, good selection of Shan dishes, run by a friendly family; ♦***Lashio Lay***, 65, 23rd St, between 83rd and 84th sts, good local food; ♦***Marie-Min***, down alley off 27th St (between 74th and 75th sts), excellent vegetarian food, good value, nice atmosphere, friendly staff, menu in 8 languages, 'Richard' – the owner – is also a guide (one of the best in Mandalay) and is very informative about trekking, there is also a comments book here for trekking information, rec. ***Ya Manya***, opp railway station on 30th Rd, rec by locals for its Burmese breakfast, *Mo Hen Ngar*, comprised of hot-and-sour vegetable soup with onion and rice noodles laced with fish paste.

Chinese: (The whole of central Mandalay is now Chinatown since the Sino-Burmese drug war lords moved in.) ♦♦♦♦***Honey***, 70th St, (between 28th and 29th sts – N side of soccer stadium), the *Honey restaurant* – which advertises with big hand-painted pictures of 'honeys' is reckoned to be about the best in town with prices to match, outside eating area; ♦♦♦♦***Lucky Hotel***, 84th St, nr 35th St, the first Chinese high-rise hotel, a roof-top restaurant has a bar, cabaret and sky-high prices (1 dish min); ♦♦♦♦***The Peking***, attached to *Mandalay Swan Hotel*, well located, Chinese-style dining room, a/c, very clean, attentive service, good Chinese food; ♦♦♦♦-♦♦♦***Pyigyimon Royal Barge***, SE corner of moat, Chinese food, lots of fish, government-run, not rated by locals, a restaurant for tourists, with great outlook, indifferent food and poor service; ♦♦♦♦-♦♦ ***Htaw Yin***, 396 81st St (between 30th and 31st sts), large menu and big helpings, ask to sit upstairs; ♦♦♦***Shwe Nung Daw***, 110 73rd St (between 28th and 29th sts), clean, rec by locals; ♦♦♦***Zaw Gji Inn***, 26, 65th St, a/c, clean, good classic Chinese restaurant; ♦♦♦-♦♦***Rainbow***, 23rd St (corner of 84th St), clean and cheap Chinese restaurant on 2 storeys with an upper floor terrace overlooking the city; ♦♦***Min Min***, 194 83rd St, between 26th and 27th sts, Chinese and Burmese dishes, no beer; ♦♦***Shwe Let Yar***, 226 83rd St (between 27th and 28th sts), rec by travellers, average Chinese nosh, serves beer.

Indian: ♦♦*Everest*, 27th Rd (next to temple), good vegetarian Pungabi dishes, no beer; ***Punjab Eating House***, nr the Sikh Temple on 27th at corner of 80th; ***Taj***, 194 83rd St (between 26th and 27th sts), Biriyani, Chinese dishes and Burmese food to order, friendly owner and reasonable nosh.

International: ♦♦♦*BBB European Restaurant*, 292 76th St (between 26th and 27th sts), just about the only place in Mandalay serving decent Western food incl steaks, Western tourists starved of home cuisine come here to recharge their gastronomical batteries.

Shan: ♦♦♦*Shan Family*, 80th St, between 28th and 29th sts, rec by locals; ***Lashio Shan***, 23rd St, between 84th and 85th sts, full of Shan gem dealers, try the water lily root and a variety of sausages.

Snacks: *Nylon Ice Cream*, 83rd St, between 25th and 26th sts, home-made custard rec; ***Flowers World Ice Cream***, 84th St, nr Mahamuni Pagoda; ♦♦***Shells***, 26th St (between 81st and 82nd sts), good breakfasts.

Foodstalls: next to the railway station; 26th St nr Zegyo market; ***Hpeq-Htouq-Kyaw***, corner of 30th and 80th sts, outdoor stall specializing in *hpeq-htonq-kyaw*, pork wrapped in dough and fried, then dipped in sauce of ginger and corriander, very popular in evenings, rec, (kosher versions available), 15 kyat/plate; 82nd St, between 26th and 28th St and 83rd St, between 24th and 27th sts.

● Airline offices

Myanmar Airways office on corner of 25th Rd and 80th St; ***Air Mandalay***, 23 82nd St (between 26 and 27 sts), T 27439.

● Banks & money changers

Mandalay Hotel for currency exchange (official rate). The black market rate in Mandalay is often as good as or better than Yangon's and money changers abound. Electrical stores seem to be recommended as a place to change money. **Myanma Economic Bank** is on 26th St (at the SW corner of the palace wall).

● Entertainment

State School of Fine Art, Music and Drama, just off the E Moat Rd, dances often based on stories from the life of Buddha and from the Hindu epic, the Ramayana, visitors can watch students practising, closed Apr; ***J Mandalay Marionettes***, Garden Villa Theatre, 66th St (between 26th and 27th sts).

Puppet shows: *Garden Villa Theatre*, 66th St, between 26th and 27th sts, T 24581, shows nightly at 2030, admission 300 kyat, the show lasts 1 hr.

● Hospitals & medical services

Mandalay's People's Hospital is one block from the railway station, nr 77th St and 30th Rd.

● Post & telecommunications

Area code: 02.

General Post Office: nr the intersection of 81st and 22nd sts.

Telephone Office: for international calls on 25th between 80th and 81st.

● Shopping

Mandalay has a strong tradition of handicrafts which originally supplied the royal courts. Many of the cottage handicraft industries are run by the same families.

Buddha images: in the area around Mahamuni Pagoda.

Film: plenty of photo processing shops in town. Price and quality of film is very variable – check for expiry date.

Gold Leaf & Ivory Workshops: group on 36th St, between 77th and 78th sts.

Handicrafts: most handicraft stalls are found around the Mahamuni temple. ***Mann Shwe Gon***, 86 between 26th and 27th St on 74th St – a craft shop with a range of *kalaga* (tapestry), puppets, teak opium-scale boxes. Bargain hard or barter Western goods. ***Win Shwe Yee***, 85/2, 28th St, between 73rd and 74th sts, good stock at reasonable prices.

Marble: most of the marble-carvers are found on 84th St on the way out to Amarapura, about 1 km from the city centre.

Markets: *Zegyo Market*, on 84th St, 3 km N of Mahamuni Pagoda; one of Myanmar's biggest markets, designed by an Italian, Count Caldrari, who was first Secretary of the Mandalay municipality, in 1903. Primary market for Chins, Kachins and Shans. Local produce, hardware and black-market goods from Thailand, but most of the old market has been knocked down or swallowed up in a modern new market with low tenancy. There's a small, but lively, market – ***Mingala Market*** – on the corner of 73rd and 30th sts, it gets very busy in the evening. ***Night market*** on 84th St (between 26th and 28th sts), on the W side of the railway yard, starts 1800.

Precious stones: second rate stones in ***Zegyo Market*** (all the best stones are exported or sold to the Diplomatic Store in Yangon for US dollars).

Silk weaving: Mandalay and Amarapura are the most important weaving centres in Burma and produce the famous *acheik* – horizontal weave patterned silk which was popular with royalty – and a highly prized silk (about 9,000 kyats for a length). ***Daw Supplies & Son***, Eastern Town Nandawshei, Sagaingdan Quarter, factory and shop. Gets many VIP visitors. ***Acheik Lunyargyaw*** on 62nd St, off 19th St, T 22617, fine textiles; silk weavers in the street opp the E entrance to Mandalay Palace. Or at Amarapura.

Tapestry (*kalaga*): ***Tin Maung Oo***, 26, 72nd St (W of Municipal Office) workshop and shop, good quality; ***U Sein Myint***, 42 Sangha University Rd (62nd St), made *kalaga* for the UN HQ in New York, his house is a miniature museum for Burmese handicrafts; ***Sein Win Myint***, 273 St (between 26th and 27th sts and 83rd and 84th sts), owner speaks good English.

Woodcarving: most of the woodcarvers are on 84th St, on the road out to Amarapura, close to the marble-carving area. Most of the carvings are sold in stalls around the Mahamuni Pagoda. ***Pam Mya***, on road from Mandalay to Sagaing is renowned as a woodcarver and sculptor in Mandalay. Specializes in Buddha images. ***U Win Maung***, 181/47 Htidan, Tampawaddy (just S of the Mahamuni) is directing the restoration of the palace and is probably the best wood carver.

● Tour companies & travel agents

Diethelm, 5 29th St, between 62nd and 63rd sts, F 32140, ***Trade Express***, 200 82nd St (between 27 and 28th sts).

● Tourist offices

MTT desk at the railway station, T 22541 (open 1400-1600 Mon-Sun) and at the airport, the main office is in the *Mandalay Hotel*, 26th St/3rd St, T 22540, open 0800-2000 Mon-Sun, ticket sales until 1400, bookings, travel information and currency exchange. Many independent tourist guides also offer their services.

● Transport

580 km N of Yangon.

Local Bicycle rental: Mr Ko Ko Gyi, Bagan Tea Shop, 184 83rd St (between 25 and 26 sts), 150 kyat/day. Also shop on 26th St (between 80 and 81st sts) which hires bikes. **Bicycle rickshaw**: prices negotiable, same price to take 2 people on one rickshaw, as 2 rickshaws with one on each. Rickshaw driver, Maung Maung Toe, based outside the *Mandalay Hotel* is a good source of information. Bargain on basis of 150 kyat/day; 20-30 kyat for trips from main hotels into town. Note that rickshaws cannot travel on all the roads. **Buses**: buses around town are very crowded. Most leave from Zegyo Market for areas surrounding Mandalay. Public buses going up Mandalay Hill leave from Mahamuni Pagoda (5 kyat). The buses stop running at 1700. **Car hire**: ask at hotels – especially cheaper ones around the market. Independent guides with cars – there are many of them – charge about US$25/day. **Pony cart**: best way to get around town; cheap: approximately 75 kyat for half a day. Drivers often act as guides. **Taxi**: there are usually taxis outside the main hotels and Zegyo market. Always negotiate fare in advance (around 60 kyat/hour). Probably the best way to see sights around Mandalay. ***Thoun-bein*** literally means '3 wheels' (like Thai *saamlor*) they are the small orange taxis which make a terrible noise – they have been banished from Rangoon because of the noise and air pollution they caused. Cheaper than taxis – about 500 kyat/day, dawn to dusk. **Tram**: a new tram system, opened in 1990, runs around the city. It was built at the instigation of General Ne Win who decided that the project would be sufficiently grandiose to upset an astrologer's prediction that his time in power would end after 26 years.

Air Airport is on the S side of town, on the Yangon road. It is currently being upgraded to take wide-bodied jets. Regular connections with Yangon and Nyaung-U, Bagan. Flights to Heho (for Inle Lake area), every Mon, Thur, Sat.

Train Station is in the S of Mandalay Palace area, on 78th St. Ordinary trains leave for Yangon daily; smarter 'special' trains leave on Mon, Thur, Sat. Leave Yangon at 1700 and arrive Mandalay early the next morning (14 hrs). Trains N to Myitkina, 23 hrs (US$27) in very uncomfortable, ancient carriages. Some private trains ply this route, 25 hrs (US$30 or US$60 for a sleeper), restaurant attached. Private trains need to be booked 3 days in advance, same day for state-owned trains.

Road Bus: comfortable overnight connections with Yangon, leaving daily at 1700 (1,000 kyat or 10 FEC) incl dinner and breakfast. **Myanmar Arrow Express**, 337, corner of 83rd and 32nd sts, T 23404; **Leo Express**, 388, 83rd St, between 32nd and 33rd sts, T 31885;

New Orient Express, 404, 83rd St, between 23rd and 33rd sts, T 31553; **Trade Express**, 82nd St, between 27th and 28th sts. Buses to Bagan leave from the terminal on 82nd St and 26th St, daily at 0400-0900 and at 1600. A 25-seater minibus takes 8 hrs (450 kyat). Connections with Taunggyi from terminal on 82nd and 26th sts daily at 0430, 8 hrs on a bad road (800 kyat). **Tiger Head Express** is the only company with a licence to take foreigners to the Taunggyi/Inle area – other companies may take you for less money. Connections with Pyin U Lwin (2 hrs by pick-up). Pick-ups to Sagaing-Ava-Amapura daily from 0600-1600 every hour, last bus back at 1600. **Taxi**: a taxi to Bagan from Mandalay should cost about US$60. The journey takes about 7 hrs and the road is in good repair – for Myanmar.

Boat The downriver trip from Mandalay to Bagan takes 2 days on the slower daily local boat, with an overnight stay at **Myingyan** (see page 177) or at Pakkoku, on the W bank (see Excursions from Bagan, page 199). Pakkoku is by no means half way, as the journey the following day to Nyaung U takes about 2 hrs. It might be worth having a little extra time here; there are plenty of boats stopping here on their way S. Not advisable during the dry season as boats can be marooned on sandbanks; others have sunk on collision with sandbanks in the dark. The 'express' boat leaves Mandalay from Minbu on Tues, Thur, Sat at 0600 and arrives at Bagan around 1830 (US$10-16), the boat is clean and the food is adequate. Deck chairs are available in the tourist section for pampered foreigners. There are also smaller boats, with deck-only seats. Private ferries often leave on days the government ferry does not, and cost a few dollars less – ask at the pier, pay on the boat. Boats to Mingun leave every hour between 0630 and 1600 (15 kyat), last boat back 1600. Tickets available from MTT.

AROUND MANDALAY

AMARAPURA အမရပူရ

When King Bodawpaya came to the throne in 1782, he dismantled his capital at Ava and founded Amarapura on the advice of court astrologers. His grandson and successor, Bagyidaw, moved back to Ava in 1823. King Tharawaddy (1837-1846), who succeeded Bagyidaw, took the capital back to Amarapura and then Mindon Min founded Mandalay in 1857. One reason for his moving the capital from Amarapura was its susceptibility to flooding; boats could sail straight up to the city putting the royal capital within range of British artillery fire.

Unlike Mandalay, there is little indication of where the royal city once stood and all that remains are the four pagodas which marked the four corners of the city walls, the watch tower and the treasury building. The military now occupies the site of the original palace. The city was laid out in a square, with a moat surrounding the brick walls. There were 12 gates in the city walls, above which there would have been wooden pavilions. Most of the palace buildings were removed, in their entirety, to Mandalay by King Mindon. Even the bricks of the fort walls have been used for building roads and railway tracks locally.

Today Amarapura has been swallowed up by the southern suburbs of Mandalay. The main industry is weaving cotton and silk.

Places of interest One of the main sights at Amarapura is the **U Bein Bridge** – a 1.2 km-long wooden bridge over the seasonal **Taungthaman Lake**, to the S of the city. It was built by the city's mayor, U Bein, in 1784 and used to have rest houses along its length. It is mainly constructed of teak planks salvaged from the ruins of the royal city of Ava. The lake dries up in winter, leaving fertile arable land for paddy farming and

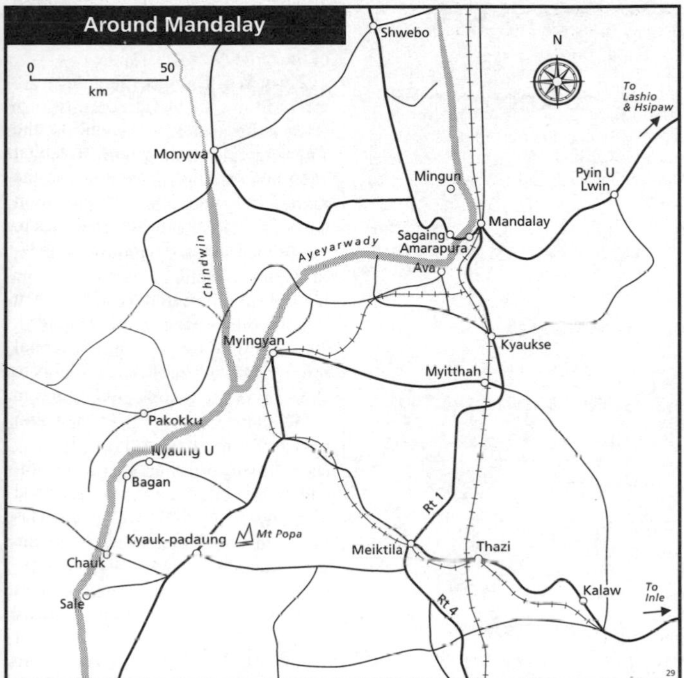

temporary brick factories. When the lake is full, the walkway is only a few feet above the surface. The sturdy teak pillars and the structural timbers are still strong, considering their age, although some of the planks are in need of replacement. King Pagin Min ordered the bridge to be built but charged the 'contractor', U Bein, with fraud for cutting corners by using beams and pillars from the former palace at Ava, which were abandoned when the capital moved to Amarapura. The bridge is an excellent place to meet monks from the nearby monastery and to sample toddy, a spirit distilled from the toddy palm and sold in the shelters. During the rainy season (Jul-Sep), it is possible to walk across the bridge and hire a rowing boat back. In the dry season a local delicacy, roasted paddy field rats, are sold from stalls in the shade of the trees beyond the bridge.

Beyond the rat stalls stands **Kyauktawgyi Pagoda**. It was built in 1847 by King Pagan Min and modelled on the Ananda Pagoda in Bagan. It is now in a rural area but the pagoda once marked the edge of Amarapura. There is one Buddha image inside carved from a single block of Sagyin marble, which looks almost like jade. Within the shrine there are 88 statues of the Buddha's disciples, as well as 12 *manusihas* – or mythical figures, half-man, half-beast. The walls of the porches are covered with 18th century paintings depicting scenes from Burmese life and other religious buildings from around the country. Taungthaman village is a typical Burmese village, without electricity,

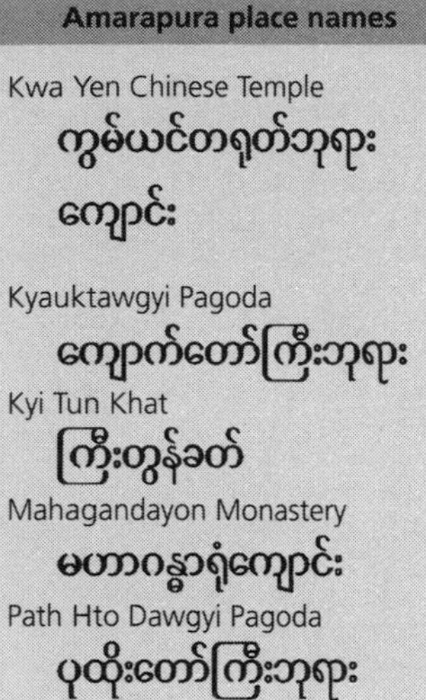

Amarapura place names

Kwa Yen Chinese Temple
ကွမ်ယင်တရုတ်ဘုရားကျောင်း

Kyauktawgyi Pagoda
ကျောက်တော်ကြီးဘုရား

Kyi Tun Khat
ကြီးတွန်ခတ်

Mahagandayon Monastery
မဟာဂန္ဓာရုံကျောင်း

Path Hto Dawgyi Pagoda
ပုထိုးတော်ကြီးဘုရား

Shwekyet Kya
ရွှေကြက်ကျ

Shwekyet Yet
ရွှေကြက်ယက်

Taungthaman Lake
တောင်သမန်အင်း

whose inhabitants make a living from weaving and selling toddy.

On the other side of the bridge is the **Mahagandayon Monastery**, the largest in Myanmar with over 1,000 monks during lent and about 700 at other times. It was founded in the early 1950s and follows the original teachings of the Buddha and has very high academic standards. Monks come from all over the country to study here.

The **Path Hto Dawgyi Pagoda**, near the S wall, outside the city, was built by King Bagyidaw in 1819. Scenes from the jataka stories cover the three lower terraces. There is also a large bronze bell in the precincts. Apart from this pagoda's size, it does not contain any relics and is not particularly noteworthy other than for the fact that it marks the SW corner of the old city of Amarapura.

Kwa Yen Chinese Temple nearby was built in 1773 by Chinese missionaries on a site granted to them by the king. The original building burned down in 1810 and its replacement went up in flames 19 years later. This structure dates from 1847. Its ornate classical Chinese-style roofs are typically gaudy but there is a collection of rather nice marble-topped tables in the courtyard. The temple is maintained by Mandalay's 20,000-strong Chinese business community. It is not necessary to take your shoes off in the temple precincts.

All that remains of the former royal palace of Amarapura is the yellow stuccoed treasury building and record office, which was built during the reign of King Tharrawaddy (1837-1846). Formerly it had been topped by a gilt pavilion which served as a belvedere – a room with a view. Nearby is the old watchtower and the tombs of King Bodawpaya and his grandson, King Bagyidaw.

Some of the villages around Amarapura are known for their weaving; the village of **Kyi Tun Khat** is renowned for its bronze Buddha statues.

Excursions On the road S from Mandalay there is a turn-off to the right just before the Ava bridge, which leads to the **Shwekyet Yet** (Golden Cock Scratches) and **Shwekyet Kya** (Golden Cock Falls) pagodas, so called because the Buddha is reputed to have lived there in a previous incarnation. The Shwekyet Yet pagoda is a cluster of stupas clinging to a high cliff over the Irrawaddy. It is most beautiful at sunset when a boat can be hired (for about 30 kyat) to go on the river and watch the sun set behind the Ava bridge and Sagaing hills.

• **Transport** 12 km S of Mandalay. **Local Pony traps**: can be hired for 75-100 kyat for a half-day. **Road Bus**: bus 8 leaves from the Zegyo market (B Rd/84th St, Mandalay) every half-hour.

AVA (IN-WA) အင်းဝ

Located at the confluence of the Ayeyarwady and the Myitnge (Dokhtawadi) rivers, Ava lies to the SW of Amarapura. The city was founded by the Shan King Thadominbya in 1364 and it remained a royal capital for a good part of the next 5 centuries, until it was finally abandoned in favour of Amarapura in 1782. During its first 300 years, Ava continually came under attack from the Mon from Pegu and the Burmans from Toungoo, and was occupied, for a time, by both. Ava's classical name is Ratnapura, the 'City of Gems', and locally it is known as In-Wa.

After founding the city in 1364, King Thadominbya led an expedition against the Mon, who had established themselves at Bago (Pegu) after the fall of Bagan in 1287, but he died on the way. Ava's war of attrition with the Mon of Bago became a recurring theme. Thadominbya was succeeded by Minkyiswa-sawke, a descendant of Bagan's Anawrahta Dynasty, who extended Ava's suzerainty as far as Pyay (Prome). He launched another invasion of Bago – but it failed too and there followed decades of continued struggle between the two kingdoms, with the Burmans of Taungoo caught in the middle. Today, Burmese traditional drama still re-enacts these epic struggles between kings Minkhaung, his son Minye-kyawswa of Ava and King Razadarit of Bago. Minkhaung died in 1422 and shortly afterwards, King Razadarit was killed on a hunting expedition; after their deaths there was a lull in the struggle for supremacy.

In the meantime the Burman kingdom of Taungoo was on the ascendency: it emerged as an important kingdom when Tabengshweti came to the throne in 1530. He led a successful attack on Bago in 1533 and the Mon king fled to Pyay. But King Tabinshweti followed up with a raid on Pyay, and when it fell he was recognized as the undisputed ruler of Lower Myanmar. 22 years later, his son, King Bayinnaung went on to capture Ava, breaking the power of the Shan kings. Ava became a tributary state of the Burman Empire. Then, in 1636, Taungoo's King Thalun moved to Ava, and it became the capital of the Burman Kingdom. But their power lasted just over a century: the Mon sacked and destroyed Ava in 1752, carrying off its king as captive to Bago, marking the end of the Taungoo Dynasty.

The following year, Alaungpaya, a deputy in Shwebo, to the N of Ava, gathered local support in defiance of Ava's Mon conquerors, and retook the capital, sending the Mons fleeing for their lives. Alaungpaya declared himself king and founded the third and final Burmese Dynasty, which he ruled from Shwebo and then Ava. His son, Hsinbyushin, made Ava his capital as did his successor, King Singu Min. When Bodawpaya came to the throne in 1782, he moved the capital to Amarapura, but the next king, Bagyidaw, moved back to Ava

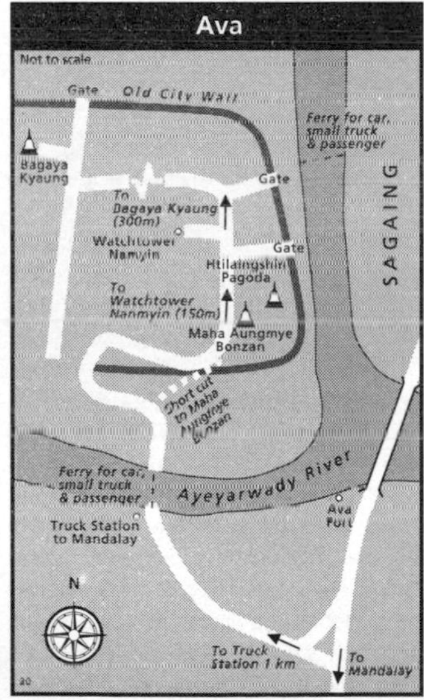

again. On many old European maps from this period, Myanmar was known as Ava. In 1838, the city was virtually destroyed by an earthquake and it was finally abandoned 3 years later by Shwebo Min, in favour of Amarapura.

The city is bounded on the N by the Ayeyarwady and on the E by the Myitnge. On the S and W, a canal links the two rivers. Ava's fortifications are unlike those of any other Burmese city in that its walls are zig-zagged. The royal palace was not in the middle either – it was positioned in the NE quarter of the city. There were three periods of building at Ava, first by King Nyaungyan Min in 1597, then by King Hsinbyushin in 1763 and finally by King Bagyidaw in 1832. Today, there are villages within the city area and most of the ruins are overgrown. The remains of the moat and the fort walls can still be seen as can a small part of the palace and several pagodas.

Ava (In-Wa) place names

Ava Fort
အင်းဝခံတပ်

Bagaya Kyaung Monastery
ဗားဂရာကျောင်း

Gaung Say Daga
ခေါင်းဆေးတံခါး

Htilaingshin Pagoda
ထီးလိုင်ရှင်ဘုရား

Maha Aungmye Bonzan
မဟာအောင်မြေဘုံစံကျောင်း

Nanmyin
နန်းမြင့်

Places of interest

The **Nanmyin**, in the NE section of the old city, is all that remains of Bagyidaw's palace. The upper part of the 30m-high masonry watch tower was destroyed by the 1838 earthquake. The lower part leans to one side, lending it the nickname of the 'leaning tower of Ava'. It is possible to climb the tower; most steps are outside the tower except for the last section (20 kyat ferry ride back to Mandalay).

The **Maha Aungmye Bonzan** monastery, was built by King Bagyidaw's chief queen for the royal abbot Nyaunggan Sayadaw (rumoured to have been her lover) in 1818. Constructed of brick and stucco, its design simulates that of wooden monasteries, with multiple roofs and a prayer hall with a 7-tiered superstructure. It has fine decorations and carvings. It was also damaged by the 1838 earthquake but was repaired by one of King Mindon's wives in 1873. Within the compound is the Adoniram Judson Memorial. Dr Judson was an American missionary who compiled the First Anglo-Burmese Bible. He was jailed on the site of the memorial stone during the First Anglo-Burmese War in 1824 – the Burmese did not distinguish between Americans and British – and was tortured during his captivity. His name lives on in the Judson Baptist Church in Mandalay, which – according to the sign outside – 'opposes liberalism, modernism, ecumenism, formalism and worldliness'.

The city walls are in good repair near the **Gaung Say Daga**, or N gate. This 'Gate of the Hair-Washing', was where the king had his hair washed in a ceremony of public purification during the Thingyan Festival in Apr.

The **Bagaya Kyaung Monastery** has ornate wood carvings, and is built of 267 teak posts. The main hall stands on a raised platform, separate from the monk's quarters, and is designed so that the space between the walls and roof allows air to circulate. It is set in the middle of the Le Daw Gyee – the royal ricefields.

Htilaingshin Pagoda was built by

King Kyanzittha of Bagan.

A 15-mins walk S of the old walled city are the ruins of the **Ava Fort**, built during the reign of King Mindon. It forms a triad with the Sagaing Fort on the opposite bank and the Thabyedan Fort near the Ava bridge. An old brick causeway leads from the S city gate towards the town of Tada-U, which is near Panya, and which, for a short time, was the capital of the early Shan Kingdom.

Local information

● Shopping

Lacquerware: there is a small factory within the old walled city, where black begging bowls are made.

● Transport

20 km SW of Mandalay.

Road Bus: bus 8 goes to Sagaing and passes through Amarapura and Ava.

SAGAING စစ်ကိုင်း

Sagaing is on the right bank of the Ayeyarwady, on the other side of the river from Ava, and is widely regarded as the religious centre of Myanmar. It is popularly known as 'Little Bagan' as the Sagaing ridge is crowded with around 600 pagodas and monasteries in which there are more than 3,000 monks. There are nearly 100 meditation centres in the Sagaing area.

After the fall of Bagan, Athinkhaya Sawyun, a Shan chieftain, founded Sagaing in 1315. It was the Shan capital for just 49 years, as King Thadominbya moved to Ava in 1364. Naungdawgyi, King Alaungpaya's eldest son, moved back to Sagaing for 4 years in the early 1760s but when he died, Ava reverted to being the capital. Many Burmese fled into the hills and caves in and around Sagaing when the Japanese invaded in 1942. The people – and monks – of Sagaing also suffered at the hands of the military in the brutal clamp-down on the 1988 anti-government demonstrations. Countless unidentified bodies were dumped in the Ayeyarwady.

Places of interest The 732m-long **Ava Bridge** was long the only bridge in the whole country to cross the Ayeyarwady River. Even though it is called the Ava Bridge it does not actually pass through Ava, but goes from Amarapura to Sa-

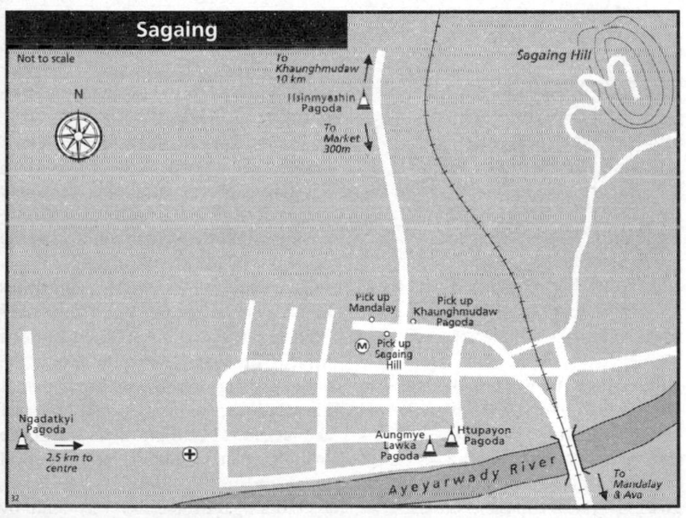

Sagaing place names

Aungmyelawka Pagoda
အောင်မြေလောက

Ava Bridge
အင်းဝတံတား

Hsinmyashin Pagoda
ဆင်များရှင်ဘုရား

Htupayon
ထူပါရုံ

Khaunghmudaw Pagoda
ကောင်းမှုတော်ဘုရား

Ngadatkyi Pagoda
ငါးထပ်ကြီးဘုရား

Ohnmin Thonze
ဥမင်သုံးဆယ်

Padamya Zedi
ပတ္တမြားစေတီ

Pon Nya Shin
ပုညရှင်

Ponnyashin Zedi
ပုညာရှင်စေတီ

Shin Bin Min Kai
ရှင်ပင်မင်ကိုင်း

Thabyedan Fort
သပြေတန်းခံတပ်

Tilawkaguru cave temple
တိလောကဂုရု

gaing. It was built by the British in 1934 and was then blown up by them 8 years later – the central portion was sabotaged in a bid to stop the Japanese advance in 1942, leaving many Allied soldiers on the wrong side, with no way to cross to relative safety. This section was rebuilt, the two sides rejoined and the bridge reopened in 1954. It connects Ava with Sagaing, affording a good view of Ava's white pagoda, and the hills on the far bank. Photographing the bridge itself is strictly prohibited.

At the foot of the bridge are the ruins of **Thabyedan Fort**. Burmese forces mounted their final resistance here against British forces in the Third Anglo-Burmese war in 1886.

There is a good view of Sagaing from the bridge but the best vantage point to view Sagaing's sprawling forest of pagodas is from **Shin Bin Min Kai**, a hill overlooking the Ayeyarwady, on which stands **Pon Nya Shin**, a golden pagoda. The hill can be climbed from a village known as Sagaing's Hton Bo Quarter – a good spot for sunset.

Htupayon was built by Narapatigyi (1443-1469) of Ava. Destroyed by the earthquake of 1838, King Pagan Min began reconstruction in 1849, but it was left unfinished when he was dethroned. It has a circular plan, with three concentric storeys with arched niches. In a nearby hut are a collection of stone engravings, which include the history of the Shan Prince Thonganbwa.

Aungmyelawka Pagoda is on the river by the hospital and close to the Htupayon. It was erected by Bodawpaya (1782-1819) on the site of his home before he became king. It is built of sandstone and based on Shwezigon Pagoda at Bagan. It is also known as the Eindawya Pagoda.

Ngadatkyi Pagoda, to the W of town, was built in 1657 by Pindale, who succeeded his father King Thalun and contains a large seated Buddha image. Pindale was unceremoniously dethroned by his brother in 1661 and a few weeks later was drowned together with his whole family. This was a fairly standard method of putting royalty to death so that no blood was spilt on the soil. The practice of disposing of all rival heirs was also fairly commonplace throughout

Burmese history (see page 38).

Hsinmyashin Pagoda, the 'Elephant Pagoda', between Sagaing and Kaungmudaw, enshrines some relics from Ceylon (Sri Lanka) and was built by King Monhyin of Ava in 1429. Its gates are guarded by 6m-high pachyderms, which failed to protect it from an earthquake in 1485 (after which it was repaired) and another, which totally destroyed the pagoda in 1955. Its reconstruction has been progressing in recent years. The contents of its relic chamber – votive tablets and Buddha images – are on display.

There are hundreds of pagodas scattered over the Sagaing hills; some of the other more noteworthy ones are: the **Ponnyashin Zedi**, said to contain two relics of Buddha (admission $3), the **Padamya Zedi**, built by a monk called Padugyi Thingayaza in 1300 and the **Ohnmin Thonze** (Thirty Caves) pagoda which enshrine a large collection of Buddha images in a crescent-shaped colonnade on the hillside. The **Tilawkaguru cave temple** is said to have been built in 1672 by King Narawara of the second dynasty of Ava and contains rare mural paintings depicting scenes from the former incarnations of the Buddha.

Khaunghmudaw Pagoda is 10 km to the N of the town and is Sagaing's most important temple. It was built by King Thalun in 1636 and styled after a Ceylonese (Sri Lankan) pagoda in commemoration of the re-establishment of Ava as the royal capital. It was constructed to house tooth and hair relics formerly kept in the Mahazedi Pagoda in Bago. It is composed of three circular terraces and a huge, brightly whitewashed dome, which – at 46m high – is the biggest in the country. In local lore, the well-proportioned dome is said to represent the ample bosom of Thalun's chief queen. A marble inscription, 2.6m high, which records the details of the pagoda's construction, is well preserved in a masonry shed. In niches around the outside of the base are 120 images of nats. The main hall is like a Buddhist disco. Each entrance is studded with mirrors and coloured tiles and the images – which come from ruins in the area – are adorned with flashing green and red neon haloes.

In Nov, at the full moon, people come from 60 villages in the area to celebrate the Khaunghmudaw annual festival. There is a colourful pageant and involves lots of dressing-up. Pilgrims also come to celebrate the end of Buddhist lent at the pagoda. But apart from the occasional festival, the Khaunghmudaw is usually deserted; there is a Burmese saying which goes: "People prefer to worship in golden pagodas." Admission US$3. Pick-ups available from town centre, 20-30 mins (10 kyat).

The Sagaing area – especially in Ywataung – is renowned for its silversmiths. **U Ba Thi Silversmith factory**, on the road from Sagaing to Khaungmudaw (just before the 53rd Light Infantry Battalion camp) has a workshop and shop specializing in the crafting of ceremonial silver bowls. U Ba Thi also has a shop at the *Inya Lake Hotel* in Yangon.

• **Places to eat** The *Lucky Restaurant* is rec.

• **Transport** 21 km SW of Mandalay. **Local** To get from Sagaing Centre to the hills, there are regular pick-ups every 30 mins from 0730-1600 (10 kyat). It takes 20-30 mins to get to the various temples. Last pick ups leave the hills around 1530. **Road Bus**: from various stops in Mandalay, 29th St/83rd St.

MINGUN မင်းကွန်း

Having enlarged his kingdom to include Rakhine (Arakan), captured the Mahamuni Image and founded the capital at Amarapura, King Bodawpaya set about constructing the biggest pagoda in the world on the banks of the Ayeyarwady. But on his death, in 1819, his project was abandoned. Bodawpaya's vast building site is now the main sight at Mingun, which is a favourite destination for locals

Mingun place names

Hsinbyume Pagoda
ဆင်ဖြူဘုရား
Mingun Pagoda
မင်းကွန်းဘုရား
Settawya Pagoda
စက်တော်ရာဘုရား

from Mandalay. It is an enjoyable river trip. In the dry season there are fishing communities on the islands and the river is busy with boats transporting sand to Mandalay for building, and bamboo rafts floating downstream from the Chinese border areas for sale as roofing material. An 'entrance' fee is now charged – $3.

Places of interest Mingun is situated on the W bank of the Ayeyarwady. Most boats land to the N of the Mingun Pagoda (the main attraction) close to the **Mingun Bell**. This bell, weighing 90 tonnes, was cast by the lost-wax process on Nandaw Island, and commissioned by King Bodawpaya in 1790 for his big new pagoda. It was transported across the Ayeyarwady on two boats (now in the Sagaing Fort Museum). The bell was originally hung on teak uprights, but these gave way during the 1838 earthquake. It is said to be the largest uncracked bell in the world – the biggest, although flawed, is in Moscow.

To the N of the bell is the **Hsinbyume Pagoda** (or the Myatheindan Pagoda), built by Bagyidaw (Bodawpaya's grandson) in 1816 in memory of his wife, Hsinbyume. It is in the form of the Sulamani Pagoda resting on Mount Meru, the centre of the earth according to Buddhist cosmography. The seven terraces represent the seven seas of Buddhist cosmology and around the terrace base are niches housing nats, ogres and nagas. The modern-looking image in the main shrine at the top of the pagoda hides a much older one.

Walk S back through the village to the main attraction – the **Mingun Pagoda**. This pagoda (also known as the Mantara Gyi Pagoda) would have been the biggest in Myanmar if it had been completed – it was to be 150m high. It was the brainchild of the mad King Bodawpaya (4th son of Alaungpaya) but was left unfinished after his death in 1819; it was also damaged by the 1838 earthquake. Even as it stands, it is the largest brick base in the world, the bottom terrace being a square, each side being 137m long. More than 20,000 Arakanese slaves were put to work on the pagoda. Each side is hollowed out to accommodate a small shrine in an archway. The only one now used faces the river. The terraces above the obelisk have small square panels which were intended to have glazed plaques on them showing scenes from the five Buddhist synods. About 500m S of the Mingun Pagoda is a small model (5m high), the Bodawpaya, designed as a working model for the real one. The remains of two huge **chinthes** stand guard to the E of the Mingun Pagoda. They too were damaged by earthquake; they must have been most imposing when complete.

On the river bank to the S is the **Settawya Pagoda**, which contains a marble footprint of the Buddha. Completed in 1811, it was the first pagoda built by King Bodawpaya in Mingun. There are several large monasteries at Mingun, one of which supports elderly men and women with no families (nearest the village jetty).

• **Transport** 12 km N of Mandalay. **Boat** Public boats depart hourly until around 1600 from the Ma Yan Chan jetty at the end of B Rd (26th St), for Mingun, 1-1½ hrs (15 kyat). Or you can hire your own boat for 700 kyat. There are two landing places; one is a 15 mins walk across a field, the other is in the middle of the village. Last boat back to Mandalay departs 1600.

PYIN U LWIN (MAYMYO)

ဖမြို့

Pyin U Lwin, far better known as Maymyo is Burma's best known colonial hill station and dates from the 1900s. The British called it Maytown, after Colonel May, who crushed a rebellion in the area after the Third Anglo-Burmese War in 1886. Pyin U Lwin served as the British colonial summer capital and the town was almost exclusively British. It stands on a plateau, 1,000m up in the Shan Hills, and is still a popular retreat for senior ministers and generals – Ne Win, for example, the old dictator of Burmese politics, has a summer house here. The Burmese army maintains a large garrison in Pyin U Lwin. A number of Indian and Nepali Gurkhas who entered the country with the British-Indian army live in Pyin U Lwin. The town is growing fast as it is on the main road to Lashio, the capital of northern Shan State and more significantly on the China road. With the increased trade with China, it is now an important outpost.

Some parts of the town were badly damaged during WW2 and have not been rebuilt; the rest of the town, with its brick and timber houses – complete with English-style gables, turrets and chimneys – remains as a ghost-like memento of empire. Most of the houses are mock-Tudor and have names like 'The Gables' and 'Fernside'. **Candacraig**, on a hill above the town, is the central attraction; it was the old R&R centre for the Bombay Burmah Trading Company, which logged teak in Upper Burma, and was built in 1905. It is often called the

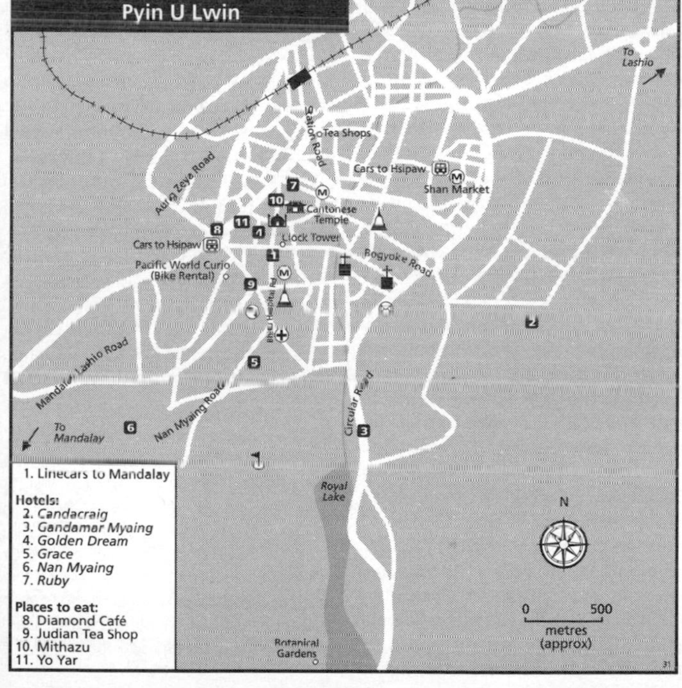

'Thiri Myaing' or 'Magnificent corpse', and still serves English food including early morning tea. Even Pyin U Lwin's churches are classically designed and there are miniature stagecoaches acting as taxis around town. In some respects, it seems like the British never left.

The British planted petunias and hollyhocks in neat gardens while the rugby fields, botanical garden and a golf course were carved out of the jungle. The 140 ha **Botanical Gardens**, to the S of town, were laid out by Sir Harcourt Butler, former Governor of Burma. Turkish prisoners-of-war during the Crimean War were used to create the now very pleasant gardens of mature trees on slopes above the two lakes. The plants and trees are labelled in Latin and Burmese. A tranquil spot, except on high days and holidays when the gardens are crowded with locals. A sign on the main gate 'create garden promote happiness' prompts you to buy seeds from the small shop by the entrance.

Pyin U Lwin's temperate micro-climate means a wide range of fruit (including strawberries), vegetables and coffee can be grown – it is an important market gardening centre. Locals say the climate has changed over the last 10 years; this cool retreat from the Burmese plains is becoming hotter, presumably as a result of deforestation. The variety of the produce in the daily **Pyin U Lwin market** is matched by the mixture of ethnic backgrounds of the traders. The covered area is full of stalls selling Chinese and Thai imports but behind this is a mass of smaller stalls with colourful displays of local produce. Stall 401 in the main market is run by Soe Moe a trader with perfect English. He buys antiques from hill villages and has collected an array of old watches, clocks, opium weights, puppets, tapestries and knives. He also fixes local trips for tourists. The **Taungaungyi Pagoda** next door is surprisingly neglected.

North on Circular Rd, over the railway line, is octagonal **Naung Kan Gyi Pagoda**, situated on a hill; a track leads to the covered steps which climb to the top, from which there are good views.

Excursions

Pwe Kauk Falls are 8 km NE of town on the Lashio Rd – not at all spectacular, although a favourite picnic spot for the locals. There's a good swimming spot with crystal clear water a bit further up river.

Anisakan Falls are 8 km SW of Maymyo; they are more impressive than Pwe Kauk and it is possible to swim. The walk back to Pyin U Lwin is a stiff uphill climb, taking about 1½ hrs from the bottom of the hill to Anisakan and probably another 2 hrs back up the road to Pyin U Lwin. Or take a horse and cart from the clocktower.

Shibaa, a Shan village, 20 km out of town, is renowned for its puppet shows. Trips can be arranged by Soe Moe, stall 401, main market.

Local information

● Orientation

Pyin U Lwin is very spread although the market, train station, buses and restaurants are all central. Even in high season, hotel occupancy is low and you should be able to get rooms at the private hotels for significantly less than the listed price.

● Accommodation

Candacraig and the '*myaing*' hotels used to be government resthouses, where the British Civil Service lived for half the year.

A-B *Nanmyaing*, by the checkpoint on the way into Pyin U Lwin, T 22112, hot water, restaurant, is a more modern-looking and larger version of the *Candacraig*, it has marginally better service but is short on atmosphere.

B-C *Thiri-myaing* (*Candacraig*), Anawrahta Rd, T 22047, restaurant, tennis court, large garden, the house had its heyday during the colonial period – it was built to resemble a scaled-down English mansion, used by the Bombay Burmah Trading Company as a 'chummery' – or bachelor quarters, log fires are still lit in the lounge, still the best place to stay in Pyin U Lwin, often full as it only has 9 rm so it's worth making a reservation.

There are 4 other government hotels but they are only used when the above are full: **A** *Cherry Myaing*, Aing Daw Rd; **B** *Gandamar Myaing*, Yuga St, T 22007, most similar in style to the *Candacraig*, but run down; **B** *Thazin Myaing*, Aing Daw Rd; **B** *Yuzana Myaing*, Aing Daw Rd.

The **D** *Grace*, 114a Nanmyaing St, T 21230, is a cheaper option without side toilets and showers, it is quiet but 10 mins' walk from town and has none of the hill station atmosphere; **D** *Ruby Guesthouse*, unfriendly, concrete floors, not rec; **D-E** *Golden Dream*, 42 Lashio Rd (nr Purcell Tower) T 22142, h/w, noisy but cheap.

● Places to eat

♦♦*Family*, nr the clock tower, Indian food – good but not very clean.

Burmese, family restaurant, 13 Block 4 in the market, popular with locals, owner speaks good English. The *Nanmyaing Hotel* serves English food (incl roast beef and potatoes) as well as Burmese dishes; ♦*Mithaza*, excellent Burmese food, very cheap (see map), *Yu Yar Chinese-Thai Restaurant*, sign on main road.

There are also a couple of reasonably priced Chinese: the *Shanghai*, Lashio Rd; the *Layngoon*, Lashio Rd, and *Mg Sein*. Various yoghurt products can be obtained from the Indian shops in town.

Noodles: the best Shan noodles are found in the market.

Teashops: the most popular teashops for young people to spend the evening at are on Station Rd.

● Shopping

Markets: *Pyin U Lwin market* is in the middle of town and offers everything from fresh strawberries to tribal souvenirs. The small shop by the clock tower sells interesting knick-knacks. *Dream Merchant*, 4 Main Rd, Block 6, has good selection of souvenirs, as does *Soe Moe*, 40 Textile Block. Closed on day of new moon. *Shan Market*, N of town on Lashio road, open 0730-1000, good selection of local produce.

● Sports

Pyin U Lwin Golf Club 18-hole course; another colonial relic. Golfers must produce evidence of their handicap; green fees: 100 kyat, clubs 100 kyat, shoes 50 kyat.

● Tour companies & travel agents

Pacific World Curio, 4 Main Rd (nr *Shanghai Restaurant*) run by Mr Slim; *Soe Moe*, 40 Textile Block, main market (also called Mohamed Ali), more expensive, speaks good English.

● Tourist offices

MTT office at *Nanmyaing*.

● Transport

67 km E of Mandalay.

Local *Myin-hle* are a peculiarity of Pyin U Lwin; they are brightly coloured horse-drawn carriages, probably a descendant of the Victorian cab. Expect to pay 300-400 kyat for an hour's trip. **Bicycles**: can be hired from *Pacific World Curio*, or from stalls at the back of the market (10 kyat/hr).

Train Takes several hours from Mandalay on a very windy track: daily connection leaves Mandalay 0445. All payment on this line (which continues to Hsipaw and Lashio) in FEC.

Road Linecar: taxis leave from Zegyo Market (84th St), Mandalay but the drivers wait until they have a load (usually every hour), last leaves about 1500, 2-3 hrs; hairpins and low gears but good scenery. If you are continuing to Hsipaw and Lashio, wait at the *Diamond Cafeteria* (see map) between 0700 and 1000, to take the place of someone disembarking. To Hsipaw (150-250 kyat), or book a place on the scheduled car at the Shan market.

MANDALAY DIVISION

MEIKTILA မိတ္ထီလာ

Meiktila is a major trading centre about 166 km from Bagan situated on the banks of Meiktila Lake. The lake was developed into a reservoir during the Bagan period and the influence of Bagan can be seen in the town's pagodas which are richly decorated. The city lays claim to an even longer history though; the Buddha is said to have come here during his time of wandering and bathed in the lake (see Nagayoun Pagoda, below).

As yet Meiktila is not a regular stop on the tourist itinerary – largely because it has been decided that there is not enough here to sufficiently interest the easily bored foreigner. That, though, is itself sufficient reason to make some people catch the next possible bus to Meiktila and the large market and peaceful lakeside pagodas do make the town a good place to take a break between more heavily touristed destinations nearby.

Places of interest

Nagayoun Pagoda is on the bank of Meiktila Lake, at the spot where, it is said, the Buddha came to bathe during his years of wandering. According to legend, naga (mythical sea serpents) came out of the lake to bring him offerings of fruit. When a heavy rainstorm lashed the shore, one of the nagas protected the Buddha from the storm by spreading his cobra-like hood over the meditating holy man. (Similar stories are told in many other countries of Southeast Asia, and statues of the Buddha being protected by the naga, often sitting on the coils of the snake, are comparatively common.) A display at the pagoda commemorates this event. The pagoda is said to have been founded during the Buddha's lifetime, but historically this can be thought to have little veracity and, in any case, the original pagoda has been built over with newer structures. The latest stupa has an unusual tower design. Recent renovations have been carried out with the help of the Japanese Asai Buddhist Association. The fact that the father of the Association's secretary-general hid from the Allies in one of the monastery's caves might have had something to do with the choice of the project. The plaques on the walls have inscriptions commemorating Japanese soldiers who died during WW2.

The **Shwemyinmi** and **Htithounzin** pagodas are in a compound between the clocktower and the bridge, W of the market. In the dark, cobwebbed buildings surrounding the stupas stand hundreds of alabaster tablets with inscriptions from the Buddhist scriptures. The **Shwemyintin Pagoda** is near the edge of town, on the Yangon road. It is more elegant than most of Meiktila's pagodas, with no mirrors but a ring of ferocious guardian spirits in gold around the stupa. There are eight entrances, leading to shrines dedicated to the 8 days of the Buddhist week. The first pagoda at this site is thought to have been erected soon after the time of the Buddha. It was neglected and fell into disrepair but was not forgotten. King

Meiktila place names

Htithounzin Pagoda
ထီးသုံးစင်းဘုရား

Moundain Pagoda
မုန်တိုင်းဘုရား

Nagayoun Pagoda
နဂါးရုံဘုရား

Shwemyinmi Pagoda
ရွှေမြင်မိဘုရား

Shwemyintin Pagoda
ရွှေမြင်တင်ဘုရား

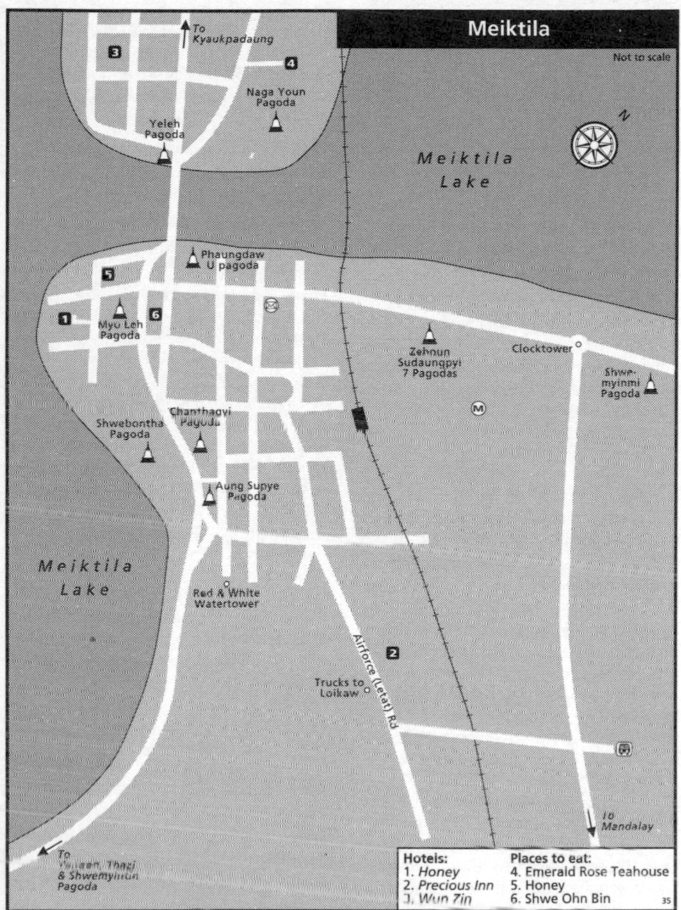

Anawratha (1044-1077) set out to find it with the help of some relics of the Buddha given to him by the monk Shin Arahan. The King put the hair and bone of the Buddha in a basket of flowers, which was loaded onto a royal elephant. He then made a solemn wish that the elephant should go to the lost pagoda. With the guidance of a giant golden fly (the brass replicas at Thursday's shrine are 2 ft long), the elephant went directly to the site where the pagoda was hidden under thick vegetation. It was quickly rebuilt with the assistance of the guardian spirits of the lake. For 108 kyat, visitors can assist in the latest renovations by having a marble tile added to the terrace. For this act of generosity donors receive a certificate of the event and the tile is added in the donor's name.

Excursions

For an appetiser before visiting Bagan,

visit 'second Bagan' – the **Moundain pagoda** and monastery complex. *Getting there*: 16 km W of Meiktila on the Kyaukpadaung road. Catch a linecar heading out of town.

Local information

● Accommodation

B *Meiktila*, off the Mandalay-Yangon highway, to N of town, T 21892, 3 classes of rooms, all the same except for extras like a balcony, fridge, TV etc, a/c, hot water, private bathrooms, restaurant (popular with tour groups at lunchtime), attractive setting in parkland.

C-D *Wun Zin Hotel*, Nandawkon Quarter (northern edge of town), T 21848, 21559 some a/c, restaurant, the economy rooms in a separate building in the garden have the most character, fan cooled, the standard and suite rooms in the main building are newer, more comfortable, but have less character, with a/c, fridge and carpet, upstairs rooms have large balconies, Burmese or Western breakfast (US$2) and dinner (US$6) available, very quiet lakeside location in large garden, with outdoor dining, friendly, English-speaking staff, recently privatized.

D *Honey Hotel*, Pan Chan St, T 21588, 21847, some a/c, large old house with high ceilings, breakfast is incl in the room rate for the more expensive a/c rooms with attached bathrooms and hot water showers, cheaper fan rooms with shared facilities, fairly basic rooms, enjoys a lakeside location and is set in a small garden, English-speaking owner; **D** *Precious Inn*, No 131 Air Force St, Yadana Man Aung Quarter, near large red and white chequered water tower, T 21818, concrete, characterless but where most people stay because a single is half the price of a room at the *Honey* and the hotel is conveniently located for the market and bus station, kind owner who speaks English, toilet/shower down the hall, not very clean, Western toilets – for cheaper rooms, more expensive rooms have a/c, bathroom and TV, mediocre, relatively expensive attached restaurant (100 kyat/dish – double what's on offer in town), but nice dark teashop beyond, breakfast not incl in room rate.

● Places to eat

Meiktila is thickly strewn with eateries in the main part of town. Perhaps best known, if only because bus passengers pile out of their vehicles to eat here, is the ***Shwe Ohn Pin*** which serves good Indian, Burmese and Chinese dishes. Across the lake just W of the Nagayoun pagoda, the ***Emerald Rose Cold and Tea Garden*** is particularly rec as a nice place to drink tea (hot or cold); it also has very good samosas and other snacks.

● Post and telecommunications

Area code: 064.

● Transport

96 km from Kyaukpadaung, 145 km from Yenangyaung, 166 km from Pagan and 190 km from Magwe.

Local Horsecarts and trishaws. **Bus**: the main bus station is N of the market. Connections with Pagan (3 hrs), Mandalay, Yangon, Thazi, Loikaw (afternoons only, arriving midmorning), Kyaukpadaung (connection to Popa), Yenangyaung and Magwe. Tour bus companies including Skyline and Trade Express pick up passengers from the *Shwe Ohn Pin* restaurant on the main through road in the centre of town at about 1700. Tickets available from *Diamond World Express* at the restaurant. Other express buses stop at restaurants a little out of town on the Mandalay road between about 2200 and 2400. No advance tickets available – prospective passengers just have to wait and see if there is space. There are several trucking companies just N of the *Precious Inn* which will take some passengers along with goods to Loikaw. They usually leave town between 1500 and 1800. Ask at *Precious Inn*, or look where goods are being loaded. **NB** Many of the companies at the station try hard to overcharge tourists by up to 4 times the normal fare. A linecar to Mandalay should cost 50 kyat, Kyaukpadaung (for Popa) 40 kyat.

Train There is a station here but connections are infrequent and inconvenient – in that they do not co-ordinate with trains on the main Mandalay-Yangon line.

THAZI သာစည်

There is very little to see in Thazi and for most travellers it is a stopping off point and way station between Bagan and Inle Lake. It is often necessary to spend the night in this non-descript town.

● **Accommodation D-E** *Wonderful Guesthouse*, brand new place, quiet, polite and helpful manager; **E** ***Red Star restaurant annex (Moonlight)***, T 56, main street (close to the railway station), friendly but basic.

• **Transport Train** Thazi is on the Yangon-Mandalay line. Regular connections with both cities. **Road Bus**: from Thazi there are regular connections by bus/pick-up to Inle Lake and Bagan.

MYINGYAN မြင်းခြံ

Situated on the Ayeyarwady S of Mandalay, this is an important trading stop, being at the junction of roads to Mandalay, Bagan, Meiktila and Myitthah. It seems that the inhabitants, too preoccupied with trading and other entrepreneurial activities, have not yet found time to leave their mark on the place and there is little to entice the visitor to tarry a while. The town's main sight, if it can be called such, is the bustling **market**. Of macabre interest are the **remains of Sun Lu Sayadaw** a highly revered local abbot who died around independence and are enshrined in **Sun Lu Kyaung Pagoda** to the S of town. Rather than cremating the monk, his body has been preserved for posterity.

• **Accommodation** Foreigners are not officially allowed to stay here, but as with most things in Myanmar this seems to be flexibly interpreted and in any case by the time this book reaches the shelves licences may have been awarded to at least one of the several (basic) guesthouses here.

• **Transport Train** There is a rail link with Thazi, one train a day, 6 hrs. **Road Linecar**: connections with Mandalay, 3 hrs; Nyaung U, 3 hrs; Yangon, 15 hrs; and Magwe, 4 hrs. **River Boat**: the boat between Mandalay and Bagan stops at Myingyan.

PAKKOKU ပခုက္ကူ

On the W bank of the Ayeyarwady, this small town is unremarkable – it is really just an agricultural marketing centre – but is the closest settlement to **Pakhangyi**, an abandoned 19th century town which lies around 20 km to the NE. Not much of the town is said to remain barring the city walls, and a wonderful old wooden monastery supported on a mass of teak pillars.

Local festivals *Thihoshin* (May-Jun): this festival, which is held at the pagoda of the same name in town, honours the holy Thihoshin Buddha image. The *pwe* performances (see page 76) are highly regarded.

• **Accommodation** There are 3 or 4 guesthouses in town, all priced at around the same level and all willing to accept foreigners. **E** *Myayatanar Inn*, the best of the guesthouses, simple rooms but friendly and helpful.

• **Shopping** There is a good spot to buy longyis and the distinctive Burmese checked blanket, both of which are sold by street hawkers at the ferry jetty. Jaggery and tobacco are both produced in the area around Pakkoku.

• **Transport** Pakkoku is much closer to Bagan than it is to Mandalay, but it is easier to reach from Mandalay. **Road Linecar**: from Mandalay from the main bus terminal at 0700 and 1100. **River Boat**: by the slow ferry from Mandalay (see page 162).

BAGAN (PAGAN)
ပုဂံ

Sprawling across the arid flood plain of the Ayeyarwady River, in the dusty heat haze of central Myanmar, stands Bagan – much better known as Pagan – one of the most remarkable archaeological sites in Southeast Asia. As 2 centuries' accumulation of architectural masterpieces, Bagan ranks on a par with the region's other awe-inspiring religious monuments: Cambodia's Angkor Wat and Borobudur in Java. But at Bagan, there are 2,217 pagodas still standing and another 2,000-odd ruined temples – the remains of Myanmar's architectural Golden Age. Bagan was Myanmar's capital for 230 years, between the 11th and 13th centuries, and in those days there would also have been thousands of secular buildings such as palaces and houses. But because these were built of wood, all have long-since rotted away, leaving only the brick temples and pagodas.

Amazingly, all Bagan's monuments are concentrated in just 42 sq km on the left bank of the Ayeyarwady River, known as the Bagan Plain. Through these temples and pagodas it is possible to trace the evolution of distinct architectural styles – from early Mon and Indian-inspired shapes (after the Late Pala style) to the classic Burmese stupa-design and the light and airy post-Mon temples. Bagan's documented history begins with its most famous temple-building king, Anawrahta, who came to the throne in 1044. He introduced Theravada Buddhism to the city – before the state religion was a mixture of Mahayana Buddhism and Brahmanism. Bagan's glory days ended abruptly with the invasion of the Mongul emperor Kublai Khan in 1287, after which the city was abandoned. Marco Polo, who arrived with the Tatar and Mongul raiders, was probably the first Westerner to set eyes on the city.

The Bagan plain is in the dry zone with only 640 mm of rain per year – and only supports a small population. Local farmers cannot grow rice but after the rains reap harvests of sesame, peanuts, corn and vegetables.

History

Bagan – whose name is thought to be a corruption of the Burmese *Pyu Ga Ma*, settlement of the Pyu – was most probably founded in 849 AD, at about the same time as many other Pyu cities in Upper and Middle Myanmar. There is thought to have been an even older Pyu city on the site though – legend has it that Bagan was settled from early in the first millenium. However, there are no architectural remains of the old Pyu pagodas. The earliest structure, dating from the late 9th century, is the Sarabha Gate (see page 186). The Buhpaya was the oldest surviving temple until it collapsed into the river in 1975. Architecturally, the city began to blossom in the reign of **King Anawrahta** (1044-1077), the 42nd ruler of the Bagan Dynasty. Bagan occupied a strategic location on the Ayeyarwady and was an important crossroads for Mon, Chinese and Indian traders. The core of the city occupied a commanding position on the inside bend of the river, which formed part of Bagan's defences and flooded the moat – still visible around the Sarabha Gate.

From his base at Bagan, Anawrahta unified the whole country, conquering the Mon kingdom of Thaton in Lower Myanmar in 1057. Anawrahta had earlier become a zealous convert to Theravada Buddhism (see page 36), having met Shin Arahan, a missionary monk from Thaton. By besieging and destroying the Mon capital, Anawrahta obtained the Tripitaka scriptures of Theravada Buddhism which he had long coveted. Manuha, the deposed Mon king, had earlier refused to hand them over – Manuha and the rest of the Talaing royal family ended their lives as pagoda slaves in Bagan. The 30 sets of the Tripitaka were said to have been brought back to Pagan on 32 white elephants. Thaton's 30,000 inhabitants were also marched N to Bagan. Anawrahta then set about converting his own people – who were mainly Mahayana Buddhists, Hindus and spirit worshippers – to Theravada Buddhism, with the help of orthodox monks from Thaton. He also used Mon architects and artists to build many of Bagan's great pagodas; Anawrahta's most famous monument is the Shwezigon Pagoda.

20 years after his victory over the Mon, Anawrahta was gored and killed by a wild buffalo. His son, **Sawlu**, succeeded him, but reigned just 7 years before he was killed and his half brother, **Kyanzittha**, seized the throne. Thousands of monuments were erected during Kyanzittha's 28-year reign. His grandson **Alaungsithu**, who succeeded him as King of Bagan, ruled for 45 years. A highly developed system of irrigation canals was built, allowing the 17 surrounding villages to grow enough rice to feed the capital. The empire began to weaken during the 13th century as the neighbouring Shan states grew in

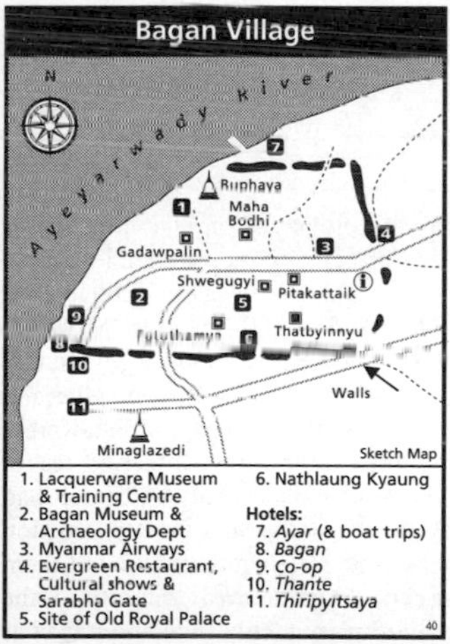
Bagan Village
N
Ayeyarwady River
Buphaya
Maha Bodhi
Gadawpalin
Shwegugyi
Pitakattaik
Thatbyinnyu
Walls
Minaglazedi
Sketch Map
1. Lacquerware Museum & Training Centre
2. Bagan Museum & Archaeology Dept
3. Myanmar Airways
4. Evergreen Restaurant, Cultural shows & Sarabha Gate
5. Site of Old Royal Palace
6. Nathlaung Kyaung
Hotels:
7. Ayar (& boat trips)
8. Bagan
9. Co-op
10. Thante
11. Thiripyitsaya

strength and **Kublai Khan** built up his Mongul army to the N. The Mongul Emperor – Genghis Khan's grandson, who had overthrown China's Sung Dynasty 8 years earlier – finally stormed and took Bagan in 1287. **King Narathihapati**, the last king of Bagan, is said to have pulled down 10,000 buildings, so as to leave little for the Mongul invaders. As they approached the city, Narathihapati earned himself the epithet 'He who fled from the Chinese'. The once-great capital was plundered, then abandoned to stand as a monument to the Buddhist renaissance.

Seven uneventful centuries after Kublai Khan's army overran and plundered Bagan, the city suffered another catastrophe. In 1975, Bagan – which stands on a geological fault-line – was at the epicentre of a major earthquake, measuring 6.5 on the Richter scale. The quake – and subsequent tremors – destroyed many of the smaller temples and most of the larger ones were damaged. As stupas cracked and crumbled, relic chambers were split open, exposing gold and jewels and priceless Buddha images. The army was quickly dispatched to guard against looters and a curfew was imposed. The treasures that were removed and smuggled out of the country kept Bangkok's antiques market in business for over a decade. Even today, in Bangkok's River City shopping centre (see page 308), items from some of Bagan's pagodas and temples are for sale. The damaged temples were quickly restored and reconstructed, using traditional materials and skills, with UNESCO assistance. The latest tragedy to afflict Bagan – this time a human one – has been the forced relocation of the population of 'Old' Bagan to a new town, 'New' Bagan (see box page 183).

Architecture

For Buddhists, the best way to make merit is to build a temple or stupa. The kings, noblemen and monks of Bagan,

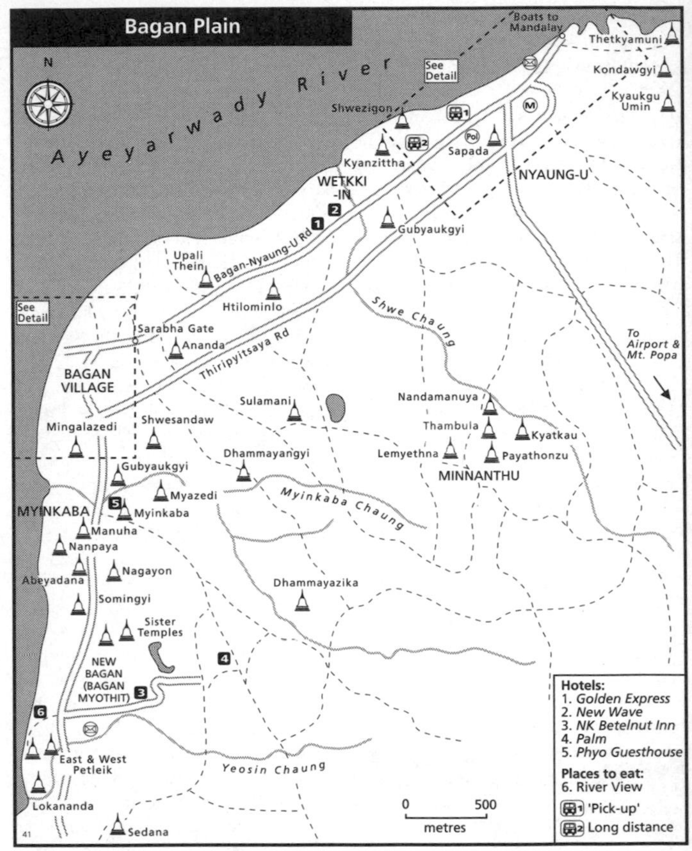

however, appear to have been obsessed with the idea. Royal temple-building, according to inscriptions, secured merit for the king's subjects as well as the king himself, guaranteeing them a shortcut to nirvana. Most of the monuments that have survived into the 20th century are religious structures built of brick and stucco. Much of Bagan's original vegetation would have been cut down to fire the brick kilns for the temples and stupas. The interiors of many of these monuments also contain intricate murals. There is plenty of evidence that there were once hundreds – if not thousands – of other, secular wooden buildings, which have now decayed. Dedicatory inscriptions in some of Bagan's temples, mention palaces, libraries and congregation halls.

Stupas – also known as ceityas or zedis (chedis) – are solid structures enshrining sacred relics, precious stones and images of the Buddha. The domes are tall, bell-shaped cylinders often with bands of ornamental moulding, and crowned with a *hti*, or umbrella. The ground plan is usually square although

Main periods of temple building in Bagan

Early Period: *circa* 850-1120

It is thought that Bagan was built on the site of an earlier Pyu city and prototypes of the early temples at Bagan have been found at the old Pyu capital of Thiri Kettaya (Sri Ksetra) (near Pyay, further S on the Ayeyarwady River). The latter years of the early period are sometimes referred to as the Mon Period, as the temple and stupa designs were heavily influenced by the Mon artists and craftsmen captured by King Anawrahta following his conquest of Thaton in 1057.

King	Temples
PYUSAWATI c. 850	Buphaya, Sarabha Gate
THUGYI 931-964	Nathlaungkyaung
ANAWRAHTA 1044-1077	East & West Petleik, Kyaukgu Umin (added to by Narapatisithu), Lokananda, Manuha, Myinkaba*, Myazedi, Nanpaya, Pitakattaik, Shwesandaw, Shwezigon (finished by Kyanzittha)
KYANZITTHA 1084-1113	Abeyadana, Ananda, Kyanzittha Cave, Nagayon, Myinkaba Gabyaukgyi (built by Kyanzittha's son, Patothamya*

Middle Period: *circa* 1120-1170

By the end of the Early Period, builders were already experimenting with upper storeys. During the middle period, the multi-storey temple was further developed, with the inclusion of upper-level sanctuaries. The earlier Pyu and Mon influences gradually disappeared and a true 'Burmese' style of art and architecture began to develop.

ALAUNGSITHU I 1113-1169	Sister Temples, Shwegugyi, Thatbyinnyu
NARATHU (also known as Kalakya) 1169-1174	Dhammayangyi

Late Period: *circa* 1174-1300

Innovation and experimentation continued throughout the Late Period and the novel 5-faced ground plan was introduced. Bagan also remained open to N Indian influences – such as that of the Maha Bodhi Temple. The fascination with elevation ceased as builders tried to create something different.

NARAPATISITHU II 1174-1211	Gwadapalin (finished by Htilominlo), Hmyathat cave temple*, Sapada, Somingyi Monastery*, Sulamani, Thamiwhet cave temple*
HTILOMINLO (or Nadaungmya) 1211-1234	Htilominlo, Lemyethna, Maha Bodhi, Upali Thein, Wetkkyi-in Gubyaukgyi
KYAZWA 1235-1249?	Nandamanuya
UZANA 1249?-1255	Thambula
NARATHIHAPATI 1248-1287	Mingalazedi

Late 1200s

Kondawgyi*, Pyathonzu, Thetkyamuni*

* Denotes those whose dates of construction are uncertain.

a 5-sided type developed in the late Pagan period. The terraces, designed to allow pilgrims to circumambulate the stupa, symbolize the tiered slopes of the cosmic Mount Meru. The terraces were also for pilgrims to view pictorial depictions of Buddhist texts emblazoned on glazed terracotta plaques – known as jataka plaques. These terraced plinths became increasingly elaborate over the centuries and the shape of the stupas evolved from early bulbous domes to the tall, tapered ones of later periods. The sealed relic chamber, or spiritual centre of the stupa, lies at the core of the stupa, below ground level. The whole religious complex, and individual buildings within it, whether based around a stupa or a temple (see below) is known as a pagoda in Myanmar.

Temples evolved out of the solid mass of the stupa, the interior of which was opened up to house images of the Buddha, while the stupa itself was raised on a high plinth with staircases in the middle of each of the four sides. Temples come in two main types: the hollow square design and the central pillar design. Those built around a **hollow square** have just one entrance, usually a vaulted chapel and one Buddha image at the far end. They were the earliest types of temple and most are just one storey high. They mimicked the early Indian cave temples, which served as places for devotion, ritual and meditation.

The later temples had a square plan and were built around a **central pillar**. A Buddha image was placed around each side of the pillar, facing the four entrances. The walls of these temples are usually very thick to support the heavy superstructure. The later temples are better lit and have vaulted corridors around the central pillar, around which pilgrims would walk. The later ones were also higher and often had monastic complexes attached to them. Their exteriors were decorated with bold stucco carvings on friezes and cornices, scrollwork on pilasters and flamboyant pediments on arches. The interiors were embellished with elaborate murals and the corridors lit by perforated windows. The remains of brick monasteries, or *okkyaung*, which would originally have had wooden porches, are found within the precincts of larger temples.

Art

The exterior decoration of temples was an integral architectural feature at Bagan. Large areas of wall are left bare but the plinth, frieze, pilasters and the pediments above the archways are often elaborately decorated with stucco. Makaras are a common form of decoration, as are the half-human half-bird Hintha. Flame-arch pediments were frequently used to give an impression of greater elevation.

The main Buddha images are made of brick and stucco (the Thandawgya Image is a classic example, see page 187). Most of the stone sculptures were crafted to occupy the niches in the temple walls. Much of Bagan's sculpture was influenced by the Indian art of Bengal and Bihar of the 8th-12th centuries. It is possible to identify common features in many of the Bagan figures:

- Buddha images are seated cross-legged on a stylized lotus throne.
- Their hair is represented by spiral (or snail-shell) curls.
- The robe is lightly defined, the body is plump and the waist thin.

Images modelled in the pure Burmese style have a more drooping head, a short neck, thick torso and fingers of uniform length. Their ear-lobes touch the shoulders. Precious stones were often placed within the spiritually sensitive areas of the body – the head, chest, abdomen and upper arms – which accounts for the widespread vandalism of the statues. Images have been plundered for centuries: many statues have gaping holes in the stomach area. Bagan's archaeological office has, in recent years, removed many of the smaller remaining images from the temples and moulded replicas in concrete. The originals are now in the museum to prevent further thefts and vandalism.

The terracotta plaques found in many of Bagan's temples, depict episodes from the jataka stories. These record the previous lives of the Buddha, and the art form was of Indian origin – though developed by the Burmese into a distinctive style of their own. The plaques are different from the relief work found in other great Buddhist temples in the region. The earliest plaques are unglazed (eg those at the E and W Petleik), while the later ones are finished with a green glaze and a beaded border (eg those at the Ananda Temple). A total of 547 jatakas represent the previous

New Bagan, *circa* 1990: a moving story

Until 1990 the main village on the Bagan Plain was Bagan itself – a small settlement inside the old city walls. To create a pristine, peasant-free, historical environment for tourists, and for 'archaeological reasons', Bagan's 5,000-7,000 residents were given one week's notice and then forcibly relocated to New Bagan (Bagan Myothit), a soulless and treeless wilderness 5 km S of the old city. The government was good enough to lend the entire village one truck for a week; most people had to hire other vehicles, at considerable expense, to move the contents of their homes. To encourage the people to move, the government first cut electricity supplies to the village, then water supplies. After they had cut off the road to the local market, the military supervised the removals at gunpoint. Bagan's residents lost many years' worth of investments in hotel premises, restaurants, shops, lacquerware workshops and cellars, and houses. At least 4 people, who wrote letters of complaint to the Township Law and Order Restoration Council (the local version of the Slorc), were arrested and jailed; they were not given access to lawyers.

In compensation for the inconvenience of moving, the government gave each of the 1,000-odd families a rocky plot of land, 10 bags of cement, 30 sheets of corrugated tin roofing and 300 kyats. These materials were promptly resold on the black market to help finance the construction of traditional grass-roofed bamboo huts in New Bagan. The old settlement was razed to the ground – only the water tanks remain. The offices of Myanmar Travels & Tours and Myanmar Airways and one handicraft shop were allowed to stay put. Given such harsh conditions, local people have been remarkably resilient. When the editors first visited Bagan in 1991, it was a bleak, depressing place. Now, however, it is a hive of activity with new guesthouses and other tourism-related enterprises springing up. The people who have been forced to live here have obviously decided that life must go on.

The reason behind the forced resettlement was ostensibly to allow the archaeological excavation of the site of the royal palace. The excavation of the site had been suggested by UNESCO (the United Nations Educational, Scientific and Cultural Organization) which met at Bagan in 1988. The actual village, however, was not on the site of the palace; since 1990, there has been no archaeological activity on the land formerly occupied by the village. Other explanations as to why the government was so keen to demolish the village have been suggested. Following the demonstrations and the military clamp-down in 1988 (there were protests both in Bagan and at nearby Nyaung-U), the military junta was not keen to have tourists mixing with or talking to locals.

Bagan highlights

Ananda Temple, built by Bagan's prolific temple-builder, King Kyanzutha, in 1091, see page 185.
Thatbyinnyu Temple, dating from 1144; beautiful temple with views over the plain (most popular sunset spot), see page 187.
Bagan Museum, Buddha images and treasures from Bagan's stupas and temples, see page 189.
Gawdawpalin Temple, upper terraces are a good spot to watch the sunset over the Ayeyarwady, see page 190.
Upali Thein, despite some deterioration, beautiful interior painting, see page 191.
Shwezigon Pagoda, with its golden stupa, is Bagan's biggest and most important temple, see page 191.
Mingalazedi Pagoda, built 3 years before the Mongul invasion; beautifully proportioned, with gentle flowing lines, see page 194.
Nanpaya Temple, for beautiful stone carving on interior pillars, see page 196.
Dhammayangyi Temple, one of the most imposing buildings on the plain, known for its fine brickwork, see page 198.
Sulamani Temple, a fine example of Bagan's Late Period, see page 198.

- Best views at sunset: Htilominlo, Shwesandaur, Gawdawpalin, Thatbyinnyn.
- Most of the main temples are signposted off the roads with yellow signs and the archaeology department's white plaques give basic information on the most important sites.
- Many of the temples are now locked to protect against thieves; some have watchmen who look after the key, or it is kept in the nearby village. For other temples, the key must be collected in advance from the Department of Archaeology next to the museum.
- Admission: US$10 to the archaeological zone, good for 3 days. No one checks tickets, but if you are found without one, your hotel will be fined. As a result most hotels and guesthouses insist that visitors buy a ticket before checking in (they are sold at all hotels). Tickets available at hotels, MTT offices and museums.

lives of the Buddha.

Nearly all of Bagan's temples would originally have had wall paintings; many still survive. Most are murals, actually painted on the wall, rather than frescoes, which are painted on wet plaster. Typically, all the forms are outlined in black or red and the paintings have little or no perspective. Most depict the Jataka tales but some are also valuable historical records, portraying secular buildings as well as fashion, jewellery and furnishings of the period. The tops and bottoms of walls were often decorated with floral and geometric designs. Some of the best murals of the Bagan period can be seen at Gubyaukkyi, while the Abeyadana is distinctive with its Mahayanist paintings, which include portrayals of Vishnu, Siva and Indra.

Places of interest

The central area, in and around the old walled city of Bagan, has many of the most important and impressive temples – they are also the most accessible temples from the main hotels. The route starts with the Ananda temple, just outside the old walls, then follows around the inside of the city in a clockwise direction. Temples and pagodas spread across the Bagan plain, and are divided into those NE of Bagan proper; N and E of Nyaung-U; S of Bagan to Myinkaba; further S around Thiripyitsaya; and E of Bagan around Minnanthu.

In and around the city walls

The **Ananda Temple**, just E of the city wall, is distinguished by its golden stupas; as it is in constant use, it is kept in good repair. The British colonial official Sir Henry Yule, who visited Pagan in 1858 talked of the "sublimity" of the Ananda's architecture, which, he said excited "wonder, almost awe". Started in 1091 by King Anawrahta and finished by Kyanzittha, the Ananda inspired the temple-building of later Burmese kings. It is a central pillar-type temple: the central portion is a square block, each side of which is 53m long and 10.7m high. There are four large gabled portico entrances, giving the temple a cruciform structure. Above the base there are six receding terraces, crowned with a beehive-like spire called a *sikhara*. The pinnacle is a tapering pagoda with a hti. Four smaller stupas, all copies of the central spire, are at the roof's corners. Two tiers of windows admit light into the interior, illuminating the narrow corridors inside the temple. The Ananda initiated the 'double terrace' style of temple at Bagan.

The Ananda's inner and outer corridors are full of niches, in which there are 1,424 Buddha statues in various postures. The most notable sculptures in the temple are the series of 80 reliefs in the two lower tiers of niches in the outer corridor, which illustrate the life of the Bodhisattva. On each face of the central cube there is a tall, arched alcove, each enshrining an imposing standing Buddha; the four Buddhas represent the Buddha's incarnations: Gautama faces W, Kakusandha N, Konagamana E and Kassapa S. Two of them date from the construction of the temple; the images on the E and S sides were destroyed in the 17th century and later rebuilt.

The W sanctum also enshrines life-size statues of King Anawrahta, and the missionary monk Shin Arahan from Thaton, who converted the king to Theravada Buddhism and died at the age of 81. In the porch on the S face, on a pedestal, there are stone footprints of the Buddha. The entrance to each porch is guarded by two door-keepers, seated on pedestals, in arched niches, topped

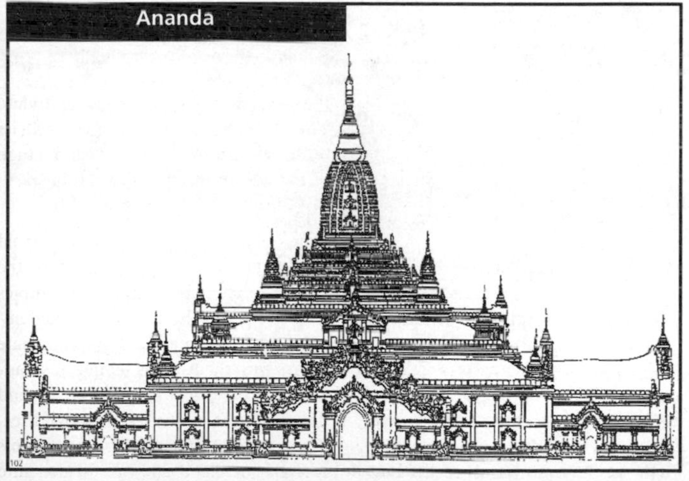

In and around the city walls

Ananda Temple
အာနန္ဒာ
Bagan Museum
ပုဂံပြတိုက်
Buphaya Temple
ဗူးဘုရား
Gawdawpalin Temple
ဂေါ်တော်ပလ္လင်
Maha Bodhi Temple
မဟာဗောဓိ
Nathlaung Kyaung
နတ်လှောင်ကျောင်း
Patothamya
ပုထိုးသားများ
Pitakattaik
ပိဋကတ်တိုက်
Shwegugyi Temple
ရွှေဂူကြီး
Thatbyinnyu Temple
သဗ္ဗညု

with miniature spires. Each entrance to the main building is also guarded by another set of door-keepers, in plaster-work, standing on low pedestals. The temple's lavish interior walls have been painted ochre and gold.

The base and terraces on the outside of the temple are ornamented with green-glazed terracotta tiles relating the jataka stories. Those on the W half of the base depict various monsters of Mara's army; the ones on the E side show devas, holding auspicious symbols, who are celebrating the Buddha's conquest of Mara. The jataka plaques on the lower terraces show just one scene, but the ones on the four upper-terraces are decorated with 389 different scenes, and are inscribed in Mon; these terraces are closed to the public to prevent theft. Inside the aisles of the four porches are stone sculptures depicting the eight principle scenes of the Buddha's life. The *Ananda Pagoda festival* is during the full moon in Jan. Camera fee 5 kyat.

Within the Ananda Temple compound is a small red-brick building, which is the monastery, or **Ananda Okkyaung**. Its walls are covered in well-preserved 18th century wall paintings depicting scenes from the Buddha's life and scenes from Bagan's history. Unlike Bagan's earlier temple painters, these painters made much more use of colour combinations, light, shadow and perspective.

The **Sarabha Gate** (to the W of Ananda) and a few ruined walls are among the only surviving remnants of Bagan's secular architecture. The *Mahgiri nats*, Pagan's guardian spirits, still have their prayer niches in the gateway. These two nats, *Nga Tinde* (Mr Handsome) or the *Mahagiri Nat* and his sister, *Shwemyethna* (Golden Face) or *Hnamadawgyi Nat*, are called Lords of the Great Mountain because they are believed to live on the sacred Mount Popa (see page 200). Originally the city wall had 12 gates, one for each month of the year, built by King Pyusawati in 850. The Department of Archaeology is rebuilding parts of the city wall and moat.

According to an 11th century Mon inscription – known as Kyanzittha's inscription – there was a royal **palace**, composed of a main pavilion surrounded by four minor ones, together with a throne room and audience hall. The archaeology department has excavated the site, which is close to the Pitakattaik (below), just within the city walls. The foundations are believed to date from the Early Bagan Period, but there are also remnants of some later building.

The Mudras of the Bagan Buddhas

Most of Bagan's Buddha images can be classified into 6 main attitudes or mudras:

- Buddha in a sitting position, attaining enlightenment with the left hand in the lap, palm upward and the right hand touching the earth.
- Buddha in a sitting position, preaching his first sermon, with the thumb and index finger of the right hand touching a finger of the left hand (turning the Wheel of Law).
- Buddha meditating with both hands turned upwards, resting in his lap.
- Buddha in a standing position with the left hand extended in the posture of bestowing gifts and the right hand with palm outwards in the gesture of reassurance.
- Buddha in a standing position in the gesture of turning the Wheel of Law.
- Buddha reclining with his head supported by his right hand, representing his attainment of 'the point of final liberation'.

For more information on the mudras, see page 54.

The **Pitakattaik**, or library, is just off the main road, W of Sarabha Gate. It is said to have been built to house the 32 elephant-loads of scriptures bought by King Anawrahta from Thaton in 1057. It is 15m square and 18m high, with three entrances on the E side – two of which are now blocked up – and windows on the other sides. It is built like a temple, with a central cell, and is surrounded by a processional corridor. From this library it is possible to get an idea of what some of the other secular buildings must have looked like, although the Pitakattaik was altered by King Bodawpaya in 1783, who added finials to the corners of the five multiple roofs and plaster carvings above the entrances. Many of the monasteries of Bagan would have had similar libraries attached to them.

The 6m-high Buddha image just to the S of the Pitakattaik is known as the **Thandawgya Image**, which means 'within earshot of the royal voice' – it was close to the palace. It shows how most of the images in Bagan were built: the bulk of the statue was made from brick and stucco with a wooden shaft through the centre of the torso to fix it to the temple wall. The image was then covered in stucco, painted and sometimes gilded.

The **Shwegugyi Temple**, just to the W of the Pitakattaik, was built by King Alaungsithu in 1131 and straddles the earlier and middle periods of Bagan's architecture. Both the hall and the inner corridor have doorways and open windows, making it airy and well-lit. The arch-pediments, pilasters, plinth and cornice mouldings are decorated with fine stucco carvings. Inside there is a Pali inscription recording King Alaungsithu's religious aspirations and that the temple was completed in 7 months.

Thatbyinnyu, to the S of the Pitakattaik and the Thandawgya Image, was also built by King Alaungsithu in 1144. The magnificent temple stands within the old city walls (to the SW of the Ananda) and is made up of two large storeys, the upper one set back above three intermediate terraces. Thatbyinnyu introduced the idea of putting a smaller 'hollow cube' on top of a larger Burman-style structure – earlier Mon-style temples were just one storey high. The main (E) entrance is unusually larger than the other three; from it a stairway – guarded by two standing figures – leads to a corridor, which runs round the central core. At the top of the next flight of steps, which are built into the thick wall, more steps scale the outside of the temple to the

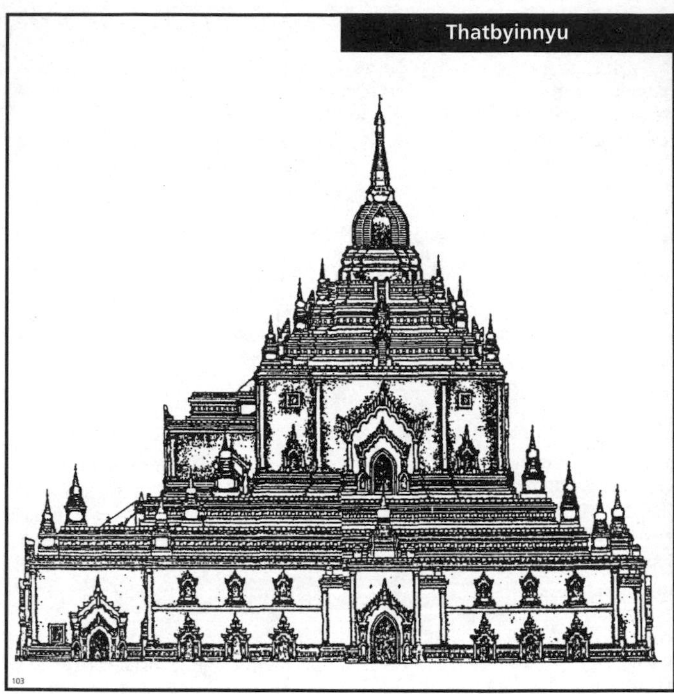

upper storey. There is an enormous seated Buddha image in the upper sanctuary, which despite appearances, dates from the temple's construction. It has been continually re-gilded and rebuilt over the centuries. Thatbinnyu is famous for its fine brickwork, which is best exemplified by the wall at the back of the statue. The 1st and 2nd levels were once the residence of monks, the 3rd level housed Buddha images and the 4th, a library.

Access to the top of the upper storey is by another narrow flight of steps to the left of the shrine. The pinnacle consists of the usual sikhara, with a tapering stupa on top, which reaches to 62m – Bagan's highest. The mini-stupas, at the corners of the terraces, were badly damaged in the 1975 earthquake, but they have been well restored. There are spectacular views from its wide terraces – it is said to be possible to see 1,500 temples from the top – which makes the temple Bagan's most popular sunset spot. The Tuyan hills are clearly visible in the distance (beyond the fertilizer plant), and 60 km to the SE, is Mount Popa. For every 10,000 bricks used in the construction of Thatbinnyu, King Alaungsithu kept one aside, with which he built the little temple next door. Camera fee 5 kyat.

From the top of Thatbinnyu it is possible to see the **Nathlaungkyaung Temple** to the SW. It is Bagan's only Hindu Vaishnavite temple and was probably built in the 10th century to serve Bagan's Indian community of merchants and craftsmen. Little is left of the original

structure but inside there are alcoves which originally held brick and stucco images of Vishnu – the remains of one of these statues are in the main alcove. Some of the sculptures from this temple are in the Bagan Museum.

Patothamya, to the W of Thatbyinnyu and Nathlaungkyaung, is thought to date from the 10th century, although it is attributed to King Kyanzittha (1084-1113). It has a square main block and a rectangular vaulted hall on the E. The hall has three doorways with elegant pediments on the arches while each side of the main block has five perforated windows. The sanctuary is lit by skylights through shrines on the terraces above. In the corridor walls are niches enshrining stone Buddhas. The paintings of the *jataka* tales (stories from the Buddha's previous incarnations) on the walls of the sanctuary have Mon captions below them. The temple is often locked to protect the murals and inscriptions. Above, there are three terraces; the bulbous dome has 12 vertical ribs and on top is the harmika – the casket containing the holy relics – and a 12-sided tapering finial.

Bagan Museum, to the W of Thatbyinnyu and near the Gawdawpalin, was built in 1979 and preserves many of the images and treasures exposed or damaged during the 1975 earthquake. In the main gallery is the **'Rosetta Stone'**, dating from 1113, which is inscribed in Pyu, Mon, Pali and Burmese allowing scholars to decode the Pyu script for the first time – it was previously indecipherable. It is also known as the **Myazedi Pillar** and was found at the pagoda of the same name, next to the Gubyaukgyi temple (see page 195) in 1917 by the German superintendent of archaeology in Bagan. One of the most interesting exhibits is a bronze lotus bud which opens up to reveal a tiny stupa with delicately carved figures of the Buddha at its base. Bagan was also famous for its dolomite carvings on display in the main room.

The museum houses a collection of 10th and 11th century Buddha images in the Statue Gallery. The Chinese-influenced pot-bellied Buddhas are a source of much amusement to visiting Burmese. It is said there are over 4 million Buddha images in Bagan – it is not hard to see why, if the scores of tiny images in relief on the stone slabs are included in the Buddha-count. A selection of jataka plaques are also on display. All items are labelled in English and dated. Next door to the Statue Gallery, replicas of particularly valuable statues are moulded from the originals; these will replace the originals in Bagan's temples to prevent theft.

The Department of Archaeology is attached to the museum; its superintendent and staff can update visitors on plans for restoration and renovation and on the progress of various archaeological digs. Since 1982, when restoration work began, most has been funded by the government and public donations, with United Nations agencies supplying technical assistance. Occasionally bilateral donations are received for particular projects – Germany, for example, has funded restoration work on the Ananda Pagoda. Archaeological digs on the E side of the city began in 1989, and excavations on the mound site of what is presumed to be one of the wooden palaces got underway in May 1990. Despite the mass-relocation of 5,000-7,000 of Bagan's residents in 1990 (see page 183), there still appear to be no plans to start archaeological excavations on the site of the old village. Admission US$4. Open 0900-1630 Tues-Sun.

The **Gawdawpalin Temple**, to the N of the museum, was mostly built during the reign of King Narapatisithu but was finished by his son, King Htilominlo. The Gawdawpalin may have been built for the purpose of royal ancestor worship as *gawdawpalin* means "platform to which respect of homage is paid". The temple is an example of the late period of Bagan architecture and, like Thatbyinnu, it is double-storeyed with the main shrine on the upper level. A curvilinear spire rises above the upper terraces and is crowned by a slim tapering stupa. Unfortunately the temple was near the epicentre of the 1975 earthquake and was badly damaged – its restoration work is rather obvious. The Gawdawpalin is a good place to watch sunrises and sunsets, with its views over the Irrawaddy. Camera fee 5 kyat.

The **Maha Bodhi Temple**, NE of the Gawdawpalin and just off the main road, is a replica of the temple of the same name at Bodhgaya in India's Bihar state, which was built in 500 AD at the site where the Buddha achieved enlightenment. The Bagan version is typical of India's Gupta Period and it is quite different from the standard bell-shaped Burmese temples. There are very few temples of this kind in Myanmar and was built during the reign of King Htilominlo (or Nadaungmya). It was the first temple in which a large number of Buddha images were placed in exterior niches – previously they had been confined to interior chambers. Most of these images are crude and rather disappointing close up: the whole temple is more impressive from a distance.

The **Bagan Lacquerware Museum & Training Centre** is on the way down to the river and the Buphaya. The museum has good examples of early lacquerware: 15th century gilded glass mosaic boxes and carved wooden doors. Visitors can look around the training centre to watch how lacquerware is made. Closed Apr. The shop has a good selection of items made by the students, all traditional designs. Well worth a visit. If the museum is locked, the office has a key.

According to legend, the **Buphaya Temple**, which sits above the riverbank, was built by the third king of Bagan, Pyusawti (c.850 AD), who found a way to get rid of the *Bu* plant which infested the riverbanks. He was rewarded by the then King Thamuddarit, with the hand of his daughter and the inheritance of the throne. In commemoration of his good fortune Pyusawati had the Buphaya pagoda built. The bulbous shape of the stupa is suggestive of its Pyu origins but it was totally destroyed in the 1975 earthquake. The temple has been reconstructed according to the original design. It is not particularly impressive.

Northeast of Bagan

The **Htilominlo**, NE of Bagan proper, is a 2-storey red-brick temple built by King Htilominlo around 1211. He was King Narapatisithu's son, which explains the similarity in style to the Sulamani temple (see page 198). It is one of the larger temples of Bagan, reaching 46m and commands the road from Bagan to Nyaung-U. Like the Sulamani it is orientated E. There is an ambulatory at the base – the arched doorways and windows of which catch the morning and evening sunlight – and on the upper level, from which there are excellent views of the plain. The steps to the top are built into the thick walls on the E side. There are good examples of the original stucco decoration on the exterior.

Upali Thein, close to Htilominlo, on the other side of the road, is a good example of a sima or ordination hall. It is thought to have been founded in the mid-13th century and named after the monk, Upali. It is rectangular with a vaulted hall and an image of the Buddha at the W end. Its design is said to resemble many of Bagan's former wooden buildings. The low parapets, arch pediments and interior paintings date from the 18th century. Unlike the early panelled paintings, these are vivid murals – large and continuous, showing the renunciation of the world by past Buddhas and depicting the consecration of the hall by the king. It is closed to visitors, but special permission to visit it can be obtained from the Department of Archaeology (next to the museum).

The **Wekkyi-in Gubyaukgyi Temple**, with its pyramidal spire, lies S of the Shwezigon. It was known for its interior jataka paintings – some were removed by an archaeologist in 1899 – and dates from the early 13th century. Most temples in Bagan would have been painted inside as this one. This temple should not be confused with the Gubyaukgyi Temple near Myinkaba village.

Northeast of Bagan

Htilominlo Temple
ထီးလိုမင်းလို
Kyanzittha Cave Temple
ကျန်စစ်သားဥမင်
Shwezigon Temple
ရွှေစည်းခုံဘုရား
Upali Thein
ဥပါလိသိမ်
Wekkyi-in Gubyaukgyi Temple
ဝက်ကြီးအင်း
ဂူပြောက်ကြီး

The **Shwezigon Pagoda**, N of Bagan, about 500m from Nyaung-U, is the main centre of pilgrimage in Bagan. It is the greatest temple of King Anawrahta's reign. A sacred relic of the Buddha is supposed to have been put on the back of a white elephant by the king and the Shwezigon marks the spot where the elephant knelt down on the river bank (Shwezigon means golden stupa on a sandbank). Anawrahta is reputed to have started the building of this pagoda, but it was finished by his son, King Kyanzittha. It was repaired over the years by several kings but never very much altered – although pilgrims' donations have funded many additions to the temple platform. The Shwezigon is one of the most important pagodas in Myanmar as it is believed to contain the Buddha's collar bone, his 'frontlet' bone and one of his teeth. It is also the first major monument built in Burmese, rather than the earlier Mon style, and the first pagoda to have nat images allowed within its precincts. The Shwezigon was a prototype for many later Burmese stupas.

Villages

Myinkaba

Myinkaba, to the S of Bagan, is well known for its bamboo 'cottage-industry'. The bamboo is floated down the Ayeyarwady in the wet season from N Myanmar and made into walls for houses, roofing and is also used in Bagan's lacquerware industry.

Minnanthu

Minnanthu, to the E of Bagan, is an agricultural village which specializes in the production of sesame and peanut oil. The village is well worth a look around, if only to view its cow-driven sesame seed grinders.

Nyaung U

Nyaung U (also spelt Nyaung-Oo) is NE of Bagan, and the main settlement on the Bagan plain. Visitors arriving from the airport will drive through Nyaung-U – and past the nearby Shwezigon – on the way to hotels around Bagan itself. Nyaung-U is a busy, modern untidy town with a few friendly tea-shops and a big market every day.

New Bagan

New Bagan, see page 183, small morning market.

The golden stupa rises from five terraces (three square, two round) each symbolizing a different state of nirvana. Stairways from all sides lead to the top of the 3rd terrace. The terrace plinths are decorated with green-glazed jataka plaques – most of which are now weathered – which illustrate the former lives of the Buddha. The terraces are closed to the public to prevent theft of the plaques. The main stupa was partially destroyed by the earthquake in 1975 and the old *hti* sits at the right of the entrance – it now rotates electronically with flashing lights and wishing bowls. Pilgrims armed with coins aim at the various bowls in the hope that they might win the lottery, become learned or pass their exams. On the N side there is a tiny hole in the pavement between the temple and the stupa which reflects the stupa when filled with water. The story goes that this little hole enabled visiting kings to view the top of the stupa without losing their ornate headgear.

On each of the four sides of the stupa, King Anawrahta built a small square temple for worshippers; each of these houses a standing Buddha in bronze – the largest surviving bronzes from Bagan. Anawrahta ordered all pagan statues to be brought into the temple to convert villagers to Buddhism. The 37 nats – many of which are riding mythological animals – are housed in an insignificant-looking building at the N-E corner of the pagoda precinct – originally they were on the lower terraces (almost Inca-looking). This building is also home to the earliest known figure of the god Indra in Myanmar. On the S side of the stupa there is a small pavilion with two statues of the local nats, Shwenyothin and his son Shwesaka. If you throw your coins into the bowls on the lucky 'merry-go-round' you can free yourself 'from five enemies': water, fire, the king, thieves, and those who hate you. In front of them is a wishing stone: when you pick it up the first time it should feel light; if it feels heavy the second time you pick it up, your wish will come true. The Shwezigon Pagoda's annual festival takes place in Nov during the full moon – it is a particularly exciting time to visit the temple. There are several stalls on the S and E sides. The *best time to visit* the Shwezigon is at

Source: Ecole Françals d'Extrême-Orient

about 1800. During the day, the 'shops' are a bit of a nuisance.

A stone's-throw from the Shwezigon is the simple **Kyanzittha Cave Temple**, which served as a place of lodging for monks. Its long dark corridors are painted with murals, some of which depict the Mongul soldiers who invaded Bagan in 1287. The temple is believed to date from Anawrahta's or Kyanzittha's reign.

Close to Nyaung-U itself is the **Sapada Stupa**, a monument to Myanmar's good relations with Ceylon (Sri Lanka). Sapada, a Burmese monk, travelled to Ceylon for ordination and on his return to Bagan in 1181 erected this stupa to commemorate his visit. It is distinctively Sinhalese in style with its box-like relic chamber and circular stem.

North and East of Nyaung-U

Kyaukgu Umin Temple – or Rock Cave Tunnel – is to the E of Nyaung-U. This early temple is built into the side of a cliff, with a high archway forming the main entrance. Around the entrance are impressive friezes and decorated door jambs. Opposite, at the back of a large square hall, is a large statue of the Buddha seated on a lotus throne. There are also niches with stone reliefs and painted panels. A series of tunnels with meditation chambers have been excavated deep into the hillside. The main temple dates from the 11th century but the terraces and small stupa are believed to have been built by King Narapatisithu. It is dark inside; visitors should bring a torch.

The **Kondawgyi Temple** or 'Great Royal Mound' overlooks the Kyaukgu

North and East of Nyaung-U

Kondawgyi Temple
ကုန်းတော်ကြီး
Kyaukgu Umin Temple
ကျောက်ဂူဥမင်
Thetkyamuni Temple
သကျမုနိ
Thamihwet Temple
သမီးဝှက်

Umin. Similar in date and style to the Thetkyamuni temple, it is a square block with receding terraces mounted by a large stupa.

Close-by is the **Thetkyamuni Temple**; it has entrances on all four sides, but the main porched entrance is orientated to the W. The temple dates from the late 13th century and has some decipherable examples of contemporary wall paintings, based on the Jataka tales. The shrine paintings are not in such good condition.

Southeast of Nyaung-U are the **Thamihwet** and **Hmyathat Cave Temples**: formed by the excavation of hillsides during the 12th and 13th centuries. The complex of passages and cells were created for monks as they were supposed to be conducive to prayer and meditation.

South of Bagan to Myinkaba

The **Mingalazedi Stupa**, S of Bagan and close to the *Thiripyitsaya Hotel*, with its soft, fluid lines, represents the height of Burmese pagoda architecture. It was built by King Narathihapati – 'the king who ran away from the Chinese' – in 1284, 3 years before Kublai Khan's invasion and the fall of Bagan. It is a well-proportioned pagoda and is noted for its beautiful terracotta jataka plaques around the terraces, which have been heavily eroded over the years. They are prized by the art world and many have been stolen; some are still for sale in antique shops in Bangkok's River City shopping complex. The small stupas at the corners of the stepped terraces are in the form of the *kalasa* – or sacred pot. On the top of the third terrace the four larger stupas balance the central stupa, which tapers to a pinnacle above the bell. The stairways enhance the soaring effect of the stupa.

The **Shwesandaw**, to the W of the Mingalazedi, was built by Anawrahta and has a strong Mon influence. The stupa has a more cylindrical bell, topped by moulded rings. The five receding terraces are accessible on all four sides by long flights of steps. There are also two octagonal bases immediately below the bell. It is believed to enshrine some sacred hairs of the Buddha, obtained from Bago (Pegu). It is also known as the Ganesh Pagoda as a stone figure of the Hindu elephant-god, Ganesh (the patron god of the Mons), was originally

South of Bagan

Abeyadana Temple
အပယ်ရတနာ
Gubyaukgyi Temple
ဂူပြောက်ကြီး
Manuha Temple
မနူဟာ
Mingalazedi Temple
မင်္ဂလာစေတီဘုရား
Nagayon Temple
နဂါးရုံ
Nanpaya
နန်းဘုရား
Shwesandaw Temple
ရွှေဆံတော်ဘုရား

placed at each corner of the stone terraces. A local monk donated money to have this stupa whitewashed, making it stand out rather too dramatically on the Bagan plain. (The only other white washed pagodas are the series of stupas which make up Min O Chan Tha.) Nearby is a brick building (Shinbinthalyaung temple) containing a reclining Buddha which is thought to date from the 11th century.

The **Gubyaukgyi Temple** on the N side of Myinkaba was built by Prince Rajakumar in 1113 and dedicated to his father, King Kyanzittha. Rajakumar commissioned a quadrilingual inscription in which he gave an account of his meritous deeds and listed a chronology of the Bagan kings in Mon, Pali, Burmese and Pyu. The Rosetta Stone (also known as the Myazedi Pillar) was found near the Myazedi Stupa, next to the temple, in 1917. It is now in the Bagan Museum (see page 189). The Gubyaukgyi has the characteristics of the earlier Mon temples, with a dark central shrine, a corridor lit by perforated stone windows and a large hall with its entrance facing E. The spire is straight-sided and tapered like that of the Maha Bodhi. The exterior is decorated with exquisite plaster carvings and the interior contains paintings of the jataka tales, including one of Gautama Buddha during his incarnation as a hermit. They are some of the earliest surviving paintings in Bagan, but many have been removed by collectors. There are 28 Buddhas, each sitting under a different tree. Each incarnation of the Buddha is believed to have achieved enlightenment under a different species of tree. The temple is

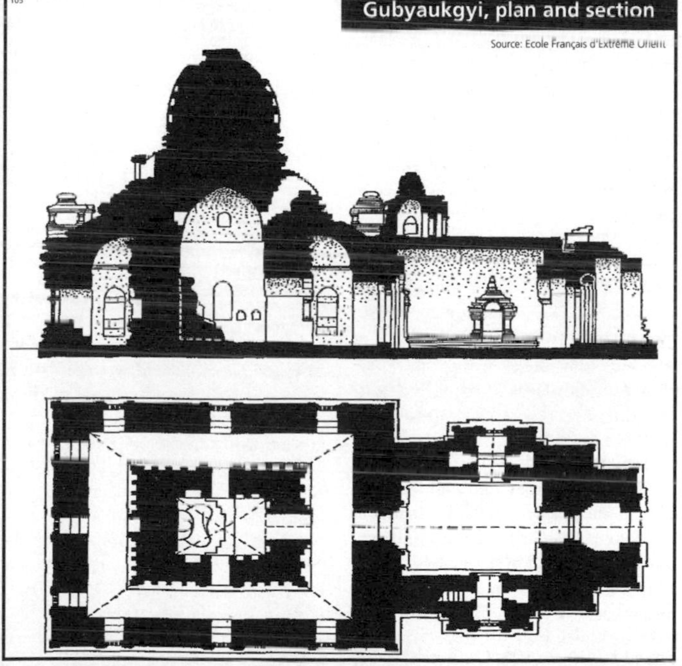

Gubyaukgyi, plan and section

Source: Ecole Français d'Extrême Orient

often locked, but permission to visit it can be obtained from the Department of Archaeology, next to the museum.

The **Myazedi**, next to the Gubyaukgyi, is said to have been built by Anawrahta in order to atone for the crime of killing his predecessor and half brother, Sokkade, in a duel for the throne in 1044. The low round terraces and an elongated bell show that it was built before the Mon-Buddhist influence on Bagan. It has been restored by donations but is heavily whitewashed and with a gilded stupa.

The **Manuha Temple**, just off the road on the S side of Myinkaba, was built by the captive King Manuha of Thaton, brought to Pagan by King Anawrahta in 1057 after his conquest of the Mon Kingdom. Manuha is supposed to have sold his last jewels to build the temple. Inside are three Buddha images, cramped into a small space, symbolizing the king's captivity. The main gold statue has a 'heavy' chest, which is thought to represent the vanquished Manuha's misery. The reclining Buddha at the back of the main shrine lies in the death position, with the head to the N. The upper storey collapsed during the 1975 earthquake.

Next to the Manuha is the Hindu **Nanpaya Temple**. Some believe this was the prison of the captive Mon king, who is thought to have worked as a temple slave. Others attribute it to one of Manuha's descendants, who built it during the reign of King Narapatisithu on the site of Manuha's residence, in memory of him. It was obviously designed by Mon architects and craftsmen and is the only temple in Bagan built in sandstone and brick. It is thought to be the first free-standing 'cave' (or hollow square) temple at Bagan. The perforated windows are set in frames of pilasters on which rest arch-pediments, each enclosing a *kalasa* pot. Within the main shrine are four square stone pillars; two sides of each are carved with fantastic figures of seated Brahmas and the two other sides with ornate floral designs. Prior to their adoption of Theravada Buddhism, the Mon had been Hindu, hence the strong Brahman influence, particularly in the interior stone relief carvings. The Mon were well known for their stone carving, much of it is so intricate that it could have been carved from wood. Unfortunately the Brahmas have had their stomachs gouged out by treasure hunters. In the centre is a low square pedestal – there is no indication of what it originally supported.

The **Abeyadana Temple**, on the W side of the Myinkaba road S of the village, is ascribed to King Kyanzittha (1084-1113). It is believed to have been built on the spot where his wife, Abeyadana, came and waited for him when he was in hiding, after Kyanzittha had incurred the wrath of his half-brother, King Sawlu (1077-1084), whom he eventually deposed. It resembles the Nagayon (see below), but has three perforated windows on the walls of the main block and a bell-shaped stupa above the terraces instead of a *sikhara*, like that of the Nagayon. The bell is topped by a prominent *harmika* – or reliquary casket – and an octagonal tapering spire. A miniature stupa resembling the main spire stands at each corner of the first terrace; a *kalasa* pot stands on the second terrace and a corner crest on the upper terrace. In the sanctuary is a large image of a seated Buddha in brick. The paintings on the outer wall of the corridor represent Bodhisattvas while on the inner walls there are figures of Brahma, Vishnu, Siva and Indra. There are some surviving jataka paintings on the walls of the front hall. It is necessary to bring a torch to inspect these paintings; the temple is usually locked, but permission to visit it can be obtained form the Department of Archaeology.

Legend has it that the **Nagayon Temple** was built by King Kyanzittha on the spot he was given protection by a *naga* (water serpent) in the course of his flight from King Sawlu, who he later overthrew. The temple has the usual hall, facing N, a dark corridor and an inner chamber. The pinnacle, in the shape of a mitre, stands above curvilinear roofs and square terraces with corner stupas. The main entrance has double pedimented gables. Within the hall are niches containing stone reliefs of the life of the Buddha. The hall and the corridor are paved with green-glazed stones. The corridor is ventilated with five perforated windows on each side. The outer walls of the shrine and the corridor walls have niches housing stone sculptures, depicting scenes from the Buddha's life. Paintings in the corridor depict similar scenes. Inside, there is a stucco image of the Buddha, double life size, under the hood of a huge naga. It is characteristic of the Mon style and is very similar to temples in India's Orissa region. The Nagayon was badly renovated after the 1975 earthquake.

Further south to Thiripyitsaya

The **Somingyi Monastery** is on the road between Myinkaba and New Bagan. It is one of the few brick-built monasteries on the Bagan plain – most were built of wood and did not survive. The ruined complex consists of a main hall, surrounded by a lobby to the E, a chapel to the W and small cells to the N and S. The chapel is a small, square, 2-storeyed building with a door opening on the E side, connecting it with the central hall by a passage.

Just S of the Somingyi are the **Sister Temples**. The elder sister, Sein Nyet Ama, built the temple in the 12th century. It is a typical square temple with entrances on all four sides, the E entrance being the main one. There are remnants of ornate stucco work. The younger sister, Sein Nyet Nyima, built the stupa, complete with guardian lions on the corners.

The **Lokananda** was built by King Anawrahta in 1059 and marks the S boundary of Bagan; Anawrahta built four stupas at the four corners of the city. It has a tall cylindrical bell similar to the Pyu-style stupa, and three octagonal terraces; the lower two can be reached by flights of steps on all four sides. Below the pagoda, there used to be an anchorage for large trading vessels, which was used when the water level was too low for them to dock at Bagan proper. The Lokananda has a modern compound, whitewashed stupa but good views of the river.

South to Thiripyitsaya

East Petleik Temple
အရှေ့ဖက်လိပ်
Lokananda Temple
လောကနန္ဒာ
Sister Temples
ညီအစ်မဘုရား
Somingyi Monastery
စိုးမင်းကြီးကျောင်း
West Petleik Temple
အနောက်ဖက်လိပ်

The twin Petleik pagodas, **East Petleik** and **West Petleik** are also attributable to King Anawrahta. These were half-buried by debris but when excavated, two tiers of unglazed terracotta tiles illustrating scenes from the jataka tales were recovered from around their bases. Originally, all 550 plaques were found in these temples, but many have been stolen over the years. The W Petleik is better-preserved. A vaulted corridor would originally have led around the base to house the jataka plaques (which have now been touched-up and repaired) and an entrance chamber facing E at both pagodas. Both temples are usually locked, but tour guides normally bring keys with them.

East of Bagan

The **Dhammayangyi Temple**, to the SE of Bagan, is similar to the Ananda in plan, but is even bigger. It is an impressive structure and looks magnificent in the evening light. The temple was built by the notorious King Narathu. There are four main entrances, but only the outer corridors are accessible as the interior is blocked by brickwork for an unknown reason. Like the Ananda, the Dhammayangyi has large porticoes in the centre of all four sides, forming the shape of a Greek cross. The top of the central stupa crumbled in the 1975 earthquake; the staircase to the top is on the E side.

The **Sulamani Temple** is just beyond the Dhammayangyi and was built by King Narapatisithu. It is one of the first examples of the Late Period of temple architecture and, like the Dhammayangyi, has no dark chambers or deep alcoves. It is characterized by the use of smaller bricks, the perfection of its arches and its elaborate stucco-work. The Sulamani consists of two storeys, each crowned by terraces ornamented with parapets and small stupas at the corners. Each storey is a square with four porches facing the cardinal points; the porch on the E face is larger than the rest and was reserved for royalty. The upper storey is almost the same height as the lower storey and access is via two narrow flights of steps.

East of Bagan and excursions

Dhammayangyi Temple
ဓမ္မရံကြီး
Lemyethna Temple
လေးမျက်နှာ
Kyatkau
ကျုတ်ကောင်
Mount Popa
ပုပ္ပားတောင်
Nandamanuya Temple
နန္ဒာမည
Nat Htaunt Kaung Monastery
နတ်ထောင့်ကောင်ကျောင်း
Sulamani Temple
ရူဠာမနိ
Thambula Temple
သမ္ဗူလ

A vaulted corridor runs round the central pillar with a statue of the Buddha on each side. There is an image chamber in a recess on the E side of the central block, with another vaulted corridor running around it. The walls and vaults were originally covered with murals; those remaining mostly date from the 18th century, although the paintings on the ceiling are older. The building is well lit with doorways ornamented with flame arches – the stucco work at the Sulamani is some of the best in Bagan. An enormous treasure-trove was discovered in the stupa of this temple following the 1975 earthquake. Unlike treasure from many of Bagan's other stupas which, along with Buddha heads and jataka plaques, has been smuggled out of the country and sold, the Sulamani's treasure has now been re-enshrined.

Around Minnanthu Village

The first temple to the N of Minnanthu is the whitewashed **Lemyethna**, meaning 'Temple of the Four Faces'. The bright and airy temple was built in the early 13th century by a minister at the court of King Htilominlo in the style of Bagan's later temples. Unfortunately the original wall paintings have been whitewashed and modern murals painted over the top. This temple is still in regular use by local villagers.

The next temple N of the village is **Thambula**. It is thought to have been built by Queen Thambula, wife of King Uzana. This later style temple is also well lit, making it easy to see the Chinese-influenced murals – note the Chinese-looking Buddhas, the ladies with Chinese hair styles and eyes, and the use of yellow.

A bit further N is the **Nandamanuya Temple** built by King Kyazwa. Some of the exterior stucco-work is still in good condition – such as the monster head on the left side of the entrance. There is a Mahayana influence in the paintings and many of these floral designs are used on lacquerware. The paintings are very complete and the colour has survived well in many of the panels. The temple is usually locked.

The **Dhammayakacedi** is a large temple in a pentagonal shape, and the **Tayobpyaymin** provides panoramic views from its summit.

Kyatkau is a cave monastery next door to Nandamanuya temple. A maze of tunnels and cells, the temple is still in use. A monk, U Narada, meditated in here for 40 years. He was highly respected locally and there are pictures of his funeral in 1988 in the monastery.

Excursions

The most popular excursion is up the Ayeyarwady to **Nat Htaunt Kaung Monastery**. It is still inhabited by monks and has good woodcarvings, although much

King Narathu

It is difficult to imagine a nastier piece of work than King Narathu, the man responsible for the construction of the imposing Dhammayangyi temple, whose powerful shape dominates the Bagan plain. He ascended to the throne by murdering his father, King Alaungsithu, and then his older brother, Minthinsaw. He then executed one of his wives – a beautiful Hindu princess from India – after she had displeased him. The homicidal Narathu built the temple as an act of atonement and in an effort to make some much-needed merit. Nonetheless, he decided to kill the architect once the temple had begun to take shape, to ensure that he could never build another like it.

According to Burmese chronicles, Narathu was assassinated before the Dhammayangyi was completed, just 2 years after he had seized the throne. His past misdeeds had finally caught up with him, for his assassins were 8 Indians, dispatched by his late wife's father. They came to Bagan disguised as Brahmin priests to avenge the execution of the princess. Narathu was remembered as *Kalagya Min* – 'He who was slain by Indians'. The Dhammayangyi temple he left behind is notable for its fine brickwork. But the temple's bricklayers fared only slightly better than the architect. King Narathu is said to have inspected their brickwork by testing the gaps with a pin; if it did not measure up to his standards he had the bricklayer's hands chopped off.

The Mahagiri Nats – a fairy tale from old Bagan

Once upon a time, during King Thinlikyaung of Thiripyitsaya's reign – in the 4th century – there was a good-looking blacksmith called Nga Tinde. He lived with his sister outside the capital. He was known as 'Mr Handsome' and was very popular with the locals, which made the king very jealous. The wicked king sent his men to kill Mr Handsome, but the blacksmith was warned in the nick of time and escaped into the woods. The king fell in love with Nga Tinde's beautiful sister, Ma Sawme or Shwemyethna (Golden Face). He soon married her and tricked her into persuading her brother to come out of hiding. But when Mr Handsome emerged, he was immediately captured by the king's guards, tied to a saga tree and burned alive. In despair, Golden Face threw herself into the flames and perished with her brother.

Following their violent deaths, the siblings became mischievous nats and lived in the saga tree. To pre-empt their mischief-making, King Thinlikyaung ordered the tree to be chopped down and thrown into the Ayeyarwady. But this made his subjects very angry and they forced the king to fish the tree-trunk out of the river. Statues of Mr Handsome and Golden Face were carved from the saga wood and these were carried, with great pomp and ceremony, to the top of Mount Popa. For the next 700 years, every king, on his coronation, would climb Mount Popa and visit the 2 nats to appease them. Today the images of Mr Handsome and Golden Face, the Lords of the Great Mountain and the guardian spirits of Bagan, stand in the prayer niches that flank the ancient Sarabha Gate, at the entrance to the old walled city. Neither image does particular justice to the good-looking couple.

has been stolen. En route is **Selen** village, standing on another island in the middle of the Ayeyarwady. *Getting there*: rowing boat (50 kyat pp); motor boat (500 kyat); the monastery can be reached by boat from the river bank, *Ayeyar Hotel*.

Another riverside village is **Pakkoku** (see page 157). **Mount Popa** known as Myanmar's Olympus, lies 85 km SE of Bagan. *Popa* means 'flower' in Sanskrit and is believed to be the sacred home of the nats. See page 205 for Mount Popa entry, and page 67 for background to the nats and nat worship.

Local festivals

Jan: *Ananda Pagoda's annual festival* (movable) with dancing, music and stalls.

Nov: *Shwezigon Pagoda's annual festival* (movable) – pilgrims travel from all over Myanmar; dancing, music and stalls.

Dec: *Annual Festival of the Spirits* – festivities in honour of the Mahagiri nats, Nga Tinde and Shwemyethana, whose home is Mount Popa (see above).

Local information

● Orientation

Bagan is 42 km square with several small villages. Nyaung-U is the main centre where buses and boats stop; the airport is close by. Hotels are situated in three distinct areas: Nyaung U/Wetkki-In, Old Bagan and New Bagan (or Bagan Myothit). Nyaung U is popular with backpackers, Old Bagan is for tour groups and tourist-class travellers. Visitors must pay US$10 entrance fee to site when checking into hotel.

● Accommodation

Price guide

A+	over US$200	**C**	US$25-50
A	US$100-200	**D**	US$10-25
B	US$50-100	**E**	under US$10

NB All telephone calls must be directed through an operator. During 1996 all Bagan telephone numbers changed; the six figure numbers listed below should be correct, but two and three digit numbers may have changed.

A *Irrawaddy Princess*, floating hotel, restaurant, hot water (can be booked in Yangon T 220854).

B-C *Thiripyitsaya*, on the riverfront to the S side of the city wall, government owned, a/c, h/w, restaurant, pool (dirty), money-changing facilities (official rate), this is also where black market money changers hang out (see **Banks & money changers**), gift shop, bungalows/chalets, promoted as the 'best hotel in Myanmar' which is obviously untrue, not well maintained, it seems older than it is, IDD phones (immediate connection).

C *Aung Mingala*, opp The Shwezigon Pagoda, T 240018, small guesthouse with a/c and cold water showers, has character; **C** *Ayar*, nr Buphaya Temple and the boat landing in old Bagan, T 24, some a/c, more expensive rooms are upstairs with hot water and wooden floors, new rooms being built, price incl breakfast; **C** *Bagan (or Thante)*, beyond the *Co-operative Hotel*, T 2240143, F 6663307, some a/c, some h/w, restaurant, choice of rooms/guesthouse 'block' and two lots of 'chalets', landscaped grounds on the banks of the Ayeyarwady, surrounded by stupas, some wooden, some brick accommodation, rooms are badly soundproofed, bathrooms not very clean, poor breakfast, newer riverfront chalets have a fine view, good value; **C** *NK Betelnut Inn*, Khayea Pin St, Ryansittharr Quarter, New Bagan, T 25, a/c, price incl breakfast, 8 very small cottages; **C-D** *Golden Express*, on the main road between Nyaung-U and Old Bagan, T 37, a/c and fan, friendly and well-run with clean rooms, garden, restaurant, serves European and Chinese food, breakfast incl, good value, rec; **C-D** *Palm*, 9 Thamudarit Ward, E of New Bagan, T 90589, a/c, private bathrooms (hot water), restaurant, car, boat, bike and pony trap hire, lovely little hotel lost in the ruins, local style, with bamboo roof; **C-D** *Zar Chi Win 2*, Nyaung U, T 334, same family as *Zar Chi Win* in Yangon, some rooms with a/c and bathrooms, price incl breakfast, laundry service available, friendly.

D *Co-Operative*, Old Bagan, fan only and mosquito nets, restaurant (not rec), unkempt and basic, popular with travellers; **D** *Eden*, Nyaung U, a/c, bathroom with hot water, fridge, clean rooms, breakfast incl; **D** *Golden Myanmar*, Nyaung U, T 240046, restaurant, more expensive rooms have a/c, bathroom with hot water, cheaper rooms are basic, price

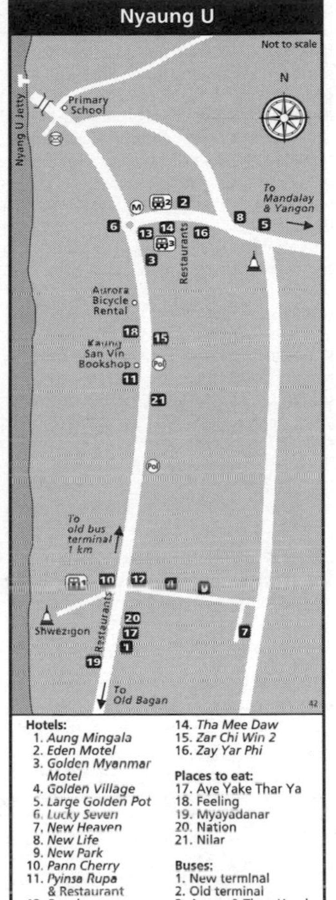

incl breakfast, friendly establishment, free transport to airport or ferry; **D** *Lucky Seven*, Nyaung U, T 77, basic guesthouse with fan rooms and shared bathrooms, clean rooms and good breakfast incl; **D** *Myathidar Guesthouse*, New Bagan, family-run, will make evening meals on request, bicycle hire; **D** *New Heaven*, Thiripyitsaya, Block No 5, Nyaung U, T 240061, all 10 rm with a/c, own bathroom and hot water, breakfast incl, a pleasant, quiet guesthouse, tours and transport organized, rec; **D** *New Wave*, on main road nr *Golden*

Express, T 218, a/c, some rooms with own bathroom (cold water showers), good location, friendly and clean, breakfast incl, laundry service; **D** ***Pann Cherry***, nr Shwezigon Pagoda, Nyaung U, T 228, some a/c and private bathrooms (cold water only), breakfast incl, 11 rm in a cool house; **D** ***Phyo Guesthouse***, Myinkaba, S of Old Bagan, fan, no hot water, outside toilets/showers, bikes for hire, breakfast, good position for sightseeing, surrounded by pagodas but some distance from town and the better restaurants (to get around this, the owner drives guests to the restaurant of their choice – no charge), Aung Mye, the owner, is friendly and informative, simple meals available, evening meal on request, good breakfast; **D** *Viewpoint Guesthouse*, on road between Nyaung U and Bagan, a/c, breakfast; **D-E** ***Pyinsa Rupa***, Nyaung U, T 240067, restaurant, some rooms with a/c and own bathroom, very clean good rooms, breakfast incl, friendly, helpful staff; **D-E** ***Royal***, nr Shwezigon Pagoda, Nyaung U, T 285, fairly clean but small rooms, not well decorated, some rooms with attached cold water shower.

E *Large Golden Pot*, nr airport road and Thiripyitsaya Rd crossing, friendly, only 6 rm, Burmese guests also, helpful owner; **E** *New Life*, nr airport road and Thiripyitsaya Rd crossing, T 240164, some a/c, some bathrooms attached with hot water, plain, clean, rather hot, no breakfast; **E** *New Park*, Thiripyitsaya, Block No 4, T 240122, fan only rooms, very helpful 'madam', quiet and clean, all rooms with attached bathroom, bicycles for hire; **E** *Shwe Li*, close to market in Nyaung U, on the Bagan-Nyaung U road, T 291, room with fan and attached bathroom, basic and clean; **E** *Tha Mee Daw*, Nyaung U, all rooms with bathroom, some with a/c, clean and basic, breakfast incl, friendly place; **E** ***Winner Guesthouse***, Wetkyi-In, next to *New Wave Guesthouse*, free bicycles, sidecar from bus terminal, complimentary breakfast, noisy, only tourist restaurants nearby.

● Places to eat

Price guide

♦♦♦♦	over US$15+	(over 180 kyat)
♦♦♦	US$5-15	(120-180 kyat)
♦♦	US$2-5	(60-120 kyat)
♦	under US$2	(under 60 kyat)

Restaurants in all the hotels provide standard Burmese/European fare.

Bagan: ♦♦***Mya Ye Da Nar***, Wetkyi-in village (formerly in Old Bagan), Burmese/Chinese dishes; ♦♦***Ever Queen***, Old Bagan, friendly and the travellers hang out, mainly Chinese dishes, outside tables.

Between Nyaung-U and Bagan: ♦♦♦*Aye Yake Thar Yar*, opp the Shwezigon just outside Nyuang-U, Burmese (2 hrs notice) and Chinese, rec; ♦♦***Myayadanar***, classic travellers fare – omelettes, shakes, toast and honey, also serves Chinese dishes and Burmese if ordered 1 hr in advance, small handicraft stall inside; ♦♦***Sarabha***, by Sarabha Gate, outside eating area under the trees, excellent food, very friendly welcome, rec; ♦***Nation***, opp Shwezigon, Chinese dishes and Burmese if pre-ordered, very good food, friendly staff, good value, rec.

Nyaung U: *Aye Yake Thar Ya*, next to *New Heaven Hotel*, good restaurant with views of Shwezigon. ♦♦♦***Pyinsa Pura***, good food, friendly service; ♦♦***Nilar***, good food; ♦***Pyi Sone***, next to *New Wave Guesthouse*, good food.

New Bagan: ♦♦*River View Restaurant*, Chinese and Burmese dishes to order, fabulous views over the river.

● Airline offices

Air Mandalay, Main Rd, T 289001.

● Banks & money changers

At MTT next to Sarabha Gate, Bagan and at the *Thiripitsaya Hotel*. Black market rates are about 10 kyat/$; lower than in Yangon – after some bargaining.

● Entertainment

Cultural Show, in hall just outside city walls, starts 1830ish; **Zaw Gyi**, Pyan Saya Hla, next to *Ever Queen* restaurant, traditional puppet show, 1830. Marionette plays in a small theatre on 66th St (close to the intersection with 28th St).

● Post & telecommunications

It is possible to phone overseas from the *Thiripyitsaya Hotel* – at exorbitant rates.

● Shopping

There are small stalls selling lacquerware and antiques outside all the main temples, hotels, restaurants and the airport. Bagan is known for its lacquerware; you'll find the finest pieces here as well as a good range of antique items. Stalls also sell small antiques: tattoo sticks, door knockers, opium weights, betel nut cutters, bells and small brass statues. **NB** If you're taken to a lacquerware shop by locals they will take 20% commission.

Lacquerware: *Maung Aung Myan*, nr Gubyaukgyi, Myinkaba. Family lacquerware shop, good quality and large range. *Pagan Lacquerware School and Museum*, on road to the Irra Inn/Buphaya temple, high quality pieces made by the students can be bought at reasonable prices (not always open); *Shweae-insi*, next to MTT, Bagan, lacquerware and handicrafts, run as a cooperative but buys from other shops, so more expensive; *Thayar-Aye monastery*, Bagan, good selection at reasonable prices. *The Golden Tortoise*, New Bagan, the best in the area, selling top quality lacquerware, but as much of it is made to order there is often little choice at the shop, visitors can order items which the shop will pack for export, it is also a good place to see all the different stages of lacquerware production, fixed price; *Shwe Sin*, next to *Golden Express Hotel*, good range and good quality; *U Ba Nyein & Son*, family shop nr Ananda Pagoda, the shop was previously in the old town and they have plans to open a shop in New Bagan; *U Kan Htun-Daw Hla Myaing and Ma Moe Moe*, Ywar Thit Quarter, Bagan; family workshop – planning to open in New Bagan. Probably the best shop for smaller, more portable wares. There are several small modern and antique lacquerware shops around Bagan's temples: the ones outside Thatbinnyu are reckoned to be the best but there are others around the Nanpaya and Manuha temples in **Myinkaba** and outside the Buphaya, Bagan.

Antique lacquerware: there are quite a few places scattered about, but beware; the quality is very variable. *U Ba Nyein*, on the Main Rd (see above), is a good price and friendly. *Ma Khin Aye Han*, nr Thatbinnyu. *Muang Muang*, Wetkyiginn village on way to Nyaung-U.

Handicrafts & antiques: there are stalls in the main entrances of the Ananda, Shwezigon, Nanpaya and Htiminlo and outside Thatbinnyu (which are probably the best). 'Antiques' should be treated with a measure of suspicion. Tourists buying from stalls in the main temples are at risk of attack from manic salespeople; most are keen to engage in barter, exchanging statues or paintings for Bangkok T-shirts and copy-watches.

Markets: *Nyaung-U market* open all day every day.

● Tour companies & travel agents

Mr Aung Than Kyaw at *New Heaven Hotel* can organize car rental and taxis to almost anywhere. *Diethelm*, Airport Rd, 5 Myay Tha Q, Nyaung U.

● Tourist offices

MTT, next to Sarabha Gate, old Bagan, T 228900.

● Transport

193 km from Mandalay, 690 km from Yangon.

Local Bicycle hire: many places hire out bikes; it is still the cheapest way to get around. For instance – outside *Myayadanar Restaurant*, *Ayeyar Hotel*, *Golden Express Hotel*, *Phyo Guesthouse* (100 kyat/day for regular bike, 150 kyat/day for mountain bike). Bicycling is the cheapest and most flexible way to get around the temples; many are not accessible by vehicle. **Boats**: small boats for hire from the jetty of the *Ayeyar Hotel* (200-300 kyat/hour). **Buses & pickups**: from Nyaung-U to New Bagan but the service is irregular and unpredictable. **Car hire**: some guesthouses have cars for charter. The *Phyo Guesthouse* charges US$20 for a trip with 4 people to Mount Popa. **Horse & cart**: 500 kyat/day (dawn to dusk – with a generous siesta but much the easiest way to get around). MTT guides can help find an English-speaking driver.

Air Airport is at Nyaung-U, 10 km N of Bagan. Regular connections with Mandalay and Yangon, Heho and Chiang Mai, Thailand.

Train Nearest station on the Mandalay-Yangon line is Thazi. Regular buses leave Thazi for Bagan via Meiktila, (see below). But the nearest station is in Kyaukpadaung, 56 km away – however this line is only from Pyinmana-Taungdwingyi-Kyaukpadaung. From Kyaukpadaung there are bus connections to Mandalay, Pyay, Yangon, Meiktila etc. Construction on an extension to Nyaung U has begun.

Road Bus: buses leave from Nyaung-U. Connections with Mandalay and Taunggyi via Meiktila (6-7 hrs). The local bus leaves Nyaung-U at 0400 and arrives in Mandalay at 1400 (250 kyat). It is crowded. There are direct buses from Nyaung-U to Thazi (250 kyat) and Taunggyi (500 kyat), leaving at 0400, 10 hrs, and pick-ups to Magwe (350 kyat). The journey from Bagan to Inle Lake can take a nightmarish 19 hrs or so; be warned! More comfortable express services are springing up; the Mandalay and Yangon services are quite good; *Tiger Head Express*, *Pagan Express*, *Poda Dagon Express*, *Arrow Express*, *Mann Transport*. The trip to Yangon leaves at about 1600, depending on which company you use it takes 15 hrs (1,000 kyat) – a/c but no food although they do provide noisy videos! *Arrow Express* provide food for another 200 kyat. **NB** Buses to/from Bagan are gaining a reputation for thievery – watch your belongings, especially on the overnight trips. **Linecars**: to Kyaukpadaung (change for Popa). **Taxi**: taxis can be chartered for the journey to Inle Lake and Mandalay – much quicker and more comfortable. Expect to pay US$60 for the 7-hr journey; not bad if split 4 ways.

Boat It only makes sense to travel downriver from Mandalay to Bagan as it can take anything from 2 to 3 days upstream. Boats to Pyay leave on Tues, Wed, Fri and Sun at 0700, US$10, 2 days.

MAGWE DIVISION

KYAUKPADAUNG
ကျောက်ပန်းတောင်း

Very few tourists stay overnight in Kyaukpadaung. However the town lies on a major junction, within a few hours or less of Meiktila, Pagan, Magwe, Yenangyaung and Popa. Travellers are sometimes forced to spend a night here; it is also worth stopping off at Kyaukpadaung for a couple of hours, if only to sample the delectable and extensive selection of Indian snacks cooked at the roadside.

In the SW quarter of the town are several Pagan-era pagodas, including **Myatshwegu**, **Thettoyat**, **Sudaungpye** and **Shwedaung U**. Some are unusual architecturally and all have views of the other pagodas and the surrounding area. **Shwedaung U** is the castle-like pagoda to the E. Its story is bound up in the legend of the founding of Kyaukpadaung itself, which means Stone Flower Hill. It is said that King Alaungsithu could travel anywhere he desired by boat as a waterway would magically open up wherever he pointed. One day he sailed to the hill where Shwedaung U now stands and there saw the nat princess Shwemyintin. The King worshipped the nat and she bade him bring her some stone flowers. Alaungsithu bowed to her wishes and brought the nat princess a basket of stone flowers and built a pagoda on the hill in her honour. Shwemyintin now protects the town.

The mountain to the SE of Kyaukpadaung is called Minpoundaung – King Hiding Mountain. Before King Anawrahta – the first of Myanmar's truly great kings – ascended to the throne in 1044 his animist brother tried to kill him. (This became a well-established tradition in Myanmar as the most effective means of preventing any pretenders usurping the throne.) Anawrahta hid here and survived to become

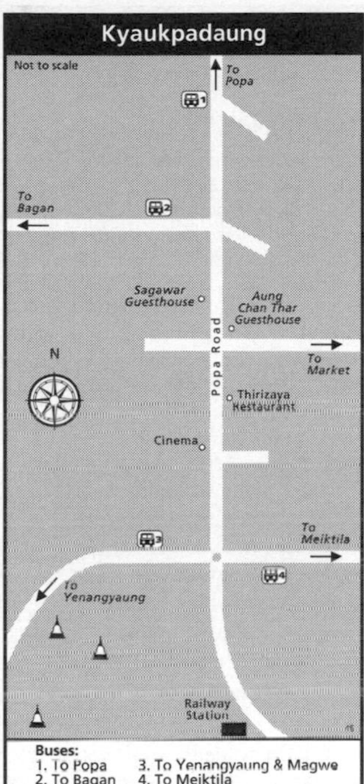

Pagan's greatest pagoda-builder.

• **Accommodation** There are three guesthouses in town but none, as yet, has a license to take foreigners. They are all close to each other, N of the cinema on Popa Rd. Ask at the *Thirizaya Restaurant* to be shown the 'guesthouse': it will take visitors (**E**), but is a brothel and very dirty. The other two guesthouses may also take foreigners but this requires offering far more than the going rate for a room – **D**; they are the ***Aung Chan Thar*** (no indication that it is more than a restaurant) and the ***Sagawar Lodging House***.

• **Transport** 56 km from Bagan, 96 km from Meiktila and Magwe and 19 km from Popa. **Local Linecar**: linecar connections with Bagan, Meiktila, Magwe and Popa from various areas of town (see map).

POPA, MOUNT POPA AND TOUNG KALAT

There is often some confusion over

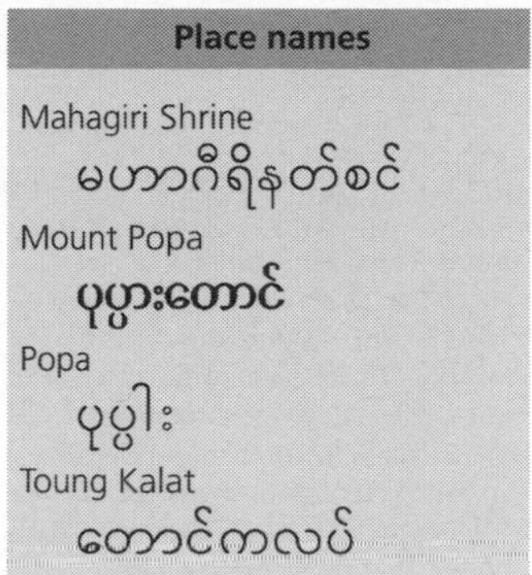

Mount Popa and Toung Kalat, or Temple Hill. Toung Kalat is a comparatively modest volcanic plug thickly clothed, as the name suggests, in temples and shrines. It is sometimes referred to as Mount Popa. But not far away is the real Mount Popa – a mountain in the true sense, rising to over 1,500m. Just to make things even more confusing, there is also Popa town.

Popa is just 5 km from **Toung Kalat**, or **Temple Hill**, the sacred mountain and home of the nats. The Toung is an ancient volcanic plug and its summit is swathed in pagodas and shrines, themselves swarming with monkeys. The temples are of assorted styles and sizes and there are shrines to nats (spirits) as well, with some of their stories in English. The steep climb to the summit takes around 20-30 mins and on a clear day the views can be breathtaking. If it is hazy, though, expect to be rather disappointed at the view.

Across the street from the entrance to the hill's main staircase is a temple to all the 37 nats – the **Mahagiri shrine**. Enjoyable but extremely noisy nat seances (*nat pwe*) are frequently held here. Sometimes they are to thank the nats for good fortune, sometimes to ask advice. Anyone can go in to watch. If the nat *kadaw* or medium commands anyone to do something, they must obey. Some of the transvestite *nat pwe* dancers are among the best traditional dancers in Myanmar.

Between Popa and the Temple Hill there is a fork in the road. The left fork leads to a national park which includes **Mount Popa**, an extinct volcano that rises to 1,518m. Visible from Bagan almost 100 km distant, this is the most magical of Burmese mountains and has been a pilgrimage site for at least 700 years as successive Burmese kings have climbed to the summit to receive the blessings of the nats. Despite the efforts of some Buddhist 'fundamentalists' to stamp out nat worship as an irrational 'superstition' few Burmese would ever knowingly offend a nat and there are various prohibitions that pilgrims to the mountain observe as they make their ascent: they do not wear red or black, they avoid cursing, and they do not take meat with them on the climb. It is possible to climb the mountain in about 4 hrs; the descent takes about 3 hrs. Mount Popa is the celebrated home of Myanmar's ever-meddling guardian Mahagiri Nat.

Local festivals May-Jun: *Festival of spirits* (full moon of Nayon, movable) Scores of pilgrims climb Mount Popa to honour the nats. **Nov/Dec**: *Nat festival* (full moon of Nadaw, movable) Thousands of Burmese from the area climb Mt Popa together. An occasion for general ribaldry and excess.

• **Accommodation** It is possible to stay at the **monastery** about 5 km out of Popa, close to Temple Hill. All visitors are introduced to the *sayadaw*, or abbot, if he is available, rooms are simple and rather dirty, but sleeping mats are provided and clean sheets, the bathroom also leaves a little to be desired in terms of cleanliness, for payment, make a donation to the *sayadaw* the following morning, to get to the monastery take a linecar and ask to be let off at *hpongyi gyaung*. **C** ***Popa Guesthouse***, at the edge of town on Temple Hill road, overpriced, caters largely for visitors on bus tours; **D** ***Shwe Metta***, is the best guesthouse in the area. It is marked by a small sign in Burmese only, next to an iron gate in a whitewashed concrete wall, on the right towards the monastery, clean rooms with a large, quiet garden, modern concrete building with separate showers/baths.

• **Transport** 85 km SE of Bagan. Occasional linecars run between Popa and the cluster of houses and restaurants at the base of the Temple Hill. Most tourists visit Popa from Bagan in a taxi or chartered pick-up, but it is possible to get here by public transport: take a linecar to Kyaukpadaung and from there another linecar on to Popa.

CHAUK ချောက်

50 km S of Nyaung U, Chauk lies on the river, ringed by slow-pumping oil wells. Not much of the oil wealth seems to have spread into the town, nor have the tourist dollars seeped down this way, but people manage to get along. After Pagan, it may seem unremarkable – indeed it is – but it is a typical central Burmese town that can provide other types of enjoyment.

Places of interest

Chauk has a **working waterfront** which is particularly picturesque at sunset. In some of the sandy cliffs near the river you can see caves the Japanese dug to protect their supplies from Allied air raids. Across the street from the large **market** (which sells the usual array of Burmese goods), is a small stationers and bookshop with a few books in English. If you loiter in this shop in the morning, the owner, an English teacher, may turn up for a talk if he is available.

In the evening, people go to the **Maha Aye Zedi Pagoda** to cool their bodies and minds. The pagoda is on a small hill, and catches the breeze. The stupa has a very unusual design, with a small stupa centred under a larger one on a roof. The pagoda museum includes the upper jaw of a stegadon among its treasures. There are unusually life-like sculptures of devout monks and scenes from the life of the Buddha. At the ring of Buddhas to be bathed, you should choose the one for your day of the week (see symbols, page

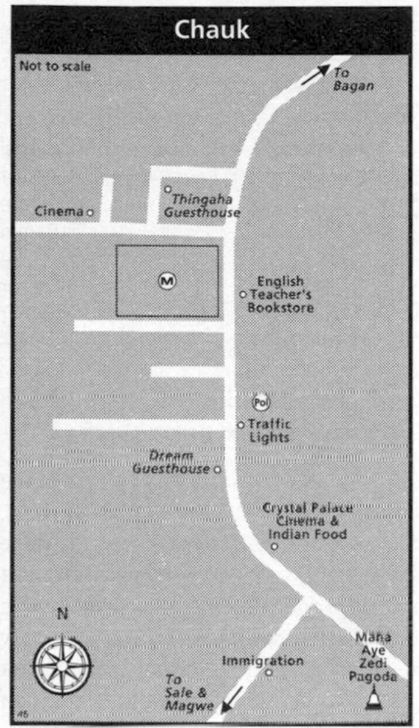

108) and pour one cup of water for each year of your life.

Excursions

Sale, 15 km SW of Chauk, is close to a large collection of Bagan-era monuments (see page 207). *Getting there*: linecars to Sale leave from near the Crystal Palace Cinema.

Local information

● Accommodation

E ***Dream Guesthouse***, on the main road, sign in English, small rooms, clean enough, fan, no mosquito net (screen on window), **E** ***Thingaha Guesthouse***, nr the market, sign in English, small rooms, fan, mosquito net, reasonably clean.

● Places to eat

Burmese food available everywhere. Indian food at the cafe at the ◆◆*Crystal Palace cinema*, some English spoken, great lassis with sprinkling of coconut.

• Transport 50 km S of Nyaung U. **Road Bus**: buses leave for different destinations from different parts of town. Connections to Bagan/Nyaung U, Kyaukpadaung (Popa), Magwe, Meiktila, Mandalay, Yangon.

SALE (SALAY) စလေ

About 15 km SW of Chauk is the town of Sale, on the banks of the Ayeyarwady. Relatively few tourists make it to Sale because, for most, it seems that it is just more of the same. Or rather, just an extension of Bagan, and not as spectacular at that. What Sale has – or rather lacks – which makes it worth the trouble to visit is a general absence of tourists. Sale is a quiet town, one where if you narrow your eyes and imagine hard enough it is possible to think you are back in British-era Burma.

The 100-odd **ruins** scattered outside town are much more modest constructions than those in Bagan. This gives them a homely charm which is absent from the grandiose structures upstream. Who built them and what role Sale played in relation to Bagan is not known. Comparatively little research has been undertaken and the monuments are largely unrenovated. It is sometimes assumed that they were built by 'commoners' rather than royalty but this seems hard to reconcile with evidence from elsewhere in Southeast Asia. It is possible they were the monuments of some minor princely dynasty, but buildings in stone were nearly always reserved for the great and the good – commoners built from wood, and wooden structures from this era have not survived the intervening years.

Sale, unlike Bagan, has continued to be a religious centre and there are several venerable working monasteries in town. There are also a smattering of colonial buildings still standing in the town. Sale is famous for its views and it has a resort here for the 'big people' – but nowhere for foreigners to stay.

Excursions Around 5 km from Sale is an **ancient monastery** which has been in continuous use for several hundred years. It is locally famous for its views, and has a resort where 'big people' relax. *Getting there*: by pony trap.

• **Accommodation** There are no hotels or guesthouses in Sale but visitors stuck here can probably spend the night in town either at one of the town's monasteries or in a local restaurant. The nearest places with accommodation are Chauk (see page 207) and Kyaukpadaung (see page 205).

• **Transport** 15 km from Chauk. From Bagan, the best way to see Sale and the other towns in the area is to travel by boat from Nyaung U to Sale, then take a pickup to either Kyaukpadaung or Chauk (and spending the night in one of these two towns), and then return to Nyaung U by bus the following day. **Road Bus**: travelling by public transport to Sale and back in a day from Nyaung U is tight. Catch the first linecar to Kyaukpadaung and then an onward pickup to Sale. This should allow 3 or 4 hrs in Sale before catching the last bus back at around 1600. The alternative is to hire a car in Nyaung U. From Kyaukpadaung or Chauk it is much easier to visit Sale, and it is worth spending a night in either town. **River** The 0500 ferry from Nyaung U to Pyay stops at Sale as it travels (slowly) downriver, arriving at around 1200.

MAGWE AND MINBU
မကွေး မင်းဘူး

Minbu is in the hot zone and in the evening, people congregate at the Setkaindeh pagoda, overlooking the river, to catch the breezes and sit on the cool stones. As the heat dissipates, young men come out and sit on the bridges and under the trees, playing guitars and singing. Others stroll around, listening to the music and visiting friends.

The **market** to the N of town, near the bus station, is large but unexceptional. In general, the town is somewhat ramshackle, but appealing. It makes a good base from which to explore Magwe (which is more expensive, noisier and less comfortable), and visit the Shwesetdaw and Kyaungdawya pagodas (see **Excursions**, below).

The legend of **Setkaindeh Paya**, at the southern edge of the town, is that the Buddha slept here one night. Afterwards, ogres carried the bed across the river, where you can now see the golden **Myathaloun Pagoda** just N of Magwe. (Myathaloun means 'emerald bed'.) In return, they got a certain sort of fruit. This is what you see demonstrated on the mechanical musical scene in the main building. The pagoda itself is quite large, and is designed to be climbed, with stairs and several terraces running around it. It provides many places for people to sit, pray, meditate and socialize. The tea house at the base of the pagoda is open late. It has particularly good *letpet thout* (pickled tea leaves served with roasted nuts and oil, and, in this case, garlic).

Excursions

Shwesetdaw Pagoda is 50 km from Minbu and easily accessible as a day trip (see page 209). *Getting there*: by linecar.

Kyaungdawya Paya is only 33 km N of Minbu, but there is no direct transport, so getting there takes time. The route passes many old and little-visited pagodas and fords a river. The pagoda is most beautiful at night, and it is possible to sleep at the monastery. Kyaungdawya is a large complex much beloved by the local people. The Buddha is rumoured to have slept a week here, in a sandalwood temple. Many years later, so the legend goes, bandits tried to steal the valuable temple. They were foiled when the Buddha's power made it disappear. Inevitably, a pagoda was built on the site to commemorate the miraculous event. The graceful main stupa is surrounded by a crowd of smaller ones, and a marble terrace, Shwedagon-style. There are many pavilions strewn about to explore or cool off in. People donate their hair in the room next to that showing the Buddha cutting his own locks. From Jul to Sep, enormous fish swim up to the monastery to be fed and petted. *Getting there*: you will need to take a linecar from Minbu to the village of Lehkain (45 kyat). There you can hire a pony trap for the last 7 km, or wait at the three-way crossing for a linecar to the pagoda.

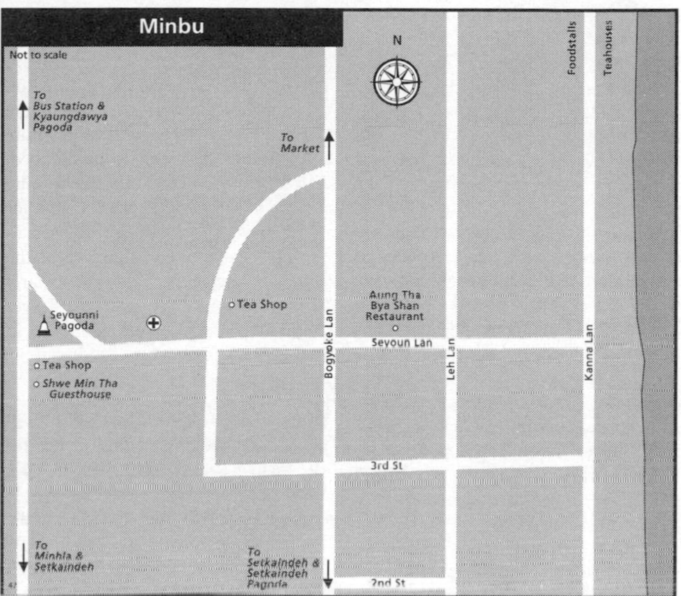

Local information

● Accommodation

F ***Shwe Min Tha Guesthouse***, accepts foreigners, fan, no mosquito net (but screens), more expensive rooms have a/c, the hotel staff are extremely friendly, helpful and funny, with some, limited English, no rooms with attached bathroom, satellite TV in lounge (onto which non a/c rooms open) makes aircon rooms somewhat quieter, however, the TV disappears at about 2200.

● Places to eat

♦♦♦***Aung Tha Bya Shan*** (sign in Burmese only – a low building with wooden lattice-work front), in the centre of town, may charge you triple the going price, but has good Chinese-style food; ♦♦♦-♦♦***Jine restaurant*** (sign in Burmese only) at the bus station has good food and a huge variety of condiments, but tends to overcharge.

Stall food: ♦Along Kanna Lan are simple stalls selling fish and rice.

● Transport

50 km from Padan, 50 km to Shwesetdaw and 150 km from Ann.

Local For transport around town there are pony traps for hire (5-20 kyat) but everything is within walking distance.

Road Trucks to Padan (150-200 kyat), Ann (300-400 kyat), linecars and buses to Shwesetdaw (150 kyat), buses to Yangon (150 kyat), also connections to Taungdwingyi and Mandalay.

River Long-distance transport is irregular. Ferries to Magwe leave from near Setkaindeh pagoda (10 kyat). 400 kyat for a whole boat after 1700 (usually they wait for 10 people).

SHWESETDAW PAGODA
ရွှေစက်တော်ဘုရား

Shwesetdaw Pagoda attracts pilgrims from all over Myanmar. It is especially busy in Mar and Apr. In this dry country of scrubby secondary growth, Shwesetdaw is like an oasis, sitting by a river, in the midst of pretty, green woods. Here are two of the Buddha's footprints left in stone, the only ones in Myanmar. The one down by the river (given to the nagas – sea serpents) is sealed with an iron cover to protect it against the floods during the rainy season. The upper footprint was found by a hunter guided by the god Indra in the form of a black dog (thus the canine motif). The pagoda was founded about 12 centuries ago by a hermit, and rediscovered during the Ava period by a monk who was the reincarnation of King Mindon.

The footprints, several feet long, are thickly covered with gold leaf. Women are not allowed to approach them, as this would damage the footprints' *phon* (see box, page 210). Along the side wall of the terrace of the upper footprint meditate the four previous Buddhas. A copy of the Mahamuni sits near the centre. Aside from the two bustling pagodas where the footprints are located on opposite sides of the river, there are many smaller pagodas, some down paths, and often very quiet among the trees.

A wide variety of curiosities are for sale on the terraces and steps of the main pagodas, from fragrant woods to carved bones. Down by the river are the stalls and restaurants. Ethnic clothing from all over Myanmar is sold here, as people often want to wear their national dress at a holy site. The river is clean and refreshing, and open for bathing. (No changing rooms; bring a longyi to undress and bathe in.)

• **Accommodation** There used to be a number of guesthouses here to provide accommodation and meals for pilgrims and other visitors. However they were all swept away in a flash flood in 1996, and it is unclear when they will be rebuilt, whether foreigners will be allowed to stay in them, and at what price. Given the paucity of accommodation most people base themselves at Minbu 50 km away and take a day trip out here. See the Minbu entry on page 208.

• **Transport** 50 km W of Minbu. **Road Bus**: linecar connections with Minbu.

PADAN ပုတၚ်

Padan is a village of 3,000 inhabitants, about 50 km W of Minbu. It has two things to recommend it: first, it is less than 20 km from Shwesetdaw Pagoda, home to not just one, but two Buddha footprints (the only ones – or at least so far discovered – in Myanmar), and is therefore an important pilgrimage centre; and second, it is on the northern road to Arakan. If you mention elephants with some enthusiasm, word may get around and you could be invited to see the pachyderms working in the forest.

Excursions To get to **Shwesetdaw** (see

Headline glory

Phon, often translated as 'glory', is a spiritual quality which only men and monks have, located around the top of the head. The Burmese word for monk, *phongyi*, means great phon. Phon is destroyed by anything related to the lower half of women. Even a woman's longyi set on a man's pillow will ruin a man's phon, which cannot be recovered. This can be an angry wife's revenge on her husband, which he can never be certain about.

Phon protection is why women's longyis and underwear are always hung lower than men's laundry in Myanmar (and never in upper storeys!), why it is very rude to touch someone's head, and why hair is usually not thrown away on the ground, but cast in water or burned. While most people say these customs are just superstition, they are almost universally followed. When General Ne Win finished the People's Park (surrounded by tall fences, with admission collected at the gate), some people boycotted it because it had been created by a dictator. To discourage people from going there, a rumour was spread that the builders had placed women's underwear in the gateway arch, destroying the phon of all men who entered.

page 208), go back to the crossroads at the E end of the village, and catch line-cars going N.

• **Accommodation** There is no guesthouse in Padan, but if you eat at the ***Aye Ya restaurant*** (on main road, blue and white sign in Burmese only) you can shower and stay upstairs, free of charge, the police and Immigration will come to register you, there is also a monastery in town: ask for the *phon gyi gyaung*, however, it is probably better to stay at the restaurant, as they will help find you a truck, here they also have the most accurate information on when the boat leaves from Ann's port – Tatdaung (one or two boats/week).

• **Transport** 50 km from Minbu. **Road** If intending to go to Rakhine, it is possible to catch a semi-scheduled Minbu-Ann truck, or hitch a lift on any vehicle that is going over the mountains. The regular Minbu-Ann service goes twice a day, passing through Padan on the way to Ann in the early morning and in the mid-afternoon. The timing will depend on how long it has taken to load and unload. The trucks tend to be rather full by the time they get to Padan. In addition, there are independent drivers who carry goods along this route, and will take passengers as well. People in town will help you find one, or you can flag a vehicle down and ask *ANN THWA th LA?* (Are you going to Ann?).

TAUNGDWINGYI AND BEIKTHANO

Taungdwingyi lies in a seemingly endless, featureless plain. It is hard to see why anyone would stop here and decide to found a city, but approximately 2,000 years ago, that is what the Pyu people did. Archaeologists presume that two millennia in the past the climate was considerably wetter and this was an agriculturally productive area. The ruins, the oldest discovered in Myanmar, are 18 km W of town, at **Beikthano** (see **Excursions**, below).

There are two extraordinary pagodas in Taungdwingyi. One of them, the **Rakhine Pagoda**, is a huge, white ruin. Said to have been built nearly 2,000 years ago by a queen who was kidnapped from Rakhine, it was badly damaged in an earthquake in the early 1980s. A small new pagoda has been built on the place where the spire used to be. People still whitewash the corner stupas which lie

Taungdwingyi place names

Beikthano
ဗိဿနိုး

Rakhine Pagoda
ရခိုင်ဘုရား

Shwe In Daung Pagoda
ရွှေအင်တောင်ဘုရား

Shwe Yaung Daw Pagoda
ရွှေရောင်တော်ဘုရား

Taungdwingyi
တောင်တွင်းကြီး

around the massive central structure. There is a monastery nearby, but the pagoda is not situated on the sanctified ground of the monastery. Therefore, you can keep your footwear on as long as you are on the grassy area surrounding the pagoda. If you climb the ruin, though, you should take off your shoes. Judging from appearances, this does not look like a pagoda built 2,000 years ago. However few people, even archaeologists working at Beikthano, seem to know the history of the Rakhine Pagoda.

The second notable pagoda is the **Shwe In Daung Pagoda**, one of Myanmar's most graceful, and the town's favourite. The stupa is built of stone instead of the usual brick, but it is covered with gilded stucco. Horizontal bands of decoration, including hundreds of miniature stupas against a deep red background, make this pagoda unusual.

Excursions

Beikthano is an archaeological site that has been reluctant to give up its secrets. Rediscovered in 1905, excavations did not begin until 1958, under the historian U Aung Thaw. Until recently, it was thought that the Pyu people, who had their capital at Thiri Kettaya near Pyay, lived here from the 1st to 5th centuries AD. However, charcoal which is thought to come from the final battle that destroyed Beikthano has been dated to the first half of the 1st century.

Little is known of its history, and little is left of the city. The inhabitants built with bricks and wood, and used nails in their construction. A large amount of iron has been found on the site. Hundreds of burial urns and thousands of pots for other uses have been unearthed, but the museum burned down in 1981, and there is still no display open to the public.

The entrance to the site is marked with a large sign in English on the Magwe-Taungdwingyi road, 18 km W of Taungdwingyi. Turning into the site, follow the road to the first milestone and turn left. You will find one cluster of three sites N of the side road, to the right. The round one is thought to be the base of a stupa, with a religious duty building to the N, and the living quarters of a monastery to the NW. Farther along, to the S of the side road is what is thought to be the ruins of the palace. Only bare bricks remain. Past the end of the road is a path that leads to a group of small pagodas on the shore of a small lake, near a village. These have been built on an ancient foundation.

Going back to the milestone, if you turn left and continue deeper into the site, the route leads to the **Shwe yaung daw Pagoda**. This pagoda was founded in the 14th century; the present stupa is over 200 years old. Inside the monastery adjoining the terrace is a large collection of curiosities, artworks and crafts, including some very fine standing Buddhas. The lowest figures guarding the steps up the side of the stupa are frogs with varied tongue positions. *Getting there*: catching a linecar to the entrance would leave a long, unshaded walk. Unless you can borrow a motorbike or bicycle, hiring a pony trap is the best option.

Local information

● Accommodation

E *Aye yadana pyo Guesthouse*, on the main street is a little hard to spot, as it is a narrow building with English on the sign only as a background pattern, relatively clean, only upper rooms have windows, fans and mosquito nets, foreigners are charged triple, very small lounge out front, with ferocious mosquitoes attacking in opaque clouds. Near the train station is the **E** *Thein Nilar*, similar, but with less of a mosquito problem.

● Transport

400 km from Yangon, 160 km from Pyay, 80 km from Magwe.

Train Taungdwingyi is on the Pyinmana-Kyaukpadaung line, which is being extended to Bagan. No direct trains to Yangon. Three trains per day going N, two S.

Road No bus station but bus companies are spread out along the main road. Linecars leave from various spots along the roads nr the train station. You have to ask where they are going.

AUNGLAN (ALLANMYO, MYAYDE)

အောင်လံ

This lovely Irrawaddy town may show up on maps as Allanmyo or Myayde. It is prosperous by Burmese standards, lying on a minor trading route and the country's most important river. Aunglan is large enough that visitors – if you hang around in public – are likely to meet some old people with an interesting history who speak English well. The E-W streets are numbered, but the signs are in Burmese numbers only.

Places of interest

An unusual pagoda on 8th St near the market area is the **Thein Koun Paya**. Within the precincts, aside from the stupas, there is an unusual tower with low, heavy arches. It is locked, but if you loiter in the main hall for a while, one of the trustees will show up with the key. (If you aren't careful, they will turn on the coloured lights around the brass and alabaster Buddhas as well.) It is possible to climb the cool staircase to the top for a

Aunglan place names

Hkan leh Paya

ခန်လည်းဘုရား

Thein Koun Paya

သိမ်ကုန်းဘုရား

good view of the town and of the stupas in the courtyard below. There is a pagoda festival here during Thadingyut month (Sep-Oct).

Hkan leh Paya lies in the middle of a pond, just as its name says in Burmese. It is a pretty wooden building in a rectangular pond N of 7th St. Ask to feed the fish.

Aunglan has two **market areas**. One is called *ze dan*, or **'market row'**. It stretches along Alehlan, between 7th and 13th streets. At the corner of 9th and Alehlan there is a stone marker engraved in Burmese and Chinese. The second market area is less well-established. It runs roughly parallel to the first, on Kanna Lan, following the waterfront. The best buy here are the textiles, especially the thick undyed hand-woven cotton blanket/sheets (very hard and rough when new, but they soften with use).

Local festivals

Sep-Oct: pagoda festival at Thein Koun Paya (Thadingyut month, movable).

Local information

● Accommodation

Only one guesthouse accepts foreigners. **E** *Aunghmala* (sign in Burmese only), the blue-green wooden building at the SW corner of the bus station (19th St and Alehlan), small room with mosquito net and fan.

● Places to eat

As usual in towns like this, Aunglan is thickly strewn with eateries with little to distinguish them. The best way to choose is to peer inside their pots and see what appeals.

Some of the tea shops have very good snacks. *Moe Gyi Tee* tea shop (red and white sign in Burmese outside, sign in Latin letters inside) at 17th and Lanmadaw has excellent *palata*, and

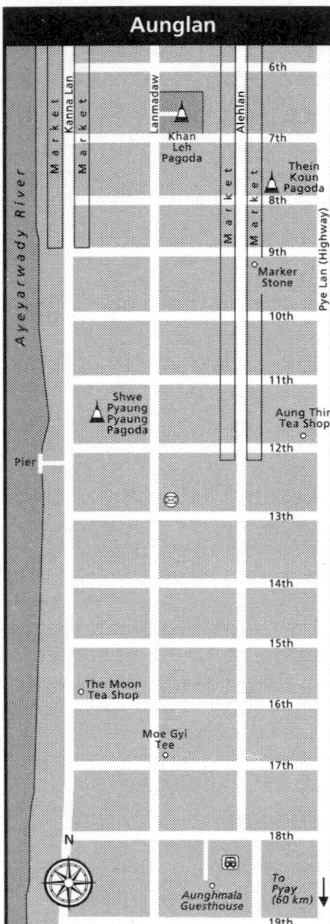

is a hangout for young people, but the video parlour opposite may not be playing your favourite music on its loudspeakers. *The Moon Tea* at Kanna and 16th is a quieter place where young people drink tea and talk. *Aung Thiri*, at the corner of 12th and Pye, is a more dignified place to imbibe.

● Post & telecommunications

Post Office: at the NE corner of Lanmadaw and 13th.

● Transport

60 km N of Pyay, 8 km and across the river from Thayet, 80 km S of Taungdwingyi.

Road Bus: connections to Pyay, Magwe, Taunggyi, Pathein, Pyinmana, Mandalay and Yangon.

Boat The pier for boats to Thayet is nr the end of 13th St, by the Shwe Pyaung Pyaung pagoda. The public boat leaves hourly around the clock and costs 7 kyat. Private boats can be hired any time for a faster, less crowded crossing for 150-200 kyat.

THAYET သရက်

Situated on the W bank of the Ayeyarwady, much of Thayet's riverfront belongs to pagodas and monasteries. It is less prosperous than Aunglan, being on the minor side of the river, with fewer road connections. This makes it quieter, but also means it has only two small guesthouses, which may be booked up if you arrive late in the day. A large cement factory S of Thayet is a major employer, and there is a prison near the town centre.

Places of interest

The untidy **market** in the S part of the town centre has less of a selection of goods than the Aunglan market. Parts of it seem to have been left largely untouched since the town was bombed towards the end of WW2. The thick-walled building, which serves as a rice warehouse, smells wonderful , even if the rice is not an obvious thing to buy and take home.

The town's prestige pagoda is definitely **Thattahtana Paya** where one of the Gautama Buddha's teeth, brought from Sri Lanka by Sayadaw U Ba Teittha is kept in a lime green room. The pagoda has several buildings; the one with the nagas at the entrance contains the tooth. To get to Thattahtana Paya from the centre of town, go S to the market and turn right past the pagoda.Then make a quick left and then right to go around the Mya Thein Deh pagoda, and continue on a few blocks until you reach the compound's walls. 10-15 mins' walk S of Thattahtana is the green **Mahamuni Pagoda**, a must for fans of nagas and folk art. A short distance N of Thattahtana

Thayet place names

Mahamuni Pagoda

မဟာမုနိဘုရား

Shyuthichamebeli

ရှိယှုသိကျမ်ဘေလိ

Thattahtana Paya

သတ္တဌာနဘုရား

Yadana Ma Aung Paya

ရတနာမအောင်ဘုရား

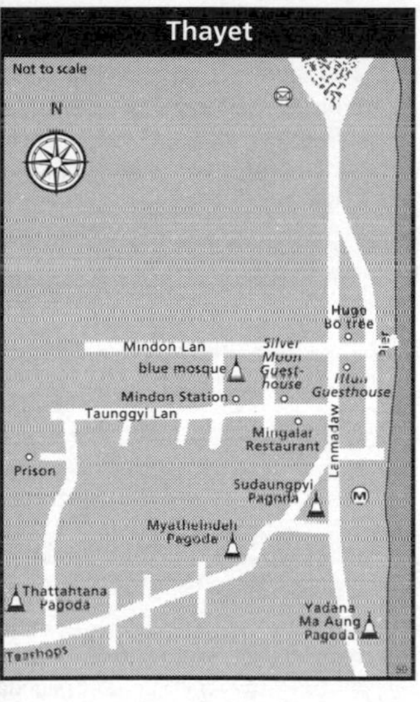

(take the small road that comes out near the eastern gate) is the **prison**, where convicts in white longyi-uniforms work the gardens in clanking leg-irons.

Just N of the market is the **Shyuthichamebeli Sunni Mosque**, built in 1838. Women cannot go inside, but everyone is welcome to sit on the cool terrace and chat while watching the river go by. All along the river are religious buildings ranging from bombed-out monasteries to gleaming new stupas. Much of the road that follows the river is tree-shaded and very pleasant to walk along. For the tourist, one of the most interesting pagodas is the **Yadana Ma Aung Paya**, on the river, S of the market. This white pagoda has steps leading up the four sides ('the way to nirvana') which provide interesting views of neighbouring pagodas.

A few minutes' walk N of the town centre is an old **park**, now nearly deserted and partially taken over by squatters. Enormous trees loom over small islands connected by wooden bridges. There is some rickety old playground equipment and what appears to be an abandoned miniature golf course. The hedges are still cut, flowers grow, and there are pavilions to sit in, but rarely anyone to enjoy them.

Local information

● Accommodation

There are only two guesthouses in town, ***Htun***, nr the pier (sign in Burmese only) and ***Ngwe La Min*** (Silver Moon) on the first block of Taunggyi Lan. Both are **E** and basic, rather dark, not particularly clean, fans and mosquito nets provided, the management of *Htun* are particularly helpful, no significant English spoken though.

● Places to eat

♦***Mingalar Restaurant***, almost opp the *Silver Moon Guesthouse*, has excellent fried rice, at night the tea shops S of the Thatahtana pagoda become quite lively.

● Post & telecommunications

Post Office: N of town, nr the park, when you reach the park take the left fork, the post office (with a small tea shop out front) will be on your left, the staff are extraordinarily friendly, but mail delivery is slow, even for Myanmar, where the postal system could hardly be described as speedy to start with (it may take a few weeks for your letter to even leave the post office).

● Transport

Road Connections to Yangon via Pyay. A daily truck goes to Mindon at 1230 (5-6 hrs).

Boat Public ferry to Aunglan, 7 kyat. Boats leave hourly around the clock. Public boats leave for Minhla, around 100 kyat. Check the schedule at the guesthouse. (Foreigners cannot stay in Minhla because of a strategic factory situated there, but can continue straight on to Minbu or Magwe.)

MINDON မင်းတုံး

Mindon is an agricultural town of 10,000 in the foothills of the Rakhine (Arakan) Yomas. The population is largely Burman, with some Chin. Frankly, there is not much here to keep the traveller loitering for long: a few crumbling pagodas whose history seems to be largely forgotten and three churches, a remarkable number considering that the town supports only a few dozen Christians. However, it is the starting point for a 3-day trek across the Rakhine Yomas to the coast, a hike which may become more popular as travel in Myanmar becomes easier (see below).

Excursions

The most compelling reason to come to Mindon is as the starting point for the **trek across the mountains to the Rakhine (Arakan) coast**. Very few foreigners have done this, and the locals say there are tigers and elephants which make the route very dangerous. However, every month or so some local people make this slightly perilous journey and it is a trek to note down for the future. While the larger beasts of the forest may seem to present the greatest danger to the intrepid traveller, it is in fact a creature so small that it can be crushed between the fingers which people should really watch out for: the mosquito. There is a very serious form of malaria endemic to the region, which requires prompt treatment. Most transmission is during the rainy season, though Dec-Jan also sees a rise in the number of malaria cases. It takes three days to get to **Letpan** on the coastal road, from where there are boats to Sittwe (see page 255). The way, which was once a surfaced road but which has since descended, like so much else in Myanmar, into decreptitude, is likely to

Mindon place names

Letpan

လက်ပန်

Ngagoun

ငါဂုံး

Sadoun

စာတုံး

be impassable during the rainy season. The first day's walk covers 25 km to **Ngagoun**, the second day, 32 km to **Sadoun**. For the third day the going is comparatively easy, and it is possible to cover all the remaining 48 km to Letpan. If you are planning on making the trek, you should have a good phrase book with you not only for being sure of the way, but in case of emergency.

Local information

● Accommodation

There are no guesthouses in Mindon. However foreigners can stay in the monastery (where the abbot is quite a character); ask the driver to let you off there: *phon-gyi-gyaung hma sin meh*. The authorities in Mindon are very friendly, and if someone invites you to stay in their house, it will probably be all right. You should still politely refuse once by saying *A na ba deh*. If your potential host responds *A ma na NEH*, then you have found a home for the night.

● Transport

50 km from Thayet, 85 km from Padan, 100 km from Pyay.

Road Connections with Thayet, Padan and Pyay. There is a new road not shown on maps connecting Pathein and Monywa. The foreign aid to construct it was cut off after the 1988 massacres, but most of the road was already built. The surface is unpaved but good. It has encouraged logging, and the landscape is unspectacular regenerating forest. The new road makes the N-S trips quick but dusty. This road intersects with the main Pyay-Taunggok road at Ohtshitbin. While buses on that route stop in the village and take on passengers, the seats are usually all occupied by the time it gets there

SAGAING DIVISION

MONYWA မုံရွာ

About 140 km W of Mandalay, Monywa is the commercial centre of the Chindwin Valley. It is an important transit point on the drug route between China and India and for goods coming down the Chindwin River. Monywa is otherwise known for the discovery of Anyatha man, believed to be as old as Peking man and is in a pretty position right on the river. **Thanbokde Pagoda**, which boasts over 6,000 Buddha images vies for importance with **Bodhitahtaung Pagoda** known for its one thousand bo trees. The former is well worth a visit. The latter now has many more than 1,000 bo trees, and there is also a huge reclining Buddha here on the hill. **Mahaleydy** is an important teaching monastery with its 806 stone slabs inscribed with the Buddhist scriptures.

Excursions 8 km out of Monywa on the Monywa-Mandalay road, you get to Myenay village. 1½ km E of Myenay you will find **Thanbodae Pagoda** with 582,357 Buddha images which were built in 1930. 6½ km further E are **Boditataung** and **Alantaye** pagodas.

Kyauka-shweguni Pagoda is 15 km E of Monywa. Each year at the end May, there is a pagoda festival here. It is the only pagoda in Monywa that faces N and is also famous for its lacquerware. Half a kilometre from the pagoda is the River Tantaluk, a local picnic spot which is all rather tacky. The government is building bungalows for tourists here.

Powintaung Across the river and 24 km to the NE, several large Buddha images have been carved directly into the stone on the Powintaung hills.

Twintaung 33 km N of Monywa you get to Budalin, 11 km W to Budalin you will reach Twintaung, an extinct volcano with a lake in the middle. The weeds that grow in the lake are turned into spirulina, a vitamin widely used in Burma.

Monywa place names

Kyauka-shweguni Pagoda

ကျောက္ကာရွှေဂူနီဘုရား

Powintaung

ဖိုးဝင်းတောင်

Thanbokde Pagoda

သမ္ဗုဒ္ဓေဘုရား

Twintaung

တွင်းတောင်

- **Accommodation** Four hotels here: **C** *Monywa*, Bogyoke Aung San Rd, T 21549, hot shower, a/c, TV, fridge, good central hotel in pretty garden, breakfast incl, good restaurant with extremely diligent service; **D** *Great Hotel*, T 21369, at bus station; **E** *Central*, in middle of town; **E** *Thein Than*, T 21275, basic but friendly, cheapest available.

- **Places to eat** **Burmese**. *Daw Tin On*, western part of town, nr the town hall. **Chinese**: *Pangyeyyi*, Bo Gyok Aung San Rd; *Paradise*, Bo Gyok Aung San Rd (middle block); *Ye Pau Restaurant* (floating restaurant), Shandaw Rd; *Shine*, Bo Gyok Aung San Rd.

- **Post & telecommunications** **Area code**: 071.

- **Transport** **Train** Trains to Myitchina can be boarded here. Price and currency depends on the whim of the station master. **Road** **Bus**: irregular connections (8 hrs). **Car**: depending on access to the area cars can be hired in Mandalay (5 hrs).

SHWEBO ရွှေဘို

At various times during the Konbaung (or Alaungpaya) Dynasty the Burmese capital was based at Shwebo: King Naungdawgyi ruled from Shwebo from 1750 to 1760, as did his successor, Naungdawgyi, from 1760 to 1763. However, Burmese kings took their palaces with them and there is little left in Shwebo to mark its previous importance.

- **Transport** **Train** Trains to Myitchina can be boarded here. Price and currency depends upon the whim of the station master.

MOGOK မိုးကုတ်

Mogok is situated within an upland valley at over 1,000m and the climate here is correspondingly cooler than on the plains. In the winter it can be cold at night and a sweater is needed. The area around the town is famous for its sapphire and ruby mines – *mogok* means ruby – and Mogok is the trading centre for the gem industry here. The principal gem deposits are found in rugged mountainous country and because of their value the government expends considerable resources and effort securing the area. Until recently Mogok was off-limits to foreigners, although it seems that access is becoming easier: check with MTT in Yangon or Mandalay to be sure.

For centuries rubies were the favoured stones of Burmese royalty, and Myanmar has some of the finest rubies in Asia. The gem was thought to have strong occult power; those who wore a ruby ring were believed to be invulnerable in battle. Today the mining at Mogok is controlled by the government under aegis of the Myanmar Gems Enterprise. The pockets of the Slorc's top brass are well known to be lined with the proceeds of gemstone smuggling. Precious stones, jade, opium and teak are among the few tangible commodities which afford Myanmar's generals an opportunity for corruption.

The town occupies a beautiful upland position and has grown up around a large lake – the Mogok Lake. There are several **gem markets** in town and the immediate vicinity: one lies NE of town and is open in the morning; another is just N of Mogok Lake and is open from midday for a couple of hours; and a third is SW of town and operates from about 1500. It is said to be a little risky buying stones here, not because of the possibility of fake gems but because not all gem sellers have the required goverment licence. Although this does not seem to worry people in Mogok particularly, customs officials at the airport in Yangon may think otherwise should they discover that you have purchased stones from a non-licensed establishment with a view to taking them out of the country.

• **Accommodation** In 1996 only one place was officially allowed to accept foreigners. However, should the *Mogok Motel* be full, the authorities allow visitors to stay at the town's cheaper guesthouses. **D** ***Mogok Motel***, hot water, private bathrooms, breakfast incl, government-run, so the service is a trifle semi-detached, electricity until 2400.

• **Shopping Gems**: Mogok is a centre of sapphire and ruby mining. See above for details on markets in the area and a warning about buying gems.

• **Transport** 200 km N of Mandalay and 150 km from Shwebo. At present the road to Mogok is closed to foreigners, but the city is open. **Air** In 1996 the only way to get to Mogok was by helicopter; US$100 pp one way from Mandalay. **Road Bus**: should the road open for travel by foreigners (which it should do given the loosening of travel restrictions in many other areas), then there are regular bus connections with Mandalay and Shwebo.

The Eastern and Northern Hills

KAYAH STATE

LOIKAW လွယ်ကော်

Loikaw is the capital of Kayah State which borders Thailand and which, save for Loikaw itself, has been off-limits to foreigners for some time. However with the ethnic insurgencies in these border highland areas under control as far as the Slorc is concerned there is every chance that other areas in Kayah, beyond the capital, will also open up for tourists. Getting to Loikaw is half the fun: the journey, whether by road or rail is spectacular, passing through upland, forested countryside. Note, though, that the rail trip is much more comfortable. It was only at the beginning of 1996 that travelling overland to Loikaw was permitted; until then tourists had to arrive by air.

Loikaw itself is set at an altitude of over 1,000m so it has a cool climate which at night can be downright chilly. The vast, main **Thirimingala market** is best on Sun when hill peoples from the surrounding area come to town to sell their goods and buy supplies. Pa O, Red Karen, White Karen and Shan all inhabit this area as well as the Padaung – better known as the 'Long-Necked Karen' (see box). The so-called **King's Palace** has long since become a monastery. However the throne and various other regalia are still kept in the monastery, along with pictures of the former royal family of Loikaw. There are various other interesting monasteries in town. **Taungkwe**, the Split Mountain Pagoda, is on the edge of town while around 7 km away is **Taung Tone Lo**, the Three Peak Pagoda whose main claim to fame is an embalmed monk. A **Kayah State Museum** was under construction in 1996 and will presumably exhibit artefacts relating to the many hill peoples who live in the area.

Loikaw place names

Taungkwe
တောင်ကွေ့

Taung Tone Lo
တောင်သုံးလုံး

Treks and trekking The *First Kayah* hotels and the *Pearl Guesthouse* organize treks to visit the famous Padaung people (see box). A 3-day trek is priced at around US$7 pp/day. Joseph at the *Pearl* has been recommended. He worked in Thailand for 7 years before returning to Loikaw and speaks a number of the local languages. Not only is he very informative about the surrounding area and its people, he is an excellent cook to boot! He has big plans to include rafting and elephant treks. Another recommended guide is Maung Maung, based at the *Best Inn*.

• **Accommodation** At the beginning of 1996 there was only one place where foreign-

Thailand: the selling of the Padaung

Forced out of Myanmar during their long struggle for autonomy, the Padaung have become refugees in Thailand and objects of tourist fascination. Their popular name – the 'Long-Necked Karen' or the 'Giraffe People' – says it all: women Padaung 'lengthen' their necks using brass rings which they add from birth. An adult Padaung can have a neck 30 cm long, and be weighed down with 5 kg or more of brass.

Why the Padaung should do this, in one sense, is clear: it is regarded as beautiful. But their explanations of how the custom arose in the first place take several forms. Some Padaung maintain that women began to add rings to their necks to protect themselves from tiger attack. Another explanation is that they were designed to disfigure the body so that Padaung women would not be taken to the Burmese court as concubines or prostitutes. A third reason relates to the myth of the origins of the Padaung people. It is said that they arose after a dragon had been impregnated by the wind, and that the lengthening of the neck is designed to mimic the dragon's long, and beautiful neck.

Sadly, Thai entrepreneurs in allegiance with the army and Karen rebels have exploited the Padaung's refugee status (they have few rights in Thailand), their relative naiveté regarding matters commercial, and their only asset from a tourist perspective – their long necks. Most tourists who take tours to the two refugee camps (paying ฿250 or US$10 to enter the villages) in Mae Hong Son Province leave disgusted at the 'selling' of these people. John Davies, a Chiang Mai resident who runs culturally-sensitive tours to the hill peoples observes: "It's a freak show brought into Thailand for commercial gain – tourism at its worst". And yet even he caved into the demands of *Asia Voyages* who insisted that the Padaung be included in his tour if they were to feed their clients into his operation. The tourist dollar speaks. But the hard fact is that the Padaung have little else to sell. One woman, Ba Nang, is paid ฿1,000 a month simply to pose for photographs. Does she like it in Thailand? "I love Thailand. Here it's easy to find food; easy living and no problems." Like so many other indigenous peoples in Southeast Asia, the Padaung find themselves caught in a web of poverty, oppression, exploitation and powerlessness.

ers were permitted to stay in Loikaw. But the middle of the year this had increased to four. If Kayah state really does open up as everyone thinks (and hopes) it will, this number will rapidly still further (and probably has done) as Loikaw has a great deal to offer. **D** ***First Kayah 1***, 34 Minsu Quarter, T 21551, the glitziest place in town, which is not saying much, room rate incl breakfast; **D-E** ***First Kayah 2***, 34 Minsu Quarter, T 21551, the cheaper half of the confusingly named *First Kayah 1*; **E-F** ***Pearl Guesthouse***, No 40 Main Rd, Min Su Quarter, T 21218, this guesthouse opened to foreigners in 1996 and for a short time was the only cheaper place to stay, Joseph, a rec guide, is based here (see above); **E** ***Best Inn***, a recently opened alternative cheap place to stay, Maung Maung, a good guide, is based here.

• **Places to eat** ***Shwe Phar Zi***, Kandarawati Rd, Chinese restaurant S of the clock tower and close to the river – tasty, cheap dishes.

• **Post and telecommunications** **Area code**: 083.

• **Transport Air** Connections on **Mandalay Airways** with Yangon and, once a week, with Heho. **Train** A line linking Aungban with Loikaw opened to foreigners in 1995. The journey takes 9 hrs. **Road Bus**: pick-ups run from Aungban and Inle to Loikaw along a poor road, 5-7 hrs (300 kyat). There are also pick-ups running from Loikaw to Mandalay (300 kyat); again the road is poor and the journey highly uncomfortable. **Boat** It is possible to take a boat from Inle all the way to Loikaw. The journey takes a full day costing a comparatively steep US$75.

KACHIN STATE

BHAMO ဗန်းမော်

Bhamo, on the road N to the Kachin State capital of Myitkyina, is reputed to be an attractive and interesting place. But like other places in the area it has been off-limits to most travellers. Check with MTT whether it is open and, if necessary, obtain a travel permit. This account is gleaned from secondary sources and should be treated accordingly.

Bhamo is an important regional market town and minorities people from the surrounding hills, including Lisu, Kachin and Shan, come here to buy necessities and sell produce. During the hot season the area can be stifling. There are several attractive pagodas in the settlement including **Theindawdye Paya**.

Excursions The city walls of the ancient city of **Sanpanago** lie about 4 km NE of Bhamo. *Getting there*: by cart.

- **Accommodation** C *Golden Dragon Hotel*, basic guesthouse, pricey given the amenities available.

- **Transport** 190 km S of Myitkyina. **Air** Myanmar Airways stops off in Bhamo between Yangon and Myitkyina. **Road** The road N from Mandalay and Lashio to Bhamo is currently closed to foreigners. **Boat** There are ferry boats between Mandalay and Bhamo. Depending on the state of the river, it takes between 1½ days (high water) and 2½ days (low water).

MYITKYINA မြစ်ကြီးနား

Kachin State is the least accessible region of Myanmar and most areas are closed to tourists. However it is sometimes possible to travel N by rail to Myitkyina, at the end of the line. Check at MTT to find out

The flight from Myitkyina

As the Japanese advanced through Burma during 1942 towards Myitkyina, thousands of refugees tried to flee the country to India taking the 500 km road through the Hukawng Valley to Margherita, just over the frontier in India. During the course of this exodus an estimated 20,000 died. At first glance this seems perplexing. They were not harassed by tribespeople, they were not strafed or ambushed by Japanese planes or soldiers, the track was not particularly challenging, and many were able to travel the first third of the way by vehicle – to Sumprabum. What killed so many was the arrival of the monsoon and with the rain, the arrival of that great killer: malaria. Within 10 days people were suffering from the fever and many just lay down, shivering in the rain and their delirium, to die. Semi-domesticated pigs began to feed on the corpses of the dead and the bodies of the almost dead. Norman Lewis, using the diary of one who survived the journey, writes in *Golden Earth*:

> "From this time until they crossed the frontier of India, a month later, they were never out of the sight and smell of death; and at this point the refugees dropped, as if with loathing, their civilized poses and pretences. Civilization provides a whalebone corseting, and when this is unfastened, the individual either turns to jelly or begins to flex unsuspected muscles. From now on Lee (the diary's author) found something exaggerated in people's conduct, including his own. They had turned into ham actors in an old-fashioned movie, either heroes or villains. It was a study in black and white, with no half-tones."

whether the town is open to foreigners and secure a travel permit if required. Register with local police (under same roof as *Popa Hotel*) on arrival. This account, however, is based on readers' comments and various secondary sources: we were not able to reach Myitkyina during our last visit.

Even when Myitkyina does open up to tourists, it is unlikely that it will become particularly popular. For although the town is attractively situated in a broad valley surrounded by hills, it is a non-descript place. Norman Lewis in *Golden Earth* describes the area as 'scorchingly' hot. Looking into the future, it may be that this area could become a trekking centre. There are numerous Kachin villages in the area, and the forested hills, fast-flowing rivers and plentiful agricultural produce – especially the fresh fruits and vegetables – could make this an area where people come to hike and relax. For the moment, however, it is one of the least secure – from the government's point of view – regions of the country and even if travellers do make it to Myitkyina it is unlikely that they will be permitted to travel much beyond 50 km from the town.

The sights of Myitkyina are thin on the ground. The **Andawshin Pagoda** is said to be attractive while the **Hsu Taungpyi** is reputed to be extremely attractive, situated on the Ayeyarwady.

• **Accommodation** In terms of services for visitors, Myitkyina is like Myanmar 5 or 6 years ago: basic and overpriced. However, new hotels and guesthouses are being mooted and the situation could have improved by the time this book goes to press. **C** *Popa Hotel*, T 21746, pretty basic place for this sort of price, plain rooms with shared facilities; **D** *Nan Thiri*, government-run but – and unusually – probably better than the privately-owned competition, large rooms with attached bathrooms; **D** *YMCA*, the cheapest rooms available but overpriced for what you get.

• **Places to eat** There is a lot of unrealized culinary potential in Myitkyina. The range of ingredients – excellent fruit and vegetable and rice which is regarded as the finest in Myanmar – means that it should be possible to produce excellent food. Searching it out is hard, though. There are several Chinese restaurants in town, but they are mediocre. New ***Garden Restaurant*** between airport and town, which serves quite good food.

• **Post & telecommunications Area code**: 074.

• **Transport** 190 km N of Bhamo. **Air Myanmar Airways** has connection with Myitkyina from Yangon, Mandalay, Bhamo and Putao. **Train** Myitkyina is at the end of the line N. There are daily departures from Mandalay but the journey time is what might be termed elastic: a scheduled 20 hrs can easily stretch to 30 or 40 hrs. Because large areas of Kachin State have been off-limits to the government until recently the line remains largely as it was at Independence. Private trains also make the journey and are more comfortable and reliable – and more expensive (US$30). An alternative to travelling the whole route by rail is to take the boat from Mandalay to Katha, and then catch the train on. **Road and river** The road N to Myitkyina is closed to foreigners. Should it open, expect a rough trip. It is also possible – should the authorities allow it – to combine a trip by bus with a journey by boat. Take the boat from Mandalay to Katha, and then catch a bus (or train) from there to Myitkyina.

PUTAO ပူတာအို

Like Myitkyina, it is hard to obtain permission to visit Putao and this account is gleaned from secondary sources. Check with MTT whether Putao is open and, if necessary, obtain a travel permit.

Putao is due N of Myitkyina on the road that the refugees took trying to escape from the advancing Japanese in 1942 (see box, page 222) and not far from Hkakabo Razi, the highest mountain in Myanmar – indeed in the whole of Southeast Asia – at almost 6,000m. (It is usually said that Mount Kinabalu in the East Malaysian state of Sabah is the highest while it is exceeded in altitude not just by this Burmese monster but also by several peaks in Indonesia's province of Irian Jaya.)

The number of tourists who have visited Putao in recent years is, by all accounts, very few. Not only is it difficult to get here – even if the authorities issue a travel permit – but there is also little reason to come. The town is rather sordid, there is little of historical interest or beauty to entreat the visitor to rest a while, and at the time of writing it was not possible to venture into the surrounding countryside. Hill tribespeople do come into town to barter and sell goods at the market and people-watching can be entertaining, but this is a long way to come for something that can be experienced in many other areas of Myanmar. The upside of a visit to Putao is that you're sure to be the only tourist and the place remains untouched by the outside world.

• **Accommodation** Accommodation is limited and expensive. This will change if the authorities make it easier for tourists to reach the town and for entrepreneurs to set up shop. **E** Two guesthouses with very limited amenities. One is run by an old Nepalese man (who lives in the shed next door). He speaks some English. Rooms are big with solid wood beds. Blankets for hire. Outside toilets, no cooking facilities. Bikes for hire. Hold onto your money here.

• **Places to eat** Very limited 'greasy spoons', closed on Sundays. Bring own food if possible. Stall food available in the evenings at the crossroads.

• **Transport Air Myanmar Airways** flies to Putao from Myitkyina, but sporadically (once a week in 1996, though the frequency may rise). **Road** The road to Putao from Myitkyina was closed to foreigners in 1996.

SHAN STATE

Shan State – the biggest state in the Burmese union, bordering Thailand, Laos and China – has a population of around 4 million people who belong to a total of 32 different tribes. The rugged and mountainous state makes up part of the Golden Triangle, the largest opium poppy-producing area in Asia (see page 86). The government has fought continual ethnic insurgencies in the state for many years (see page 61) and because of the security problems, only this small part of Shan state is open to tourists. The people can be divided into six main ethnic groups (for more details, see page 58):

- The Shan, descended from Tai-Chinese stock and traditionally traders.
- The Pa-O, a Tibeto-Burman people, living around Taunggyi.
- The Intha, residents of the Inle lake area.
- The Taungyoe, of Tibeto-Burmese stock, living around Inle and Heho.
- The Danu, also Tibeto-Burmese people, living around Pindaya.
- The Palaung, a Mon-Khmer tribal people who live around Kalaw, of which there are eight sub-groups – some also live in North Shan state.

One of the most rewarding excursions in the Inle area is to one of the **regional markets**, at which many of the tribal people come to sell their produce. There is one going on somewhere every day of the week, but they rotate between different towns on a 5-day cycle:

1) Heho, including a cattle market
2) Taunggyi (a big market), Floating Market on Inle Lake (Pa-O), Aungban (near Kalaw)
3) Pwehela (on the way to Pindaya)
4) Kalaw (Pa-O and Palaung) and Shwenyaung
5) Nyaung Shwe and Pindaya (both Pa-Oand Palaung)

Taunggyi, Shan State's administrative capital, which is perched on top of a precipitous escarpment. Inle Lake itself is reached from the town of Nyaung Shwe; the main sight is the Phaung Daw U pagoda which houses five 12th century Buddha images, although the lake is just as famous for its floating gardens and its 'leg-rowing fishermen'. To the W is Kalaw, a former British colonial hill station, which is surrounded by Palaung hilltribe villages. Pindaya, to the NE of Inle Lake, is famous for its Shweumin Pagoda – a cave temple which houses more than 6,000 Buddha images.

KALAW ကလော

"If we could take Kalaw with us, we would" the British are reported to have said when leaving Myanmar. Fortunately, they had to leave it behind and this old hill station on the rim of the Shan Plateau, in the 'Pineland', 50 km W of Inle, remains a favourite place. Many of the enormous pine trees which used to surround Kalaw were cut down during the government's long-running and multiple conflicts with Myanmar's ethnic minorities, as part of an effort to deny the rebels safe refuge. But a reforestation programme has been successful, by and large, despite a certain number of people selling scented wood by the roadside.

The main attractions of Kalaw are the town itself, with its mock-Tudor colonial bungalows, its ethnic mix of people, and its setting within trekking distance of many ethnic minority villages. Kalaw is made up of a mixture of Shan, Palaung, Burman, Indian and Nepali people. Many speak English well, having been taught in mission schools or by fluent parents. About 60,000 Palaung people inhabit the Plateau area.

The most famous cave-pagoda in the area is at Pindaya, a day trip from Kalaw, but there are many smaller caves in the surrounding hills and Kalaw has its own Shweohnmin Pagoda cave.

Win two Iberia flights to Latin America

Welcome to Footprint Handbooks - the most exciting new development in travel guides since the original South American Handbook from Trade & Travel.

We want to hear your ideas for further improvements as well as a few details about yourself so that we can better serve your needs as a traveller.

We are offering you the chance to win two Iberia flights to Latin America. Iberia is the leading airline for Latin America, currently flying to 34 destinations. Every reader who sends in their completed questionnaire will be entered in the Footprint Prize Draw. 10 runners up will win an exclusive Footprint T-shirt!

Complete in a ball-point pen and return this tear-off questionnaire as soon as possible.

1 Title of this Handbook __________

2 Age Under 21 ☐ 21 - 30 ☐ 31 - 40 ☐ 41 - 50 ☐ over 50 ☐

3 Occupation __________

4 Which region do you intend visiting next?
North America ☐ India/S. Asia ☐ Africa ☐
Latin America ☐ S.E. Asia ☐ Europe ☐
Australia ☐

5 Which country(ies) do you intend visiting next?
____

6 There is a complete list of Footprint Handbooks at the back of this book. Which other countries would you like to see us cover?
____

Please enter your name and permanent address:

Name __________

Address __________

E-mail __________

Offer ends 30 November 1997. Prize Draw winners will be notified by 30 January 1998. Flights are subject to availability.

IBERIA

Win two Iberia flights to Latin America

Footprint Handbooks
6 Riverside Court
Lower Bristol Road
Bath
BA2 3DZ
England

Affix
Stamp
Here

Footprint Handbooks

6 Riverside Court
Lower Bristol Road
Bath BA2 3DZ
T 01225 469141
F 01225 469461
handbooks@footprint.cix.co.uk

Places of interest

Kalaw's **Shweohnmin Pagoda** caves date from the Pagan era, about the same time as the Pindaya cave.The main cave is at the bottom of a small cliff. The rock above is split, but the pieces are believed to be held in place by the Buddha's power. There is an open chamber, with a tiled pathway leading deeper into the hill. The Buddha to the left of the passage has eight fingers on each hand. As you follow the path, the large standing Buddha is the one to make offerings to for prosperity. The last five Buddhas on the right of the narrow corridor are the four past Buddha and the future Buddha. The cave contains 137 images, all different, and is still being expanded. A few valuable and portable images have been moved to the monastery across the road to prevent theft. In the small space in front of the cave are 34 whitewashed pagodas,

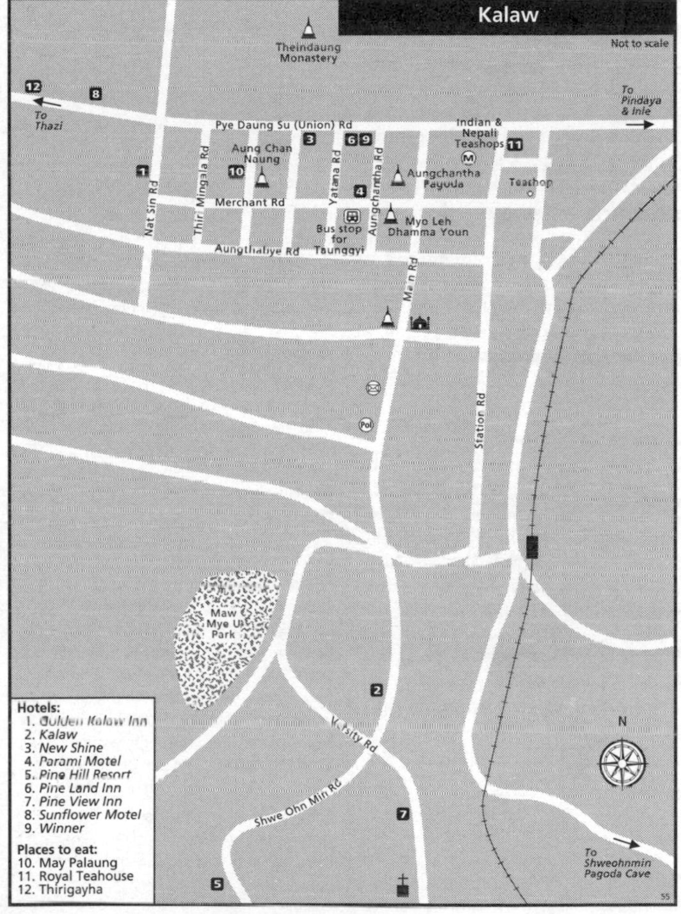

each with a different design while cut into the steep face to the left of the main cave is a stairway that leads to the entrances to other caves. Some are just small hollows, but one goes back 150m into the mountainside and can be explored (bring a torch).

In the main **monastery building** across the paved road there are several old and unusual images (take off your shoes as you reach the top of the rise by the main hall). The most famous is the Hnipaya (bamboo strip image) which is in the second rank, on the left side of the wide altar. (Wait for the *sayadaw* or one of the monks to guide you before stepping onto the altar platform.) The Hnipaya is over 1,000 years old. The woven bamboo shape has been covered in a thick lacquer, gilded, and given a coloured glass mosaic royal dress. The wooden image next to it is also portable, and was transferred here from the cave. At the opposite end of the altar are a number of roughly lacquered black images which are also ancient. A hollow wooden stupa opens to show three standing Buddhas inside. There is a **market** in town every 5 days.

Tours and trekking

The area around Kalaw is dotted with Palaung, Pa-O and Taungyoe villages and companies and guesthouse are beginning to take visitors into the hills. Robin, co-owner of the *Golden Kalaw Guesthouse* (see above), operates treks into the area S of Kalaw which is still relatively unspoilt. He speaks excellent English and his overnight treks are rec. There are other guides of who the following have been rec: 'Soe Moe', who operates from the *Kalaw Hotel* (ask at the front desk), Sam Kyaw Myint, from *Pineland Inn* – who speaks Shan, Palaung, Pa-O, Danu and Burmese, as well as excellent English, and Charles, a Burmese of Indian extraction, who is based at the *Parami Motel* and is reliable, informative and enormously polite. Expect to pay about $10/day inclusive of food – take small gifts for the villagers, if possible. Hiring a car to Inle Lake, 2½ hrs, 4,800 kyat return (3 hrs' boat trip, 900 kyat).

Local information

● Accommodation

B-D *Kalaw Hotel*, 1 km out of town, for reservations (essential) call Kalaw T 50039, Taunggyi T 22409/21425, Yangon T 6660563, a/c, hot water, privatized, the *Kalaw* is an old British building retaining much of its colonial charm, rather like the *Candacraig* in Pyin U Lwin – with a solid teak staircase and doors, cheaper rooms are available in the newer annexe and there are some more expensive rooms in a new building, their dining room is more famous for its atmosphere than its food – call a day ahead to order whatever you like for high tea, popular with tour groups, 5% discount for 3 nights, very quiet, except when trains pass, nice garden with tennis court, good English spoken.

C *Winner*, T 50021/50025, a/c, hot water, satellite TV, BBC World Service, main road, large, dull architecture; **C-E** *Parami Motel*, a/c, hot water, satellite TV, more character than the other new hotels, rooms are clean and the place quiet and friendly.

D *Golden Kalaw Inn*, T 50108, hot water, clean, friendly, family run – Lily runs the guesthouse, whilst her brother Robin arranges hill treks (see trekking below), quieter than *Pine Land*, as regards road noise, but there is little sound proofing between the rooms; **D** *New Shine*, T 50028/60015, a/c, hot water, satellite TV, clean, large, a bit noisy because it's on a main road, deferential staff, fairy lights flashing on the exterior of the building to give it that Hollywood feel; **D** *Pine Hill Resort*, T 50078 and T 50079, not yet open but looks like it will be quite good, there is a good view from here; **D** *Pine View Inn*, T (081) 50020 for reservations – no phone in the hotel (yet), a/c, hot water, new and small hotel; **D** *Sunflower Motel*, hot water, little brightly-coloured double bungalows in a garden on the main road, cute, fairly clean, little English spoken.

E *Pine Land Inn*, T 50020, hot water, undergoing improvements, which may mean that the room rate will increase, nice staff, good guides, reasonably clean, not much atmosphere.

● Places to eat

By far the best place to have Burmese food is ♦♦♦♦*Thirigayha* (variously spelt), in a house on the main road, large menu of Burmese, European, Indian and Chinese food, cooked by the Shan family in their kitchen, comparatively pricey but worth the extra, Irish grandfather, friendly people.

The ♦♦♦*Kalaw Hotel's* restaurant has some atmosphere and elaborate service but mediocre, overpriced food, however, if you order fresh fruit for high tea, you can't go wrong.

♦♦*May Palaung*, 5 Zatila St, excellent Burmese food in this restaurant tucked away off the main road, the best place to eat in Kalaw. *Soe Restaurant*, in the line S of the market is also good, it serves tea and is open late, there are many Indian and Nepali tea joints with good snacks along the N and E sides of the market and another down a side street, they serve delicious variations of chapati and falafel-like fried bean snacks. There are several good **teahouses** in town, notably *Tan E Win*, nr the market.

● Post & telecommunications

Area code: 081.

● Transport

Train There is a new train line (completed in 1994) linking Kalaw with Loikaw. The train leaves Kalaw at 0900 and takes 9 hrs to Loikaw. The mountain scenery is very alluring but there are only ordinary seats available.

Road Bus: regular connections with Taunggyi (3 hrs) and via Aungban with Pindaya – attractive road through hilly countryside. There are also bus connections with Inle (70 kyat).

PINDAYA ပင်းတယ

39 km from the Aungban junction, Pindaya is a small, charming town, centred round a lake, called Nattamiekan or Angels Lake, which looks rather like an Indian tank, with steps leading down into the murky water. The population is mainly comprised of Taungyoe and Danu people (page 59). Apart from its cool air and pretty setting, Pindaya's attraction is its cave complex.

The main sight is the **Shwe U Min Pagoda** – the 'Golden Cave Pagoda' – (also simply known as Pindaya Caves) on the steep hill behind the hotel. The limestone caves contain a maze of chambers with 6,226 Buddha statues – last counted in 1990; there are now so many that the temple has stopped accepting new ones. Some of the images are tiny, others are huge, and are made of white marble, bronze or plaster, coated with gold leaf. Most of the statues have been donated by devotees and pilgrims, and have been brought from all around the area. Behind the smaller stupa to the right of the entrance there are also several teak wood pillars, carved with small Buddhas. Some of the smaller caves within the complex serve as meditation chambers. The main stupa dates from the 12th century. It is a steep climb up to the cave but there is also a road to the entrance. The Pindaya Cave festival takes place in Mar, in which thousands of pilgrims converge on the small area below the caves. Everyone has something to sell from large watermelons to old clothes; hundreds of people spend their time standing around watching videos. There are also stage performances of traditional dancing and Western-style rock music. Local Pindaya specialities on sale at the caves and in the town are potato snacks, Shan tea (sesame flavoured) and avocados at 1 or 2 kyat each. There is also a sweet called *thagya-kwe* or twisted sugar, a bit like nougat, which can be found drying out-

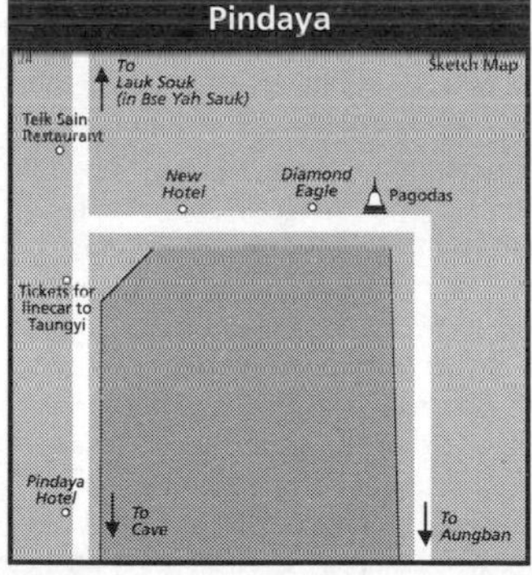

side houses in town. Take a torch. Admission to the caves US$5. **NB** The nearby Padah-Lin caves, in which traces of Neolithic settlement have been unearthed, are not accessible for tourists. Pindaya hosts a **market** every 5 days. Visit the paper and umbrella 'factory' behind the *Pindaya Hotel*.

Excursions A new pagoda and monastery has been built, about 15 km beyond Pindaya.

• **Accommodation** **C** *Pindaya*, Main St, 5 mins' walk from town on the road towards the caves, good tranquil position on the lake, a/c, irregular supplies of hot water, good restaurant, friendly place; **D** *Diamond Eagle*, will bargain. Another hotel is due to be finished in late 1996 – **D-E**.

• **Places to eat** ♦♦♦*Kyanlike*, nr the banyan tree on the road into town, Chinese, reasonable. *Teik Sain* for best Shan food in town.

• **Transport** See Inle Lake, page 232. **Road Linecar**: the linecar from Taunggyi stops at the Aungban junction at 0900. Wait at the *Mekhaing restaurant*. (Other traffic may take you along but there is little.) 90 mins (40-50 kyat). The last linecar leaves Pindaya at 1300 for Taunggyi (80 kyat). If you take a pony trap to the cave (70 kyat return if the driver waits) this leaves you approximately 2 hrs in the cave. To go to Kalaw, get off in Aungban and walk 5 mins S to the *Khitlite Restaurant* to flag down a linecar.

NYAUNG SHWE AND INLE LAKE
ညောင်ရွှေ အင်းလေးကန်

The lake is about 40 km N to S but only 5 km wide and there are more than 200 villages on or around it, supporting a population of about 150,000. Most are Intha people (*Intha* means 'sons of the lake') who are of Mon rather than Shan descent, originally from SE Myanmar (see page 58). It is a charming place to relax for several days.

The main lake town is **Nyaung Shwe** (Yaunghwe), 11 km from the Shwe Nyaung junction on the Heho-Taunggyi road and 1 km from the lake – although the main part of town is a bit further from the lake. 15 mins from the market is an old **Shan Palace**, beautifully carved and constructed of teak. There is very little left of the interior, however. It is under the supervision of the Ministry of Culture, but is more like a performance art piece on the fate of aristocracy in Myanmar than a maintained museum. Admission about US$3. Open 0900-1700 Mon-Fri.

Inle Lake place names

Floating gardens
ကျွန်းမျော
Nankand Canal
နန်းကန့်တူးမြောင်း
Phaung Daw U Pagoda
ဖောင်တော်ဦးဘုရား

Yadanamanaung Pagoda, also not far from the market, has been one of the beneficiaries of Nyaung Shwe's newfound prosperity. Deep red and gold inside and out, the artwork is very fine. There are many curious non-pecuniary donations displayed in cabinets in the pagoda's various rooms.

The **Nankand Canal** from Nyaung Shwe goes down to the lake, which is only 4m deep. Inle's central portion is devoted to floating gardens and newly reclaimed land (see below). Travelling in a boat, parts of Inle seem more like a network of canals than an open lake. These channels are continually redredged by villagers and the army which co-opts local dredging parties every weekend. All the waterways are marked with whitewashed wooden railings and the round mile posts give it the appearance of a giant, flooded racecourse. With the mountains as a backdrop, Inle bears comparison with Kashmir's Dal Lake in India. Admission US$3 (5 FEC).

Inle's most unusual feature is its extraordinary **'leg-rowing fishermen'**,

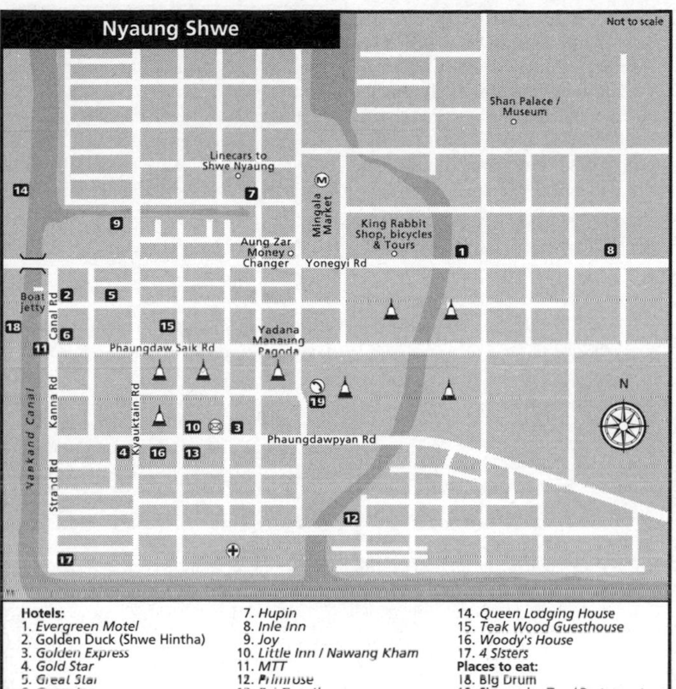

who have developed an original, eccentric method of rowing with one leg. With the other, they balance precariously on the back of their sampans, leaving their hands free to drop their tall conical nets over passing fish, which they can spot in the shallow lake. Another of Inle's unusual claims to fame is its **floating gardens**, which are built-up from strips of water hyacinth and mud, dredged from the lake bed, which breaks down into a rich humus; it take 50 years to produce a layer 1m thick. The floating allotments are anchored to the bottom with bamboo poles. Land is also reclaimed in this way, and parts of the lake have been reduced to a maze of canals around these plots. Most of the produce grown on the lake gardens is vegetables – mainly tomatoes and beans – and the codia leaf, which is used to roll tobacco and make cheroots. As well as being accomplished fishermen and market gardeners, the Intha are talented metalworkers, carpenters and weavers.

The best time to visit Inle Lake is during the Phaung Daw U festival (see below) or in Nov and Dec when the water lilies are flowering and the Hazy Blue Mountains surrounding the lake are not quite as hazy.

The main sight is **Phaung Daw U Pagoda** on the lake, one of the principal shrines in Myanmar (24 km from Nyaung Shwe). Phaung Daw is the name of the royal bird. The building dates from the 18th century but has been greatly altered over the years, and plans are afoot to further enlarge the complex (see model inside). It houses five 12th century Buddha images, which have completely lost their shape due to the fact that devotees are constantly plastering them with gold leaf. To the right of the main shrine there are two golden pedestals used to transport the images during the festival (the smaller one takes them to the **floating market** and the larger one carries them on the lake).

The boat used in the procession is housed in a shed in the complex. In 1965 at the annual Phaung Daw U festival, the royal boat capsized in a storm and the four images sank – this is all documented in a series of photographs in the

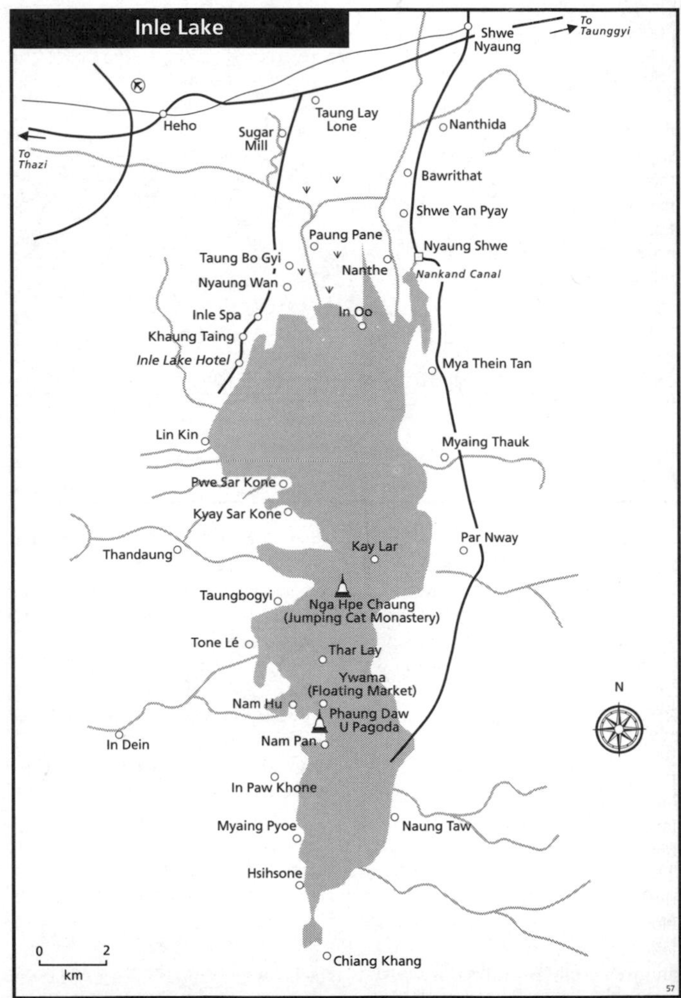

Inle in bloom

From Jan to Apr, Myanmar blossoms. Nowhere are flowering trees more dramatic than in the Inle area, where they line roadsides, provide startling splashes of colour in far-off fields, and grace the shores of the lake itself. First to flower is the tiger claw, with its orange blossoms, and the bompax trees which turn bright red: bompax flowers are boiled and eaten with Shan noodles. In Mar the jacaranda bursts into lilac blossom, followed closely by the flame of the forest (*Butea frondosa*), with its hanging clusters of scarlet flowers. The bougainvillaea blossom in Mar, as do white bohemia – the 'Hong Kong orchids', which are eaten as a salad (mixed with ground peanuts) after being boiled and chopped. In an explosive finale, the pink cassia blossoms – often mistaken for cherry – also come out in Mar.ch

pagoda. They were all salvaged and a statue of the royal bird was erected in the lake at the disaster site. There is a market beneath the pagoda selling local textiles, knives and assorted domestic wares and some antiques. Inle's famous floating market, at nearby **Ywama**, is held every 5 days. On the off days, there is a floating souvenir market your boatman may try to take you to. Just N of Ywama is the **Nga Hpe Chaung Monastery**, an old wooden building where the monks have trained their cats to show jump (it is known locally as Jumping Cat Monastery).

Inle Spa, N of the *Inle Hotel*, has a modest hot spring. Admission: US$1 for bath, 15 kyat for changing room. Open daily.

There is a **Cheroot factory** here which might be worth a visit.

Local festivals

Oct: *Phaung Daw U festival* (movable), four of the Buddha images from the Phaung Daw U Pagoda are rowed round the lake (one remains behind to guard the pagoda) in a copy of a royal *karaweik* on a tour of other pagodas around the lake. The barge is in the shape of the royal bird (which is akin to a giant chicken). There are boat races on the lake during the festival.

Nov: *Full moon of Tazaungmon* (movable), following the harvest festival, donations are given to the local temples. Large procession; biggest in Taunggyi.

Local information

● Accommodation

It is also possible to stay in Aungban, where there are numerous unlicenced guesthouses which offer wildly fluctuating prices in dollars and kyat. As there are so many, there is plenty of room to bargain.

Nyaung Shwe: **C** *Gold Star*, corner of Phaungdawpyan and Kyauttain rds, T 21635, new, very Chinese-style, 2-storey building, dining room on 2nd floor and a large terrace on the top, rooms in blocks all around, a/c, TV (CNN), fridge, clean, good value, popular tour group hotel; **C** *Hupin*, No 66, Kantar Quarter, W of Market Bazaar, T 23/25, very good restaurant, big new hotel, no balconies, no views, family run, clean; **C-D** *Evergreen*, Yonegyi Rd, T 79, by canal, clean, relatively new place, hot water, balcony; **C-D** *Golden Express*, 19 Phaungdawpyan Rd, T 37, T Mandalay 70382, F Yangon 221479, F Yangon 27636, clean, no character, all with bathrooms and hot water; **C-D** *Gypsy Inn*, 82 Canal Rd, T 84, new inn on the canal; nice location but no atmosphere, desultory service; **C-E** *Inle Inn*, Yonegyi Rd, T 16, restaurant, friendly, well-run and nice rooms, popular with travellers so advisable to book, put on traditional puppet shows, serve Shan food and organize trips.

D *Golden Duck Guest House* (*Shwe Hintha*), T 62, run by the father of the owner of the *Joy Hotel*, this place comes rec too as a clean, well-run and friendly guest house, great views over the canal to the hills, price incl breakfast; **D** *Joy Guest House*, T 83, just off main canal, friendly, very clean, will arrange boat trips and book bus tickets, best rooms have balconies overlooking the canal, pleasant roof terrace where backpackers congregate for breakfast and evening beers, good breakfast incl in price, rec; **D** *Little Inn* (*Nawang*

Kham), Phaungdawpyan Rd, T 21448, 7 double rooms, courtyard with plants, cheesy cultural shows, willing to halve prices in off-season; **D** ***Primrose***, modern bungalows next to trees and a stream, kind staff, mostly populated by tour groups; **D** ***Pyi Guesthouse***, 35 Phaungdawpyan Rd, T 76, restaurant, garden; **D-E** ***Woody's House***, 2 Phaungdawpyan Rd, T 22066, bamboo house, some bathrooms ensuite, friendly, courtyard, good coffee, will serve Burmese breakfast upon request.

E ***Queen Lodging House***, nice location on far side of canal in front of *Golden Duck Guesthouse*, basic rooms with fan and hot water shower attached in a rustic bungalow with a small verandah looking out onto a badly maintained garden and the canal, noisy in the morning with all the long-tail boat traffic; **E** ***Teak Wood Guesthouse***, very clean, quite large rooms, quiet location, open area on upper floor to eat/relax in, can arrange trips, cheapest and best deal in town.

Khaung Taing and Shwe Nyaung: **C** ***Inle Lake***, T Taunggyi 21374, fan rooms only, restaurant, electricity 1800-2300, magnificent views across the lake, only 4 rm, a bar and a swimming pool are being constructed in the lake below the hotel; **C** ***Remember Inn***, this excellent little hotel lies about 10 km N of Inle Lake, but staying here is certainly worth considering, the owner is immensely hospitable, the rooms are large and clean, breakfast is included in the room rate, they also have a boat for charter, rec.

● Places to eat

Burmese: ♦♦♦***Daw Aye Hla***, at the lake-end of Nyaung Shwe, nr the teacher training school and the Russian hospital, rec by locals; ***Inle Inn***, nr the market, Burmese food and puppet show; ♦♦♦***Khine Thazin***, nr the teacher training school and Russian hospital; ♦♦♦***4 Sisters*** (although one of the four sisters is now married), last house at end of Canal Rd, best food in town, stacks of atmosphere, simple cuisine (and mounds of it), no menu – eat what is served to everybody, guests pay what they think is fair (except fixed price beer) – also a very good source of information on the area, popular with younger people; ♦♦***Big Drum***, attached to *The Queen*, over the bridge opp the *Golden Duck*), Burmese, European, Shan set dinner, good, reasonable dishes, the Shan fish is rec, order in advance for some dishes, pleasant tables set under a bamboo and palm thatched hut with a view of the canal; ***Shwe Pyisu***, nr Yadana Manaung, very good Burmese food, best tea in town.

Chinese: ♦♦♦***Naung Shwe***, on the Nankand Canal, government run, necessary to order in advance; ♦♦♦-♦♦***Hu Pin***, Inle Lake, very popular with locals and backpackers alike, serves excellent Chinese food made with fresh ingredients, the hot and sour Inle Lake fish is particularly rec, cold beers, open until 2000-2100, rec; ♦♦***Inn Thar Lay***, nr Phaung Daw U Pagoda, fish and rice; ***Inle Hotel Restaurant***, Burmese curries, standard dreadful food in a beautiful setting, overlooking the lake. There are long-term plans to build a floating restaurant on the lake below the hotel.

● Admission fees

Visitors must pay US$5 admission fee at MTT office to see the lake.

● Banks & money changers

It is possible to change money at the official rate at government run hotels and MTT offices. Black market rates in the Inle area are considerably lower than in Rangoon, and unlike Rangoon, you have to go in active pursuit of business.

● Entertainment

The ***Inle Inn*** puts on puppet shows.

● Post & telecommunications

Area code: 081.

● Tour companies & travel agents

4 Sisters, last house at end of canal road (also see **Places to eat**, above) arrange boat trips and are an excellent source of information. ***Big Drum Restaurant***, ***King Rabbit Tours***, Yonegyi Rd and most hotels/guesthouses organize walking trips to Shan villages.

● Tourist offices

Heho Airport, Nyaung Shwe, Inle Lake and Taunggyi. Naungshwe, Nankand Canal.

● Transport

Local There are local laws supposedly restricting tourists from using transportation here – but vehicles are still for rent. **Bicycles**: available for hire from many guesthouses and hire shops are prominently advertised on street corners. **Boats**: motorized long boats/canoes can be hired from hotels/guesthouses for 700-800 kyat (boats take up to 7 people) for most of the day. The *4 Sisters Restaurant*, *Joy Guest House*, *Remember Inn*, and *Golden Duck*

Guest House all run or can help to charter boat trips for tourists. Expect to pay about 700 kyat for a full day excursion incl stops at the Ywama floating market and Jumping Cat Monastery or Nga Hpe Chaung Monastery. There are also local ferries which criss-cross the lake. **NB** The boatmen have a very strong tendency to go to only certain places, incl souvenir shops. It is worth investing some time at the outset, with a translator if necessary, to make clear where you want to go. Although the boatman may say otherwise, the whole Inle area is open for tourists to visit. Some of the surrounding towns are on the market circuit, others are accessible up small rivers. **Bus**: regular buses/pickups from Taunggyi to Nyaung Shwe (30 kyat); Pindaya (40 kyat); Kalaw (70 kyat). **Linecars**: these are now monitored by a private tour company ensuring that tourists are not overcharged. Linecars will drop passengers at their lodging place, after letting other passengers off at the market. **Car hire**: it is possible to hire cars or 4WD vehicles in Taunggyi.

Air Heho is the regional airport, 40 km from Taunggyi. Regular connections with Yangon, Mandalay and Bagan. **Air Mandalay** and **Myanmar Airways** both serve the airport, **Myanmar Airways** being somewhat cheaper (US$70 versus US$105 to Yangon (Rangoon) but with a somewhat disturbing safety record.

Train The nearest train station to Inle is Shwe Nyaung. Regular connections from here with Thazi, and from Thazi with Yangon, Mandalay and Taungoo. It is sometimes difficult to get a seat at Thazi making for a long and uncomfortable journey standing or squatting in the aisles. Regular overnight connections with Yangon and Mandalay. There are additional trains every Sun, Tues and Fri.

Road Bus: regular public buses run from Taunggyi to Yangon, 14-20 hrs, Thazi 5 hrs, Mandalay 8 hrs, Meiktila 4 hrs and Bagan 8 hrs (on a good day, can be up to 20 hrs). Most travellers returning to Yangon take the bus that leaves Inle Lake/Shwe Nyaung daily in the mid-afternoon and arrives in Yangon at 0900 the following day (1,300-1,500 kyat). Prices fluctuate according to the cost of petrol. There are 'Express' buses to Mandalay, Bagan and overnight expresses to Yangon. **Taxi**: taxis are available for long-distance charter. To Bagan expect to pay about US$60, which split 4 ways is reasonable. The journey takes about 9 hrs by taxi, as opposed to as much as 20 hrs by bus.

TAUNGGYI တောင်ကြီး

The administrative capital of Shan state, 28 km NE of Inle Lake, has a population of about 150,000. The people of Taunggyi – who are predominantly Shan – regard themselves as so distinct from the Burmans that they talk about 'going down to Myanmar' (and the Burmans talk of going 'up to the highlands'). The town has mushroomed into the country's 4th largest centre after Yangon, Mandalay and Mawlamyine. *Taunggyi* literally means 'big hill' – an understated description of the dramatic scarp slope on which the town stands. It was founded by Sir George Scott, superintendent of the Shan states in the early 1900s, as a hill station for over-heated colonial officials and their families; a few colonial buildings

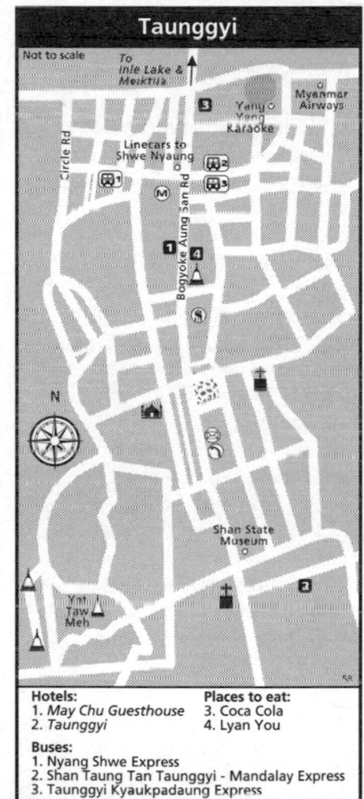

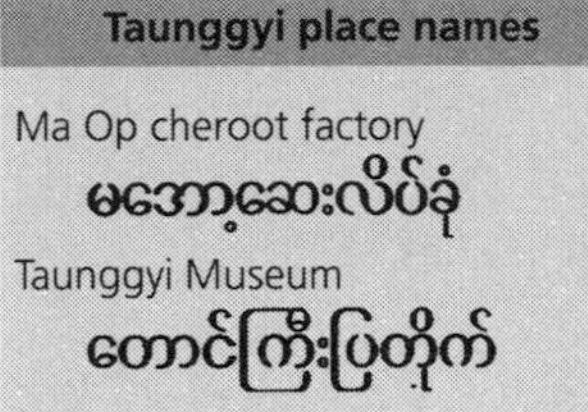

remain. Sited at 1,430m it has a much more temperate climate than the sultry plains below.

Shan princes came to Taunggyi to get a British education and Christian missionaries, who headed into the hilltribe areas, used Taunggyi as their base. Today there are said to be more than 32,000 Roman Catholics in the diocese and the bishop is an old Italian Priest. Despite the fact that Myanmar was officially 'closed' from 1962, there were Western Catholic priests working at Taunggyi's St Joseph's Cathedral throughout. Two of them are buried in the graveyard; one had lived there for 64 years, the other for 47.

The town has a hectic daily market and a bigger regional market once every 5 days. Huge piles of *thanaka* bark (from the acacia tree) are sold in small packets; it is ground into a paste and worn by many Burmese women on their faces, who often apply it in intricate patterns. It protects the face from the sun and is the Burmese equivalent of vanishing cream, make-up and sun-tan lotion, all rolled into one. In Mar, the market sells huge avocados and strawberries. Mingala Market, to the S of Taunggyi's Russian Hospital, is a well known source of smuggled goods.

The **Taunggyi Museum** or **Shan State Museum** as it is officially named, is on the Main St near the *Taunggyi Hotel* and is in need of a good spring clean. It contains a small but good collection of tribal costumes, weapons and artifacts as well as a collection of antique opium weights and musical instruments (including a snakeskin guitar). Next to the entrance there is a large ethnographic map 'showing the dwelling places of the natives' of Shan State which borders China, Laos and Thailand. Tourists are unlikely to get another chance to see the costumes of many of the more remote hilltribes as they are not allowed access to most of the war-torn state. A second, more interesting room, upstairs, has old Shan royal costumes and furniture, as well as portraits of previous kings on display. It also has a copy of the 1947 Panglong Agreement, a treaty of peace and co-operation between the interim government, headed by national hero Aung San, and the hilltribes. Admission US$2. Open 0900-1600 Mon-Fri. Next to the museum is a good library with many books and periodicals in English and helpful staff.

Ma Op cheroot factory is near the Nyaung Shwe pool, N of the market. Taunggyi is the Havanna of Myanmar: its tobacco is sweet and is known throughout the country; the town's tobacco traders are among its wealthier residents. Ma Op is the number one brand and the factory produces over a million a year. Ma Op herself is a rich and jolly Intha lady in her 60s. She employs 50 women who roll about 1,000 cheroots each and every day. They work 7 days a week (except for special market and full moon days) and get paid 2 kyat for every 100 produced – roughly the retail cost of four big cheroots. The cheroots are made from a mixture of dried tobacco and woodchips and are flavoured with tamarind and dried banana. Their filters are made from maize husks wrapped in old copies of the *Working People's Daily*, and finally they are rolled in dried green codia leaves. They are a surprisingly mild and aromatic smoke and burn for more than half an hour. Ma Op welcomes visitors to the factory and is likely to dispatch men with a bundle of her best cheroots which would take several weeks to smoke. There is an interesting **gem market** in town, which is open daily and another market which is open every 5 days.

Local information

● Accommodation

There are several smaller hotels in the centre of town but at present only the *Taunggyi* and *May Chu* are open to foreigners, many are considerably cheaper than the *Taunggyi Hotel* but facilities are very basic.

C ***Duwon***, 122 Mahabandoola St, T 21166; **C** ***Taunggyi***, Shu Myaw Kin Rd, T 21127, just off the main street at the S end of town (nr the museum), restaurant, pleasant old fashioned hotel in wooded grounds, the *Taunggyi* employ a few Padaung women in a mock village to pose for tourists who want to photograph their brass-armoured long-necked selves (the Padaung people are native to Kayah State); **E** ***May Chu***, very dirty and basic, cold shower.

● Places to eat

Chinese: ***♦♦♦Coca Cola***, nr Nan film studio at N end of town; ***♦♦Lyan You Hotel Restaurant***, Main St, mainly noodles, good selection of Burmese liquor; ***♦♦♦Maw Shwe Synn Restaurant***, Main St, good menu; ***♦♦♦♦Summer Prints***, E of Nan film studio, rec by locals.

International/Burmese: ***♦♦♦Taunggyi Hotel Restaurant***, European, Burmese and Chinese food, good spot for breakfast as it is one of the few places in Myanmar not serving insipid coffee.

Shan: ***Daw Htwan*** (or *Htun's*), noodle shop, Thida St, Nyun Shwe Haw Gone quarter (behind the market), highly rec for breakfast or lunch, Shan exiles in Yangon dream of Daw Htwan's Shan *hkankswe* (noodles), fried tofu and *weq-tha-kyin* (rice and pork).

● Post & telecommunications

It is possible to make international phone calls here at rates slightly higher than in Yangon.

● Tourist offices

MTT, *Taunggyi Hotel*.

● Transport

See Inle Lake, page 232.

Local Taxis: small green taxis, cost around 20 kyat from the *Taunggyi Hotel* to the centre of town. **Pony & cart**: 20 kyat for short ride.

KENGTUNG (CHIANG TUNG) ကျိုင်းတုံ

The Mae Sai-Tachilek border was previously only accessible for Thais and Burmese but it has recently opened to foreigners. The Burmese Government has officially sanctioned the border crossing to Tachilek, but the Thais have not, so your passport is not officially stamped as having left Thailand. The Burmese allow tour groups of up to 10 people to make the 167 km journey to Kengtung. The visa is only for a maximum of 4 days/3 nights and is liable to change at a moment's notice. Visitors must leave the border before 1000 so they reach Kengtung by nightfall. The border is open 0600-1800 Mon-Sun. It is obligatory to exchange US$100 into FECs on the border.

The road to Kengtung is in bad condition – a 4WD is advisable. However, the Thais are building a new road which is intended to eventually connect Thailand with China's Yunnan Province. It is the only way visitors can reach the otherwise inaccessible Burmese territory within the *Golden Triangle*. The road, which winds precipitously through the mountain ravines on rock-cut shelves, is a major smuggling route, not only for heroin and opium, but for Chinese and Shan girls, many of whom end up in Bangkok brothels. James Pringle, one of the few Western journalists to have made the trip to Kengtung, reported seeing chain gangs of shackled prisoners breaking stones to be used for building the road to China. Some of the prisoners are reported to be students, arrested during the 1988 uprising. Pringle quotes a Myanmar specialist in Bangkok as saying: "The Burmese military is so out of touch with the real world it does not seem to realize it is doing anything wrong, and is even allowing tourists to see this".

A smugglers outpost, the city is often compared to Chiang Mai 50 years ago before it was hit by tourism. It is and was an important Shan stronghold. Next to the main hotel, originally named *The Kengtung*, is the site of an old Shan palace demolished by the military in 1992 to build a car park. The Buddha image, Maha Myat Muni is the most sacred but other important temples are the Sun

Sali, Sun Taung and Sun Lwe. The town is a treasure trove of traditional architecture with old-style houses with intricately designed wooden balconies so characteristic of Shan architecture.

• **Accommodation** Military governor, Brigadier Kyaw Win, believes there is future in tourism here and has turned his residence into a guesthouse. So, too, has the local police chief who lives next door. The ***Kyaingtong Hotel*** has also recently been refurbished but the rooms are said to be pricey.

• **Tour companies & travel agents** Several Thai tour companies run trips to the border: ***Dits Travel***, Baanboran Hotel, Sop Ruak, T 716678, F 716680; ***Diethelm***, Kian Gwan Bldg II, 140/1 Wireless Rd, Bangkok 10330, T 2559150, F 2560248.

• **Transport Road Car**: 6-7 hrs; petrol is available along the route.

HSIPAW (THIBAW)

A cool Shan valley contains Hsipaw (in Shan pronunciation; in Burmese, *Thibaw*) and many small Shan and other national minority villages. The town makes a good base for getting acquainted with northern Shan State, as it has a large market, cheap and decent accommodation, plenty of sights and excursions, and very friendly people. There are minority villages nearby, and a number of cottage industries in town. The noodle factory is a great asset – fresh Shan sticky noodles are available all around town. A number of Hsipaw residents have made it a mission to show tourists around town while answering all their questions about the area, the country and current events.

This is the town Inge Sargent came to live in after marrying a man who turned out to be a Shan prince. She wrote about her experiences in *Twilight over Burma*. The prince's niece and nephew now live in her house, and receive interested visitors.

It may not be apparent to the casual visitor, but there is some ethnic tension in Hsipaw, where many Burmans live. There are distinct Shan and Burman monasteries, for example. Socially the various ethnic groups (including Chinese, Indian and Palaung people, among others) have a tendency to separate. Many of the people from local ethnic groups feel exploited and oppressed by the arbitrary ways of the Yangon-based government and its local representatives. However, the NLD and the Shan party are strong in this area, which helps release political frustration in a useful way, and few people talk seriously of total independence from Myanmar.

Places of interest

Ko Zaw Tun's ('Mr Book') bookstall on the main road near the market is open early and late. Ko Zaw Tun and friends have bicycles to lend, will arrange trips to nearby towns, and will ensure you get good bus tickets. In fact, several of the excursions can be made only with their help, as they know the villagers and drivers whose cooperation you need. All payment and gifts of value will be refused. At the bookstall you will also find the latest information about what towns and routes are open and closed. This is a good first stop in Hsipaw.

The **Bawgyo Pagoda**, 7 km out of Hsipaw on the Mandalay road, was a simple Shan-style pagoda until recently. For years it suffered the indignity of being repainted periodically in the favourite colour of newly assigned Burmese army area commanders. In 1995 the ancient Bawgyo was Burmanized by the addition of elaborate layers of red and gold ornamentation. Many local Shans resent the change, but they had no recourse to stop it. Now they joke that the result looks like the historical general Maha Bandoola's helmeted head. Maha Bandoola's killing by the British during the First Anglo-Burmese War crippled Lower Burma's resistance to the colonizers. Now, however, his head seems to be resurrected in the service of other oppressors.

Shan-style chedis can still be seen in

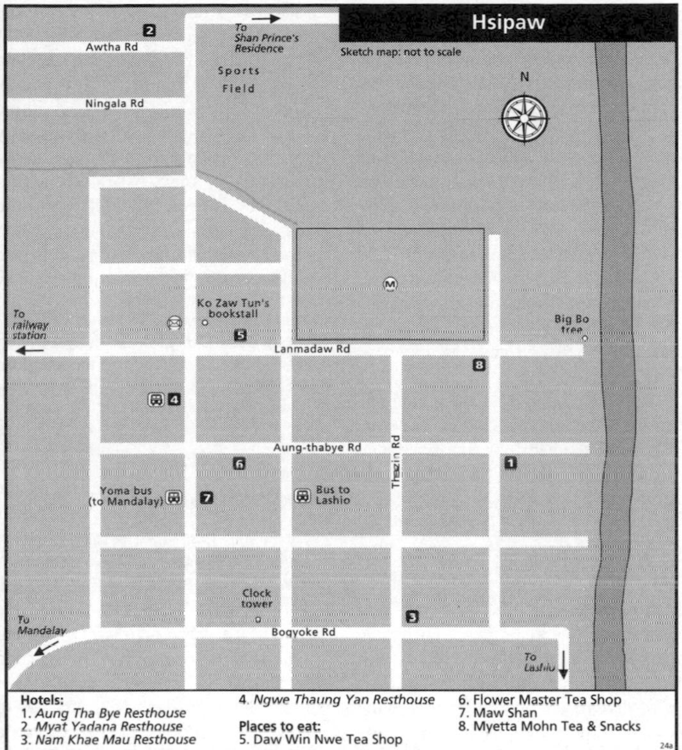

Hsipaw. There is one near the large bo tree (with a nat shrine) after the turnoff from the main road, on the way to the prince's residence. Another is in the **Aungzedi Monastery** (just opposite the lane to the residence), among a crowd of other structures.

In the **prince's English-style residence** live three generation of Shan aristocracy. The last Shan-style *haw* in the area was burnt down during WW2, but the prince's meditation house is built in the traditional style. The Shan princes gave up their ruling power in exchange for seats in Parliament in 1959, but the royal families still enjoy great respect in the area. Some members stood for election in 1990, and others are watching the situation and waiting for a better time to get involved; still others live a more private life. Most of the Shan royalty's property was nationalized in 1964. In Hsipaw, cash crops now grow where the lawn once spread, the tennis courts are cracked, and there has long not been enough electricity available to pump the swimming pool full. The family, however, have lost none of their dignity. They graciously show unannounced visitors around, and tell the history of their family and Shan State. As you are visiting their home, there is no entrance fee, but there is a box for donations.

Further N is the town's nat shrine,

under a large tree. Turn left (W) and follow the lane to visit the 19th century **Kantha Monastery**. One of the Buddha images here is made of lacquered bamboo.

In the centre of town is a **large market**. Various minority village residents come down in the morning to sell their goods and buy supplies. Local wares include Shan longyis with fine stripes, pack baskets worn low on the back and large sheets of handmade paper. Two blocks S of the market is a shoulder-bag weaving workshop; a short distance farther S is a longyi-weaving workshop. Both can be visited any day, but have little action on Sun.

The whole valley can be seen from the hillside **Theindaung Pagoda**, 30 mins walk from the centre of Hsipaw, along the Lashio road. Ko Zaw Tun often gathers people to go together to watch the sunset, but as the hill is E of the town, the view at sunrise is the most striking and photogenic.

Excursions

Excursions to nearby villages can include watching a traditional water-driven rice mill and a less traditional water-driven battery recharger; observing the weaving of items from bamboo ranging from baskets to houses; seeing Shan spirits ferment; and floating down a small river on large inner tubes.

Local information

● Accommodation

All guesthouses are in our **E** category and have simple facilities.

Aungthabye, away from all the main roads, is the quietest, it has a garden, is fairly clean, but all the rooms are on the ground floor, so there is little privacy, singles, doubles, triples, all beds have mosquito nets, good English spoken; ***Myatyadana***, N of the centre of town, past the sports field, T 105, the green propaganda sign reads 'Myanma sports must overwhelm the world' in Burmese, friendly, good English, few mosquito nets, mattresses on floor, clean, one block off noisy road, most foreigners stay here; ***Nam Khae Mao***, nr the clock tower, on Mandalay-Lashio road, T 88, noisy, a bit dirty, English spoken; ***Aung Chan Tha***, a few minutes out of town on the Mandalay road, T 84, larger rooms than other guesthouses, airy, view of paddy fields, little English; ***Ngwe Thaung Yan***, at the bus stop in the heart of town, often full, noisy, mostly Burmese guests, little English; ***Duhtawaddy***, in the S part of town on the Lashio road, mainly truck drivers and therefore very noisy in the morning, doubles as a brothel.

● Places to eat

Particularly good Shan noodles are served all over town all day. In and around the market are other Shan specialities, incl *tahubyaw*, a savoury bean dish with a custard-like texture, and fried squares of yellow-bean tofu served with hot sauce. Shan rice dishes are served at ***Maw Shan***, on the main road. (Two signs in Burmese only. It is the northernmost room in the long woven-bamboo row.) Most of the restaurants in town serve the Burmese version of Chinese food.

Tea and snacks: in the afternoon and early evening, fruit and Shan snacks are sold at tables set up nr the cinema on the main road. The best *nan-bya* (Indian-style nan bread) and *palata* are served at ***Myetta Mohn*** (blue sign in Burmese only) on the corner SE of the market. All tea shops and restaurants close by 2100.

● Transport

200 km from Mandalay, 70 km from Lashio.

Train FEC fares are collected all along this rail line. The 0445 train from Mandalay stops in Pyin U Lwin between 0830 and 0930, and generally reaches Hsipaw by mid-afternoon.

Road Bus: the fastest transport is by road, but it is 6-9 rough hrs from Mandalay. Linecars leave from 84th St, nr the Zegyo market (250-350 kyat). From Pyin U Lwin, one car leaves at 0600 from the Shan market (300 kyat). Here a car and driver can also be chartered for approximately US$45. Or, wait at the *Diamond Cafeteria* between 0730 and 0900 for a seat on the cars coming from Mandalay (150-250 kyat).

NAMHSAN နမ့်ဆန်

Namhsan, a tea-growing village, is one day's rough ride from Hsipaw. As is typical for a Palaung village, it is stretched out along a ridge top, with pagodas on nearby hills. Although Namhsan has been officially open to foreigners for some time, the local officials were in the habit of sending away the rare foreigner who arrived. In 1996 some local NLD (National League for Democracy) members and a few determined tourists conducted a letter-writing and visiting campaign which has succeeded in smoothing later arrivals.

Namhsan bureaucrats are still a bit stiff in their welcome. Permission is required to go more than 8 km out of the town. Daw Aye Wun, the guesthouse proprietor, or Sayamagyi (a retired administrator) usually accompany tourists everywhere, partly out of friendliness, partly to keep an eye on them. They are a good source of information about local culture. However, Sayamagyi is prone to repeating the latest propaganda line.

Places of interest The last person who makes **traditional glittering Palaung overshirts** lives in Namhsan. The sequined garments are worn at weddings and other special occasions. The patterns are related to the Palaungs' legends about the beginning of their people, as children of a naga (water serpent). Daw Aye Wun or Sayamagyi will introduce you to the woman, who works in her home. She may also have unusual longyis to sell.

There are **numerous pagodas** in gorgeous hilltop locations within strolling or hiking distance of the centre of town. None of them has particular architectural or historic interest, but all are pretty and have friendly monks. Thanks to geography and Palaung culture – the roads have been built along the lines of ridges – it is impossible to lose one's way.

To one side of town is an old British tea factory which has been nationalized, and is now run by the military. The road past it is closed at 1800. Normally when roads are closed after dark, it is because of insurgent activity, but the insurgents in this area had a stable cease-fire with the Burmese army at the end of 1996 when this book went to press. You may see some of them around town, with different uniforms or insignia from the Tatmadaw troops.

Although this area grows the finest tea in Myanmar, as is evident in the tea-shop quality, *lephet-thouk* (pickled tea leaves) is not available in restaurants and tea shops.

Palaung villages usually have a wooded knoll with a large shrine to the local spirits. Check to be sure it is all right to go near these shrines before starting up the steps or path toward the sacred site, as it may be off limits to strangers, or to all when no ceremony is in progress.

- **Accommodation** Someone from the truck that brings you to Namhsan will deliver you to the only place to stay: Daw Aye Wun's converted shop on the main road, nr the 3-way crossing. She has beds for 5 people in her attic (plus extra mats for overflow) and cold, rather dirty showers in her basement. 70 kyat pp; watch out for rats. Daw Aye Wun is kind, and speaks quite a bit of English. She can arrange for a rather tough massage, which may relieve or exacerbate the effects of the journey.

- **Transport** The only way to get to Namhsan is an all-day truck ride from Hsipaw. There is no regular public transport, but Ko Zaw Tun can contact the drivers and arrange a ride (250 kyat). Availability is unpredictable, ranging from near-daily to once or twice per week. During tea harvesting times, it is possible to go all the way to Mandalay in approximately 24 hrs on early-morning trucks which stop for a few hours of sleep on the road. However, even during peak transport periods, there may not be daily departures.

LASHIO လားရှိုး

Lashio is at the Burmese end of the Burma Rd to Kunming, and was built to supply the Kuomintang during China's civil war. Lashio is often spoken of dismissively as "just a Chinese town" but these are not the same Chinese who are buying Burmese citizenship and transforming Mandalay. Many of the families have lived in this area for generations, and have mixed with the Shans.

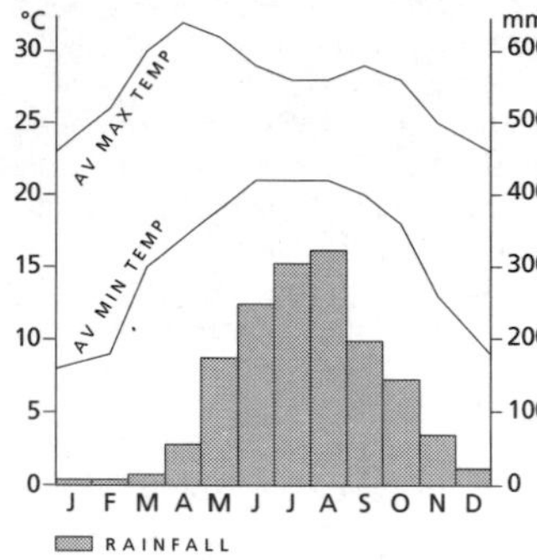

Climate: Lashio

Lashio is near areas which have never been under firm government control. Many smugglers and others connected with trade have prospered here. The town is surrounded by tempting green hills and numerous minority villages, but as yet tourists are not allowed to leave Lashio proper, though a few have made it to some nearby hotsprings. It is also possible to visit the border town of **Museh** if one is coming in from China. However, at present it is not possible to leave Myanmar this way, and local immigration is a bit nervous about tourists trying it. (In the past, people have been known to get permission to enter Myanmar at the border post, but it is better to arrange the trip in Kunming.)

Places of interest A **Chinese monastery** sits on a hillside 15 mins walk from the centre of town founded about half a century ago, it is still the site of fresh building. From the forbidding gateway guardians to the dragons on the roof it is typically Chinese, and a good place to see that population in action.

The **Thathana 2500 pyelon paya**, commemorating the halfway mark to the emergence of the next Buddha, is on a hilltop N of town. The old Buddha image is said to date from the Pagan era. The pagoda itself is standardly pretty; the real attraction is the sweeping view of the whole valley.

• **Accommodation** Three hotels accept foreigners. **E** *Lashio*, T 21702, a/c, hot water shower, TV, breakfast incl; **E** *New Asia*, not very friendly staff.

• **Transport Train** Connections from Mandalay, Pyin U Lwin and Hsipaw (14 hrs from Mandalay). **Road Car**: see Travel Agents in Pyin U Lwin, page 173. **Linecars**: from Pyin U Lwin, Hsipaw and Mandalay.

The West Coast

RAKHINE AND CHIN STATES

Getting to Rakhine (Arakan)

If you ask MTT how to get to Rakhine, they will tell you to fly. Indeed, Rakhine is not easy to get to by land, some say by design. For decades after independence, it looked quite possible that Rakhine would split off from central Myanmar. Therefore the Yangon government saw no reason to invest in infrastructure or industry beyond what it needed to extract raw materials for its own use. Hospitals, schools and other government services are extremely poor even today. However, Rakhine has a lot to offer the visitor, and there are more interesting ways of getting there than Myanmar Airlines.

Ship to Sittwe: the least strenuous of them is to take a 2½-day sea passage. Ships leave Yangon for Sittwe on an irregular schedule, as they are primarily for goods, not people, but they usually number around one a month. *5 Star Lines* (corner of Theinbyu and Merchant streets) provide information on when the next ship is leaving. The one way fare is US$60. The seas may be rough during the rainy season, which hits Rakhine particularly hard. To inquire, go in the back entrance of the building, upstairs to the first floor, and straight ahead into the office. The manager speaks English well.

Bus to Taunggok and boat to Sittwe: the next easiest way is to take a bus from Pyay to Taunggok. In Taunggok make your way to the port and ask the boats when they are leaving and for where. Passage to Sittwe (2 days) is 600 kyat. Boats anchor at night.

Bus to Minbu, Ann and Tatdaung and boat to Sittwe: there is a second, rougher road from Minbu on the Ayeyarwady to Ann (Am). From Ann continue another 40 km to Tatdaung on the coast to catch the weekly boat to Sittwe (see page 255 for details). However, this route is sometimes arbitrarily closed by the army, even when it is officially open.

Bus to Mindon and then trek to the coast: finally, a 3-day trek will take you from Mindon (W of Thayet) to Letpan on the coastal road, where there are boats to Sittwe. For details on this hike see pages 216 and 255.

THANDWE (SANDOWAY)
သံတွဲ

Thandwe, which the British corrupted into Sandoway, has been an important trading centre for centuries but today seems to have fallen on thin times. The town is marvellously undeveloped and most of the buildings date from before (or shortly after) independence. The **market** in the centre of town, housed in what used to be the local jail during the British era, is a throng of stalls and hawkers selling mostly dry goods from cloth to metal tools. Outside town, built on low hills, are three **stupas** which, though not particularly notable, make for a rewarding walk and climb. Most people who come to Thandwe, though, do not linger long but merely stop off en-route to Ngapali Beach (see the next entry).

• **Accommodation** Perhaps because so few people stay here, the town's guesthouses have not yet been granted permission to accept foreigners. However, there are two places, both in our **D** category, which might allow you to stay: the ***San Yeik Nyein Guesthouse*** and the ***Mla Guesthouse***. The former is said to be the more pleasant.

• **Transport Air** Myanmar Airways operated flights between Thandwe and Yangon and Mandalay. **Road Bus**: there are daily bus connections between Yangon and Thandwe, but it requires an overnight stop in Pyay or Sinde and the journey is pretty gruelling. It is much better to stop off en-route, either in Pathein, Pyay or Hinthada. The Pyay route is most convenient. The road is good as far as Pyay but deteriorates over the Rakhin Yoma towards Thandwe. From Pyay catch a bus to Taunggok and then a connection onto Thandwe – old and cramped buses leave at 1200 and 1400 along the pot-holed road.

NGAPALI ငပလီ

Just S of Thandwe is Myanmar's best known resort, although all along this coast are unspoilt sandy beaches fringed with coconut groves. It has not changed much since Maurice Collis' visit in 1923 on his way to take up his post as Deputy Commissioner of Thandwe for the Indian Civil Service: "The pleasures of Sandaway were very simple. The chief was to drive down to Ngapali beach and bathe... By the edge of the beach was a bungalow on posts with coconut palms waving over it, where you could stay as long as you liked. There was, however, nothing to do except bathe, walk along an incomparable sand, and sit in an armchair on the bungalow's veranda, dozing in the warm wind." (*Into Hidden Burma*). Most of the local villages thrive from the good fishing off the coast. Many wealthy Burmese generals and government ministers have holiday homes in Ngapali. The best time to go is between Oct and May during the rainy season, the hotels close.

• **Accommodation B** ***New Ngapali Beach Hotel***, T 27, a newer but less attractive version of *Ngapali Beach Hotel*, 2-storey buildings with no trees to provide shade and sporadic electrical supply for the a/c, hot water; **C *Ngapali Beach Hotel***, T 28, beachside restaurant, bungalows with balconies on the beach, mosquito nets, cold water only, electricity at night only; **D *Lintha Oo Lodge***, Lintha Village, bungalows on the beach and trips to the islands.

• **Places to eat** ♦***Hokkay***, Ngapali Village, fresh seafood; ♦***Reik***, small restaurant serving seafood, Chinese and Burmese food, modest but friendly.

• **Transport Local Bicycles**: for rent from *Ngapali Beach Hotel* or *Lintha Oo Lodge* (150 kyat/day). **Air** There are regular flights between Yangon and Thandwe (1 hr) and there is also a service between Thandwe and Mandalay. **Road Bus**: to get to Ngapali it is first necessary to get to Thandwe. See the previous entry for bus details. From Thandwe take a taxi to Ngapali. **Boat** Boats can be hired for trips to the nearby islands either from *Lintha Oo Lodge* or *Zaw Restaurant*, opp *Ngapali Beach Hotel*.

MRAUK-U (MYOHAUNG) မြောက်ဦး

The last royal capital of Rakhine is renowned for its archaeological remains, wall paintings of Indian influence and scenic beauty. It is popularly known as the 'Golden City'. It lies at the head of a tributary of the Kaladan River, about 60 km from Sittwe on the coast. Myohaung, as it is known today, is a simple market town, although 'Myohaung' actually means 'ancient city'. In the Myohaung area you may come across local hill tribe people called the *thet* who can be recognized by their large earrings.

History

The first kingdom of the Rakhine (Arakan) Dynasty was based ruled by King Vasudeva. He married a local princess and became the head of a powerful kingdom. His son, Marayu, conquered Vesali and founded Dhanyawaddy on the Thari River in 3000 BC. Several dynasties were based on this site until 326 AD.

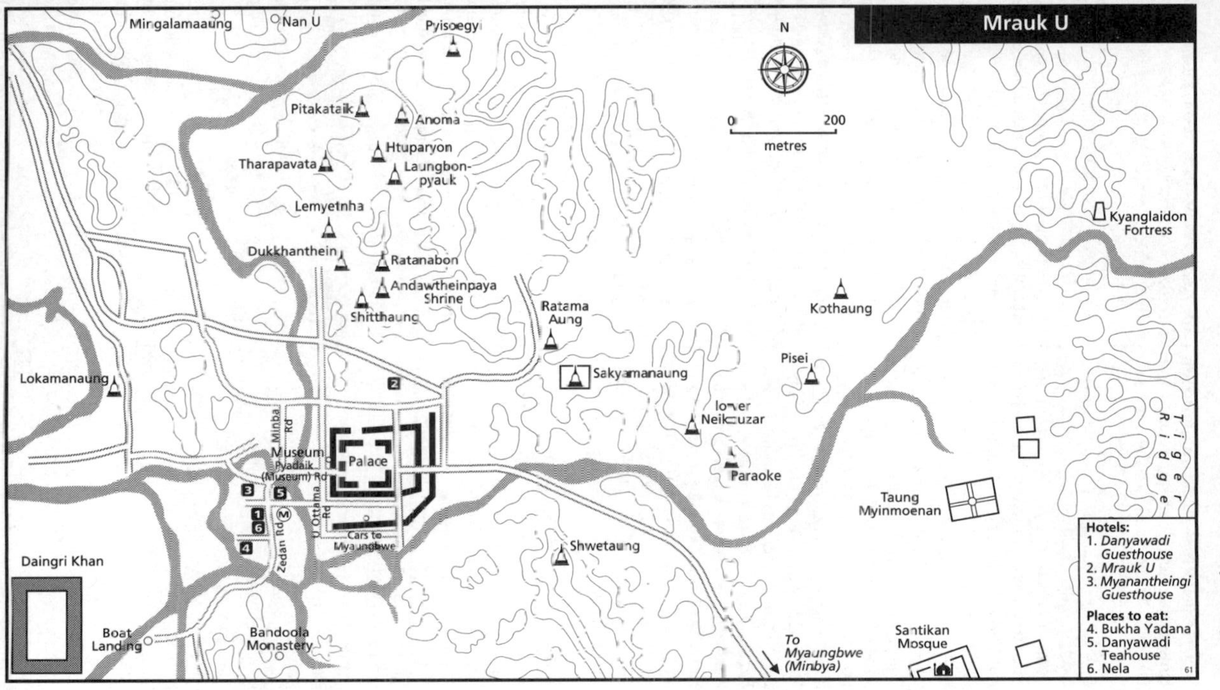
Mrauk U
N
0 200
metres
Mingalamaaung
Nan U
Pyisoegyi
Pitakataik
Anoma
Htuparyon
Tharapavata
Laungbon-pyauk
Lemyetnha
Dukkhanthein
Ratanabon
Andawtheinpaya Shrine
Shitthaung
Ratama Aung
Kothaung
Kyanglaidon Fortress
Pisei
Sakyamanaung
lower Neikuzar
Paraoke
Lokamanaung
Minba Rd
Museum
Pyadaik (Museum) Rd
Palace
U Ottama Rd
Zedan Rd
Cars to Myaungbwe
Shwetaung
Taung Myinmoenan
Tiger Ridge
Daingri Khan
Boat Landing
Bandoola Monastery
To Myaungbwe (Minbya)
Santikan Mosque
Hotels:
1. Danyawadi Guesthouse
2. Mrauk U
3. Myanantheingi Guesthouse
Places to eat:
4. Bukha Yadana
5. Danyawadi Teahouse
6. Nela

The Chandra Dynasty, founded by King Mahataing Chandra, moved from Dhanywaddy to Vesali on the advice of his astrologers in 327 AD. The city prospered as a river port and established foreign trade. Local legends tell of thousands of vessels laden with merchandise calling at Vesali annually. The kingdom was Buddhist and the Mahamuni image formed the centre of religious worship. Early inscriptions also tell of two missionaries introducing a new religion and images of Brahma, Vishnu and Siva have also been found in local shrines at Vesali. Despite invasions by the Shans, Vesali continued to flourish until 1018. King Minbeeloo was assassinated by a noble in 1078 and the royal family fled to Pagan. According to tradition a large army was sent from Bagan to restore King Letyaminnan, the true descendant, to the throne in 1103. He built a temporary city at Launggret and then settled at nearby Parein. In 1251, on the advice of his astrologers, King Alawmarphyu, reinstated Launggret reinstated as the capital of his kingdom.

The Kaladan River was originally navigable to this area, and it was a meeting point of roads E and W. With high rainfall the surrounding area was also a rich rice growing region. Launggret was based on the plains but King Minsawmon decided its position was indefensible and the city had been ruined by invaders. Mrauk-U was an obvious choice, naturally well defended by surrounding ridges and the king's astrologers foretold the prosperity of the site. The city was founded in 1430 AD. City walls were built in the gaps between the natural barriers and a maze-like chain of lakes and moats were constructed for protection and to supply fresh drinking water. The city became an important commercial centre and the seat of the Rakhine Dynasty until it was annexed by the Burmese in 1785. In 1826 it was taken by the English.

Rakhine is predominantly Muslim; its people were the focus of international concern in 1992 when 200,000 of them fled into neighbouring Bangladesh, to refugee camps at Cox's Bazar.

Places of interest

Beside the pagodas, the city walls, moats, ramparts, watch towers and forts are still visible. If you get a chance, the **Archaeological Museum** is worth a visit for its 15th and 16th century Buddha images. Take off your shoes when entering the room with the Buddha images. The museum also has some old musical instruments and pieces of the intricately decorated blue-and-white floor tiles from the Ratanabon Temple. Open Mon-Fri, 0900-1630.

The palace was the centre of the

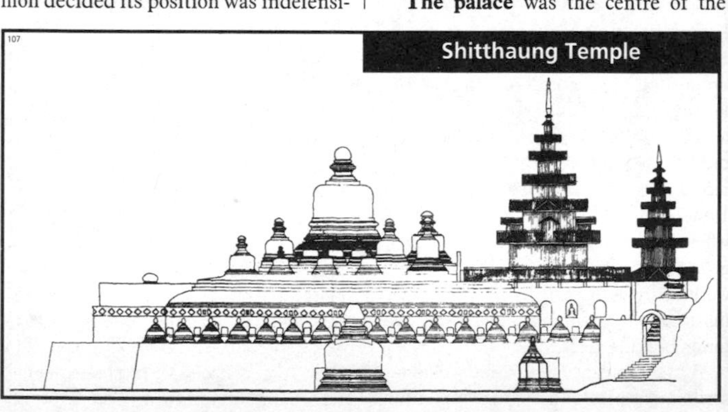
107

Shitthaung Temple

ancient city and was built to the same traditional pattern as Burmese palaces. The walls can be seen today but the original teak buildings have long since disappeared. The stone walls were erected by King Minbin (1531-53). According to Father Manrique, a Portuguese monk, "there were three enclosures which rose in tiers, each bounded by a thick stone wall. ... The main audience hall and the private apartments were situated in the innermost square. ... They were of teakwood, lacquered and gilded, the roofs carved with figures and rising in spires. ... The audience hall with its great wooden pillars of such length and symmetry that one would be astonished that trees so lofty and straight could exist." Manique was conducted into a room "which was panelled with scented timber, such as sandalwood and eagle-wood". Passing through these perfumed chambers he came to a pavilion known as the 'House of Gold', the walls of which were plated with gold. Along the ceiling was a golden creeper with many gourds moulded in the same metal and leaves of emeralds and grapes of garnets. In the same chamber were seven idols of gold.

Northern side

About 1 km N of the palace site is the **Shitthaung Temple**, or the shrine of 80,000 images. It was built in 1535 by King Minbin, one of the most powerful rulers of the Mrauk-U Dynasty, in celebration of the successful defeat of the Portuguese. The king is said to have collected 80,000 Buddha images from formerly Buddhist territory which he reconquered, and enshrined the images in 108 relic chambers underneath the temple, where they remain. It is said that the pagoda was built by 1,000 architects and workmen over a year. It is probably the most famous temple here and renowned for its Buddha images and reliefs.

By the entrance is a stone pillar inscribed with Rakhine characters and a

Mrauk-U northern side

Andawtheinpaya Shrine
အံတော်စေတီ

Anoma Pagoda
အနော်မာဘုရား

Dukkhanthein Temple
ဒုက္ကံသိမ်ဘုရား

Htupayon Pagoda
ထူပါရုံဘုရား

Laungbonpyauk Pagoda
လောင်ပုံပြောက်ဘုရား

Lemyetnha Pagoda
လေးမျက်နှာဘုရား

Ne Htwet Para
နေထွက်ဘုရား

Pitakattaik
ပိဋကတ်တိုက်

Pysisoegyi Pagoda
ပြည်စိုးကြီးဘုရား

Ratanabon Pagoda
ရတနာပုံဘုရား

Shitthaung Temple
သျှစ်သောင်းဘုရား

Shitthaung Pillar
သျှစ်သောင်းကျောက်တိုင်

Tharapavata Pagoda
သာရပဗ္ဗတဘုရား

statue of King Minbin. There are two small sandstone pagodas on the first platform: the octagonal **Ne Htwet Para** (Sun Rise Pagoda) and the stupa **Ne Win Para** (Sun Set Pagoda). The central platform is dominated by a wooden prayer

Dukkhanthein Temple cross section

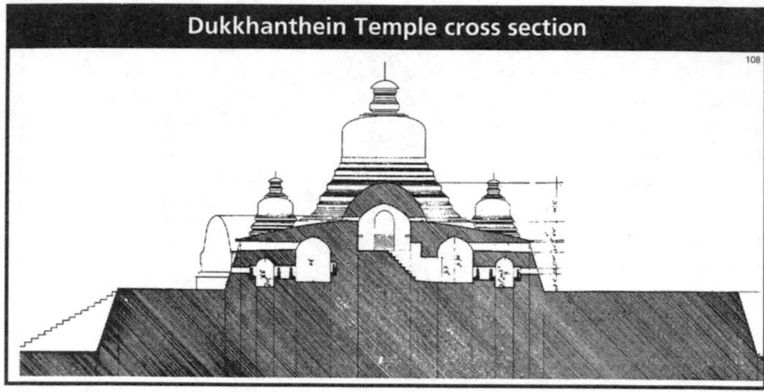

hall, which housed innumerable Buddha images. The third Buddha at the top of the stairs is carved out of a single piece of stone, pedestal and all. The central pagoda is 27m high and is surrounded by smaller copies between which were a stone slab sculpted with nagas, mythical birds and beasts. The shrine is surrounded by a gallery with Buddha images in the outer wall.

The Buddha in the altar room off the main room inside the temple is also carved of a single piece of stone. He is in the classic Arakanese style, with an unadorned forehead, ears stopping short of shoulders, eyes looking downward, legs folded on each other (not crossed) and a spark, in the shape of a flower, in the open hand in his lap.

The temple's real attraction, however, is the layered corridor system. The outermost layer contains representations of hundreds of scenes from the jataka tales and other educational fables. The highest row of figures depict kings and queens worshipping. The figures of Ganesh at the corners are meant to ensure that the building endures – elephant-headed Ganesh is the god of arts and architecture. The carvings have certainly endured very well. The paint you see on them, though, is from British times. Originally they were glazed, but only a small area of glazing remains, on the 3-headed elephant, Erawan, at the corner near the main room.

The outer corridor is connected to the outside world by open arches with back-to-back Buddhas in them, and the eyes and mind are kept busy by the many carvings. Take a sharp turn into the doubled-back inner corridors, and everything changes. The air is cooler, the corridor's smooth arch is complicated only by a row of smooth-faced Buddhas. An inner chamber holds four more images. One is wearing trappings imitating the 16th century prime minister who donated the image.

If the corridors are dark (the original lighting system, cups in the wall filled with oil, and a lighted wick, has been abandoned for electric lights), you can make a donation to the trustees in the main room and they will turn on the lights for an hour.

The **Shitthaung Pillar** is to the N of the Shitthaung Pagoda and is said to have been brought here by King Minbin from Vesali, an earlier Rakhine capital. Three sides of the pillar are inscribed with Sanskrit and list the kings who ruled ancient Rakhine. It is believed to have been a lintel.

The **Andawtheinpaya Shrine** is to the NE of the Shitthaung. It was built by King Min Hla Raza in 1521 to enshrine a tooth-relic of the Buddha, which was bought from Sri Lanka by King Minbin. King Minrazagyi rebuilt

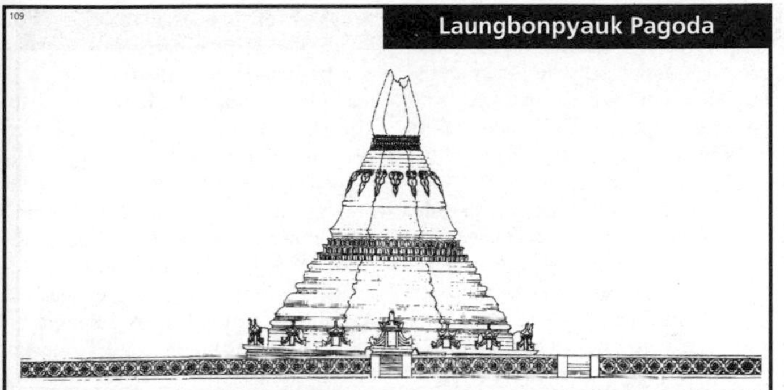

the shrine in 1596. The sandstone shrine is octagonal and encircled by smaller brick pagodas. A gallery runs round the main shrine with thousands of niches with Buddha images carved into the walls. On the E side is the main prayer hall.

Further N stands the **Ratanabon Pagoda**, built by King Minkhamaung and his chief queen Shin Htway in 1612, and is impressive by its massiveness. Unfortunately, the central sandstone stupa, and surrounding stupas, were badly damaged in WW2. It is completely undecorated, uncharacteristic for Rakhine. The lions protecting the outer pagoda walls are still standing.

King Minphalaung built the **Dukkhanthein** (or Htaukkanthein) **Temple** in 1571 to the W of Ratanabon. It is approached by massive stone stairways on all four sides. The bell-shaped central dome is similar to the Shitthaung but an arch on the eastern side admits light into the central chamber. The pagoda is renowned for its sculpture in the inner passages – especially the seated ladies offering lotus buds to the Buddha. These ladies have 64 different kinds of hairstyles and were modelled on the wives of noblemen. These inner walls are also punctuated with 140 niches holding Buddha statues. This temple also has a double corridor design, with a narrow outer passage and a spacious inner one. During WW2, the Japanese took refuge in the inner corridor.

To the NW is the **Lemyetnha** (or Four Faced) **Pagoda**, built by King Minsawmon (the first king of Mrauk U Dynasty) in 1430. Along with the nearby Myatanzaung pagodas and the Mokseiktaw, it was built when the city was established. The Mokseiktaw has a well preserved library and a famous footprint of the Buddha.

The **Laungbonpyauk Pagoda** was built in 1525 by King Minkhaungraza. The sculptures on the inner wall are particularly fine: at the centre of each is a rosette containing eight coloured clay tablets. The façade also has exquisite carvings.

According to local records, the rather neglected **Htupayon Pagoda** was erected by King Minranaung, the sixth king of the Mrauk-U Dynasty in 1494. It was rebuilt in 1613 by King Minkhamaung. The four corners are guarded by manotethiha, or lions with two heads. It was an important pagoda – the site of victory and prosperity – and was traditionally visited by kings after their coronations.

On a hill between Htuparyon and Mokseiktaw is the **Tharapavata Pagoda**. A buddha image was found here with inscriptions dating back to the 4th century. Just to the N is the **Pitakattaik**, or library, donated by King Minphalaung in 1591. It housed the Buddhist scriptures, supposedly the 30 sets of the Triptika which King Narapatigyi (1638-1645) received from Sri Lanka. Just to the N of the library are remains of the old city wall and moat.

Further E is the **Pyisoegyi Pagoda**, which also has a library decorated with fine sculptures. Pyisoegyi means 'head of state' and it was believed to have been donated. Further E is the Minthami water gate, which was opened to fill the Tharikonboung moat in times of war.

All that remains of the **Anoma Pagoda** is a Buddha statue and a finely decorated pedestal. The original pagoda was donated by Princess Anowzaw, daughter of King Salingathu (1494-1501). The Minpaung Pagoda to the S was built by King Minkhamaung and his chief queen, Shin Htway, in 1640. The pagoda walls are decorated with fantastic figures of dragons. The bell-shaped temple to the S is the Mahabodhi Shwegu and is renowned for the carving in its inner corridors. The stone sculptures around the pedestal of the main image are held to be some of the best Rakhine sculpture. The two temples to the S, Ratanasanraway and Ratanamhankin, were built by King Basawphyu in 1468. The latter is renowned for its carvings of birds, ogres, lotus and griffin. Further E is the Ratanmanaung donated in 1652 by King Candathudhammaraza.

110

The Pitakataik Façade

The field to the E is called Laykhinpyin meaning archery. It was the training ground for the Rakhine archers.

Eastern side

The **Sakyamanaung Pagoda**, NE of the palace site, stands out because of its unusual shape and the two giants which guard the western gate. On a hill to the S is the Wuninattaung, the oldest site in Mrauk-U. The Wuntinattaung inscription found here is an important cultural link as the script resembled the Pali inscriptions found at Thiri Kittaya (Sri Ksetra) from the 6th and 7th century. To the E is the Winmana paddy storehouse, one of 40 in the inner city used to store rice; it was originally surrounded by walls and moats. The Neikbuza pagodas on the hill to the E were all built by King Min Saw Oo in 1527.

To the N is the **Ratanama Aung Pagoda**, where the king and queen had meditation chambers. The queen's is to the left of the road on the way to Ratanabon from Sakyamanaung. The king's is near the main stupa, and is thought to have one of the (unexcavated) exits to the palace's tunnel system. It was damaged in WW2, and the larger Buddhas are replacements, but the smaller ones are thought to be original.

To the SE of the lower Neikbuzar Pagoda is the **Paraoke Pagoda** built by King Minphalaung in 1571. After building the Dukkhanthein Pagoda the king was advised by astrologers to donate another pagoda to prevent disintegration of his kingdom. 'Oake' means to control the whole country.

The **Pisei Pagoda** to the NE was built in 1123 by King Kawliya and houses a

Sakyamanaung Pagoda (northern side)

Mrauk-U eastern side

Kothaung Pagoda
ကိုးသောင်းဘုရား
Paraoke Pagoda
ဘုရားအုတ်
Pisei Pagoda
ပိစေးဘုရား
Ratanama Aung Pagoda
ရတနာမအောင်ဘုရား
Sakyamanaung Pagoda
စကြာမာန်အောင်ဘုရား
Santikan Mosque
စန်တိကန်
Taung Myinmoenan
တောင်မြင့်မိုးနန်း

relic of the Buddha. It is an important Buddhist shrine.

Kothaung means 90,000 and the **Kothaung Pagoda** to the N is supposed to have contained a large number of Buddha images. It was built by King Mintaikkha, son of King Minbin, in 1553. It is one of the largest temples at Mrauk-U. The images were on glazed tiles covering the walls of the corridors inside the thick walls of the temple. These corridors have caved in, but pieces of the tiles can be seen among the rubble.

The central chamber of the temple is also open to the sky now, but there are still Buddhas on the main altar. Several of them are a demonstration in how the heads get knocked off by thieves in order to get at the hollows with gold or jewels inside. Secretary I Khin Nyunt has declared that 1.1 million kyat will be spent on Kothaung's renovation, but work had not yet begun in 1996. If forced labour is used on the project, it may be off-limits to tourists.

Traditionally the kings celebrated their head washing in a small tank, Udawsaykan, to the NE. Kings usually stayed in a small temporary palace originally on the site. On the W side was the elephant training camp for the Rakhine elephant army. Kyanglaidon Fortress on Tiger Ridge parallel to the Lemro River was one of the most important defence points.

To the E of the palace site are the remains of the **Taung Myinmoenan**, another palace. Within the palace walls were five islands, each surrounded by a small moat. The palace or 'Golden House' was on the central island. It is called the Golden House as the central hall was supposed to have been gilded. The king and his chief queen stayed here for important ceremonies. The governors from the provinces stayed on the surrounding islands and were taken in to the Golden House in a gilded boat. They drank the sacred water in the presence of the king to show their loyalty. The nearby **Santikan Mosque** was built by Muslim followers of King Minsawmon in 1429 after campaigns abroad.

Southern side

On top of a small hill, the **Shwetaung Pagoda** is one of the most prominent temples to the S of the palace site. It is believed to have been built by King Mindon in 1531. Nearby are some remaining Burmese fortifications from the first Anglo-Burmese War in 1824. Beyond this temple to the S is a large man-made lake called Anomakan. It was originally a moat but now supplies fresh water to the area. Beyond the lake are the Myataung and Laythataung fortresses and another lake – Letsekan. To the N of the lake is the largest Buddha image in Mrauk-U, all of 4m high. It was donated by King Tazarta in 1515. King Minbin built a shrine to cover the image before one of his military campaigns in India. Unfortunately the shrine is now in ruins.

Southern & western sides
Bandoola Monastery
ဗန္ဓုလကျောင်း
Lokamanaung Pagoda
လောကမာန်အောင်ဘုရား
Shwetaung Pagoda
ရွှေတောင်ဘုရား

Western side

The **Lokamanaung Pagoda** was built by King Candathudhammaraza in the late 17th century. It was an important pagoda as it was at the start of the 'gold' and 'silver' roads to Vesali and Mahamuni. The nearby Parabaw got its name from the image it houses. According to legend the image was salvaged from the river, hence the name Parabaw meaning 'out of water'. The Daingripet, a former European settlement, is on the other bank of the Aungdat Creek. The European Quarter was outside the city walls and flour ished from the 16th to the 17th centuries. King Thirithudhammaraza even allowed Father Manrique to build a Christian church in the area.

The area to the SW of the palace site was protected by a narrow ridge and the Launggret Creek. Ramparts and forts, such as Aungmingala, were built along the slope. The Thongyaiktaau Shrine on the ridge has good views over the Letsekan Valley.

South of the village is the **Bandoola Monastery**, near the site of a First Anglo-Burmese War massacre. In the main building is a good museum with many ancient Buddha images, and a few Buddhas-in-a-bottle. The gilded pillars give an idea of what the palace might have looked like.

In another building nearby is the Mahagyan image, a large Buddha made from the scraps left over from the making of the original Mahamuni image. Its parts are made from alloys of seven metals – gold, three grades of silver, copper, bronze, iron, lead and zinc – with the most precious used for the head. It is a copy of the Mahamuni, stripped to the waist, as was the original before the royal robes were added.

On a hilltop by the nearby lake is a large, free-standing image which is said to be naked. It is no longer visited, and there is no path up the thorny brush covered hillside.

Excursions

30 km from Mrauk-U are the remains of the old Rakhine capitals, **Launggret** and **Parein**. Most of the buildings have disappeared but there is a huge stone slab on top of Taungmawtaung Hill. The inscriptions on the slab describe King Kawliya's (1118-1123) donations. Although the slab is nothing much to look at, the view from the top of the hill is worth the climb. From here you can see the original palace site, the Nandawgon, and city of Launggret to the S. As of mid-1996 these areas are off-limits to foreign tourists.

About 16 km S of Launggret is the **Kadothein Shrine**, discovered in the jungle in 1890. Kadothein was built by King Candavizaya in 1720 and is covered in ornamental designs. There are eight huge boulders engraved with figures, the only ones of this kind in the area.

10 km to the N of Mrauk-U is one of the earliest Rakhine cities, **Vesali**. It was founded by King Mahataing Candra in 327. According to local inscriptions it was called Vesali Kyaukhlayga, the City with Stone Stairs. The city was an important river port and the stairs led to the docks on the river; they can still be seen at low tide. The present village of Vesali is on the original palace site, which remains unexcavated. To the N of the village is the Vesali image, donated by the chief queen, Thupabadevi, in 327. There are few remains of other impor-

Mrauk-U excursions

Dhanyawaddy
ဓညဝတီ
Kadothein Shrine
ကုတိုးသိမ်
Launggret
လောင်ဂရက်
Parein
ပုရိမ်
Vesali
ဝေသာလီ

tant sites in the area: the Shwedaunggyi, or great golden hillock to the N; Sanghayana Hill, supposedly the site of the fourth Buddhist Synod; and Thingyaingtaung, an old burial site.

Dhanyawaddy, 34 km N of Mrauk-U, is another ancient Rakhine city. Its heyday was from 580 BC to 326 AD. It was believed to have been founded by King Sandasuriya but there is some disagreement between archaeologists. There are walls and fortifications still remaining. The city had an inner and outer area. The inner city was a special site for the royal family. The outer walls enclosed the paddy fields so that in times of siege there was an assured food supply. The fields were irrigated by a complex system of tanks and channels, which can be seen in aerial photographs of the region.

The Mahamuni Shrine, one of the most renowned Buddhist sites in Burma, is at the NE corner of the old palace site. It was built to house the Mahamuni image (now in Mandalay, see page 155), believed to be an actual likeness of the Gautama Buddha. Because of its religious importance, it was sought as a prize by neighbouring kings and after several attempts was finally captured by King Bodawpaya in the 18th century. On the first platform you can still see the library built by King Minkhari in 1439, a tank dug by King Sandasuriya and an ordination hall. The Buddha is believed to have rested under the Banyan tree on the second platform, and so it is surrounded by small shrines. On the central platform is the chamber where the Mahamuni image was once kept.

• **Accommodation** *Myanantheingi* and *Danyawadi* guesthouses used to be in the **E** category. However, there is a strong rumour that once the government ***Mrauk-U Hotel*** is finished – which it should be by the time this book goes to press – foreigners will be required to stay there (**C-D**).

• **Places to eat** *Danyawadi Teahouse*, has the best tea and snacks in town; ***Bukhayadana Restaurant***, which does not get much business until night-time, has the best food in town.

• **Transport Local** Most of the pagodas can be visited by foot or on **horse and cart** but for trips further afield hire a **jeep**. **Boat** There are big old government boats which travel upriver from Sittwe to Mrauk-U on Mon, Tues, Thur, Fri and Sat and private ferries (not much better) on Wed and Sun. It is also possible to charter a boat for 15,000 kip. 4½-5 hrs journey time.

SITTWE (AKYAB) စစ်တွေ

Sittwe is an improbable provincial capital. It is a Muslim city in a largely Buddhist country and stands on a small island at the end of a spit of land jutting into the Bay of Bengal. It was originally built by the British after the annexation of Arakan in 1826 and has several buildings dating from that period. Bureaucrats on poverty wages choke the plentiful grand and spacious stucco government buildings, with their large gardens and verdant lawns. The vast majority of the traffic is sidecars and bicycles slaloming around the potholes. Thanks to Sittwe's comfortable sprawl, sidecar drivers get a lot of business, and charge even less than elsewhere in Myanmar. Goods, however, tend

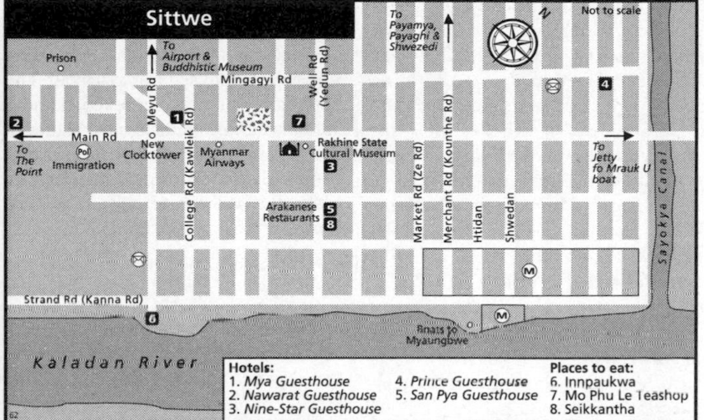

to have rather high prices, often twice what is paid in Yangon. There is little manufacturing in Arakan, so everything must be brought in from elsewhere in Myanmar, or from their neighbours to the W. A highway linking Yangon and Sittwe is under construction (via Ann, and possibly the reason for that district's 'sensitivity'). It will bridge some rivers for the first time, and is due to be completed in 1999.

Places of interest

Sittwe has two museums. The rather clumsily named **Buddhistic Museum**, once housed in a monastery, has been moved to a new building on the airport road. Take off your footwear before going up the steps. Thousands of Buddha images are lined up in glass cases. Most of the figures are only a few centimetres high. These are 'lifetime Buddhas' which have been taken out of the relic chambers of Mrauk-U pagodas. When the pagodas were being built, donors invited others to share in their merit making by offering one image for each year of their life, plus one more for long life. There are also a few bowls containing relics (bones) of the Buddhas. These small images form a backdrop to the larger images which are 10-15 cm high. Many are in unusual postures, such as sitting with hanging legs, or rarely seen hand gestures or grins. Admission free, there is a box for donations.

The **Rakhine State Cultural Museum** is in the centre of town, in a large and ugly purpose-built box. The museum contains a scale model of the Mrauk-U royal palace and some temples. Ancient Arakanese musical instruments have been recreated based on temple carvings. There are also displays of clothing and artefacts of Arakan's seven major minorities. The staff do not speak much English, but they smile prettily when crowding around to take your hard currency. Admission $3 for foreigners (exact change required).

Near the crossing of Sayung and Kounthe roads are several monasteries. Furthest N is the popularly-known **Payagyi Pagoda**, although pedantics may wish to curl their lips around its full name: Atulamarazei Pyilonchantha Payagyi. The 'Payagyi' in the name refers to the monastery's popular 'large Buddha image', a sitting Buddha with a golden face. It is about 100 years old. Inside the Payagyi's shelter, on the S side (to the image's right) in a small glass case, is the Sutaungbyi Buddha, from

Vesali. Just S of the Payagyis is the **Shwezedi Monastery**. U Ottama, the monk who was one of the leaders of the anti-colonial movement in the 1920s and 1930s, was a monk here. The monastery is called 'Golden Chedi', after the square, Indian-inspired shrine on the grounds, which was once covered in gold. Since it was damaged during WW2, however, it has been whitewashed. This hollow shrine and the round ochre and gold one next to it were built by a sister and brother respectively, for their father and grandfather. Both contain Buddha images or fragments of them. The third old shrine on the monastery grounds has a painted interior. However, its history has been lost – beyond the belief that it is only about 100 years old.

Across the street to the W is the **Payamya Monastery**. The main monastery to the N has an old domed library and a chedi that is thought to be about 400 years old, but it is the study compound on the corner of the main streets that is most interesting to look around.

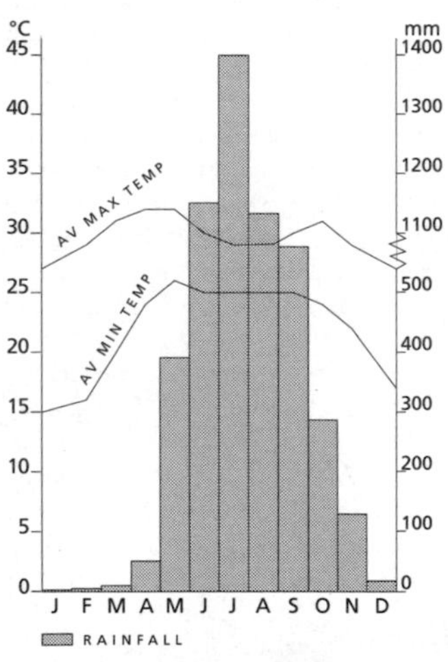

Climate: Sittwe

The compound's main gates, with mini Kyaikhtiyos in silver on the gateposts, are locked to prevent theft, but the N side gate (opposite the main monastery entrance) is usually unlocked. A small study room with evidence of WW2 bomb damage is in the centre of the compound. Behind it is a diverse collection of gravestones of especially holy monks. Between the study room and the street are some chedis in the thickset style typical of the area. Many are hollow with a Buddha image inside.

The Point (*Pwaint* in Burmese pronunciation) is at the southernmost extremity of Sittwe town, where the Kaladen River meets the sea. The quiet Strand Rd that lies between the Point and the centre of Sittwe is the best place to watch the giant fruit bats that wake at sunset and fly off for the night. The Point is a small area with a nominal admission charge. It has been partitioned off from the Navy barracks to the N. There is a snack stand and a former lighthouse which you can climb for better views and to catch all the available breeze. The Point is a favourite hangout of students and lecturers from Sittwe Degree College. Much posed photography is perpetrated here, sometimes on foreigners.

The **riverfront market** is the best place to look for fine Arakanese longyis. These are distinguished by their geometric patterns in dark thread, with the warp and weft of the background in different colours, giving the cloth a shimmering appearance as it is turned in the light and the colours change. The market is otherwise poorly stocked unless you are considering a dried fish purchase.

Local information

● Accommodation

The **B** *Sittwe* has been undergoing renovation and may, by the time this book goes to print, be the only hotel that foreigners are allowed to stay at, however it may be possible to get permission from immigration to stay at one of the guesthouses, government owned, small swimming pool, a/c, hot water.

D-E *Nine Star Guesthouse*, 354 Well St, T 21927, fans, mosquito net, clean, small rooms, helpful, English speaking staff, rec.

E *Mya*, nr college, T 21888, fans, mosquito net, garden, attached teahouse, a little English spoken but the otherwise acceptable rooms are none too clean; **E** *Nawarat*, single to triple rooms, fan, mosquito net, inconvenient location; **E** *Prince*, 27 Main Rd, T 21395, one room with a/c but not much good when the power's off, the other fan rooms are a trifle noisy but quite reasonable; **E** *San Pya*, Well St, T 21884, fans, net, little English.

● Places to eat

The lane behind the cultural museum has a row of Arakanese food rice shops. These range in quality and atmosphere from fairly clean and well-lit family places to sand floored grimy joints, with unlabelled bottles of rum at most tables. Most of the Chinese restaurants are in the neighbourhood just to the N of the museum. ◆◆*Seikkantha* on Well St. At the time of writing, the ◆◆*Innpaukwa* on the river bank was the finest restaurant in town, pink tablecloths, Chinese and Burmese food. However, when the *Sittwe Hotel* opens, its second-floor restaurant with a/c and a view of the sea is likely to become the leading dinery. The two tea shops across the road from the college (on the main road just N of the new clock tower) are naturally the students' favourite place to spend the evening. *Mo Pu Leh*, across the main road from the cultural museum is also a favourite among young people.

● Post & telecommunications

Area code: 043.

Post Office: the main post office is on the seafront, nr the southern edge of the town.

● Transport

There are more ways, and more varied (or complicated, depending how you look at it) ways to get to Sittwe than just about anywhere else.

Air Connections with Yangon 3 days a week, $90.

Road **Truck, foot and boat**: from Thayet there are trucks to Mindon. There is no guesthouse in Mindon but it is possible to stay in the monastery (phongyi gyaung). From here it is a 3-day walk to Letpan: 1st day, 25 km to Mga Koun; 2nd day, 34 km to Sadoun; 3rd day, 50 km to Letpan on the coast (see page 216 for further information). There you catch a boat.

Road Truck and boat: from Minbu it is possible to take a truck to Ann (300 kyat, 6 hrs), two scheduled trucks make this trip each day, plus others carrying goods. From Ann you need to go 43 km further to Tattaung on the coast. At the time of writing, the boat for Sittwe left Tatdaung on Tues mornings but you will want to check this several times in Minbu and in Padan, where the trucks stop for a meal.

This route is officially open, but may be arbitrarily closed by the army. If you plan to use it, it may be worth trying to get a paper from MTT pointing out that it is open (and checking to see whether it's been officially closed).

Boat There is approximately one boat per month from Yangon ($60 one way). This is not a scheduled passenger boat, so departure times and days are irregular. Ask at *Five Star Lines* in Yangon, at the intersection of Theinbyu and Merchant sts. Go in the entrance at the back of the building, into the office on the 1st floor. The manager speaks English well. From Pyay it is possible to take a bus to Taunggok on the coast and from there a weekly boat, which takes approximately 3 days and costs under l00 kyat. Alternatively, ask in the harbour about cargo boats, which are generally faster and cost 600 kyat. There are usually cargo boats leaving every day in the early morning. *Getting to the harbour*: the harbour is about 3 km from the bus station. Pony traps and sidecars are available.

The South

MON AND KAYIN STATES AND TANINTHAYI DIVISION

KYAIKTIYO ကျိုက်ထီးရိုး

Kyaiktiyo Pagoda, 65 km E of Bago on the railway line to Mawlamyine (Moulmein), is 20 km from Kyaiktiyo town. The 'Golden Rock' pagoda is in a spectacular location, perched on a huge, seemingly precarious boulder on the edge of a cliff. A hair of the Buddha is said to be enshrined in the pagoda, which was supposed to have been given to a hermit monk, who kept it in his top-knot. His last request was that the hair should be enshrined in a pagoda built on a rock, resembling his head. There are numerous legends about the pagoda, and the path up is lined with nat shrines. It is a tough 3-4 hr climb to the top of the hill, but there is a popular belief that those who reach the top will grow rich, and the views are magnificent. There are porters at the bottom of the hill who will carry bags for 50 kyat. An alternative is to take one of the pickups which take less enthusiastic, or less fit, pilgrims to within 45 mins' walk of the summit. *Best time to visit*: Kyaiktiyo is only accessible in the dry season (Oct-Apr) and the extreme heat of Mar/Apr reduces the number of pilgrims who undertake the 8-hr climb. Admission: $6, pay at the office at the foot of the mountain. There are food and drink stalls along the route and more substantial restaurants at the foot and summit.

• **Accommodation** Confusingly, there are two *Kyaiktiyo Hotels*, one at the summit and one at the foot of the mountain. The one on the summit (**C-D**) is the better place to stay and not just because of its position. Rooms are clean and it has a welcoming atmosphere. To book a room T (Yangon) 31563. The only visitors who are permitted to camp out on the summit are pilgrims – and by definition, foreigners do not fulfill this categorization. The **D** *Kyaiktiyo Hotel* at the foot of the mountain is much the second best option, but many are forced to stay here because the mountain-top hotel books up quickly.

• **Transport** By train from Bago to Kyaiktiyo town (US$3). From the train station there are buses and pick-ups running to the foot of the mountain. From Yangon it is a 6-hr taxi/car ride.

THATON သထုံ

Thaton was the first great capital of the Mon Kingdom and there are still some remains of the medieval fortifications. The **Shwezayan Pagoda** is thought to date back to the 5th century BC. The **Thagyapaya Pagoda** is known for its terracotta glazed tiles dating from the 11th and 12th centuries – the best examples are in the Kalyani Sima (ordination hall).

• **Accommodation** *No Name*, off N side of main road, T 186, shared bathrooms, clean rooms, friendly management, not licenced, but the management seem to be able to 'sort' it.

• **Transport Train** Connections with Yangon (10 hrs).

PA-AN ဘားအံ

One might never guess, from the easy atmosphere of the town, that Pa-an was the capital of Karen State. Karen State, after all, is a place where a sizeable

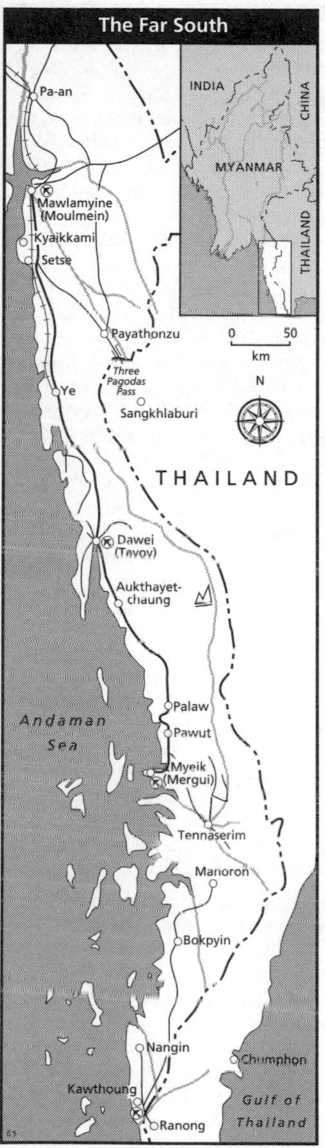

proportion of the territory is under the control of the Karen National Union (KNU). Out in the villages, horrific human rights violations are said to be frequent – and certainly the evidence seems pretty compelling. Needless to say, though, foreigners are not allowed near the more sensitive areas and there is little indication of the disturbances in Pa-an itself – although it does have more than its share of red and white propaganda signboards and soldiers on leave wandering about with impressively large weaponry.

Putting aside the soldiers and the disturbances in the surrounding countryside, first impressions of Pa-an are of a friendly and peaceful town. It is only over the course of a few days that this calm façade is penetrated and the disquiet beneath the surface is revealed. The Slorc's flexible laws on subversion are made with people like this in mind, so visitors must be careful about what they talk about with whom and where. Five to 20 years imprisonment can be the result of loose talk or unauthorized literature – not for the foreign visitor of course, but for the unwary Burmese. One reason for the town's 'sensitivity' is Aung San Suu Kyi's connection to the Thamanya sayadaw – his monastery was the first place outside Yangon that she went after being released from house arrest.

About half of Pa-an's population is Karen, mostly Sgaw and Pwo, a quarter is Burman, and the rest comprise small numbers of Mon, Indian Muslims, Tamils, Chinese, and others.

Pa-an town is situated on an alluvial plain, but around it are dotted numerous steep limestone hills. These hills are riddled with caves, which are some of the major sights in the area. In fact, there are so many day trips to make from here that it is easy to stay for some time.

Pa-an only opened to foreigners in 1995/96 and officials here are still rather restrictive. First, foreign travellers have to register at a checkpoint outside town. Once settled at a hotel,

Pa-an place names

Kawgungu Cave
ကော်ကွန်ဂူ

Payinnyigu Cave
ပုရင်ယိဂူ

Sandangu
စန်တန်ဂူ

Shweyinmyaw Pagoda
ရွှေရင်မြော်ဘုရား

Taung Gale Monastery
တောင်ကလေးကျောင်း

Thamanya Monastery
သာမန်ရာကျောင်း

Thetama Aung Pagoda
သက်တမာအောင်ဘုရား

Zwagabin Daung
ဇွာကာပင်တောင်

the polite Immigration officer will then come to seek you out – either there or around town – and will try to make conversation with you daily in order to discover where you have been and where you are planning to go. On your way to some of the outlying sights, travellers are also sometimes asked to show their passports or register again. Mae Sot, in Thailand, is only about 150 km away, but foreigners are not allowed to travel along most of the road, and are not likely to be allowed to, even if a ceasefire is signed with the KNU insurgents. Many of the local people have been to Mae Sot, and many have worked in Thailand and Thai-speakers may find some opportunity to use the language.

Places of interest

The large **main market** on Thitsa Rd is not as lively as one might hope. However, it has a large selection of Karen textiles. The two main pagodas in town are the unusual ancient-style Thetama Aung Pagoda on Bogyoke Rd and Shweyinmyaw Pagoda on the riverfront. Neither is very impressive, as the main Buddhist excitement is located out of town in Thamanya and Taung Gale monasteries, with their charismatic sayadaws.

Thetama Aung Pagoda has a design rare to see in modern pagodas: a tall, smooth whitewashed mound, with a small pagoda perched on top. The pagodas of Thiri Kittaya (outside Prome) might have looked much like this when new. This pagoda, though, is less than 100 years old. The gilt **Shweyinmyaw Pagoda** is the favourite picture-taking spot in Pa-an. Its large frog and views over the river make a backdrop for many a posed shot. The dramatic hills surrounding the town are well viewed from here. Architecturally, however, the pagoda is not particularly interesting.

The **Karen State Museum** is S of the centre of town. It chiefly contains Karen clothing, musical instruments, and artefacts from daily like. It is a shady 20-min walk from the main part of the town, or a short sidecar ride. Open Mon-Fri 0900-1600. No English signs. The museum is the last building, at the lake. There is a path all the way around the small lake in front of the museum and a park with two teashops at the SW part of the shore.

Pa-an College is about 15 mins' walk E of the centre of town. Naturally there are some teashops next to the entrance. The **Baptist Church** is probably the best place to meet old people who are fluent in English. Many students took their subjects in English language in mission schools before the government nationalized the schools and determined the curriculum in the 1960s. Decades later the former pupils haven't lost their language skills.

Excursions

The attraction of the **Thamanya Mon-**

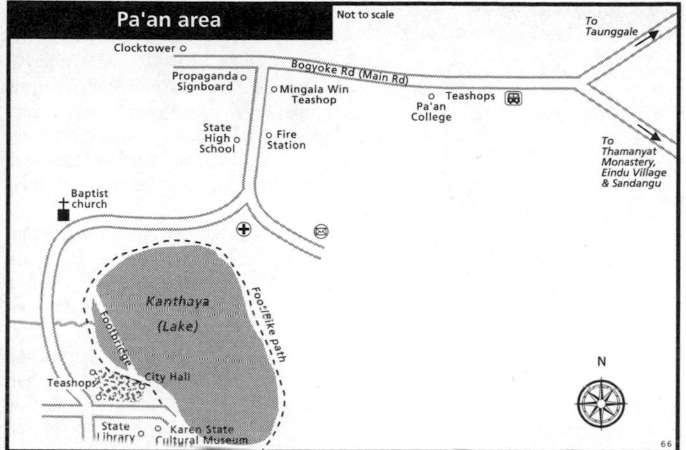

astery is its venerated *sayadaw*, or abbot, U Winaya. The monastery where he lives is 40 km outside Pa-an, at one of the limestone hills that punctuate the plain. Among local Buddhists, the sayadaw is rumoured to be able to fly to foreign lands during meditation, and talk with people there. Also, they say, fairies keep his storehouses full of rice, so he can feed however many people come to the monastery. The dining room is in a building near the top of the hill, to the right of the stairway, just where the pipes that serve as a bannister dive back into the ground. All are welcome to eat the vegetarian food. It is also possible for foreigners to spend the night at the monastery. Once you find an Enlish-speaking monk this is easily arranged. At noon the sayadaw comes up the hill to meet the people who have come to visit him. From the top of the hill, there is a sweeping view of the hills and plains. The way there is also attractive, running through attractive countryside and past villages whose wooden houses show their relative prosperity. *Getting there*: there are frequent linecars running between Pa-an and Thamanya from the base of the riverside Shweyinmyaw pagoda, near the jetty. For the larger linecars, buy a ticket at the booth where they are parked. If you take one of the smaller pickups, you will pay on the way. The linecars leave when they are full, which is several times per hour in the morning, less often in the afternoon (1 hr, 40 kyat, 60 kyat to sit in front).

Sandangu (Sandan cave) is the best cave on the Pa-an side of the river, but also the hardest to get to, as there is no public transport for the last 15 km. The spacious cave stretches all the way beneath a limestone karst formation, with openings on both sides. There is a monastery at the 'front', and some religious sculptures in the wide entrance. From here, walk past the stalactites and stalagmites to the idyllic scene at the back. A monk will show you through the cave, in a walk that takes half an hour each way. The only alterations beyond the sculptures at the front and an inscription at the back are some stairs – you will need to bring a torch. The sheltered area on the far side of the hill where the cave comes out is a great place to meditate or picnic. (Picnic elements are available at the market in Eindu, where visitors alight from the Thamanya linecar.) Visitors must enter the cave barefoot, as it

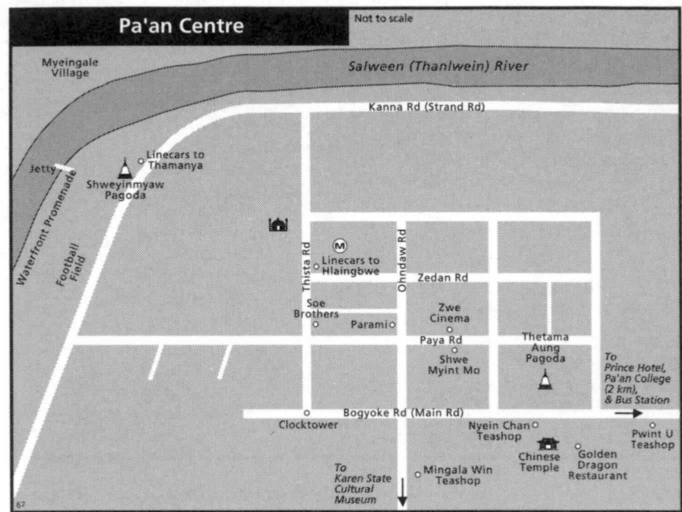

lies within the sanctified grounds of the monastery, but beyond the entrance room you can wear shoes again – follow the example of the guide. There is a children's tale associated with the cave, about an elephant king who lived here until a hunter killed him for his tusks, to make a crown for a queen. Various rock formations are called the elephant's mosquito net, corpse, and so on. Most visitors are spared this story, as the monks who guide people do not speak English. In the building to the left of the cave as you emerge, for 10 kyat, visitors can buy small packets of red gummy material called 'rock blood' which is supposed to cure cuts and scratches. Buy a laminated photo of the sayadaw, or make a donation to the monastery. *Getting there*: it is only possible to get to the monastery when the weather is dry, which is obviously most likely during the dry season. But even during the rainy season it is still feasible on days when it does not rain. Take a Thamanya linecar (see getting to Thamanya monastery, above) but get out at Eindu village, well before Thamanya. Passengers for Sandangu are let off at a fork in the road where the market is located. Take the right fork, and alongside the market you will find pony traps to take you the last 15 km to Sandangu and back for a few hundred kyat. The last few kilometres are unpaved and rather rough.

If your preference is for the top of a karst formation, rather than its bowels, the highest hill near Pa-an is **Zwagabin Daung**, at over 1,000 metres. It is a tough climb to the pagodas at the top and once there, monkeys are rather a pest. However, the view of the river and landscape is worth a little sweat and simian scorn. *Getting there*: the hill is a short way off the main road to Thamanya, so hiring a pony trap in Pa-an is the best way to get there.

The young *sayadaw* at **Taung Gale Monastery** is famous for being able to see into the future. His star feat is telling all seven numbers of the Thai lottery, the last three numbers of which are played in the Burmese 'Yodaya hti' (Yodaya=Ayutthaya, still one of the Burmese ways to refer to Thailand). He speaks English well. The monastery is about 10 km from the centre of Pa-an.

Getting there: take the 0800 linecar for Hlaingbwe, which leaves from the SW corner of the main market, and ask for *Taung Gale Phongyi Gyaung*, or hire a pony trap. The monastery is 8 km from Pa-an. Returning linecars are infrequent.

Kawgungu and **Payinnyigu**, two large caves, are on the other side of the river. They are within 15 km of the village of Myein Gale and are likely to be accessible to foreign travellers soon. The town's Immigration officer will have the latest information.

Local information

● Accommodation

Three guesthouses in Pa-an are currently licensed to accept foreigners.

D ***Prince***, nr the main bus station (cross the main road and go left, toward the centre of town), T (035) 21458, a/c, clean, hot water, featureless place, little English spoken.

E ***Parami***, in the centre of town, T 21647, some a/c, other rooms with fans and mosquito nets, baths down the hall, clean and quiet with helpful management; **E** ***Soe Brothers Guesthouse***, nr the market, T 21372, cheapest, dirtiest and most fun of the lot, no a/c or mosquito nets (screens on the windows), bath down the hall, not disgustingly dirty but certainly not the place to choose for an invasive surgical operation, thin walls, but quiet street, good English spoken, very friendly staff, international phone calls can be attempted from here (with no mark up).

● Places to eat

♦♦***Golden Dragon***, in the grounds of a run down Chinese temple, fairly simple but good Chinese food, the staff will show you the temple if you ask – good English spoken.

♦***Nyein chan*** (sign in Burmese only) is the place for young people to meet in the evenings, and has very good snacks; ♦***Pwint U*** (sign in Burmese only) is favoured in the evenings by some of the local-level bureaucrats, some of whom speak English; ♦***Shwe Myint Moe*** (sign in Burmese only), opp the cinema on Paya Rd, easily recognized by long row of covered pots out front, good Burmese food.

Tea shops: as usual there are plenty of places to get a cup of tea and a snack. ***Mingala win*** has especially good breakfast selection, and a helpful, English-speaking owner.

There are also some simple cheap 'rice shops' by the waterfront.

● Post and telecommunications

Area code: 035.

● Transport

Road Linecars and buses: leave from the main bus station. As well as several buses during the day, there is a night bus from Yangon, which stops to let passengers sleep for a few hours on the way. There is no night bus returning to Yangon. From Pego, there are two direct early morning linecars at 0400 and 0500. It is also possible to take a bus to Thaton and continue from there.

Boat Two boats daily to and from Mawlamyine's (Moulmein) Pa-an Jetty (2½-4 hrs), 17 kyat ordinary class, 70 kyat for a cabin. From Mawlamyine the boats leave at 0700 and 1300. There are also vessels to Yangon, 78 hrs (300 kyat). The **car ferry** at Pa-an does not operate often, but in the afternoon it is possible to go to Myein Gale, directly across the river from Pa-an, by taking one of the small boats making frequent crossings for 10 kyat.

MAWLAMYINE (MOULMEIN) မော်လမြိုင်

On the Tennasserim coast, Mawlamyine was once an important teak port but has been superseded by Yangon and Pathein. Most of Myanmar's teak was exported from here and some of the timber yards are still working. Evidence of the town's more glorious past can be seen in the moulding colonial buildings and in terms of population it remains Myanmar's third city with over a quarter of a million inhabitants. It is also one of the friendliest cities, with the children finding tourists a great source of entertainment.

The city is renowned for its seafood and beautiful pagodas. The **Uzina Pagoda** has exquisitely carved life-sized figures depicting Buddha's enlightenment. The **Kyaikthanlan Pagoda** was – in colonial times – better known as 'Kipling's Pagoda' after his lines:

> By the old Moulmein Pagoda lookin' lazy at the sea,
> There's a Burma girl a-settin, and I know she thinks o' me;

Mawlamyine place names

Kyaikthanlan Pagoda
ကျိုက်သံလန်ဘုရား
Mon Cultural Museum
မွန်ယဉ်ကျေးမှုပြတိုက်
Uzina Pagoda
ဦးဇိနဘုရား

It has good views over the town. The **Mon Cultural Museum** has an eclectic collection of Mon musical instruments, 18th and 19th century statues and an old carved wooded screen from Myeik (Mergui). Admission free. Open Wed-Sun, 0930-1600.

Another sight worth visiting in the city is the **First Baptist Church** – or **Judson's Church** – on Dawei Jetty Road near the corner of Upper Main Road. This church was founded 150 years ago by an American missionary who went by the glorious name of Mr Adoniram Judson and seems to have changed little since both in terms of its outside appearance and its interior fittings and fixtures. The warden who lives on the church compound will open the building to visitors.

• **Accommodation** In mid-1996 only one hotel – the *Mawlamyine* was licensed to accept foreigners. However, by the time this book is published other places are likely to have received their licenses too. **B-C** *Mawlamyine*, Strand Rd, T 22560, a/c, nice restaurant with terrace. **E** *Breeze*, adequate.

• **Places to eat** *Min Thin*, on the jetty, Chinese fare.

• **Transport Air** Two flights a week on Myanmar Airways, one via Dawei (Tavoy). **Road Bus**: regular connections from Yangon's Highway Bus Centre but the journey is long and arduous even by usual Myanmar standards. Only some buses continue all the way to Mawlamyine; most terminate at Mottama on the far bank of the Thanlwin and passengers then take one of the ferries across the river to the city. There are onward buses from the bus terminal on the southern edge of town to Dawei (Tavoy), Kyaikkami (Amherst) and other southern towns. **Train** The railway station is N of the city centre and the river, so a ferry takes passengers across the town (20 mins). There are two express trains daily from Yangon, and it is both quicker (at 7-8 hrs) and more comfortable than taking the bus. Connections with Bago (7½ hrs). **Boat** There are a half a dozen jetties where boats serving various ports dock. From the N, S they are as follows: Thaton Jetty (just N of the central market) for Mottama (car ferry); Mottama Jetty (just S of the central market) for Mottama (pedestrian ferry); Pa-an Jetty (on Strand Rd) for Pa-an (pedestrian ferry at 0700 and 1300); and Dawei Jetty (at the end of Dawei Jetty Rd) for Dawei (Tavoy).

KYAIKKAMI (AMHERST) ကျိုက္ခမိ

Until recently tourists were forbidden to venture beyond Mawlamyine (Moulmein). Kyaikkami was originally a seaside resort during the British colonial period. It is renowned for its pagoda which is separated from the mainland at high tide. The **Thanbyuzayat war cemetery**, 64 km S of Mawlamyine and not far from the beach resort of Setse, is the resting place of many prisoners of war forced by the Japanese to build the Myanmar-Thailand railway during WW2. Dawei (Tavoy), the capital of Tenasserim, lies on the Thalween River. 20 km S is one of Myanmar's most beautiful stretches of beach. There are no hotels but tour companies organize stays in government bungalows

SETSE စက်စဲ

There is a long sandy beach here; the water is muddy from the Salween River.

DAWEI (TAVOY) ထားဝယ်

Dawei, better known by its old name Tavoy, is off the tourist route and has been largely out-of-bounds to foreigners since the late 1980s. It seems that the authorities are becoming slightly more flexible about granting travel permits and more may begin to make it down here. But even should Dawei open up, it is doubtful that many tourists will travel down here – unless they are allowed to use the port as an entry/exit point to and from Thailand – as it lies at the very end of the road and rail network and the only option open to visitors is to retrace their steps N.

One of the reasons that Dawei has been off-limits is because there are a number of sensitive projects underway in the area. The French and US-based oil companies Total and Unocal are building an important pipeline from Myanmar to Thailand which will carry natural gas from wells in the Andaman Sea to Thailand's energy-hungry industries. Amnesty International, the Burma Action Group and various other organizations have consistently claimed that the pipeline is being built using slave labour – a claim that the oil companies, unsurprisingly, flatly reject. Nonetheless, Unocal have had to deal with embarrassing interrogations at their AGMs and activists in California have tried to encourage the boycotting of their petrol stations.

Like many other towns, the charm of Dawei is rather hard to pin down. There is nothing here of note in the sense that it should be recorded for posterity, yet the coastal position, the pace of life, and the friendliness of the people leave a marked impression. There are several notable *paya* in town. Perhaps most important from an artistic point of view is

Bird's nest soup

The tiny nests of the brown-rumped (*Collocalia esculenta*) and grey-rumped (*Collocalia francica*) swift, also known as the edible-nest swiftlet or sea swallow, are collected for bird's nest soup, a Chinese delicacy, throughout Southeast Asia. The semi-oval nests are made of silk-like strands of saliva secreted by the birds which, when cooked in broth, softens and becomes a little like noodles. Like so many Chinese delicacies, the nests are believed to have aphrodisiac qualities, and the soup has even been suggested as a cure for AIDS. The red nests are the most highly valued, and the Vietnamese Emperor Minh Mang (1820-1840) is said to have owed his extraordinary vitality to his inordinate consumption of bird's nest soup. This may explain why restaurants serving it in Southern Thailand are usually also associated with a plethora of massage parlours.

The swifts nest in the limestone caves of the Myeik Archipelago and the nests have been collected for centuries. The Thai name for the bird – 'wind-eating bird' – apparently refers to the belief that these creatures took their sustenance from the air, and never alighted to feed. Although the King of Siam claimed the right to harvest the nests, such was their value that poaching quickly took hold. Norman Lewis recounts in his book *Golden Earth* (1952) how he stayed in the Mergui (Myeik) lodging house of Yok Seng, a Chinese gentleman who by chance happened to be in the nest exporting business. He records that an early Chinese scientific expedition analysed the constituents of the life-giving nests and concluded that they were composed of 'solidified sea foam', which is rather more appetizing than the saliva explanation. Yok Seng also told the inquisitive travel writer that unscrupulous individuals had taken to selling fake nests composed of jelly made from seaweed. "Be sure", Yok Seng warned, "that when you order bird's nest soup in a restaurant, it will be a fake you will be served". Collecting the nests is a precarious business. The collectors climb flimsy bamboo poles into total darkness, with candles strapped to their heads. In Hong Kong a kilo of nests may sell for US$2,000 and nest-concessions are vigorously protected.

Shinmokhti Paya which dates from the 15th century. **Lyaung Daw Mu** may not be as old, it dates from the 1930s, but it contains what is said to be the largest – or perhaps the second largest – reclining Buddha in Myanmar.

Excursions In theory, Dawei would be an ideal spot for a beach resort. As yet there are no hotels or guesthouses and the beaches – especially those to the W – remain unmarred by foreigners. Even more enticing are the islands that lie off-shore, but these too remain closed and undeveloped.

• **Accommodation** **E** *Sibin Guesthouse*, government-run and simple.

• **Transport** **Air** *Myanmar Airways* flies to Dawei from Yangon daily and also has connections with Mawlamyine and Myeik. **Road** **Bus**: there are 'direct' buses to Dawei all the way from Yangon, but the journey is said to take between 2 and 3 days. It is best to get here in stages, stopping off en-route. **Sea** **Boat**: **Myanmar Five Star Lines** operate ships between Yangon and Dawei, calling at ports en-route.

MYEIK (MERGUI) မြိတ်

During 1996 Myeik was off-limits to most foreigners and this account is collated from secondary sources. Myeik is the capital of Tanintharyi (Tenasserim) Division and has served an important trading function for centuries. During the Ayutthaya period in Siam (Thailand, 1350-1767) many travellers, rather than sail S through the Melaka Strait and then N through the Gulf of Thailand would alight here and continue their journey overland. In a sense this role of old continues to be acted out, but surreptitiously. Smugglers carry gems and other goods to Thailand, exchanging them for consumer goods. One high value product for which the area is famous are its birds' nests used in the cooking of birds' nest soup (see box). The grey-rumped swifts that produce the supposed delectable nests nest in the caves and caverns of the limestone islands that make up the Myeik Archipelago.

Tour operators and tourist planners must become slightly moist with excitement when they read of Myeik and the surrounding area. There are hundreds of pristine islands strung like gems through the iridescent sea. As yet, though, this can only be enjoyed by the Burmese and local aquatic life.

There are several attractive paya in town. The **Theindawgyi Pagoda** is the most revered. A short distance off-shore on **Pataw Patit Island** are a monastery, several shrines and various images of the Buddha.

• **Accommodation** Reportedly there are no hotels or guesthouses licensed to take foreigners although if the authorities grant you a travel permit to get here then local officialdom will be likely to let you stay at one of the guesthouses. The *Annawa* is said to be the best.

• **Transport** **Air** Myanmar Airways flies to Myeik daily from Yangon. There are also connections with Dawei and Kawthoung. **Road** **Bus**: there are buses to Myeik from Dawei but foreigners are not allowed to travel overland between the two towns. **Sea** **Boat**: **Myanmar Five Star Lines** operate ships between Yangon and Myeik, calling at ports en-route.

KAWTHOUNG

Kawthoung, at the southern tip of Myanmar, is just a few kilometres from the Thai fishing port of Ranong. In Ranong, Burmese trawlers fishing the Andaman Sea dock to unload their catch and regular ferries ply the waters between Ranong and Kawthoung. As at some other crossings between Myanmar and Thailand, it is possible to secure a day visa, or an even longer visa, at the immigration office at Kawthoung Pier. However, the visa only allows people to travel in the immediate area. The road N is off-limits to foreigners – and in any case it is little more than a track – and though there are flights to Yangon it is not clear whether people arriving in Myanmar from Ranong would be permitted to board.

Because of Kawthoung's close links

with Thailand, the town feels comparatively wealthy by Burmese standards. Many people work in Ranong, while others travel all the way to Bangkok to secure work. Growing numbers of girls in Bangkok's brothels come from Myanmar and many of these are said to enter the country via Ranong. Whatever work these international labour migrants secure, some filters back to Kawthoung in the form of cash and consumer goods.

• **Accommodation** C *Kawthoung Motel*, slightly better than many of the hotels in out-of-the-way spots like this with attached facilities and a reasonable level of service, still pretty spartan though, considering the rates that are charged.

• **Transport Air** **Myanmar Airways** flies to Kawthoung from Yangon. There are also connections with Dawei and Myeik. **Road** **Bus**: the road N is a track and not only are foreigners not permitted to travel along it, but there is no regular bus service in any case. **Sea** **Boat**: **Myanmar Five Star Lines** operate ships between Yangon and Kawthoung, calling at ports en-route. **International connections with Thailand** There are regular ferry connections between Kawthoung and the Thai port of Ranong from early morning to mid-afternoon. On arrival in Kawthoung visitors should report to the immigration office at the jetty where they will be issued with a day visa.

Bangkok

กรุงเทพมหานคร

MANY people visiting Myanmar pass through Thailand en route. Bangkok has the greatest concentration of companies offering tours to Myanmar and it is also the best place to obtain a visa. There are regular air connections between Bangkok's Don Muang and Yangon's airport and there are also air connections between Chiang Mai in Northern Thailand and Myanmar. This section of the book provides a basic guide to Bangkok and Chiang Mai. There is also a short **Information for travellers** section providing some general practical background. The information has been condensed from the *Thailand Handbook* also published by Footprint Handbooks. Please note that the information here is not comprehensive: much of the background material, details on the more obscure sights, and practicalities have been either omitted or substantially edited. Those wishing to spend any length of time in Thailand are strongly advised to buy a dedicated guide to the country. We, naturally enough, would recommend the *Thailand Handbook*.

BANGKOK

Bangkok is not a city to be trifled with: a population of 11 million struggle to make their living in a conurbation with perhaps the worst traffic in the world; a level of pollution which causes some children, so it is (rather improbably) said, to lose four intelligence points by the time they are seven; and a climate which can take one's breath away. (The *Guinness Book of Records* credits Bangkok as the world's hottest city because of the limited seasonal and day-night temperature variations.) As journalist Hugo Gurdon wrote at the end of 1992: "One would have to describe Bangkok as unliveable were it not for the fact that more and more people live here". But, Bangkok is not just a perfect case study for academics studying the strains of rapid urban growth. There is charm and fun beneath the grime, and Bangkokians live life with a *joie de vivre* which belies the congestion. There are also numerous sights, including the spectacular Grand Palace, glittering wats (monasteries) and the breezy river, along with excellent food and good shopping.

The official name for Thailand's capital city begins Krungthep – phramaha – nakhonbawon – rathanakosin – mahinthara – yutthayaa – mahadilok – phiphobnobpharaat – raatchathaanii – buriiromudomsantisuk. It is not hard to see why Thais prefer the shortened version – Krungthep, or the 'City of Angels'. The name used by the rest of the world – Bangkok – is derived from 17th century Western maps, which referred to the city (or town as it then was) as Bancok, the 'village of the wild plum'. This name was only superseded by Krungthep in 1782, and so the Western name has deeper historical roots.

In 1767, Ayutthaya, then the capital of Siam, fell to the marauding Burmese for the second time and it was imperative that the remnants of the court and army find a more defensible site for a new capital. Taksin, the Lord of Tak, chose Thonburi, on the western banks of the Chao Phraya River, far from the Burmese and from Phitsanulok, where a rival to the throne had become ensconsed. In 3 years, Taksin had established a kingdom and crowned himself king. His reign was short-lived, however; the pressure of thwarting the Burmese over three arduous years caused him to go mad and in 1782 he was forced to abdicate. General Phraya Chakri was recalled from Cambodia and invited to accept the throne. This marked the beginning of the present Chakri Dynasty.

Bangkok highlights

Temples Bangkok's best known sight is the temple of ***Wat Phra Kaeo***, situated within the grounds of the ***Grand Palace*** (page 274). Other notable temples include ***Wat Pho*** (page 272), ***Wat Arun*** (page 283), ***Wat Suthat*** (page 278) and ***Wat Traimitr*** (page 280).

Museums Bangkok's extensive ***National Museum*** houses the best collection in the country (page 277); other notable collections include those in ***Jim Thompson's House*** (page 286), the ***Suan Pakkard Palace*** (page 286) and ***Vimanmek Palace*** (page 283).

Markets The sprawling ***Chatuchak Weekend market*** (page 288), ***Nakhon Kasem*** or Thieves' market (page 280), ***Pahurat Indian market*** (page 279) and Chinatown's ***Sampeng Lane*** (page 280).

Boat trip On ***Bangkok's canals*** (page 282).

Excursions Day trips to the ***floating market at Damnoen Saduak*** (page 289).

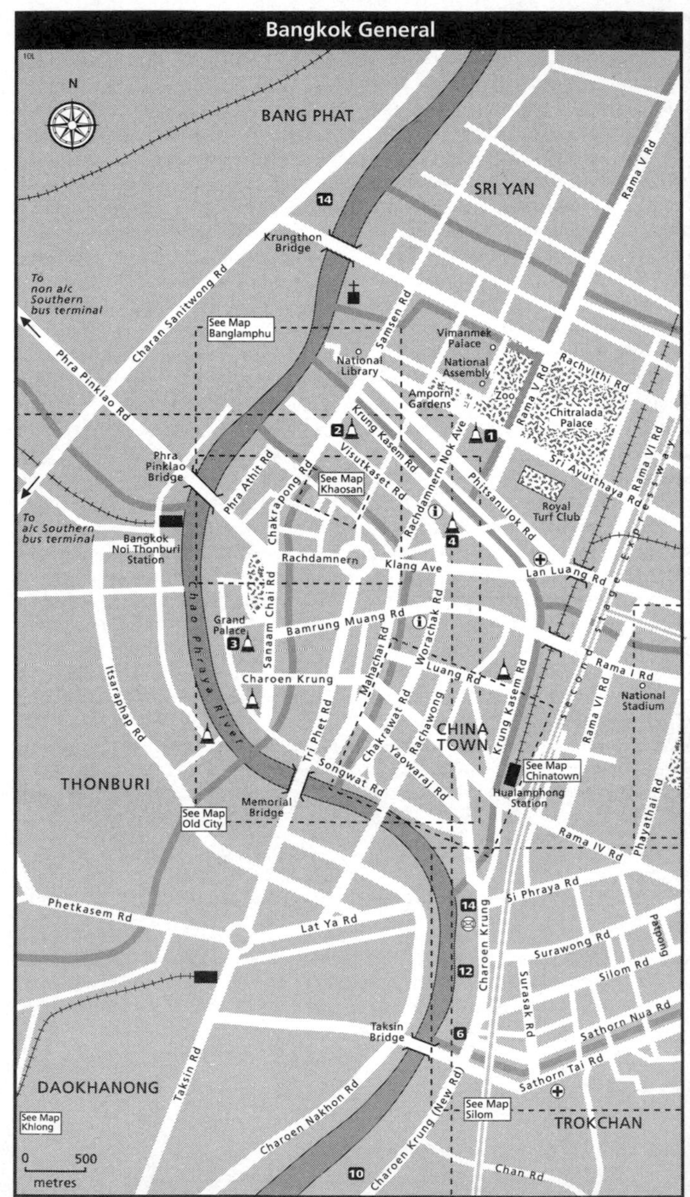
Bangkok General
N
BANG PHAT
SRI YAN
Rama V Rd
Krungthon Bridge
To non a/c Southern bus terminal
Charan Sanitwong Rd
Samsen Rd
See Map Banglamphu
Vimanmek Palace
National Library
National Assembly
Phra Pinklao Rd
Rachvithi Rd
Amporn Gardens
Zoo
Rama V Rd
Chitralada Palace
Krung Kasem Rd
Rachdamnern Nok Ave
Phra Pinklao Bridge
Visutkaset Rd
Sri Ayutthaya Rd
Rama VI Rd
Phra Athit Rd
Chakrapong Rd
See Map Khaosan
Phitsanulok Rd
Royal Turf Club
To a/c Southern bus terminal
Bangkok Noi Thonburi Station
Chakrapong Rd
Rachdamnern
Klang Ave
Lan Luang Rd
Second Stage Expressway
Sanaam Chai Rd
Chao Phraya River
Bamrung Muang Rd
Grand Palace
Mahachai Rd
Worachak Rd
Rama I Rd
Luang Rd
Krung Kasem Rd
Charoen Krung
Rama VI Rd
National Stadium
Itsaraphap Rd
Tri Phet Rd
Chakrawat Rd
Rachawong
CHINA TOWN
Yaowaraj Rd
See Map Chinatown
Songwat Rd
THONBURI
Memorial Bridge
Hualamphong Station
Phayathai Rd
See Map Old City
Rama IV Rd
Si Phraya Rd
Phetkasem Rd
Lat Ya Rd
Patpong
Surawong Rd
Silom Rd
Charoen Krung
Surasak Rd
Sathorn Nua Rd
Taksin Bridge
Taksin Rd
Sathorn Tai Rd
DAOKHANONG
See Map Silom
TROKCHAN
See Map Khlong
Charoen Nakhon Rd
Charoen Krung (New Rd)
0 500
metres
Chan Rd

Wat:
1. Benchamabophit (The Marble Temple)
2. Indraviharn
3. Phra Kaeo
4. Sonnakviharn

Hotels:
5. *Dusit Thani*
6. *Hilton*
7. *Imperial*
8. *Intercontinental*
9. *Le Meridien*
10. *Menam*
11. *Novotel*
12. *Oriental*
13. *Regent*
14. *Royal Orchid* & River City Shopping Complex
15. *Royal River*
16. *Siam City*

Chatuchak Weekend Market
Northern bus terminal
To Airport
SAPHANKHWAI
HUAY KHWANG
DIN DAENG
ASOKE
THUNG MAHAMEK
Second Stage Expressway
Rama VI Rd
Phahonyothin Rd
Expressway
Victory Monument
Phayathai Rd
Rachprarop Rd
Suan Pakkard Palace
See Map Siam Sq
Pratunam Market
Phetburi Rd
New Phetburi Rd
Siam Square
Ploenchit Rd
Erawan Shrine
Soi Nana Nua
Siam Society & Kamthieng house
Soi Asoke
See Map Sukhumvit
Chulalongkorn University
Henri Dunant Rd
Rachdamri Rd
Vietnam Embassy
Witthayu (Wireless) Rd
Snake Farm
Lumpini Park
Sukhumvit Rd
To Eastern bus terminal
Rama IV Rd
Lumpini Boxing Stadium
Rachdaphisek Rd
Soi 26
Sathorn Nua Rd
Sathorn Tai Rd
Soi Sribamphen
Immigration Dept
Soi Ngam Duphli
Nang Linchi Rd

In 1782, Chakri (now known as Rama I) moved his capital across the river to Bangkok (an even more defensible site) anticipating trouble from King Bodawpaya who had seized the throne of Burma. The river that flows between Thonburi and Bangkok and on which many of the luxury hotels – such as *The Oriental* – are now located, began life not as a river at all, but as a canal (or *khlong*). The canal was dug in the 16th century to reduce the distance between Ayutthaya and the sea by shortcutting a number of bends in the river. Since then, the canal has become the main channel of the Chao Phraya River. Its original course has shrunk in size, and is now represented by two khlongs, Bangkok Yai and Bangkok Noi.

This new capital of Siam grew in size and influence. Symbolically, many of the new buildings were constructed using bricks from the palaces and temples of the ruined former capital of Ayutthaya. But population growth was hardly spectacular – it appears that outbreaks of cholera sometimes reduced the population by a fifth or more in a matter of a few weeks. An almanac from 1820 records that "on the 7th month of the waxing moon, a little past 2100 in the evening, a shining light was seen in the N-W and multitudes of people purged, vomited and died". In 1900 Bangkok had a population of approximately 200,000. By 1950 it had surpassed 1 million, and in 1992 it was, officially, 5,562,141. Most people believe that the official figure considerably understates the true population of the city – 10-11 million would be more realistic. By 2010, analysts believe Bangkok will have a population of 20 million. As the population of the city has expanded, so has the area that it encompasses: in 1900 it covered a mere 13.3 sq km; in 1958, 96.4 sq km; while today the Bangkok Metropolitan region extends over 1,600 sq km and the outskirts of the city sprawl into neighbouring provinces. Such is the physical size of the capital that analysts talk of Bangkok as an EMR or Extended Metropolitan Region.

In terms of size, Bangkok is at least 23 times larger than the country's second city, Chiang Mai – 40 times bigger, using the unofficial population estimates. It also dominates Thailand in cultural, political and economic terms. All Thai civil servants have the ambition of serving in Bangkok, while many regard a posting to the poor NE as (almost) the kiss of death. Most of the country's industry is located in and around the city (the area contributes 45% of national GDP), and Bangkok supports a far wider array of services than other towns in the country. Although the city contains only 10% of the kingdom's population, its colleges of higher education graduate 71% of degree students, it contains 83% of pharmacists, and has 69% of Thailand's telephone lines. It is because of Bangkok's dominance that people often, and inaccurately, say 'Bangkok is Thailand'.

The immediate impression of the city to a first-time visitor is bedlam. The heat, noise, traffic, pollution – the general chaos – can be overwhelming. This was obviously the impression of Somerset Maugham, following his visit in 1930:

> 'I do not know why the insipid Eastern food sickened me. The heat of Bangkok was overwhelming. The wats oppressed me by their garish magnificence, making my head ache, and their fantastic ornaments filled me with malaise. All I saw looked too bright, the crowds in the street tired me, and the incessant din jangled my nerves. I felt very unwell ...'

It is estimated that over 1 million Bangkokians live in slum or squatter communities, while average traffic speeds can be less than 10 km/hour. During peak periods the traffic congestion is such that 'gridlock' seems inevitable. The figures are sometimes hard to believe: US$500mn of petrol is consumed each year while cars wait at traffic lights; one day in Jul 1992 it took 11 hrs for some motorists to get home after a monsoon storm; and the number of cars on the capital's streets increases by 800 each day (the figure for the country is 1,300); while traffic speeds are snail pace – and expected to fall further. For those in Bangkok who are concerned about their city and the environment, the worst aspect is that things will undoubtedly get worse before they get any better – despite the plethora of road building programmes the car and truck population is growing faster than the roads to accommodate them. The government of former Prime Minister Anand did give the go-ahead to a number of important infrastructural projects, but many would say a decade too late. As one analyst has observed: "Bangkok is only just beginning to happen". Even editorial writers at the *Bangkok Post* who, one might imagine, are used to the traffic find it a constant topic for comment. At the end of 1993 the newspaper stated: "Bangkok's traffic congestion and pollution are just about the worst in the world – ever. Never in history have people had to live in the conditions we endure each day".

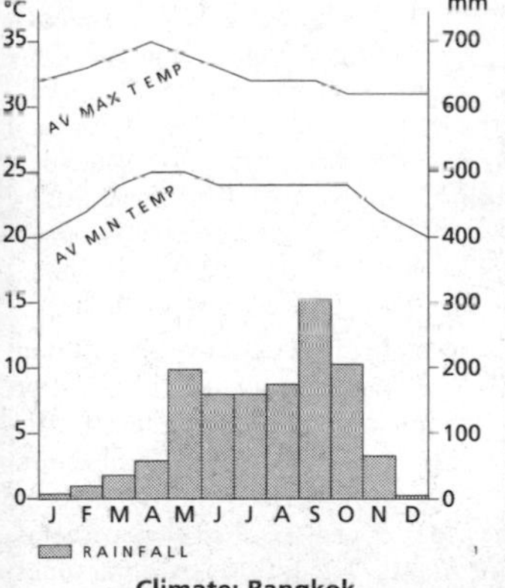

Climate: Bangkok

PLACES OF INTEREST

This section is divided into five main areas: the **Old City**, around the Grand Palace; the **Golden Mount**, to the E of the Old City; **Chinatown**, which lies to the S of the Golden Mount; the **Dusit** area, which is to the N and contains the present day parliament buildings and the King's residence; and **Wat Arun** and the **khlongs**, which are to the W, on the other bank of the Chao Phraya River in Thonburi. Other miscellaneous sights, not in these areas, are at the end of the section, under Other places of interest.

GETTING AROUND THE SIGHTS

Buses, both a/c and non-a/c, travel to all city sights (see Local transport, page 310). A taxi or tuk-tuk for a centre of town trip should cost ฿50-100. Now that taxis are almost all metered visitors may find it easier, and more comfortable (they have a/c) – not to mention safer – than the venerable tuk-tuk, although a ride on one of these three-wheeled machines is a tourist experience in itself. If travelling by bus, a bus map of the city – and there are several, available from most bookshops and hotel gift shops – is an invaluable aid. The express river taxi is a far more pleasant way to get around town and is also often quicker than going by road (see map **page** 285 for piers, and box page 284).

THE OLD CITY

The Old City contains the largest concentration of sights in Bangkok, and for visitors with only one day in the capital, this is the area to concentrate on. It is possible to walk around all the sights mentioned below quite easily in a single day. For the energetic, it would also be possible to visit the sights in and around the Golden Mount. If intending to walk around all the sights in the old city start from Wat Pho; if you have less time or less energy, begin with the Grand Palace.

Wat Phra Chetuphon

(Temple of the Reclining Buddha) or **Wat Pho**, as it is known to Westerners (a contraction of its original name Wat Potaram), has its entrance on Chetuphon Rd on the S side of the complex. It is 200 years old and the largest wat in Bangkok, now most famous for its 46m long, 15m high gold-plated reclining Buddha, with beautiful mother-of-pearl soles (showing the 108 auspicious signs). The reclining Buddha is contained in a large viharn built during the reign of Rama III (1832).

The grounds of the wat contain more than 1,000 bronze images, rescued from the ruins of Ayutthaya and Sukhothai

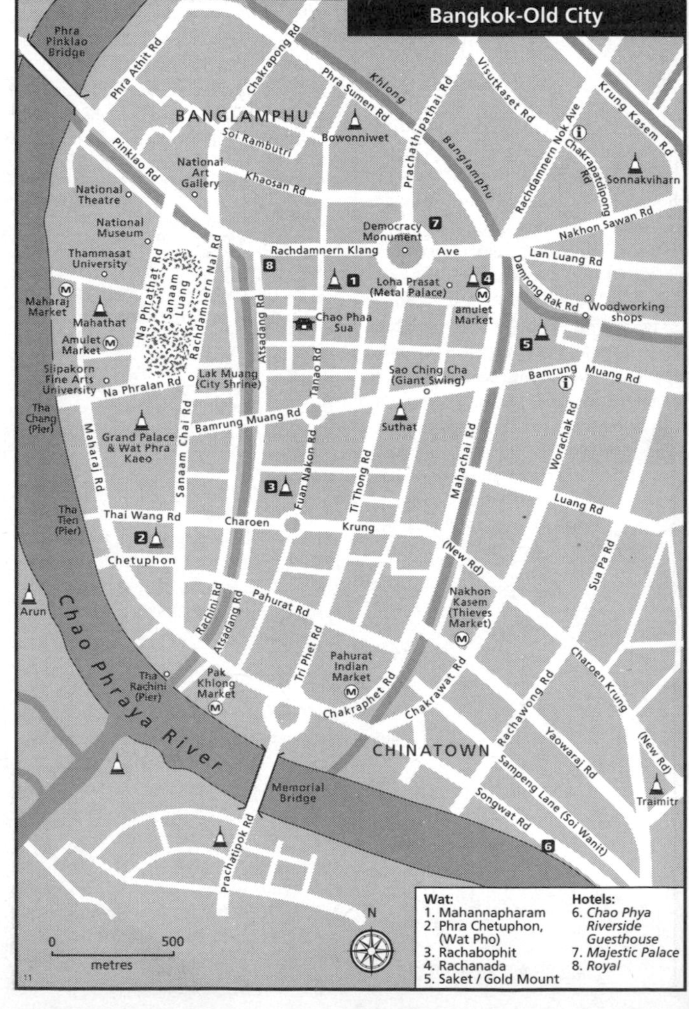

Old City place names

Grand Palace

พระบรมมหาราชวัง

National Museum

พิพิธภัณฑสถานแห่งชาติ

Wat Phra Chetuphon/ Wat Pho

วัดพระเชตุพน วัดโพธิ์

Wat Phra Kaeo

วัดพระศรีรัตนศาสดาราม

by Rama I's brother. The bot, or ubosoth, houses a bronze Ayutthayan Buddha in an attitude of meditation and the pedestal of this image contains the ashes of Rama I. Also notable is the 11-piece altar table set in front of the Buddha, and the magnificent mother-of-pearl inlaid doors which are possibly the best examples of this art from the Bangkok Period (depicting episodes from the Ramakien). The bot is enclosed by two galleries which house 394 seated bronze Buddha images. They were brought from the N during Rama I's reign and are of assorted periods and styles. Around the exterior base of the bot are marble reliefs telling the story of the Ramakien as adapted in the Thai poem the *Maxims of King Ruang* (formerly these reliefs were much copied by making rubbings onto rice paper). The 152 panels are the finest of their type in Bangkok. They recount only the second section of the Ramakien: the abduction and recovery of Ram's wife Seeda. The rather – to Western eyes – unsatisfactory conclusion to the story as told here has led some art historians to argue they were originally taken from Ayutthaya. Thai scholars argue otherwise.

A particular feature of the wat are the 95 chedis of various sizes which are scattered across the 20-acre complex. To the left of the bot are four large chedis, memorials to the first four Bangkok

Wat Phra Chetuphon (Wat Pho)

1 *Sala kan parian* or study hall
2 *Viharn* of the reclining Buddha
3 Enclosure of the royal *chedis*
4 *Ubosoth* (*bot*) or ordination hall
5 Cloister or *phra rabieng*

Source: adapted from a drawing by Kittisak Nualvilai based on aerial photographs and reproduced in Beek, Steve van andTettoni, L. (1991) *The arts of Thailand*, Thames & Hudson: London

12

The Emerald Buddha

Wat Phra Kaeo was specifically built to house the Emerald Buddha, the most venerated Buddha image in Thailand, carved from green jade (the emerald in the name referring only to its colour), a mere 75 cm high, and seated in an attitude of meditation. It is believed to have been found in 1434 in Chiang Rai, and stylistically belongs to the Late Chiang Saen or Chiang Mai schools. Since then, it has been moved on a number of occasions – to Lampang, Chiang Mai and Laos (both Luang Prabang and Vientiane). It stayed in Vientiane for 214 years before being recaptured by the Thai army in 1778 and placed in Wat Phra Kaeo on 22 March, 1784. The image wears seasonal costumes of gold and jewellery; one each for the hot, cool and the rainy seasons. The changing ceremony occurs 3 times a year in the presence of the King.

Buddha images are often thought to have personalities. The Phra Kaeo is no exception. It is said, for example, that such is the antipathy between the Phra Bang in Luang Prabang (Laos) and the Phra Kaeo that they can never reside in the same town.

kings. The library nearby is richly decorated with broken pieces of porcelain. The large top-hatted stone figures, the stone animals and the Chinese pagodas scattered throughout the compound came to Bangkok as ballast on the royal rice boats returning from China. Rama III, whose rice barges dominated the trade, is said to have had a particular penchant for these figures, as well as for other works of Chinese art. The Chinese merchants who served the King – and who are said to have called him *Chao Sua* or millionaire – loaded the empty barges with the carvings to please their lord. Rama III wanted Wat Pho to become known as a place of learning, a kind of exhibition of all the knowledge of the time and it is regarded as Thailand's first university. Admission ฿20. Open 0900-1700 Mon-Sun. **NB** From Tha Tien pier at the end of Thai Wang Rd, close to Wat Pho, it is possible to get boats to Wat Arun (see page 282). Wat Pho is also probably Bangkok's most respected centre of traditional Thai massage, and politicians, businessmen and military officers go there to seek relief from the tensions of modern life. Most medical texts were destroyed when the Burmese sacked the former capital, Ayutthaya, in 1776 and in 1832 Rama III had what was known about Thai massage inscribed on stone and then had those stones set into the walls of Wat Pho to guide and teach. For Westerners wishing to learn the art, special 30-hrs courses can be taken for ฿3,000, stretching over either 15 days (2 hrs/day) or 10 days (3 hrs/day). The centre is located at the back of the Wat, on the opposite side from the entrance. A massage costs ฿100 for 30 mins, ฿180 for 1 hr. With herbal treatment, the fee is ฿260 for 1.30 hr. For other centres of Thai Traditional massage see page 310.

Grand Palace and Wat Phra Kaeo

About 10-15 mins walk from Wat Pho northwards along Sanaam Chai Rd is the entrance to the **Grand Palace** and **Wat Phra Kaeo**. (**NB** The main entrance is the Viseschaisri Gate on Na Phralan Rd.) The Grand Palace is situated on the banks of the Chao Phraya River and is the most spectacular – some might say 'gaudy' – collection of buildings in Bangkok. The complex covers an area of over 1.5 sq km and the architectural plan is almost identical to that of the Royal Palace in the former capital of Ayutthaya. It was started in 1782 and was subsequently added to. Initially, the palace was the city,

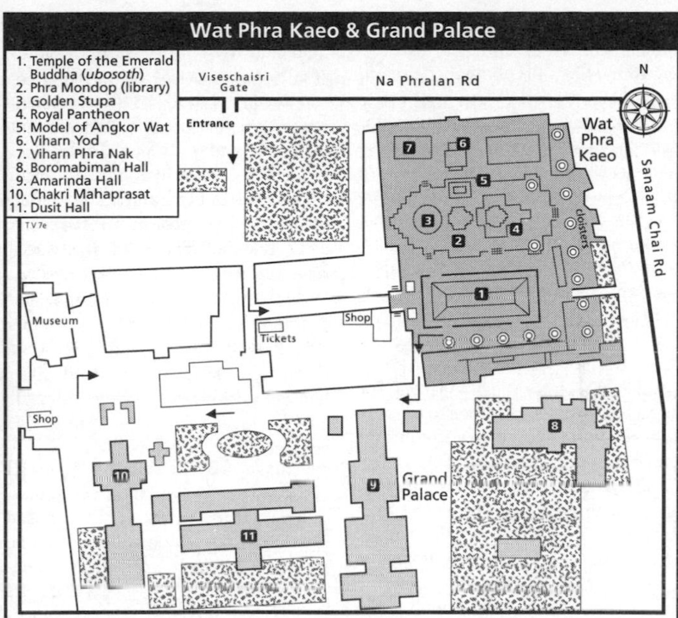

the seat of power, surrounded by high walls and built to be self-sufficient.

The buildings of greatest interest are clustered around **Wat Phra Kaeo**, or the 'Temple of the Emerald Buddha'. On entering the compound, the impression is one of glittering brilliance, as the outside is covered by a mosaic of coloured glass. The buildings were last restored for Bangkok's bicentenary in 1982 (the Wat Phra Kaeo Museum shows the methods used in the restoration process). Wat Phra Kaeo was built by Rama I in imitation of the royal chapel in Ayutthaya and was the first of the buildings within the Grand Palace complex to be constructed. While it was being erected the king lived in a small wooden building in one corner of the palace compound.

The ubosoth is raised on a marble platform with a frieze of gilded figures of garudas holding nagas running round the base. Bronze singhas act as door guardians. The door panels are of inlaid mother-of-pearl and date from Rama I's reign (late 18th century). Flanking the door posts are Chinese door guardians riding on lions. Inside the temple, the Emerald Buddha (see box) sits high up, illuminated above a large golden altar. In addition, there are many other gilded Buddha images, mostly in the attitude of dispelling fear, and a series of mural paintings depicting the jataka stories. Those facing the Emerald Buddha show the enlightenment of the Buddha when he subdues the evil demon Mara. Mara is underneath, wringing out his hair, while on either side, the Buddha is surrounded by evil spirits. Those on one side have been subjugated; those on the other have not. The water from the wringing out of Mara's hair drowns the evil army, and the Buddha is shown 'touching ground' calling the earth goddess Thorance up to witness his enlightenment. No photography is allowed inside the ubosoth.

Around the walls of the shaded cloister that encompasses Wat Phra Kaeo, is a continuous mural depicting the Ramakien – the Thai version of the Indian Ramayana. There are 178 sections in all, which were first painted during the reign of King Rama I but have since been restored on a number of occasions.

To the N of the ubosoth on a raised platform, are the **Royal Pantheon**, the **Phra Mondop** (the library), two gilt stupas, a model of Angkor Wat and the **Golden Stupa**. At the entrance to the Royal Pantheon are gilded kinarees. The Royal Pantheon is only open to the public once a year on Chakri Day, 6 Apr (the anniversary of the founding of the present Royal Dynasty). On the same terrace there are two gilt stupas built by King Rama I in commemoration of his parents. The Mondop was also built by Rama I to house the first revised Buddhist scriptural canon. To the W of the mondop is the large Golden Stupa or chedi, with its circular base, in Ceylonese style. To the N of the mondop is a model of Angkor Wat constructed during the reign of King Mongkut (1851-1868) when Cambodia was under Thai suzerainty.

To the N again from the Royal Pantheon is the **Supplementary Library** and two viharns – **Viharn Yod** and **Phra Nak**. The former is encrusted in pieces of Chinese porcelain.

To the S of Wat Phra Kaeo are the buildings of the **Grand Palace**. These are interesting for the contrast that they make with those of Wat Phra Kaeo. Walk out through the cloisters. On your left can be seen **Boromabiman Hall**, which is French in style and was completed during the reign of Rama VI. His three successors lived here at one time or another. The **Amarinda Hall** has an impressive airy interior, with chunky pillars and gilded thrones. The **Chakri Mahaprasart** (the Palace Reception Hall) stands in front of a carefully manicured garden with topiary. It was built and lived in by Rama V shortly after he had returned from a trip to Java and Singapore in 1876, and it shows: the building is a rather unhappy amalgam of colonial and traditional Thai styles of architecture. Initially the intention was to top the structure with a Western dome, but the architects settled for a Thai-style roof. The building was completed in time for Bangkok's first centenary in 1882. King Chulalongkorn (Rama V) found the overcrowded Grand Palace oppressive and after a visit to Europe in 1897, built himself a new home at Vimanmek (see page 283) in the area to the N, known as Dusit. The present King Bhumibol lives in the Chitralada Palace, built by Rama VI, also in the Dusit area. The Grand Palace is now only used for state occasions. Next to the Chakri Mahaprasart is the raised **Dusit Hall**; a cool, airy building containing mother-of-pearl thrones. Near the Dusit Hall is a **museum**, which has information on the restoration of the Grand Palace, models of the Palace and many Buddha statues. There is a collection of old cannon, mainly supplied by London gun foundries. Close by is a small café selling refreshing coconut drinks. All labels in Thai, but there are free guided tours in English throughout the day. Admission ฿50. Open: Mon-Sun 0900-1600.

ADMISSION to the Grand Palace complex ฿125, ticket office open 0830-1130, 1300-1530 Mon-Sun except Buddhist holidays when Wat Phra Kaeo is free but the rest of the palace is closed. The cost of the admission includes a free guidebook to the palace (with plan) as well as a ticket to the *Coin Pavilion*, with its collection of medals and 'honours' presented to members of the Royal Family and to the Vimanmek Palace in the Dusit area (see page 283). **NB** Decorum of dress is required (trousers can be hired for ฿10 near the entrance to the Grand Palace) which means no shorts, and no singlets or sleeveless shirts.

The National Museum

On the N edge of Sanaam Luang is the **National Museum**, reputedly the largest museum in Southeast Asia. It is an excellent place to view the full range of Thai art before visiting the ancient Thai capitals, Ayutthaya and Sukhothai.

Gallery No 1, the gallery of Thai history, is interesting and informative, as well as being air-conditioned, so it is a good place to cool-off. The gallery clearly shows Kings Mongkut and Chulalongkorn's fascination with Western technology. The other 22 galleries and 19 rooms contain a vast assortment of arts and artefacts divided according to period and style. If you are interested in Thai art, the museum alone might take a day to browse around. A shortcoming for those with no background knowledge is the lack of information in some of the galleries and it is recommended that interested visitors buy the 'Guide to the National Museum, Bangkok' for ฿50 or join one of the tours. Admission ฿20, together with a skimpy leaflet outlining the galleries. Open 0900-1600, Wed-Sun, tickets on sale until 1530. For English, French, German, Spanish and Portuguese-speaking tour information call T 2241333. They are free, and start at 0930, lasting 2 hrs (usually on Wed and Thur).

The Buddhaisawan Chapel, to the right of the ticket office for the National Museum, contains some of the finest Bangkok period murals in Thailand. The chapel was built in 1795 to house the famous Phra Sihing Buddha. Folklore has it that this image originated in Ceylon and when the boat carrying it to Thailand sank, it floated off on a plank to be washed ashore in Southern Thailand, near the town of Nakhon Si Thammarat. This, believe it or not, is probably untrue: the image is early Sukhothai in style (1250), admittedly showing Ceylonese influences, and almost certainly Northern Thai in origin. There are two other images that claim to be the magical Phra Buddha Sihing, one in Nakhon Si Thammarat and another in Chiang Mai. The chapel's magnificent murals were painted between 1795 and 1797 and depict stories from the Buddha's life. They are classical in style, without any sense of perspective, and the narrative of the Buddha's life begins to the right of the rear door behind the principal image, and progresses clockwise through 28 panels. German-speaking tours of the chapel are held on the third Tues of the month (0930).

THE GOLDEN MOUNT, GIANT SWING AND SURROUNDING WATS

From the Democracy Monument, across Mahachai Rd, at the point where Rachdamnern Klang Ave crosses Khlong Banglamphu can be seen the **Golden Mount** (also known as the Royal Mount), an impressive artificial hill nearly 80m high. The climb to the top is exhausting but worth it for the fabulous views of Bangkok. On the way up, the path passes holy trees, memorial plaques and Chinese shrines. The construction of the mount was begun during the reign of Rama III who intended to build the greatest chedi in his kingdom. The structure collapsed before completion, and Rama IV decided merely to pile up the rubble in a heap and place a far smaller golden chedi on its summit. The chedi contains a relic of the Buddha placed there by the present king after the structure had been most recently repaired in 1966. Admission ฿5. Open 0800-1800 Mon-Sun.

Wat Saket

This lies at the bottom of the mount, between it and Damrong Rak Rd – the mount actually lies within the wat's compound. Saket means 'washing of hair' – Rama I is reputed to have stopped here and ceremoniously washed himself before being crowned King in Thonburi (see Festivals, Nov). The only building of

Golden Mount place names

Amulet market
ตลาดพระเครื่อง
Golden Mount
ภูเขาทอง
Wat Rachabophit
วัดราชบพิธ
Wat Rachanada
วัดราชนัดดา
Wat Saket
วัดสระเกศ
Wat Suthat
วัดสุทัศน์เทพวราราม

real note is the *library* (*hor trai*) which is Ayutthayan in style. The door panels and lower windows are decorated with woodcarvings depicting everyday Ayutthayan life, while the window panels show Persian and French soldiers from Louis XIV's reign. Open 0800-1800 Mon-Sun.

Also in the shadow of the Golden Mount but to the W and on the corner of Rachdamnern Klang Ave and Mahachai Rd lies Wat Rachanada and the Loha Prasat. Until 1989 these buildings were obscured by the Chalerm Thai movie theatre, a landmark which Bangkok's taxi and tuk-tuk drivers still refer to. In the place of the theatre there is now a neat garden, with an elaborate gilded **sala**, which is used to receive visiting dignitaries. Behind the garden the strange looking **Loha Prasat** or Metal Palace, with its 37 spires, is easily recognizable. This palace was built by Rama III in 1846, and is said to be modelled on the first Loha Prasat built in India 2,500 years ago. A second was constructed in Ceylon in 160 BC, although Bangkok's Loha Prasat is the only one still standing. The palace was built by Rama III as a memorial to his beloved niece Princess Soammanas Vadhanavadi. The 37 spires represent the 37 Dharma of the Bodhipakya. The building, which contains Buddha images and numerous meditation cells, has been closed to visitors for many years, although it is possible to walk around the outside.

Next to the Loha Prasat is the much more traditional **Wat Rachanada**. Wat Rachanada was built by Rama III for his niece who later became Rama IV's queen. The main Buddha image is made of copper mined in Nakhon Ratchasima province to the NE of Bangkok, and the ordination hall also has some fine doors. Open 0600-1800 Mon-Sun. What makes the wat particularly worth visiting is the **Amulet market** to be found close by, between the Golden Mount and the wat. The sign, in English, below the covered part of the market reads 'Buddha and Antiques Centre'. The market also contains Buddha images and other religious artefacts and is open every day.

Wat Suthat

A 5 min walk S of Wat Rachanada, on Bamrung Muang Rd, is the **Sao Ching Cha** or **Giant Swing**, consisting of two tall red pillars linked by an elaborate cross piece, set in the centre of a square. The Giant Swing was the original centre for a Brahmanic festival in honour of Siva. Young men, on a giant 'raft', would be swung high into the air to grab pouches of coins, hung from bamboo poles, between their teeth. Because the swinging was from E to W, it has been said that it symbolized the rising and setting of the sun. The festival was banned in the 1930s because of the injuries that occurred; prior to its banning, thousands would congregate around the Giant Swing for 2 days of dancing and music. The magnificent **Wat Suthat** faces the Giant Swing. The wat was begun by Rama I in 1807, and his intention was to build a temple that would equal the most glorious in Ayutthaya. The wat was not finished until the end of the reign of Rama III in 1851.

The viharn is in early-Bangkok style and is surrounded by Chinese pagodas. Its six pairs of doors, each made from a single piece of teak, are deeply carved with animals and celestial beings from the Himavanta forest. The central doors are said to have been carved by Rama II himself, and are considered some of the most important works of art of the period. Inside the viharn is the bronze Phra Sri Sakyamuni Buddha in an attitude of subduing Mara. This image was previously contained in Wat Mahathat in Sukhothai, established in 1362. Behind the Buddha is a very fine gilded stone carving from the Dvaravati Period (2nd-11th centuries AD), 2.5m in height and showing the miracle at Sravasti and the Buddha preaching in the Tavatimsa heaven.

The bot is the tallest in Bangkok and one of the largest in Thailand. The murals in the bot painted during the reign of Rama III are interesting in that they are traditional Thai in style, largely unaffected by Western artistic influences. They use flat colours and lack perspective. The bot also contains a particularly large cast Buddha image. Open 0900-1700; the viharn is only open on weekends and Buddhist holidays 0900-1700.

Wat Rachabophit

The little visited Wat Rachabophit is close to the Ministry of the Interior on Rachabophit Rd, a few minutes walk S of Wat Suthat down Ti Thong Rd. It is recognizable by its distinctive doors carved in high relief with jaunty looking soldiers wearing European-style uniforms. The temple was started in 1869, took 20 years to complete, and is a rich blend of Western and Thai art forms (carried further in Wat Benchamabophit 40 years later, see page 286). Wat Rachabophit is peculiar in that it follows the ancient temple plan of placing the Phra Chedi in the centre of the complex, surrounded by the other buildings. It later became the fashion to place the ordination hall at the centre.

The 43m high gilded chedi's most striking feature are the five-coloured Chinese glass tiles which richly encrust the lower section. The ordination hall has 10 door panels and 28 window panels each decorated with gilded black lacquer on the inside and mother-of-pearl inlay on the outside showing the various royal insignia. They are felt to be among the masterpieces of the Rattanakosin Period (1782-present). The principal Buddha image in the ordination hall, in an attitude of meditation, sits on a base of Italian marble and is covered by the umbrella that protected the urn and ashes of Rama V. It also has a surprising interior – an oriental version of Italian Gothic, more like Versailles than Bangkok. Admission ฿10. Open 0800-1700 Mon-Sun.

From Wat Rachabophit, it is only a short distance to the **Pahurat Indian Market** on Pahurat Rd, where Indian, Malaysian and Thai textiles are sold. To get there, walk S on Ti Thong Rd which quickly becomes Tri Phet Rd. After a few blocks, Pahurat Rd crosses Tri Phet Rd. **Pak Khlong Market** is to be found a little further S on Tri Phet Rd at the foot of the Memorial Bridge. It is a huge wholesale market for fresh produce, and a photographer's paradise. It begins very early in the morning and has ended by 1000. The closest pier to the Pak Khlong Market is Tha Rachini, which is remembered for a particularly nasty episode in Thai history. It is said that in the 1840s a troublemaking upcountry *chao* or lord was brought to Bangkok and sentenced to death. His eyes were burnt out with heated irons and then the unfortunate man was suspended above the river at Tha Rachini in a cage. The cage was so positioned that the *chao* could touch the water with his finger tips but could not cup water to drink. He died of thirst and sunstroke after 3 days and for years afterwards people would not live near the spot where he died.

CHINATOWN AND THE GOLDEN BUDDHA

Chinatown covers the area from Charoen Krung (or New Rd) down to the river and leads on from Pahurat Rd Market; cross over Chakraphet Rd and immediately opposite is the entrance to Sampeng Lane. A trip through **Chinatown** can either begin with the Thieves Market to the NW, or at Wat Traimitr, the Golden Buddha, to the SE. An easy stroll between the two should not take more than 2 hrs. This part of Bangkok has a different atmosphere from elsewhere. Roads become narrower, buildings smaller, and there is a continuous bustle of activity. There remain some attractive, weathered examples of early 20th century shophouses. The industrious Sino-Thais of the area make everything from offertory candles and gold jewellery to metalwork, gravestones and light machinery.

Nakhon Kasem, or the Thieves Market, lies between Charoen Krung and Yaowaraj Rd, to the E of the khlong that runs parallel to Mahachai Rd. Its boundaries are marked by archways. As its name suggests, this market used to be the centre for the fencing of stolen goods. It is not quite so colourful today, but there remain a number of second-hand and antique shops which are worth a browse – such as the *Good Luck Antique Shop*. Amongst other things, musical instruments, brass ornaments, antique (and not so antique) coffee grinders are all on sale here.

Just to the SE of the Thieves Market are two interesting roads that run next to and parallel with one another: Yaowaraj Road and Sampeng Lane. **Yaowaraj Road**, a busy thoroughfare, is the centre of the country's gold trade. The trade is run by a cartel of seven shops, the Gold Traders Association, and

Chinatown place names

Wat Traimitir

วัดไตรมิตรวิทยาราม

Woeng Nakhon Kasem

เวิ้งนครเกษม

the price is fixed by the government. Sino-Thais often convert their cash into gold jewellery, usually bracelets and necklaces. The jewellery is bought by its 'baht weight' which fluctuates daily with the price of gold (most shops post the price daily). Should the owner need to convert their necklace or bracelet back into cash it is again weighed to determine its value. The narrower, almost pedestrian **Sampeng Lane**, also called **Soi Wanit**, is just to the S of Yaowaraj Rd. This road's history is shrouded in murder and intrigue. It used to be populated by prostitutes and opium addicts and was fought over by Chinese gangs. Today, it remains a commercial centre, but rather less illicit. It is still interesting (and cool, being shaded by awnings) to walk down, but there is not much to buy here – it is primarily a wholesale centre specializing in cloth and textiles although it is a good place to go for odd lengths of material, buttons of any shape and size, and things like costume jewellery.

The most celebrated example of the goldsmiths' art in Thailand sits within **Wat Traimitr**, or the **Temple of the Golden Buddha**, which is located at the E edge of Chinatown, squashed between Charoen Krung, Yaowaraj Rd and Traimitr Rd (just to the S of Bangkok's Hualamphong railway station). The Golden Buddha is housed in a small, rather gaudy and unimpressive room. Although the leaflet offered to visitors says the 3m-high, 700 year-old image is 'unrivalled in beauty', be prepared to be disappointed. It is in fact rather featureless, showing the Buddha in an attitude of subduing Mara. What makes it special, drawing large numbers of visitors each day, is that it is made of 5.5 tonnes of solid gold. Apparently, when the East Asiatic Company was extending the port of Bangkok, they came across a huge stucco Buddha image which they obtained permission to move. However, whilst being moved by crane in 1957, it fell and the stucco cracked open to reveal a solid gold image. During the Ayutthayan Period it was the custom to cover valuable Buddha images

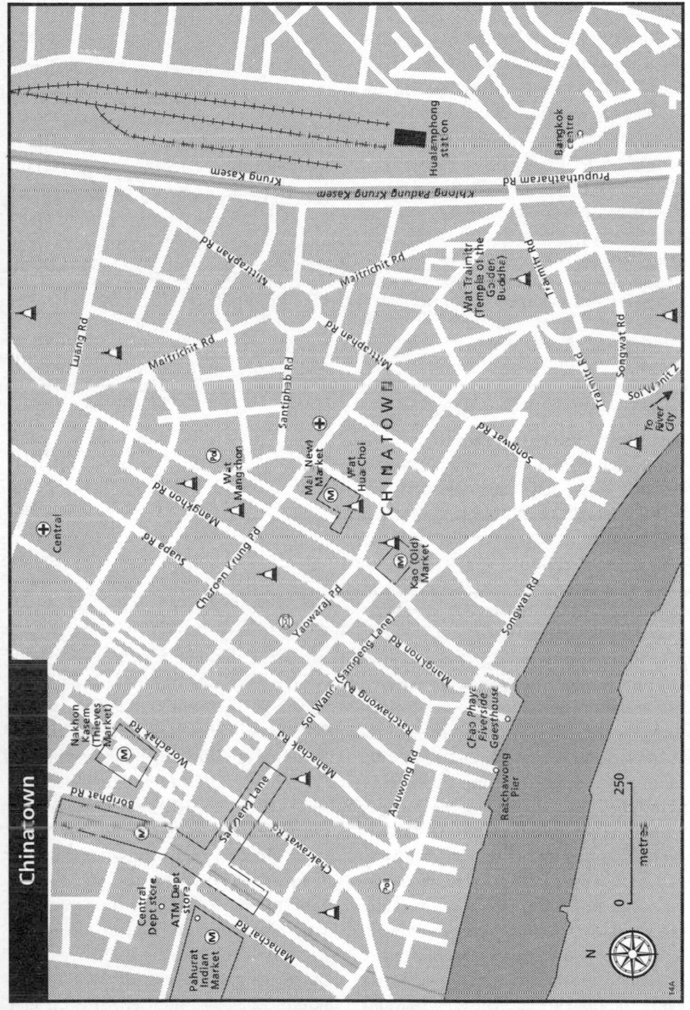

in plaster to protect them from the Burmese, and this particular example stayed that way for several 100 years. In the grounds of the wat there is a school, crematorium, foodstalls and, inappropriately, a money changer. Admission ฿10. Open 0900-1700 Mon-Sun. Gold beaters can still be seen at work behind Suksaphan store.

Between the river and Soi Wanit 2 there is a warren of lanes, too small for traffic – this is the Chinatown of old. From here it is possible to thread your way through to the River City shopping complex which is air-conditioned and a good place to cool-off.

RECOMMENDED READING Visitors wishing to explore the wonders of Chinatown more thoroughly, should buy Nancy Chandler's *Map of Bangkok*, a lively, detailed (but not altogether accurate) map of all the shops, restaurants and out of the way wats and shrines. ฿70 from most bookstores.

WAT ARUN AND THE KHLONGS

One of the most enjoyable ways to see Bangkok is by boat – and particularly by the fast and noisy ***hang yaaws*** (**long-tailed boats**). You will know them when you see them; these powerful, lean machines roar around the river and the khlongs at break-neck speed, as though they are involved in a race to the death. There are innumerable tours around the khlongs of Thonburi taking in a number of sights which include the floating market, snake farm and Wat Arun. Boats go from the various piers located along the E banks of the Chao Phraya River. The journey begins by travelling downstream along the Chao Phraya, before turning 'inland' after passing underneath the Krungthep Bridge. The route skirts past laden rice-barges, squatter communities on public land and houses overhanging the canals. This is a very popular route with tourists, and boats are intercepted by salesmen and women marketing everything from cold beer to straw hats.

Wat Arun place names

Royal Barges National Museum
พิพิธภัณฑสถานแห่งชาติเรือพระราชพิธี

Wat Arun
วัดอรุณราชวราราม

You may also get caught in a boat jam; traffic snarl-ups are not confined to the capital's roads. Nevertheless, the trip is a fascinating insight into what Bangkok must have been like when it was still the 'Venice of the East', and around every bend there seems to be yet another wat – some of them very beautiful. On private tours the first stop is usually the **Floating market** (*Talaat Nam*). This is now an artificial, ersatz gathering which exists purely for the tourist industry. It is worth only a brief visit – unless the so-called 'post-tourist' is looking for just this sort of sight. The nearest functioning floating market is at Damnoen Saduak (see excursions from Bangkok, page 289). The **Snake Farm** is the next stop where man fights snake in an epic battle of wills. Visitors can even pose with a python. The poisonous snakes are incited, to burst balloon with their fangs, 'proving' how dangerous they are. There is also a rather motley zoo with a collection of crocodiles and sad-looking animals in small cages. The other snake farm in Central Bangkok is (appropriately) attached to the Thai Red Cross and is more professional and cheaper (see page 288). Admission ฿70, shows every 20 mins. Refreshments available. On leaving the snake farm, the boat will join up with Khlong Bangkok Yai at the site of the large **Wat Paknam**. Just before re-entering the Chao Phraya itself, the route passes by the impressive **Wat Kalaya Nimit**.

Wat Arun

North on the Chao Phraya River is the famous Wat Arun, or the Temple of the Dawn, facing Wat Pho across the river. Wat Arun stands 81m high, making it the highest prang (tower) in Thailand. It was built in the early 19th century on the site of Wat Chaeng, the Royal Palace complex when Thonburi was briefly the capital of Thailand. The wat housed the Emerald Buddha before the image was transferred to Bangkok and it is said that King Taksin vowed to restore the wat after passing it one dawn. The prang is completely covered with pieces of Chinese porcelain and includes some delicate gold and black lacquered doors. The temple is really meant to be viewed from across the river; its scale and beauty can only be appreciated from a distance. Young, a European visitor to the capital, wrote in 1898: 'Thousands upon thousands of pieces of cheap china must have been smashed to bits in order to furnish sufficient material to decorate this curious structure ... though the material is tawdry, the effect is indescribably wonderful'.

Energetic visitors can climb up to the halfway point and view the city. This is not recommended for people suffering from vertigo; the steps are very steep – be prepared for jelly-like legs after descending. Admission ฿10. Open 0830-1730 Mon-Sun. The men at the pier may demand ฿10 to help 'in the maintenance of the pier'. **NB** It is possible to get to Wat Arun by water-taxi from Tha Tien pier (at the end of Thai Wang Rd near Wat Pho), or from Tha Chang (at the end of Na Phralan near Wat Phra Kaeo) (฿1). The best view of Wat Arun is in the evening from the Bangkok side of the river when the sun sets behind the prang.

After visiting Wat Arun, some tours then go further upstream to the mouth of Khlong Bangkok Noi where the **Royal Barges** are housed in a hangar-like boathouse. These ornately carved boats, winched out of the water in cradles, were used by the king at 'krathin' (see OK Phansa festival, page 347) to present robes to the monks in Wat Arun at the end of the rainy season. The ceremony ceased in 1967 but the Royal Thai Navy restored the barges for the revival of the spectacle, as part of the Chakri Dynasty's bicentennial celebrations in 1982. The oldest and most beautiful barge is the Sri Supannahong, built during the reign of Rama I (1782-1809) and repaired during that of Rama VI (1910-1925). It measures 45m long and 3m wide, weighs 15 tonnes and was created from a single piece of teak. It required a crew of 50 oarsmen, and two coxwains, along with such assorted crew members as a flagman, a rhythm-keeper and singer. Its gilded prow was carved in the form of a *hamsa* (or goose) and its stern, in the shape of a *naga*. Admission ฿10. Open 0830-1630 Mon-Sun (see Festivals, Sep, page 290).

Arranging a boat tour

Either book a tour at your hotel, or go to one of the piers and organize your own customized trip. The most frequented piers are located between the Oriental Hotel and the Grand Palace (see map, or ask at your hotel). The pier just to the S of the Royal Orchid Sheraton Hotel is recommended. Organizing your own trip gives greater freedom to stop and start when the mood takes you. It is best to go in the morning (0700). For the trip given above (excluding Wat Rakhang and Wat Suwannaram), the cost for a hang yaaw which can sit 10 people should be about ฿600 for the boat for a half-day. If visiting Rakhang and Suwannaram as well as the other sights, expect to pay about another ฿200-300 for the hire of a boat. Be sure to settle the route and cost before setting out.

THE DUSIT AREA

The Dusit area of Bangkok lies N of the Old City. The area is intersected by wide tree-lined avenues, and has an almost European flavour. The **Vimanmek Palace** lies off Rachvithi Rd, just to the N of the National Assembly. Vimanmek is the largest golden teakwood mansion in the world. It was built by Rama V in 1901 and designed by one of his brothers. The palace makes an interesting contrast to Jim Thompson's House (see page 286) or Suan Pakkard (page 286). While Jim Thompson was enchanted by Thai arts, King Rama V was clearly taken with Western arts. It seems like a large Victorian hunting lodge – but raised off the ground – and is filled with china, silver and paintings from all over the world (as well as some gruesome hunting trophies). The photographs are fascinating – one shows the last time elephants were used in warfare in Thailand. Behind the

The Chao Phraya River Express

One of the most relaxing – and one of the cheapest – ways to see Bangkok is by taking the Chao Phraya River Express. These boats (or *rua duan*) link almost 40 piers (or *tha*) along the Chao Phraya River from Tha Wat Rajsingkorn in the S to Tha Nonthaburi in the N. The entire route entails a journey of about 1¼-1½ hr, and fares are ฿4, ฿6 or ฿8. Adjacent to many of the piers are excellent riverside restaurants. At peak periods, boats leave every 10 mins, off-peak about every 15-25 mins. Note that boats flying red or green pennants do not stop at every pier; they also exact a ฿1 surcharge. Also, boats will only stop if passengers wish to board or alight, so make your destination known.

Selected piers and places of interest, travelling upstream

Tha Orienten By the *Oriental Hotel*; access to *Silom Road*.

Tha River City In the shadow of the *Royal Orchid Hotel*, on the S side and close to *River City* shopping centre.

Tha Ratchawong *Rabieng Ratchawong Restaurant*; access to *Chinatown* and *Sampeng Lane*.

Tha Saphan Phut Under the *Memorial Bridge* and close to *Pahurat Indian market*.

Tha Rachini *Pak Khlong Market*; just upstream, the *Catholic seminary* surrounded by high walls.

Tha Tien Close to *Wat Pho*; *Wat Arun* on the opposite bank; and just downstream from Wat Arun the *Vichaiprasit fort* headquarters of the Thai navy), lurking behind crenellated ramparts.

Tha Chang Just downstream is the *Grand Palace* peeking out above white-washed walls; *Wat Rakhang* with its white corn-cob prang lies opposite.

Tha Maharat *Lan The Restaurant*; access to *Wat Mahathat* and *Sanaam Luang*.

Tha Phra Arthit *Yen Jai Restaurant*; access to *Khaosan Road*.

Tha Visutkasat *Yok Yor Restaurant*; just upstream the elegant central *Bank of Thailand*.

Tha Thewes *Son Ngen Restaurant*; just upstream are *boatsheds* with royal barges; close to the *National Library*.

Tha Wat Chan Just upstream is the *Singha Beer* Samoson brewery.

Tha Wat Khema *Wat Khema* in large, tree-filled compound.

Tha Wat Khian *Wat Kien*, semi-submerged.

Tha Nonthaburi Last stop on the express boat route .

palace is the Audience Hall which houses a fine exhibition of crafts made by the Support Foundation, an organization set up and funded by Queen Sirikit. Support, rather clumsily perhaps, is the acronym for the Foundation for the Promotion of Supplementary Occupations and Related Techniques. Also worth seeing is

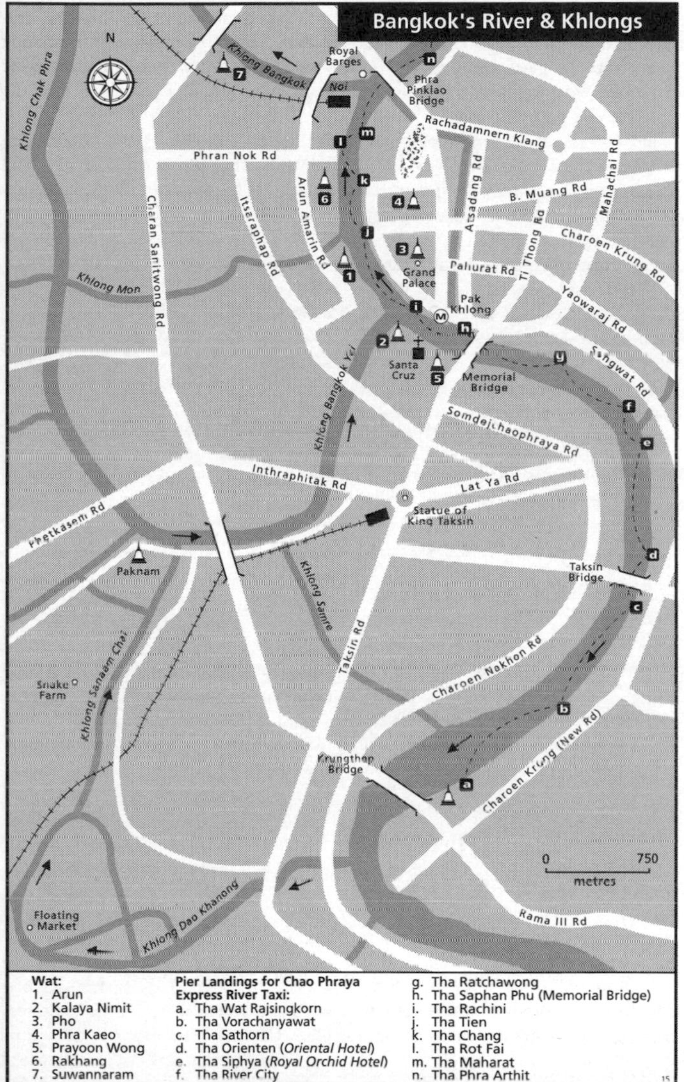

Dusit area place names

Vimanmek Palace

พระที่นั่งวิมานเมฆ

the exhibition of the king's own photographs, and the clock museum. Dance shows are held twice a day. Visitors are not free to wander, but must be shown around by one of the charming guides who demonstrate the continued deep reverence for King Rama V (tour approx 1hr). Admission ฿50, ฿20 for children. Note that tickets to the Grand Palace include entrance to Vimanmek Palace. Open 0930-1600 (last tickets sold at 1500) Mon-Sun. Refreshments available. **NB** Visitors to the palace are required to wear long trousers or a skirt; sarongs available for hire (฿100, refundable). Buses do go past the palace, but from the centre of town it is easier to get a tuk-tuk or taxi (฿50-60).

Wat Benchamabophit

Or the **Marble Temple**, is the most modern of the royal temples and was only finished in 1911. It is of unusual architectural design (the architect was the king's half brother, Prince Naris), with carrara marble pillars, a marble courtyard and two large singhas guarding the entrance to the bot. Rama V was so pleased with the marble-faced ordination hall that he wrote to his brother: 'I never flatter anyone but I cannot help saying that you have captured my heart in accomplishing such beauty as this'. The interior is magnificently decorated with crossbeams of lacquer and gold, and in shallow niches in the walls are paintings of important stupas from all over the kingdom. The door panels are faced with bronze sculptures and the windows are of stained-glass, painted with angels. The cloisters around the assembly hall house 52 figures (both original and imitation) – a display of the evolution of the Buddha image in India, China and Japan. The Walking Buddha from the Sukhothai Period is particularly worth a look. The rear courtyard houses a large 80-year-old bodhi tree and a pond filled with turtles, released by people hoping to gain merit. The best time to visit this temple complex is early morning, when monks can be heard chanting inside the chapel. Admission ฿10. Open 0800-1700 Mon-Sun.

OTHER PLACES OF INTEREST

In addition to the Vimanmek Palace, Bangkok also has a number of other beautiful Thai-style houses that are open to the public. **Suan Pakkard Palace** or Lettuce Garden Palace is at 352-354 Sri Ayutthaya Rd, S of the Victory Monument. The five raised traditional Thai houses (domestic rather than royal) were built by Princess Chumbhot, a great-grand-daughter of King Rama IV. They contain her fine collection of antiquities, both historic and prehistoric (the latter are particularly rare). Like the artefacts in the National Museum, those in Suan Pakkard are also poorly labelled. The rear pavilion is particularly lovely, decorated in black and gold lacquerwork panels. Prince Chumbhot discovered this temple near Ayutthaya and reassembled and restored it here for his wife's 50th birthday. The grounds are very peaceful. Admission ฿80 – including a fan to ward off the heat. Open 0900-1600, Mon-Sat. All receipts go to a fund for artists.

Jim Thompson's House is on the quiet Soi Kasemsan Song (2), opposite the National Stadium on Rama I Rd. It is an assemblage of traditional teak Northern Thai houses, some more than 200 years old, transported here and reassembled (these houses were designed to be transportable, consisting of five parts – the floor, posts, roof, walls and decorative elements constructed without the use of nails). Jim Thompson arrived in Bangkok as an intelligence officer attached to the United States' OSS (Office of Strategic Services) and then made his name by reinvigorating the Thai silk industry after

Other area place names

Chatuchak Weekend Market
ตลาดนัดสวนจัตุจักร
Jim Thompson's House
บ้านจิม ทอมป์สัน
Siam Square
สยามสแควร์
Suan Pakkard Palace
วังสวนผักกาด

WW2. He disappeared mysteriously in the Malaysian jungle on 27 March 1967, but his silk industry continues to thrive. (The *Jim Thompson Silk Company*, selling fine Thai silk, is at the NE end of Surawong Rd. This shop is a tourist attraction in itself. Shoppers can buy high-quality bolts of silk and silk clothing here – anything from a pocket handkerchief to a silk suit. Prices are top of the scale.) Jim Thompson chose this site for his house partly because a collection of silk weavers lived nearby on Khlong Saensaep. The house contains an eclectic collection of antiques from Thailand and China, with work displayed as though it was still his home. Shoes must be removed before entering; walking barefoot around the house adds to the appreciation of the cool teak floorboards. Bustling Bangkok only intrudes in the form of the stench from the khlong that runs behind the house. Compulsory guided tours around the house and no photography allowed. Admission ฿100 (profits to charity). Open 0900-1630, Mon-Sat. Getting there: bus along Rama 1 Rd, taxi or tuk-tuk.

A 10 mins' walk E along Rama I Rd is the shopping area known as **Siam Square** (or *Siam Sa-quare*). This has the greatest concentration of fast food restaurants, boutiques and cinemas in the city. Needless to say, it is patronized by young Thais sporting the latest fashions and doing the sorts of things their parents would never have dreamed of doing – girls smoking and couples holding hands, for instance. For Thais worried about the direction their country is taking, Siam Square encapsulates all their fears in just a few *rai*. This is crude materalism; this is Thais aping the West; this is the erosion of Thai values and culture with scarcely a thought to the future. Because of the tourists and wealthy Thais who congregate around Siam Square it is also a popular patch for beggars. It seems that over the last few years the number of beggars has increased – which may seem odd given Thailands's rapid economic growth. It may be that this economic expansion hasn't reached the poor in rural areas (Thailand has become a more unequal society over the last decade or so); or it maybe that with greater wealth, begging has become a more attractive – in terms of economic return – occupation.

East of Siam Square is the **Erawan Shrine** on the corner of Ploenchit and Rachdamri rds, at the Rachparasong intersection. This is Bangkok's most popular shrine, attracting not just Thais but also large numbers of other Asian visitors. The spirit of the shrine, the Hindu god Thao Maha Brahma, is reputed to grant people's wishes – it certainly has little artistic worth. In thanks, visitors offer garlands, wooden elephants and pay to have dances performed for them accompanied by the resident Thai orchestra. The popular *Thai Rath* newspaper reported in 1991 that some female devotees show their thanks by covorting naked at the shrine in the middle of the night. Others, rather more coy about exposing themselves in this way, have taken to giving the god pornographic videos instead. Although it is unlikely that visitors will be rewarded with the sight of naked bodies, the shrine is a hive of activity at most hours, incongruously set on a noisy, polluted intersection tucked into a corner, and in the shadow of the Sogo Department Store.

One other traditional house worth visiting is the home of the **Siam Society**, off Sukhumvit Rd, at 131 Soi Asoke. The Siam Society is a learned society established in 1904 and has benefited from almost continual royal patronage. The **Kamthieng House** is a 120-year-old N Thai house from Chiang Mai. It was donated to the society in 1963, transported to Bangkok and then reassembled a few years later. It now serves as an ethnological museum, devoted to preserving the traditional technologies and folk arts of Northern Thailand. It makes an interesting contrast to the fine arts displayed in Suan Pakkard Palace and Jim Thompson's house. The Siam Society houses a library, organizes lectures and tours and publishes books, magazines and pamphlets. Admission ฿25, ฿10 for children. Open 0900-1200, 1300-1700, Tues-Sat, T 2583491 for information on lectures.

For those with a penchant for snakes, the **Snake Farm** of the Thai Red Cross is very central and easy to reach from Silom or Surawong rds. It was established in 1923, and raises snakes for serum production, which is distributed worldwide. The farm also has a collection of non-venomous snakes. During showtime (which lasts 30 mins) various snakes are exhibited, and venom extracted. Visitors can fondle a python. The farm is well maintained and professional. Admission ฿70. Open 0830-1630 Mon-Fri (shows at 1100 and 1430), 0830-1200 Sat/Sun and holidays (show at 1100). The farm is within the Science Division of the Thai Red Cross Society at the corner of Rama IV and Henri Dunant rds.

Slightly further out of the centre of Bangkok is the **Chatuchak Weekend Market** which is off Phahonyothin Rd, opposite the Northern bus terminal. Until 1982 this market was held at Sanaam Luang, but was moved because it had outgrown its original home and also because the authorities wanted to clean up the area for the Bangkok bicentenary celebrations. It is a huge conglomeration of 8,672 stall-holders spread over an area of 28 acres, selling virtually everything under the sun, and an estimated 200,000 people visit the market over a weekend. It is probably the best place to buy handicrafts and all things Thai in the whole Kingdom. There are antique stalls, basket stalls, textile sellers, shirt vendors, carvers, painters ... along with the usual array of fish sellers, vegetable hawkers, butchers and candle-stick makers. In the last couple of years a number of bars and food stalls geared to tourists and Thai yuppies have also opened so it is possible to rest and re-charge before foraging once more. Definitely worth a visit – and allocate half a day at least. In addition to the map below, Nancy Chandler's Map of Bang-

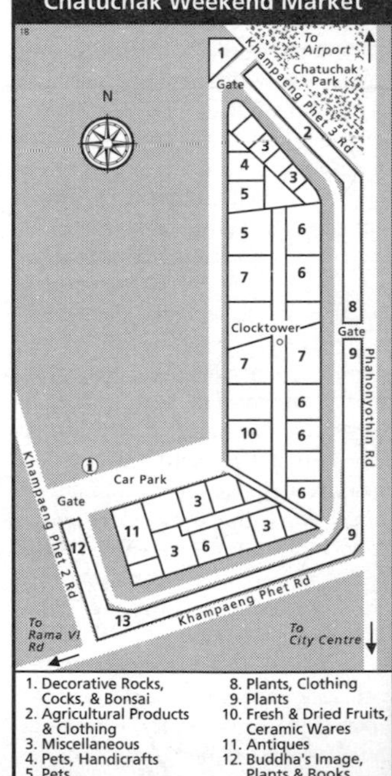

kok has an inset map of the market to help you get around. Believe it or not, the market is open on weekends, officially from 0900-1800 (although in fact it begins earlier around 0700). It's best to go early in the day. In 1994 plans were announced to transform the market by building a three-storey purpose-built structure with car parking and various other amenities. Such has been the outcry that the planners have retired to think again. But the fear is that this gem of shopping chaos will be re-organized, sanitized, bureaucratized and, in the process, ruined. **Beware pick-pockets**. There is a tourist information centre at the entrance gate off Kamphaeng Phet 2 Rd, and the Clock tower serves as a good reference point should visitors become disoriented. Getting there: a/c buses 2 (from Silom Rd), 3, 10, 13 and 29 go past the market, and non-a/c buses 8, 24, 26, 27, 29, 34, 39, 44, 59, and 96. Or take a taxi or tuk-tuk.

EXCURSIONS

FLOATING MARKET AT DAMNOEN SADUAK

Ratchaburi Province, 109 km W of Bangkok. Sadly, it is becoming increasingly like the Floating Market in Thonburi, although it does still function as a legitimate market. **Getting there**: catch an early morning bus (No 78) from the Southern bus terminal in Thonburi – aim to get to Damnoen Saduak between 0800-1000, as the market winds down after 1000, leaving only trinket stalls. The trip takes about 1½ hrs. A/c and non-a/c buses leave every 40 mins from 0600 (฿30-49) (T 4355031 for booking). The bus travels via Nakhon Pathom (where it is possible to stop on the way back and see the great chedi – see Nakhon Pathom). Ask the conductor to drop you at Thanarat Bridge in Damnoen Saduak. Then either walk down the lane

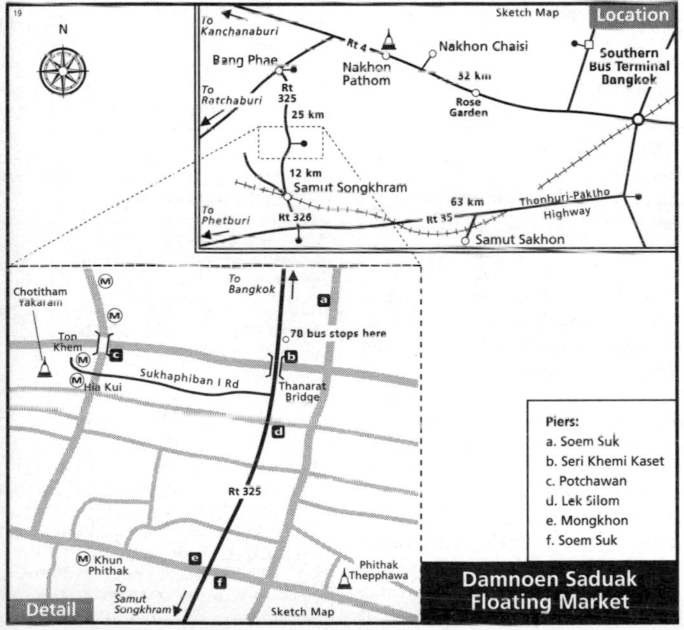

Other area place names

Floating market at Damnoen Saduak
ตลาดน้ำดำเนินสะดวก

(1.5 km) that leads to the market and follows the canal, or take a river taxi for ฿10, or a mini-bus (฿2). There are a number of floating markets in the maze of khlongs – Ton Khem, Hia Kui and Khun Phithak – and it is best to hire a hang yaaw to explore the back-waters and roam around the markets, about ฿300/hour (agree the price before setting out). Tour companies also visit the floating market.

TOURS

Bangkok has innumerable tour companies that can take visitors virtually anywhere. If there is not a tour to fit your bill – most run the same range of tours – many companies will organize one for you, for a price. Most top hotels have their own tour desk and it is probably easiest to book there (arrange to be picked up from your hotel as part of the deal). Prices per person are about ฿250-500 for a half day tour, ฿600-1,000 for a full day (incl lunch).

FESTIVALS AND MAJOR EVENTS

Jan: *Red Cross Fair* (movable), held in Amporn Gardens next to the Parliament. Stalls, classical dancing, folk performances etc.
Feb: *Chinese New Year* (movable), Chinatown closes down, but Chinese temples are packed. *Handicraft Fair* (mid-month), all the handicrafts are made by Thai prisoners.
Mar-Apr: *Kite Flying* (movable, for 1 month), every afternoon/evening at Sanaam Luang there is kite fighting. An *International Kite Festival* is held in late Mar at Sanaam Luang when kite fighting and demonstrations by kite-flyers from across the globe take place.
May: *Royal Ploughing Ceremony* (movable), this celebrates the official start of the rice-planting season and is held at Sanaam Luang. It is an ancient Brahman ritual and is attended by the king.
Sep: *Swan-boat races* (movable), on the Chao Phraya River.
Nov: *Golden Mount Fair* (movable), stalls and theatres set-up all around the Golden Mount and Wat Saket. Candles are carried in procession to the top of the mount. *Marathon* road race, fortunately at one of the coolest times of year.
Dec: *Trooping of the Colour* (movable), the élite Royal Guards swear allegiance to the king and march past members of the Royal Family. It is held in the Royal Plaza near the equestrian statue of King Chulalongkorn.

LOCAL INFORMATION

● Accommodation

Bangkok offers a vast range of accommodation at all levels of luxury. There are a number of hotel areas in the city, each with its own character and locational advantages. Accommodation has been divided into five such areas with a sixth – 'other' – for the handful situated elsewhere. A new type of hotel which has emerged in Bangkok in recent years is the 'boutique' hotel. These are small, with immaculate service, and represent an attempt to emulate the philosophy of 'small is beautiful'.

For the last few years Bangkok has had a glut of hotel rooms – especially 5-star – as hotels planned during the heady days of the late 1980s and early 1990s have opened. Room rates at the top end fell around 50% between 1991 and 1996, so there are bargains to be had.

NB For business women travelling alone, the *Oriental*, *Dusit Thani* and *Amari Airport* hotels allocate a floor to women travellers, with all-female staff.

Many of the more expensive places to stay are on the **Chao Phraya River** with its views, good shopping and access to the old city. Running eastwards from the river are **Silom** and **Surawong** rds, in the heart of Bangkok's business district and close to many embassies. The bars of Patpong link the two roads. This is a good area to stay for shopping and bars, but transport to the tourist sights can be problematic. A more recently developed area is along **Sukhumvit Rd** running E from Soi Nana Nua (Soi

Price guide		
	US$	**Baht**
L	200+	5,000+
A+	100-200	2,500-5,000
A	50-100	1,250-2,500
B	25-50	625-1,250
C	15-25	375-625
D	8-15	200-375
E	4-8	100-200
F	<4	<100

3). The bulk of the accommodation here is in the **A-B** range, and within easy reach is a wide range of restaurants, 'girlie' bars, and reasonable shopping. But, the hotels are a long taxi or tuk-tuk ride from the sights of the old city and most of the places of interest to the tourist in Bangkok. In the vicinity of **Siam Square** are two deluxe hotels and several 'budget' class establishments (especially along Rama 1 Soi Kasemsan Nung). Siam Square is central, a good shopping area, with easy bus and taxi access to Silom and Sukhumvit rds and the sights of the old city. Guesthouses are to be found along and around **Khaosan Rd** (an area known as Banglamphu); or just to the N, at the NW end of **Sri Ayutthaya Rd** there is a small cluster of rather friendly places. **Soi Ngam Duphli**, off Rama IV Rd, is the other big area for cheap places to stay. These hotel areas encompass about 90% of Bangkok's accommodation, although there are other places to stay scattered across the city; these are listed under **Other**.

● Silom, Surawong and the River

L ***Dusit Thani***, 946 Rama IV Rd, T 2360450, F 2366400, a/c, restaurants, pool, when it was built it was the tallest building in Bangkok, refurbished, still excellent and has been continually refurbished and upgraded, though disappointing pool, rec; **L** ***Montien***, 54 Surawong Rd, T 2348060, F 2365219, a/c, restaurants, pool, one of the first high-rise hotels (opened 1967) with good location for business, shopping and bars, slick service, and continuing good reputation with loyal patrons; **L** ***Oriental***, 48 Soi Oriental, Charoen Krung, T 2360400, F 2361939, a/c, restaurants, pool, one of the best hotels in the world, beautiful position overlooking the river, superb personal service despite its size (400 rm). The hotel claims that Joseph Conrad, Somerset Maugham and Noel Coward all stayed here at one time or another, although the first of these probably did not – he lived aboard his ship or, perhaps, stayed in the now defunct *Universal Hotel*. Good shopping arcade, good programme of 'cultural' events, and 6 excellent restaurants, some of the equipment and bathrooms could be said to be a little old, however it still comes highly rec; **L** ***Royal Orchid Sheraton***, 2 Captain Bush Lane, Si Phraya Rd, T 2345599, F 2368320, a/c, restaurants, pool, at times strong and rather unpleasant smell from nearby khlong, lovely views over the river, close to River City shopping centre (good for antiques), rooms are average at this price but service is very slick; **L** ***Shangri-La***, 89 Soi Wat Suan Plu, Charoen Krung, T 2367777, F 2368570, a/c, restaurants, lovely pool, great location overlooking river, sometimes preferred to *Oriental* but some consider it dull and impersonal, recently upgraded and extended, rec; **L** ***The Western Banyan Tree***, 21/100 Sathorn Tai Rd, T 6791200, F 6791199, a/c, restaurant, pool, new hotel and the tallest in Bangkok. It is targeting the business traveller, all rooms are suites with working area, in room fax and copier, computer port and voice mail, good position for many offices; **L-A+** ***Sukhothai***, 13/3 Sathorn Tai Rd, T 2870222, F 2874980, a/c, restaurants (especially good poolside Italian restaurant), pool, beautiful rooms and excellent service, in Thai postmodern style, clean and elegant, there are those who say it is even better than such established hotels as *The Regent*, even *The Oriental*, rec; **L-A+** ***Holiday Inn Crowne Plaza***, 981 Silom Rd, T 2384300, F 2385289, a/c, restaurants, pool, vast, pristine marble-filled hotel, all amenities, immensely comfortable, minimum atmosphere and character.

A+ ***Marriott Royal Garden Riverside Hotel***, 257/1-3 Charoen Nakorn Rd, T 4760021, F 4761120, a/c, restaurant, large pool, situated on the river but on the Thonburi bank, attractive low rise hotel with some attempt to create Thai-style and ambience; **A+** ***Monarch Lee Gardens***, 188 Silom Rd, T 2381991, F 2381999, a/c, restaurants, pool, opened 1992, stark and gleaming high-tech high-rise, all facilities, still trying hard to attract custom, discounts available; **A+** ***Pan Pacific Hotel***, 952 Rama IV Rd, T 6329000, F 6329001, a/c, restaurant, pool, 235 rm hotel, good central position for business and shopping.

A ***Mandarin***, 662 Rama IV Rd, T 2380230, F 2371620, a/c, restaurant, small pool, friendly atmosphere, comfortable rooms, popular

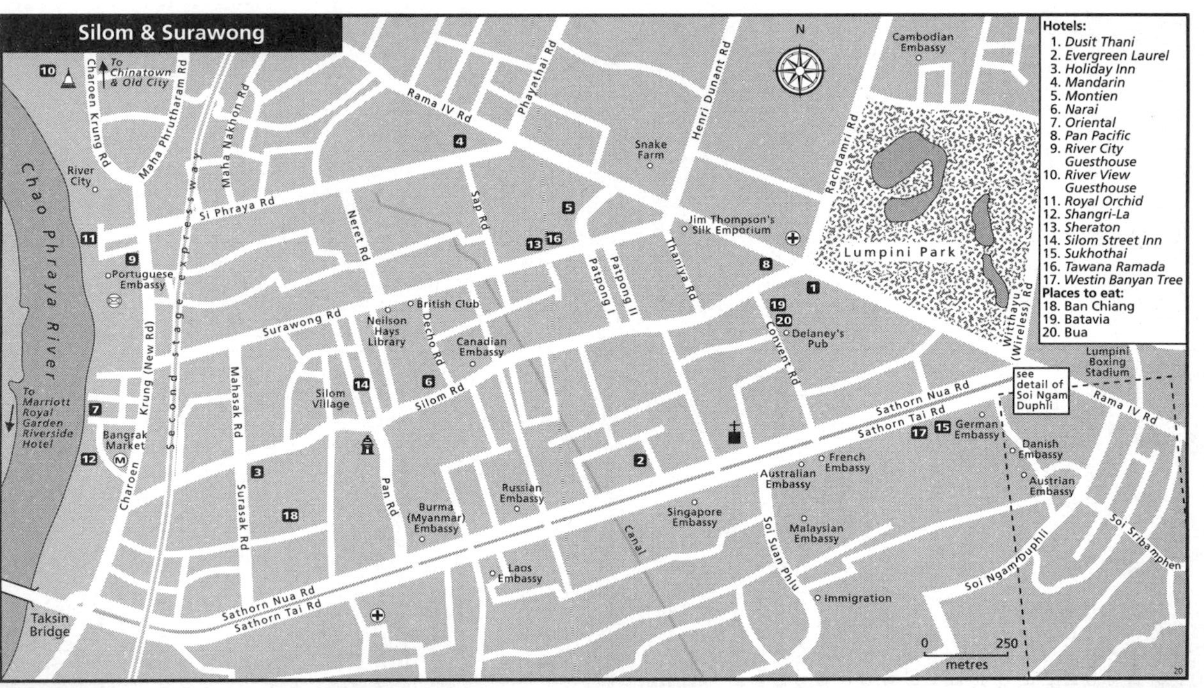
Silom & Surawong
Hotels:
1. Dusit Thani
2. Evergreen Laurel
3. Holiday Inn
4. Mandarin
5. Montien
6. Narai
7. Oriental
8. Pan Pacific
9. River City Guesthouse
10. River View Guesthouse
11. Royal Orchid
12. Shangri-La
13. Sheraton
14. Silom Street Inn
15. Sukhothai
16. Tawana Ramada
17. Westin Banyan Tree
Places to eat:
18. Ban Chiang
19. Batavia
20. Bua
To Chinatown & Old City
Charoen Krung Rd
Maha Phrutharam Rd
Maha Nakhon Rd
Rama IV Rd
Phayathai Rd
Henri Dunant Rd
N
Cambodian Embassy
Rachdamri Rd
Snake Farm
River City
Chao Phraya River
Si Phraya Rd
Neret Rd
Sap Rd
Jim Thompson's Silk Emporium
Lumpini Park
Portuguese Embassy
Patpong I
Patpong II
Thaniya Rd
British Club
Surawong Rd
Neilson Hays Library
Decho Rd
Canadian Embassy
Delaney's Pub
Convent Rd
Witthayu (Wireless) Rd
Lumpini Boxing Stadium
see detail of Soi Ngam Duphli
Second stage expressway
Krung (New Rd)
Silom Village
Silom Rd
Sathorn Nua Rd
Sathorn Tai Rd
Rama IV Rd
German Embassy
To Marriott Royal Garden Riverside Hotel
Bangrak Market
Mahasak Rd
Danish Embassy
French Embassy
Australian Embassy
Austrian Embassy
Charoen
Surasak Rd
Pan Rd
Russian Embassy
Burma (Myanmar) Embassy
Singapore Embassy
Malaysian Embassy
Soi Suan Phlu
Canal
Soi Sribamphen
Laos Embassy
Soi Ngam Duphli
Immigration
Taksin Bridge
0 250 metres

nightclub; **A** ***Silom Street Inn***, 284/11-13 Silom Rd, opp the junction with Pan Rd (between sois 22 and 24), T 2384680, F 2384689, a/c, restaurant, pool, small new hotel, small, comfortable, 30 well-equipped rm with CNN News, grubby rather seedy lobby, set back from road; **A** ***Tower Inn***, 533 Silom Rd, T 2344051, F 2344051, a/c, restaurant, pool, simple but comfortable hotel, with large rooms and an excellent roof terrace, good value.

B ***River City Guesthouse***, 11/4 Charoen Krung Soi Rong Nam Khang 1, T 2351429, F 2373127, a/c, not very welcoming but rooms are a good size and clean, good bathrooms, short walk to River City and the river; **B** ***Rose***, 118 Surawong Rd, T 2337695, F 2346381, a/c, restaurant, pool, opp Patpong, favourite among single male visitors, but getting seedier by the month; **B** ***Swan***, 31 Charoen Krung Soi 36, T 2348594, some a/c, great position, clean but scruffy rooms.

C ***Chao Phya Riverside***, 1128 Songward Rd (opp the Chinese school), T 2226344, F 2231696, some a/c, old style house overlooking river, clean rooms, atmospheric, unusual location in commercial Chinatown with *sip lors* (ten-wheelers) loading rice, and metal workers fashioning steel, seems to be a little more run-down than a few years back and characteristically brusque management but worth considering for its position and character; **C** ***River View Guesthouse***, 768 Songwad Soi Panurangsri, T 2345429, F 2375771, some a/c, the restaurant/bar is on the top floor and overlooks the river, food is mediocre, but the atmosphere is friendly, rooms are large, clean, some with balconies, some hot water, difficult to find but in a central position in Chinatown and overlooking (as the name suggests) the river, professional management, Khun Phi Yai, the owner, is a pharmacist, so can even prescribe pills.

● Soi Ngam Duphli

Soi Ngam Duphli is much the smaller of Bangkok's two centres of guesthouse accommodation. Locationally, the area is good for the shopping and bars of Silom Rd but inconvenient for most of the city's main places of interest in the old city. Guesthouses tend to be quieter and more refined than those of Khaosan Rd –

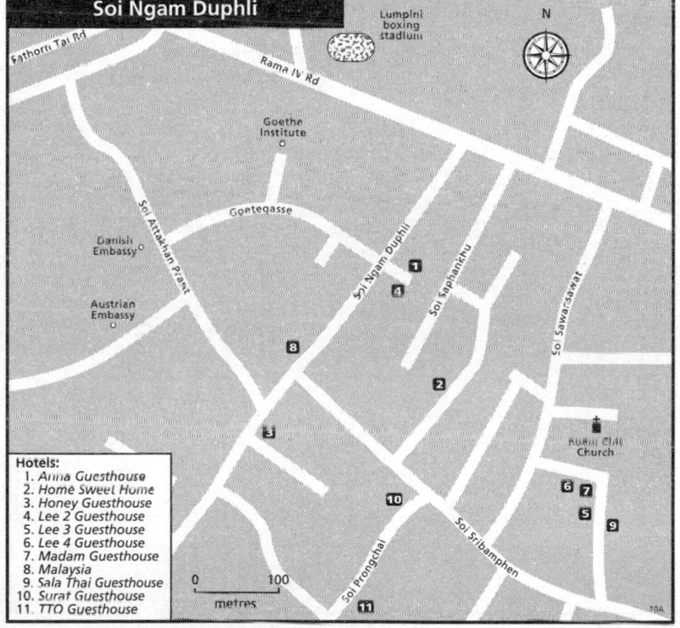

and therefore more expensive too. See the Soi Ngam Duphli map for locations.

B ***Malaysia***, 54 Rama IV Soi Ngam Duphli, T 2863582, F 2493120, a/c, restaurant, pool, once a Bangkok favourite for travellers.

C ***TTO***, 2/48 Soi Sribamphen, T 2866783, F 2871571, a/c, well-run and popular, homely atmosphere, rooms a little small; **C-D** ***Honey***, 35/2-4 Soi Ngam Duphli, T 2863460, some a/c, large rooms, in a rather rambling block, clean and good value, service can be rather surly, no hot water.

D ***Sala Thai Guesthouse***, 15 Soi Sribamphen, T 2871436, at end of peaceful, almost leafy, soi, clean rooms, family run, good food, but shared bathroom, rec; **D-E** ***Anna***, 21/30 Soi Ngam Duphli, clean rooms, some with bathrooms; **D-E** ***Home Sweet Home***, 27/7 Soi Sribamphen (opp Boston Inn, down small soi, so relatively quiet, average rooms with attached bathrooms; **D-E** ***Lee 3***, 13 Soi Saphan Khu, T 2863042, some a/c, wooden house with character, down quiet soi, rooms are clean but with shared bathrooms, rec; **D-E** ***Madam***, 11 Soi Saphan Khu, T 2869289, wooden house, friendly atmosphere, attached bathrooms, no hot water, quiet, rec.

E ***Lee 2***, 21/38-39 Soi Ngam Duphli, T 2862069, clean, friendly, rec; **E** ***Lee 4***, 9 Soi Saphan Khu, T 2867874, spotless rooms and bathrooms, some with balconies and views over city, rec; **E** ***Surat***, 2/18-20 Sribumphen Rd, T 2867919, some a/c, own bathroom, no hot water, clean and well-run, rec.

● Siam Square, Rama I, Ploenchit and Phetburi roads

L ***Grand Hyatt Erawan***, 494 Rachdamri Rd, T 2541234, F 2535856, the replacement hotel for the much-loved old *Erawan Hotel*, towering structure with grandiose entrance and a plastic tree-filled atrium plus sumptious rooms and every facility but has lost atmosphere in the process; **L** ***Hilton***, 2 Witthayu Rd, T 2530123, F 2536509, a/c, restaurants, attractive pool, excellent hotel set in lovely grounds with a remarkable garden feel for a hotel that is so central, comparatively small for such a large plot and first class service; **L** ***Novotel***, Siam Sq Soi 6, T 2556888, F 2551824, a/c, restaurant, pool, undistinguished but commendably comfortable; **L** ***Siam Intercontinental***, 967 Rama I Rd, T 2530355, F 2532275, a/c, restaurants, small pool, relatively low-rise hotel, set in 26 acres of grounds, good sports facilities, excellent service;

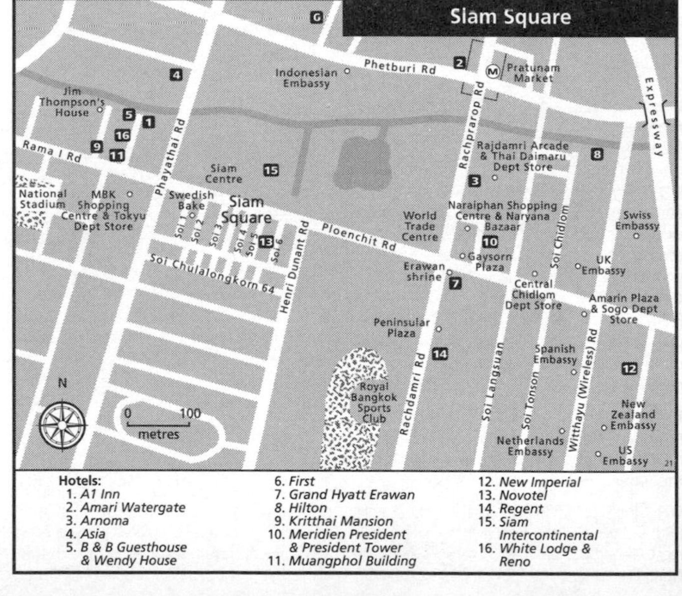

L-A+ *Imperial*, 6-10 Witthayu Rd, (on the edge of Siam Sq area), T 2540023, F 2533190, a/c, restaurants, pool, lovely grounds but hotel seems rather jaded next to Bangkok's newer upstarts, 370 rm and numerous bars and restaurants where, apparently, it is possible to rub shoulders with the city's 'beautiful people', walls are very thin and recent visitors have been disappointed at how this hotel has declined in quality; **L-A+** *Regent Bangkok*, 155 Rachdamri Rd, T 2516127, F 2539195, a/c, restaurants (see Thai Restaurants, page 303), pool (although rather noisy, set above a busy road), excellent reputation amongst frequent visitors who insist on staying here, stylish and postmodern in atmosphere with arguably the best range of cuisine in Bangkok. It is also perhaps the most impressive piece of modern hotel architecture in Bangkok – which admittedly isn't saying much, rec.

A+ *Amari Atrium Hotel*, 1880 Phetburi Rd, T 7182000, F 7182002, a/c, restaurant, pool, Clark Hatch fitness centre, opened early 1996, 600 rm, all facilities, reasonably accessible for airport but not particularly well placed for the sights of the old city, nor for the central business district for that matter; **A+** *Amari Watergate*, 847 Phetburi Rd, T 6539000, F 6539045, a/c, restaurants, pool, fitness centre, squash court, situated close to the Pratunam market, great curvey pool (which makes swimming lengths a little tricky), but close to 600 rm makes this a hotel on a grand scale, lots of marble and plastic trees, uninspired block, good facilities; **A+** *Le Meridien President*, 971 Ploenchit Rd, T 2530444, F 2549988, pool, health club, 400 rm in this, one of the older but still excellent luxury hotels in Bangkok (it opened in 1966), tranquil atmosphere, good service, excellent French food, a new sister hotel, *The President Tower* is due for completion in late 1996 and will tower 36 storeys skywards, the original hotel is still rec; **A+** *Siam City*, 477 Sri Ayutthaya Rd, T 2470120, F 2470178, a/c, restaurants, pool, stylish hotel with attentive staff, large rooms with in-house movies, all facilities (gym etc) and well managed, good Mediterranean restaurant and bakery, rec.

B *Florida*, 43 Phayathai Rd, T 2470990, a/c, restaurant, pool, one of Thailand's first international hotels and it shows, average even at this price.

C *A-1 Inn*, 25/13 Soi Kasemsan Nung (1), Rama I Rd, T 2153029, a/c, well run, intimate hotel, rec; **C** *Bed and Breakfast*, 36/42 Soi Kasemsan Nung (1), Rama 1 Rd, T 2153004, F 2152493, a/c, friendly efficient staff, clean but small rooms, good security, bright 'lobby', price includes breakfast, rec; **C** *Muangphol Building*, 931/9 Rama I Rd, T 2150033, F 2168053, a/c, pool, hot water, good sized rooms, reasonable rates; **C** *Wendy House*, 36/2 Soi Kasemsan Nung (1), Rama I Rd, T 2162436, F 2168053, a/c, spotless, but small rooms with eating area downstairs, hot water; **C** *White Lodge*, 36/8 Soi Kasemsan Nung (1), Rama I Rd, T 2168867, F 2168228, a/c, hot water, airy, light reasonably sized rooms, rec; **C-E** *Alternative Tour Guesthouse*, 14/1 Rachaprarop Soi Rachatapan, T 2452963, F 2467020, friendly, excellent source of information, attached to *Alternative Tour Company*, promoting culturally and environmentally sensitive tourism, clean.

● Sukhumvit Road

L *Imperial Queen's Park*, Sukhumvit Soi 22, T 2619000, F 2619530, massive new 37-storey hotel with a mind boggling 1,400 rm, how service can, in any sense, be personal is hard to imagine, but all possible facilities, location is away from most sights and the main business district so means guests have to battle with the traffic to do most things; **L** *Windsor Plaza Embassy Suites*, 8 Sukhumvit Soi 20, T 2580160, F 2581491, a/c, restaurants, pool, next door to the *Windsor Hotel*, 460 suites, health centre.

A+ *Delta Grand Pacific*, 259 Sukhumvit Rd, T 2544998, F 2552441, a/c, restaurants, pool, almost 400 rm in this large high-rise hotel, all facilities but characterless for the price; **A+** *Rembrandt*, 15-15/1 Sukhumvit Soi 20, T 2617040, F 2617017, a/c, restaurants, pool, new hotel with lots of marble and limited ambience; **A+-A** *Somerset*, 10 Sukhumvit Soi 15, T 2548500, F 2548534, a/c, restaurant, tiny enclosed pool, small hotel, rather ostentatious, rooms are nondescript but comfortable, baths are designed for people of small stature.

A *Amari Boulevard*, 2 Sukhumvit Soi 5, T 2552930, F 2552950, a/c, restauarant, roof top, pool, good mid-range hotel, over 300 rm, fitness centre, nothing to mark it out as particularly Thai – generic tropical feel; **A** *Ambassador*, 171 Sukhumvit Rd, T 2540444, F 2534123, a/c, restaurants, pool, large, impersonal rather characterless hotel, with great food hall (see restaurants); **A** *Manhattan*, 13 Sukhumvit Soi 15, T 2550166, F 2553481, a/c, restaurant, pool, recently renovated high-rise, lacks character but rooms are comfortable and competitively priced although some are rather shabby so ask to inspect; **A** *Tai-pan*,

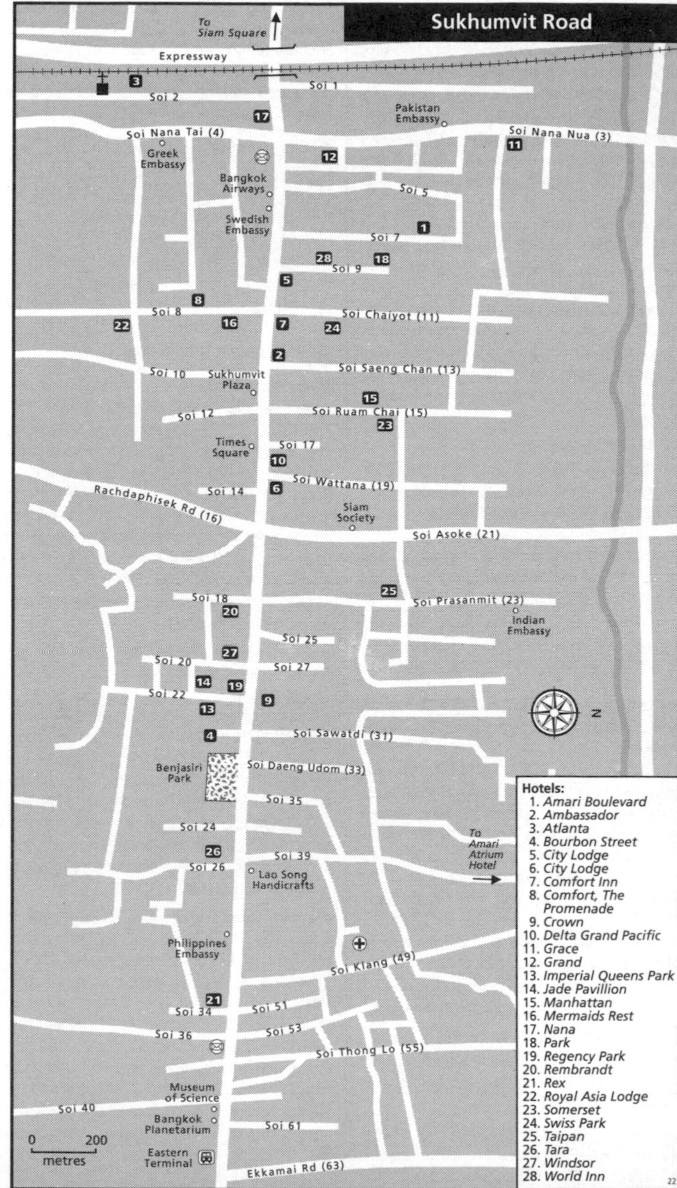
Sukhumvit Road
To Siam Square
Expressway
Soi 1
Soi 2
Pakistan Embassy
Soi Nana Tai (4)
Soi Nana Nua (3)
Greek Embassy
Bangkok Airways
Soi 5
Swedish Embassy
Soi 7
Soi 9
Soi 8
Soi Chaiyot (11)
Soi 10
Sukhumvit Plaza
Soi Saeng Chan (13)
Soi 12
Soi Ruam Chai (15)
Times Square
Soi 17
Soi 14
Soi Wattana (19)
Rachdaphisek Rd (16)
Siam Society
Soi Asoke (21)
Soi 18
Soi Prasanmit (23)
Indian Embassy
Soi 25
Soi 20
Soi 27
Soi 22
Soi Sawatdi (31)
Benjasiri Park
Soi Daeng Udom (33)
Soi 35
Soi 24
To Amari Atrium Hotel
Soi 39
Soi 26
Lao Song Handicrafts
Philippines Embassy
Soi Klang (49)
Soi 34
Soi 51
Soi 36
Soi 53
Soi Thong Lo (55)
Museum of Science
Soi 40
Bangkok Planetarium
Soi 61
0 200 metres
Eastern Terminal
Ekkamai Rd (63)
N
Hotels:
1. Amari Boulevard
2. Ambassador
3. Atlanta
4. Bourbon Street
5. City Lodge
6. City Lodge
7. Comfort Inn
8. Comfort, The Promenade
9. Crown
10. Delta Grand Pacific
11. Grace
12. Grand
13. Imperial Queens Park
14. Jade Pavillion
15. Manhattan
16. Mermaids Rest
17. Nana
18. Park
19. Regency Park
20. Rembrandt
21. Rex
22. Royal Asia Lodge
23. Somerset
24. Swiss Park
25. Taipan
26. Tara
27. Windsor
28. World Inn
22

25 Sukhumvit Soi 23, T 2609888, F 2597908, a/c, restaurant, pool, tasteful new hotel; **A** *Windsor*, 8 Sukhumvit Soi 20, T 2580160, F 2581491, a/c, restaurant, pool, tennis.

B *Bourbon Street*, 29/4-6 Sukhumvit Soi 22 (behind Washington Theatre), T 2590328, F 2594318, a/c, small number of rooms attached to this Cajun restaurant, well run and good value, rec; **B** *China*, 19/27-28 Sukhumvit Soi 19, T 2557571, F 2541333, a/c, restaurant, a small hotel masquerading as a large one, but rooms are up to the standard of more expensive places, so good value; **B** *Comfort Inn*, 153/11 Sukhumvit Soi 11, T 2519250, F 2543562, a/c, restaurant, small hotel, friendly management, rec; **B** *Crown*, 503 Sukhumvit Soi 29, T 2580318, F 2584438, a/c, clean, good service; **B** *Grand*, 2/7-8 Sukhumvit Soi Nana Nua (Soi 3), T 2533380, F 2549020, a/c, restaurant, small hotel with friendly staff, good value.

C *Atlanta*, 78 Sukhumvit Soi 2, T 2521650, a/c, restaurant, large pool, left-luggage facility, poste restante, daily video-shows, good tour company in foyer, rec.

D *Chu's*, 35 Sukhumvit Soi 19, T 2544683, restaurant, one of the cheapest in the area, good food, rec; **D** *Happy Inn*, 20/1 Sukhumvit Soi 4, T 2526508, some a/c, basic rooms, cheerful management; **D** *SV*, 19/35-36 Sukhumvit Soi 19, T 2544724, some a/c, another cheap hotel in this area, musty rooms, shared bathrooms and poor service; **D-E** *Disra House*, 593/28 Sukhumvit Soi 33-33/1, T 2585102, some a/c, friendly and well run place which comes highly recommended, rather out-of-the way but good value a/c rooms.

Banglamphu (Khaosan Road) and surrounds

Khaosan Rd lies NE of Sanaam Luang, just off Rachdamnern Klang Ave, close to the Democracy Monument. It is continually expanding into new roads and sois, in particular the area W of Chakrapong Rd. The sois off the main road are often quieter, such as Soi Chana Songkhran or Soi Rambutri. Note that rooms facing on to Khaosan Rd tend to be very noisy. Khaosan Rd is not just a place to spend the night. Also here are multitudes of restaurants, travel and tour agents, shops, stalls, tattoo artists, bars, bus companies – almost any and every service a traveller might need. They are geared to budget visitors' needs and more than a few have dubious reputations, in general the guesthouses of Khaosan Rd itself have been eclipsed in terms of quality and cleanliness by those to the N, closer to the river. The useful little post office that used to be at the top of Khaosan Rd and operated a poste restante service and a fax facility has recently closed. Whether it will re-open is not certain.

A+ *Royal Princess*, 269 Lan Luang Rd,

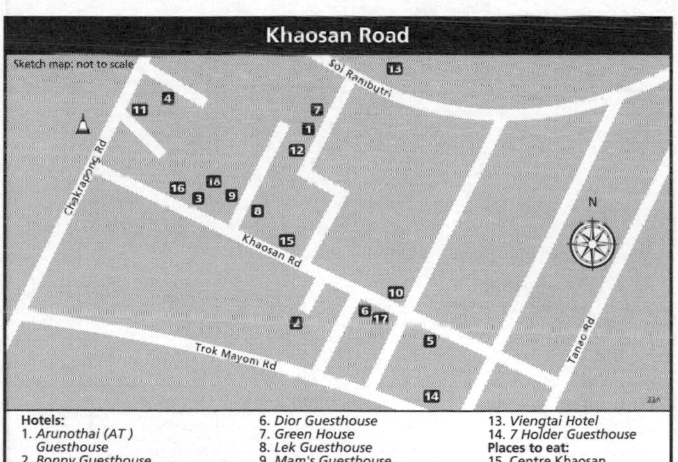

T 2813088, F 2801314, a/c, restaurants, pool, newish addition to Dusit chain of hotels, good facilities.

A ***Majestic Palace***, 97 Rachdamnern Klang Ave (opp Democracy Monument), T 2805610, F 2800965, a/c, restaurant, pool, old hotel given half-hearted face-lift, good location but rooms overpriced and limited facilities; **A** ***Royal***, 2 Rachdamnern Klang Ave, T 2229111, F 2242083, a/c, restaurant, pool, old (by Bangkok standards) hotel which acted as a refuge for demonstrators during the 1991 riots, rooms are dated and featureless; **A** ***Viengtai***, 42 Tanee Rd, Banglamphu, T 2815788, a/c, restaurant, pool, rooms are very good, clean relatively spacious, with all the advantages of this area in terms of proximity to the Old City.

B ***Trang Hotel***, 99/1 Visutkaset Rd, T 2811402, F 2803160, a/c, restaurant, pool, clean and friendly mid-range hotel which comes rec by regular visitors to Bangkok, discount voucher available from *Vieng Travel* in the same building.

C ***New World Apartment and Guesthouse***, 2 Samsen Rd, T 2815596, F 2815596, some a/c, good location for the Old City yet away from the hurly-burly of Khaosan Rd, rooms are

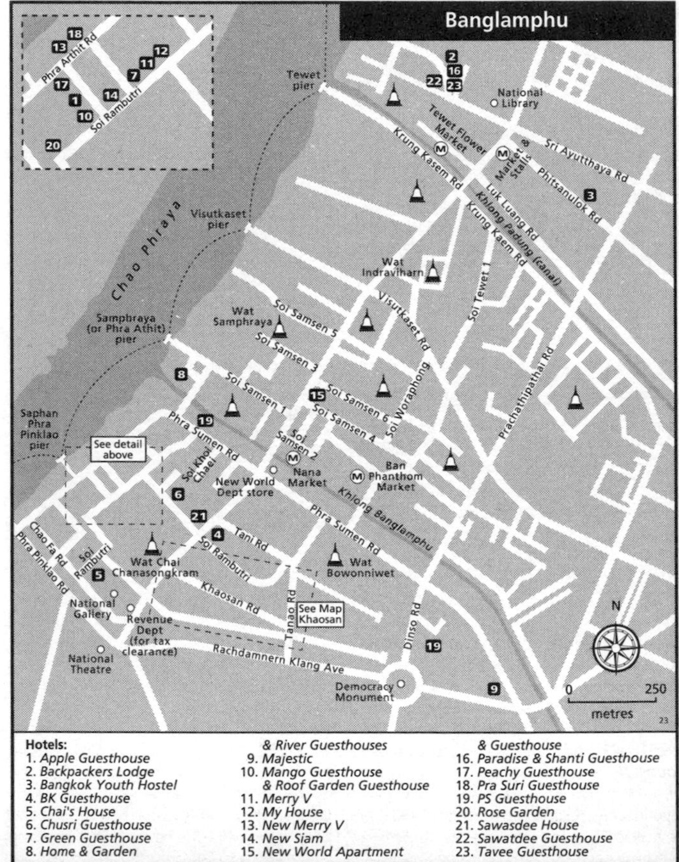

clean and good value even if the overall atmosphere is rather institutional; **C** *Pia Arthit Mansion*, 22 Phra Arthit Rd, comfortable rooms, hot water, a/c, carpeted, bath tubs, pleasant communal sitting area; **C-D** *7 Holder*, 216/2-3 Khaosan Rd, T 2813682, some a/c, clean, friendly, located on the narrow soi behind Khaosan Rd, so quieter than those places situated right on the street; **C-D** *New Siam*, Phra Athit 21 Soi Chana Songkram, T 2824554, F 2817461, some a/c, good restaurant, modern and clean, friendly helpful staff, airy rooms, but featureless block, tickets and tour information, fax facilities, lockers available, overpriced; **C-E** *Chart*, 58 Khaosan Rd, T 2803785, restaurant, some a/c, small but clean rooms, some have no windows; **C-E** *Green House*, 88/1 Khaosan Soi Rambutri, T 2819572, some a/c, ask for rooms away from street, for an extra ฿100 they will flip the switch for a/c, rec; **C-E** *Peachy*, 10 Phra Athit Rd, T 2816659, some a/c and more expensive rooms with hot water, recent visitors have reported a deterioration in quality and cleanliness, but still has pleasant restaurant area.

D *My House*, 37 Phra Athit Soi Chana Songkram, T 2829263, management are a little offhand but the rooms are well maintained and loos are kept clean, remains popular; **D** *Pra Suri*, 85/1 Soi Pra Suri (off Dinso Rd), 5 mins E from Khaosan Rd not far from the Democracy Monument, fan, restaurant, own bathrooms (no hot water), clean and quiet, very friendly and helpful family-run guesthouse, rec; **D-E** *BK*, 11/1 Chakrapong Soi Sulaow, T 2815278, some a/c, in busy area of Banglamphu, but guesthouse is set back from road, so not too noisy, clean but dark rooms, shared bathrooms, good information; **D-E** *Buddy*, 137/1 Khaosan Rd, T 2824351, off main street, some a/c, rooms are small and dingy but it remains popular, large open restaurant area bustles with people exchanging information; **D-E** *CH*, 216/1 Khaosan Rd, T 2822023, some a/c, good reputation, left luggage (฿5/day, ฿30/week); **D-E** *Chai's House*, 49/4-8 Chao Fa Soi Rongmai, T 2814901, F 2818686, some a/c, friendly atmosphere, clean and colourful with borgainvillea growing from the balconies and bamboos and orchids in the restaurant, last house down Soi Rambutri, so away from the others, rec; **D-E** *Hello*, 63-65 Khaosan Rd, T 2818579, some a/c, popular; **D-E** *Privacy Tourist House*, 69 Tanow Rd, T 2827028, popular, quiet, rec; **D-E** *Sawasdee House*, 147 Chakrapong Soi Rambutri, T 2818138, bit of a warren of a place and feels like a cross between a guesthouse and a hotel, shared loos and showers are kept clean, and rooms though box-like are fine. Out the front is a sitting area and what is rather optimistically called a beer 'garden'.

E *Apple 2*, 11 Phra Sumen Rd, T 2811219, old-time favourite, very small rooms, basic, but friendly and characterful; **E** *Arunothai (AT)*, 90/1, 5, 12 Khaosan Soi Rambutri, T 2826979, friendly owner, situated in a quiet little courtyard with 4 or 5 other guesthouses, good place to start looking for a room as it is easy to check them all out; **E** *Bonny*, 132 Khaosan Rd, T 2819877, quiet, situated down a narrow alley off Khaosan itself, reports of bed bugs; **E** *Chuanpis*, 86 Chakrapong Rd (nr intersection with Khaosan Rd, down small soi opp Wat Chanasongkhram), popular, geared particularly to Israeli visitors, good food, average rooms, often full; **E** *Democratic*, 211/8 Rachdamnern Ave, T 2826035, F 2249149, set back, opp the Democracy Monument, 4-storey concrete house with friendly management but small rooms and grubby stairwell; **E** *Dior*, 146-158 Khaosan Rd, T 2829142, small but clean rooms and bathrooms, quiet, as set back from road, 'family' atmosphere, rec; **E** *Green Guesthouse*, 27 Phra Athit Soi Chana Songkram, T 2828994, not to be confused with the *Green House*, rooms are fine and competively priced; **E** *Home and Garden*, 16 Samphraya Rd (Samsen 3), T 2801475, away from main concentration of guesthouses, down quiet soi (quite difficult to find), good location for river taxi, rooms are small and basic but clean, well run and friendly, rec; **E** *Lek*, 90/9 Khaosan Soi Rambutri, T 2812775, popular; **E** *Mam's*, 119 Khaosan Rd, friendly, homely atmosphere, rec; **E** *Merry V*, 33-35 Phra Athit Soi Chana Songkram, T 2829267, some a/c, large place, some rooms with balconies although interior rooms have no outside windows and are dark, lockers available, friendly and well run with good information; **E** *Nat*, 217 Khaosan Rd, brusque management but clean, larger than average rooms with fan, rec; **E** *New Merry V*, 18-20 Phra Athit Rd, T 2803315, new guesthouse with clean but very small rooms, pleasant place to stay, friendly, with a good travel service; **E** *PS*, 9 Phra Sumen Rd, T 2823932, spotlessly clean, rooms with no windows, but satellite TV and free tea and coffee, rec; **E** *The River Guest House*, 18/1 Samphraya Rd (Samsen 3), T 2800876, next to the *Home and Garden* and very similar, good location, quiet but accessible by express boat, friendly, rec. (**NB** There is a third guesthouse on Samphraya Rd, *The Clean and Calm* about which we have received disturbing reports.) **E** *Rose Garden*, 28/6 Phra Athit Soi Trok

Rongmai, T 2818366, friendly although rooms are a bit dark; **E** *Siam*, 76 Chakrapong Rd, T 2810930, rooms facing onto the street are noisy, small rooms but good clean bathrooms; **E** *Suneeporn*, 90/10 Khaosan Soi Rambutri, T 2826887, popular; **E** *Sweety*, 49 Thani Rd, clean, rec; **E-F** *Uimol Guesthouse*, Soi 2 Samsen Rd, clean relaxing and friendly guesthouse, good eating places in vicinity.

F *KC*, 60-64 Phra Sumen Rd Soi Khai Chae, T 2820618, friendly management, clean rooms, rec.

● Sri Ayutthaya Road

Sri Ayutthaya is emerging as an 'alternative' area for budget travellers. It is a central location with restaurants and foodstalls nearby, but does not suffer the over-crowding and sheer pandemonium of Khaosan Rd and so is considerably quieter and more peaceful. It is also close to the Tewet Pier for the express river boats (see the Banglamphu map). The guesthouses are perhaps a little more expensive but the rooms are better and the places seem to be generally better managed. One family runs four of the guesthouses which means if one is full you will probably be moved on to another.

D *Shanti Lodge*, 37 Sri Ayutthaya Rd, T 2812497, restaurant with extensive menu, very popular, rooms nicely done up, rec.

E *Backpackers Lodge*, 85 Sir Ayutthaya Rd, Soi 14, T 2823231, restaurant, rooms with fans, small patio, quiet and friendly, large python (*ngulaam*) keeps watch at the bottom of the stairs, fortunately caged, rec; **E** *Paradise*, 57 Sri Ayutthaya Rd, T 2828673, some fans, small guesthouse, rooms with no outward-looking windows, friendly management; **E** *Sawatdee*, 71 Sri Ayutthaya Rd, T 2810757, Western menu, pokey rooms, popular with German travellers, management rather brusque and off-hand; **E** *Tavee*, 83 Sri Ayutthaya Rd, Soi 14, T 2801447, restaurant, fan, small garden, clean and pleasant, rooms and shared showers and loos are kept spotless, down a quiet little soi, has been operating since 1985 and has managed to maintain a very high standard, rec; **E-F** *Bangkok Youth Hostel*, 25/2 Phitsanulok Rd (off Samsen Rd), T 2820950, N of Khaosan Rd, away from the bustle, dorms available.

● Others

A+ *Central Hotel*, 1695 Phahonyothin Rd, T 5411234, F 5411087, a/c, restaurant, pool, out of town, close to w/e market, efficiently run, but inconveniently located and recently taken over by the Central Department Store group.

A+ *Marriot Royal Garden*, Riverside Resort, 257/1-3 Charoen Nakrom Rd, T 4760021, F 4761120, a/c, restaurant, excellent swimming pool,almost resort-like, very spacious surrounding, opp the *Oriental*, nr the Krung Thep Bridge, free shuttle-boat service every 30 mins between hotel and the *Oriental* and River City piers.

A *Sunroute Bangkok*, 288 Rama IX Rd, T 2480011, F 2485990, a/c, restaurants, pool, part of a Japanese chain, markets itself as the 'route to satisfaction', located away from most sights and shopping; Dusit Riverside, over Sathorn Bridge in Thonburi (opening late 1992); **A-B** *Ramada Renaissance Bridgeview*, 3999 Rama III Rd, T 2923160, F 2923164, a/c, numerous restaurants, pools, tennis, squash, new 476 room high-rise overlooking Chao Phraya River, all facilities, poor location for sights, shopping and business.

C-E *The Artists Club*, 61 Soi Tiem Boon Yang, T 4389653, some a/c, run by an artist, this is a guesthouse cum studio cum gallery in Thonburi (ie the other side of the river), clean rooms and a real alternative place to stay with concerts and drawing lessons, away from the centre of guesthouse activity.

● Places to eat

Bangkok has the largest and widest selection of restaurants in Thailand – everyone eats out, so the number of places is vast. Food is generally very good and cheap – this applies not just to Thai restaurants but also to places serving other Asian cuisines, and Western dishes. Roadside food is good value – many Thais eat on the street, businessmen and civil servants rubbing shoulders with factory workers and truck drivers. **NB** Most restaurants close between 2200 and 2230. For a fuller listing of places to eat see *Bangkok Metro Magazine*, published monthly. The magazine is also good for bars, music venues, shopping etc.

Afternoon tea: *The Authors Lounge*, *Oriental Hotel*; the **Bakery Shop**, *Siam Intercontinental Hotel*; **The Cup**, second floor of Peninsula Plaza, Rachdamri Rd; *The Regent Hotel* lobby (music accompaniment), Rachdamri Rd; the *Dusit Thani Hotel* library, Rama IV Rd.

Bakeries: Bangkok has a large selection of fine bakeries, many attached to hotels like the *Landmark*, *Dusit Thani* and *Oriental*. There are also the generic 'donut' fast food places although few lovers of bread and pastries would

Price guide

	US$	Baht
♦♦♦♦♦	20	500+
♦♦♦♦	15+	375+
♦♦♦	5-15	125-375
♦♦	2-5	50-125
♦	under 2	under 50

want to lump the two together. ***The Bakery Landmark Hotel***, 138 Sukhumvit Rd, many cakes and pastry connoiseurs argue that this is the best of the hotel places, popular with expats, wide range of breads and cakes; ***Basket of Plenty***, Peninsula Plaza, Rachdamri Rd (another branch at 66-67 Sukhumvit Soi 33), bakery, deli and trendy restaurant, very good things baked and a classy (though expensive) place for lunch; ***Bei Otto***, Sukhumvit Soi 20, a German bakery and deli, makes really very good pastries, breads and cakes; ***Cheesecake House***, 69/2 Ekamai Soi 22, rather out of town for most tourists but patronized enthusiastically by the city's large Sukhumvit-based expat population, as the name suggests cheescakes of all descriptions are a speciality – and are excellent; ***Folies***, 309/3 Soi Nang Linchee (Yannawa), T 2869786, French expats and bake-o-philes maintain this bakery makes the most authentic pastries and breads in town, coffee available, a great place to sit, eat and read; ***Jimmy***, 1270-2, nr Oriental Lane, Charoen Krung, a/c, cakes and ice creams, very little else around here, so it's a good stopping place; ***La Brioche***, ground flr of *Novotel Hotel*, Siam Sq Soi 6, good range of French patisseries; ***Sweet Corner***, *Siam Intercontinental Hotel*, Rama I Rd, one of the best in Bangkok; ***Swedish Bake***, Siam Square Soi 2, good Danish pastries.

Chinese: most Thai restaurants sell Chinese food, but there are also many dedicated Chinese establishments. **Siam Square** has a large number, particularly those specializing in shark's fin soup. For shark's fin try the ***Scala Shark's Fin*** (reputed to be the best of the bunch), ***Bangkok Shark's Fin***, and the ***Penang Shark's Fin*** all opp the Scala Cinema, Siam Square Soi 1. ♦♦♦♦-♦♦♦***Kirin***, 226/1 Siam Square Soi 2, over 20 years old, traditional Chinese decor, good atmosphere; ♦♦♦***Art House***, 87 Sukhumvit Soi 55 (Soi Thonglor), country house with traditional Chinese furnishings, surrounded by gardens, particularly good seafood; ♦♦♦***China***, 231/3 Rachdamri Soi Sarasin, Bangkok's oldest Chinese restaurant, serving full range of Chinese cuisine; ♦♦♦***Chinese Seafood Restaurant***, 33/1-5 16 Wall St Tower, Surawong Rd, Cantonese and Szechuan; ♦♦♦***Joo Long Lao***, 2/1 Sukhumvit Soi 2, spacious, with wide choice of dishes, rec; ♦♦♦***Lung Wah***, 848/13 Rama III Rd, large restaurant, with good reputation, serves shark's fin and other seafood, also serves Thai; ♦♦♦***Pata***, 26 Siam Square Soi 3; ♦♦♦***Shangarila***, 154/4-7 Silom Rd, T 2340861, bustling Shanghai restaurant with dim sum lunch; ♦♦♦***Sunshine Noodle Square***, 392/27-30 Siam Square Soi 5, opened in 1996, clean and cool design and nouvelle Chinese cuisine – open 24 hrs; ♦♦***Tongkee***, 308-314 Sukhumvit Rd (opp Soi 19), Kwangtung food, popular with Thais.

Fast Food: Bangkok now has a large number of Western fast food outlets, such as *Pizza Hut, McDonalds, Kentucky Fried Chicken, Mister Donut, Dunkin' Donuts, Shakey's, Baskin Robbins* and *Burger King*. These are located in the main shopping and tourist areas – Siam Square, Silom/Patpong rds, and Ploenchit Rd, for example.

Foodstalls: scattered across the city for a rice or noodle dish, where a meal will cost ฿15-30 instead of a minimum of ฿75 in the restaurants. For example, on the roads between Silom and Surawong Rd, or down Soi Somkid, next to Ploenchit Rd, or opp on Soi Tonson.

Italian: ♦♦♦♦***L'Opera***, 55 Sukhumvit Soi 39, T 2585606, Italian restaurant with Italian manager, conservatory, good food (excellent salted baked fish), professional service, lively atmosphere, popular, booking essential, rec; ♦♦♦♦***Paesano***, 96/7 Soi Tonson (off Soi Langsuan), Ploenchit Rd, T 2522834, average Italian food, sometimes good, in friendly atmosphere, very popular with locals; ♦♦♦***Gino's***, 13 Sukhumvit Soi 15, Italian food in bright and airy surroundings, set lunch is good value; ♦♦♦***Ristorante Sorrento***, 66 North Sathorn Rd, excellent Italian food; ♦♦♦***Roberto's 18***, 36 Sukhumvit, Soi 18, Italian; ♦♦♦***Terrazzo***, *Sukhothai Hotel*, 13/3 South Sathorn Rd, T 2870222, stylish al fresco Italian restaurant overlooking the pool, wonderful Italian breads and good pasta dishes, rec; ♦♦♦***Trattoria Da Roberto***, 37/9 Plaza Arcade, Patpong 2 Rd, T 2336851, authentic Italian setting; ♦♦♦***Vito's Spaghetteria***, Basement, Gaysorn Plaza, Ploenchit Rd (next to *Le Meridien Hotel*), bright and breezy pasta bar, make up your own dish by combining 10 types of pasta with 12 sauces and 29 fresh condiments, smallish servings but good for a hurried lunch.

French: ♦♦♦♦*Beccassine*, Sukhumvit, Soi Sawatdee, English and French home cooking, rec; ♦♦♦♦*Diva*, 49 Sukhumvit Soi 49, T 2587879, excellent French restaurant, with very good Italian dishes and crepe suzette which should not be missed, friendly service, attractive surroundings, good value, rec; ♦♦♦♦*La Grenouille*, 220/4 Sukhumvit Soi 1, T 2539080, traditional French cuisine, French chef and manager, small restaurant makes booking essential, French wines and French atmosphere, rec; ♦♦♦♦*Le Banyan*, 59 Sukhumvit Soi 8, T 2535556, excellent French food; ♦♦♦♦*L'Hexagone*, 4 Sukhumvit Soi 55 (Soi Thonglor), T 3812187, French cuisine, in 'posh' surroundings; ♦♦♦*Brussels Restaurant*, 23/4 Sukhumvit Soi 4, small and friendly, also serves Thai food; ♦♦♦*Chez Daniel Le Normand*, 1/9 Sukhumvit Soi 24, top class French restaurant; ♦♦♦*Classique Cuisine*, 122 Sukhumvit Soi 49, classic French cuisine; ♦♦♦*Le Bordeaux*, 1/38 Sukhumvit Soi 39, T 2589766, range of French dishes; ♦♦♦*Le Café Français*, 22 Sukhumvit Soi 24, French seafood; ♦♦♦*Le Café de Paris*, Patpong 2, traditional French food, rec; ♦♦♦*Restaurant Des Arts Nouveaux*, 127 Soi Charoensuk, Sukhumvit Soi 55, art nouveau interior, top class French cuisine; ♦♦♦*Stanley's French Restaurant*, 20/20-21 Ruamrudee Village, good French food, special Sun brunch, closed Mon.

Other International: ♦♦♦♦*Neil's Tavern*, 58/4 Wittayu, Soi Ruamrudee, T 2566644, best steak in town, popular with expats; ♦♦♦♦*Wit's Oyster Bar*, 20/10 Ruamrudee Village, T 2519455, Bangkok's first and only Oyster Bar, run by eccentric Thai, one of the few places where you can eat late, good salmon fishcakes, international cuisine; ♦♦♦*Bei Otto*, 1 Sukhumvit Soi 20, Thailand's best known German restaurant, sausages made on the premises, good provincial food, large helpings; ♦♦♦*Bobby's Arms*, 2nd Flr, Car Park Bldg, 114/1-4 Patpong 2 Rd, T 2336828, British pub food; ♦♦♦*Bourbon Street*, 29/4-6 Sukhumvit Soi 22 (behind Washington Theatre), Cajun specialities including gumbo, jambalaya and red fish, along with steaks and Mexican dishes, served in a/c restaurant with VDOs and central bar – good for breakfast, excellent pancakes; ♦♦♦*Den Hvide Svane*, Sukhumvit Soi 8, Scandinavian and Thai dishes, former are good, efficient and friendly service; ♦♦♦*Gourmet Gallery*, 6/1 Soi Promsri 1 (between Sukhumvit Soi 39 and 40), interesting interior, with art work for sale, unusual menu of European and American food; ♦♦♦*Hard Rock Café*, 424/3-6 Siam Sq Soi 11, home-from-home for all burger-starved farangs, overpriced, videos, live music sometimes, and all the expected paraphernalia, a couple of Thai dishes have been included, large portions and good atmosphere. ♦♦♦*Haus Munchen*, 4 Sukhumvit Soi 15, T 2525776, German food in quasi-Bavarian lodge, connoisseurs maintain cuisine is authentic enough; ♦♦♦*Longhorn*, 120/9 Sukhumvit Soi 23, Cajun and Creole food; ♦♦♦*Senor Pico*, *Rembrandt Hotel*, 18 Sukhumvit Rd, Mexican, pseudo-Mexican decor, staff dressed Mexican style, large, rather uncosy restaurant, average cuisine, live music; ♦♦♦*Tia Maria*, 14/18 Patpong Soi 1, best Mexican restaurant in Bangkok; ♦♦*Caravan Coffee House*, Siam Sq Soi 5, large range of coffee or tea, food includes pizza, curry and some Thai food; ♦♦*Crazy Horse*, 5 Patpong 2 Rd, simple decor, but good French food, open until 0400; ♦♦*Harmonique*, 22 Charoen Krung, small elegant coffee shop with good music, fruit drinks and coffee.

South Asian (Indian): ♦♦♦♦*Rang Mahal*, *Rembrandt Hotel*, Sukhumvit Soi 18, T 2617100, best Indian food in town, very popular with the Indian community and spectacular views from the roof top position, sophisticated, elegant and ... expensive; ♦♦♦*Himali Cha Cha*, 1229/11 Charoen Krung, T 2351569, good choice of Indian cuisine, mountainous meals for the very hungry, originally set up by Cha Cha and now run by his son – 'from generation to generation' as it is quaintly put; ♦♦♦*Moghul Room*, 1/16 Sukhumvit Soi 11, wide choice of Indian and Muslim food; ♦♦♦*Mrs. Balbir's*, 155/18 Sukhumvit Soi 11, T 2532281, North Indian food orchestrated by Mrs Balbir, an Indian originally from Malaysia, regular customers just keep going back, chicken dishes are succulent, Mrs Balbir also runs cookery classes; ♦♦*Bangkok Brindawan*, 15 Sukhumvit Soi 35, S Indian, Sat lunch set-price buffet; ♦♦*Nawab*, 64/39 Soi Wat Suan Plu, Charoen Krung, N and S Indian dishes; ♦*Samrat*, 273-275 Chakraphet Rd, Pratuleck Lek, Indian and Pakistani food in restaurant down quiet lane off Chakraphet Rd, cheap and tasty, rec; ♦*Tamil Nadu*, 5/1 Silom Soi (Tambisa) 11, T 2356336, good, but limited South Indian menu, cheap and filling, *dosas* are rec, there are 4 or 5 **Indian** restaurants in a row on Sukhumvit Soi 11.

Vietnamese: ♦♦♦♦*Pho*, 2F Alma Link Building, 25 Soi Chidlom, T 2518900 (another branch at 3rd floor, Sukhumvit Plaza, Sukhumvit Soi

12, T 2525601), supporters claim this place serves the best Vietnamese in town, modern trendy setting, non-smoking area; ♦♦♦*Le Cam-Ly*, 2nd Flr, 1 Patpong Bldg, Surawong Rd; ♦♦♦*Le Dalat*, 47/1 Sukhumvit Soi 23, T 25841912, same management as *Le Cam-Ly*, reputed to serve the best Vietnamese food in Bangkok, arrive early or management may hassle; ♦♦♦*Sweet Basil*, 1 Silom Soi Srivieng (opp Bangkok Christian College), T 2383088, another branch at 5/1 Sukhumvit Soi 63 (Ekamai), T 3812834; ♦♦*Saigon-Rimsai*, 413/9 Sukhumvit Soi 55, Vietnamese and some Thai dishes, friendly atmosphere.

Japanese and Korean: ♦♦♦*Akamon*, 233 Sukhumvit Soi 21, Japanese; ♦♦♦*Kobune*, 3rd Fl, Mahboonkhrong (MBK) Centre, Rama 1 Rd, Japanese, Sushi Bar or sunken tables, rec; ♦♦♦*Otafuku*, 484 Siam Sq Soi 6, Henry Dunant Rd, Sushi Bar or low tables, Japanese; ♦♦*New Korea*, 41/1 Soi Chuam Rewang, Sukhumvit Sois 15-19, excellent Korean food in small restaurant, rec.

Indonesian and Burmese: ♦♦♦*Bali*, 20/11 Ruamrudee Village, Soi Ruamrudee, Ploenchit Rd, only authentic Indonesian in Bangkok, friendly proprietress; ♦♦♦*Batavia*, 1/2 Convent Rd, T 2667164, 'imported' Indonesian chefs, good classic dishes like *saté*, *gado-gado* (vegetable with peanut sauce and rice) and *ayam goreng* (deep fried chicken); ♦♦♦*Mandalay*, 23/17 Ploenchit Soi Ruamrudee, authentic Burmese food, most gastronomes of the country reckon the food is the best in the capital, rec.

Middle Eastern: ♦♦♦*Akbar*, 1/4 Sukhumvit Soi 3, T 2533479, Indian, Pakistani and Arabic; ♦♦♦*Nasir al-Masri*, 4-6 Sukhumvit Soi Nana Nua, T 2535582, reputedly the best Eastern (Egyptian) food in Bangkok, *felafal, tabouli, humus*, frequented by large numbers of Arabs who come to Sayed Saad Qutub Nasir for a taste of home.

Asian: ♦♦*Ambassador Food Centre*, *Ambassador Hotel*, Sukhumvit Rd. A vast self-service, up-market hawkers' centre with a large selection of Asian foods at reasonable prices: Thai, Chinese, Japanese, Vietnamese etc, rec.

Lao/Isan food: ♦♦♦♦*La Normandie*, *Oriental Hotel*, 48 Oriental Ave, T 2360400, despite many competitors, *La Normandie* maintains extremely high standards of cuisine and service, guest chefs from around the world, jacket and tie required in the evening, very refined (and expensive); ♦♦♦*Bane Lao*, Naphasup Ya-ak I, off Sukhumvit Soi 36, Laotian open-air restaurant (doubles as a travel agent for Laos), Laotian band, haphazard but friendly service; ♦♦♦*Sarah Jane's*, 36/2 Soi Lang Suan, Ploenchit Rd, T 2526572, run by American lady, married to a Thai, best Thai salad in town and good duck, Isan food especially noteworthy, excellent value, rec; ♦♦*Isn't Classic*, 154 Silom Rd, excellent BBQ, king prawns and Isan specialities like spicy papaya salad (*somtam*).

Vegetarian: ♦♦♦*Whole Earth*, 93/3 Ploenchit Soi Lang Suan, T 2525574 (another branch at 71 Sukhumvit Soi 26, T 2584900), Thailand's best known vegetarian restaurant, eclectic menu from Thai to Indian dishes, live music, ask to sit at the back downstairs, or sit Thai-style upstairs.

Thai: ♦♦♦♦♦*Dusit Thani Thai Restaurant*, 946 Rama IV Rd, beautiful surroundings – like an old Thai palace, exquisite Thai food, very expensive wines; ♦♦♦♦♦*Spice Market*, *Regent Hotel*, 155 Rachdamri Rd, T 2516127, Westernized Thai, typical hotel decoration, arguably the city's best Thai food – simply delectable; ♦♦♦♦*Bussaracum*, 35 Soi Phiphat off Convent Rd, T 2358915, changing menu, popular, rec; ♦♦♦♦*D'jit Pochana Oriental*, 1082 Phahonyothin Rd, T 2795000, extensive range of dishes, large and rather industrial but the food is good; ♦♦♦♦-♦♦♦there are several excellent restaurants in *Silom Village*, a shopping mall, on Silom Rd (N side, opp Pan Rd), excellent range of food from hundreds of stalls, all cooked in front of you, enjoyable village atmosphere, rec; ♦♦♦♦-♦♦♦*Once Upon a Time*, 67 Soi Anumanrachaton, T 2338493, set in attractive traditional Thai house (between Silom and Surawong rds); ♦♦♦♦-♦♦♦*Bua Restaurant*, Convent Rd (off Silom Rd), classy post-modern Thai restaurant with starched white table linen and cool, minimalist lines, the food also reflects the decor (or the other way around?): refined and immaculately prepared; ♦♦♦*Ban Chiang*, 14 Srivdieng Rd, T 2367045, quite hard to find – ask for directions, old style Thai house, large menu of traditionally-prepared food; ♦♦♦*Ban Khun Phor*, 458/7-9 Siam Square Soi 8, T 2501732, good Thai food in stylish surroundings; ♦♦♦*Ban Krua*, 29/1 Saladaeng Soi 1, Silom Rd, simple decor, friendly atmosphere, a/c room or open-air garden, traditional Thai food; ♦♦♦*Ban Thai*, Soi 32 or Ruen Thep, Silom Village, Silom Rd, T 2585403, with classical dancing and music; ♦♦♦*Banana Leaf*, Silom complex (basement floor), Silom Rd, T 3213124, excellent and very popular Thai restaurant with some unusual dishes, including *kai manaaw* (chicken in lime sauce), *nam tok muu* (spicy pork salad, Isan style) and fresh spring rolls 'Banana Leaf', booking recommended for lunch; ♦♦♦***Garden Restaurant***, 324/1 Phahonyothin Rd, open-air restaurant or the air-conditioned comfort of a wood panelled room, also serves Chinese, Japanese and International; ♦♦♦***Kaloang***, 2 Sri Ayutthaya Rd, T 2819228. Two dining areas, one on a pier, the other on a boat on the Chao Phraya River, attractive atmosphere, delicious food, rec.; ♦♦♦***Lemon Grass***, 5/1 Sukhumvit Soi 24, T 2588637, Thai style house, rather dark interior but very stylish, one step up from Cabbages and Condoms, rec; ♦♦♦***Moon Shadow***, 145 Gaysorn Rd, good seafood, choice of dining-rooms – a/c or open-air; ♦♦♦***Seafood Market***, Sukhumvit Soi 24, this famous restaurant has recently moved to new premises, and is said to be both larger and better, "if it swims we have it", choose your seafood from the 'supermarket' and then have it cooked to your own specifications before consuming the creatures at the table, popular; ♦♦♦***Seven Seas***, Sukhumvit Soi 33, T 2597662, quirky 'nouvelle' Thai food, popular with young sophisticated and avant garde Thais; ♦♦♦***Side Walk***, 855/2 Silom Rd (opp Central Dept Store), grilled specialities, also serves French, rec; ♦♦♦***Tum Nak Thai***, 131 Rajdapisek Rd, T 2746420, 'largest' restaurant in the world, 3,000 seats, rather out of the way (฿100 by taxi from city centre), classical dancing from 2000-2130; ♦♦♦-♦♦***Ban Somrudee*** 228/6-7 Siam Square Soi 2, T 2512085; ♦♦***Ban Bung***, 32/10 Mu 2 Intramara 45, Rachadapisek, well known garden restaurant of northern-style pavilions, row around the lake to build up an appetite; ♦♦***Ban Mai***, 121 Sukhumvit Soi 22, Sub-Soi 2, old Thai-style decorations in an attractive house with friendly atmosphere, good value; ♦♦***Cabbages and Condoms***, Sukhumvit Soi 12 (around 400m down the soi), Population and Community Development Association (PDA) restaurant so all proceeds go to this charity, eat rice in the Condom Room, drink in the Vasectomy Room, good *tom yam kung* and honey-roast chicken, curries all rather similar, good value, rec; ♦♦***Princess Terrace***, Rama I Soi Kasemsan Nung (1), Thai and French food with BBQ specialities served in small restaurant with friendly service and open terrace down quiet lane, rec; ♦♦***Puang Kaew***, 108 Sukhumvit Soi 23, T 5238172, large, unusual menu, also serves Chinese; ♦♦***Rung Pueng***, 37 Saladaeng, Soi 2, Silom Rd, traditional Thai food at reasonable prices; ♦♦***Sanuk Nuek***, 397/1 Sukhumvit Soi 55 (Soi Thonglor), T 4935590, small restaurant with unusual decorations, live folk music, well priced; ♦♦***September***, 120/1-2 Sukhumvit Soi 23, art nouveau setting, also serves Chinese and European, good value for money; ♦♦***Suda***, 6-6/1 Sukhumvit Rd, Soi 14, rec; ♦♦***Wannakarm***, 98 Sukhumvit Soi 23, T 2596499, well established, very Thai restaurant, grim decor, no English spoken, but rated food.

Travellers' food available in the guesthouse/travellers' hotel areas (see above). ***Hello*** in Khaosan Rd has been recommended, the portions of food are a good size and they have a useful notice board for leaving messages. Nearly all the restaurants in Khaosan Rd show videos all afternoon and evening. If on a tight budget it is much more sensible to eat in Thai restaurants and stalls where it should be possible to have a good meal for ฿10-20.

● Bars

The greatest concentration of bars are in the two 'red light' districts of Bangkok – Patpong (between Silom and Surawong rds) and Soi Cowboy (Sukhumvit). Patpong was transformed from a street of 'tea houses' (brothels serving local clients) into a high-tech lane of go-go bars in 1969 when an American made a major investment. In fact there are two streets, side-by-side, Patpong 1 and Patpong 2. Patpong 1 is the larger and more active, with a host of stalls down the middle at night (see page 308); Patpong 2 supports cocktail bars and, appropriately, pharmacies and clinics for STDs, as well as a few go-go bars. The ***Derby King*** is one of the most popular with expats and serves what are reputed to be the best club sandwiches in Asia, if not the world. Opposite Patpong, along Convent Rd is ***Delaney's*** (see Silom map), an Irish pub with draft Guinness from Malaysia (where it is brewed) and a limited menu, good atmosphere and well-patronized by Bangkok's expats – sofas for lounging and reading (upstairs). Soi Cowboy is named after the first bar here, the ***Cowboy Bar***, established by a retired US Airforce officer. Although some of the bars obviously also offer other forms of entertainment (something that quickly becomes blindingly obvious), there are, believe it or not, some excellent and very reasonably priced bars in these two areas. A small beer will cost ฿45-65, with good (if loud) music and perhaps videos thrown in for free. However, if opting for a bar with a 'show', be prepared to pay considerably more.

Warning Front men will assure customers

that there is no entrance charge and a beer is only ฿60, but you can be certain that they will try to fleece you on the way out and can become aggressive if you refuse to pay. Even experienced Bangkok travellers find themselves in this predicament. Massages and more can also be obtained at many places in the Patpong and Soi Cowboy areas. **NB** AIDS is a significant and growing problem in Thailand so it is strongly recommended that customers practice safe sex.

A particularly civilized place to have a beer and watch the sun go down is on the verandah of the *Oriental Hotel*, by the banks of the Chao Phraya River, expensive, but romantic; ♦♦♦***Basement Pub*** (and restaurant), 946 Rama IV Rd, live music, also serves international food, open 1800-2400; ♦♦♦***Black Scene***, 120/29-30 Sukhumvit Soi 23, live jazz, also serves Thai and French food, open 1700-1300; ♦♦♦***Bobby's Arms***, 2nd Flr, Car Park Bldg, Patpong 2 Rd, English pub and grill, with jazz on Sun from 2000, open 1100-0100; ***Gitanes***, 52 Soi Pasana 1, Sukhumvit Soi 63. Live music, open 1800-0100; ***King's Castle***, Patpong 1 Rd, another long-standing bar with core of regulars; ***Royal Salute***, Patpong 2 Rd, cocktail bar where local farangs end their working days.

Hemingway Bar and Grill, 159/5-8 Sukhumvit Soi 55, live jazz and country music at the w/e, plus Thai and American food, open 1800-0100; ♦♦***Old West Saloon***, 231/17 Rachdamri Soi Sarasin, live country music, also serves international and Thai food, open 1700-0100. ♦♦***Picasso Pub***, 1950-52 Ramkamhaeng Rd, Bangkapi. Live music, also serves Thai food, open 1800-0300; ♦♦***Round Midnight***, 106/12 Soi Langsuan, live blues and jazz, some excellent bands play here, packed at weekends, good atmosphere and worth the trip, also serves Thai and Italian food, open 1700-0400; ***Trader Vic's***, *Royal Marriott Garden Hotel*; ♦♦***Trumpet Pub*** (and restaurant), 7 Sukhumvit Soi 24, live blues and jazz, also serves Thai food, open 1900-0200. **Note** For bars with live music also see *Music*, below, under **Entertainment**, page 306.

● Airline offices

For airport enquiries call, T 2860190. **Aeroflot**, Regent House, 183 Rachdamri Rd, T 2510617; **Air China**, 2nd Flr, CP Bldg, 313 Silom Rd, T 6310731; **Air France**, Grd Flr, Charn Issara Tower, 942 Rama IV Rd, T 2339477; **Air India**, 16th Flr, Amarin Tower, 500 Ploenchit Rd, T 2350557; **Air Lanka**, Grd Flr, Charn Issara Tower, 942 Rama IV Rd, T 2369292; **Alitalia**, 8th Flr, Boonmitr Bldg, 138 Silom Rd, T 2334000; **American Airlines**, 518/5 Ploenchit Rd, T 2511393; **Asiana Airlines**, 14th Flr, BB Bldg, 54 Asoke Rd, T 2607700; **Bangkok Airways**, Queen Sirikit National Convention Centre, New Rajdapisek Rd, Klongtoey, T 2293434; **Bangladesh Biman**, Grd Flr, Chongkolnee Bldg, 56 Surawong Rd, T 2357643; **British Airways**, 2nd Flr, Charn Issara Tower, 942 Rama IV Rd, T 2360038; **Canadian Airlines**, 6th Flr, Maneeya Bldg, 518/5 Ploenchit Rd, T 2514521; **Cathay Pacific**, 11th Flr, Ploenchit Tower, 898 Ploenchit Rd, T 2630606; **China Airlines**, 4th Flr, Peninsula Plaza, 153 Rachdamri Rd, T 2534242; **Continental Airlines**, CP Tower, 313 Silom Rd, T 2310113; **Delta Airlines**, 7th Flr, Patpong Bldg, Surawong Rd, T 2376838; **Egyptair**, CP Tower, 313 Silom Rd, T 2310504; **Finnair**, 12 Flr, Sathorn City Tower, 175 Sathorn Tai Rd, T 6396671; **Garuda**, 27th Flr, Lumpini Tower, 1168 Rama IV Rd, T 2856470; **Gulf Air**, Grd Flr, Maneeya Bldg, 518 Ploenchit Rd, T 2547931; **Japan Airlines**, 254/1 Ratchadapisek Rd, T 2741411; **KLM**, 12th Flr, Maneeya Centre Bldg, 518/5 Ploenchit Rd, T 2548325; **Korean Air**, Grd Flr, Kong Bunma Bldg (opp *Narai Hotel*), 699 Silom Rd, T 2359220; **Kuwait Airways**, 12th Flr, RS Tower, 121/50-51 Ratchadapisek Rd, T 6412864; **Lao Aviation**, 491 17 Ground Flr, Silom Plaza, Silom Rd, T 2369822; **Lufthansa**, 18th Flr, Q-House (Asoke), Sukhumvit Rd Soi 21, T 2642400; **MAS** (*Malaysian Airlines*), 20th Flr, Ploenchit Tower, 898 Ploenchit Rd, T 2630565; **Myanmar Airways**, Charn Issara Tower, 942 Rama IV Rd, T 2342985; **Pakistan International**, 52 Surawong Rd, T 2342961; **Philippine Airlines**, Chongkolnee Bldg, 56 Surawong Rd, T 2332350; **Qantas**, 11th Flr, Charn Issara Tower, 942 Rama IV Rd, T 2675188; **Royal Brunei**, 4th Flr, Charn Issara Tower, 942 Rama IV Rd, T 2330056; **Royal Nepal Airlines**, Sivadon Bldg, 1/4 Convent Rd, T 2333921; **Sabena**, 3rd Flr, CP Tower, 313 Silom Rd, T 2382201; **SAS**, 8th Flr, Glas Haus I, Sukhumvit Rd Soi 25, T 2600444; **Saudi**, 3rd Flr, Main Bldg, Don Muang Airport, T 5352341; **Singapore Airlines**, 12th Flr, Silom Centre, 2 Silom Rd, T 2360440; **Swissair**, 2nd Flr, 1-7 FE Zuellig Bldg, Silom Rd, T 2332930; **Thai**, 485 Silom Rd, T 2333810; **TWA**, 12th Flr, Charn Issara Tower, 942 Rama IV Rd, T 2337290; **Vietnam Airlines**, 584 Ploenchit Rd, T 2514242.

● Banks & money changers

There are countless exchange booths in all the tourist areas open 7 days a week, mostly 0800-1530, some from 0800-2100. Rates vary only marginally between banks, although if changing a large sum, it is worth shopping around.

● Embassies

Australia, 37 Sathorn Tai Rd, T 2872680; **Brunei**, 154 Ekamai Soi 14, Sukhumvit 63, T 3815914, F 3815921; **Cambodia**, 185 Rachdamri Rd, T 2546630; **Canada**, 12th Flr, Boonmitr Bldg, 138 Silom Rd, T 2341561/8; **Denmark**, 10 Sathorn Tai Soi Attakarnprasit, T 2132021; **Finland**, 16th Flr, Amarin Plaza, 500 Ploenchit Rd, T 2569306; **France**, 35 Customs House Lane, Charoen Krung, T 2668250. (There is also a French consulate at 29 Sathorn Tai Rd, T 2856104.) **Germany**, 9 Sathorn Tai Rd, T 2132331; **India**, Sukhumvit Rd Soi 23, T 2580300; **Indonesia**, 600-602 Phetburi Rd, T 2523135; **Israel**, 25th Flr, Ocean Tower II, 75 Soi Wattana, Sukhumvit 19, T 2604850; **Greece**, 79 Sukhumvit Soi 4, T 2542936, F 2542937; **Italy**, 399 Nang Linchi Rd, T 2854090; **Japan**, 1674 New Phetburi Rd, T 2526151; **Laos**, 502/1-3 Soi Ramkhamhaeng 39, T 5396667; **Malaysia**, 15th Flr, Regent House, 183 Rachdamri Rd, T 2541700; **Myanmar** (Burma), 132 Sathorn Nua Rd, T 2332237; **Nepal**, 189 Sukhumvit Soi 71, T 3917240; **Netherlands**, 106 Witthayu Rd, T 2547701; **New Zealand**, 93 Witthayu Rd, T 2518165; **Norway**, 1st Flr, Bank of America Bldg, Witthayu Rd, T 2530390; **People's Republic of China**, 57 Ratchadapisek Rd, Dindaeng, T 2457032; **Philippines**, 760 Sukhumvit Rd, T 2590139; **Singapore**, 129 Sathorn Tai Rd, T 2862111; **South Africa**, 6th Flr, Park Place, 231 Soi Sarasin, Rachdamri Rd, T 2538473; **Spain**, 93 Witthayu Rd, T 2526112; **Sweden**, 20th Flr, Pacific Place, 140 Sukhumvit Rd, T 2544954; **UK**, 1031 Witthayu Rd, T 2530191/9; **USA**, 95 Witthayu Rd, T 2525040; **Vietnam**, 83/1 Witthayu Rd, T 2515835.

● Church services

Evangelical Church, Sukhumvit Soi 10 (0930 Sun service); the *International Church* (interdenominational), 67 Sukhumvit Soi 19 (0800 Sun service); *Baptist Church*, 2172/146 Phahonyothin Soi 36 (1800 Sun service); *Holy Redeemer*, 123/19 Wittayu Soi Ruam Rudee (Catholic, 5 services on Sun); *Christ Church*, 11 Convent Rd (Anglican – Episcopalian – Ecumenical) (3 Sun services at 0730, 1000 and 1800).

● Entertainment

Art galleries: *The Artist's Gallery*, 60 Pan Rd, off Silom, selection of international works of art. *The Neilson Hays Library*, 195 Surawong Rd, has a changing programme of exhibitions.

Buddhism: the headquarters of the World Fellowship of Buddhists is at 33 Sukhumvit Rd (between Soi 1 and Soi 3). Meditation classes are held in English on Wed at 1700-2000; lectures on Buddhism are held on the first Wed of each month at 1800-2000.

Cinemas: most cinemas have daily showings at 1200, 1400, 1700, 1915 and 2115, with a 1300 matinee on weekends and holidays. Cinemas with English soundtracks include *Central Theatre 2*, T 5411065, *Lido*, T 2526729, *Pantip*, T 2512390, *Pata*, T 4230568, *Mackenna*, T 2517163, *Washington 1*, T 2582045, *Washington 2*, T 2582008, *Scala*, T 2512861, *Villa*, T 2589291. *The Alliance Française*, 29 Sathorn Tai Rd, T 2132122 shows French films. Remember to stand for the National Anthem, which is played before every performance. Details of showings from English language newspapers.

Cultural centres: **British Council**, 254 Chulalongkorn Soi 64 (Siam Square), T 6116830, F 2535311, for films, books and other Anglocentric entertainment; Check in 'What's On' section of *Sunday Bangkok Post's* magazine for programme of events; **Alliance Française**, 29 Sathorn Tai Rd; **Goethe Institute**, 18/1 Sathorn Tai Soi Atthakan Prasit; **Siam Society**, 131 Soi 21 (Asoke) Sukhumvit, T 2583494, open Tues-Sat. Promotes Thai culture and organizes trips within (and beyond) Thailand.

Meditation: *Wat Mahathat*, facing Sanaam Luang, is Bangkok's most renowned meditation centre. Anyone interested is welcome to attend the daily classes – the centre is located in Khana 5 of the monastery. Apart from Wat Mahathat, classes are also held at *Wat Bowonniwet* in Banglamphu on Phra Sumen Rd (see the Bangkok – Old City map), and at the *Thai Meditation Centre* in the World Fellowship of Buddhists building on 33 Sukhumvit Rd, T 2511188.

Music: (see also **Bars**, page 304, for more places with live music): *Blues-Jazz*, 25 Sukhumvit Soi 53, open Mon-Sun 1900-0200, three house bands play really good blues and jazz, food available, drinks a little on the steep side. *Blue Moon*, 73 Sukhumvit 55 (Thonglor), open Mon-Sun 1800-0300, for country, rhythm, jazz and blues – particularly Fri and Sun for jazz – some food available. ***Brown Sugar***, 231/20 Sarasin Rd (opp Lumpini Park), open Mon-Fri 1100-0100, Sat and Sun 1700-0200, five regular bands play excellent jazz, a place for Bangkok's trendies to hang out and be cool. ***Cool Tango***, 23/51 Block F, Royal City Av (between Phetburi and Rama IX rds), open Tue-Sat 1100-0200, Sun 1800-0200, excellent resident rock band, great atmosphere, happy hour(s) 1800-2100. ***Front Page***, 14/10 Soi Saladaeng 1, open Mon-Fri 1000-0100, Sat and Sun 1800-0100, populated, as the name might suggest, by journos who like to hunt in packs more than most, music is country, folk and blues, food available. ***Hard Rock Café***, 424/3-6 Siam Sq Soi 11, open Mon-Sun 1100-0200, speaks for itself, burgers, beer and rock covers played by reasonable house band, food is expensive for Bangkok though. ***Magic Castle***, 212/33 Sukhumvit Plaza Soi 12, open Mon-Thu 1800-0100, Fri and Sat 1800-0200, mostly blues, some rock, good place for a relaxed beer with skilfully performed covers. ***Picasso Pub***, 1950-5 Ramkhomhaeng Rd (close to Soi 8), open Mon-Sun 1900-0300, house rock band, adept at playing covers. ***Round Midnight***, 106/12 Soi Langsuan, open Mon-Thu 1900-0230, Fri and Sat 1900-0400, jazz, blues and rock bands.

Thai Performing Arts: classical dancing and music is often performed at restaurants after a 'traditional' Thai meal has been served. Many tour companies or travel agents organize these 'cultural evenings'. ***National Theatre***, Na Phrathat Rd, (T 2214885 for programme). Thai classical dramas, dancing and music on the last Fri of each month at 1730 and periodically on other days. ***Thailand Cultural Centre***, Rachdaphisek Rd, Huai Khwang, T 2470028 for programme of events. ***College of Dramatic Arts***, nr National Theatre, T 2241391. ***Baan Thai Restaurant***, 7 Sukhumvit Soi 32, T 2585403, 2100-2145. ***Chao Phraya Restaurant***, Pinklao Bridge, Arun Amarin Rd, T 4742389; ***Maneeya's Lotus Room***, Ploenchit Rd, T 2526312, 2015-2100; ***Piman Restaurant***, 46 Sukhumvit Soi 49, T 2587866, 2045-2130; ***Ruen Thep***, Silom Village Trade Centre, T 2339447, 2020-2120; ***Suwannahong Restaurant***, Sri Ayutthaya Rd, T 2454448, 2015-2115; ***Tum-Nak-Thai Restaurant***, 131 Rachdaphisek Rd, T 2773828 2030-2130.

● Hospitals & medical services

Bangkok Adventist Hospital, 430 Phitsanulok Rd, Dusit, T 2811422/2821100; *Bangkok General Hospital*, New Phetburi Soi 47, T 3180066; *Bangkok Nursing Home*, 9 Convent Rd, T 2332610; *St. Louis Hospital*, 215 Sathorn Tai Rd, T 2120033. **Health clinics**: *Dental Polyclinic*, New Phetburi Rd, T 3145070; *Dental Hospital*, 88/88 Sukhumvit 49, T 2605000, F 2605026, good, but expensive; *Clinic Banglamphu*, 187 Chakrapong Rd, T 2827479.

● Immigration

Sathorn Tai Soi Suanphlu, T 2873101.

● Libraries

British Council Library, 254 Chulalongkorn Soi 64 (Siam Square). Open Tue-Sat 1000-1930, membership library with good selection of English language books. **NB** In Oct 1996 Queen Elizabeth II opened the new British Council offices and it was rumoured that the library had been cut in the interests of economy; *National Library*, Samsen Rd, close to Sri Ayutthaya Rd, open Mon-Sun 0930-1930; *Neilson Hays Library*, 195 Surawong Rd, T 2331731, next door to British Club. Open: 0930-1600 Mon-Sat, 0930-1230 Sun. A small library of English-language books housed in an elegant building dating from 1922. It is a private membership library, but welcomes visitors who might want to see the building and browse; occasional exhibitions are held here. Open 0930-1600 Mon-Sat, 0930-1230 Sun; *Siam Society Library*, 131 Sukhumvit Soi 21 (Asoke), open Tue-Sat 0900-1700, membership library with excellent collection of Thai and foreign language books and periodicals (especially English) on Thailand and mainland south east Asia.

● Meditation and Yoga

The *Dharma Study Foundation*, 128 Soi Thonglor 4, Sukhumvit Soi 55, T 3916006, open 0900-1800 Mon-Fri and the *World Fellowship of Buddhists*, 33 Sukhumvit Rd (between sois 1 and 3), T 2511188, open 0900-1630 Mon-Fri, both offer classes in meditation and some religious discussions. Yoga classes available at *Sunee Yoga Centre*, 2nd Flr, Pratunam Centre, 78/4 Rachprarop Rd, T 2549768, open 1000-1200 and 1700-1900 Mon-Sat.

● Post & telecommunications

Area code: 02.

Central GPO (*Praysani Klang* for taxi drivers): 1160 Charoen Krung, opp the *Ramada Hotel*. Open 0800-2000 Mon-Fri and 0800-1300 weekend and holidays. The money and postal order service is open 0800-1700, Mon-Fri, 0800-1200 Sat. Closed on Sun and holidays. 24 hrs telegram and telephone service (phone rates are reduced 2100-0700) and a packing service.

● Shopping

Most shops do not open until 1000-1100. Nancy Chandler's *Map of Bangkok* is the best shopping guide. Bangkok still stocks a wonderful range of goods, but do not expect to pick up a bargain – prices are high. Stallholders, entirely understandably, are out for all they can get – so bargain hard here. The traditional street market, although not dying out, is now supplemented by other types of shopping. Given the heat, the evolution of the air conditioned shopping arcade and air conditioned department store in Bangkok was just a matter of time. Some arcades target the wealthier shopper, and are dominated by brand name goods and designer ware. Others are not much more than street side stalls transplanted to an arcade environment. Most department stores are now fixed price.

Bangkok's main shopping areas are:

1. Sukhumvit: Sukhumvit Rd, and the sois to the N are lined with shops and stalls, especially around the *Ambassador* and *Landmark* hotels. Many tailors and made-to-measure shoe shops are to be found in this area.

2. Central: 2 areas close to each other centred on Rama I and Ploenchit rds. At the intersection of Phayathai and Rama I rds there is Siam Square (for teenage trendy Western clothing, bags, belts, jewellery, bookshops, some antique shops and American fast food chains) and the massive – and highly popular – Mah Boonkhrong Centre (MBK), with countless small shops and stalls and the Tokyu Department Store. Siam Square used to be great for cheap clothes, leather goods etc, but each year it inches further up market: there are now branches of ***Timberland***, the ***Body Shop***, ***Kookäi*** and various designer outlets here. Peninsular Plaza, between the *Hyatt Erawan* and *Regent* hotels is considered the smartest shopping plaza in Bangkok. For those looking for fashion clothes and accessories, this is probably the best area. A short distance to the E, centred on Ploenchit/Rachprarop rds, are more shopping arcades and large department stores, including the World Trade Centre, Thai Daimaru, Robinsons, Gaysorn Plaza (exclusive shopping arcade), Naraiphan shopping centre (more of a market stall affair, geared to tourists, in the basement) and Central Chidlom (which burnt down in a catastrophic fire in 1995 but which should be rebuilt/renovated – although in 1996 it was still waiting for work to begin). North along Rachprasong Rd, crossing over Khlong Saensap, at the intersection with Phetburi Rd is the Pratunam market, good for fabrics and clothing.

3. Patpong/Silom: Patpong is more of a night market (opening at 2100), the streets are packed with stalls selling the usual array of stall goods which seem to stay the same from year to year (fake designer clothing, watches, bags etc). **NB** Bargain hard. The E end of Silom has a scattering of similar stalls open during the day time, and Robinsons Department Store. Surawong Rd (at the other end of Patpong) has Thai silk, antiques and a few handicraft shops.

4. West Silom/Charoen Krung (New Rd): antiques, jewellery, silk, stamps, coins and bronzeware. Stalls set up here at 2100. A 15 min walk N along Charoen Krung (close to the *Orchid Sheraton Hotel*) is the River City Shopping Plaza, specializing in art and antiques.

5. Banglamphu/Khaosan Road: vast variety of low-priced goods, such as ready-made clothes, shoes, bags, jewellery and cassette tapes.

6. Lardphrao-Phahonyothin: some distance N of town, not far from the Weekend Market (see page 288) is the huge Central Plaza shopping complex. It houses a branch of the Central Department Store and has many boutiques and gift shops.

Department Stores: *Central* is the largest chain of department stores in Bangkok, with a range of Thai and imported goods at fixed prices; credit cards are accepted. Main shops on Silom Rd, Ploenchit Rd (Chidlom Branch – which burnt down in 1995 but should be renovated), and in the Central Plaza, just N of the Northern bus terminal. Other department stores include ***Thai Daimaru*** on Rachdamri and Sukhumvit (opp Soi 71), ***Robinson's*** on corner of Silom and Rama IV rds, Sukhumvit (nr Soi 19) and Rachdamri rds, ***Tokyu*** in MBK Tower on Rama I Rd, ***Sogo*** in the Amarin Plaza on Ploenchit Rd, and ***Zen***, World Trade Centre, corner of Rama I and Rajdamri rds.

Supermarkets: *Central Department Store* (see above), ***Robinsons*** – open until midnight (see above), ***Villa Supermarket***, between Sois 33 and 35, Sukhumvit Rd (and branches elsewhere in town) – for everything you are unable to find anywhere else, ***Isetan***, (World Trade Centre), Rachdamri Rd.

Markets: the markets in Bangkok are an excellent place to browse, take photographs and pick up bargains. They are part of the life blood

Buying gems and jewellery

More people lose their money through gem and jewellery scams in Thailand than in any other way (60% of complaints to the TAT involve gem scams). **DO NOT** fall for any story about gem sales, special holidays, tax breaks – no matter how convincing. **NEVER** buy gems from people on the street (or beach) and try not to be taken to a shop by an intermediary. **ANY** unsolicited approach is likely to be a scam. The problem is perceived to be so serious that in some countries Thai embassies are handing out warning leaflets with visas.

Rules of thumb to avoid being cheated

- Choose a specialist store in a relatively prestigious part of town (the TAT will informally recommend stores).
- Note that no stores are authorized by the TAT or by the Thai government; if they claim as much they are lying.
- It is advisable to buy from shops who are members of the Thai Gem and Jewellery Traders Association.
- Avoid touts.
- Never be rushed into a purchase.
- Do not believe stories about vast profits from re-selling gems at home. They are lies.
- Do not agree to have items mailed ("for safety")
- If buying a valuable gem, a certificate of identification is a good insurance policy. The Department of Mineral Resources (Rama VI Rd, T 2461694) and the Asian Institute of Gemological Sciences (484 Rachadapisek Rd, T 5132112) will both examine stones and give such certificates.
- Compare prices; competition is stiff among the reputable shops; be suspicious of 'bargain' prices.
- Ask for a receipt detailing the stone and recording the price.

For more information (and background reading on Thailand) the *'Buyer's Guide to Thai Gems and Jewellery'*, by John Hoskin can be bought at Asia Books.

of the city, and the encroachment of more organized shops and the effects of the re-developer's demolition ball are eating away at one of Bangkok's finest traditions. Nancy Chandler's map of Bangkok, available from most bookshops, is the most useful guide to the markets of the capital. The largest is the ***Weekend Market*** at Chatuchak Park (see page 288). The ***Tewes Market***, nr the National Library, is a photographers dream; a daily market, selling flowers and plants. ***Pratunam Market*** is spread over a large area around Rachprarop and Phetburi rds, and is famous for clothing and fabric. Half of it was recently bulldozed for redevelopment, but there is still a multitude of stalls here. The *Bai Yoke Market* is next door and sells mostly fashion garments for teenagers – lots of lycra. A short distance S of here on Rachprarop Rd is the ***Naraiphan Shopping Centre and Narayana Bazaar*** an indoor stall/shopping centre affair (concentrated in the basement) geared to tourists and *farang* residents. ***Nakhon Kasem*** known as the ***Thieves Market***, in the heart of Chinatown, houses a number of 'antique' shops selling brassware, old electric fans and woodcarvings (tough bargaining recommended, and don't expect everything to be genuine – see page 280). Close by are the stalls of ***Sampeng Lane*** (see page 280), specializing in toys, stationery, clothes and household goods, and the ***Pahurat Cloth Market*** (see page 279) – a small slice of India in Thailand, with mounds of sarongs, batiks, buttons and bows. ***Bangrak Market***, S of the General Post Office, nr the river and the *Shangri-La Hotel*, sells exotic fruit, clothing, seafood and flowers. ***Pak Khlong Market*** is a wholesale market selling fresh produce, orchids and cut flowers and is situated nr the Memorial Bridge (see page 279). ***Phahonyothin Market*** is Bangkok's newest, opp the Northern bus terminal, and sells potted plants and orchids. ***Banglamphu Market*** is close to Khaosan Rd, the backpackers' haven, on Chakrapong and Phra Sumen rds. Stalls here sell clothing, shoes, food and household goods. The nearby ***Khaosan Road Market*** (if it can be called such) is much more geared to the needs and desires of the foreign tourist. CDs and cassettes, batik shirts, leather goods and so on. ***Patpong Market***, arranged down the middle of Patpong Rd, linking Silom and Surawong rds, opens up about 1700 and is geared to tourists, selling handicrafts, T-shirts, leather goods, fake watches, cassettes and VDOs. ***Penang Market***, Khlong Toey, situated under the expressway close to the railway line specializes in electronic equipment from hi-fis to computers, with a spattering of other goods as well. A specialist market is the ***Stamp Market*** next to the GPO on Charoen Krung which operates on Sun only. Collectors come here to buy or exchange stamps.

● Tour companies & travel agents

Travel agents abound in the tourist and hotel areas of the city – Khaosan Rd/Banglamphu, Sukhumvit, Soi Ngam Duphli, and Silom (several down Pan Rd, a soi opp Silom Village). All major hotels will have their own in-house agent. Most will book airline, bus and train tickets, arrange tours, and book hotel rooms. Because there are so many to choose from, it is worth shopping around for the best deal. For companies specialising in tours and other travel arrangements to Burma, see page352).

● Tourist offices

Tourist Authority of Thailand (TAT), Rachdamnern Nok Ave (at intersection with Chakrapatdipong Rd), T 2815051. There is also a smaller office at 372 Bamrung Muang Rd, T 2260060. Open Mon-Sun, 0830-1630. **NB** The main office on Rachdamnern Nok Ave opened after some delay in mid-1996. For the time being the TAT are also keeping their office on Bamrung Muang Rd open, although it may close and/or be relocated in 1997 or 1998. In addition there is a counter at Don Muang airport (in the Arrivals Hall, T 5238972) and offices at 1 Napralarn Rd, T 2260056, and the Chatuchak Weekend Market (Kampaeng Phet Rd). The main office is very helpful and provides a great deal of information for independent travellers – certainly worth a visit.

A number of good, informative, English language magazines providing listings of what to do and where to go in Bangkok have started up recently. The best is undoubtedly *Bangkok Metro*, published monthly (฿80). It is well designed and produced and covers topics from music and nightlife, to sports and fitness, to business and children. Less independent, and with less quality information, is the oddly named *Guide of Bangkok* or GoB. Its advantage is that it is free.

● Tourist Police

Unico House, Ploenchit Soi Lang Suan, T 1699 or 6521721. There are also dedicated tourist police offices in the main tourist areas.

● Traditional Thai Massage

Many hotels offer this service; guesthouses also, although most masseuses are not trained. The most famous centre is at Wat Pho (see page 274), a Mecca for the training of masseuses. Wat Pho specializes in the more muscular Southern style. The Northern-style is less exhausting, more soothing. Other centres offering quality massages by properly trained practioners include: *Marble House*, 37/18-19 Soi Surawong Plaza (opp Montien Hotel), T 2353519, open 0100-2400 Mon-Sun, ฿300 for 2 hrs, ฿450 for 3 hrs and *Vejakorn*, 37/25 Surawong Plaza, Surawong Rd, T 2375576, open Mon-Sun 1000-2400, ฿260 for 2 hrs, ฿390 for 3 hrs.

● Transport

Local Bus: this is the cheapest way to get around town. A bus map marking the routes is indispensable. The ***Bangkok Thailand*** map and ***Latest tours guide to Bangkok and Thailand*** are available from most bookshops as well as many hotel and travel agents/ tour companies. Major bus stops also have maps of routes and instructions in English displayed. Standard non-a/c buses (coloured blue) cost ฿2.50. Beware of pickpockets on these often crowded buses. Red-coloured express buses are slightly more expensive (฿3.50), slightly less crowded, and do not stop at all bus stops. A/c buses cost ฿6-16 depending on distance. Travelling all the way from Silom Rd to the airport by a/c bus, for example, costs ฿14; most inner city journeys cost ฿6. There are also smaller a/c 'micro buses' (a bit of a misnomer as they are not micro at all, not even 'mini'), which follow

Thai Airways: sample domestic routes and fares

Route	Mins	Fare (baht)*
Bangkok to:		
Chiang Mai	65	1,650
Khon Kaen	55	1,060
Korat	40	555
Ubon Ratchathani	65	1,405

* late 1996 fares quoted, one way (return fares are double)

the same routes but are generally faster and less crowded because officially they are only meant to let passengers aboard if a seat is vacant. They charge a flat fare of ฿25. **NB** More people have their belongings stolen on Bangkok's city buses than almost anywhere else.

Elevated railway: an elevated railway being built by Ital-Thai is under construction and should be opened in 1997/1998.

Express boats: travel between Nonthaburi in the N and Wat Rajsingkorn (nr Krungthep bridge) in the S. Fares are calculated by zone and range from ฿4-15. At peak hours boats leave every 10 mins, off-peak about 15-25 mins (see map, page 285 for piers). The journey from one end of the route to the other takes 75 mins. Note that boats flying red or green pennants do not stop at all piers (they also exact a ฿1 express surcharge). Also, boats will only stop if passengers wish to board or alight, so make your destination known.

Ferries: small ferries take passengers across the Chao Phraya River, ฿1 (see map on page 285 for piers).

Khlong or long-tailed boats: can be rented for ฿200/hour, or more (see page 283).

Motorcycle taxi: a relatively new innovation in Bangkok (and now present in other towns in Thailand) they are the fastest, and most terrifying, way to get from A to B. Riders wear numbered vests and tend to congregate in particular areas; agree a fare, hop on the back, and hope for the best. Their 'devil may care' attitude has made them bitter enemies of many other road users. Expect to pay ฿10-20.

Taxi: most taxis are metered (they must have a/c to register) – look for the 'Taxi Meter' illuminated sign on the roof. There are a number of unmarked, unofficial taxis which are to be found around the tourist sites. Flag fall is ฿35 for a journey of 2 km or less and it should cost ฿40-100 for most trips in the city. If the travel speed is less than 6 km/hr – always a distinct possibility in the traffice choked capital – a surcharge of ฿1 per minute is automatically added. Sometimes taxis refuse to use the meter – insist they do so. Taxi drivers should not be tipped. For most tourists the arrival of the metered taxi has lowered prices as it has eliminated the need to bargain – check, though, that the meter is 'zeroed' before setting off.

Tuk-tuk: the formerly ubiquitous motorized saamlor is rapidly becoming a piece of history in Bangkok, although they can still always be found nr tourist sites. Best for short journeys, they are uncomfortable and, being open to the elements, you are likely to be asphyxiated by car fumes. Bargaining is essential and the fare must be negotiated before boarding, most journeys cost at least ฿40. Both tuk-tuk and taxi drivers may try to take you to restaurants or shops – do not be persuaded; they are often mediocre places charging high prices.

Long distance Bangkok lies at the heart of Thailand's transport network. Virtually all trains and buses end up here and it is possible to reach anywhere in the country from the capital. Bangkok is also a regional transport hub, and there are flights to most international destinations. For international transportation, see page 341.

Air Don Muang Airport is 25 km N of the city. Regular connections on **Thai** to many of the provincial capitals. For airport details see page 343. There are a number of Thai offices in Bangkok, Head Office for domestic flights is 89 Vibhavadi Rangsit Rd, T 5130121, but this is inconveniently located N of town. Two more central offices are at 6 Lan Luang Rd (T 2800070) and 485 Silom Rd. Tickets can also be bought at most travel agents. **Bangkok Airways** flies to Koh Samui, Hua Hin, Phuket, Sukhothai, Chiang Mai, Ranong, Hat Yai, U-Tapao (Pattaya) and Mae Hong Son. They have an office in the domestic terminal at Don Muang, and two offices in town: Queen Sirikit National Convention Centre, New Rachadapisek Rd, T 2293456; and llll Ploenchit Rd, T 2542903.

Train Bangkok has two main railway stations. The primary station, catering for most destinations, is Hualamphong, Rama IV Rd, T 2237010/2237020; condensed railway timetables in English can be picked up from the information counter in the main concourse. Trains to Nakhon Pathom and Kanchanaburi leave from the Bangkok Noi or Thonburi station on the other side of the Chao Phraya River.

Road Bus: there are three main bus stations in Bangkok serving the N and NE, the E, and the S and W. Destinations in the Central Plains are also served from these terminals – places N of Bangkok from the northern bus terminal, SW of Bangkok from the southern terminal, and SE from the eastern bus terminal. The **Northern bus terminal** or *Mor Chit*, Phahonyothin Rd, T 2712961, serves all destinations in the N and NE as well as towns in the Central Plains that lie N of Bangkok like Ayutthaya and Lopburi. Getting to *Mor Chit* by public transport is comparatively easy as many a/c (Nos 2, 3, 9, 10, 29 and 39) and non-a/c buses travel along Phahonyothin Rd. The new non-a/c **Southern bus terminal** is on Phra Pinklao Rd (T 4110061) nr the intersection with Route 338. Buses for the W (places like Nakhon Pathom and Kanchanaburi) and the S leave from here. A/c town bus No 7 travels to the terminal. A/c buses to the S and W leave from the terminal on Charan Santiwong Rd, nr Bangkok Noi Train Station in Thonburi, T 4351199. The **Eastern bus terminal**, Sukhumvit Rd (Soi Ekamai), between Soi 40 and Soi 42, T 3912504 serves Pattaya and other destinations in the Eastern region.

Buses leave for most major destinations throughout the day, and often well into the night. There are overnight buses on the longer routes – Chiang Mai, Hat Yai, Chiang Rai, Phuket, Ubon Ratchathani. Even the smallest provincial towns such as Mahasarakham have deluxe a/c buses connecting them with Bangkok. Note that in addition to the government-operated buses there are many private companies which run 'tour' buses to most of the major tourist destinations. Tickets bought through travel agents will normally be for these private tour buses, which leave from offices all over the city as well as from the public bus terminals listed above. Shop around as prices may vary. Note that although passengers may be picked up from their hotel/guesthouse therefore saving on the ride (and inconvenience) of getting out to the bus terminal the private buses are generally less reliable and less safe. Many pick-up passengers at Khaosan Rd, for example.

CHIANG MAI
เชียงใหม่

HISTORY

Around 1290 King Mengrai succeeded in annexing Haripunjaya (Lamphun), the last of the Mon kingdoms. Up until that point, the capital of his kingdom had been Chiang Rai, but with the defeat of Lamphun he decided to move his capital S to a more central location. In 1296 he chose a site on the banks of the Ping River and called his new capital, Nopburi Sri Nakawan Ping Chiang Mai, later shortened to Chiang Mai or 'New City'. It is said that he chose the site after seeing a big mouse accompanied by four smaller mice scurry down a hole beneath a holy Bodhi tree (*Ficus religiosa* – the tree under which the Buddha attained enlightenment). This he took to be a good omen, and with his friends King Ramkhamhaeng of Sukhothai and King Ngarm Muang of Phayao who agreed with thc portents, he made this the heart of his kingdom of Lanna (*laan naa*) or a 'million rice fields'. Through his reign, Mengrai succeeded in expanding his kingdom enormously: in 1259 he became King of

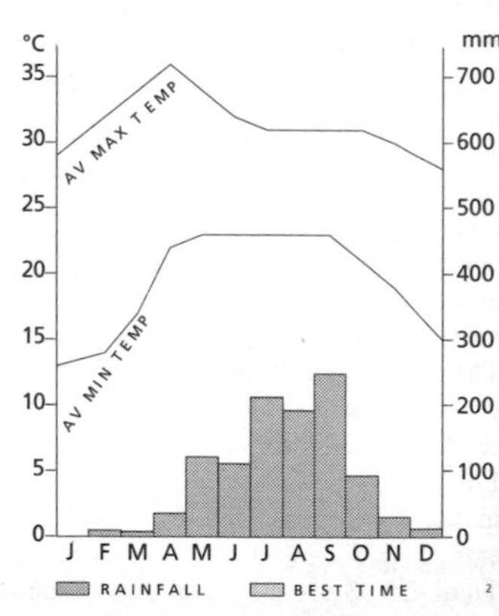

Climate: Chiang Mai

Chiang Saen; from there he extended the areas under his control to Fang and Chiang Rai; and then, finally, to Haripunjaya. The land in itself was unimportant; King Mengrai was concerned with the control of people, and he spent much of his reign founding new towns which he would settle with people who would then owe him allegiance.

Like his friend King Ramkhamhaeng, Mengrai was a great patron of Theravada Buddhism. He brought monks from Ceylon to unify the country through promoting this religion of both King and commoner. From Mengrai's reign up until the 15th century, Chiang Mai flourished. Towards the end of the 15th century, during the reign of King Tiloka (1442-1488), relations with up-and-coming Ayutthaya became strained. The two kingdoms engaged in a series of wars with few gains on either side, although many stories recount the bravery and cunning of each side's warriors. Muen Loknakorn, one of Tiloka's most skilful commanders, is said to have defeated the Ayutthayan army on one occasion by creeping into their camp at night, and cutting the tails off their elephants. With the elephants rampaging around the camp in pain, the Ayutthayans thought they were being attacked, and fled in confusion.

Although relations between Chiang Mai and Ayutthaya were fractious, it was actually the Burmese who eventually captured the city of Chiang Mai in 1556. King Bayinnaung, who had unified all of Burma, took Chiang Mai after a battle of 3 days and the city remained a Burmese regency for the next 220 years. There was constant conflict during these years and by the time the Burmese succeeded in overthrowing Ayutthaya in 1767, the city of Chiang Mai was decimated and depopulated. In 1775, General Taksin united the kingdom of Thailand and a semi-autonomous prince of the Lampang Dynasty was appointed to rule the N. It was not until 1938 that Chiang Mai lost its semi-independence and came under direct rule from Bangkok.

Today, Chiang Mai is possibly the second largest city in Thailand with a population of between 250,000 (the official figure) and 500,000 (the unofficial, and more likely, figure), a thriving commercial centre as well as a favourite tourist destination. The TAT estimates that 12% of Thailand's tourists travel to Chiang Mai. Its attractions to the visitor are obvious: the city has a rich and colourful history, still evident in the architecture of the city which includes over 300 wats; it is manageable and still relatively 'user friendly' (unlike Bangkok); it has perhaps the greatest concentration of handicraft industries in the country; and it is also an excellent base from which to go trekking and visit the famous hilltribe villages in the surrounding highlands. Chiang Mai has developed into a major tourist centre with a good infrastructure including excellent hotels and restaurants in all price categories.

In pursuing the tourist dollar, some long-time visitors argue that the city may have lost some of its charm in the process. Bangkok's problems of traffic congestion, pollution and frantic property development have arrived in Chiang Mai – albeit on a smaller scale. This is rather ironic in that part of the cause is people escaping congestion, pollution and development in Bangkok – and in so doing bringing the problems with them. Various tax breaks have attracted more than 80 companies to Chiang Mai and the surrounding area which is dotted with industrial estates, factories and warehouses.

In Dec 1995 Chiang Mai hosted the Southeast Asian Games and in 1996 the city celebrated its 700th anniversary. Although all this attention was intended to mark Chiang Mai's 'coming of age', some locals and long time visitors regret the attention that it has received. In

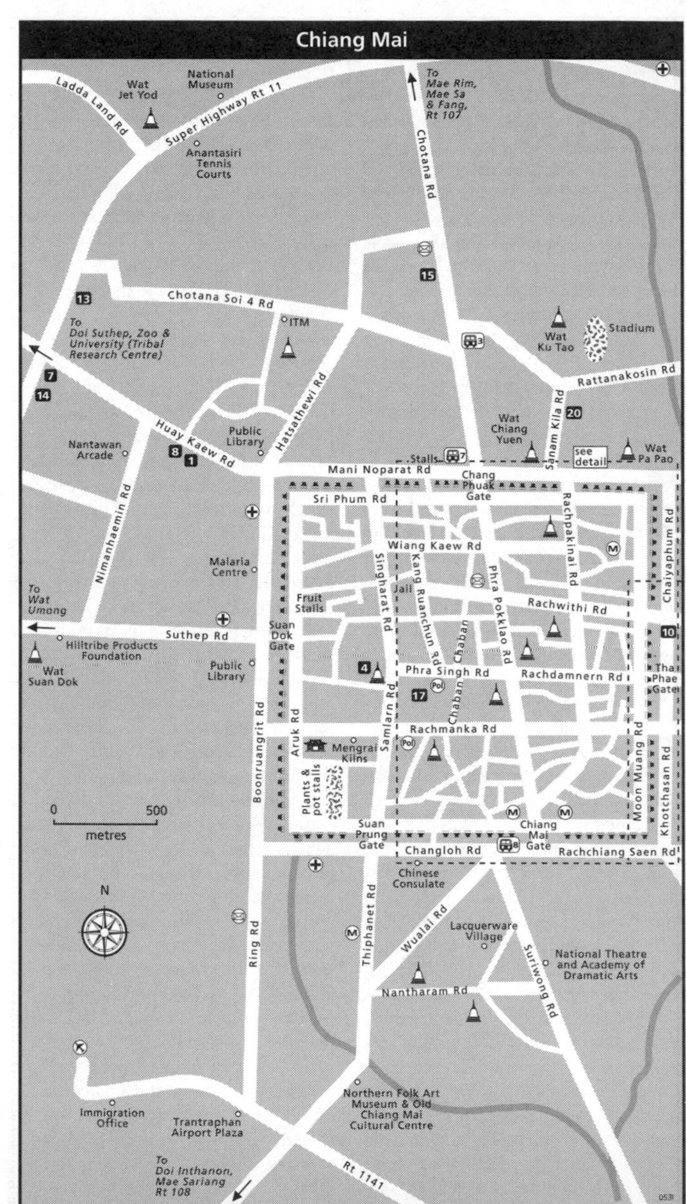
Chiang Mai
Ladda Land Rd
Wat Jet Yod
National Museum
Super Highway Rt 11
Anantasiri Tennis Courts
To Mae Rim, Mae Sa & Fang, Rt 107
Chotana Rd
15
13
Chotana Soi 4 Rd
To Doi Suthep, Zoo & University (Tribal Research Centre)
ITM
3
Wat Ku Tao
Stadium
Rattanakosin Rd
7
14
Hatsathewi Rd
Sanam Kila Rd
20
Wat Chiang Yuen
Huay Kaew Rd
Public Library
Nantawan Arcade
8
1
Stalls
see detail
Wat Pa Pao
Mani Noparat Rd
Chang Phuak Gate
Sri Phum Rd
Rachpakinai Rd
Chaiyaphum Rd
Nimanhaemin Rd
Wiang Kaew Rd
Singharat Rd
Kang Ruanchun Rd
Phra Pokklao Rd
Malaria Centre
Jail
To Wat Umong
Fruit Stalls
Rachwithi Rd
Chaban
Suthep Rd
Suan Dok Gate
10
Hilltribe Products Foundation
Wat Suan Dok
Public Library
4
Phra Singh Rd
Rachdamnern Rd
Tha Phae Gate
Pol
17
Boonruangrit Rd
Aruk Rd
Samlarn Rd
Rachmanka Rd
Mengrai Kilns
Moon Muang Rd
Khotchasan Rd
Plants & pot stalls
0
500
metres
Suan Prung Gate
Chiang Mai Gate
8
Changloh Rd
Rachchiang Saen Rd
Chinese Consulate
N
Thiphanet Rd
Ring Rd
Wualai Rd
Lacquerware Village
Suriwong Rd
National Theatre and Academy of Dramatic Arts
Nantharam Rd
Northern Folk Art Museum & Old Chiang Mai Cultural Centre
Immigration Office
Trantraphan Airport Plaza
To Doi Inthanon, Mae Sariang Rt 108
Rt 1141

1. Wat Bupharam
2. Wat Chedowan
3. Wat Mahawan
4. Wat Phra Singh
5. Wat Saen Fang

Hotels:

6. *Hotel* & Central Dept Store & Kad Suan Kaew Shopping Plaza
7. *Amari Rincome*
8. *Chiang Mai Orchid*
9. *Chiang Mai Plaza*
10. *Darets Guesthouse*
11. *Diamond Riverside*
12. *Felix City Inn*
13. *Holiday Inn Green Hills*
14. *Lotus*
15. *Novotel*
16. *President*
17. *Riverfront Resort*
18. *River Ping Palace*
19. *River View Lodge*
20. *SSS Guesthouse*

Places to eat:

21. Bain Garden
22. Le Coq d'Or
23. The Gallery
24. The Riverside & Good View Bar & Restaurant
31. Westin

Buses:

1. Arcade Bus Station (long distance)
2. Buses to Bor Sang & San Kampaeng
3. Chang Puak Bus station; Bus & Minibus to Mae Rim & Chiang Dao
4. Bus to Lamphun & Pasang
5. Songthaews to Lamphun (blue)
6. Songthaews to Mae Rim (yellow)
7. Minibus to Doi Sep
8. Minibus to Rang Dong & Chom Thong

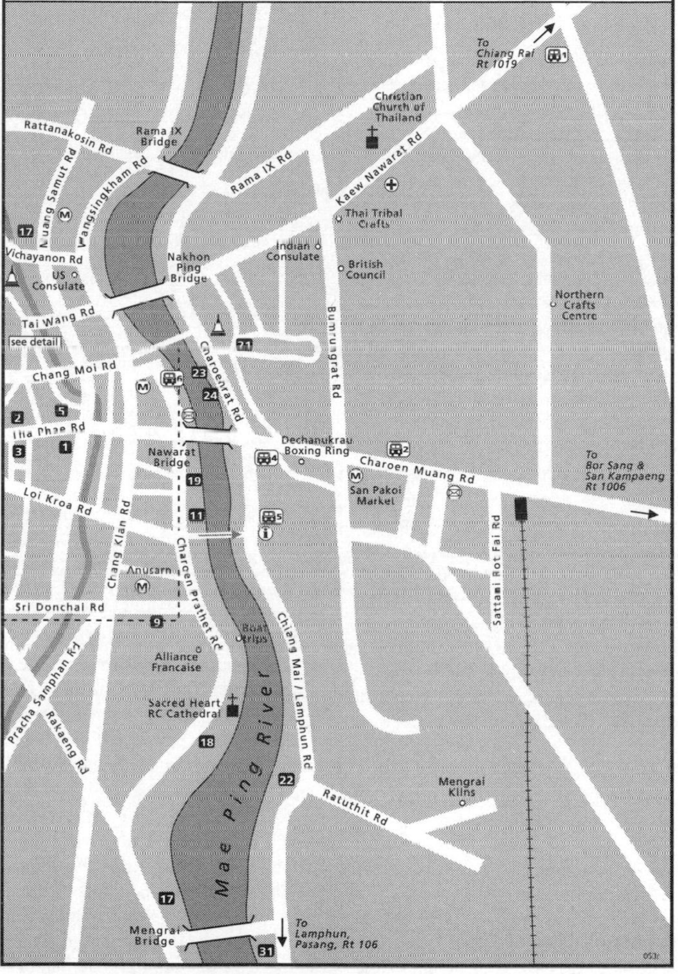

1993, 2.2 million tourists visited the city – over four times more than its total population – and some tourists are returning disappointed that "What was clearly once a beautiful place ... is now a concrete wilderness of ... bleak treeless highways, snarling exhausts ... and very few Thai smiles" (letter from a foreign tourist to the *Bangkok Post*). Nonetheless, Reginald Le May's observations of 1938 are not entirely redundant:

> "Chiangmai possesses a singular beauty. I was stationed there in 1913, and again in 1915, and completely succumbed to its charms; and when I visited it afresh in 1927, after twelve years' absence, I found it more enchanting than ever, with its brick-red palace-fort surrounded by a lotus-filled moat dating from about 1350, its shady avenues, its broad flowing river, and its innumerable temples each within its leafy garden, where the tiled roofs and stately stupas, the swept courtyards, the green mango trees and the heavenly blue sky above all combined to induce a feeling of such peace and happiness as it would be hard to match elsewhere."

PLACES OF INTEREST

Chiang Mai is centred on a square moat and defensive wall built during the 19th century although their origins lie in the late 13th century. The four corner bastions are reasonably preserved (although parts of the wall have been rather insensitively rebuilt) and are a useful reference point when roaming the city. Much of the rest of the towns walls were demolished during WW2 and the bricks used for road construction. Not surprisingly, given Chiang Mai's turbulent history, many of the more important and interesting wats are located within the city walls which is – surprisingly – the least built-up part. Modern commercial development has been concentrated to the E of the city, and now well beyond the Ping River.

Wat Chiang Man, situated in the NE of the walled town, is on Rachpakinai Rd within a peaceful compound. The wat is the oldest in the city and was built by King Mengrai soon after he had chosen the site for his new capital in 1296. It is said that he resided here while waiting for his new city to be constructed and also spent the last years of his life at the monastery. The wat is Northern Thai in style, most clearly evident in the gilded woodcarving and fretwork which decorate the various pavilions. The gold-topped chedi *Chang Lom* is supported by rows of elephants, similar to those of the two chedis of the same name at Si Satchanalai and Sukhothai. Two ancient Buddha images are contained behind bars within the viharn on the right-hand side as you enter the compound. One is the tiny crystal Buddha, *Phra Sae Tang*

Chiang Mai place names

Folk Art Museum
พิพิธภัณฑ์ศิลปพื้นบ้าน

Wat Chedi Luang
วัดเจดีย์หลวง

Wat Chiang Man
วัดเชียงมั่น

Wat Duang Dii
วัดดวงดี

Wat Jed Yod
วัดเจ็ดยอด

Wat Ku Tao
วัดกู่เต่า

Wat Phra Singh
วัดพระสิงห์

Wat Suan Dok
วัดสวนดอก

Wat Umong
วัดอุโมงค์

Chiang Mai: within the Old City

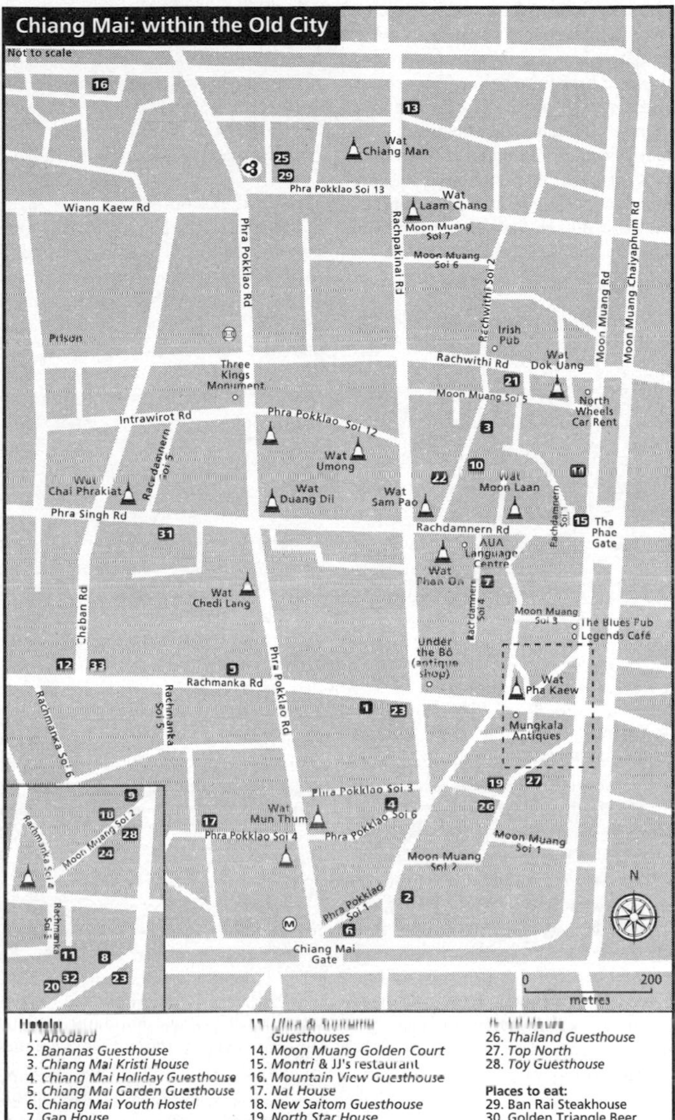

Hotels:
1. *Anodard*
2. *Bananas Guesthouse*
3. *Chiang Mai Kristi House*
4. *Chiang Mai Holiday Guesthouse*
5. *Chiang Mai Garden Guesthouse*
6. *Chiang Mai Youth Hostel*
7. *Gap House*
8. *Jame House*
9. *John's Place*
10. *Kavil House*
11. *Kent Guesthouse*
12. *La Maloon Guesthouse*
13. *[illegible] Guesthouses*
14. *Moon Muang Golden Court*
15. *Montri & JJ's restaurant*
16. *Mountain View Guesthouse*
17. *Nat House*
18. *New Saitom Guesthouse*
19. *North Star House*
20. *Pathara House*
21. *Rama Guesthouse*
22. *Rendezvous Guesthouse*
23. *Rose Guesthouse*
24. *Somwang's Guesthouse*
25. *[illegible]*
26. *Thailand Guesthouse*
27. *Top North*
28. *Toy Guesthouse*

Places to eat:
29. Ban Rai Steakhouse
30. Golden Triangle Beer Garden Bar & Restaurant
31. La Villa Italian
32. Pum Pui Italian
33. Uan Phuan

55A

Tamani (standing 10 cm high). This image, possibly originally from Lopburi, is thought to have been brought to Chiang Mai from Lamphun by King Mengrai in 1281, where it had already resided for 600 years. The second is the stone Buddha, *Phra Sila* (literally, 'Stone Buddha'), in bas-relief, believed to have originated in India or Ceylon about 2500 years ago. It is supposed to have been made by Ajatacatru at Rajagriha in India, after the death of the Buddha and contains his relics. From India it was taken to Ceylon, and from there was brought by monks to Chiang Mai after first residing at both Sukhothai and Lampang. The image is carved in a dark stone, later gilded over, and shows the Buddha taming the wild elephant Nalagiri, sent to kill him by Ajatacatru. Both the Phra Sae Tang Tamani and the Phra Sila are believed to have the power to bring rain and are paraded through the streets of Chiang Mai and drenched in water during the Songkran Festival in Apr at the end of the dry season. Wat Chiang Man is an excellent place to see the full range of wat buildings, and how architectural designs have evolved. The largest structure is an extensively renovated viharn – gaudy to most Western tastes. Behind it is the Chedi Chang Lom; to the left of the chedi, a raised *hor trai* or scripture library (raised to protect the scriptures from pests and flooding); to the left of this a fine, old *bot* or ordination hall, identifiable from the *bai sema* that surround it. On the right hand side of the compound are monks' dormitories or *kutis*, the abbot's own abode, a second, smaller viharn and a bell tower. Taken together, these structures make up the main elements of a large monastery.

Wat Phra Singh, the 'Temple of the Lion Buddha', is arguably Chiang Mai's most important and certainly its largest wat. It is situated in the W quarter of the old city and is impressively positioned at the end of Phra Singh Rd. The wat was founded in 1345 and contains a number of beautiful buildings decorated with fine woodcarving. Towards the back of the compound is the intimate *Lai Kham Viharn*, which houses the venerated Phra Buddha Singh image. It was built between 1385 and 1400 and the walls are decorated with early 18th century murals. Two walls are painted in the more rustic Lanna Thai style, and depict women weaving and the traditional costumes of the N. Another two walls are printed in central Thai style: here there are Burmese noblemen, central Thai princes, court scenes and battles. The two sets of murals make a fascinating contrast. The former concentrate on the lives of ordinary people; the latter on the élites. The *Phra Buddha Sihing* is yet another image with a colourful and rather doubtful provenance. It is said to have come from Ceylon by a rather roundabout route, but as art historians point out, is Sukhothai in style. The head, which was stolen in 1922, is a copy. Among the other buildings in the wat is an attractive *raised library* (*hor trai*), with intricate carved wood decorations, inset with mother-of-pearl.

Wat Chedi Luang, on Phra Pokklao Rd, to the E of Wat Phra Singh, is a 500-year-old ruined chedi which once stood some 90m high. Built initially in 1401 and then substantially enlarged between 1475 and 1478 by King Tiloka, the chedi was partially destroyed during an earthquake in 1545 and never rebuilt. Now the Fine Arts Department, after an interlude of a mere 450 years, are attempting to restore it. Judging by the remains, it must have been an impressive monument, especially as the entire chedi was encased in metal plates, covered with gold leaf. The wat has two particular claims to fame: during the 15th century, the E niche of the chedi housed the famous Emerald Buddha, now in Bangkok, and second, King Mengrai is believed to have been killed by a bolt of lightning in the temple compound. The airy viharn

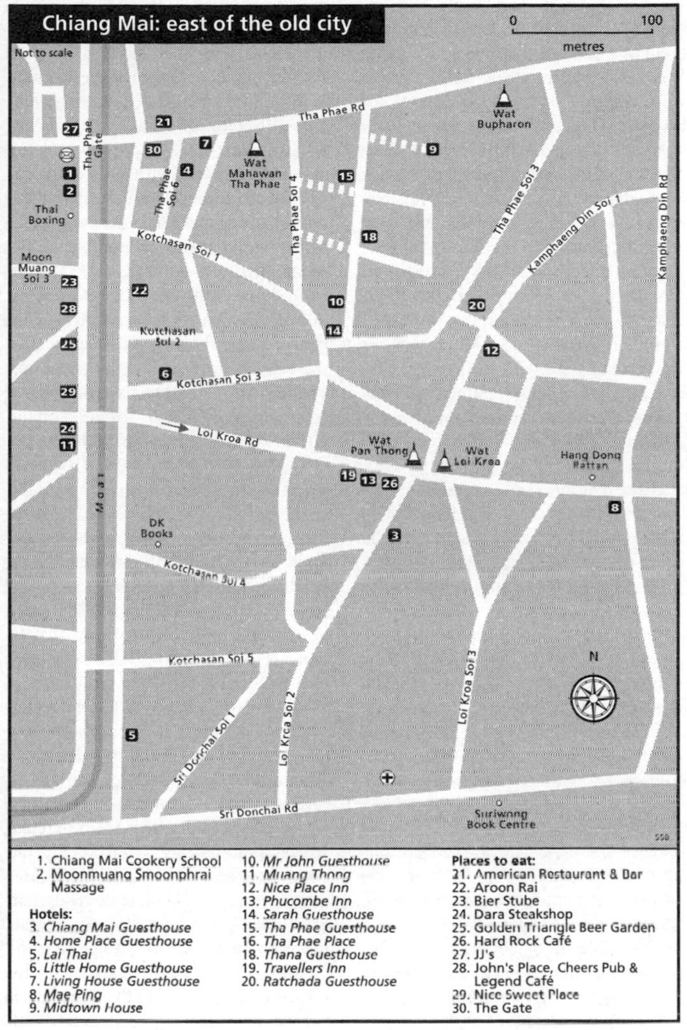

still contains a mid-15th century standing Buddha, along with a series of framed paintings depicting some of the jataka stories. Chiang Mai's rather uninteresting **Lak Muang**, or city pillar, is to be found within the compound.

Also within the city walls, just N of the intersection of Rachdamnern and Phra Pokklao rds, is a haven of peace at **Wat Duang Dii**. The compound contains three Northern Thai wooden temple buildings with fine woodcarving and attractively weathered doors. Note the small, almost Chinese-pagoda roofed, structure to the left of the gate with its meticulous stucco work. Behind the viharn and bot is a square-based chedi with elephants at each corner, and topped with copper plate. Close by is the less attractive **Wat Umong** with a pair of formerly stucco-clad chedis, now weathered down to brick. **Wat Mengrai**, is situated in the S quarter of the city.

Outside the walls, **Wat Suan Dok** (or **Wat Bupharam** [not to be confused with the monastery of the same name on Tha Phae Rd]), lies to the W of town on Suthep Rd. Originally built in 1371 but subsequently much restored and enlarged, the wat contains the ashes of Chiang Mai's royal family housed in many white, variously-shaped, mini-chedis. Much of the monastery was erected during the reign of King Kawila (1782-1813). Not content with just one relic, the large central chedi is said to house eight relics of the Lord Buddha. On the sides of its base are four finely moulded brick and stucco naga slipways and gates. The large, open-walled viharn which confronts the visitor on entering the complex displays some good woodcarving on its exterior walls. The two large Buddha images, seated back-to-back at one end of the building, are regarded by art historians as artistically inferior. Behind the viharn is the bot which houses a 6m gilded bronze Buddha image in the Chiang Saen style, seated in an attitude of subduing Mara. The walls are decorated with lively, if rather too gaudy for Western tastes, scenes from the jataka stories. The wat is also a centre of Thai traditional massage – ask one of the monks for information.

Continuing W on Suthep Rd, is the turn-off for **Wat Umong**, about 1 km off the road down a narrow lane. The wat was founded in 1371 by King Ku Na (1355-1385) who promoted the establishment of a new, ascetic school of forest dwelling monks. In 1369 he brought a leading Sukhothai monk to Chiang Mai – the Venerable Sumana – and built Wat Umong for him and his followers. Sumana studied here until his death in 1389. The wat features a statue of the fasting Buddha, reduced to skin and bones. Also here is a garden and lake as well as the tunnels after which the wat is named. From the trees hang Thai proverbs and sayings from the Buddhist texts extolling pilgrims to lead good and productive lives. Vivid, almost lurid, murals decorate one building and the wat is a centre for meditation. To get there take a songthaew or bus (Nos 1 and 4) along Suthep Rd and ask to be let off at the turning for Wat Umong.

The beautiful **Wat Jet Yod** (literally, 'seven spires'), is just off the 'superhighway' at the intersection with Ladda Land Rd, NW of the city and close to the National Museum. It was begun in 1453 and contains a highly unusual square chedi with seven spires. These represent the 7 weeks the Buddha resided in the gardens at Bodhgaya, after his enlightenment under the Bodhi tree. According to the chronicles the structure is a copy of the 13th century Mahabodhi temple in Pagan, Burma, which itself was a copy of the famous temple at Bodhgaya in Bihar (although it is hard to see the resemblance). On the faces of the chedi are an assortment of superbly modelled, stucco figures in bas relief, while at one end is a niche containing a large Buddha image, dating from 1455, in an attitude of subduing Mara (now protected behind steel bars). The stucco work represents the 70 celestial deities and are among the finest works from the Lanna School of art. They are wonderfully modelled, flying, their expressions serene. At the back of the compound is the small **Phra Chedi** and associated bot, both raised off the ground on a small brick platform. Next to this is a much larger chedi with four niches containing images of the Buddha subduing Mara.

Unfortunately, the wat was ransacked by the Burmese in 1566 and its buildings were badly damaged. The stucco facing of the original structures has in large part disappeared, leaving only attractively weathered brick. A new, gaudy, gold and red viharn rather detracts from the 'lost city' atmosphere of the compound.

The National Museum lies just to the E of Wat Jet Yod on Highway 11. It is a cool relief from 'Wat spotting' and has a fine collection of Buddha images and Sawankhalok china downstairs, as well as some impressive ethnological exhibits upstairs. Admission ฿10. Open 0900-1600 Wed-Sun.

Wat Ku Tao, to the N of the city off Chotana Rd, dates from 1613. It is situated in a leafy compound and has an unusual chedi, shaped like a pile of inverted alms bowls.

Given that Chiang Mai has over 300 wats, there are a great many to choose from. Others worth a fleeting visit for those not yet 'watted out' include: **Wat Chiang Yeun** and **Wat Pa Pao** just outside the N walls of the city; and **Wat Chedowan**, **Wat Mahawan**, **Wat Saen Fang** and **Wat Bupharam** – all on Tha Phae Rd – between the E walls of the city and the Ping River. **Wat Mahawan** displays some accomplished woodcarving on its viharn, washed in a delicate yellow, while the white stupa is guarded by a fearsome array of singhas – mythical lions – some with bodies hanging from their gaping jaws. **Wat Bupharam** has two, fine old viharns (*viharn yai* [big] and *lek* [small]), a new and rather gaudy raised viharn, a small bot and a white stupa. Of the viharns, the finest is the viharn lek, built about 300 years ago in Lanna Thai style. The small 'nave' is crowded with Buddha images and features Chinese plates, adhered to the wooden ceiling. The façade of the viharn – which is in need of funds for renovation – has some fine woodcarving. Also impressive are the carved doors of the viharn yai: note the carving of the Buddha subduing the wild elephant Nalagiri, sent to attack him.

The **Folk Art Museum** (or Lanna Folk Museum) is just S of the junction of Thiphanet and Wualai rds and is housed in a traditional Northern Thai house (130 years old) with a modest collection of kitchenware, betel nut and tobacco holders, ceramics etc. Admission ฿20. Open 1000-1600 Fri-Wed. The **Tribal Research Centre** on Chiang Mai University's campus is worth visiting for those intending to go trekking (see page 325).

The **Night Market** dominates the W side of Chang Klan Rd; it consists of a number of purpose built buildings with hundreds of stalls selling a huge array of tribal goods as well as clothing, jewellery, tapes etc (see page 335). For a completely different atmosphere, walk through Chiang Mai's 'Chinatown' which lies to the N of Tha Phae Rd, between the moat and the river. True to form, this area buzzes with business activity. Small workshops run by entrepreneurial Sino-Thais jostle between excellent small restaurants serving reasonably priced Thai and Chinese food. Few tourists explore this area.

The **Chiang Mai Zoo** is to be found at the end of Huay Kaew Rd, W of town at the foot of Doi Suthep. The animals here are better cared for than in many SE Asian zoos, although that may not be saying a great deal. The new aviary is worth seeing. The zoo occupies an attractive position on a hillside overlooking the Chiang Mai Valley, and covers 85 ha of parkland. *Best time to visit*: is in the cool of the early morning, as there's not much shade. Admission ฿10. Open 0800-1700 Mon-Sun. There is an Arboretum and Fitness Park next to the zoo. *Getting there*: No 3 bus from Chang Puak Gate, or songthaew.

EXCURSIONS

Doi Suthep is a hill overlooking the town, 16 km to the NW. A steep winding road climbs 1,000m to the base of a 300 step naga staircase which in turn leads up to **Wat Phrathat** (usually known by visitors simply as Doi Suthep [*doi* is the Northern word for mountain; in Thai, *Khao*]), a very popular pilgrimage spot for Thais, perched on the hillside, and offering spectacular views of the city and plain below. Avoid the climb by taking the cable car which has a suggested ฿5 donation charge. A white elephant is alleged to have collapsed here, after King Kuena (1367-1385) gave it the task of finding a propitious site for a shrine to house a holy relic of the Lord Buddha. A chedi was built to house the relic, which was embellished and extended two centuries later.

The 24m high chedi, recently replated, is topped with a 5-tiered honorific parasol. There are a number of Buddha images in both Sukhothai and Chiang Saen styles arrayed in the gallery surrounding the chedi. The whole compound is surrounded by bells (which visitors can ring) and meditation instruction is available at the wat. When James McCarthy visited Chiang Mai and Doi Suthep at the end of the 19th century (he was employed by the government of Siam as a surveyor and adviser) the city had just suffered a prolonged dry spell. As water was channelled the 12 km from the hill, it was assumed that the chief of Chiang Mai had somehow offended the spirits of the chedi. An angel, allegedly, appeared to the man and insisted he surmount it with a new, precious stone-encrusted finial. He was then enjoined to parade around the city with his finest elephants to propitiate the offended spirits. *Getting there*: songthaew from Mani Noparat Rd, by Chang Puak Gate (฿30 up, ฿20 down), or take bus No 3 to the zoo and then change onto a minibus. A taxi should cost about ฿200 return. The temple is closed after 1630.

Chiang Mai excursions

Bor Sang
บ่อสร้าง
Chiang Dao Caves
ถ้ำเชียงดาว
Doi Pui
ดอยปุย
Doi Suthep
ดอยสุเทพ
Mae Sa Valley
แม่สาวาเลย์
Pasang
ป่าซาง
Phu Ping Palace
พระราชตำหนักภูพิงค์ราชนิเวศน์
Wiang Kum Kam
เวียงกุมกาม

Phu Ping Palace, 5 km past Wat Phrathat, is the winter residence of the King. The immaculate gardens are open 0830-1630 Fri-Sun and public holidays when the Royal Family is not in residence. *Getting there*: the Doi Suthep minibus continues on to the Phu Ping Palace.

Doi Pui, 4 km past Phu Ping Palace, down a deteriorating track, is a rather commercialized Meo village. Nonetheless, it is worth a visit for those unable to get to other, more traditional, villages. There are two second-rate museum huts, one focusing on opium production, the other on the different hilltribes. On the hillside above the village is a rather unexpected English flower garden (in full bloom in Jan). *Getting there*: charter a songthaew or take a minibus

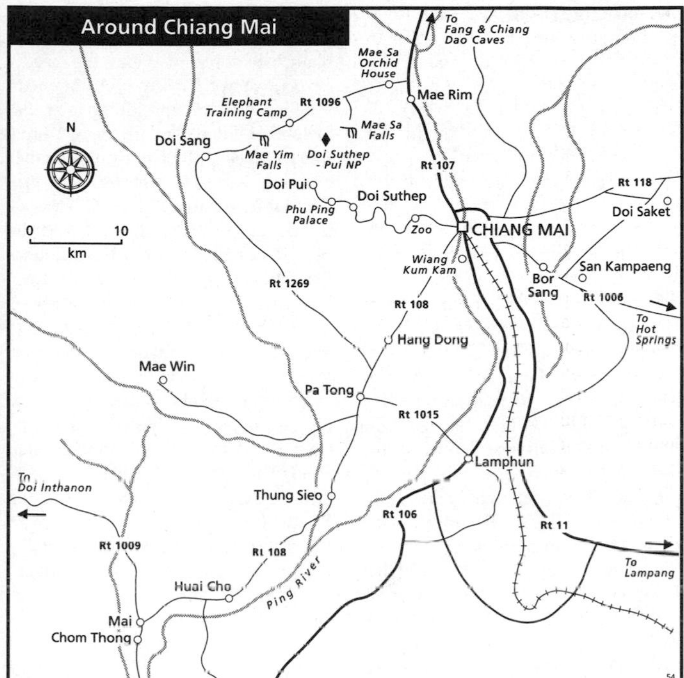

from Mani Noparat Rd, by Chang Puak Gate, and then charter a songthaew from Doi Suthep.

Wiang Kum Kam is a ruined former city 5 km S of Chiang Mai. A *wiang* is a fortified site, and Wiang Kum Kam was an outlier of the Mon Haripunjaya Kingdom which had its capital at Lamphun. The city was established by the Mon in the 12th or 13th centuries and was not abandoned until the 18th century. Today, archaeologists are gradually beginning to uncover the site which covers an area of about 9 sq km and contains the remains of at least 20 wats. The most complete monument is **Wat Kan Thom** (in Thai, Wat Chang Kham) which has a marvellous bronze naga outside. Behind the Wat is the spirit chamber of the great King Mengrai (?-1317) who founded the city of Chiang Mai and who through military prowess and diplomatic verve substantially enlarged the kingdom of Lanna Thai. It is believed his spirit still resides here and consequently is a highly revered place. The gardens and ruins are very beautiful and peaceful, dotted with bodhi trees. Nearby are the ruins of **Wat Noi** and two dilapidated chedis; also notable is the chedi of **Si Liam** which takes the form of a stepped pyramid – a unique Mon architectural style (the best example hereabouts is at Wat Phra That Haripunjaya in Lamphun). However the most important archaeological discovery has been a series of inscriptions which seem to indicate that King Ramkhamhaeng was not the 'inventor' of the Thai script, but rather made adaptations to a script that was already in use. *Getting there*: accessible by bicycle or motorbike, or by tuk-tuk. Take Route 106 S towards Lamphun; the ruins are signposted off to the right about 3 km from Chiang Mai – but only in Thai – from where it is another 2 km. Look out for a ruined chedi on the right and ask along the way for confirmation.

Bor Sang, the Umbrella Village, lies due E of the city. This 15 km stretch of road, from Chiang Mai to San Kampaeng, has become a ribbon development of numerous 'workshops' and showrooms. It is worth heading out here if you are looking for things to buy (see Shopping), although local residents now avoid the area as being too touristed. It is best known for its paper umbrellas, made by hand and then painted. The shaft is made from local softwood, the ribs from bamboo, and the covering from oiled rice paper. *Getting there*: take a bus from the N side of Charoen Muang Rd, just E of Nawarat Bridge.

Mae Sa Valley orientated E-W, lies off Route 107, N of town. It has a number of attractions along with a selection of 'back-to-nature' resorts (popular with Thais). The newly opened **Queen Sirikit Botanical Gardens** is a pleasure to visit. The **Sai Nam Phung Orchid and Butterfly Farm** (among others) is a kilometre off Route 1096, about 4 km from the intersection with Route 107. It has the best selection of orchids in the area as well as a small butterfly enclosure (unusual jewellery for sale). Admission ฿10. Open 0700-1700. A short distance further on is a **Snake Farm** (shows 0700-1415, ฿80). The **Mae Sa Waterfall** is located in the **Doi Suthep-Pui National Park**, a kilometre off Route 1096 and about 3 km on from Maesa House. The waterfall is in fact a succession of mini-falls – relatively peaceful, with a visitors' centre and a number of stalls. Special parking for 'Royal' cars. Admission ฿3 pp, ฿20/car. Open 0800-1800, Mon-Sun. Most popular of all in the valley is the **Elephant Training Camp**, 3 km further on from the waterfall. Visitors can watch elephants bathing, dragging logs and perform other feats – are the mahouts really necessary, or could the pachyderms do it by themselves? At the end of the show visitors can indulge in an elephant ride. There is a daily show. Admission ฿40, 0940-1100. Continuing further on along Route 1096 there are, in turn, the **Mae Yim Falls** (17 km), **Doi Sang** – a Meo tribal village (25 km), and the **Nang Koi Falls** (34 km). **Accommodation B** *Samoeng Resort*, Route 1096, T 487072, F 487075, restaurant, pool, jacuzzi, hot water. *Getting there*: a half to one day trip from Chiang Mai on a chartered songthaew, or hired motorbike or car. Alternatively take a public bus/songthaew to Mae Rim from the Chang Puak bus station and then catch a songthaew on. The valley lies 16 km N of town on Route 107, and then W on Route 1096. Route 1096 links up with Route 1269 and emerges again at the town of Hang Dong, a 'basket village', 15 km S of Chiang Mai. The entire circular route is some 110 km.

Chiang Dao Caves lie 78 km N of Chiang Mai on Route 107 (almost 6 km off the main road – turn left in the town of Chiang Dao, just after the 72 km marker). The caves penetrate deep into the limestone hills which represent the E extension of the Himalayas and are associated with a wat, **Wat Chiang Dao**. They are amongst the most extensive in Thailand and are a popular pilgrimage spot for monks. The caverns contain an assortment of Buddha and hermit images as well as some impressive natural rock formations. Guides with kerosene lamps show visitors around, although it is only possible to explore a small part of the system. Admission ฿5. **Accommodation F** (dorm) **D** (Bungalow) *Malee's Nature Lovers Bungalows*, 144/2 Mu 5, Chiang Dao, T 01 (mobile) 9618387, these bungalows are about 1 km from the caves, it can be cold at night and in the early morning, especially between Nov and Feb, restaurant and dormitory beds as well as bungalows available, good for trekking and walking. *Getting there*: catch a bus to Fang from the Chang Puak bus station on Chotana Rd and get off at Chiang Dao. Songthaews take visitors the final 6 km from the main road to the caves. A taxi to the caves and back should cost about ฿1,000 (1½ hrs each way) which, shared four ways, is an easier and reasonable alternative.

Lamphun, a historic city, lies 26 km S of Chiang Mai. *Getting there*: buses leave regularly from the Old Lamphun-Chiang Mai Rd, just over the Nawarat Bridge and near the TAT office, 30-40 mins (฿7). The route is along a beautiful 15 km avenue of massive *yang khao* trees (*Dipterocarpus alatus*). The latex from these trees is used for waterproofing and as a fuel for torches (it is flammable). A few years ago there were suggestions that the road would be widened and the *yang* trees felled. Environmentalists, appalled at the prospect, solicited the help of local activist monks to ordain (*buat*) the trees by wrapping lengths of saffron cloth around them. Every tree on a 10 km stretch from just outside Chiang Mai is ordained and the development plans have been shelved.

Lampang lies 93 km S of Chiang Mai and is easily visited on a day trip. Outside Lampang is the incomparable **Wat Phra That Lampang Luang**. **The Young Elephant Training Centre** en route to Lampang is also worth a visit. *Getting there*: by bus from Nawarat Bridge or from the Arcade terminal.

Cotton weaving centre of Pasang is 12 km SW of Lamphun. *Getting there*: regular songthaews from Lamphun and from Chiang Mai (same stop as for Lamphun).

TREKKING

There are scores of trekking companies in Chiang Mai and hundreds of places selling trekking (this includes Kodak shops, launderettes, restaurants). Not many places actually organize the trek themselves and it is rare to meet the guide – or other people in the group – before leaving for the trek. Competition is stiff, and most provide roughly the same assortment of treks, ranging from 1 night to over a week. Treks can also incorporate raft trips and elephant rides. Motorcycle trekking is also becoming popular, although it is environmentally destructive bringing noise to otherwise quiet areas and promoting soil erosion. Some companics, in order to convince potential customers that they will be pioneers, offer a money-back guarantee should they come into contact with other trekkers. The TAT office distributes a list of recommended trekking operators and a leaflet on what to look out for when choosing your trip. **The Tribal Research Institute**, situated at the back of the Chiang Mai University campus on Huay Kaew Rd provides information on the various hilltribes, maps of the trekking areas, and a library of books on these fascinating people. Open 0900-1600 Mon-Fri. There is a small ethnographic museum attached to the centre, open 0830-1200, 1300-1630 Mon-Fri. An informative book on the hilltribes can be bought here for ฿35.

Choosing a trekking company and guide When choosing a guide for the trip, ensure that he can speak the hilltribe dialect as well as good English (or French, German etc). **NB** Guides must hold a **'Professional Guide Licence'**. Treks must be registered with the Tourist Police; to do this the guide must supply the Tourist Police with a photocopy of the Identity page of your passport and your date of entry stamp. You can check on a company's reputation by contacting the police department. **Beware of leaving valuables** in guesthouses in Chiang Mai; however reliable the owner may appear, it is always safer to deposit valuables such as passport, jewellery and money in a bank (banks on Tha Phae Rd have safety deposits and charge about ฿200/month). **Insects**: remember to take protection against mosquitoes; long trousers and long-sleeved shirts are essential for the night-time. **Prices** for treks start at about ฿1,200 for a single night, and increase by ฿200 for each additional night. Elephant treks are more expensive. Nonetheless, it is possible to book a 3 day/4 night trek, with rafting and an elephant ride for about ฿1,500 pp. There are scores of trekking companies in Chiang Mai (a list can be obtained from the TAT office) and guesthouses also often provide a trekking service. Many of the companies are concentrated along Tha Phae, Chaiyaphum, Moon Muang and Kotchasan rds. We have decided to stop recommending companies because standards change so very rapidly. Note that it is the guide, rather than the company, who is important in determining a 'successful' trek, and guides swop allegiances constantly; as noted above, many are freelance in any case. A recommendation from another visitor is hard to beat.

TOURS

A range of day tours run from Chiang Mai to such sights as Wat Phrathat Doi Suthep, the Phu Ping Palace and a Meo village (฿250); the Mae Sa Valley to visit a waterfall, orchid farm and elephants at work (฿450); Doi Inthanon National Park (฿850); Bor Sang (the Umbrella village) and San Kampaeng (฿100); Chiang Rai and the Golden Triangle (฿900), even the Sukhothai historical park over 200 km S (฿1,500). A ride on an elephant, some bamboo rafting and a visit to an orchid farm cost about ฿600. Tour operators are to be found concentrated along Tha Phae, Chang Klan and Moon Muang rds. See Tour companies and travel agents for listings. A notable operator is *Chiang Mai Green Tour and Trekking*, which tries to provide eco-friendly and culturally-sensitive tours. However, they also run motorbike treks which can hardly be said to be the former.

Many of the larger tour companies and travel agents will also arrange visas and **tours to Myanmar as well as Cambodia, Laos and Vietnam**. For Laos, some agents can arrange visas in 24 hrs (฿1,200).

LOCAL FESTIVALS

Jan: *Chiang Mai Winter Fair* (movable), a 10-day festival held late Dec/early Jan, based in the Municipal Stadium. Exhibitions, Miss Beauty Contest, musical performances; *Bor Sang Umbrella Fair* (outside Chiang Mai, mid-month) celebrates traditional skill of umbrella making, and features contests, exhibitions and stalls selling umbrellas and other handicrafts. Miss Bor Sang, a beauty contest, is also held.

Feb: *Flower Festival* (1st Fri, Sat and Sun) floral floats, flower displays, handicraft sales and beauty contests.

Apr: *Songkran* (13th-16th public holiday) traditional Thai New Year celebrated with more enthusiasm in Chiang Mai than elsewhere. Boisterous water-throwing, particularly directed at farangs; expect to be soaked to the skin for the entire four days. Given that it is the hottest time of year, no bad thing – unless you are going out for a business lunch or dinner (leave your camera in your hotel).

Nov: *Yi Peng Loi Krathong* (mid-month) the ritual of the lighted balloon. Colourful balloons are launched into the sky, in order to banish troubles. In the evenings, homes and shops are lit up with lanterns, and balloons are floated on the rivers.

LOCAL INFORMATION

● Accommodation

Chiang Mai has a vast range of accommodation to choose from, mostly concentrated to the E of the old walled city although there is a significant group of guesthouses to be found W of Moon Muang Rd, S of Tha Phae Gate. There are over 110 guesthouses and 97 hotels at the last count, so below is only a selection. Stiff competition, a proliferation of new hotels and a stagnant industry mean room rates are slashed in many instances. It is rare for visitors to have to pay the set room rate. Some guesthouse owners complain that tourists have moved on to other pastures – notably Myanmar and the countries of Indochina.

● **Within the Old City Walls**

Within the old city walls and the moat is the greatest concentration of guesthouses plus one or two small(ish) mid-range places. Most are to be found in the eastern half of the old city, and many of these in the south-eastern quarter. The old city is quiet and tree-filled and away from the main centre of commercial activity. It is about a 15-min walk to the night market although there are a number of bars and restaurants in the area as welll as tour operators and motorbike and jeep rental outfits.

B ***Felix City Inn***, 154 Rachmanka Rd, T 270710, F 270709, a/c, restaurant, 137 rm hotel opened in 1991, mediocre, mid-range place situated within the city walls in a quiet location but away from most of the action E of the moat.

C ***Gap House***, 3 Soi 4 Rachdamnern Rd, T 278140, restaurant, incl breakfast, positioned down a quiet soi in the heart of the walled city (turn off Rachdamnern Rd after the offices of the American Universities Alumni Language Centre [AUA]), attractive rooms, good value, rec; **C** ***Montri***, 2-6 Rachdamnern Rd, T 211070, F 217416, some a/c, restaurant, clean, good central position nr Tha Phae Gate, large rooms sparsely furnished, the restaurant here (*JJ's*) is one of Chiang Mai's more popular places – but rooms tend to be very noisy due to hotel's position on an intersection; **C-D** ***Anodard***, 57 Rachmanka Rd, T 270755, F 270759, restaurant, pool, one of Chiang Mai's older large hotels and there is no attempt in terms of design to make the place in any sense 'Thai', rooms in this classic 60s-style concrete block are functional but it is the only large place within the old city walls – erected before restrictions pushed developers to build elsewhere; **C-D** ***Top North***, 15 Soi 2 Moon Muang Rd, T 278900, F 278485, some a/c, pool, modern concrete block, well-run but rather sterile, check rooms as cleanliness varies, pool usually crowded, popular but needs to maintain standards, slightly overpriced – largely because people are willing to pay extra for access to a pool.

D ***Kavil House***, 10/1 Rachdamnern Soi 5, T 224740, some a/c, quiet place down a long narrow soi, attached bathrooms with hot water, good food; **D** ***Pathara House***, 24 Moon Muang Soi 2, T 206542, F 206543, some a/c, new small hotel-cum-guesthouse, rooms are clinically clean, and also clinically bare, attached bathrooms with hot water, raised rather exposed patio, beer 'garden', the a/c rooms are well priced and considerably cheaper than the *Top North* just up the soi – but then there's no pool; **D-E** ***Moon Muang Golden Court***, 95 Moon Muang Rd, T 212779, some a/c, set back from the road, large hotel at this price bracket, dark, gloomy corridors, rooms OK but bare and very plain, bathrooms with hot water, discounts for long stay; **D-E** ***North Star***, 38 Moon Muang Soi 2, T 278190, some a/c, much like the *Thailand Guesthouse* over the road, though perhaps with a touch more character, good food and relaxing eating area, clean rooms; **D-E** ***Rama Guesthouse***, 8 Moon Muang Soi 5 (in fact on Rachwithi Rd), T 216354, some a/c, a well run place, rooms are set back from the road, nice garden, good food, clean. Treks and various rental services, rec; **D-E** ***Rendezvous Guesthouse***, 3/1 Rachdamnern Soi 5, T 213763, F 217229, some a/c, situated down a quiet soi, good rooms – though a little gloomy because arranged around a covered lobby – with clean bathrooms, close to Wat Sam Pao, attractive atmosphere with relaxing plant-filled lobby, satellite TV, books and comfy chairs, rec; **D-E** ***Thailand***, 38/2 Moon Muang Soi 2, T 274592, some a/c, bright and airy rooms in otherwise featureless block, some rooms beginning to become a tad shabby, but management is enthusiastic and friendly, own bathroom, hot water.

E ***Bananas Guesthouse***, 4 Rachpakinai Rd (nr intersection with Phra Pokklao Soi 1), T 278458, set on a rather noisy road and almost irritatingly cool and trendy with lots of signs stating how hip the management are, that aside, the rooms are OK and the food here is good; **E** ***Chiang Mai Garden Guesthouse***, 82-86 Rachmanka Rd, T 278881, F 278455, good food (homemade yoghurt), very clean large rooms with bathroom, second floor rooms are better than first floor, their trekking guide, Piroon, has been rec; **E** ***Chiangmai Kristi House***, 14/2 Rachdamnern Soi 5, T 418165, a largish place with over 30 rm, down quiet soi, rooms are a good size with very clean attached bathrooms, hot water, and

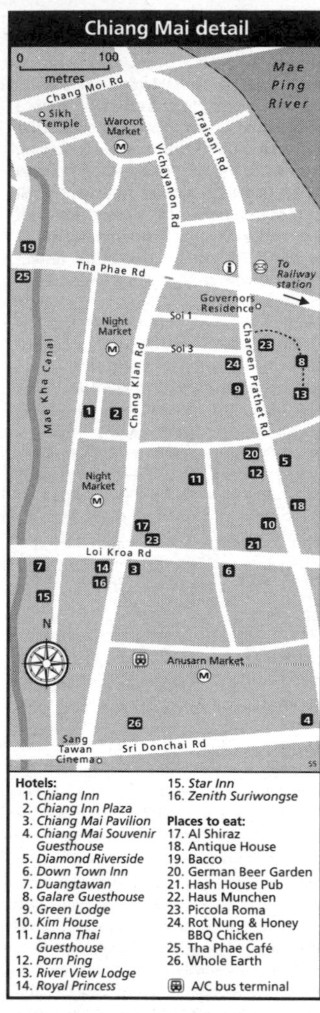

a well in the lobby for some reason; **E** ***Jame House***, 22 Moon Muang Soi 2, T/F 278344, rooms are OK with attached bathrooms but a little overpriced compared with other places in this part of town; **E** ***Johnny Boy Guesthouse (JB House)***, 7-3 Rachdamnern Soi 1, T 213329, small restaurant, no hot water, clean, quiet and friendly, good trekking from here; **E** ***Kent Guesthouse***, 5 Rachmanka Soi 1, T 217578, one of the more peaceful guesthouses in this area, house in large, leafy compound down a quiet dead end soi, the rooms are well maintained with attached bathrooms; **E** ***La Maloon***, 1 Chaban Rd, T 271001, stylish and (usually) peaceful little guesthouse away from the mass of other places, set in large compound but next to a car shop so can be noisy; **E** ***Libra***, 28 Moon Muang Soi 9, T 210687, number of good reports concerning this place, large, clean rooms, hot water showers, welcoming owners and good treks arranged, friendly owners; **E** ***Nice Apartment***, 15 Rachdamnern Soi 1, T 210552, clean but bare and rather sterile in feel, fine for a short stay but lack of character could be rather disturbing long-term; **E** ***Rama House***, Rachwithi Rd (100m from intersection of Rachwithi and Moon Muang rds), large, clean rooms with attached bathrooms, restaurant, laundry and left luggage facilities, good value; **E** ***SB House***, 1/1 Phra Pokklao Soi 13 (not far from Wat Chiang Man), T 210644, some a/c, this is one of the few places to stay well within the city walls, almost like someone's home in atmosphere, rooms are fine, bathrooms larger than is usual, a/c rooms a bargain – quiet; **E** ***Supreme House Guesthouse***, 44/1 Moon Muang Rd Soi 9, T 222480, F 218545, friendly and helpful place with cosmopolitan mix of guests and rooftop restaurant, rec; **E** ***Thong Koon House***, 27/5 Moon Muang Rd Soi 9, T 418174, F 418161, a/c, hot showers and private bathrooms, small, very clean guesthouse, friendly set up and good information about trekking; **E** ***VIP House***, 1 Rachdamnern Soi 1, T 419199, F 418970, opened in 1995 and immaculately clean with good hot water showers (attached) and large rooms, friendly and welcoming but whether they will maintain standards is the key issue, rec if they do; **E-F** ***Chiang Mai Holiday Guesthouse***, 31 Phra Pokklao Soi 3, T 278455, quite a wide range of services provided here incl bicycle and motorbike rental, and tours and trekking, the rooms are nothing special (attached bathrooms, hot water) but the dorm beds (฿40) are a good deal; **E-F** ***Chiang Mai Youth Hostel***, 63A Bamrungburi Rd (by Chiang Mai Gate), T 276737, F 279043, rooms are clean, dorm beds available (discounts for YH and ISIC cardholders), rather close to a busy road and the mangement during our last visit were rather lacking in enthusiasm; **E-F** ***NAT***, 7 Phra Pokklao Soi 6, T 277878, run by an Israeli woman (Kosher food available) who has made this one of the best guesthouses in the area, rooms are clean with some attempt to create a local feel, small balconies, clean attached bathrooms with hot water, views over the old city to Doi Suthep from upper floor, rec; **E-F** *New Saitum*, 21 Moon Muang Soi 2, T 278575, rooms in a group of traditional wooden houses in large compound, peaceful and a refreshing absence of concrete – although the bathrooms could be cleaner; **E-F** *Somwang Guesthouse*, Moon Muang Soi 2, T 278505, cheaper and older rooms with shared bathrooms, the friendly owner has built a new, rather uninspired concrete block with more expensive rooms, they are clean, with attached bathrooms (Asian style downstairs, Western commodes upstairs, though bare and characterless).

F *Rose Guesthouse*, 87 Rachmanka, T 273869, large guesthouse at an intersection of two quite busy roads, rooms are very plain, slightly scruffy, although the shared bathrooms (hot water showers) are kept clean, not much provincial charm here, but the rooms are well priced; **F** *Toy*, 45/1 Moon Muang Soi 1, over-enthusiastic use of concrete has created a bare, almost naked guesthouse, rooms are dark and dingy, but with attached bathroom, well priced.

● Between the eastern city wall and Chang Klan Rd

This area of town includes two sections of hotels and guesthouses. On Chang Klan Rd and close by are a number of large, up-market hotels. This is the shopping heart of Chiang Mai with the night market and many other stalls and shops. It is busy and noisy (although the hotels need not be) with a good range of restaurants. West of here, down the sois or lanes between Loi Kroa and Tha Phae rds are a number of guesthouses and small mid-range hotels. This area, though quiet and peaceful (usually) is still close to many restaurants and the shops and stalls of Chiang Klan Rd.

A+-A *Chiang Inn*, 100 Chang Klan Rd, T 270070, F 274[illegible], a/c, restaurant (rec, particularly good Western breakfasts), pool, one of Chiang Mai's older first class hotels, but kept up-to-date and pristine, very central in the heart of the night market area, still a good match in terms of price and quality with more recent upstart hotels; **A+-A** *Mae Ping*, 153 Sri Donchai Rd, T 270160, F 270181, a/c, restaurant, large ugly tower block in big plot, Chinese in character, popular with Asian tourists, at this price there are other places with more style and finesse; **A+-A** *Zenith Suriwongse*, 110 Chang Klan Rd, T 270051, F 270063, a/c, good restaurants, pool, all facilities, the slightly frayed exterior betrays a renovated interior, central, rec although some rooms look out directly onto neighbouring blocks; **A** *Chiang Mai Plaza*, 92 Sri Donchai Rd, T 270040, F 272230, a/c, restaurant, pool, large (444 rm), impersonal but central to night market and restaurants; **A** *Duangtawan*, 132 Loi Kroa Rd, T 270384, F 275304, a/c, restaurants, pool, high rise hotel, luxurious but rather sterile and indistinguishable – even the rooms might as well be in Spain or Tokyo. Recently expanded facilities, and a new conference centre. Convenient for Night Market, no charge for children under 12. **NB** There seems to be some confusion over whether this hotel is actually open at present. **A** *Royal Princess* (formerly the *Dusit Inn*), 112 Chang Klan Rd, T 281033, F 281044, a/c, restaurant, small pool and gym, part of the Dusit chain of hotels, central (right by the night market), quite noisy (on the main road), 200 rm which though in places a little tatty still have more style than most places, excellent service, rec.

B *Star Inn Hotel*, 36 Loi Kroa Soi 4, T 270310, F 270371, a/c, restaurant, smallish tourist hotel geared to East Asian market, no pool but guests can use the pool at the *Duangtawan* next door free of charge, central with good discounted rates; **B** *Tha Phae Place*, 2 Tha Phae Soi 3, T 270159, F 271982, a/c, restaurant next to Wat Bupharam, small hotel in the mid-range bracket, refined for a place in this price category and surprisingly stylish, good central location but set off the busy Tha Phae Rd – no pool, though.

C *Lai Thai*, 111/4-5 Khotchasan Rd, T 271725, F 272724, some a/c, restaurant, good clean pool, free baby cots, spotless rooms, cross between a N Thai house and Swiss chalet, popular and well-run, good facilities, attractive surroundings, tours, trekking and motorbike rental, note that the cheaper rooms at the back are noisy so expect an early wake up, nonetheless rec; **C** *Phucome Inn*, Loi Kroa Rd, T 206390, a/c, restaurant, small modern hotel in central location, rooms are on the small side but come with hot water bathrooms and cable television, reasonable at the price; **C** *Riverfront Resort*, 43/3 Chang Klan Rd, T 275125, F 282988, some a/c, restaurant, Lanna Thai house on the banks of the Ping

River, live Northern Thai music in restaurant at night; **C** ***Traveller Inn***, 40 Loi Kroa Rd, T 208484, F 272078, a/c, restaurant, small modern hotel with hot water bathrooms, cable TV and minibar in each room, comfortable enough and keenly priced but not much atmosphere; **C-D** ***Home Place***, 9 Tha Phae Soi 6, T 273493, F 273494, some a/c, clean, quiet, good service, helpful advice, clean rooms of a good size with some attempt to infuse the place with Thai-ness, central location, rec; **C-D** ***Nice Place Inn***, 77/1 Kampaeng Din Soi 1, T 272919, some a/c, a guesthouse with pretensions of hotel grandeur, for an extra ฿150 they will turn the a/c on, rooms are plain but clean, quiet but central location, trekking company attached, hot water.

D ***Fang Guesthouse***, 46-48 Kamphaeng Din Soi 1, T 282940, some a/c, quiet place in good central location, attached restaurant, rooms are very clean although a little dark, good attached bathrooms (some with hot water), a/c rooms are an especially good deal; **D** ***Little Home Guesthouse***, 1/1 Kotchasarn Soi 3, T 273662, F 273662, large, clean rooms in a peaceful guesthouse down a quiet Soi within a leafy compound, Roger, the Dutch manager, has insisted on no TV, no videos and no music – well run, rec; **D-E** ***Living House***, 4 Tha Phae Soi 5, T 275370, some a/c, hot water, rooms with bathrooms, clean and quiet, but at our last visit rather unenthusiastic reception – probably just a bad day, as it has been rec by visitors.

E ***Midtown***, 7 Tha Phae Soi 4, T 209062, F 273191, clean, plain rooms with hot water, centrally located down quiet soi nr Wat Mahawan, rather listless service, trekking, motorbike and car rental; **E** ***Sarah's***, 20 Tha Phae Soi 4, T 208271, F 279423, run by an English woman married to a Thai, this is a marvellously quiet place with trees and orchids in a largish compound, the 12 rm are clean, sizeable and good value, with attached bathrooms and shared hot water showers, trekking and tour services available, friendly family atmosphere, rec. **E** ***Thana Guesthouse***, 27/8 Tha Phae Soi 4, T 279794, F 272285, this is a better place than it looks at first sight, the rooms have been redecorated and the attached bathrooms refitted with hot water showers – such investment is not common in many guesthouses, recent visitors have rec it, a particular favourite with Israeli visitors as it serves kosher food, jeeps for hire, trekking organized; **E-F** ***Mr John Guest House***, 16/1 Tha Phae Soi 4, T 208228, small guesthouse, rather ramshackle but has a certain charm, people who stay here seem to be loyal fans; **E-F** ***Ratchada Guest House***, 55 Tha Phae Soi 3, T 275556, friendly guesthouse with reasonable attached bathrooms, can be a little fusty but welcoming, treks arranged, well run.

● On the W bank of the river and off Charoen Prathet Road

This area includes a number of mid- and upper-range hotels on the river. Some of the smaller places are particularly rec. They are peaceful, often on large plots of land, and have the added bonus of the Ping River. They are within easy walking distance of many restaurants and not too far from the markets and shops of Chang Klan Rd.

A ***Diamond Riverside***, 33/10 Charoen Prathet Rd, T 270081, F 271482, a/c, restaurant, pool, large high rise hotel, river views from rather spartan rooms, riverside pool and verandah, discounts available, good value; **A** ***Pornping Tower***, 46-48 Charoen Prathet Rd, T 270099, F 270119, a/c, restaurant, this towering block is built onto one of Chiang Mai's older hotels built in the 1970s, there's not much to set it apart from other similar places across the world – there's not even a pool; **A-C** ***River Ping Palace***, 385/2 Charoen Prathet Rd, T 274932, F 2338493, some a/c, restaurant, traditional northern Thai teak buildings on the banks of the river, rooms with four poster beds and mosquito nets, very romantic, highly rec.

B ***Downtown Inn***, 172/1-11 Loi Kroa Rd, T 270662, F 272406, a/c, 72 rm in this hotel close to the night market, rooms are a good size, discounts available; **B** ***River View Lodge***, 25 Soi 2 Charoen Prathet Rd, T 271109, F 279019, a/c, restaurant, pool, small, quiet, riverside hotel with large, rather plain rooms, some with wonderful views, attractive verandah and pool overlooking the Mae Ping, breakfast incl, the hotel is run by very friendly Thai family, who have good English, and the place is small enough to feel personal and have such amenities as a book lending service, rec.

C ***Galare***, 7 Soi 2 Charoen Prathet Rd, T 273885, F 279088, some a/c, restaurant, small hotel in leafy compound, lovely position on the river, large, clean rooms, and efficient service, the open air restaurant overlooks the Ping and serves simple but tasty food, rec; **C** ***Green Lodge***, 60 Charoen Prathet Rd,

T 279188, F 279188, some a/c, clean rooms with attached bathrooms in small, but featureless hotel on busy road; **C** *Kim House*, 62 Charoen Prathet Rd, T 282441, F 274331, some a/c, small hotel down small, secluded soi, with clean rooms and welcoming atmosphere, rec.

D *Ratana Guesthouse*, 3/5 Charoen Prathet Rd, T 272716, some a/c, clean; **D-E** *Lanna Thai Guesthouse*, 48/1 Loi Kroa Rd, Soi 6, T 275563, some a/c, good central location in the Anusarn market area, rooms are rather drab, bathrooms clean though.

E *Chiang Mai Souvenir*, 118 Charoen Prathet Soi Anusarn, T 282335, good sized rooms but shared hot water bathrooms, in converted private house with large leafy garden and peaceful atmosphere (apart from the dogs barking and the traffic!), early check-out at 0900, popular, rec.

● On the E bank of the river

E *Hollanda Montri*, 265 Charoenrat Rd, T 242450, a/c, hot water, coffee shop, same Dutch management as *The Riverside* restaurant.

● Elsewhere in the city

A+ *Novotel*, 183 Chang Puak Rd, T 225500, F 225505, a/c, restaurants, pool, a new addition to Chiang Mai.

C *Chatree*, 11/10 Suriwong Rd, T 279179, F 279085, some a/c, coffee shop, good pool, good rates, hot water, popular with long-term visitors during the winter, relaxed atmosphere.

E *Daret's*, 4/5 Chaiyaphum Rd, T 235440, popular restaurant, good source of information, although standards have declined, rooms can be grubby, check out time 1000, rather detached service, good trekking centre, motorbikes and bicycles for hire, **E** *Lek House*, 22 Chaiyaphum Rd, T 252686, quiet compound down narrow Soi, rooms are good on the upper floor, slightly murky below, small bathrooms in need of upkeep, but good information and peaceful atmosphere, rec; **E-F** *SSS*, 48/3 Sanam Kila Rd, T 217424, F 217424, restaurant, very basic but clean, friendly staff, good atmosphere, tours and treks organized, great place to meet other travellers, highly rec.

● Huay Kaew Rd (W of city towards Doi Suthep)

There are a number of large hotels on Huay Kaew Rd which runs NW towards Doi Suthep from the north western corner of the city walls. Until a few years ago this area of the city was comparatively quiet – Huay Kaew now has a string of shopping plazas and other developments along its length. It is some distance from the shops and markets of the town centre – too far to walk with any ease – but some people prefer to be away from the bustle of the commercial heart of the city in any case.

A+-A *Amari Rincome*, 301 Huay Kaew Rd, T 221130, F 221915, W of town, a/c, restaurant, pool, tennis court, popular with tour groups, a little frayed at the edges, set price buffet lunch, out of town centre but with friendly staff and still one of the better places to stay, also has 14 apartments that can be rented on a monthly basis; **A+-A** *Chiang Mai Orchid*, 23 Huay Kaew Rd, T 222099, F 221625, W of town, a/c, restaurants, large pool, large but attractive hotel recently expanded, health club, efficient service, relatively peaceful, very good Chinese restaurant, rec; **A** *Holiday Inn Green Hills*, 24 Chiang Mai – Lampang Super Highway, T 220100, F 221602, a/c, 4 restaurants, pool, tennis, golf, business centre, new hotel on edge of town – not well placed for exploring the city on foot; **A** *Lotus Pang Suan Kaew Hotel*, 99/4 Huay Kaew Rd, T 224333, F 224493, a/c, restaurants, pool, gym, large new hotel to the W of town, attached to a shopping centre and rather hard to navigate around, though they've invested in lots of teak cladding, it still lacks ambience, while some of the brick laying seems to have been done in the dark! – in late 1996 competitive rates were a plus and the rooms are large and so is the pool, lots of conference activity.

Outside the City: **A+** *Chiangmai Sports Club*, 284 Moo 3, Don Kaew, Mae Rim (7 km from the city on the Chiang Mai-Mae Rim road), T 298330, F 297897, a/c, restaurant, pool, this sports club on a 10 ha site also has 45 rm and excellent facilities incl squash and tennis clubs, horse riding and a large pool, free shuttle service to town – an alternative hotel for people keen on sports and not wishing or needing to be in the city; **A+** *Westin Chiang Mai*, 318/1 Chiang Mai-Lamphun Rd, T 275300, F 275299, a/c, restaurant, all facilities, over 500 rm in this luxurious high rise hotel on the E bank of the Ping River, its main disadvantage is being 2 km or so S of town which means that any trip really requires transport.

● Places to eat

For listing of where to have a Northern Kantoke meal plus cultural show, see Entertainment. Some of the best Thai food, particularly seafood, is served from numerous small and large restaurants, and countless stalls, in the ***Anusarn market*** area. The best place to see what is on offer in a small area; food available all day but best at night when there is a cacophony of talking, frying and chopping.

Thai: ♦♦♦***The Gallery***, 25-29 Charoenrat Rd, T 248601, quiet and refined Thai restaurant on the Ping River in a century-old traditional Thai house, superb food, highly rec for a special night out, art gallery attached, either sit in a leafy verandah overlooking the river or inside; ♦♦♦***The Good View Bar and Restaurant***, 13 Charoenrat Rd, T 302764, opened at the beginning of 1996 and early reports are excellent – situated on the Ping River, good music and food and very reasonably priced, the owner/manager is Khun Chawal and it looks like his restaurant will give the better-known *Riverside* next door a good run for its money; ♦♦♦***New Krua Thai***, 87/2 Oom Muang Rd, also serves Chinese, open-air, good seafood; ♦♦♦***Riverside***, 9-11 Charoenrat Rd, T 243239, also serves International food, very popular restaurant overlooking the Ping River, live music, good service, good food and value for money, booking advised, rec; ♦♦♦***Whole Earth***, 88 Sri Donchai Rd, also serves Indian, traditional house, situated in lovely garden, very civilized, with unobtrusive live Thai classical music, rec; ♦♦♦-♦♦***Antique House***, 71 Charoen Prathet Rd (next to the *Diamond Riverside Hotel*), well prepared Thai food in wonderful garden with antiques and an old teak house, built in 1894, very nice candlelit ambience, tasty but small servings and rather slow service, live music – though a busy road can be intrusive; ♦♦***Aroon Rai***, 43-45 Kotchasan Rd, very big restaurant, good value Thai food, N Thai specialities, popular with tourists but don't be put off, this is a good place to eat Thai food; ♦♦***Galae***, 65 Suthep Rd, T 278655, in the foothills of Doi Suthep on the edge of a reservoir, Thai and N Thai dishes in garden setting; ♦♦***Honey BBQ Chicken***, Charoen Prathet Rd, northeastern food, excellent 'Chiang Mai' chicken, open-air restaurant, popular with locals; ♦♦***Nang Nuan Seafood***, 27/2-5 Kuan Klang Rd, on the Ping River, also serves Chinese and International food, popular with tour groups; ♦♦-♦***Rot Nung***, Charoen Prathet Rd (opp the *Diamond Riverside Hotel*), excellent Thai noodle soup (*kwaytio*) in a restaurant almost entirely frequented by Thais – few sacrifices to *farang* taste here; ♦♦-♦***Uan Phen***, Rachmanka Rd (at T-junction with Chaban Rd), excellent Thai restaurant with some of the best curries in Chiang Mai, basic open air place and the sign is only in Thai – but worth rooting out; ♦***Chang Moi***, Boonruangrit Rd, just N of Malaria Centre, excellent *kuay tiaw* (noodle soup), rec; ♦***Thanom Pochana***, 8 Chaiyaphum Rd, clean, 'dress appropriate', full of locals, probably better than *Aroon Rai*; ***Krua Thai***, S side of town, on Route 106, nr junction with super highway. A new branch of ***Ta-Krite*** is opening in the shopping and restaurant area opp the *Chiang Mai Orchid Hotel*.

Other Asian cuisines: ♦♦♦♦***Jasmine***, *Royal Princess Hotel*, Chang Klan Rd, excellent Chinese food (*dimsum* at lunchtime); ♦♦♦♦***White Orchid***, in the *Diamond Hotel*, 33/10 Charoen Prathet Rd, Chinese, on the banks of the Ping River, also serves seafood and Thai food, rec; ♦♦***Shere Shiraz***, Charoen Prathet Soi 6, popular Indian restaurant, rec; ♦***Sophia***, Charoen Prathet Soi I (down narrow soi between the night market and the river road), cheap and very popular Muslim restaurant, this soi also usually supports a number of stalls serving Malay/Muslim dishes from *roti* to mutton curry.

International: ♦♦♦♦***Le Coq d'Or***, 68/1 Koh Klang Rd, T 282024, a long established international restaurant set in gardens S of town, excellent food, refined, prices to match; ♦♦♦***Bacco***, 158 Tha Phae Rd, opp Tantraphan Dept Store, Italian restaurant in restored teak house, the chef and manager is an Italian and though the food is just mediocre by the standards set by officials it has style, with rattan chairs, white table linen and soothing lighting and music; ♦♦♦***Chez Daniel Le Normand***, 68/68-1 Chiang Mai Lamphun Rd, T 248840, next door to Kazoo Discotheque, good French food – home-made charcuterie, big choice of French wine, French music in the background, Daniel has cooked for the Queen of Thailand and members of the Royal Family, who frequent this restaurant; ♦♦♦***Daret's***, 4/5 Chaiyaphum Rd, good travellers' food and fruit shakes, very popular but rather smug, slow service; ♦♦♦***German Beer Garden***, 48 Charoen Prathet Rd (opp *Diamond Riverside Hotel*), German specials served in roadside 'garden', good BBQ; ♦♦♦***Hard Rock Café***, Loi Kroa Rd, burgers, fries etc but not the original — good music, reasonable food; ***JJ Bakery*** (*Montri Hotel*), Tha Phae Gate and in the *Chiang Inn Plaza*, Chang

Klan Rd, good breakfasts and sandwiches, own bakery, but don't come here for the Thai food which is only average, very popular, a/c so an excellent place to cool off, note that unlike *Daret's* opp, this is not just a traveller's place – locals also meet here; ♦♦♦***La Villa***, 145 Rachdamnern Rd, T 277403, Italian, mostly pizza, but good pasta dishes too, traditional wooden house in large garden compound, great atmosphere, service can be slow though; ♦♦♦***Le Chalet***, Charoen Prathet Rd, French, nice building, rec; ♦♦♦***Piccola Roma***, 3/2-3 Charoen Prathet Rd, T 271256, good Italian food prepared by the Italian chef and owner Angelo Faro, excellent wine cellar; ♦♦♦-♦♦***America Bar and Restaurant***, 402/2-3 Tha Phae Rd (close to Tha Phae Gate), a welcoming retreat for homesick travellers, excellent Mexican food and great apple pie, as well as pizzas, bagels, deli food and breakfast, although not cheap; ♦♦♦-♦♦***Ban Rai Steak House***, Wiang Kaew Rd, situated within the city walls behind Wat Chiang Man, microwaved food, not rec; ♦♦***Bier Stube***, Moon Muang Rd, reasonable German restaurant serving wurst, home baked breads, smoked ham, salads; ♦♦***The Gate***, 291 Tha Phae Rd (on the corner facing Tha Phae Gate), menu of Thai and western dishes, new so very keen; ♦♦***Haus Munchen***, Loi Kroa Rd (nr Chang Klan Rd), popular German restaurant; ♦♦***Pizza Hut***, Chang Klan Rd (nr night market); ♦♦***Pizza Peacock***, 138 Tha Phae Rd, fondu, kebabs, pizza and some Thai dishes; ♦♦***Pum Pui Restaurant and Bar***, 24/1 Moon Muang Soi 2, traditional Thai house with large garden converted into an Italian restaurant – reasonable Italian, good value and pleasant location; ♦♦***Tiramisu***, Tha Phae Rd (opp Wat Mahawan Tha Phae), looks rather like a Parisian café from the outside (well, that's the idea), good for breakfast with croissants, pastries, and aromatic coffee, also good fruit shakes and travellers' food; ♦♦-♦***Legends Café***, Moon Muang Rd, good capuccino, baguettes as well as beer, serves breakfast; ♦♦-♦***Nice Sweet Place***, 27/1 Moon Muang Rd, a/c restaurant with attached bakery, good pastries, serves breakfast; ♦***Dara Steak Shop***, 1 Rachmanka Rd, good breakfast stop – yoghurts and lassis; ♦***Tha Phae Café***, 79/81 Tha Phae Rd, cheap place but good for simple dishes and coffee; ♦***Thai-German Dairy Products***, Rachdamnern Rd, delicious yoghurt and muesli, rec; ***Lek House***, 22 Chaiyaphum Rd, yoghurts, fruit shakes, steaks.

Fast food: ***Burger King, Pizza Hut, Svenson's Icecream*** and ***Mister Donut*** have opened outlets in the new, vast, *Chiang Inn Plaza*, nr the night market on Chang Klan Rd. ***McDonald's*** in the *Chiang Mai Pavilion* on corner of Chang Klan and Loi Kroh rds. Other fast food outlets in the ***Lotus Pang Suan Kaew*** shopping centre on Huay Kaew Rd.

Foodstalls: ***Anusarn Market*** (SE of the Night Market) stalls mostly at night but also smaller number throughout the day, cheap (฿10-15 single dish meals), lively and fun, rec; stalls along Chang Klan Rd sell delicious pancakes ฿3-7; ***Somphet market*** on Moon Muang Rd for takeaway curries, fresh fish, meat and fruit. North of ***Chang Phuak Gate***, outside the moat, is another congregation of good foodstalls.

● Bars

Many of the bars are concentrated around the SE wall of the city. See under **Music** (page 334) for more bars with live music. There is a group of bars within leafy gardens at the entrance to Moon Muang Soi 2 – ***Golden Triangle Beer Garden***, ***John's Place***, ***The Blue's Pub***, and ***Cheers Pub***. The *Golden Triangle Bar* serves reasonable food (♦♦) and is set within and without a teak house; while the ***Cheers Pub*** is down a narrow soi and serves pub food like pork pies and pea and ham soup (♦♦). Upstairs at *John's Place*, on the balcony is the best place to be voyeuristic; ***Black Cat***, 25 Moon Muang Rd, open 1300-0100, happy hour 1700-1900; ***Byblos***, *Rincome Hotel*, Huay Kaew Rd; ***Nina Pub***, 95/25 Nantawan Arcade, Nimanhemin Rd; ***Pleuk Mai Tai***, beside Tanam on Chang Klan Rd; ***The Pub***, 88 Huay Kaew Rd, quasi-English replica, food overpriced (♦♦♦) and still relaxing in the after-glow of a decade-old review in *Newsweek*; Amarit beer on draught is the main attraction, run by a charming Thai woman with excellent English, only worth a visit if you're after the company of other 'farangs' (rumour is that it is now – to the horror of purists – under German management). ***Overlander Bar***, Moon Muang Rd (facing the moat), good atmosphere, extremely cold beer. ***Irish Pub***, Rachwithi Rd, good atmosphere and food available (♦♦), name speaks for itself – management help to organize the (small) annual St Patrick's Day parade.

● Airline offices

Air Mandalay (*Skybird Tour*), 92/3 Sri Donchai Rd, T 818049; **Bangkok Airways**, Chiang Mai International Airport, T 281519, F 281520; **Cathay Pacific**, Rachawong Rd; **Japan Airlines**, 62/6 Charoen Prathet Rd; **Lao Aviation**, 840 Phra Pokklao Rd, T 418258;

Malaysian Airlines (MAS), *Mae Ping Hotel*, 153 Sri Donchai Rd, T 276523; **Orient Express Air**, *Zenith Suriwongse Hotel*, Chang Klan Rd, T 272040 (airport T 201566), F 818092; **Silk Air**, *Mae Ping Hotel*, 153 Sri Donchai Rd, T 276495; **Thai**, 840 Phra Pokklao Rd, T 211044, open Mon-Sun, 0830-1630.

● **Banks & money changers**

Several banks on Tha Phae Rd and plenty of exchange services along Chang Klan and Tha Phae rds. Many exchange booths open Mon-Sun, 0800-2000. Most banks offer a safety deposit service (useful for leaving valuables when embarking on a trek), expect to pay about ฿200/month. Good rates at **SK**, 73/8 Charoen Prathet Rd.

● **Cultural centres**

Alliance Française, 138 Charoen Prathet Rd, T 275277 presents French cultural (and some Northern Thai) activities. French films with English subtitles are screened on Tues (1630) and Fri (2000). Entrance to non-members, students ฿10, public ฿20; **AUA (American University Alumni)**, 24 Rachdamnern Rd, T 278407, F 211973, library open 1200-1800 Mon-Fri, 0900-1200 Sat. English and Thai classes; films and other shows; **British Council**, 198 Bumrungrat Rd, T 242103, F 244781.

● **Embassies & consulates**

British, Airport Business Park, T 203405; **French Honorary Consulate**, 138 Charoen Prathet Rd, T 281466; **India**, 344 Charoenrat Rd, T 243066; **Japanese**, 8 Soi 1 Na Wat Kate Rd, T 302042; **People's Republic of China**, 111 Changlor Rd, T 276125; **Sweden**, YMCA International, 11 Sermsuk Rd, T 222366; **Sweden**, YMCA Building, 2/4 Mengrai-Sami Rd, T 210877, open 1400-1600 Mon-Fri; **USA**, 387 Vichayanon Rd, T 252629.

● **Entertainment**

Cinema: *Sang Tawan*, corner of Chang Klan and Sri Donchai rds. *Mahanakorn*, Chang Puak Rd; *Chotana*, Chotana Mall, Chang Puak Rd.

Cookery: there are many cooking schools of equal reputation. One is at the *Chiang Mai Thai cookery school*, 1-3 Moon Muang Rd (by Tha Phae Gate), T 206388. The courses run over 1, 2 or 3 days between 1000 and 1600. Contact Samphon and Elizabeth Nabnian at the above address. Another is *Old Lanna Thai Cooking School*, 17/3 Moon Muang Rd Soi 9, T 213787, or *VIP House Cooking School*, 1 Rachdamnern Soi 1.

Cultural shows: *Khun Kaew Palace*, 252 Phra Pokklao Rd (N end), T 214315, admission ฿180 (book in advance), open 1900-2200 Mon-Sun; *Old Chiang Mai Cultural Centre*, 185/3 Wualai Rd, T 275097, admission ฿180 (book in advance), Khantoke dinner, followed by hilltribe show, Mon-Sun 1900-2200; the *Diamond Riverside Hotel* on Charoen Prathet Rd and the *Galare Food Centre* in the Night Bazaar, Chang Klan Rd, also organize Kantoke dinners, 1900. ฿180.

Discos: *Bubble*, Pornping Tower Hotel, 46048 Charoen Prathet Rd, T 270099, very popular, admission ฿100; *Kazoo*, 68/2 Lamphun Rd, T 240880, 300m from TAT office, open daily, very popular. *Porn Ping Hotel*, Charoen Prathet Rd, *Chiang Mai Orchid Hotel*, Huay Kaew Rd.

Kantoke dinners: (northern food served on low tables to diners who sit uncomfortably on the floor), to the accompaniment of rather tacky music.

Meditation and yoga: *Raja Yoga Meditation Centre*, 218/6 Chotana Rd, T 214904.

Music: *Early Times*, Kotchasan Rd, open-air and live heavy metal music; *Baritone*, 96 Praisani Rd, live jazz from 2100; *Riverside Bar and Restaurant*, 9-11 Charoenrat Rd, assorted music from blues to Thai rock; *The Good View Bar*, next door also offers live music, usually rock covers; *The Hill*, 122 Bumrungburi Rd, Thai rock and heavy metal – more of a venue than a bar.

Thai boxing: *Dechanukrau boxing ring*, S of San Pakoi market, on Bumrungrat Rd. Matches every w/e at 2000 (฿20/70).

Traditional Thai massage: there are a number in town; *Baan Nit*, Soi 2 Chaiyaphum Rd, ฿100/hour, welcoming atmosphere, professional, coffee and snacks available, rec; *Rinkaew Povech*, 183/4 Wualai Rd, T 234565; *Tha Phae Moonmuang Smoonphrai*, 2-3 Chaiyaphum Rd, T 234655 (nr *Daret's*, opp Tha Phae Gate), open 0830-2400, ฿100/hr, also herbal sauna; *Moonmuang Smoonphrai 2*, 57 Moon Muang Rd, T 279749, open 0830-2400, sister establishment to *Moonmuang Smoonphrai I*, also provides lessons in Thai massage. *Lek Chaiya with herbs*, 44 Old Sanambin Rd, Suthep, T 809023, is considered the best place to learn about Thai massage, the course includes a video, small classes and friendly capable English speaking teachers. Other courses available: ***ITM (Institute of Thai Massage)***, 17/7 Morokot Rd, T 218632, F 224197, 5-10 day courses in basic, intermediate and advanced Thai massage, 0900-1600; courses begin on Mon and cost ฿1,500 – the 'Master Teacher' Chongkol Setthakorn is well qualified. Courses are also available at the ***Moh Shivagakomarpaj Foundation***, Old Chiang Mai Traditional Hospital, 78/1 Soi Moh Shivagakomarpaj (opp Old Chiang Mai Cultural Centre, Chiang Mai-Hod Rd), T 275085. Courses last 11 days (fee ฿2,770) and run from the beginning and middle of each month; ***Moon Muang Smoonphrai 2*** also give lessons – see above for address.

● Hospitals & medical services

Chiang Mai Ram Hospital, Boonruangrit Rd; *McCormick Hospital*, Kaew Nawarat Rd, T 241107, Mon-Fri 1700-2000; *Suandork Hospital*, Suan Dok Rd, T 221122, good facilities, not too expensive; *Malaria Centre*, Boonruangrit Rd, N of Suan Dok Gate.

● Libraries

21/1 Rachmanka Rd, ***Soi 2***. Open 0800-1700 Mon-Sat. Advice on routes, books on Thailand and novels available. Chiang Mai University's Tribal Research Institute is a useful information source for people going trekking – see page 325.

● Places of worship

Churches: *Chiang Mai Community Church*, Charoen Rasada Rd, services on Sun at 1700 (nursery and kindergarten available) in English, also at the Chiang Mai International School auditorium on the first Sun of the month at 0930 (also in English). *Christian Church of Thailand*, Kaew Nawarat Rd, English service on Sun 1700. *Seven Fountains Catholic Chapel*, 97 Huay Kaew Rd, English service on Sun 0930.

● Post & telecommunications

Area code: 053.

General Post Office: Charoen Muang Rd (W of the railway station), telegram counter open daily 24 hrs, T 241056. Chiang Mai's other main post office is the new **Mae Ping Post Office** on Praisani Rd nr the Nawarat Bridge. This post office has a packing service and is more conveniently situated than the GPO out nr the train station. It also offers an international telephone facility. Other post offices incl the **Phra Singh Post Office**, nr Wat Phra Singh, **Sriphum Post Office** on Phra Pokklao Rd, **Night Bazaar Post Office**, in the basement of the bazaar, Chang Klan Rd, open until 2300. **Rachdamnern Post Office** (opp *JJ's*, by Tha Phae Gate), convenient for many guesthouses on Moon Muang Rd, packing service available, open 0830-2200 Mon-Sun, run by Mi Tui, who speaks perfect English and some French, very reliable. Post Office at the airport offers telegram and international telephone services. Many travel agents in town offer overseas call and fax services.

Telephone: international calls can be made from many tour companies; the post offices on Charoen Muang and Praisani rds also have international telephone services.

● Shipping & packing companies

Packers available around the Post Offices; shippers along Wualai Rd, many S from the Superhighway.

● Shopping

The **Night Markets**, situated on the W and E sides of Chang Klan Rd, are now a major tourist attraction in Chiang Mai and consist of 2 or 3-storey purpose-built buildings containing countless stalls. The set up is no longer a ramshackle affair and many would say the whole area has been rather sanitized. However, it is an excellent place to browse and, along with a wide range of tribal handicrafts, it is possible to buy T-shirts, watches, cheap tapes, leather goods, children's clothes and Burmese 'antiques'. Beware of wood carved products which may well be made of polymer resin. In addition, there are some better quality shops selling jewellery, antiques and silks (both ready-made and lengths) on the first floor of the Viang Ping Building. Most stalls and shops open at about 1800 and close around 2300. ***Warorot Market***, N of Tha Phae Rd for clothing, fabric, sportswear, hilltribe handicrafts. Open 0700-1600. ***Fruit stalls and market*** on both sides of moat N of Tha Phae Gate. Some tuk-tuk drivers are subsidized by factories, so will take you to see silver, silk, enamel factories for about ฿20 each, with no obligation to buy.

Antiques: beware of fakes. There are a number of shops in Tha Phae Rd and opp the *Rincome Hotel* in the Nantawan Arcade. Another good road to wander along is Loi Kroa which supports a large number of antique and hilltribe handicraft shops. ***Oriental Spirit***, 28 Rachmanka Rd; ***Mungkala Antiques***, Rachmanka Rd (by Soi 3), run by a friendly woman, some handicrafts plus old pieces – specializes in Chinese antiques; ***Under the Bô***, Rachmanka Rd (nr intersection with Rachpakinai Rd), good collection of pieces, especially wood carvings, incl old looms, *galae* and *nagas*; ***Antique House***, 71 Charoen Prathet Rd; ***Oriental Style***, 36 Charoenrat Rd, rec; ***Banmai***, 37/5 Charoenmuang Rd (see below for suppliers outside Chiang Mai).

Books and maps: *Nancy Chandler* and *DK Maps* are both good sources of information on Chiang Mai; ***Welcome to Chiang Mai & Chiang Rai***, is the best magazine on the market with information on what's on, where to go, Thai customs, Thai culture and the environment; ***DK Bookstore***, Kotchasarn Rd; ***Suriwong Book Centre***, 54/1-5 Sri Donchai Rd (most extensive collection of books in English on Thailand in Chiang Mai); ***Book Exchange***, 21/1 Soi 2 Rachmanka, books bought and sold, guidebooks and maps available.

Ceramics: 6 km N of Chiang Mai on the Mae Rim Rd, factory producing Thai Celadon, modelled on Sawankhalok pottery; ***Mengrai Kilns***, 31/1 Ratuthit Rd, 2 km SE of Nawarat Bridge. Open 0800-1700 Mon-Sun; ***Suan Buak Haad*** in the SW corner of the city on Aruk Rd has a good selection of rustic pottery, large tongs and baskets; ***Naiyana***, 283-286 Chang Moi Rd for large pottery tongs.

Clothing: huge assortment of T-shirts, cotton clothing and tribal clothing in the 3 Night Markets on Chang Klan Rd.

Furniture: see **Woodcarving and furniture**.

Handicrafts: Chiang Mai is the centre for hilltribe handicrafts. There is a bewildering array of goods, much of which is of poor quality. Bargain for everything. ***Co-op Handicraft***, next to *Thai Farmer's Bank* on Tha Phae Rd; ***Hilltribe Products Foundation***, next to *Wat Suan Dok* on Suthep Rd; ***Thai Tribal Crafts***, 208 Bumrungrat Rd, nr McCormick Hospital – run by Karen and Lahu church organizations on a non-profit basis, good selection, quality and prices. The ***night market*** on Chang Klan Rd also has a lot on offer, although generally of poor quality; better pieces can be found at the more exclusive shops on Loi Kroa Rd.

Honey: good range of local honeys from ***Bees Knees***, 17 Chang Klan Rd.

Jewellery: ***Shiraz Co***, 170 Tha Phae Rd.

Lacework: ***Sarapee Handmade Lace***, 2 Rachwithi Rd, claims to be the only workshop in SE Asia using silk thread.

Lacquerware: ***Vichaikul***, nr *Wat Nantharam*; ***Masusook Antiques***, 263/2-3 Tha Phae Rd.

Paper: ***Mountain Products***, 252 Nimanhaemin Rd Soi 6, for Sa Paper, a local handmade paper, made from the bark of the Sa tree.

Rattanware: ***Hang Dong Rattan***, Loi Kroa Rd (nr intersection with Kampaeng Din Rd), high quality rattan products.

Silverwork: hilltribe jewellery particularly. Wualai Rd to the S of the city, and the roads roundabout have the biggest concentration of shops; ***Charoen Panich***, 244-248 Tha Phae Rd has a selection; ***Siam Silver Ware***, 5 Wualai Soi 3; ***Sipsong Panna***, 95/19 Nimanhaemin Rd, opp *Rincome Hotel*, selection of Thai, Lao and Burmese silverware; ***Narinthip Tour***, 59/3 Loi Kroa Rd, for silver and hilltribe silver; ***Tada Silverware*** on Huay Kaew Rd; ***Lanna House***, Mae Rim, Samoeng Rd, Km 4.5 (just beyond Shell petrol station).

Supermarkets/department stores: ***Rimping Superstore***, Lamphun Rd and 171 Chotana Rd, ***7 Eleven stores*** on Huay Kaew, Chotana and Chang Klan rds. The largest department store is the ***Central Department Store*** supermarket in the ***Kad Suan Kaew*** shopping complex on Huay Kaew Rd, not far from the *Chiang Mai Orchid Hotel*. ***Tantraphan Airport Plaza***, at the intersection of Hang Dong Rd and the Ring Rd, good selection of Western food, clothing and household goods.

Tailors: ***Far Mee***, 66 Square U Pakut, Tha Phae Rd; many of the stalls in and around Warorot Market will make up clothes.

Terracotta: plaques, murals, statues, pots at ***Ban Phor Liang Meun***, 36 Phra Pokklao Rd, a factory showroom.

Textiles: ***Pothong House***, 4 Moon Muang Soi 5 for Khmer, Lao and hilltribe fabrics; ***Chatraporn***, 194 Tha Phae Rd, for silks, cotton and made-up garments; ***Shinawatra Silk***, Huay Kaew Rd (opp the *Chiang Mai Orchid Hotel*); ***Studio Naenna***, 138/8 Soi Changkhian, Huay Kaew Rd, T 226042, handwoven cloth, made up; ***Le Bombyx***, 3 km out of town on the San Kampaeng Rd, ready to wear and made to measure silk and cotton clothing; ***Folk Art***, 326 Tha Phae Rd for textiles, *matmii*, handwoven cotton.

Woodcarving and furniture: ***Banyen***, 201/1 Wualai Rd, just to the S of the Superhighway on road 108. Wholesale furniture suppliers can be found off the roads to Hang Dong and also en route to Bor Sang, although much may not be to Western tastes. Also furniture available, including custom-made pieces, from *Chiangmai Sudaluck*, 99/9 Chiang Mai-San Kamphaeng Rd. *Lanna House*, Km 4.5, Mae Rim-Samoeng Rd (just beyond Shell petrol station).

Outside Chiang Mai: travelling E on Route 1006, towards San Kampaeng, there is a ribbon of shops, (often with factories and display rooms attached) selling umbrellas (at Bor Sang), jewellery, handicrafts, lacquerware, woodcarvings, 'antiques', cotton and silk (at San Kampaeng, 15 km), ceramics. The Umbrella Fair, in Jan, has a colourful display of every size and shape of umbrella. *Getting there*: bus from N side of Charoen Muang Rd (฿4). **Hang Dong** is a basket area S of town on Route 108. *Getting there*: buses leave from Chiang Mai Gate. **Pasang** is a cotton-weavers village, 36 km S of the city on Route 108. *Getting there*: buses leave from E side of Charoenrat Rd, nr the TAT office, ฿5.

● Sports

Latest information on sports listed in most free newspapers and newsletters, available from many shops, hotels and guesthouses.

Club House Inn Chiang Mai Sports Club, Km 10 Mae Rim Rd (Rt 107), large pool, tennis, squash, badminton, gym, aerobics.

Fitness park: *Huay Kaew Fitness Park* is on Huay Kaew Rd at the bottom of Doi Suthep nr the zoo. *Hillside Fitness Centre*, 4th Flr, Hillside Plaza 4, Huay Kaew Rd, T 225984, fitness centre, sauna and herbal steam rooms, beauty treatment.

Go-kart racing: *Chiang Mai Speedway*, 8 km out of town on Route 108, racing every Sat and Sun afternoons, open Mon-Sun; *Chiang Mai Gokart*, San Kampaeng Rd, nr Bor Sang intersection.

Golf: *Lanna Public Golf Course*, Chotana Rd (at Nong Bua, 4 km N of the city). Green fee ฿400, ฿600 at weekends, club hire ฿250. Open 0600-1800. There is also a driving range here. *Gymkhana Club*, Chiangmai-Lamphun Rd, 9 hole course, green fees ฿100 weekdays, ฿400 weekends; *Chiang Mai Golf Driving Range* opp *Banyen*, where Route 108 meets the superhighway; *Mae Sa Resort*, km 3, Mae Sa Waterfall Rd, T 222203; *Green Valley Golf Club*, green fees ฿500 weekdays, ฿1,500 weekends.

Hash House Harriers: hashes are fortnightly, Sat evening for men and women, Mon evening for men. Contact either David or Martin on T 278503, or John on T 271950, or the *Domino Bar*, T 278503.

Horse racing: next to the *Lanna Public Golf Course*, Chotana Rd (4 km N of the city), races every Sun from 1200-1730.

Horse Riding: *Lanna Sports Centre*, Chotana Rd (N of town), ฿250/hr, call Janet on T 217956 for details. *The Chiang Mai Sports Club* on the Chiang Mai-Mae Rim Rd (T 298327) also offers riding (see the entry in Accommodation under 'Outside the city'). *The Army Horseriding Club*, Km 10 Mae Rim Rd, the hourly rate is a very competitive ฿100 but not much English spoken.

Squash: *Gymkana Club*, Chiang Mai-Lamphun Rd, T 247352, every Thur 1730.

Swimming: *Amari Rincome Hotel*, Huay Kaew Rd, ฿60; *Top North Guesthouse*, 15 Moon Muang Rd Soi 2, ฿50; *Anodard Hotel*, 57 Rachmanka Rd; *Padungsilpa Sports Club*, Rasada Rd, large pool, clean with snack bar, open 0830-2030; *Pang Suan Kaew Hotel* on Huay Kaew Rd – large pool. Numerous others; public pools listed in most free magazines.

Tennis: Fees are about ฿100/hr; rackets for hire. *Amari Rincome Hotel*, Huay Kaew Rd. *Anantasiri Courts*, Superhighway, (nr the National Museum). *Kaeo Kasem Courts*, Canal Rd (off Huay Kaew Rd), not far from the strawberry fields. *Padungsilpa Sports Club*, Rasada Rd (฿40/hr, ฿80/hr under floodlights).

Yoga: *Khun Wai*, Huay Kaew Rd, Mon-Sat 0800-1800, ฿100/hour.

● Tour companies & travel agents

There are numerous travel agents along Tha Phae, Chang Klan and Moon Muang (in the vicinity of Tha Phae Gate) rds, most of whom will offer tours and treks over the N. They will also book air, train and bus tickets out of Chiang Mai. **NB** The TAT recommend that services should only be bought from companies that register with the tourist Business and Guide Registration Office; they provide a list of all such companies. As noted in the trekking section (see page 325) we have decided not to list or recommend companies because standards vary between treks (and guides) within individual outfits and because standards change rapidly. Word of mouth is the best guarantee. **Visas**: can be arranged in Chiang Mai for Laos, Myanmar (Burma), Vietnam and Cambodia. There are direct flights to Mandalay and Yangon (Rangoon) in Myanmar and to Vientiane in Laos.

● **Tourist offices**

TAT, 105/1 Chiang Mai-Lamphun Rd, T 248604, F 248605 (open 0830-1630 Mon-Sun). Helpful and informative, with a good range of maps and leaflets, including information on guesthouses and guidelines for trekking. Areas of responsibility are Chiang Mai, Lamphun, Lampang and Mae Hong Son. **Chiang Mai Municipal Tourist Information Centre** corner of Tha Phae and Charoen Prathet rds. The only one of its type in Thailand, good maps and some other handouts, but not yet up to TAT standard and at our last visit at the end of 1996 distinctly unenthusiastic. Open Mon-Fri 0830-1200, 1300-1630. In addition to these tourist information offices, there are also a number of free tourist-oriented magazines, namely: *Trip Info*, *Chiang Mai This Week*, *Le Journal* (in French), *Guidelines Chiang Mai*, *Chiang Mai Newsletter* and *Welcome to Chiang Mai and Chiang Rai*. These are regularly updated and, although not very selective or critical, have good maps. The *Chiang Mai Newsletter* has the most informed articles.

● **Useful addresses**

Fire Emergency: T 199.

Immigration: Fang Rd, 300m before the entrance to the airport, T 277510. Open Mon-Fri 0830-1200, 1300-1630 (visa extensions possible, see page 340).

Police Main Police station: corner of Phra Singh and Jhaban rds. **Police Emergency**: T 191. **Tourist Police**: in the same building as the TAT office on the Chiang Mai-Lamphon Rd, T 248974, at the Arcade Bus Station, the Night Market and at the airport.

NB Chiang Mai's several local English newsletters have useful community services pages, listing such things as yoga classes, women's groups, Alcoholics Anonymous meetings, and meditation sessions.

● **Transport**

697 km from Bangkok.

Local Bicycle hire: from Chang Phuak Gate and at the S end of Moon Muang Rd, ฿20-60/day, or on Nakhon Ping Bridge, plus some guesthouses (eg *Chiang Mai Holiday Guesthouse*) and from *Fame Tree* at the intersection of Rachwithi and Moon Muang rds. A deposit of ฿500 or your passport will probably be required. Mountain bikes should be locked up and always tie your bag to the basket. **Bus**: ฿3-5 (the latter is for a/c) anywhere in town (the bus routes are given in Nancy Chandler's Map of Chiang Mai). **Car or jeep hire**: there are numerous places to hire vehicles and motorbikes and rates start at ฿800-1500/day, ฿6000/week. Many guesthouses will arrange rental or there are many outfits along Chaiyaphum and Moon Muang rds. **Hertz** and **Avis** are slightly more expensive, but are more reliable. **Hertz**, 90 Sri Donchai Rd (main office – next to *Chiang Mai Plaza Hotel*), T 279474, 12/3 Loi Kroa Rd, T 279473, *Novotel Suriwongse Hotel*, T 270058 and *Chiang Mai Plaza*, T 270040; **Avis**, 14/14 Huay Kaew Rd (opp *Chiang Mai Orchid Hotel*), T 21316, *Royal Princess Hotel*, T 281033 or the airport, T 222013. **SMT Rent-a-car**, *Amari Rincome Hotel*, 301 Huay Kaew Rd, T 221044, F 210118. **North Wheels** 127/2 Moon Muang Rd, T 216189, seems reliable. There are plenty of others, but check insurance cover and the car before setting off. It is even possible to hire a self-drive tuk-tuk from **PC Service**, 56 Chaiyaphum Rd. **Motorbike hire**: along Chaiyuphum and Moon Muang rds and at many guesthouses. Rates start at around ฿120 for a Honda Dream. Insurance is not available for small motorbikes, eg ***Ladda Motorcycle Rental***, Moon Muang Soi 2 (at the *Panda Guest House*); ***POP***, 51 Kotchasan Rd, T 276014, ฿250 for 24 hrs. **NB** At the end of Jun 1995 the wearing of helmets in Chiang Mai city became mandatory. Some places include a helmet in the rental rate; others charge an additional fee; still others don't have helmets at all. **Saamlor**: ฿5-10 within city, ฿20 for longer distances. **Sii-lor** ('four wheels'): these converted red pick-ups are known as songthaews ('two rows') in most other towns, but in Chiang Mai they are usually referred to as sii-lors. They are the most common means of transport around town. Travelling on regular routes costs ฿5, ฿10 if you want them to take you somewhere off their route. Before boarding, tell the driver where you want to go and he will either say 'yes' or, if it's not on his route, he will quote you a price for the trip. Use landmarks (such as hotels, bridges, gates etc) rather than street names as a guide for where you want to go. **Tuk-tuk**: minimum ฿20/trip, ฿30-40 for longer journeys.

Air The airport is 3 km SW of town. It contains a bank (currency exchange vans also park outside the terminal building), post office, Avis rent a car counter, tourist information counter, hotels counter, and snack bar. Regular connections on **Thai** with Bangkok, 1 hr. Also flights to Chiang Rai 40 mins, Mae Hong Son 30 mins,

Nan 45 mins, Mae Sot 50 mins, Phuket 2 hrs, Phitsanulok 35 mins and Khon Kaen 1 hr 25 mins. **Bangkok Airways** also operate a service to Bangkok and Sukhothai, with connections on to Koh Samui. A new airline is **Orient Express Air** which is competitively priced and flies to Surat Thani, Khon Kaen, Udon Thani, Ubon Ratchatani and Hat Yai. **International air connections** with Hong Kong, Singapore, Pagan and Mandalay in Myanmar (Burma); Kunming in S China; and Vientiane in Laos (twice a week). Lao Aviation, Air Mandalay, Silk Air and Malaysian Airlines all serve Chiang Mai. **Transport to town**: taxis to town cost ฿80 (fixed price from the taxi booking counter). Thai Airways operate a shuttle bus service between the airport and their office in town (but you can get off anywhere in town), ฿40. **Airport information**: T 270222.

Train Station is in the E of the town, on Charoen Muang Rd, across the Ping River, ticket office open 0530-2100. Left luggage 0600-1800, ฿5/bag for first 5 days, ฿10/bag from then on. Regular connections with Bangkok's Hualamphong station and towns along the route, 11-15 hrs. The overnight express train leaves Bangkok at 1800 (13½ hrs), the Special express leaves at 1940 (12 hrs).

Road Bus: the long distance bus station or Bor Kor Sor (BKS) is at the **Chiang Mai Arcade**, on the corner of the super highway and Kaew Nawarat rds, NE of town, T 242664. Most companies will provide a transfer service to the station: pick-up points are Anusarn Market, Narawat Bridge, Sang Tawan Cinema and Chiang Inn Hotel Lane. Tuk-tuks and siilors wait at the station to take passengers into town. There is an information desk within the main terminal building with information on all departure times and prices. The tourist police also have a desk here. Regular connections with Bangkok's Northern bus terminal 9-12 hrs, Phitsanulok 6 hrs, Sukhothai 5 hrs, Chiang Rai 3-4 hrs, Mae Sariang 4-5 hrs, Mae Hong Son 8-9 hrs, Pai 4 hrs, Nan 6 hrs and other Northern towns. A number of tour companies organize coaches to the capital; these are concentrated in the **Anusarn market** area and usually provide transport to the Arcade terminal, from where the buses depart. Buses to closer destinations (such as Mae Rim, Phrao, Chiang Dao, Fang, Thaton, Bor Sang, San Kampeang, Lamphun and Pasang) go from Chotana Rd, N of Chang Puak Gate.

THAILAND – INFORMATION FOR TRAVELLERS

BEFORE TRAVELLING

ENTRY REQUIREMENTS

● Visas

All tourists must possess passports valid for at least 6 months longer than their intended stay in Thailand.

30 day visa exemptions No visa is required for tourists arriving by air, holding a confirmed onward air ticket and who intend to stay for up to 30 days (not extendable). (Until 1995 tourists were only permitted to stay for 14 days.) Visitors are fined ฿100/day each day they exceed the 30 day limit. The same applies to tourists who arrive via the Thai-Malaysian border by sea, rail or road. This applies to nationals of the following countries: Algeria, Argentina, Australia, Austria, Bahrain, Belgium, Brazil, Brunei, Canada, Denmark, Djibouti, Egypt, Fiji, Finland, France, Germany, Greece, Iceland, Indonesia, Ireland, Israel, Italy, Japan, Kenya, Kuwait, Luxembourg, Malaysia, Mauritania, Mexico, Morocco, Myanmar (Burma), Netherlands, New Zealand, Oman, Papua New Guinea, Philippines, Portugal, Qatar, Republic of Korea, Saudi Arabia, Senegal, Singapore, Slovenia, South Africa, Spain, Sweden, Switzerland, Tunisia, Turkey, UAE, UK, USA, Vanuatu, Western Samoa, Yemen. Malaysian nationals arriving by road from Malaysia do not need evidence of onward journey.

Visas on arrival There is now a new visa booth at Don Muang (Bangkok) Airport itself, at customs control. Visitors without visas can have one issued here and there is even a photo booth to provide passport snaps (one photograph required). However, the desk only provides tourist visas valid for 15 days (฿300), which nationals of many countries do not require in any case (see above). The facility is only useful for nationals of those countries which are not exempted from having an entry visa. These number 76 in total. Applicants must also have an outbound (return) ticket. There are similar desks at Chiang Mai, Phuket and Hat Yai airports.

3 month visa exemptions Nationals from South Korea, New Zealand, Sweden, Denmark, Norway and Finland visiting as a tourist do not require a visa for visits of up to 3 months, and those from Hong Kong for a visit of up to 15 days.

Tourist visas These are valid for 90 days from date of entry (single entry); **transit visas** for 30 days (single entry). **Visa extensions** are obtainable from the Immigration Department in Bangkok (see below) for ฿500. The process used to be interminable, but the system is now much improved and relatively painless. Extensions can also be issued in other towns, such as Koh Samui and Chiang Mai. Applicants must bring two photocopies of their passport ID page and the page on which their tourist visa is stamped, together with three passport photographs. It is also advisable to dress neatly. It may be easier to leave the country and then re-enter having obtained a new tourist visa. Visas are issued by all Thai embassies and consulates.

Passport control at Don Muang Airport during peak arrival periods (usually 1200-1400) can be choked with visitors – be prepared for a wait of an hour or more before reaching the arrivals hall.

90-day non-immigrant visas These are also issued and can be obtained in the applicant's home country (about US$30). A letter from the applicant's company or organization guaranteeing their repatriation should be submitted at the same time.

In the UK there is now a visa information line, operating 24 hrs a day, T 01891 600 150.

● Procedure for lost or stolen passport

1. File a report with the local police.

2. Take the report to your local embassy or consulate and apply for a new travel document or passport. (If there is no representation, visit the Passport Division of the Ministry of Foreign Affairs.)

3. Take the new passport plus the police report to Section 4, Subdivision 4, Immigration Bureau, room 311 (3rd floor), Old Building, Soi Suan Plu, Sathorn Tai Rd, Bangkok, T 2873911, for a new visa stamp.

● Immigration Department

Soi Suan Plu, Thanon Sathorn Tai, Bangkok 10120, T 2873101. Open: 0930-1630 Mon-Fri, 0830-1200 Sat (tourists only).

● Vaccinations

No vaccinations required, unless coming from an infected area (if visitors have been in a yellow fever infected area in the 10 days before arrival, and do not have a vaccination certificate, they will be vaccinated and kept in quarantine for 6 days, or deported. See health section below for details.

● Representation overseas

Australia, 111 Empire Circuit, Yarralumla, Canberra, ACT 2600, T (06) 2731149, 2732937; **Austria**, Weimarer Strasse 68, 1180 Vienna, T (0222) 3103423; **Belgium**, Square du Val de la Cambre 2, 1050 Brussels, T 2 6406810; **Canada**, 180 Island Park Drive, Ottawa, Ontario, K1Y 0A2, T (613) 722 4444; **Denmark**, Norgesmindevej 18, 2900 Hellerup, Copenhagen, T (31) 6250101; **France**, 8 Rue Greuze, 75116 Paris, T 47043222; **Germany**, Uberstrasse 65, 5300 Bonn 2, T (0228) 355065; **Italy**, Via Nomentana, 132, 00162 Rome, T (396) 8320729; **Japan**, 3-14-6, Kami-Osaki, Shinagawa-ku, Tokyo 141, T (03) 3441-1386; **Laos**, Route Phonekheng, PO Box 128, Vientiane, T 2508; **Malaysia**, 206 Jl Ampang, 50450 Kuala Lumpur, T (03) 2488222; **Myanmar**, 91, Pyay Rd, Rangoon, T 21713; **Nepal**, Jyoti Kendra Building, Thapathali, PO Box 3333, Kathmandu, T 213910; **Netherlands**, 1 Buitenrustweg, 2517 KD, The Hague, T (070) 3452088; **New Zealand**, 2 Cook St, PO Box 17-226, Karori, T 768618; **Norway**, Munkedamsveien 59B, 0270 Oslo 2, T (02) 832517-8; **Spain**, Calle del Segre, 29, 20 A, 28002 Madrid, T (341) 5632903; **Sweden**, Sandhamnsgatan 36 (5th Floor), PO Box 27065, 10251 Stockholm, T (08) 6672160; **Switzerland**, Eigerstrasse 60 (3rd Floor), 3007 Bern, T (031) 462281; **UK**, 29-30 Queens Gate, London, SW7 5JB, T 0171 589 0173; **USA**, 2300 Kalorama Rd NW, Washington, DC 20008, T (202) 4837200.

HEALTH

Vaccinations: no vaccinations are required, but cholera immunization and a tetanus booster are advisable. A gamma globulin injection (against hepatitis) is also recommended. There is a vaccination clinic in the Science Division of the Thai Red Cross Society, at the corner of Rama IV and Henri Dunant rds, Bangkok, T 2520161.

● Medical facilities

For full listing of hospitals, check the Yellow Pages, or listings under Useful addresses in each town. Hospitals in Bangkok are of a reasonable (Western) standard.

● Food and water

Tap water is not recommended for drinking.

Cut fruit or uncooked vegetables from roadside stalls may not always be clean.

● Travelling with children

(For more information and a check-list, see the Rounding Up section.) Disposable nappies are now widely available in Thailand, although they are expensive. Powdered milks and a good range of powdered foods are on sale in most supermarkets. Bottled water is available everywhere. Fruit is a good source of nutrition and is also widely available. Anti-malarials are recommended (quarter to half dosage by some doctors) if travelling outside the main cities and tourist destinations although opinions – as on most issues connected with malaria – seem to differ. Check with your doctor or telephone your country's centre for tropical diseases.

MONEY

● ATMs (cash dispensers)

American Express can be used at Bangkok Bank, JCB at Siam Commercial Bank, Master Card at Siam Commercial, Visa at Bangkok Bank.

● Credit cards

Major credit cards such as American Express, Visa, Diners Club, Carte Blanche, Master Charge/Access are accepted in leading hotels, restaurants, department stores and several large stores for tourists. Visitors may have some problems upcountry where the use of credit cards is less common. Generally, Visa and Mastercard are more widely accepted than American Express; the Bangkok Bank takes Amex, but several banks accept Visa and Mastercard. Amex's higher commission also puts off many shopkeepers. **Notification of credit card loss**: American Express, IBM Bldg, Phahonyothin Rd, T 2730022; Diners Club, Dusit Thani Bldg, Rama IV Rd, T 2332645, 2335775; JCB T 2561361, 2561351; Visa and Master Card, Thai Farmers Bank Bldg, Phahonyothin Rd, T 2701801-10.

Exchange rates: Jan 1997

Currency	Baht
US$	25
£	41
DM	16
¥	0.23
Malaysian $	10
Singapore $	18
Hong Kong $	3.3
Swiss Franc	19
Dutch Guilder	15
French Franc	4.8
Lire	0.016
Australian $	20
New Zealand $	18

● Cost of living

Visitors staying in first class hotels and eating in hotel restaurants will probably spend a minimum of ฿1500/day. Tourists staying in cheaper air-conditioned accommodation, and eating in local restaurants will probably spend about ฿500-750/day. A backpacker, staying in fan-cooled guesthouses and eating cheaply, might expect to be able to live on ฿200/day. In Bangkok, expect to pay 20-30% more.

● Currency

The unit of Thai currency is the **baht** (฿), which is divided into 100 **satang**. Notes in circulation include ฿20 (green), ฿50 (blue), ฿100 (red), ฿500 (purple) and new ฿1,000 (orange and grey). Coins include 25 satang and 50 satang, and ฿1, ฿5, and ฿10. The two smaller coins are gradually disappearing from circulation and the 25 satang coin, equivalent to the princely sum of US$0.001 (1 cent), is rare.

● Exchange rates

It is best to change money at banks or money changers which give better rates than hotels. First class hotels have 24 hrs money changers. There is a charge of ฿13/cheque when changing TCs (passport required). Indonesian Rupiah and Nepalese Rupees cannot be exchanged for Thai currency.

GETTING THERE

AIR

The majority of visitors arrive in Thailand through Bangkok's Don Muang airport. There are also international chartered flights to Chiang Mai in the N and to Phuket in the S (see below). More than 35 airlines and charter companies fly to Bangkok, and Thailand is easily accessible from Europe, North America, Australasia and the Middle East as well as from other Asian countries. **Thai International** is the national airline.

● Links with Indochina and Myanmar (Burma)

Bangkok is a transport hub for air connections with Phnom Penh, Yangon – (Rangoon, Myanmar/Burma), Vientiane (Laos), and Hanoi and Ho Chi Minh City/Saigon (Vietnam). Partly as a result it also has a concentration of tour companies specializing in Indochina/Myanmar and is a good place to arrange a visa.

TRAIN

Regular rail services link Singapore and Bangkok, via Kuala Lumpur, Butterworth and the major southern Thai towns. Express a/c trains take two days from Singapore, 34 hrs from Kuala Lumpur, 24 hrs from Butterworth (opp Penang). The *Magic Arrow Express* leaves Singapore on Sun, Tues and Thur, Bangkok-Singapore (฿899-1,965), Bangkok-Kuala Lumpur (฿659-1,432) and to Ipoh (฿530-1,145). An additional train from Butterworth departs at 1340, arriving Bangkok 0835 the next day. The train from Bangkok to Butterworth departs 1515, arriving Butterworth 1225 (฿457-1,147). All tickets should be booked in advance. The most luxurious way to journey by train to Thailand is aboard the *Eastern & Oriental (E&O) Express*. The a/c train of 22 carriages including a salon car, dining car, bar and observation deck and carrying just 132 passengers runs once a week from Singapore to Bangkok and back. Luxurious carriages, fine wines and food designed for European rather than Asian sensibilities make this not just a mode of transport but an experience. The journey takes 43 hrs with stops in Kuala Lumpur, Butterworth and Padang Besar. But such luxury is expensive: US$1,130-2,950. For information call Bangkok 2514862; London (0171) 9286000; US (800) 5242420; Singapore (065) 2272068.

ROAD

The main road access is to and from Malaysia. The principal land border crossings into Malaysia are nr Betong in Yala Province and from Sungei Golok in Narathiwat Province. In Apr 1994 the Friendship Bridge linking Nong Khai with Laos opened – and became the first bridge across the Mekong River. To cross into Laos here foreigners need to obtain a visa in Bangkok – although a consulate is due to open in Nong Khai.

BOAT

No regular, scheduled cruise liners sail to Thailand any longer but it is sometimes possible to enter Thailand on a freighter, arriving at Khlong Toey Port. The *Bangkok Post* publishes a weekly shipping post with details on ships leaving the kingdom.

CUSTOMS

● Duty free allowance

250 gr of cigars or cigarettes (or 200 cigarettes) and 1 litre of wine or spirits. One still camera with five rolls of film or one movie camera with three rolls of 8mm or 16mm film.

● Currency regulations

Non-residents can bring in up to ฿2,000 pp and unlimited foreign currency although amounts exceeding US$10,000 must be declared. Maximum amount permitted to take out of the country is ฿50,000 pp.

● Prohibited items

All narcotics; obscene literature, pornography; fire arms (except with a permit from the Police Department or local registration office).

Some species of plants and animals are prohibited, for more information contact the Royal Forestry Department, Phahonyothin Rd, Bangkok, T 5792776. Permission of entry for animals by air is obtainable at the airport. An application must be made to the Department of Livestock Development, Bangkok, T 2515136 for entry by sea. Vaccination certificates are required; dogs and cats need rabies certificates.

ON ARRIVAL

● Airport information

Don Muang airport lies 25 km N of Bangkok. There are two international terminals (adjoining one another) and one domestic terminal. Terminal 1 serves Asia, and Terminal 2 the rest of the world. A 0.5 km-long covered walkway links the domestic and international terminals. Facilities include: banks and currency exchange, post office, left luggage (฿20/item/day – max 4 months), hotel booking agency, airport information, airport clinic, lost and found baggage service, duty-free shops, restaurants and bars including a whole slate of newly-opened fast food outlets – Burger King, Svensson's, Pizza Hut and Upper Crust. **NB** Food is expensive here – cheap food is available across the footbridge at the railway station. The *Airport Hotel* is linked to the international terminal by a walkway. It provides a 'ministay' service for passengers who wish to 'freshen-up' and take a room for up to 3 hrs between 0800 and 1800 (฿400 T 5661020/1). **International flight information**: T 5351386 for departures, T 5351301 for arrivals. **Domestic flight information**: T 5351253. The new domestic terminal has a hotel booking counter, post office, currency exchange counters, restaurant and bookshop. An elevated a/c walkway connects the international and domestic terminals; a shuttle bus is sometimes available, beware – taxis grossly overcharge for a drive of under 1 km.

Airport accommodation: **A** *Amari Airport*, 333 Chert Wudthakas Rd, T 5661020, F 5661941, a/c, restaurants, pool, connected to airport by foot-bridge; rooms look onto attractive gardens, useful hotel for transit passengersm short-term stays for wash and rest available; **A** *Rama Gardens*, 9/9 Vibhavadi Rangsit Rd, Bangkaen (7 km from the airport), T 561002, F 5611025, a/c, restaurants, two attractive, large pools, out of town on road to airport, inconvenient for most except those merely stopping-over for a few hours, but spacious grounds with fitness centre, tennis, squash, golf, putting.

Transport to town **By taxi**: official taxi booking service in the arrivals hall. There are two desks. One for the more expensive official airport taxis (newer, more luxurious vehicles); one for public taxis. The former cost ฿400 downtown; ฿300 to the northern bus terminal; ฿450 to the southern bus terminal; ฿1,500 to Pattaya. Note that airport flunkies sometimes try to direct passengers to this more expensive 'limousine' service: walk through the barriers to the public taxi desk. A public taxi to downtown should cost about half these prices – roughly ฿150-200 with ฿50 extra if using the new elevated expressway. Note that there are both metered and unmetered public taxis; the fare for the latter will be quoted when you state your destination at the desk. If taking a metered taxi, the coupon from the booking desk will quote no fare – ensure that the meter is used or you may find that the trip costs ฿300 instead of ฿200, keep hold of your coupon – some taxi drivers try to pocket it – as it details the obligations of taxi drivers. **Warning** There have been cases of visitors being robbed in unofficial taxis. To tell whether your vehicle is a registered taxi, check the colour of the number plate. Official aiport limousines have green plates, public taxis have yellow plates – and a white plate means the vehicle is not registered as a taxi. The sedan service into town costs ฿500-650. Cars are newer, more comfortable and better maintained than the average city taxi. It takes 30 mins to 1 hr to central Bangkok, depending on the time of day and the state of the traffic. The new elevated expressway reduces journey time to 20 mins – ask the taxi driver to take this route if you wish to save time but note that there is a toll fee – ฿20 and ฿30 for the two sections of this elevated road. Also note that there have been some complaints about taxi drivers at the domestic terminal forming a cartel, refusing to use their meters and charging a fixed rate considerably above the meter rate.

By bus: until 1996 buses were the cheapest but also the slowest way into town. But in Apr a new a/c airport bus service was introduced – ฿70 to Silom Rd (service A1), Sanaam Luang (service A2) (most convenient for Khaosan road guesthouses) and Phra Khanong (service A3). The service operates every 15 mins, 0500 2300. **Stops are as follows**: **Silom service (A1)**: Don Muang Tollway, Din Daeng, Pratunam, Lumpini Park, Silom. **Sanaam Luang service (A2)**: Don Muang Tollway, Din Daeng, Victory Monument, Phayathai, Phetburi, Lan Luang, Democracy Monument, Sanaam Luang. **Phra Khanong service (A3)**: Don Muang Tollway, Din Daeng, Sukhumit, Ekamai, Phra Khanong. While hotel stops are: **Silom service (A1)**: *Century, Indra, Anoma, Grand*

Arranging visas for Myanmar and Indochina

	LENGTH OF VISA	WORKING DAYS TO ARRANGE	COST
Myanmar (Burma)	4 weeks	2 days	฿300-500
Vietnam	4 weeks	4 days	฿1,100-1,300
Laos	2 weeks	7 days	฿1,300-1,600
Cambodia	4 weeks	7 days	฿500-800

NB Above details were collected in Oct 1996. With easing of travel restrictions, the advantages of paying for a tour company to arrange a visa to Myanmar or Indochina are becoming less.

Hyatt, *Erawan*, *Regent*, *Dusit Thani*, and *Narai* hotels. **Sanaam Luang service (A2)**: Victory Monument, *Siam City Hotel*, Soi King Phet, Saphan Khao, *Majestic* and *Rattanakosin* hotels. **Phra Khanong service (A3)**: Amari Building, *Ambassador* and *Delta Grand Pacific* hotels, Bang Chan Glass House, *Novotel*, Soi Ekkamai (Sukhumuit). **NB** Return buses have slightly different stops.

Although many visitors will see ฿70 as money well spent there will still be the hardened few who will opt for the regular bus service, which is just as cheap and slow as it ever was, 1½-3 hrs (depending on time of day) (฿7-15). The bus stop is 50m N of the arrivals hall. Buses are crowded during rush-hours and there is little room for luggage. Bus 59 goes to Khaosan Rd, bus 29 goes to Bangkok's Hualamphong railway station, via the Northern bus terminal and Siam Square. A/c bus 10 goes to Samsen Rd and Silom Rd via the Northern bus terminal, a/c bus 4 goes to Silom Rd, a/c bus 13 goes to Sukhumvit Rd and the Eastern bus terminal, a/c bus 29 goes to the Northern bus terminal, Siam Square and Hualamphong railway station. **By minibus**: ฿100 to major hotels, ฿60 shuttle bus to the *Asia Hotel* on Phayathai Rd. ฿50-80 to Khaosan Rd, depending on the time of day. Direct buses to Pattaya at 0900, 1200 and 1700, ฿180. **By train**: the station is on the other side of the N-S highway from the airport. Regular trains into Bangkok's Hualamphong station, ฿5 for ordinary train, 3rd clas (the cheapest option). But only 6 ordinary trains per day. For 'rapid' and 'express' a supplementary charge of ฿20-50 is levied. The State Railways of Thailand runs an 'Airport Express' 5 times a day (but not on Sat and Sun), with a/c shuttle bus from Don Muang station to airport terminal, 35 mins (฿100). **Hotel pick-up services**: many of the more expensive hotels operate airport pick-up services if informed of your arrival ahead of time.

● Airport tax

Payable on departure – ฿250 for international flights, ฿30 for domestic flights.

● Clothing

In towns and at religious sights, it is courteous to avoid wearing shorts and singlets (or sleeveless shirts). Visitors who are inappropriately dressed may not be allowed into temples. Thais always look neat and clean. *Mai rieb-roi* means 'not neat' and is considered a great insult. Beach resorts are a law unto themselves – casual clothes are the norm, although nudity is still very much frowned upon by Thais. In the most expensive restaurants in Bangkok diners may well be expected to wear a jacket and tie.

● Conduct

Thais are generally very understanding of the foibles and habits of foreigners (*farangs*) and will forgive and forget most indiscretions. However, there are a number of 'dos and don'ts' which are worth observing:

Common greeting *Wai*: hands are held together as if in prayer, and the higher the wai, the more respectful the greeting. By watching Thai's wai it is possible to ascertain their relative seniority. Again, foreigners are not expected to conform to this custom – a simple wai at chest to chin height is all that is required. When *farangs* and Thais do business it is common to shake hands.

Heads, heart and feet Try not to openly point your feet at anyone – feet are viewed as spiritually the lowest part of the body. At the same time, never touch anyone's head which is the holiest, as well as the highest, part. Among Thais, the personal characteristic of ***jai yen*** is very highly regarded; literally, this means to have a 'cool heart'. It embodies calmness, having an even temper and not displaying emotion. Although foreigners generally receive special dispensation, and are not expected to conform to Thai customs (all *farang* are thought to have 'hot hearts'), it is important to try and keep calm in any disagreement – losing one's temper leads to loss of face and subsequent loss of respect.

The monarchy Never criticize any member of the royal family or the institution itself. The monarchy is held in very high esteem.

Monastery (*wat*) **etiquette** Remove shoes on entering, do not climb over Buddha images or have pictures taken in front of one. Wear modest clothing – women should not expose their shoulders or wear dresses that are too short (see below, clothing). Females should never hand anything directly to monks, or venture into the monks' quarters.

Smoking Prohibited on domestic flights, public buses and in cinemas.

Further reading A useful book delving deeper into the do's and don'ts of living in Thailand is Robert and Nanthapa Cooper's *Culture shock: Thailand*, Time Books International: Singapore (1990). It is available from most bookshops.

● **Emergencies**
Police 191, 123; **Tourist Police** 195; **Fire** 199; **Ambulance** 2522171-5. **Tourist Police head office**: Unico House, Ploenchit Soi Lang Suan, Bangkok, T 6521721-6. **Tourist Assistance Centre**, Rachdamnern Nok Ave, Bangkok, T 2828129.

● **Hours of business**
Banks: 0830-1530 Mon-Fri. **Currency exchange services**: 0830-2200 Mon-Sun in Bangkok and Pattaya, 0830-1930 in Phuket and 0830-1630 Mon-Fri in other towns. **Government offices**: 0830-1200, 1300-1630 Mon-Fri. **Tourist offices**: 0830-1630 Mon-Sun. **Shops**: 0830-1700, larger shops: 1000-1900 or 2100.

● **Official time**
7 hrs ahead of GMT.

● **Tipping**
Generally unnecessary. A 10% service charge is now expected on room, food and drinks bills in the smarter hotels as well as a tip for any personal service. Increasingly, the more expensive restaurants add a 10% service charge; others expect a small tip.

● **Voltage**
220 volts (50 cycles) throughout Thailand. Most first and tourist class hotels have outlets for shavers and hair dryers. Adaptors are recommended, as almost all sockets are two pronged.

WHERE TO STAY

As a premier tourist destination and one of the world's fastest-growing economies, Thailand has a large selection of hotels – including some of the very best in the world. However, outside the tourist centres, there is still an absence of adequate 'Western style' accommodation. Most 'Thai' hotels are distinctly lacking in character and are poorly maintained. Due to the popularity of the country with backpackers, there are also a large number of small guesthouses, geared to Westerners serving Western food and catering to the foibles of foreigners.

● **Hotels**
Hotels are listed under eight categories, according to the *average* price of a double/twin room for one night. It should be noted that many hotels will have a range of rooms, some with air-conditioning (a/c) and attached bathroom facilities, others with just a fan and shared facilities. A service charge of 10% and government tax of 11% will usually be added to the bill in the more expensive hotels (categories B-L). Ask whether the quoted price includes tax when checking-in. **NB** During the off-season, hotels in tourist destinations may halve their room rates so it is always worthwhile bargaining.

FOOD AND DRINK

FOOD

Thai cuisine is an intermingling of Tai, Chinese, and to a lesser extent, Indian cuisines. This helps to explain why restaurants produce dishes which must be some of the (spicy) hottest in the world, as well as some which are rather bland. Despite these various influences, Thai cooking is distinctive. Thais have managed to combine the best of each tradition, adapting elements to fit their own preferences. Remarkably, considering how ubiquitous it is in Thai cooking, the chilli pepper is a New World fruit and was not introduced into Thailand until the late 16th century (along with the pineapple and papaya).

When a Thai asks another Thai whether he has eaten he will ask, literally, whether he has 'eaten rice' (*kin khaaw*). Similarly, the accompanying dishes are referred to as food 'with the rice'. A Thai meal is based around rice, and many wealthy Bangkokians own farms up-country where they cultivate their favourite variety. A meal usually consists (along with the rice) of a soup like *tom yam kung* (prawn soup), *kaeng* (a curry) and *krueng kieng* (a number of side dishes). Generally, Thai food is chilli-hot, and aromatic herbs and grasses (like lemon grass) are used to give a distinctive flavour. *Nam pla* (fish sauce) and *nam prik* (nam pla, chillies, garlic, sugar, shrimps and lime juice) are two condiments that are taken with almost all meals. Food is eaten with a spoon and fork, and dishes are usually served all at once; it is unimportant to a Thai that food be hot. Try the open-air foodstalls to be found in every town which are frequented by middle-class Thais as well as the poor and where a meal costs only ฿15-20. Many small restaurants have no menus. Away from the main tourist spots, 'Western' breakfasts are commonly unavailable, so be prepared to eat Thai-style (noodle or rice soup or fried rice). Finally, due to Thailand's large Chinese population (or at least Thais with Chinese roots), there are also many Chinese-style restaurants whose cuisine is variously 'Thai-ified'.

Tourist centres also provide good European, American and Japanese food at reasonable prices. Bangkok boasts some superb restaurants. Less expensive Western fastfood restaurants can also be found – McDonalds, Pizza Hut, Kentucky Fried Chicken and others.

DRINK

● Drinking water

Water in smaller restaurants can be risky, so many people recommend that visitors drink bottled water (widely available) or **hot tea**.

● Soft drinks

Coffee is also now consumed throughout Thailand (usually served with coffeemate or *creamer*). In stalls and restaurants, coffee come with a glass of Chinese tea. Soft drinks are widely available. Many roadside stalls prepare **fresh fruit juices** in liquidizers (*bun*) while hotels produce all the usual cocktails.

● Alcohol

Spirits Major brands of spirits are served in most hotels and bars, although not always off the tourist path. The most popular spirit among Thais is ***Mekhong* – local cane whisky** – which can be drunk straight or with mixers. It can seem rather sweet to the Western palate but it is the cheapest form of alcohol.

Beer The most popular local beer is *Singha* beer brewed by Boon Rowd. It's alcohol content is high of 6% must be partly to blame. Among expatriates, the most popular Thai beer is the more expensive *Kloster* brand (similar to a light German beer) with an alcohol content of 5.7%. *Singha* introduced a light beer called *Singha Gold* a few years ago which is quite similar to *Kloster*. *Amarit* is a third, rather less widely available, brand but popular with foreigners. Two new 'local' beers (in the sense that they are locally brewed) to enter the fray are *Heineken* and *Carlsberg*. The beer is sweeter and lighter than *Singha* and *Kloster* but still strong with an alcohol content of 6%. Yet another new local beer, although it appears to have only a very small segment of the market (as yet), and is hard to find is: *Bier Chang* or *Elephant Beer*. Beer is relatively expensive in Thai terms as it is heavily taxed by the government. In a café, expect to pay ฿30-50 for a small beer, in a coffee shop or bar ฿40-65, and in a hotel bar or restaurant, more than ฿60.

Wine Thais are fast developing a penchant for wines. Imported wines are expensive by international standards and Thai wines are pretty ghastly – overall. An exception is *Chateau de Loei* which is produced in the northeastern province of Loei by Chaijudh Karnasuta with the expert assistance of French wine maker.

COMMUNICATIONS

● Postal services

Local postal charges: ฿1 (postcard) and ฿2 (letter, 20 g). **International postal charges**: Europe and Australasia – ฿9 (postcard), ฿12.50 (letter, 10 g); US – ฿9 (postcard), ฿14.50 (letter, 10 g). Airletters cost ฿8.50. Poste Restante: correspondents should write the family name in capital letters and underline it, to avoid confusion.

Outside Bangkok, most post offices are open from 0800-1630 Mon-Fri and only the larger ones will be open on Sat.

Fax services: now widely available in most towns. Postal and telex/fax services are available in most large hotels.

● Telephone services

From Bangkok there is direct dialling to most countries. Outside Bangkok, it is best to go to a local telephone exchange for 'phoning outside the country.

Codes: local area codes vary according to province, they are listed under "Post & telecommunications" in each town; the code can also be found at the front of the telephone directory.

Directory inquiries: domestic long distance including Malaysia and Vientiane (Laos) – 101, Greater Bangkok BMA – 183, international calls T 2350030-5, although hotel operators will invariably help make the call if asked.

Callboxes cost ฿1. All telephone numbers marked in the text with a prefix 'B' mean that they are Bangkok numbers.

ENTERTAINMENT

● Newspapers

Until recently there were two major English language daily papers – the *Bangkok Post* and the *Nation Review* (known as *The Nation*). They provide good international news coverage and are Thailand's best known broadsheets.

● Television and radio

Five TV channels, with English language sound track available on FM. Channel 3 – 105.5 MHz, Channel 7 – 103.5 MHz, Channel 9 – 107 MHz and Channel 11 – 88 MHz. The *Bangkok Post* stars programmes where English soundtrack is available on FM. Shortwave radio can receive the BBC World Service, Voice of America, Radio Moscow, see page 372.

HOLIDAYS AND FESTIVALS

Festivals with month only are movable; a booklet of holidays and festivals is available from most TAT offices.

Jan: *New Year's Day* (1st: public holiday).

Feb: *Magha Puja* (full-moon: public holiday) Buddhist holy day, celebrates the occasion when the Buddha's disciples miraculously gathered together to hear him preach. Culminates in a candle-lit procession around the temple *bot* (or ordination hall). The faithful make offerings and gain merit. *Chinese New Year* (movable, end of Jan/beginning of Feb) celebrated by Thailand's large Chinese population. The festival extends over 15 days; spirits are appeased, and offerings are made to the ancestors and to the spirits. Good wishes and lucky money are exchanged, and Chinese-run shops and businesses shut down.

Apr: *Chakri Day* (6th: public holiday) commemorates the founding of the present Chakri Dynasty. *Songkran* (movable: public holiday) marks the beginning of the Buddhist New Year and is particularly big in the N (Chiang Mai, Lampang, Lamphun and Chiang Rai). It is a 3 to 5 day celebration, with parades, dancing and folk entertainment. The first day represents the last chance for a 'spring clean'. Rubbish is burnt, in the belief that old and dirty things will cause misfortune in the coming year. The wat is the focal point. Revered Buddha images are carried through the streets, accompanied by singers and dancers. The second day is the main water-throwing day (originally an act of homage to ancestors and family elders). Young people pay respect by pouring scented water over the elders heads. The older generation sprinkle water over Buddha images. Gifts are given. This uninhibited water-throwing continues for all 3 days (although it is now banned in Bangkok). On the third day birds, fish and turtles are all released, to gain merit and in remembrance of departed souls.

May: *Coronation Day* (5th: public holiday) commemorates the present King Bhumibol's crowning in 1950. *Ploughing Ceremony* (movable: public holiday) performed by the King at Sanaam Luang near the Grand Palace in Bangkok. Brahmanic in origin, it traditionally marks the auspicious date when farmers could begin preparing their riceland. Impressive bulls decorated with flowers pull a sacred gold plough.

Jun: *Visakha Puja* (full-moon: public holiday) holiest of all Buddhist days, it marks the Buddha's birth, enlightenment and death. Candle-lit processions are held at most temples.

Aug: *The Queen's Birthday* (12th: public holiday). *Asalha Puja and Khao Phansa* (full-moon: public holiday) – commemorates the Buddha's first sermon to his disciples and marks the beginning of the Buddhist Lent. Monks reside in their monasteries for the 3 month Buddhist Rains Retreat to study and meditate, and young men temporarily become monks. Ordination ceremonies all over the country and villagers give white cotton robes to the monks to wear during the Lent ritual bathing.

Oct: *Ok Phansa* (3 lunar months after Asalha Puja) marks the end of the Buddhist Lent and the beginning of Krathin, when gifts – usually a new set of cotton robes – are offered to the monks. Particularly venerated monks are sometimes given silk robes as a sign of respect and esteem. Krathin itself is celebrated over two days. It marks the end of the monks' retreat and the re-entry of novices into secular society. Processions and fairs are held all over the country; villagers wear their best clothes and food, money, pillows and bed linen are offered to the monks of the local wat. *Chulalongkorn Day* (23rd: public holiday) honours King Chulalongkorn (1868-1910), perhaps Thailand's most beloved and revered king.

Nov: *Loi Krathong* (full-moon) a *krathong* is a small model boat made to contain a candle, incense and flowers. The festival comes at the end of the rainy season and honours the goddess of water. The little boats are pushed out onto canals, lakes and rivers. Sadly, few krathongs are now made of leaves: polystyrene has taken over and the morning after Loi Krathong lakes and river banks are littered with the wrecks of the night's festivities. **NB** The 'quaint' candles in flower pots sold in many shops at this time, are in fact large firecrackers.

Dec: *The King's Birthday* (5th: public holiday). Flags and portraits of the King are erected all over Bangkok, especially down Rachdamnern Ave and around the Grand Palace. *Constitution Day* (10th: public holiday). *New Year's Eve* (31st: public holiday).

NB Regional and local festivals are noted in appropriate sections.

ပြည့်အင်အားသည်ပြည်တွင်းမှာသာရှိသည်
THE STRENGTH OF THE NATION
LIES ONLY WITHIN.

Information for travellers

BEFORE TRAVELLING

Regulations for tourists and businessmen have been easing over the last few years. To give an indication: In 1988 foreign tourists were allowed to stay for just 7 days and all travel within the country was closely controlled. Large swathes of Myanmar were off-limits to tourists. In 1990 the 7-day visa was extended to 14 days but independent travel was still not permitted – all visitors arrived on pre-arranged tours. In 1992 independent travellers were allowed into the country, but still for only 14 days, and in 1994 the 14-day visa was extended to 28 days. The advice given below was checked in 1996, but visitors must be ready for the possibility that new, or altered, regulations have come into force since then.

ENTRY REQUIREMENTS

● **Tourist visas**

At the time of going to press, tourists were eligible for a 28 day visa to Myanmar. Visas cost around US$10 (฿250) and are processed on the day of application at the Burmese Embassy in Bangkok (within 1 hr if you arrive before 1000).

Visas can be obtained at any of Myanmar's consulates or embassies abroad, the Bangkok Embassy (132 Sathorn Nua Rd) being the one most frequently used by tourists. Procuring a visa can take anything up to 48 hrs from embassies outside the region. Two copies of the application form are required along with three passport photographs; occasionally tourists are also asked to show their return ticket. Extended stays are rarely given – you must have a good reason such as joining a Burmese language course or going to a meditation centre. Meditation visas for foreign yogis can be obtained by writing to: Buddhasana, Niaggaha Organization, Mahasi Meditation Centre, 16 Thatana Rd, Yangon. This organization organizes full-time meditation courses which run for 6-12 weeks. **Visa extensions**: visas can be extended by 30 days in Yangon; it costs 36 US$/FECs from the MTT Tourist Office, 77-91 Sule Pagoda Rd, T 2753828, F 282535. Five photocopies of your passport and 5 of your visa and entry stamp are required. It takes 3 working days. After that, visitors must take the paperwork to the Immigration Office on Strand Rd (between Sule Pagoda and Shwebontha roads). Another form needs to be filled in here (5 kyat) and 2 photos are required. After a 30-min wait, you may get your extension. Note, though, that if intending to extend your stay then it is likely that you will be asked to provide proof that you exchanged US$300 into Foreign Exchange Certificates (FECs) at the airport on arrival (see page 354). For longer stays, a business visa needs to be applied for. **Visa overstays**: some visitors find that rather than go through the hassle of dealing with the Immigration Office it is easier simply to overstay their visas and pay the fine at the airport on departure (in 1996, US$3/day). Signs indicate this at immigration. **Visas for other countries in the region**: visas for **Vietnam**, cost US$45, for 1 month, 2 photos required and 2 working days. Transit visas for **Laos** (Vientiane only),

US$43, 2 photos and 2 working days. Visas for **Nepal**, US$25 for 1 month, 2 photos and 10 mins. For Embassy addresses in Yangon see page 121.

● Travel permits

Travelling to the major tourist sites does not require any additional documentation beyond a regular visa. However, to visit some towns off the main tourist route and especially those in what are regarded as sensitive areas may require a travel permit issued by MTT (Myanmar Travel and Tours) and approved by the Ministry of Defence. We say 'may' because there is no definitive list of places which require such permits. It seems to depend partly on conditions in Myanmar generally and in that particular area, and partly on who happens to be sitting at a desk at a particular time. It is not unusual for tourists to be stopped and their passports scrutinized by the security forces, and sometimes for tourists to be sent back. Our researcher for example had this happen to her when she was visiting the Shwesetdaw Pagoda in Magwe Division. The reason? It happened to coincide with a visit to the pagoda by a phalanx of high ranking police officers from Yangon (who had two helicopter landing pads specially constructed for their visit – not the privations of the road for the military!). For further advice on travelling to the more out-of-the-way spots see box, page 352.

● Vaccinations

Cholera and yellow fever vaccinations are required if you have been in an affected area in the 9 days prior to arrival. A vaccination against typhoid is advisable. Anti-malarial drugs are essential, although much of Myanmar is said to be malaria-free. The border areas, however, have particularly dangerous strains.

● Travelling in Myanmar

In 1992 the military junta decided that the tourist industry was to be the panacea for Myanmar's economic ailments. In a bout of perhaps misplaced optimism, the year from Oct 1996 was declared Visit Myanmar Year and the target raised to 500,000 tourists per year. Few believe that the tourist infrastructure can absorb these numbers: in 1994, arrivals totalled just 60,000 visitors. Visitors are put off not just by the limited infrastructure, but also by the poor international reputation of the military junta. Pressure groups like the Burma Action Group attempt of dissuade visitors and in 1995 the Swiss Federation of Travel Agents, apparently succumbing to such pressure, recommended to their members that they not push Visit Myanmar Year 1996.

With the gradual opening of Myanmar to tourists, the government has been forced to free-up the tourist market. Guesthouses and small, mid-range family hotels are sprouting up across the country, private tour companies are flourishing, and entrepreneurs are setting up and operating increasingly efficient transport services. Backpacking is back, alive and kicking, after a desultory period of heavy-handed government control.

It is now possible to travel to many destinations in Myanmar without special permission. You may find that in 'sensitive' areas you will be followed and questioned as to where you plan to go. There are still Immigration Officers in these towns and you must check-in upon arrival.

It is no longer necessary to travel as part of a tour, although some travellers may find it easier. Travelling on a tour in Myanmar does not mean that you have to put up with 10 or 20 other tourists; it is possible to go alone with a registered guide. However, the fewer the people, the more expensive the tour. Registered guides all have to undergo a 6 month government training and usually know their 'stuff'. They will also interpret in places where English is not spoken. See **Tours** below for examples of prices.

In main towns such as Yangon, Mandalay, Pyin U Lwin (Maymyo) and Taunggyi travellers will often come across a 'Mr Fixit' who will be able to organize trips to restricted areas. He will, depending on the situation, be able to grease the right palms and always has a 'friend' with a car for hire.

To save hassles with transport, travellers often hire cars in Mandalay to get around the main sights in Bagan and the Inle Lake area. This is a good way to travel if you want flexibility and to save time. It should cost around US$100 for a car from Mandalay to Bagan but prices vary according to the cost of petrol and various other factors – like the age of the vehicle.

● Private v Government

The government is trying to eke dollars out of tourists to Myanmar to fill its coffers. If you don't want to support the current regime there are ways of putting your money into private hands. It is also worth emphasizing that private operators usually provide a better and more efficient service more cheaply:

- Stay in private hotels/guesthouses rather

than government-run institutions (they are often better anyway, see page 362);

- Eat in private restaurants rather than government-run ones (the food tends to be authentic and fresh in private restaurants);
- Travel by bus, linecar or hire cars where possible; Myanmar Airways and trains are run by the government;
- Use private-run tour operators as opposed to MTT (privately organized tour companies are usually more efficient and less restrictive);
- Buy from private shops/stalls rather than government-run shops (you cannot bargain in government shops, so it is usually cheaper to buy from private operators).

If you want to find out more about the situation in Myanmar, contact the **Burma Action Group (BAG)**, Collins Studio, Collins Yard, Islington Green, London N1 2XU, UK, T +44171 3597679. The Burma Action Group suggest travellers interested in making an anti-government statement while in Myanmar should: visit U Thant's tomb and leave flowers; wear Aung San Suu Kyi T shirts; bring books, magazines and medicines (with careful instructions). They also publish *Burma: the alternative guide*. In late 1996, as this guide went to press, the BAG recommended, however, that people not visit Myanmar at all, see page 9 for the arguments for and against going to Myanmar.

● Entry points

Yangon is the main point of entry, although there are also flights to Mandalay from Chiang Mai. In theory it should be easy to cross into Myanmar overland from Thailand. However, over the last few years these potential border crossings have been usually closed to all except Thai and Burmese nationals. However, regulations change month by month and it may be worth checking in Bangkok whether any of the Thai-Myanmar border crossing points are open to foreign tourists. The one most likely to be open is the **Mae Sai-Tachilek** (Kengtung) crossing, which reopened in 1996. The new bridge crossing the Moei River linking **Mae Sot** with **Myawaddi** was completed in early 1996 but by the end of the year was still not open to foreign tourists. The same was true of the crossing at the **Three Pagodas Pass** in Thailand's Kanchanaburi province.

Visiting Rural Myanmar: some pointers

The smaller market towns and villages are the real Myanmar – the vast majority of the population live in rural areas and for them places such as Mandalay and Yangon are a world away. With deep shade, slow pace, cheap guesthouses, and lack of people calling 'hello', they also make a good place to stop for a while to relax and reflect. Travelling to towns and villages can be highly rewarding or extremely frustrating, depending largely on your knowledge, attitude and patience. The local people will be delighted to see you; though the reactions of the local authorities are likely to be mixed. Here are some things you should know and some pointers:

- Almost all of Myanmar excepting border regions is open to tourism. However, the local authorities, even Immigration, do not always know this. (Immigration deals mostly with the internal movements of Burmese, who are not free to travel at will in their country.) Even in fairly remote villages, Immigration officers will usually be able to speak English. If you are planning to go somewhere unusual, MTT in Yangon can read you the latest list of open and closed areas. Don't believe what the people at the front counter tell you from memory. The list changes every few months.
- It is useful to arrive during business hours and to have the phone number of MTT in Yangon with you. A phone call will normally clear things up. You may need to be delicate to avoid causing loss of face. Remember, it is not their fault they have not been promptly informed of changing policies. If you arrive in the evening, you will be allowed to stay the night in any case.
- If you are seeking physical comfort, you've come to the wrong country. This is even more true in the countryside, where some small towns have electricity for only a few hours a day, and some have no running water. Guesthouses will probably have rats, but may not have mattresses (but you will always get clean sheets to put on your straw mat). However, they cost only 50-100 kyat per person, and the

TOURS

It is possible to purchase Myanmar package tours in the US, Europe and Australasia, but they are cheaper to organize in Bangkok or through agents in Yangon.

The cheapest 7-night tours, which include the return flight from Bangkok to Yangon cost around US$400-500 and take in the main tourist attractions – Yangon, Mandalay and Bagan. Bangkok-based travel agents offer short tours (5-6 days) from Chiang Mai to Bagan and Mandalay. Tours to 'restricted' areas in Myanmar tend to be more expensive. A 5 day tour to Rakhine (better known as Arakan) from Yangon for a single traveller with a guide costs US$500, including return flight to Sittwe, inclusive of all transport, hotels and food. A 14-day tour arranged in Bangkok and staying in good hotels is likely to cost anywhere from US$1,000 up; and if travelling from the US or Europe (with airfare included), US$2,000 or more.

● Tourist information

The main tourist office in the country is Myanmar Travels & Tours (MTT) in Yangon (77-79 Sule Pagoda Rd, T 278376, F 289588, on the corner, to the SE of Sule Pagoda). There are branch offices in Mandalay, Nyaung Shwe (Inle Lake) Bagan and Taunggyi. MTT is state-run and only provides basic information (street plans of Yangon and Mandalay) much of which is incorrect; some of the MTT tour guides, however, are very well informed. They can also be useful for finding out the latest information on which areas are open to foreigners and for obtaining travel permits to restricted areas. MTT sells tickets for main sights, which are paid for in US$/FECs (or the kyat equivalent at the official rate) and also for express trains on the Yangon-Mandalay line and express boats between Mandalay and Bagan. Government-run hotels and the museums in Yangon and Mandalay also sell tickets for main sights.

management is usually charming however sordid the conditions.

- Some guesthouses close at 2200 or 2300 at night. If you arrive later, you can still get a room by knocking (hitting the padlock against the gate is most effective) and calling 'manager'. On subsequent nights, you will be expected to be back by closing time. The same people who close at night must open in the morning, often 7 days a week.
- If there is no guesthouse in a village, you can stay at the monastery. Sometimes people will invite you to sleep at their house. It is very important that you refuse at first, as they may not know the trouble this may cause them. (*m-YA. BU tin deh* is the simplest way to express this: 'That's not all right, I think'. Two straightened fingers tapped across the shoulder represent the stripes of police and military, and explains why. It is best to do this when there are several people around, to get a number of opinions.) If people understand you and persist with their invitation, then they know the authorities (or they are the authorities!) and know there will be no problems. A chorus of *YA. deh, YA. ba deh* means 'everything will be all right'.
- You will usually have to register separately with the police, Immigration and MI (Military Intelligence). Normally they will come to you for information, but sometimes they will get it from your guesthouse. All are unfailingly polite and you should be in return.
- The authorities will likely be rather puzzled at why you are not in Bagan or other tourist destinations, where most Burmese would like to travel. They may also be embarrassed at their lack of development. While it is helpful for you to have responses to these queries in the authorities' minds, they will probably have you followed just to make sure. This is often because they fear the consequences of getting it wrong (see the box 'Being followed by Military Intelligence: how to tell and what to do about it' on page 358).

WHEN TO GO

Best time to visit

Nov to the end of Feb, in the cool season, when temperatures are around 16-21°C and it is dry. But because this is the most popular time to go, it is also difficult to confirm bookings for hotels and flights. Hill stations are quite cool at this time. Tourists should also note that Yangon's annual International gem fair in Feb/Mar regularly results in an accommodation crisis (see page 216). Mar and Apr are dry but very hot – temperatures rise as high as 45°C in Bagan. **NB** Do not arrive in Bangkok during Chinese New Year, hoping to get a Burmese visa in 48 hrs. Many Bangkok travel agents close for the duration of the festivities. For monthly rainfall and temperature graphs, see page 106 (Yangon), page 145 (Mandalay), page 240 (Lashio), and page 254 (Sittwe).

Clothing

Shorts and short skirts are considered immodest forms of dress. Cool trousers and longish skirts are recommended – as is a hat. Sweaters might be needed for the evenings in the hill stations. Traditional dress is the *longyi* (see **Shopping**, above), similar to the Malaysian *sarong*, and a blouse called the *eingyi*. The longyi is worn shorter in the countryside for working in the ricefields. Traditional male headwear, the *gaung-baung*, is only worn on special occasions.

The women's longyi is tucked in at the side whereas the men's longyi is twisted and tucked in the middle. The women's ceremonial longyi is called a *hta-mein*. It is similar to an orthodox longyi but overlaps at the front and has a train at the back. The graceful management of this train while walking and dancing was considered an important accomplishment for women. It is now only worn by female Burmese dancers. Since there are no pockets in a longyi, a shoulder bag, often of handwoven cloth, is a universal accessory.

HEALTH

See the health section beginning on page 383 Rounding Up for more detailed advice on health and staying healthy.

● Vaccinations

Hepatitis, typhoid, tetanus and polio vaccinations are recommended. It is necessary to have evidence that you have been vaccinated against yellow fever if coming from an infected area.

● Malaria

Malaria is endemic in much of Myanmar; anti-malarial medication and mosquito repellents are strongly recommended. High resistance to traditional medications like Paludrine and Nivaquine is reported in some areas. Check on recommended medications before leaving.

● Food and water

Do not eat raw vegetables, or fruit which you cannot peel yourself. It is highly inadvisable to drink tap water unless it has been boiled for at least 15 mins. Dehydration can be a problem; visitors are advised to bring some electrolyte rehydration powder with them. Bottled drinking water is available everywhere but the tiniest villages for 20-30 kyat per bottle. Hot tea is safe to drink.

● Medical facilities

Although Burmese doctors are well-trained, drug stocks are poor. It is advisable for tourists to contact their embassies, should they suddenly fall ill. Some (such as the Australian Embassy) have their own clinics and a nurse. They will always be able to recommend the best course of action. Unofficial medical care like this must be paid for in US dollars. Health insurance with emergency air ambulance provision is worthwhile. The main hospitals in Yangon are *Diplomatic Hospital*, Kyaikkasan Rd, T 50149; *Yangon General Hospital*, Bogyoke Aung San St, T 81722 (ask for medical superintendent); *Infectious Disease Hospital*, Upper Pansodan St, T 72497.

MONEY

● Currency

Myanmar's currency unit is the kyat (pronounced 'chat'); notes come in unhelpful (but cosmologically sound) denominations of 1, 5, 10, 15, 20, 45, 50, 90, 100, 200 and 500. There are 100 pyas to the kyat but the coins are virtually worthless and rarely seen. In the past the government has periodically demonetized particular denominations of notes. There seem to be two explanations why it has felt it necessary to do this. One is that the government was attempting to stamp out the black market, and the second that the manically superstitious Ne Win had been told by his astrologers that certain numbers were lucky (see box, page 355). What it means for the unsuspecting visitor, though, is that some money changers try to palm foreigners off with worthless notes. As a general rule of thumb, if the note is labelled 'Central Bank of Myanmar', then it is kosher.

Blissful economic mismanagement has meant that while the official exchange rate is pegged at around 5.9 kyat to US$1 (Nov 1996), the purchasing power of the dollar on the black market can be much more. At the end of 1996, kyat were changing hands on the free market at up to 160 to US$1.

What is surprising, given Myanmar's Mickey Mouse economy, is that the value of the kyat on the black market should have remained so stable for so long. Economists see the hand of the Slorc maintaining some semblance of order even here while they officially quote a ludicrous exchange rate up to 25 times greater. The demand for hard currency has resulted in what economists call 'the dollarization' of the urban economy. Almost no one changes money at the farcical official rate. Generally, larger bills and large sums mean a better rate of exchange.

Currency regulations Foreign currency is accepted from the following countries: USA, United Kingdom, Canada, Germany, France, Switzerland, Australia, Singapore, Malaysia, Hong Kong and Japan. However, black market exchange dealers have a preference for US dollars. Tourists are (officially) expected to exchange US$300 in Myanmar into Foreign Exchange Certificates or FECs (see below).

● US$/FECs

Fortunately, the booming black market is relatively painless and profitable and nobody seems to get into trouble for using it. But tourists confronted by ominous-looking currency exchange control forms on entering Myanmar and the requirement listed on the visa application form that they exchange US$300 may be liable to worry about bending or breaking rules. Foreign independent travellers are supposed to exchange a minimum of US$300 (or the equivalent) at the official rate on arrival in Yangon. These have to be paid for in US$

Red faces on the black market

Faced with a massive counterfeit operation, the government withdrew all 100 kyat notes from circulation in 1985. Because little advance notice was given and communications in Myanmar are so poor, many people lost a fortune, having been left with their life savings in worthless bills. Many families now prefer to protect their savings by investing in gemstones. In 1987, following demonetization, the government abolished 25, 35 and 75 kyat notes and introduced 45 and 90 kyat notes. Astronomers had told the superstitious General Ne Win that 9 was his lucky number. This fitted in with the general's regal pretensions: past kings of Myanmar were obsessed with the number 9 – King Mindon, for example, had 9 royal white umbrellas and 9-tiered roofs on his palace.

or £ Sterling, and TCs, cash or a credit card can be used for the transaction (see below for credit cards accepted in Myanmar). But a small bribe of US$5 will entice the FEC exchange desk to issue an exchange receipt for US$300 without ever changing the money. In any case, and increasingly, visitors are simply ignoring the requirement – confidently walking past the currency exchange desk direct to the baggage reclaim area. Note that visitors on tours with everything – transport and full board – included in the cost of a pre-paid package, do not need to change any money at the official rate on arrival.

Though FECs have had a bad press and most visitors think that by avoiding buying the requisite US$300-worth they will be saving money, it is not nearly so clear-cut. For many purchases – hotels in main cities and tourist sites, air and rail fares, tours – only US$ or FECs are acceptable and they are both worth the same amount. In addition, FECs can be exchanged on the free market into kyat at something pretty close to the free market dollar rate. In addition, while it is technically illegal for many shops and other enterprises to accept US$, they are all permitted to take FECs.

The FEC exchange rate is pegged at US$1 = 1 FEC unit = approx 125-150 kyat (it varies according to the free market US$ exchange rate). Certificates are issued in 4 denominations equivalent to US$20, US$10, US$5 and US$1. Some hotel bills in major cities and tourist sites, air fares and some rail fares have to be paid in hard currency (ie US$ or FECs); most restaurants and smaller guesthouses, though, accept kyat. Pagodas and museum entry fees may be in dollars or kyat. If you have landed up with too many FECs you may be able to exchange them with other travellers who did not buy any on arrival; it is still useful to carry some FECs, as hotels like them. Note that FECs, as well as US$, can be changed on the black market – but only changing US$ is forbidden. Rates are almost as good for FECs as for US$ cash, so many people simply accept the small rate reduction to avoid the wrath of the authorities if they get caught. Any unused FECs cannot be exchanged on departure **unless** you have bought more than US$300-worth during your trip. To do this you will need to have retained your FEC Voucher. However, FECs can be exchanged on the black market in main cities at slightly (5-10%) less than the US$ (cash) rate.

● Cash and travellers' cheques

Cash and TCs denominated in US$ and £ Sterling can be exchanged at the official rates at the airport, MTT offices and at many government-run hotels, although this is not financially worthwhile and any exchange should be kept to a minimum. Although the US$ can only legally be used in enterprises with a licence to accept the currency, most shops, guesthouses, restaurants and tour operators will happily accept US$ cash as payment. US$ can also be easily changed into kyat on the free/black market (see below). It makes no sense to change US$ at the ridiculously over-valued official exchange rate.

● Credit cards

Credit cards are now accepted in Myanmar but only in major hotels, and at MTT and Air Mandalay offices. As Myanmar reforms its economy the number of outlets accepting credit cards is likely to grow. Accepted cards are: Amex, Diners Club, MasterCard, and Visa.

● Black market

US$ are easily exchanged on the black market. Other currencies can also be exchanged on the black market, for example Thai baht and pounds Sterling, but the rates are not usually as good. You do not generally have to look far to exchange money – most people will be approached before they even leave the airport. However, you are usually better off waiting until you get into town when you know the going rate. The best place to do a quick transaction is at the Bogyoke Market or around the Sule Pagoda in Yangon, though a slightly better exchange rate can usually be found at the exchange cente on Lower Theinbyu St. Generally it is safer to change money in shops or restaurants and not out on the street where there is a greater chance that you will be shortchanged. Note that larger denominations of US$ get better rates. The black market rate is highest in Yangon but generally drops 5-10 kyat once outside the capital (the exception being Mandalay). Bundles of old notes are still occasionally touted on the black market in the hope they can be palmed off on some naive tourist (see the opening paragraph to this Money section).

NB Airport tax is FEC/US$6. Tourists who forget about this tax and change all their money on the black market are the bane of foreign consular divisions in Yangon. It is also important to avoid being left with piles of kyat after your trip. Remaining kyat must be surrendered on departure and you only get a quarter of their official value in exchange – an extremely bad deal. Because the kyat is not a convertable currency, it cannot be exchanged outside Myanmar although it might be handy to paper a large room.

A few years ago, tourists to Myanmar would arrive laden with Johnny Walker and 555 cigarettes hoping to make a killing on the black market. This is at an end: they are cheaper in Yangon than in Bangkok.

● Cost of living

The cost of visiting in Myanmar has been coming down since 1990 as a response to the opening up of the tourist industry to private enterprise. While tourism was controlled by the State, the government could set just about any tariff they liked and visitors could do little about it: there was simply no competition. Now that there are privately-run hotels and guesthouses and private tour companies there is not only more choice and higher standards, but also lower prices. This is not to say that Myanmar is cheap. Like Laos and Vietnam, and despite the fact that they are among the poorest countries in the world, it is still cheaper to travel in Thailand or Indonesia.

Visitors staying in top hotels and eating in hotel restaurants will probably spend US$200-300 per day. Those staying in standard, mid-range hotels with attached bathrooms and a/c should expect to spend around US$50-75 per day. Travellers staying in cheaper guesthouse accommodation and eating in local restaurants can live on around US$10 per day. Note that during the high season (roughly, Nov-May) prices tend to increase – even to double. Or, to put it more positively, prices may as much as halve during the low season.

CUSTOMS

Officially, all items of jewellery, cameras and foreign currency must be declared at customs and on currency declaration forms. Very occasionally, items are checked off against this list on departure, to ensure they have not been sold on the black market. This is a rare occurrence however.

● Duty-free allowance

400 cigarettes, 2 litre of spirits and half a litre of perfume. It is no longer possible to make a profit in kyat on the black market (see page 360).

● Export restrictions

Gemstones can only be bought at government-controlled outlets such as the Tourist Department Store in Yangon (where value for money is often not as good as Bangkok). It is inadvisable to smuggle black market gemstones out of the country as they will be confiscated if found. The export of Buddha images and antiques requires a special license.

GETTING THERE

AIR

Several international carriers fly to Yangon: *Myanmar Airways International* (from Hong Kong, Kuala Lumpur and Singapore), *Biman* (links with Hanoi and Dhaka), *CAAC* (from Kunming and Beijing), *Thai Airways International* (from Bangkok) and *Silk Air* (Singapore). Daily connections with Bangkok on *Myanmar Airways International* (now a joint venture with *Royal Brunei*) and *Thai*. *Myanmar Airways International*; *Thai Airways*. *Biman* operate the cheapest flights between Bangkok and Yangon but only on Thur. *Bangkok Airways* runs a direct service, 3 times a week between Chiang Mai and Mandalay. *Air Mandalay* has flights from Chiang Mai to Yangon and Mandalay. They are also planning to begin flying between Phuket in Thailand and Yangon. **NB** You must confirm your outward bound flight on arrival.

Procedure on arriving:

- Visas and passports are checked at immigration.
- Independent travellers are expected to change US$300 at the exchange desk but increasingly visitors are simply walking past the desk straight to the baggage reclaim area, apparently without being stopped, or are paying a small bribe (US$1) to be issued with a receipt confirming that the US$300 has, indeed, been changed (see page 191).
- Declaration forms are examined at customs.

Procedure on leaving:

- Pay airport tax (US$6) at counter just inside main door to airport; you will need to show your air ticket and passport.
- Check in at relevant airline counter; you will need your airport tax receipt.
- Passport and embarkation cards are checked at immigration.
- Luggage is inspected before going into waiting area.

ON ARRIVAL

● Airport information

Mingaladon Airport is 19 km NW of Yangon. The new international terminal has recently been completed. The old building is now the domestic terminal. Facilities at the airport include a MTT information office, restaurant upstairs from the arrivals area, money-changing facilities (charges 2 FECs), post office, souvenir shop. For spending your last kyat, there are a few shops and noodle stalls opposite the old airport building (domestic terminal) – on the other side of the road.

Transport to town The cheapest way to get to town is on Old Japanese Bus No 51 – the number is not in roman numerals – but most of the buses are green and yellow. Ask driver if they go to Sule Pagoda. To get to the No 51 bus stop on Pyay Rd, flag down a linecar on the airport access road. **From town**, the No 51 bus leaves from Maha Bandoola Garden St. These buses tend to be full at rush-hour time but they run from 0500-2100 every 15 mins (6 kyat). **Taxi**: taxis into Yangon cost about US$1. Representatives from the various guesthouses tout for business at the airport and quite often offer free transport to town.

● Airport tax

US$6 for all international flights.

● Conduct

Face, anger and affection: the Burmese value, above all else, a subdued, restrained and non-confrontational approach to life. Even in the heat of an argument with a Myanmar Airways official who is in the process of bumping you off a flight for which you have a confirmed seat, it is best to keep your cool. Many people will say that it gets you further in the long run in any case. To lose one's cool, even in the most trying of circumstances, is to lose face. While to maintain one's integrity is to show great – and admirable – self-restraint. That said, there are also a few expatriate residents of Yangon who maintain that as most Burmese do not expect foreigners to conform to Burmese 'type', it pays – when pushed to the very limit – to conform to the western stereotype and to argue and gesticulate – and the official or whoever concerned will comply just to be rid of you. The Burmese, though, would regard such behaviour as a gross transgression if one of their compatriots acted so and it simply confirms their view that westerners are congenitally rude and uncivilized. This 'coolness' extends from situations of frustration and anger, to open displays of affection. The opposite sexes should not kiss and hug in public; nor should they even hold hands – although members of the same sex can with impunity.

Due respect: men should treat women with respect, and younger people should pay suitable regard to their seniors. Burmese will carefully gauge the age of any person they meet for the first time, and then use the appropriate polite title – a young person would address a middle aged man using the title *U* (uncle) or a woman, *Daw* (Aunt). Though it is not unusual to see army officers behaving with over-bearing arrogance, this does not mean that it is normal behaviour and many Burmese will say that this breakdown in accepted mores is one of the reprehensible side-effects of the Slorc's rule.

Head and feet: as in the other Theravada Buddhist societies of mainland Southeast Asia, the head is regarded as holy, while the feet are both the lowest and the lowliest parts of the body. You should never touch another person – even a child – on the head. Nor should you

Being followed by Military Intelligence: how to tell and what to do about it

It is common, especially outside the main tourist areas, for foreigners to be followed by Military Intelligence (see Visiting rural Myanmar: some pointers, page 352). MI will likely claim that they are having you followed for your security, but if you actually need some help, don't expect your MI 'bodyguard' to step in! Sometimes the shadow is quite obvious, but at other times he may be far more subtle. MI is likely to interview everyone you have a conversation with, so you must warn people and be careful what you talk about in public.

Sometimes someone from MI will show up in the guesthouse and chat for a while, as another guest might. If you are friendly with the guesthouse staff, they will usually tell you who you were talking with afterwards. They might also tell you if you are being followed. (Note that MI in Magwe Division is especially strict, and will almost certainly assign someone to you.)

Identifying your 'bodyguard'

- He is invariably a man.
- He will not be in uniform, but is well-dressed.
- He may offer to show you the way to the place you want to go, and then prove impossible to get rid of. This is also true of innocent Burmese, but they are more excited about it.
- He may join your table in restaurants or tea shops, often without speaking.
- If no one in a tea shop appears interested in you, it is probably because they recognize your tail.
- Anyone sitting alone at your tea shop for a long time, especially without ordering, is very suspicious. He may arrive some time after you do, if you are not being followed closely.
- 'Where are you going' and 'where are you coming from' are normal Burmese greetings used with strangers. 'Where did you go this morning?' is not.

use your feet to point at anyone.

Dress: although visitors will have no need for formal attire in Myanmar, neatness, cleanliness and modesty of dress are expected. Do not wear shorts or revealing clothes around town. Though it may be common practice in some areas of Thailand for foreigners and Thais to dress in such a manner, remember that Myanmar has not had the hordes of tourists and remains a much more traditional place. In private homes, visitors should remove their shoes.

Paya (pagoda) etiquette: when visiting monasteries of any description, even ones which appear ruined and abandoned, you should remove your shoes. In addition, do not visit monasteries wearing shorts or singlets; women should take particular care to dress demurely – no shorts or short skirts, or revealing blouses. Some people find taking a scarf to cover the shoulders is useful. Unlike neighbouring Thailand where the shoes rule only applies within the monastery buildings, in Myanmar it applies to the whole compound. Women should observe one more aspect of monastery etiquette: they should not touch monks or hand anything directly to them.

● Hours of business

Government offices: 0930-1600 or 1630, Mon-Fri. **Banks**: 1000-1400, Mon-Fri. **Shops** in the cities are open Mon-Sun; opening and closing hours vary. **Restaurants**: most close by 2100. Many teashops are open until 2200 or 2400. They serve snacks. **Myanmar Travels & Tours (MTT)**: 0800-2000, Mon-Sun.

● Official time

6½ hrs ahead of GMT.

● Safety

Myanmar is generally a lot safer for tourists than it is for the Burmese. The government does not allow tourists to travel to areas which

Burmese names

Burmese names are usually made up of two or three syllables, eg Tin Win, or Khin Maung Aye. A few names have one or four. The syllables usually carry auspicious or affectionate meanings. Here are some favourite name syllables:

Traditional Roman Spelling	Pronounced	Meaning
Tin, Tinn	Tin	survivor
Win, Wynn	Win	radiant
Naing	Nain	victor
Thein, Thane	Thein	100,000
Than	Thán	million
Khin, Kin	Kin	loving, loved
Hla	Hlá	pretty
Myint	Myint	noble
Kyi, Kyee	Kyi	clear
Kyi, Jee	Ji	big
Shwe	Shwe	gold
Lay, Le	Le	little
Aye, E	Ei	calm, cool
Maung	Maung	little brother
Kyaw	Kyaw	famous
Sein	Sein	diamond
Mya	Mya	emerald

Burmese tradition is to have individual names, not family names. So someone named Aye Aye Shwe might have a father named Hla Maung and a mother named Khin Than Myint. A few parents adopt western customs by incorporating an element of their own name into their children's names. Sometimes children incorporate an element of a parent's name, especially when the parent dies.

Children are called by their name as it stands, and so are some young women, but normally when you talk to or about adults you put a prefix before the name:

Traditional Roman Spelling	Used For
U (pronounced *Oo*)	men
Daw	women
Ko	young men (student age)
Ma (pronounced *Ma*)	young women (student age) and girls
Maung	boys

So the members of the fictitious family mentioned above would be Ma Aye Aye Shwe, U Hla Maung and Daw Khin Than Myint, U Hla Maung and Daw Khin Than Myint.

they consider militarily insecure; tourists have rarely been victims of civil crime – other than those who have been stung on the black market; and violent crime is far rarer than in most of the countries that tourists call 'home'. As in other police states, the presence of such a large and insidious security presence makes the country usually safe.

This is not to say that tourists should leave valuables lying around: all the usual precautions are recommended. The most dangerous thing visitors are likely to encounter is Russell's Viper – one of the world's deadliest snakes. It is worth taking particular care in and around old pagodas – particularly in Bagan – where sun warmed bricks and cool crevices provide perfect living conditions for snakes. Scorpions are also a problem in Myanmar and visitors are advised to shake out shoes after leaving pagoda complexes and in the morning.

Rural Myanmar is one of the safest places on Earth – unless you are Burmese that is. Rarely, single women may be annoyed by drunken men in the evening but in most cases the drunk's friends usually call him off. In any case, Burmese do not generally drink much (this is most likely to happen during festivals when social constraints on such behaviour are more lax).

● Selling duty-free on the black market

While some precautions are necessary in informal currency transactions, officialdom turns a blind eye to the black market in spirits and cigarettes. Note that it is no longer worth taking spirits or cigarettes into the country to sell – although they may be good as gifts. Designer T-shirts, watches, cosmetics, cameras and walkmans are readily saleable or exchangeable for souvenirs. **But beware**: if you have declared any of these items on entering the country and you are found to be leaving without them, you may have to pay for them at their declared value. These forms are rarely scrupulously checked on departure though.

● Shopping

Antiques: it is possible to buy brass and bronze opium weights, folding scales, temple bells, tattoo sticks, door knockers, betel nut cutters, brass statues, wooden boxes as well as antique lacquerware; in Rangoon there are some shops selling items such as ships' clocks and gramophones (see page 123). Religious antiques cannot be shipped out of the country without obtaining proper documentation – although a large number of Burmese antiques are being smuggled out of the country and appear in Bangkok antique shops (see page 335).

Copperware and brassware: cottage industry in Mandalay.

Embroidery: the best embroidery is found in Mandalay. Burmese embroidery is now found worldwide made into baseball hats, waistcoats and cushions. Originally the sequinned, appliquéd embroidery was used in funerary ceremonies as coffin covers.

Gems: rubies, jade and sapphires mostly come from the northern mines of Mogok, 115 km NE of Mandalay and Mogaung. Also aquamarine, topaz, amethysts and lapis lazuli. Gemstones should be bought at government-approved shops only, otherwise you risk having them confiscated on leaving the country.

Lacquerware: while most articles are made for practical domestic purposes, a wide variety of products can be found. The most common are *kunit* (betel nut boxes), *lahpetok* (receptacle boxes), cheroot boxes and *bu* (storage containers), but even big *sadaik* (manuscript chests) can be bought. Burmese lacquerware is now being copied in Chiang Mai, Thailand but Thai copies tend to be heavier than Burmese pieces and are not as carefully finished.

Mother-of-pearl: originally popular for decorating palace interiors, mother-of-pearl goods – necklaces, boxes etc, come from the Tenerassim region.

Shoulder bags: can be found everywhere.

Silverware: dates back to the 13th century. Now mostly produced near Sagaing.

Textiles: local textiles now face stiff competition from cheap imported fabrics smuggled into Burma from neighbouring countries.

Weaving: silk *longyis* are often made to order. The colours in an individual's longyi is determined by his or her horoscope. Specially-made longyis are often expensive – more than 5,000 kyat. Cotton longyis are made in several patterns, which are associated with different parts of the country. The purple/green/black 'tartan' pattern comes from Kachin state and 'tartan' longyis became a uniform for politicians of the National League for Democracy in the run-up to the elections in 1990; they were worn with white shirts.

Woodcarvings: Mandalay is the main centre.

● Tipping

Tipping is not encouraged in Myanmar, although it is quite common in hotels and restaurants. Small gifts are welcomed, especially if you are invited to visit someone's home for a meal. Gifts particularly appreciated are lipsticks, ball-point pens, T-shirts, paperback books, and postcards (for Britons, pictures of Piccadilly Circus, Nelson's Column, Buckingham Palace, the Queen and Princess Diana go down very well). Disposable cameras are also highly appreciated: they cost about ฿250 in Bangkok.

It is normal to tip guides – without tips it is hard for them to make a living.

● Voltage

220 volts, 50 cycles; current fluctuates alarmingly and can cause problems with electrical equipment. In minor towns electricity may only be supplied during the evening, roughly 0600-2200 or 2300.

● Weights and measures

As in neighbouring India, the Indian-English terms *lakh* and *crore* are widely used in Myanmar – mainly in the context of money. One lakh is 100,000; a crore is 100 lakhs, or 10 million. In markets, rice and flour is usually sold by volume rather than weight; the normal standard measuring unit is an empty condensed milk can. Other commonly used weights and measures include:

viss (peith-tha) = 1,633g
1 tical =16.33g
cubit (tong) = 46 cm
1 span (htwa) = 23 cm

WHERE TO STAY

Hotels in Myanmar are generally quite expensive and the choice is limited – although this is changing month-by-month as new hotels and guesthouses open up. The scale of hotel construction, especially in Yangon, is extraordinary. Tourism is the second most important sector for foreign investment after oil and gas, and it shows. Looking at other countries – like Vietnam – where a wave of investment has led to a profusion of new hotels, one would expect room rates to fall as competition increases. However, at the time of writing, Myanmar remains comparatively expensive by Southeast Asian standards: it is cheaper to find a room in Bangkok where average incomes are many times the level of Yangon. The authorities in Myanmar also operate a 2-tier pricing system where equivalent rooms will be much cheaper for a Burmese than for a foreigner. Although it is possible to bargain in all but the upper range places, you should not expect to be able to pay the same kyat rate as the next Burmese.

All hotels have to be paid for in hard currency (US$ or FECs) – except for some of the cheapest guesthouses in our '**D**' and '**E**' categories (see below). Government hotels used to be run to the same poor standards with rarely functioning air conditioners, sporadic hot water and a hotel restaurant serving indifferent European/Burmese food. However, competition from privately-run establishments (some of the old state-run hotels have been privatized) has shaken up the system and some are now well-run and maintained. There is sometimes a small single occupancy surcharge and virtually all hotels and guesthouses add 10% government tax onto the bill as well. More expensive hotels, from our category '**B**'

Hotel classifications

A+: US$200+ Only a handful of places in Yangon fall into this category at the moment but more top international-style hotels are under construction in Yangon, Bagan and Mandalay and will have opened when this book goes to press. Other places are in the pipeline and the Burmese tourist infrastructure is entering a period of rapid expansion.

A: US$100-200 Burmese hotels backed by foreign capital, these hotels offer a/c, rooms with attached bathrooms, restaurant and bar, some business services (like a fax for guests' use), room service, laundry service, television in room showing satellite TV. Neither standards, nor facilities are as good as their Bangkok counterparts but at least the amenities and technology will tend to work – which you can't count on with cheaper places. Hotels in this bracket are concentrated in Yangon but others are beginning to open in the main tourist destinations such as Mandalay and Bagan.

B: US$50-100 Hotels in this bracket will have a/c, rooms with attached bathrooms, h/w, laundry service and a restaurant. Most government-run hotels will fall into this bracket or our 'C' category.

C: US$25-50 The more upmarket privately-run guesthouses/ hotels fall into this category and a few of the cheaper government-run places. Most will offer a/c and attached bathrooms with hot water; most will also usually have an associated restaurant. Invariably privately-run hotels will offer better value for money, although standards are very uneven and some government-managed establishments are raising their standards in response to private competition.

D: US$10-25 Guesthouses and hotels in this category are the cheapest that will provide an a/c room with attached bathroom. Sometimes cheaper rooms in more expensive hotels will fall into this category, or sometimes it will be the best room(s) in a cheaper guesthouse. As ever, standards vary enormously.

E: under US$10 Privately-run guesthouses in this category are opening up in all the main tourist destinations. They offer basic facilities (although some may have more expensive a/c rooms) but represent excellent value for money. As they are geared to backpackers they will have such additional facilities as bicycle hire, bus booking services as well as being invaluable sources of information. Food is usually but not always available.

upwards, will top this up further still by including a 10% service charge.

Note that when tourists are taken to hotels (or restaurants) by a trishaw driver or a guide, for example, they receive a commission of up to 20% from the hotel management. This additional cost to the hotel makes it difficult to bargain over the room rate. Such commission-taking is most evident in Mandalay, Bagan and Pyin U Lwin (Maymyo). Those guests staying for longer periods – more than 2 nights – can often negotiate further discounts. In all but the more expensive hotels, the room rate includes breakfast.

Travellers are only allowed to stay in hotels/guesthouses registered with MTT unless, that is, they get permission from local immigration. Tourists are able to stay in private hotels/guesthouses not registered with MTT at the discretion of hotel owners. Private hotels are usually a bit cheaper and better value than their government-run counterparts. However, they cannot afford radically to reduce their rates as government taxes are so high. There are private hotels/guesthouses practically everywhere except (at present) in Mawlmayine (Moulmein).

FOOD AND DRINK

FOOD

Although there is no doubt that Burmese restaurants and cuisine have improved tremendously over the last few years, particularly in terms of the quality of the ingredients, it is still true that Burmese food can be disappointing – especially in comparison with Thailand. Many restaurants serve Indian, Chinese or European food; Burmese restaurants tend to close early – doors are often firmly shut by 1900 or 2000. In Yangon many hotel restaurant menus are printed in English but in smaller restaurants, and especially off the tourist route, it may be necessary to point and gesticulate. Hotel food tends to be poor in government-run establishments – often a disastrous mix between Burmese and European.

In small restaurants outside Yangon and Mandalay expect to pay 50-100 kyat for a meal. The choice of restaurants outside the main cities is limited, and only Burmese and local dishes may be available (although Chinese restaurants are common in towns). However, it is usual to find a foodstall area serving hot snacks, often associated with the local market. In larger cities, like Yangon and Mandalay, there is a wide range of cuisines. The standard of restaurants is also higher, as are the prices. In top restaurants in Yangon expect to pay 200-300 kyat for a meal.

The staples of typical Burmese cuisine are rice and rice noodles; these are traditionally served in a large bowl placed in the centre of the low table. Burmese curries, unlike Indian curries, use only a few spices and herbs – garlic and onions, tomatoes, coriander, ginger, turmeric, salt and hot chilli peppers, which are all fried in peanut oil. Greater variety is provided by mixing *a-thout* (fresh, spicy combinations of herbs, onion, vegetables and spices) with the rice and curry on your plate. *Hin* is curry; *kyet tha hin* is chicken curry, *ametha hin*, beef curry and *nga hin*, fish curry. Portions of curries are often small, you are supposed to fill yourself up with rice. A clear soup, or *hingyo*, nearly always accompanies the meal. Food is always served at room temperature. Dishes are usually served with *ngapi ye* – fermented fish or shrimp paste. The more upmarket fish paste, *balachaung*, is made with dried shrimps and garlic (it is related to the Malaysian *belacan*). Balachaung is not supposed to be taken out of the country as it is red and is therefore an

Restaurant classifications

♦♦♦♦ Over 400 kyat: international restaurants offering a variety of cuisine. The top restaurants, with prices to match, like *The Strand* are superb quality. But some international restaurants lose on all accounts in that they are expensive and menus are uninteresting and food mediocre compared to cheaper outlets. You will only find international restaurants in hotels in Yangon, Mandalay, Bagan and the Inle area.

♦♦♦ 200-400 kyat: top of the range Chinese establishments fall into this bracket with large menus, little ambience and standard food. You will only find Chinese restaurants in the main towns.

♦♦ 100-200 kyat: local Indian and Burmese restaurants serving authentic dishes; these restaurants offer the best value for money.

♦ under 100 kyat: stalls offer good, fresh food on the whole although not all will be to Western tastes (barbecued rats and red ants are local delicacies). The cheapest local restaurants in smaller towns may also fall into this price bracket.

easy way to smuggle rubies. The tiny chilli-padis, which lace many dishes, are known as *kala au* – which translates as 'the chillies which make Indian men cry'. They are very hot. Seafood is exported from Myanmar and items such as *kya-bazon* (tiger prawns) regularly appear on menus even far inland.

● Meat dishes

Wet-tha kyaw – sweet pork – a favourite – pork is meant to be very good in Myanmar.
Wet-tha paung – stewed pork soup.
Kyet tha hin – chicken curry.
Kyet that kyaw – fried chicken.
Kyet tha thout – chicken salad with onions.
Sei-tha hin – goat curry.
Ameh-tha – beef, but beef is rarely served in restaurants.
Beh-tha-hin – duck curry.

● Fish dishes

Gna-talaung paung – stewed fish – typically Burmese fish, tastes a bit like Sardines, since it is stewed, the bones have gone soft and can be eaten too.
Gna-pan mwe – shredded fish (no bones at all), cooked in chilli, garlic and ginger.
Gna-min – butter fish – usually served in a spicy tomato based sauce.
Bazon si-pien – prawns in oil and onions. Prawns can be very big, usually from the river.
Bazon thot – small prawn salad.
Gna chauk kyaw – dried fried fish.
Ng pi kyaw – fried fish paste with chilli – a Burmese favourite.
Gna-talaung u – fish roe – usually cooking in oil and onions.

● Vegetable dishes

Pehgyi nat – large yellow butter beans – can be ordered as a vegetarian dish.
Cheh-hin-kha-thi kyaw – bitter gourds
Kha-yin-thi nat – aubergines.
Byan-by kyaw – corn.
Ah-lu – potatoes.
Gazon ywet – spinach-like leaf, often translated as water cress here.
Gazon ywet-hmoe – same as above with mushrooms.
Chin baung – sour leaf that tastes a bit like sorrel, often cooked with bamboo shoots.

● Salads *(thot)*

Burmese are fond of salads (*thot*), to be eaten with rice or without. The base for salad is peanuts, sesame seeds, pea powder, fried onions and garlic, peanut oil and tamarind juice.
Min-khwa-ywet thot – type of water cress.
Salad ywet thot – lettuce leaves in Burmese style (in season).
Kha-yin-kyinthi thot – tomato salad.
Lapeh thot – pickled tea leaves – only found in Burma, usually eaten after the meal, though can also be had with rice. Best in Mandalay.
Kyin thot – pickled ginger – also eaten after a meal.

● Soups

Peh-kala hin – lentil soup with vegetables.
Thi-zon-hin-jo – vegetable sour soup.
Beh-tha-paung-hin-jo – stewed duck soup.
Peh-dji-hin-jo – yellow butter bean soup.

● Noodles

Mohinga – fermented rice noodles, served in a spicy fish soup with an onion and ginger base. the Burmese love *mohinga* they eat in the street at every hour of the day.
On-no-khauk-swe – wheat noodles served in a coconut milk soup, with chicken and duck egg.

For a description of Southeast Asian fruits see page 381.

DRINK

Tap water is not safe to drink unless it has been thoroughly boiled. *Ye gnwe* – literally 'hot water', but actually green tea – is available at restaurants and teahouses; it is served free of charge. Teahouses mainly serve strong, sweet and milky tea (made with condensed milk). Pickled tea, or *lapet thek* (or *thoq*), is also popular. Pepsi and Miranda orange are now produced locally. Soda water or sickly sweet green lemonade costs 15-20 kyats a bottle. Bottled drinking water is widely available for 30-40 cents/litre.

Mandalay beer is a light but malty brew, made by the People's Brewery and Distillery in the original British-built brewery, which has been operating since 1886. The quality is said to have gone down hill since 1988 and as the country's only brewery it has also had problems meeting demand. The price of Mandalay beer varies considerably but averages 100-150 kyat/bottle; it is too expensive for the average Burmese to afford. Imported alcohol is normally only available at hotel bars, although Johnnie Walker is an ubiquitous ornament in shops, bars and private homes. **Mandalay Rum** is not very strong; it claims to be 'finely flavoured' and 'mellow throughout'. In bars and restaurants, spirits are measured in 'pegs' – a quaint colonial hangover. A peg is a double; single measures are known as smalls.

GETTING AROUND

AIR

Myanmar Airways is the country's major domestic airline and national flag carrier. The airline operates Fokker 27s (turboprops) and F-28s (jets) on internal routes – the former had a spate of fatal crashes in the mid-1980s which were attributed to pilot error, not lack of maintenance. Although their cabin fittings are falling apart, the F-28s, have a more reliable record. However, all, though, are cramped for space and service is poor, verging on the non-existent. In the early 1990s, foreign embassies in Yangon avoided flying with *Myanmar Airways* whenever possible. "Our advice", one foreign diplomat cautioned at the time "to those planning to travel by plane is 'Don't'". Fortunately, things are rather better now and there has not been a fatal accident for some years.

Tickets must be paid for in FECs or US$ cash (*Air Mandalay* – see below – also accepts major credit cards). Burmese pay considerably less than foreigners and are permitted to foot the bill in kyat. Schedules are adhered to in only the loosest of senses and flights are notoriously difficult to book. Tourists are also sometimes forced to forego their seats when government officials require them at short notice. Planes may leave early, late or not at all. Because *Myanmar Airways* tend to overbook it is best to turn up early at the airport even if that means a long wait – longer still because more often than not planes depart late. In the airline's pecking order, the independent traveller comes at the very end of the line and are therefore the very first to be bumped off a flight if seats are scarce. Return tickets can be purchased but return flights can only be confirmed at the destination. Tickets can be purchased in Bangkok but reservations can only be made in Myanmar.

In the last few years two new airlines have begun operating on domestic routes – to great sighs of relief from expats in Yangon. The first to begin operating was Singapore-based *Air Mandalay*. Australian and French pilots fly French-built ATR-72s between Yangon and Thande, Nyaung U (Bagan), Mandalay and Heho. It is a much more efficient, comfortable and, one would expect, safer airline than Myanmar Airways. Surprisingly, it is in fact a joint venture between Singapore-based *Air Mandalay Holdings* and *Myanmar Airways*. The hope seems to be that the majority of tourists, willing to pay slightly over the odds for comfortable planes with better service and a stricter timetable, will plum for *Air Mandalay*, leaving *Myanmar Airways* for the ever-patient Burmese and a handful of budget travellers. Tickets on *Air Mandalay* can be bought and seats booked in Bangkok and Singapore. Flights are around 25% more expensive than on *Myanmar Airways*.

The second, even more recent entrant is *Yangon Airways*. Like *Air Mandalay*, it offers better standards of service and comfort than *Myanmar Airways*, and newer and more modern aircraft. These fares are also higher by around 25%.

For details on fares and routes, see map and table on pages 364 and 392.

Air Mandalay routes

Yangon to:	
Bagan	3-4 departures each day
Heho	daily departures
Mandalay	3-4 departures each day
Thandwe	3, 5 and 7
Mandalay to:	
Bagan	1, 2, 4, 5, 6 and 7
Heho	1-2 departures each day
Yangon	4-5 departures each day
Bagan to:	
Heho	1-2 departures each day
Mandalay	2-4 departures each day
Yangon	2-3 departures each day
Thandwe to:	
Yangon	3, 5 and 7
Heho to:	
Bagan	3 and 7
Mandalay	1, 2, 4, 5 and 6
Yangon	2 departures each day

1 = Mon; **2** = Tues; **3** = Wed; **4** = Thur; **5** = Fri; **6** = Sat; **7** = Sun.

NB 1 Timetable correct at end of 1996. **NB 2** Air Mandalay also operate international flights between Chiang Mai in Thailand and Yangon and Mandalay.

TRAIN

Train tickets can be booked through MTT or through the main station ticket offices. In the Yangon and Mandalay train stations there are special windows reserved for foreign visitors, emblazoned with the sign 'Foreigner Ticket Centre'. In Yangon most travellers buy tickets to Thazi or Mandalay through MTT using US$ or FECs. But MTT also accept major credit cards – Amex, MasterCard and Visa. Tickets can be booked on T 274027. For other routes and at stations other than Mandalay, Yangon and Thazi, buying tickets is rather more of a hit and miss affair. There are no dedicated windows for foreigners and while some ticket offices allow tourists to pay the kyat fare (in kyat), others convert the regular fare into US$/FECs at some unrealistic exchange rate. Although there does not seem to be much pattern to this, generally the less frequented the station by foreigners the more likely you will be allowed to pay the standard fare in kyat. The same goes for booking a seat in ordinary class: on the more popular lines, foreigners are usually only permitted to book upper class tickets, but on the less frequented routes it is easier to buy ordinary class tickets.

Rail fares are cheap compared with travelling by air but the new express bus services are cheaper still – and faster. What the bus does not have though, is the atmosphere of the old, clattering trains. There are two classes: 'upper class' and 'ordinary class'. (Clearly Richard Branson visited Myanmar to get some pointers from *Myanmar Railways*.) Tourists, however, are not expected to travel by ordinary class. Upper class seats are reserved and recline; ordinary class is unreserved. Smarter 'special' trains run between Yangon and Mandalay on Mon, Thur and Sat (US$38) with a dining car.

Most tourists use just one line in the country – between Yangon and Mandalay. The other popular lines are Pyinmana to Kyauk Padaung (about 50 km from Bagan) and Thazi to Shwenyaung (for Inle Lake). As the Yangon Mandalay route is by far the best maintained line with the flashiest locos and rolling stock ('flashiest' is used advisedly), it is easy to leave the country thinking that the government has done pretty well to maintain the rail network. This, though, is a somewhat false impression. Minor lines – which is effectively all the rest of the network – are poorly maintained and investment is minimal. Travel is even slower than on the Yangon-Mandalay line, and journey times are unpredictable. They can also be dangerous – although less so than overland alternatives.

Travel agents are sometimes reluctant to sell tickets to Thazi, so travellers may have to buy a ticket to Mandalay and jump off at Thazi. There is always plenty to eat on the trains as vendors hop on and off at stations. **NB** Overnight journeys in the cool season can be cold enough to need a jumper.

For details on routes and services see map and table on page 393 and 394.

BUS

Like the rest of the transport sector, bus travel in Myanmar has undergone fundamental change over the last 5 years or so. Until then, bus services were a government monopoly and vehicles were ancient, unreliable, uncomfortable and slow. But now that private companies have been allowed to operate on many of the more popular routes, there is much more competition and choice. New express buses, some with a/c, ply between major tourist towns. *Skyline*, *Yoma Express*, *Bagan Express*, *Diamond*, *Arrow* and *Rainbow Express* are the main companies. These services are both cheaper and faster than travelling by train. Even so, many people continue to prefer the sedate rail journey over buses. Unlike rail and air, bus tickets can be purchased with kyat. In addition, although the US$/FEC fare may be quoted, this is converted from the kyat fare at the prevailing free market exchange rate.

Although the bus transport sector may be changing – and it seems likely that more and more private companies will be allowed to operate – the antique vehicles of old are still to be found trundling along most routes. There are 1940s-vintage Chevrolets with brightly painted teak bodies and other mongrel vehicles that in any other country would be sent to the bus equivalent of the knackers yard. These are overcrowded with passengers and their assorted luggage, many hanging off the sides. Needless to say, these buses are highly unreliable and slow. They can be flagged down anywhere. Travellers are advised that during the rainy season (especially Jul-Oct) poor road conditions may mean long delays.

The opening-up of the transport sector to competition has also led to the proliferation of small converted pick-up services – known as 'linecars' (see below).

For details on bus fares and travel times see table on page 395.

CAR HIRE

Self-drive car hire is not permitted for foreigners except when they are resident in the country. However, it is possible to hire a car and driver – which makes a lot of sense given the hazards of driving in the country. Hotels and tour companies in the main towns, cities and tourist destinations will invariably have cars and drivers for private charter and the price will be around US$35-50 per day. The cost tends to vary according to the age of the vehicle – it may be possible to hire a grotty, ageing car for as little as US$30/day. The price will also go up if areas are considered difficult to get to (ie 'restricted' areas) or for longer trips (ie to Bagan or Inle Lake from Mandalay). For a 5-day trip a car should cost around US$450. You are nearly always asked to pay in hard currency.

DRIVING ON MYANMAR'S ROADS

In 1974 General Ne Win decided that it would be more auspicious if Myanmar changed from driving on the left, to the right – with which, fortunately, people have decided to comply. This means that while almost all vehicles continue to be right-hand drive, they also drive on the right.

Like many other poor countries, there are far more hazards on Myanmar's roads than on highways in the developed world. For a start, only a small proportion of the country's roads are surfaced and off the main routes road conditions can be very poor. In the wet season dirt and laterite roads become more hazardous still. In addition to the poor physical condition of Myanmar's roads, there are numerous human and animal obstacles and hazards with which to contend. Many people do not have a finely-honed road sense, animals always pose a potential hazard, while carts and wagons and other road users have to be carefully watched. Foreign residents in Yangon rarely drive themselves even though they are familiar with the country: they don't believe it is worth the risk.

OTHER LOCAL TRANSPORT

● Bicycles

Bicycles can be hired from guesthouses in most towns and especially in Mandalay, Bagan, Inle Lake and Pyin U Lwin. Depending on the age and sophistication of the machine, prices range from 100-200 kyat/day. Bicycles are an ideal way to explore a town or local area at your own pace. Because traffic is generally pretty light outside Yangon, Myanmar remains comparatively bicycle-friendly.

Few visitors to Myanmar tour the country by bike. There is no reason why it shouldn't be possible though. But given the paucity of sophisticated machines it is best either to bring a bicycle with standard parts or to buy a bike in Myanmar itself.

● Horse-drawn cart

Horsecarts or *myint hlei* are mainly found in Bagan, Mandalay and Pyin U Lwin (Maymyo); they cost about 200 kyat/day to hire.

● Linecars/pick-ups

With the gradual privatization of the transport sector some areas now have pick-ups which are locally known as 'linecars' – rather like the Thai songthaew with bench seats in the back and a soft top to protect passengers against sun and rain. Linecars tend to carry people between local towns and on medium distance journeys, especially on the less frequented routes where there is not the demand for large express buses. Because they are faster and more reliable than the old buses, and usually leave at more regular intervals, they tend to charge a slightly higher fare – say 300 kyat rather than 250 kyat. People with private vehicles hoard petrol in the run-up to the water festival in Apr (those who own jeeps cruise up and down the streets for 3 days) and fares tend to escalate at that time. Bus fares can be paid for in kyat.

● Motorcycle hire

While foreigners are not permitted to drive cars in the country, for some reason this regulation does not seem to apply to motorcycles. Though few people have tried it, we have had reports of people hiring or buying motorcycles in Yangon and using them to travel independently around the country. Ask around at guesthouses and travel/tour companies and there may be someone willing to hire out or sell a motorcycle. Because any hire arrangement will be an informal one, it is likely that you will need to lay down a substantial deposit. Also see 'driving' for some of the hazards of Myanmar's roads.

● Taxis

Taxis can easily be found in most towns. Always negotiate the price before setting off; saloon taxis should cost around 200 kyat/hr. Small Mazda taxis in Yangon and *thoun-bein* (3-wheelers) in Mandalay are cheaper (about 120 kyat/hr).

● Trishaw

Bicycle trishaws (*sai kaa*) are used in Mandalay

and Yangon. Expect to pay about 250 kyat/day or 20-30 kyat for short trips around town.

Hitching

Hitchhiking in Myanmar is easy. Cars and lorries will stop with alacrity to pick up foreign travellers and few people have to wait very long. However, be aware that carrying foreigners in more sensitive areas of the country may compromise the generous driver. Buses will also stop anywhere – just flag them down.

BOAT

River

Most river boats in Myanmar are operated by the State-owned Inland Water Transport Company. A shortage of capital and rather lackadaisical management has meant that the vessels are in rather a poor state of repair, much like the rest of the country. River boats travel the entire length of the Ayeyarwady up to Myitkyina, although in the dry season, sand banks can make river journeys hazardous.

The most common river journey undertaken by tourists is from Mandalay down the Ayeyarwady to Bagan; it takes 12-15 hrs (see table and page 162). This stretch of the river is well served by vessels and there is even a tourist boat to shuttle foreigners around in more style than the average vessels can offer. Other, though less popular, river journeys include: Yangon to Thanlyin (Syriam) (see page 128); Mandalay to Mingun (see page 170); Yangon to Twante; Bagan to Yangon (although this trip is time consuming); and Yangon to Pathein.

Fares are cheap – it costs between 50-150 kyat from Mandalay to Bagan, depending which class you travel. However, as with Myanmar Railways, how foreigners are charged seems to be somewhat arbitrary. Often it is possible to pay in kyat at the Burmese rate. On other occasions the fare is quoted and has to be paid for in US$/FECs, at varying rates of exchange. There are seats and deckchairs on the upper deck (which can be reserved). Some food and drink is served and it is also possible to buy food from vendors at stops along the way.

The most luxurious way to travel the Ayeyarwady is on the Orient Express river cruiser which was brought over from the River Elbe in Germany (where it was the *Nederland*) and reincarnated as the *Road to Mandalay*. Fiendishly expensive by Myanmar standards, but the only way to travel the river in style. A 6-day cruise in a standard cabin costs around US$2,500. Contact Venice Simplon-Orient-Express, Sea Containers House, 20 Upper Ground, London SE1 9PF, T (0171) 805 5100.

Towns on rivers will always have private boats to hire for short hops. Rowing boats are cheaper than motor boats (approx 300-400 kyat/hr, depending on price of petrol) but can only be used for nearby sights.

For details on riverboat schedules, see page 396.

Sea

Myanmar Five Star Line (MFSL), another State-owned and operated concern, runs a small fleet of coastal vessels that carry cargo from town to town. Some also take fare-paying passengers. Most of the ships operate on a fortnightly timetable, leaving and returning to Yangon once every 14 days. However, there is no pattern to when they depart and so it is hard to plan ahead. In addition, buying a ticket can take some persuasion. As a result very few people have used MFSL vessels to travel along the coast and the company are not really geared up to receive inquiries from foreigners. The MFSL jetty in Yangon is W of the Pansodan St jetty and it is best to go down here to find out the latest on departures.

COMMUNICATIONS

Language

More than 80 different dialects are spoken in Myanmar, with all the different tribal minorities having their own dialects. The national language is Burmese; it uses an extraordinary-looking script which is based on strings of circles and comes from an ancient Indian script. English is no longer as widely spoken as it used to be, although in the towns and cities there is never much difficulty finding someone who speaks reasonable English. Under British colonial rule, English was the medium of instruction but following independence it was dropped from the school curriculum. In 1981 English was reinstated on the national curriculum after Ne Win's daughter Sanda failed her English examinations abroad.

Postal services

Aerograms – 3.5 kyat. Postcards or letters – 5 kyat (anywhere). Inland letters – 50 pya. Post Office hours (in theory) are 0930-1600, Mon-Fri.

Telephone services

Local: the city code for Yangon is 01; Mandalay

is 02; Bagan is 035. Local calls are free of charge from private phones, usually 10 kyat from a shop or hotel. Call 101 to book inland calls.

Local area codes

Bago (Pegu)	052
Chauk	061
Henzada (Hinthada)	044
Lashio	082
Loikaw	083
Kengtung	101
Magwe	063
Mandalay	02
Mawlamyine (Moulmein)	032
Meiktila	064
Minbu	065
Monywa	071
Pa-an	035
Pathein (Bassein)	042
Pyay (Prome)	053
Pyin U Lwin (Maymyo)	085
Sagaing	072
Sittwe	043
Taunggyi	081
Taungoo (Toungoo)	054
Thanlyin (Syriam)	065
Yangon	01

International: the country code is 95. International calls can be made from major hotels and from the Central Telegraph Office in Yangon (Pansodan/Maha Bandoola roads; open 0700-2000 Mon-Sun) and Mandalay. The international service has improved, but is still poor, due to major deficiencies in the domestic network. All international calls have to go through the operator and may be tapped: 131 to book an overseas or inland trunk call between 0700 and 1900. A connection takes 30-90 mins at a phone office and should be booked at least 3 hrs in advance from other phones. IDD microwave relay calls are available in Bagan, Pyin U Lwin, Mandalay and a few other places. Rates are approximately US$10/minute. Telex and fax facilities are also available at the Central Telegraph Office, as well as in some major hotels.

ENTERTAINMENT

● Newspapers

Newspapers are a product of Western influence. The first English-language newspaper was started in British Burma in 1836 and the first Burmese-language paper rolled off the presses in Arakan in 1873. After the 1962 military coup, the press was restricted and quickly became the mouthpiece of the government. Yangon has six daily newspapers, two of which are English-language papers: *The Working People's Daily* – which in 1993 was rechristened *Myanmar Alin*, or 'New Light of Myanmar', after a pre-1962 publication – takes most of its information from Western or Asian news agencies. Newspaper reports of events inside Myanmar are highly selective and should be taken with a pinch of salt; the pages of *Myanmar Alin* are filled with rants against the BBC and are padded out with endless transcripts of the latest landmark speech by a member of the junta.

● Nightlife

Nightlife has not really hit Myanmar yet (sighs of relief). Burmese people frequent teashops and chat with their friends until 2200-2400.

● Radio

Burmese Broadcasting Service (BBS) operates for 16 hrs of the day and has news in English at 0830, 1300 and 2115. Most of the broadcasting is in Burmese, although there are some programmes in minority dialects. Burmese themselves rely mainly on the BBC World Service and Voice of America to bring them news of what is happening in Myanmar; both of these stations have Burmese-language services which broadcast daily.

● Television

Myanmar's first TV station started operating in 1981 with the assistance of the Japanese.

Warning Many people were jailed for their links with foreign journalists in the run-up to the 1988 riots. In 1990 a Burmese Military Intelligence mole who had infiltrated the Burmese service of the BBC World Service in London was dismissed from his job. Information passed by him to MI in Yangon had been instrumental in the arrest of Nay Min, a Burmese lawyer and secret source of reports on the 1988 uprising. He was sentenced to 14 years' hard labour by a military tribunal. Foreign diplomats report that he has been badly beaten and has suffered internal injuries.

HOLIDAYS AND FESTIVALS

The government runs on the Gregorian calendar but religious and cultural festivals are regulated by the **Burmese calendar**, which is counted from 638 AD. The Burmese calendar is lunar-based. The Buddhist era dates from

544 BC, the agreed date of the Buddha's attainment of nirvana. Each pagoda has its own birthday festival and its favourite *nat* (see page 67) to honour. If a festival is due at one of the most important pagodas, pilgrims travel vast distances to attend the festival.

Myanmar still uses a lunar calendar. On the centre of the masthead of *Myanmar Alin*, for example, the date in the centre of the page might be '14th Waxing of Tagu, 1353' or '6th Waning of Tazaungmon, 1353', the year corresponding to the Buddhist Era (BE). Most festivals (*pwes*) take place on or around the full moon. Business – including MTT – fortunately operates on the Gregorian system.

Jan: *Independence Day* (4th: public holiday) week-long festivities; celebrated all over the country with boat races on the Royal Lake, Yangon and the palace moat, Mandalay.

Feb: *Union Day* (12th: public holiday) in honour of the founding of the Union of Burma in 1947. Parade in Yangon of representatives of Myanmar's various ethnic groups in traditional costumes. *Htamane* (movable: new moon) rice-harvest festival. Rice is offered to the monasteries and a special dish, *htamane*, made of rice, sesame, peanuts, sugar and coconut is eaten.

Mar: *Farmers' (or Peasants') Day* (2nd: public holiday) anniversary of General Ne Win's military take-over in 1962, marked by parades. *Dry Season Festival* (10th: public holiday). *Armed Forces (Resistance) Day* (27th: public holiday) celebrated with fireworks and parades; although the Tatmadaw (see page 80) has given the Burmese people little cause to celebrate in recent years.

Apr: *Thingyan (water festival)* (movable: public holiday) similar to Songkran in Thailand; Thagyamin, king of the nats, descends to earth to bring blessings for the new year. Buddhist New Year is celebrated by much water-throwing – a tradition most enthusiastically observed in Mandalay. Traditionally a small bowl of scented water was thrown over passers-by to 'cleanse' them; now anything goes. Revellers are armed with everything from buckets to firehoses. People from all over Burma travel to the city for the simple pleasure of getting soaked, driving around in WW2 vintage open-topped Willy Jeeps and watching traditional dancers and bad rock bands performing late into the night on street-side stages. The festival has not yet been hooliganized as it has in parts of Thailand and there are never many tourists around. At night, once the water-throwing deadline is passed at 1800 (no-one breaks this unwritten rule), the streets of Mandalay are host to a huge city-wide open-air party. A visit to Mandalay during Thingyan is highly recommended – but visitors are advised to be very careful with cameras. Buddha images and pagodas are cleaned for New Year's Day. The exact time the Lord of the Nats descends to earth is calculated by astrologers. The stars on New Year's Eve also provide the basis for predictions about the coming year – such as whether the rains will be good. There are similar festivals in Laos, Cambodia and Thailand.

May: *Workers' Day* (1st: public holiday). *Kason* (or pouring-water-on-the- banyan-tree Festival) (movable – full moon: public holiday) is the Buddha's birthday; banyan trees get a soaking to celebrate the Buddha's enlightenment under one. Procession in temples.

Jul: Waso (movable: public holiday) commemorates the Buddha's first sermon and the beginning of Buddhist lent. New robes are offered to the monks and gifts taken to pagodas. *Thadingyut* (Buddhist Lent) and the beginning of a 3-month period of prayer and contemplation by Buddhists. During this time monks are not supposed to travel and marriages and pwes should not take place. It is an auspicious time for young men to enter the monkhood, and shin-pyu, can be observed at temples all over the country. *Martyr's Day* (19th: public holiday) in memory of Bogyoke Aung San, independent Myanmar's first Prime Minister, assassinated in 1947 (see page 48).

Sep: during Sep, boat races are held on rivers and lakes throughout Myanmar: it is known as the *Tawthalin* festival and coincides with the beginning of the rains. The most spectacular procession is at Inle Lake (see page 231).

Oct: *Thadingyut* (end of Buddhist Lent) – or festival of lights (movable) celebrates the end of Buddhist lent and means weddings and other celebrations can now take place. Oil lamps are lit for 3 days. Robe-giving ceremonies throughout Oct when monks' robes are presented to monasteries.

Nov: *National Day* (11th: public holiday). *Tazaungmon* (movable: full moon); weaving festival in which teams of unmarried girls engage in weaving competitions, making new robes for monks in the light of the full moon.

Dec: *Spirit-honouring festivals* are held during the full moon. *Christmas Day* (25th, public holiday).

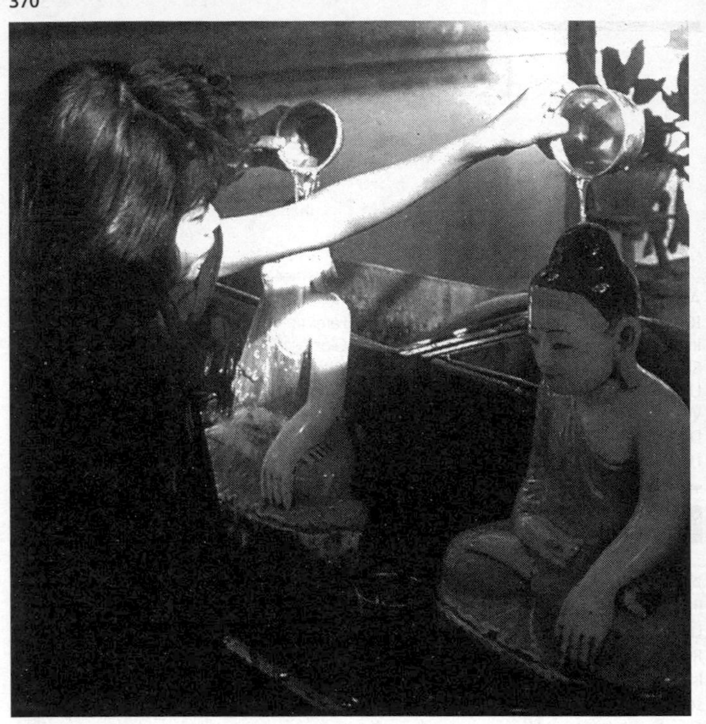

Rounding up

ACKNOWLEDGEMENTS

Angelo Borraccino, Italy; Silvia Borraccino, Italy; Phyllis McFadden, Canada; Natasha Lopez, Colombia; Eric Lammers, Holland; Rosie and Jorge, Portugal; Nigel Easton, UK; Isabella Bisaschl Caruzzo, Italy; Gillian Henson, Laos; George Kovacs, Canada; Pilou Grenié, Shang Thian Huat, Singapore; Paul Patrick, UK; Reyntiens Schaliehoevelaan, Belgium; David Steinke, Germany; Kim Umemoto, Myanmar; Peter Yore, Ireland; Tapani Mäntysaari, Finland; Peter and Bonnie Jensen, USA; Stefano Magistretti.

READING AND LISTENING

BOOKS AND MAGAZINES COVERING THE REGION

Magazines

Asiaweek (weekly). A lightweight *Far Eastern Economic Review*; rather like a regional *Time* magazine in style. *The Far Eastern Economic Review* (weekly). Authoritative Hong Kong-based regional magazine; their correspondents based in each country provide knowledgeable, in-depth analysis, particularly on economics and politics.

Books

Buruma, Ian (1989) *God's dust*, Jonathan Cape: London. Enjoyable journey through Myanmar, Thailand, Malaysia and Singapore along with the Philippines, Taiwan, South Korea and Japan; journalist Buruma questions how far culture in this region has survived the intrusion of the West.

Dingwall, Alastair (1994) *Traveller's literary companion to South-east Asia*, In Print: Brighton. Experts on Southeast Asian language and literature select extracts from novels and other books by western and regional writers. The extracts are annoyingly brief, but it gives a good overview of what is available.

Dumarçay, Jacques (1991) *The palaces of South-East Asia: architecture and customs*, OUP: Singapore. A broad summary of palace art and architecture in both mainland and island Southeast Asia.

Fraser-Lu, Sylvia (1988) *Handwoven textiles of South-East Asia*, OUP: Singapore. Well-illustrated, large-format book with informative text.

Keyes, Charles F (1977) *The golden peninsula: culture and adaptation in mainland Southeast Asia*, Macmillan: New York. Academic, yet readable summary of the threads of continuity and change in Southeast Asia's culture. The volume has been recently republished by Hawaii University Press, but not updated or revised.

King, Ben F and Dickinson, EC (1975) *A field guide to the birds of South-East Asia*, Collins: London. Best regional guide to the birds of the region.

Miettinen, Jukko O (1992) *Classical dance and theatre in South-East Asia*, OUP, Singapore. Expensive, but accessible survey of dance and theatre, mostly focusing on Myanmar, Indonesia and Thailand.

Osborne, Milton (1979) *Southeast Asia: an introductory history*, Allen & Unwin: Sydney. Good introductory history, clearly written, published in a portable paperback edition. A new revised edition is not on the shelves.

Rawson, Philip (1967) *The art of Southeast Asia*, Thames & Hudson: London. Portable general art history of Myanmar, Cambodia, Vietnam, Thailand, Laos, Java and Bali; by necessity, rather superficial, but a good place to start.

Reid, Anthony (1988) *Southeast Asia in the age of commerce 1450-1680: the lands below the winds*, Yale University Press: New Haven. Perhaps the best history of everyday life in Southeast Asia, looking at such themes as physical well-being, material culture and social organization.

Reid, Anthony (1993) *Southeast Asia in the age of commerce 1450-1680: expansion and crisis*, Yale University Press: New Haven. Volume 2 in this excellent history of the region.

Savage, Victor R (1984) *Western impressions of nature and landscape in Southeast Asia*, Singapore University Press: Singapore. Based on a geography PhD thesis, the book is a mine of quotations and observations from Western travellers.

Sesser, Stan (1993) *The lands of charm and cruelty: travels in Southeast Asia*, Picador: Basingstoke. A series of collected narratives first published in the *New Yorker* including essays on Myanmar, Singapore, Laos, Cambodia and Borneo. Finely observed and thoughtful, the book is an excellent travel companion.

Steinberg, David *et al* (1987) *In search of Southeast Asia: a modern history*, University of Hawaii Press: Honolulu. The best standard history of the region; it skilfully examines and assesses general processes of change and their impacts from the arrival of the Europeans in the region.

Tarling, Nicholars (1992) (edit.) *Cambridge History of Southeast Asia*, Cambridge: Cambridge University Press. Two volume edited study, long and expensive with contributions from most of the leading historians of the region. A thematic and regional approach is taken, not a country one, although the history is fairly conventional.

Waterson, Roxana (1990) *The living house: an anthropology of architecture in South-East Asia*, OUP: Singapore. An academic but extensively-illustrated book on Southeast Asian architecture and how it links with lives and livelihoods. Fascinating material for those interested in such things.

Radio

The BBC World Service's *Dateline East Asia* provides probably the best news and views on Asia. Also with a strong Asia focus are the broadcasts of the ABC (Australian Broadcasting Corporation).

BOOKS ON MYANMAR/BURMA

Novels

Bates, HE (1949) *The Jacaranda tree*, Michael Joseph: London. The story of a mixed marriage and the months leading up to the Japanese invasion and occupation of Myanmar.

Law-Yone, Wendy (1983) *The coffin tree*, Alfred Knopf: New York. Published in English, this novel is one of political intrigue. The first part of the book is set in Mandalay, the latter part in the US.

Michio Takeyama (1964) *Harp of Burma*, Tuttle: Vermont. For an alternative look at Myanmar, and especially at Buddhism, this book is unequalled. It describes the effects of Buddhism on the Japanese soldiers who served in the country.

Orwell, George (1934) *Burmese days*, Penguin: Harmondsworth. Perhaps the best known novel set in Myanmar, and the most easily available. It is an anti-imperialist tract, painting British officials (of which Orwell was one) as ignorant and indifferent to the Burmese and their culture. Others who, like Orwell, worked in Myanmar, understandably, refute its tone and its general thesis.

Thompson, Edward (1937) *Burmese silver*, Faber and Faber: London. A novel set in the Chindwin Valley and Conradian in tone.

Shute, Nevil (1947) *The chequer board*, William Morrow: New York. Part set in Myanmar, this tells the story of an Englishman and his Burmese wife and the problems they face when they return to England.

Travel

Collis, Maurice (1938) *Trials in Burma*, Faber and Faber: London. Collis was a magistrate in Myanmar and this tells the fascinating story of his experiences in that position.

Lewis, Norman (1952) *Golden earth: travels in Burma*, Jonathan Cape: London. Lewis is the doyenne of all travel writers on the East and with this book he made his name. It is more than a travel book: it is a thoughtful rumination on Myanmar at a critical time in its post-independence development. It has been republished on numerous occasions and is available either new or in its many guises from second-hand bookshops.

Maugham, Somerset (1930) *The gentleman in the parlour: a record of a journey from Rangoon to Haiphong*, Douleday: New York. Particularly good at describing the Irrawaddy – which seems to have changed little over the intervening 63 years.

Mirante, Edith *Burmese Looking Glass*. An adventurous tourist becomes captivated by the struggle for freedom in Myanmar and, after many adventures, dedicates herself to the cause.

O'Connor, VC Scott (1905) *The silken east: a record of life and travel in Burma*, Hutchinson: London. An enormously evocative book, recounting the author's travels and experiences in the country. Kiscadale (based in Stirling, Scotland) have recently republished it, so it is fairly easy to obtain.

Theroux, Paul (1975) *The great railway bazaar*, Hamish Hamilton: London. Most of this is based elsewhere, but it does have a chapter that deals with travel in Myanmar and is worth reading for this reason.

Biography and autobiography

Arnold, Sue (1995) *A Burmese legacy*, Hodder and Stoughton, London. The author has two Burmese grandmothers and in the mid-1980s decided to write an account of her family's history. The book trips between London and Rangoon, and from the past to the present day. Entertaining and a good insight into mixed-marriages and how the broader sweep of history affects one family.

Aung San Syu Kyi (1984) *Aung San of Burma*, University of Queensland Press: St Lucia. The story of Aung San, the father of Burmese independence who was tragically assassinated at the dawn of the country's freedom, is told by his daughter who is now probably even better known for her own fight against tyranny.

Aung San Suu Kyi with Michael Aris (1991) *Freedom from Fear*, Penguin: Harmondsworth. The tale of Myanmar's stuggle for democracy and against tyranny, by someone on the front line.

Aung San Suu Kyi (1993) *Towards a True Refuge*, Oxford.

Aye Saung (1989) *Burman in the back row: autobiography of a Burmese rebel*, White Lotus: London and Bangkok.

Collis, Maurice (1982) *Siamese white*, DD Books: Bangkok. Biographical book by one of the most knowledgeable of writers on Myanmar.

MiMi Khaing (1946) *Burmese family*. Written and originally published in English, this is an autobiographical account of the author's childhood in Myanmar, excellent vignettes of Burmese life and very informative. It can be picked up in Myanmar.

Sargent, Inge (1994) *Twilight over Burma: my life as a Shan princess*, Chiang Mai: Silkworm Books. The author married a Hsipaw prince and arrived in Myanmar in 1953. The coup of 1962 effectively ended the couple's blissful life – see the entry on Hsipaw.

History

Aung-Thwin, Michael (1985) *Pagan: the origins of modern Burma*, University of Hawaii Press: Honolulu. A good history of

Myanmar.

Cady, John F (1958) *A history of modern Burma*, Cornell University Press: Ithaca. Good on the lead up to independence and the years following but, by dint of its publication date, cannot offer an insight into recent history.

Life and livelihood

Shway Yoe (1882) *The Burman, his life and notions*. A long book and a key marker in works describing Burmese ways. Sometimes it can be picked up in second-hand book shops and it has recently been republished by Kiscadale (based in Stirling, Scotland). An excellent travel companion.

Strachan, Paul and Rodrigue, Yves (1995) *Nat-pwe: Burma's supernatural sub-culture*, Whiting Bay, Arran: Kiscadale. Glossy publication with lots of illustrations and an informative text on this uniquely Burmese spiritual practice and art form.

Art and architecture

Lowry, John (1974) *Burmese Art*, Victoria & Albert Museum: London.

O'Connor (1907) *Mandalay and other cities of the past in Burma*, Hutchinson: London.

Strachan, Paul (1989) *Pagan: art and architecture of old Burma*, Whiting Bay, Arran, Kiscadale. Well illustrated, large format book with a good text, covering Pagan's main temples.

Thaw, Aung (1972) *Historical sites in Burma*, Ministry of Union Culture: Rangoon. A good illustrated account of Myanmar's main sites – it is available in Rangoon.

Natural history and geography

Toke Gale U *Burmese timber elephant*, Trade Corporation: Rangoon.

Williams, JH (1950) *Elephant Bill*, Rupert Hart Davis: London. Colonel JH Williams lived and worked for over 20 years with elephants in the teak industry and, as they say, knew them better than most. As an elephant officer he had to know not just the elephants, but also the mahouts who looked after them. The book has since been republished but is also occasionally available in second-hand book shops.

Williams, JH (1953) *Bandoola*, Rupert Hart Davis: London. The less well known follow up to Elephant Bill. Not quite as evocative, but nonetheless a recommended read for all ele-philes.

Economics and politics

Allott, Anna (1993) *Inked over, ripped out: Burmese storytellers and the censors*, Pen American Center: New York. Anna Allott taught Burmese at the School of Oriental & African Studies in London and the title of this book really says it all: it is about the endless struggle that Burmese authors face in telling their stories.

Boucaud, Andre and Louis (1989) *Burma's Golden Triangle on the trail of the opium warlords*, Asia 2000.

Lintner, Bertil (1990) *Outrage: Burma's struggle for democracy*, White Lotus: London and Bangkok. This book, a definitive and emotive account of the 1988 uprising has been printed in Burmese and is available in Myanmar in brown paper covers – under-the-counter.

Lintner, Bertil (1990) *Land of jade: a journey through insurgent Burma*, Kiscadale: Stirling. A travel book with a political axe to grind: Lintner, journalist on Myanmar for the *Far Eastern Economic Review* describes life in and among the insurgents.

Lintner, Bertil (1995) *Burma in revolt: opium and insurgency since 1948*, Bangkok: White Lotus. Really speaks for itself – an historical analysis of Myanmar's succession of ethnic conflicts and the opium industry; draws on many first person interviews with key figures.

McCoy, Alfred W (1991) *The Politics of Heroin: CIA complicity in the global drugs trade*, Lawrence Hill Books: New York.

Smith, Martin (1991) *Burma: insurgency and the politics of ethnicity*, Zed Books: London. A very well researched investigation into Myanmar's current plight focusing on the myriad ethnic-based movements that, until recently, divided the country from top to bottom.

Steinberg, David (1982) *Burma: a socialist nation of Southeast Asia*, Westview Press:

Boulder, Colorado. Academic book, good on economics and politics, but for obvious reasons not much on recent reforms.

Taylor, Robert (1989) *The state in Burma*, University of Hawaii Press: Honolulu. Highly scholarly study of Burmese politics, written just before the democracy demonstrations of 1988 which it failed to anticipate.

Guides

Along with other travel guides like this one, a guide with a difference is Burma Action Group's *Burma: the alternative guide*. This has been published to complement their 'Don't Visit Burma' campaign. Available from BAG, Collins Studios, Collins Yard, Islington Green, London N1 2XU, T +44 (0) 171 359-7679, F +44 (0) 171-354-3897. E-mail: bagp@gn.apc.org.

Activist publications

There is probably more material produced of an 'activist' bent on Myanmar than on just about any other country.

Burma Issues, published monthly from Bangkok. For further information write to *Burma Issues*, PO Box Silom 1076, Bangkok 10504, Thailand.

Burma News, published by the Burma Action Group in the UK. Write to: BAG, Collins Studios, Collins Yard, Islington Green, London N1 2XU, T +44 (0)171 359-7679, F +44 (0)171-354-3897. E-mail: bagp@gn.apc.org.

Films

Beyond Rangoon, directed by John Boorman, released in 1995, received mixed reviews. The film tells the story of a US doctor caught up in the 1988 democracy demonstrations.

THE INTERNET

Listed below are Internet addresses which access information on Asia generally, the Southeast Asian region, or Myanmar. **News-groups** tend to be informal talking shops offering information from hotels and sights through to wide-ranging discussions on just about any topic. **Mailing Lists** have a more academic clientele, and probably are not worth plugging into unless you have a specific interest in the subject concerned. **Web sites** offer a whole range of information on a vast variety of topics. Below is only a selection.

Newsgroups on USENET with a Southeast Asian focus

Newsgroups are discussion fora on the USENET. Not every computer linked to the Internet has access to USENET – your computer needs Net News and a News reader. Newsgroups are informal fora for discussion; they are occasionally irreverent, usually interesting.

• Asia general

alt.asian.movies
alt.buddha.short.fat.guy
rec.travel.asia
soc.religion.eastern
talk.religion.buddhism

• Southeast Asia

soc.culture.asean

• Burma

soc.culture.burma

Mailing lists

These are discussion groups with a more academic content; some may be moderate – ie the content of messages is checked by an editor. Mailing lists communicate using E-mail. The focus of the groups are in brackets.

• Asia general

actmus-1@ubvm.bitnet
[Asian Contemporary Music Discussion Group]
apex-1@uheevm.bitnet
[Asia-Pacific Exchange]
buddha-1@ulkyvm.bitnet
[Buddhist Academic Discussion Forum]

• Southeast Asia

seanet-1@nusvm.bitnet
[Southeast Asian Studies List]
seasia-1@msu.bitnet
[Southeast Asia Discussion List]

Myanmar and Southeast Asia on the World Wide Web – Web sites

Web sites are on the World Wide Web. They can now be browsed using a graphical mouse-based hypertext system. The two in use are Mosaic and the newer, Netscape. They allow the user to browse through the WWW easily. Note, however, that images (especially) take time to download and if on the Web during the time of the day when the US is alive and kicking expect to spend a very long time twiddling your thumbs. The subject of the web site is in brackets after the address.

● Asia general

http://none.coolware.com/infoasia/
[run by Infoasia which is a commercial firm that helps US and European firms get into Asia]
http://www.city.net/regions/asia
[pointer to information on Asian countries]
http://www.branch.com:80/silkroute/
[information on hotels, travel, news and business in Asia]
http://www.singapore.com/pata
[Pacific Asia Travel Association – stacks of info on travel in the Pacific Asian region including stats, markets, products etc]
http://pears.lib.ohio-state.edu/asianstudies/asian studies.html
[huge range of links with information on topics from sports and travel to economics and engineering]
http://webhead.com/asergio/asiaregion.html
[travel information on Asian region]
http///www.clark.net/pub/global/asia.html
[mostly Japan and China, but also links with Southeast Asian countries]
http://www.yahoo.com/Regional Countries/[name of country]
[insert name of country to access practical information including material from other travel guides]
http://coombs.anu.edu.au/WWWVLPages/WhatsNewWWW/asian-www-news.html
[assortment of material from across Asian region]

● Southeast Asia

http://emailhost.ait.ac.th/asia/asia. html
[clickable map of mainland Southeast Asia with pointer to sources of other information on the region]
http://www.leidenuniv.nl/pun/ubhtm/mjkintro.htm
[library of 100 slides of Thailand (Phimai, Chiang Mai, Lamphun) and other mainland Southeast Asian countries]
http://libweb.library.wisc.edu/guides/SEAsia/library.htm
['Gateway to Southeast Asia' from University of Wisconsin, numerous links]
http://www.pactoc.net.au/index/resindex.htm
[covers all Pacific, but good links into Southeast Asian material; emphasis on academic issues rather than travel]

Terms

E-mail = Electronic mail
WWW = World Wide Web or, simply, the Web
HTML = Hypertext Markup Language
URL = Uniform Resource Locators

Sources: the above was collated from *Internet news* published in the *IIAS Newsletter* [International Institute for Asian Studies Newsletter], Summer 1995, updated from the *IIAS Newsletter* no 8 (Spring 1996 and from the *Asian Studies Newsletter* (June/July 1996). The IIAS publish a guide, *IIAS Internet guide to Asian Studies '96* which can be ordered from the IIAS Secretariat, PO Box 9515, 2300 RA Leiden, the Netherlands (Dfl, 20-) or accessed at: http://iias.leidenuniv.nl.

SHORT WAVE RADIO

British Broadcasting Corporation (BBC, London) *Southeast Asian service* 3915, 6195, 9570, 9740, 11750, 11955, 15360; *Singapore service* 88.9MHz; *East Asian service* 5995, 6195, 7180, 9740, 11715, 11750, 11945, 11955, 15140, 15280, 15360, 17830, 21715.

Voice of America (VoA, Washington) *Southeast Asian service* 1143, 1575, 7120, 9760, 9770, 15185, 15425; *Indonesian service* 6110, 11760, 15425.

Radio Beijing *Southeast Asian service (English)* 11600, 11660.

Radio Japan (Tokyo) *Southeast Asian service (English)* 11815, 17810, 21610.

Useful addresses

EMBASSIES AND CONSULATES

Australia
22 Arkana St, Canberra ACT 2600, T 062 733811, F 61-6 273.4357

Bangladesh
106 Gulshan Ave, Gulshan, Dhaka 1212, T 8802 601461, F 88370

Canada
85, Range Rd, Apartment No 902-903, The Sandringham, Ottawa, Ontario, KIN 816, T 613 232-6434, F 1-613 232-6435

China
No 6, Dong Zhi MenWai St, Chaoyang District, Beijing, T 861 532 1584, F 861 532.1344 or 3rd Flr Bldg 3, Camellia Hotel, Kunming, T/F 871 317 6609

France
60 Rue De Courcelles, 3rd Flr, 75008 Paris, T 1 4225 5695, F 33.1 42.56.49.41

Germany
Schumann Str 112, 53113 Bonn, T 0228 210091, F 49-228 219316

Hong Kong
Room No 2424, Sun Hung Kai Centre, No 30, Harbour Rd, Wanchai, Hong Kong, T 28277929, F 28276597

India
No 3/50 f, Nyaya Marg, Chanakyapuri, New Delhi 110021, T 11 600251, F 91-11 6877.942

Indonesia
109 Jalan Haji Agus Salim, Jakarta, T 21 327684, F 21 327204

Israel
No 26 Hayarkon St, Tel Aviv 68011, T 35170760, F 35171440

Italy
Via Vincenzo Bellini 20, Interno 1, 00198 Rome, T 6 8549374, F 39-6 8413167

Japan
8-26, 4 Chome, Kita-Shinagawa, Shinagawa-Ku, Tokyo, T 03 441-9291-5, F 81-3 447.7394

Laos
Sok Paluang Rd, PO Box II, Vientiane, T 21314910, F 21314913

Malaysia
5, Taman U Thant Satu, 55000 Kuala Lumpur, T 3 242 4085, F 60-3 2480049

Nepal
Chakupat, Patan Gate, Lalitpur, Kathmandu, T 71 521788, F 71 523402

Pakistan
No 12/1, St 13, F-7/2, Islamabad, T 51 822460, F 51 221210

Philippines
104, 4th Flr, Basic Petroleum Bldg, Carlos Palanca Jr St

Russia
41 UL Gertsena, Moscow, T 291 05 34, F 7-95 2010166

Singapore
133 Techmat Bldg, 05-04, Middle Rd, Singapore 0718, T 3388025, F 3380738

Sri Lanka
17 Skelton Gardens, Colombo 5, T 1 587 608, F 94-1 580460

Switzerland
Permanent Mission to the UN, 47, Ave Blanc, 1202 Geneva, T 022 7317540, F 41-22 7384882

Thailand
132, North Sathorn Rd, Bangkok 10500, T 02 233 2237, F 66-2 236.6898

UK
19A Charles St, London W1X 8ER, T 0171 629 6966, F 0171 629 4169

USA
2300 S St NW, Washington DC 20008, T (202) 332-9044, F (202) 332 9046, and 10 East 77th St, New York NY 10021, T (212) 535 1310

Vietnam
Building No A3, Ground Flr, Van Phuc, Diplomatic Quarters, Hanoi, T 53369, F (84-4) 52404

Useful Burmese words and phrases

MANY PEOPLE in Myanmar can speak English well, and others remember a bit from schooldays. All staff in immigration, customs, tourist shops and hotels in tourist areas are English speakers. However, everyone is appreciative if visitors show they have made an effort to learn the language. Several phrasebooks are available in Thailand and Myanmar for those who would like to learn more.

PHRASE BOOKS

There is a good little phrase book printed in Myanmar called *Practical Myanmar* (Sun Associates, 350 kyat).

SPELLING AND PRONUNCIATION

Burmese is written in its own script and there is no standard method of writing Burmese words in roman letters. In the following notes read.

i as in *magazine*
ei as in *eight*
eh as in *men*
a as in *bra*
aw as in *law*
o as in *go*
oo as in *too*
in as in *pin* (nasalized, as in French)
ai as in *Thai*
an as in *man* (nasalized, as in French)
au as in German *Autobahn* or *ou* in *sound*
u as in *put*
it as in *it*

The typical English *kpt* are about halfway between the unaspirated Burmese consonants and the heavily aspirated *kh, ph, ht*. There is also an aspirated *s*, often transcribed as *hs*. However, many Burmese are sloppy about making this distinction. *Ch* is aspirated, as in English. *Ky* is the same sound, unaspirated, which may sound like a *j* to English ears. At the end of a syllable represents a glottal stop – close in effect to an unaspirated *t*. Burmese has 3 tones – high (:), creaky (.) and low (unmarked). Give high, creaky, and glottal stop syllables more emphasis than low ones. In addition, a creaky syllable is subject to a gradual glottal choke. In syllables with nasalized *ns*, this is often represented by a *t*. *U Thant*, for example, is a high and creaky tone. In our transcription he would be *U: Than*.

HELLO AND GOODBYE

Among themselves people use a variety of greetings phrases ("Where are you going?" "I see you've arrived" etc), but in schools, and sometimes to foreigners, they may say *Min-g-la-ba*. The reply is the same. On leaving say *Thwa:-ba-on:-meh* ("I'll be getting along now") or less formally *Thwa:-meh naw* ("I'm going now – OK?"). The response is *Kaun:-ba-bi* ("Fine" "OK"). You can preface your farewell with *Thwa:-z-ya shi.-ba-deh* ("I have things to do").

USEFUL WORDS AND PHRASES

Thanks
Kyei:-zoo:-tin-ba-deh
You're welcome
Ya.-ba-deh or Keit-sa. m-shi.-ba-boa
Sorry
Saw:-ri:-beh
That's all right
Ya.-ba-deh or Keit-sa. m-shi.-ba-boa
No thanks or That's enough
Taw-ba-bi
Just a minute
K-na:-lei
Have you finished?
Pi:-bi-la:
Yes ("I have finished")
Pi:-ba-bi
No ("I haven't finished")
M-pi:-thei:-boo:
I'm happy to have met you
Twei.-ya.-da wun:-tha-ba-deh
Pleased to meet you too
Wun:-tha-ba-deh
How are you?
Nei-kaun:-yéh-là? literally ("Are you well?")
Fine
Nei-kaun:-ba-deh literally ("I am well")
What is your name?
Nan-meh beh-loh kaw-dhålèh?
It is Mary
Mary-ba
I/me (male)
Kyun-daw
I/me (female)
Kyun-ma

'ASKING FOR' WORDS

What's this?
Da-ba-leh?
It's a mango
Th-yet-thi
What's that called?
Eh:-da beh-lo-kaw-th-leh?
It's called Ee-jcha-gkwày
I-kya-kwe i:-lo.kaw-ba-deh
Please say that again
Tat-pyaw:-ba-on:

ASKING THE WAY

I want to go to ...
... thwa:-jin-ba-deh
How do I get there?
Beh-lo thwa:ya.-m-leh
Go this way
Di-bet-thwa:-ya.-deh
This way?
Di-bet-la:
That's right
Hot-ba-deh
Go straight
Teh:-deh:-thwa:-ba
Is it far?
Wei:-th-la:?
It is a bit far
Neh:-neh:wei:-ba-deh
It's not far
M-wei:-ba-boo:

RESTAURANTS

Please give me/us ...
... pei:-ba
Have you got any ...?
... shi-th-la:
Yes, I have
-shi-ba-deh
No, I haven't
-m-shi.-ba-boo:
We want to settle up
Pait-san shin:-meh
How much does it come to?
Beh-laut-kya-th-leh
I like ...
... chait-deh
Don't put in ...
... m-teh:ba neh
Does it have ... in it?
... pa-th-la:
I can't eat ...
... må sà daq boò.
meat
å thà
fish paste
ngå peè

NUMBERS

0 thon-nya
1 tit

2 hnit
3 thon:
4 lei:
5 nga:
6 chaut
7 kun-nit
8 shit
9 ko:
10 t-seh
20 hn-seh
30 thon:-zeh
40 lei:-zeh
100 t-ya
200 hu-ya
300 thon:-ya
400 lei:ya
1,000 t-htaung
10,000 t-thaung:
100,000 t-thein:
1,000,000 t-than:

COUNTING

one bottle of water
yei t boq
two cups of coffee
kaw-hpi-hn-kwet
three bottles of Coke
Kot-thon:-p-lin
two plates of fish curry
ngå-hìn hnåpwèh
one plate of rice
t-min: t-hpweh

Items without a unit of quantity are counted by -goó (sometimes pronounced koó)

two cakes
keit-mon hnkha
three dumplings
paut-si thon:-goo
four paratas
p-la-ta lei:-goo

SHOPS

How much is this?
Da beh-laut heh:
It's 8 kyat
Shit-kyat-ba
That's too expensive
Neh:neh:mya:ba deh
I'll give you 6 kyat
Chaut-kyat-pei:-meh
Would that be all right?
Ya.m-la:
OK
Kaung:-ba-bi
No it wouldn't
M-ya.-ba-boo:
It's too little
Neh:-ba-deh
Give me 7 kyat
Kun-n-kyat pei:-ba
It's too small
Thei: ba-deh
It's too big
Kyi: ba-deh
I'll look around elsewhere – OK?
Kyi.-on-meh-naw

BASIC VOCABULARY

beef u-meh-tha:
chicken kyet-tha:
curry hin:
doctor hs-ya-wun
fish gna:
fish paste ng pi:
guesthouse teh:-ko-khan:
hotel ho-dteh
hospital hsei: yon
noodles kaut-hsweh:
not spicy hot m-sat-boo:
police station yeh:-ta-na.
pork wet-thas
post office sa-dait
prawn båzun
restaurant t-min: zain
rice t-min:
room eit-khan:
toilet ein-tha
vegetarian thet-that-lot

DISTINCTIVE FRUITS

Custard apple (or sugar apple) Scaly green skin, squeeze the skin to open the fruit and scoop out the flesh with a spoon. Season: Jun-Sep.

Durian (*Durio zibethinus*) A large prickly fruit, with yellow flesh, about the size of a football. Infamous for its pungent smell. While it is today regarded by many visitors as simply revolting, early Europeans (16th-18th centuries) raved about it, possibly because it was similar in taste to Western delicacies of the period. Borri (1744) thought that "God himself, who had produc'd that fruit". But by 1880 Burbridge was writing: "Its odour – one scarcely feels justified in using the word 'perfume' – is so potent, so vague, but withal so insinuating, that it can scarcely be tolerated inside the house". Banned from public transport in Singapore and hotel rooms throughout the region, and beloved by most Southeast Asians (where prize specimens can cost a week's salary), it has an alluring taste if the odour can be overcome. Some maintain it is an addiction. Durian-flavoured chewing gum, ice cream and jams are all available. Season: May-Aug.

Jackfruit Similar in appearance to durian but not so spiky. Yellow flesh, tasting slightly like custard. Season: Jan-Jun.

Mango (*Mangifera indica*) A rainforest fruit which is now cultivated. Widely available in the West; in Southeast Asia there are hundreds of different varieties with subtle variations in flavour. Delicious eaten with sticky rice and a sweet sauce (in Thailand). The best mangoes in the region are considered to be those from South Thailand. Season: Mar-Jun.

Mangosteen (*Garcinia mangostana*) An aubergine-coloured hard shell covers this small fruit which is about the size of a tennis ball. Cut or squeeze the purple shell to reach its sweet white flesh which is prized by many visitors above all others. In 1898, an American resident of Java wrote, erotically and in obvious ecstasy: "The five white segments separate easily, and they melt on the tongue with a touch of tart and a touch of sweet; one moment a memory of the juiciest, most fragrant apple, at another a remembrance of the smoothest cream ice, the most exquisite and delicately flavoured fruit-acid known – all of the delights of nature's laboratory condensed in that ball of *neige parfumée*". Southeast Asians believe it should be eaten as a chaser to durian. Season: Apr-Sep.

Papaya (*Carica papaya*) A New World Fruit that was not introduced into Southeast Asia until the 16th century. Large, round or oval in shape, yellow or green-skinned, with bright orange flesh and a mass of round, black seeds in the middle. The flesh, in texture and taste, is somewhere between a mango and a melon. Some maintain that it tastes 'soapy'. Season: Year round.

Pomelo A large round fruit the size of anything from an ostrich egg to a football, with thick, green skin, thick pith, and flesh not unlike that of the grapefruit, but less acidic. Season: Aug-Nov.

Rambutan (*Nephelium lappaceum*) The bright red and hairy rambutan – *rambut* is the Malay word for 'hair' – with its slightly rubbery but sweet flesh is a close relative of the lychee of southern China and tastes similar. The Thai word for rambutan is *ngoh*, which is the nickname given by Thais to the fuzzy-haired Negrito aboriginals in the southern jungles. Season: May-Sep.

Salak (*Salacca edulis*) A small pear-shaped fruit about the size of a large plum with a rough, brown, scaly skin (somewhat like a miniature pangolin) and yellow-white, crisp flesh. It is related to the sago and rattan trees.

Tamarind (*Tamarindus indicus*) Brown seedpods with dry brittle skins and a brown tart-sweet fruit which grow on a tree introduced into Southeast Asia from India. The name is Arabic for 'Indian date'. The flesh has a high tartaric acid content and is used to flavour curries, jams, jellies and chutneys as well as for cleaning brass and copper. Elephants have a predilection for tamarind balls. Season: Dec-Feb.

Health

THE TRAVELLER to Myanmar is inevitably exposed to health risks not encountered in North America, Western Europe or Australasia. Myanmar has a tropical climate; nevertheless the acquisition of true tropical disease by the visitor is probably conditioned as much by the rural nature and standard of hygiene of the country than by the climate. There is an obvious difference in health risks between the business traveller staying in international class hotels and the backpacker staying in basic guesthouses in more out of the way places. There are no hard and fast rules to follow; you will often have to make your own judgements on the healthiness or otherwise of your surroundings.

Medical care

The quality of medical care in Myanmar is highly variable. Away from Yangon it is, generally speaking, very poor indeed. In Bangkok, medical care is adequate (and rapidly improving) for most exigencies, although Singapore and Hong Kong offer the best facilities for serious illness. In rural areas there are systems and traditions of medicine wholly different from the Western model and you may be confronted with less orthodox forms of treatment such as herbal medicine and acupuncture. At least you can be sure that local practitioners have a lot of experience with the particular diseases of their region. If you are in Yangon it may be worthwhile calling on your embassy to provide a list of recommended doctors.

Medicines

If you are a long way away from medical help, a certain amount of self administered medication may be necessary and you will find many of the drugs available have familiar names. However, always check the date stamping (sell-by date) and buy from reputable pharmacists because the shelf life of some items, especially vaccines and antibiotics, is markedly reduced in hot conditions. Unfortunately, many locally produced drugs are not subjected to quality control procedures and so can be unreliable. There have, in addition, been cases of substitution of inert materials for active drugs. With the following precautions and advice you should keep as healthy as usual. Make local enquiries about health risks if you are apprehensive and take the general advice of European, Australian or North American families who have lived or are living in the area.

BEFORE YOU GO

Take out medical insurance. You should also have a dental check-up, obtain a spare glasses prescription and, if you suffer from a long-standing condition, such as diabetes, high blood pressure, heart/lung disease or a nervous disorder, arrange for a check-up with your doctor who can at the same time provide you with a letter explaining details of your medical disorder. Check the current practice for malaria prophylaxis (prevention) for the countries you intend to visit.

INOCULATIONS

Smallpox vaccination is no longer required. Neither is cholera vaccination, despite the fact that the disease occurs – but not at present in epidemic form – in some of these countries. Yellow fever vaccination is not required either, although you may be asked for a certificate if you have been in a country affected by yellow fever immediately before travelling to Southeast Asia. The following vaccinations are recommended:

Typhoid (monovalent) One dose followed by a booster 1 month later. Immunity from this course lasts 2-3 years. An oral preparation is also available.

Poliomyelitis This is a live vaccine generally given orally but a full course consists of three doses with a booster in tropical regions every 3-5 years.

Tetanus One dose should be given, with a booster at 6 weeks and another at 6 months. 10 yearly boosters thereafter are recommended.

Meningitis and Japanese B encephalitis (JVE) There is an extremely small risk of these rather serious diseases; both are seasonal and vary according to region. Meningitis can occur in epidemic form; JVE is a viral disease transmitted from pigs to man by mosquitos. For details of the vaccinations, consult a travel clinic.

Children should, in addition to the above, be properly protected against diphtheria, whooping cough, mumps and measles. Teenage girls, if they have not had the disease, should be given a rubella (German measles) vaccination. Consult your doctor for advice on BCG inoculation against tuberculosis: the disease is still common in the region.

INFECTIOUS HEPATITIS (JAUNDICE)

This is common and seems to be frequently caught by travellers. The main symptoms are stomach pains, lack of appetite, nausea, lassitude and yellowness of the eyes and skin. Medically speaking there are two types: the less serious but more common is *hepatitis A* for which the best protection is careful preparation of food, the avoidance of contaminated drinking water and scrupulous attention to toilet hygiene. Human normal immunoglobulin (gammaglobulin) confers considerable protection against the disease and is particularly useful in epidemics. It should be obtained from a reputable source and is certainly recommended for travellers who intend to travel and live rough. The injection should be given as close as possible to your departure and as the dose depends on the likely time you are to spend in potentially infected areas, the manufacturers' instructions should be followed. A vaccination against hepatitis A has recently become generally available and is safe and effective. Three shots are given over 6 months and confer excellent protection against the disease for up to 10 years. Eventually this vaccine is likely to supersede the use of gammaglobulin.

The other, more serious, version is *hepatitis B* which is acquired as a sexually transmitted disease, from a blood transfusion or an injection with an unclean needle, or possibly by insect bites. The symptoms are the same as hepatitis A but the incubation period is much longer.

You may have had jaundice before or you may have had hepatitis of either type before without becoming jaundiced, in which case it is possible that you could be immune to either hepatitis A or B (or C or a number of other letters). This immunity can be tested for before you travel. If you are not immune to hepatitis B already, a vaccine is available (3 shots over 6 months) and if you are not immune to hepatitis A already, then you should consider having gammaglobulin or a vaccination.

AIDS

This is increasingly prevalent in Myanmar (and Thailand). It is not wholly confined to the well known high risk sections of the population ie homosexual men, intravenous drug abusers, prostitutes and the children of infected mothers. Heterosexual transmission is probably now the dominant mode of infection and so the main risk to travellers is from casual sex. The same precautions should be taken as when encountering any sexually transmitted disease. In Thailand and increasingly in Myanmar, almost the entire population of female prostitutes is HIV positive and in other parts intravenous drug abuse is common. The AIDS virus (HIV) can be passed via unsterile needles which have been previously used to inject an HIV positive patient, but the risk of this is very small indeed. It would, however, be sensible to check that needles have been properly sterilized or disposable needles used. The chance of picking up hepatitis B in this way is much more of a danger. Be wary of carrying disposable needles. Customs officials may find them suspicious. The risk of receiving a blood transfusion with blood infected with the HIV virus is greater than from dirty needles because of the amount of fluid exchanged. Supplies of blood for transfusion are supposed to be screened for HIV in all reputable hospitals so the risk should be small. Catching the virus which causes AIDS does not necessarily produce an illness in itself; the only way to be sure if you feel you have been put at risk is to have a blood test for HIV antibodies on your return to a place where there are reliable laboratory facilities. However, the test does not become positive for many weeks.

COMMON PROBLEMS

HEAT AND COLD

Full acclimatization to tropical temperatures takes about 2 weeks and during this period it is normal to feel relatively apathetic, especially if the humidity is high. Drink plenty of water (up to 15 litres a day are required when working physically hard in the tropics). Use salt on your food and avoid extreme exertion. Tepid showers are more cooling than hot or cold ones. Large hats do not cool you down but do prevent sunburn. Remember that, especially in highland areas, there can be a large and sudden drop in temperature between sun and shade and between night and day so dress accordingly. Loose-fitting cotton clothes are best for hot weather. Warm jackets and woollens are often necessary after dark at high altitude.

INTESTINAL UPSETS

Practically nobody escapes intestinal infections, so be prepared for them. Most of the time they are due to the insanitary preparation of food. Do not eat uncooked fish, vegetables or meat (especially pork), fruit without the skin (always peel fruit yourself), or food that is exposed to flies (particularly salads). Tap water may be unsafe, especially in the monsoon seasons and the same goes for stream water or well water. Filtered or bottled water is usually available and safe but you cannot always rely on it. If your hotel has a **central** hot water supply, this is safe to drink after cooling. Ice should be made from boiled water but rarely is, so stand your glass on the ice cubes instead of putting them in the drink. Dirty water should first be strained through a filter bag (available from camping shops) and then boiled or treated. Bringing the water to a rolling boil at sea level is sufficient. In the highlands, you have to boil the water a bit longer to ensure that all the microbes are killed (because water boils at a lower temperature at altitude). Various sterilizing methods can be used and there are proprietary preparations containing chlorine or iodine compounds. Pasteurised or heat-treated milk is now fairly widely available as is ice cream and yoghurt produced by the same methods. Unpasteurised milk products, including cheese, are sources of tuberculosis, brucellosis, listeria and food poisoning germs. You can render fresh milk safe by heating it to 62°C for 30 mins followed by rapid cooling or by boiling. Matured or processed cheeses are safer than fresh varieties.

Fish and shellfish are popular foods but can be the source of health problems. Shellfish which are eaten raw will transmit food poisoning or hepatitis if they have been living in contaminated water. Certain fish accumulate toxins in their bodies at certain times of the year, which give rise to illness when they are eaten. The phenomenon known as 'red tide' can also affect fish and shellfish which eat large quantities of tiny sea creatures and thereby become poisonous. The only way to guard against this is to keep as well informed as possible about fish and shellfish quality in the area you are visiting. Most countries impose a ban on fishing in periods when red tide is prevalent, although this is often flouted.

Diarrhoea is usually the result of food poisoning, but can occasionally result from contaminated water. There are various causes – viruses, bacteria, protozoa (like amoeba), salmonella and cholera organisms. It may take one of several forms coming on suddenly or rather slowly. It may be accompanied by vomiting or severe abdominal pain, and the passage of blood or mucus (when it is called dysentery).

All kinds of diarrhoea, whether or not accompanied by vomiting, respond favourably to the replacement of water and salts taken as frequent small sips of some kind of rehydration solution. There are proprietary preparations consisting of sachets of oral rehydration electrolyte powder which are dissolved in water, or you can make up your own by adding half a teaspoonful of salt (3.5 grams) and 4 tablespoons of sugar (40 grams) to a litre of boiled water. If it is possible to time the onset of diarrhoea to the minute, then it is probably viral or bacterial and/or the onset of dysentery. The treatment in addition to rehydration is Ciprofloxacin (500 mgs every 12 hrs). The drug is now widely available as are various similar ones.

If the diarrhoea has come on slowly or intermittently, then it is more likely to be protozoal, i.e. caused by amoeba (amoebic dysentery) or giardia, and antibiotics will have no effect. These cases are best treated by a doctor as should any diarrhoea continuing for more than 3 days. If there are severe stomach cramps, the following drugs may help: Loperamide (*Imodium*, *Arret*) and Diphenoxylate with Atropine (*Lomotil*). The drug usually used for giardia or amoeba is Metronidazole (*Flagyl*) or Tinidazole (*Fasigyu*).

The lynchpins of treatment for diarrhoea are rest, fluid and salt replacement, antibiotics such as Ciprofloxacin for the bacterial types, and special diagnostic tests and medical treatment for amoeba and giardia infections. Salmonella infections and cholera can be devastating diseases and it would be wise to get to a hospital as soon as possible if these were suspected. Fasting, peculiar diets and the consumption of large quantities of yoghurt have not been found useful in calming travellers' diarrhoea or in rehabilitating inflamed bowels. Oral rehydration has, especially in children, been a lifesaving technique and as there is some evidence that alcohol and milk might prolong diarrhoea they should probably be avoided during, and immediately after, an attack. There are ways of preventing travellers' diarrhoea for short periods of time when visiting these countries by taking antibiotics but these are ineffective against viruses and, to some extent, against protozoa. This technique should not be used other than in exceptional circumstances. Some preventatives such as Enterovioform can have serious side effects if taken for long periods.

INSECTS

These can be a great nuisance. Some, of

course, are carriers of serious diseases such as malaria, dengue fever or filariasis and various worm infections. The best way of keeping mosquitos away at night is to sleep off the ground with a mosquito net and to burn mosquito coils containing Pyrethrum. Aerosol sprays or a 'flit gun' may be effective as are insecticidal tablets which are heated on a mat which is plugged into the wall socket (if taking your own, check the voltage of the area you are visiting so that you can take an appliance that will work; similarly, check that your electrical adaptor is suitable for the repellent plug; note that they are widely available in the region).

You can, in addition, use personal insect repellent of which the best contain a high concentration of diethyltoluamide (DET). Liquid is best for arms and face (take care around eyes and make sure you do not dissolve the plastic of your spectacles). Aerosol spray on clothes and ankles deter mites and ticks. Liquid DET suspended in water can be used to impregnate cotton clothes and mosquito nets. The latter are now available in wide mesh form which are lighter to carry and less claustrophobic to sleep under.

If you are bitten, itching may be relieved by cool baths and anti-histamine tables (take care with alcohol or when driving), corticosteroid creams (great care – never use if any hint of septic poisoning) or by judicious scratching. Calamine lotion and cream have limited effectiveness and anti-histamine creams have a tendency to cause skin allergies and are therefore not generally recommended. Bites which become infected (a common problem in the tropics) should be treated with a local antiseptic or antibiotic cream such as Cetrimide, as should infected scratches. Skin infestations with body lice, crabs and scabies are unfortunately easy to pick up. Use gamma benzene hexachloride for lice and benzyl benzoate for scabies. Crotamiton cream alleviates itching and also kills a number of skin parasites. Malathion lotion is good for lice but avoid the highly toxic full strength Malathion which is used as an agricultural insecticide.

MALARIA

Malaria is prevalent in Myanmar and remains a serious disease and you are advised to protect yourself against mosquito bites as above and to take prophylactic (preventative) drugs. Start taking the tablets a few days before exposure and continue to take them 6 weeks after leaving the malarial zone. Remember to give the drugs to babies and children, pregnant women also.

The subject of malaria prevention is becoming more complex as the malaria parasite becomes immune to some of the older drugs. Nowhere is this more apparent than in Southeast Asia. In particular, there has been an increase in the proportion of cases of falciparum malaria which are resistant to the normally used drugs. It would not be an exaggeration to say that we are near to the situation where some cases of malaria will be untreatable with presently available drugs.

Before you travel you must check with a reputable agency the likelihood and type of malaria in the countries which you intend to visit. Take their advice on prophylaxis but be prepared to receive conflicting advice. Because of the rapidly changing situation in the Southeast Asian region, the names and dosage of the drugs have not been included. But Chloroquine and Proguanil may still be recommended for the areas where malaria is still fully sensitive; while Doxycycline, Mefloquine and Quinghaosu are presently being used in resistant areas. Quinine, Halofantrine and tetracycline drugs remain the mainstay of treatment.

It is still possible to catch malaria even when taking prophylactic drugs, although this is unlikely. If you do develop symptoms (high fever, shivering, severe headache, and sometimes diarrhoea) seek medical advice immediately. The risk of the disease is obviously greater the further you move from the cities into rural areas, with primitive facilities and standing water.

SUNBURN AND HEAT STROKE

The burning power of the tropical sun is

phenomenal, especially in highland areas. Always wear a wide-brimmed hat, and use some form of sun cream or lotion on untanned skin. Normal temperate zone suntan lotions (protection factors up to 7) are not much good. You need to use the types designed specifically for the tropics or for mountaineers or skiers, with a protection factor between 7 and 15 or higher. Glare from the sun can cause conjunctivitis so wear sunglasses, particularly on beaches.

There are several varieties of heat stroke. The most common cause is severe dehydration. Avoid this by drinking lots of non-alcoholic fluid, and adding salt to your food.

SNAKE AND OTHER BITES AND STINGS

If you are unlucky enough to be bitten by a venomous snake, spider, scorpion, centipede or sea creature, try (within limits) to catch or kill the animal for identification. Reactions to be expected are shock, swelling, pain and bruising around the bite, soreness of the regional lymph glands, nausea, vomiting and fever. If in addition any of the following symptoms should follow closely, get the victim to a doctor without delay: numbness, tingling of the face, muscular spasms, convulsions, shortness of breath or haemorrhage. Commercial snake-bite or scorpion-sting kits may be available but these are only useful against the specific type of snake or scorpion for which they are designed. The serum has to be given intravenously so is not much good unless you have had some practice in making injections into veins. If the bite is on a limb, immobilize it and apply a tight bandage between the bite and the body, releasing it for 90 seconds every 15 minutes. Reassurance of the victim is very important because death from snake bite is very rare. Do not slash the bite area and try to suck out the poison because this sort of heroism does more harm than good. Hospitals usually hold stocks of snake-bite serum. The best precaution is not walk in long grass with bare feet, sandals, or in shorts.

When swimming in an area where there are poisonous fish such as stone or scorpion fish (also called by a variety of local names) or sea urchins on rocky coasts, tread carefully or wear plimsolls/trainers. The sting of such fish is intensely painful. This can be relieved by immersing the injured part of the body in water as hot as you can bear for as long as it remains painful. This is not always very practical and you must take care not to scald yourself, but it does work. Avoid spiders and scorpions by keeping your bed away from the wall, look under lavatory seats and inside your shoes in the morning. In the rare event of being bitten, consult a doctor.

OTHER AFFLICTIONS

Remember that **rabies** is endemic in Myanmar. If you are bitten by a domestic or wild animal, do not leave things to chance. Scrub the wound with soap and water and/or disinfectant, try to have the animal captured (within limits) or at least determine its ownership where possible and seek medical assistance at once. The course of treatment depends on whether you have already been satisfactorily vaccinated against rabies. If you have (and this is worthwhile if you are spending lengths of time in developing countries) then some further doses of vaccine are all that is required. Human diploid cell vaccine is the best, but expensive: other, older kinds of vaccine such as that derived from duck embryos may be the only types available. These are effective, much cheaper and interchangeable generally with the human derived types. If not already vaccinated then anti-rabies serum (immúnoglobulin) may be required in addition. It is wise to finish the course of treatment whether the animal survives or not.

Dengue fever is present in Myanmar. It is a viral disease transmitted by mosquito and causes severe headaches and body pains. Complicated types of dengue known as haemorrhagic fevers occur throughout Asia but usually in persons who have caught the disease a second time. Thus, although it is a very serious type it is rarely caught by visitors. There is no treatment, you must just avoid mosquito bites.

Intestinal worms are common and the more serious ones, such as hook worm can be contracted by walking barefoot on infested earth or beaches.

Influenza and **respiratory diseases** are common, perhaps made worse by polluted cities and rapid temperature and climatic changes – accentuated by air-conditioning.

Prickly heat is a very common itchy rash, best avoided by frequent washing and by wearing loose clothing and is helped by the use of talcum powder, allowing the skin to dry thoroughly after washing.

Athlete's foot and other **fungal infections** are best treated by sunshine and a proprietary preparation such as Tolnaftate.

WHEN YOU RETURN HOME

On returning home, remember to take anti-malarial tablets for 6 weeks. If you have had attacks of diarrhoea, it is worth having a stool specimen tested in case you have picked up amoebic dysentery. If you have been living rough, a blood test may also be worthwhile to detect worms and other parasites.

FURTHER HEALTH INFORMATION

Information regarding country-by-country malaria risk can be obtained from the World Health Organization (WHO) or in Britain from the Ross Institute, London School of Hygiene and Tropical Medicine, Keppel Street, London WClE 7HT which also publishes a highly recommended book: *The preservation of personal health in warm climates*. The Centres for Disease Control (CDC) in Atlanta, Georgia, USA will provide equivalent information. The organization MASTA (Medical Advisory Service for Travellers Abroad) also based at the London School of Hygiene and Tropical Medicine (T 0171 631-4408) will provide up-to-date country-by-country information on health risks. Further information on medical problems overseas can be obtained from the new edition of *Travellers health, how to stay healthy abroad*, edited by Richard Dawood (Oxford University Press, 1992). This revised and updated edition is highly recommended, especially to the intrepid traveller. A more general publication, with hints on health and much more besides, is John Hatt's new edition of *The tropical traveller* (Penguin, 1993).

The above information has been compiled by Dr David Snashall, Senior Lecturer in Occupational Health, United Medical Schools of Guy's and St Thomas' Hospitals and Chief Medical Adviser, Foreign and Commonwealth Office, London.

Travelling with children

MANY PEOPLE are daunted by the prospect of taking a child to Southeast Asia. Naturally, it is not something which is taken on lightly; travelling is slower and more expensive and there are additional health risks for the child or baby. But it can be a most rewarding experience, and with sufficient care and planning, it can also be safe. Children are excellent passports into a local culture. You will also receive the best service, and help from officials and members of the public when in difficulty.

Children in Southeast Asia are given 24-hr attention by parents, grandparents and siblings. They are rarely left to cry and are carried for most of the first 8 months of their lives – crawling is considered animal-like. A non-Asian child is still something of a novelty and parents may find their child frequently taken off their hands, even mobbed in more remote areas (particularly in Thailand). This can be a great relief (at mealtimes, for instance) or most alarming. Some children love the attention, others react against it; it is best simply to gauge your own child's reactions.

PRACTICALITIES

Accommodation

At the hottest time of year, air-conditioning may be essential for a baby or young child's comfort. This rules out many of the cheaper hotels, but a/c accommodation is available in all but the most out-of-the-way spots. When the child is bathing, be aware that the water could carry parasites, so avoid letting him or her drink it.

Food and drink

The advice given in the health section on food and drink (see page 385) should be applied even more stringently where young children are concerned. Be aware that expensive hotels may have squalid cooking conditions; the cheapest street stall is often more hygienic. Where possible, try to watch food being prepared. Stir-fried vegetables and rice or noodles are the best bet; meat and fish may be pre-cooked and then left out before being re-heated. Fruit can be bought cheaply right across Southeast Asia: papaya, banana and avocado are all excellent sources of nutrition, and can be self-peeled ensuring cleanliness. Powdered milk is also available throughout the region, although most brands have added sugar. But if taking a baby, breast-feeding is strongly recommended. Powdered food can be bought in most towns – the quality may not be the same as equivalent foods bought in the West, but it is perfectly adequate for short periods. Bottled water and fizzy drinks are also sold widely. If your child is at the 'grab everything and put it in mouth' stage, a damp cloth and some *dettol* (or equivalent) are useful. Frequent wiping of hands and tabletops can help to minimize the chance of infection.

Transport

Public transport may be a problem; trains are fine but long bus journeys are restrictive and uncomfortable. Hiring a car is undoubtedly the most convenient way to see a country with a small child. Back-seatbelts are rarely fitted but it is possible to buy child-seats in capital cities.

ESSENTIALS

Disposable nappies

These can be bought in Thailand, but are often expensive. If you are staying any length of time in one place, it may be worth taking Terry's (cloth) nappies. All you need is a bucket and some double-strength nappy cleanse (simply soak and rinse). Cotton nappies dry quickly in the heat and are generally more comfortable for the baby or child. They also reduce rubbish – many countries are not geared to the disposal of nappies. Of course, the best way for a child to be is nappy-free – like the local children.

Baby products

Many Western baby products are now available in Southeast Asia: shampoo, talcum powder, soap and lotion. Baby wipes can be difficult to find.

HEALTH

Emergencies

Babies and small children deteriorate very rapidly when ill. A travel insurance policy which has an air ambulance provision is strongly recommended. When planning a route, try to stay within 24 hours' travel of a hospital with good care and facilities. Many expatriats fly to Singapore for medical care, which has the best doctors and facilities in the region.

Sunburn

Never allow your child to be exposed to the harsh tropical sun without protection. A child can burn in a matter of minutes. Loose cotton-clothing, with long sleeves and legs and a sun-hat are best. High-factor sun-protection cream is essential.

CHECKLIST FOR BABIES

Baby wipes
Child paracetamol
Cloth nappies
Disinfectant
First aid kit
Flannel
Immersion element for boiling water
Decongestant
Instant food for under-one-year-olds
Mug/bottle/bowl/spoons
Nappy cleanse, double-strength
ORS (Oral Rehydration Salts) such as *Dioralyte*, the most effective way to alleviate diarrhoea (it is not a cure)
Portable baby chair, to hook onto tables; this is not essential but can be very useful
Sarong or backpack for carrying child (and/or light weight collapsible buggy)
Sterilizing tablets and container
Cream for nappy rash and other skin complaints such as *Sudocrem*
Sunblock, factor 15 or higher
Sunhat
Thermometer
Zip-lock bags

FURTHER INFORMATION

Suggested reading

Pentes, Tina and Truelove, Adrienne (1984) *Travelling with children to Indonesia and South-East Asia*, Hale & Iremonger: Sydney
Wheeler, Maureen *Travel with children*, Lonely Planet: Hawthorne, Australia.

Fares and timetables

Air fares

Myanmar Airways

Yangon to:	**US$**
Bhamo	155
Dawei (Tavoy)	85
Heho*	85
Kawthoung	145
Kengtung	115
Khamti	195
Kyaukpyu	80
Lashio	145
Loikaw	60
Mandalay*	100
Mawlamyine (Moulmein)	75
Myeik (Mergui)	155
Myitkyina	180
Nyaung U (Bagan)*	90
Putao	225
Sittwe	90
Tachilek	110
Thandwe (Sandoway)*	55

* Also served by **Air Mandalay**.

Air Mandalay

Mandalay-Heho	45
Nyaung U (Bagan)-Mandalay	45
Yangon-Heho	113
Yangon-Mandalay	129
Yangon-Nyaung U (Bagan)	113
Yangon-Thandwe	75

Other routes

Bhamo-Myitkyina
Dawei (Tavoy)-Myeik (Mergui)
Heho-Kengtung
Heho-Lashio
Heho-Loikaw
Heho-Tachilek
Mandalay-Bhamo
Mandalay-Heho*
Mandalay-Kengtung
Mandalay-Khamti
Mandalay-Lashio
Mandalay-Loikaw
Mandalay-Myitkyina
Mawlamyine (Moulmein)-Dawei (Tavoy)
Myeik (Mergui)-Kawthoung
Myitkyina-Putao
Nyaung U (Bagan)-Heho
Nyaung U (Bagan)-Mandalay*
Thandwe-Mandalay

* Also served by **Air Mandalay**.

NB All fares one way on *Myanmar Airways*. Fares vary slightly on *Myanmar Airways* depending on the aircraft. Thus the Yangon-Mandalay fare can be US$90 or US$100, the Yangon-Nyaung U (Bagan) fare US$80 or US$90, and the Yangon-Thandwe fare US$50 or US$50. We have quoted the higher fare in each instance.

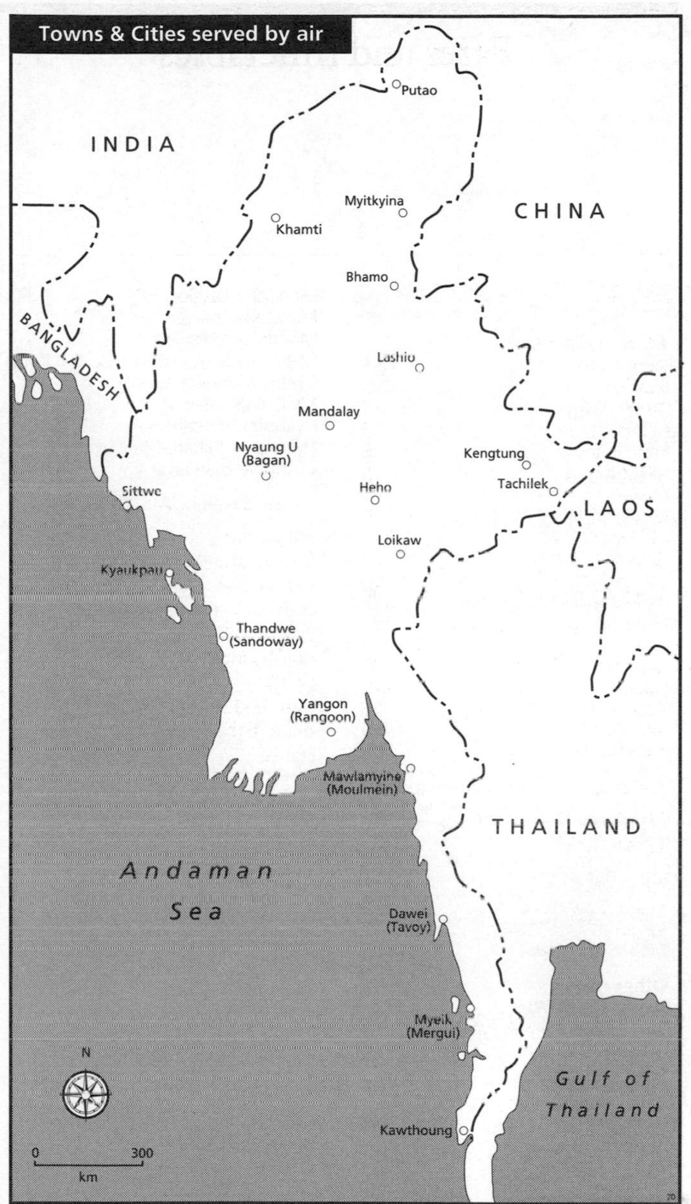
Towns & Cities served by air
INDIA
CHINA
BANGLADESH
LAOS
THAILAND
Andaman
Sea
Gulf of
Thailand
Putao
Myitkyina
Khamti
Bhamo
Lashio
Mandalay
Nyaung U
(Bagan)
Kengtung
Tachilek
Heho
Sittwe
Loikaw
Kyaukpau
Thandwe
(Sandoway)
Yangon
(Rangoon)
Mawlamyine
(Moulmein)
Dawei
(Tavoy)
Myeik
(Mergui)
Kawthoung
N
0
300
km

Train times and fares

FROM-TO:	ETD	ETA	JOURNEY TIME (hrs)	FARE (US$)
Yangon-Mandalay	0600	2110	15.10	30
	1515	0600	14.45	(Private Service)
	1700	0700	14	38
	1830	0830	14	38
	1930	1035	15.05	30
Yangon-Thazi	0600	1752	11.52	27
	1700	0414	11.14	27
	1830	0536	11.06	33
	1930	0717	11.47	27
Mandalay-Yangon	0600	2130	15.30	30
	1515	0520	14.05	30
	1615	0620	13.05	(Private Service)
	1730	0730	14	38
	1830	1000	15.30	30
Thazi-Yangon	0923	2130	12.07	27
	1800	0520	11.20	27
	2016	0730	11.14	33
	2143	1000	12.17	27

OTHER ROUTES AND FARES

FROM-TO	ETD	ETA	JOURNEY TIME (hrs)	FARE (kyat)	NOTES
Thazi-Aungban	0400	1000	6	21	
Kalaw-Aungban	0930	1000	30 mins	5	
Aungban-Loikaw	1030	2100	10.30	25	
Aungban-Pinlon	1400	2100	7	10	
Aungban-Thazi	1030/ 1130/ 1330	1630/ 1730/ 1930	6	21	
Aungban-Shwenyaung	1000/ 1400	1300/ 1800	3	12	For Inle Lake
Shwenyaung-Aungban	0830/ 1000	1130/ 1330	3	12	
Loikaw-Aungban	0400	1200	8	25	Does not always run from Loikaw; sometimes only as far as Pinlon
Pyin U Lwin (Maymyo) -Lashio	1000	2200	12	US$11	Upper class
Lashio-Mandalay	0400	2030	16½	US$12	Upper class (US$6 ordinary class)
Hsipaw-Mandalay	0830	2030	12	US$10/5	Upper/ordinary class
Kyaukme-Mandalay	1100	2030	9½	US$8/4	
Maymyo-Mandalay	1630	2030	4	US$4	Upper class
Yangon-Bago (Pegu)	-	-	-	US$2	Ordinary class
Yangon-Mawlamyine (Moulmein)	-	-	-	US$8	Ordinary class

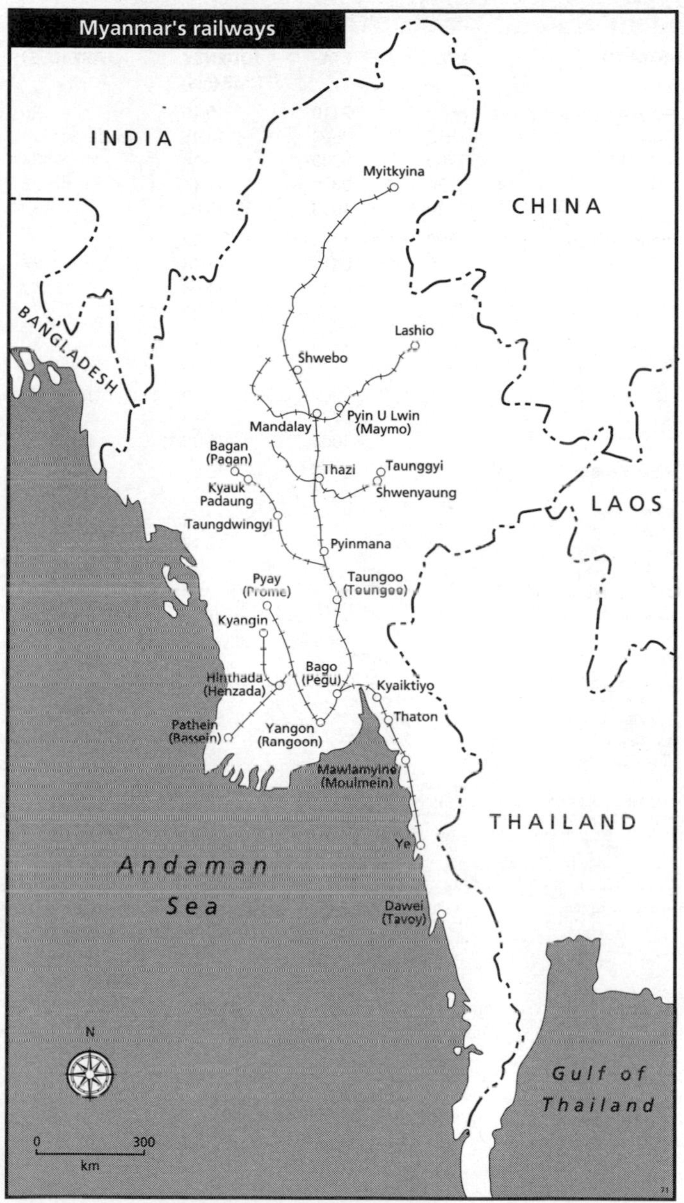
Myanmar's railways
INDIA
CHINA
BANGLADESH
LAOS
THAILAND
Andaman Sea
Gulf of Thailand
Myitkyina
Lashio
Shwebo
Pyin U Lwin (Maymo)
Mandalay
Bagan (Pagan)
Thazi
Taunggyi
Shwenyaung
Kyauk Padaung
Taungdwingyi
Pyinmana
Taungoo (Toungoo)
Pyay (Prome)
Kyangin
Bago (Pegu)
Hinthada (Henzada)
Kyaiktiyo
Thaton
Pathein (Bassein)
Yangon (Rangoon)
Mawlamyine (Moulmein)
Ye
Dawei (Tavoy)
N
0
300
km

Selected bus fares and journey times

FROM-TO:	ETD	ETA	JOURNEY TIME (hrs)	FARE (kyat)	NOTES
Yangon-Taungoo	1600	2200	6	100	
Taungoo-Meiktila	0600	1200	6	100	
Meiktila-Thazi	-	-	30 mins	15	Numerous daily departures
Meiktila-Kyaukpadung	-	-	3	70	
Kyaukpadung-Bagan	-	-	1½	-	
Bagan-Mt Popa	-	-	-	20	
Kalaw-Meiktila	-	-	4	150	Pick-up
Meiktila-Mandalay	0630/ 0730/ 0830/ 1030	-	3	70	
Meiktila-Yangon	1800	-	10	650	Yangyiaung
Meiktila-Yangon	2000/ 2100	-	10	US$10	Rainbow/Skyline
Meiktila-Yangon	1800-1900	-	10	500	Diamond
Meiktila-Kalaw-Shwenyaung-Taunggyi	0800		-	200	Pick-up
Mandalay-Bagan	0400	1100	7	300	Daily
Mandalay-Bagan	0900	1600	7	300	Sun/Wed/Fri only
Hisipaw-Kyaukme	0600	0730		50	
Mandalay-Monywa	1630	2000	3½	50	Big bus, pick-up 70 kyat
Monywa-Mandalay	1630	2000	3½	50	Big bus, pick-up 70-90 kyat
Pyay-Yangon	1600	2100	5	200	
Nyaung Shwe-Taunggyi	0600	-	40 mins	15	Pick-up
Bagan-Yangon	1700	0630	12	1,000	Bagan Express
Taunggyi-Kalaw	1000	-	2	50	
Mandalay-Pyin U Lwin (Maymyo)	-	-	3½	50	Pick-up
Pyin U Lwin (Maymyo)-Lashio	0600	-	-	250	Big bus (300 kyat pick-up)
Lashio-Hsipaw	1600	-	2	50	Pick-up
Hsipaw-Kaukme	0630	0715	45 mins	50	Yoma Express
Kaukme-Mandalay	0800	-	-	-	Yoma Express

Selected riverboat schedule and fares

	ETD	ETA	DEPARTURE DAYS	FARES
MANDALAY-BAGAN (NYAUNG U)				
MTT boat	0530	1800	Sun and Thur	US$10 deck US$30 cabin
Local boat	0530	Next morning (overnight stop at Pakoku)	Every day	US$6
YANGON-PYAY (PROME)				
Local boat	1600	-	Not everyday, depart from junction of Strand Rd, Shwedagon Pagoda Rd and Merchant St	
BAGAN (NYAUNG U)-PYAY (PROME)				
Local boat	0900 from Nyaung U	Morning of second day (2 days/2 nights journey)	2 departures/ week	300 kyat

Glossary

A

Amitabha
the Buddha of the Past (see Avalokitsvara)

Amulet
protective medallion

Arhat
a person who has perfected himself; images of former monks are sometimes carved into arhat

Avadana
Buddhist narrative, telling of the deeds of saintly souls

Avalokitsvara
also known as Amitabha and Lokeshvara, the name literally means 'World Lord'; he is the compassionate male Bodhisattva, the saviour of Mahayana Buddhism and represents the central force of creation in the universe; usually portrayed with a lotus and water flask

B

Bai sema
boundary stones marking consecrated ground around a Buddhist bot

Batik
a form of resist dyeing

Bhikku
Buddhist monk

Bilu
an ogre; Burmese version of the dvarapala

Bodhi
the tree under which the Buddha achieved enlightenment (*Ficus religiosa*)

Bodhisattva
a future Buddha. In Mahayana Buddhism, someone who has attained enlightenment, but who postpones nirvana to help others reach it.

Bonze
term for a Buddhist monk

Bot
Buddhist ordination hall of rectangular plan, identifiable by the boundary stones placed around it

Brahma
the Creator, one of the gods of the Hindu trinity, usually represented with four faces, and often mounted on a hamsa

Brahmin
a Hindu priest

Bun
to make merit (Thailand)

Byauk
'variegated'; describes a temple with a colourfully painted interior

C

Caryatid
elephants, often used as buttressing decorations

Ceityas
stupa

Chat
honorific umbrella or royal multi-tiered parasol

Chedi
from the Sanskrit *cetiya* (Pali, *caitya*) meaning memorial. Usually a religious monument (often bell-shaped) containing relics

of the Buddha or other holy remains. Used interchangeably with stupa

Chinlon
The Burmese equivalent of the Thai sport *takraw*; a rattan ball is hit over a net using any part of the body except the hands (see page 77)

Chinthe
Guardian temple lion (see page 130)

D

Deva
a Hindu-derived male god

Devata
a Hindu-derived goddess

Dharma
the Buddhist law

Dipterocarp
family of trees (Dipterocarpaceae) characteristic of Southeast Asia's forests

G

Ganesh
elephant-headed son of Siva

Garuda
mythical divine bird, with predatory beak and claws, and human body; the king of birds, enemy of naga and mount of Vishnu

Gautama
the historic Buddha

Geomancy
the art of divination by lines and figures

Gopura
crowned or covered gate, entrance to a religious area

H

Hamsa
sacred goose, Brahma's mount; in Buddhism it represents the flight of the doctrine

Hang yaaw
long-tailed boat in Thailand

Harmika
box-like part of a Burmese stupa that often acts as a reliquary casket

Hinayana
'Lesser Vehicle', major Buddhist sect in Southeast Asia, usually termed Theravada Buddhism

Hintha
mythical bird

Hti
'umbrella' surmounting Burmese temples, often encrusted with jewels

I

Ikat
tie-dyeing method of patterning cloth

Indra
the Vedic god of the heavens, weather and war; usually mounted on a 3 headed elephant

J

Jataka(s)
the birth stories of the Buddha; they normally number 547, although an additional 3 were added in Burma for reasons of symmetry in mural painting and sculpture; the last ten are the most important

K

Kala (makara)
literally, 'death' or 'black'; a demon ordered to consume itself; often sculpted with grinning face and bulging eyes over entranceways to act as a door guardian; also known as kirtamukha

Kalasa
the sacred pot from which temple plinths at Bagan often take their profile

Kathin/krathin
a one month period during the eighth lunar month when lay people present new robes and other gifts to monks

Ketumula
flame-like motif above the Buddha head

Khao
mountain (Thailand)

Khlong
canal

Kinaree
half-human, half-bird, usually depicted as a heavenly musician

Kirtamukha
see kala

Krishna
incarnation of Vishnu

Kuti
living quarters of Buddhist monks

Kyaung
monastery, or school

L

Laterite
bright red tropical soil/stone commonly used in construction of Khmer monuments

Linga
phallic symbol and one of the forms of Siva. Embedded in a pedastal shaped to allow drainage of lustral water poured over it, the linga typically has a succession of cross sections: from square at the base through octagonal to round. These symbolise, in order, the trinity of Brahma, Vishnu and Siva

Lintel
a load-bearing stone spanning a doorway; often heavily carved

Lokeshvara
see Avalokitsvara

Lungyi
Burmese sarong, worn by men and women

M

Mahabharata
a Hindu epic text written about 2,000 years ago

Mahayana
'Greater Vehicle', major Buddhist sect

Maitreya
the future Buddha

Makara
a mythological aquatic reptile, somewhat like a crocodile and sometimes with an elephant's trunk; often found along with the kala framing doorways

Mandala
a focus for meditation; a representation of the cosmos

Mara
personification of evil and tempter of the Buddha

Meru
sacred or cosmic mountain at the centre of the world in Hindu-Buddhist cosmology; home of the gods

Mon
race and kingdom of southern Burma and central Thailand from 7-11th century

Mondop
from the sanskrit, *mandapa*. A cube-shaped building, often topped with a cone-like structure, used to contain an object of worship like a footprint of the Buddha

Muang
'town' in Thai, but also sometimes 'municipality' or 'district'

Mudra
symbolic gesture of the hands of the Buddha

N

Naga
benevolent mythical water serpent, enemy of Garuda

Naga makara
fusion of naga and makara

Nalagiri
the elephant let loose to attack the Buddha, who calmed him

Nandi/nandin
bull, mount of Siva

Nat
a Burmese spirit or god. There are 37 in total, which are local spirits, famous people who have died, or are borrowed from Hindu mythology

Nirvana
release from the cycle of suffering in Buddhist belief; 'enlightenment'

P

paddy/padi
unhulled rice

Pagoda
Western term which has evolved to describe a stupa or zedi

Pali
the sacred language of Theravada Buddhism

Parvati
consort of Siva

Paya
see Pagoda

Pha sin
tubular piece of cloth, similar to sarong

Phi
spirit

Phnom/phanom
Khmer for hill/mountain

Pradaksina
pilgrims' clockwise circumambulation of holy structure

Prah
sacred

Prang
form of stupa built in Khmer style, shaped like a corncob

Prasada
stepped pyramid (see prasat)

Prasat
residence of a king or of the gods (sanctuary tower), from the Indian *prasada*

Pwe
Burmese festival (see page 76)

R

Rahu
Burmese planet which causes eclipses

Rama
incarnation of Vishnu, hero of the Indian epic, the *Ramayana*

Ramayana
Hindu romantic epic

S

Sakyamuni
the historic Buddha

Sal
the Indian sal tree (*Shorea robusta*), under which the historic Buddha was born

Sangha
the Buddhist order of monks

Sawbwas
Shan feudal lords

Seltpadi
rosary beads used by important monks

Shwe
gold

Sikhara
beehive-like spire

Singha
mythical guardian lion

Siva
the Destroyer, one of the three gods of the Hindu trinity; the sacred linga was worshipped as a symbol of Siva

Sravasti
the miracle at Sravasti when the Buddha subdues the heretics in front of a mango tree

Stele
inscribed stone panel

Stucco
plaster, often heavily moulded

Stupa
chedi

T

Tam bun
see bun

Tavatimsa
heaven of the 33 gods at the summit of Mount Meru

Tazaungs
small pavilions found within temple complexes

Thanaka
a paste worn by many Burmese women on

their faces; it is ground from the bark of the acacia tree

Thein
ordination hall

Theravada
'Way of the Elders'; major Buddhist sect also known as Hinayana Buddhism ('Lesser Vehicle')

Traiphum
the three worlds of Buddhist cosmology – heaven, hell and earth

Trimurti
the Hindu trinity of gods: Brahma, the Creator, Vishnu the Preserver and Siva the Destroyer

Tripitaka
Theravada Buddhism's Pali canon

U

Ubosoth
see bot

Urna
the dot or curl on the Buddha's forehead, one of the distinctive physical marks of the Enlightened One

Usnisa
the Buddha's top knot or 'wisdom bump', one of the physical marks of the Enlightened One

V

Vahana
'vehicle', a mythical beast, upon which a deva or god rides

Viharn
from Sanskrit *vihara*, an assembly hall in a Buddhist monastery; may contain Buddha images and is similar in style to the bot

Vishnu
the Protector, one of the gods of the Hindu trinity, generally with four arms holding a disc, conch shell, ball and club

Z

Zat
Classical Burmese dramas, usually based on the *Ramayana* (see page 76)

Zayat
prayer pavilion found in Burmese temple complexes

Zedi
Burmese term for a stupa

TEMPERATURE CONVERSION TABLE

°C	°F	°C	°F
1	34	26	79
2	36	27	81
3	38	28	82
4	39	29	84
5	41	30	86
6	43	31	88
7	45	32	90
8	46	33	92
9	48	34	93
10	50	35	95
11	52	36	97
12	54	37	99
13	56	38	100
14	57	39	102
15	59	40	104
16	61	41	106
17	63	42	108
18	64	43	109
19	66	44	111
20	68	45	113
21	70	46	115
22	72	47	117
23	74	48	118
24	75	49	120
25	77	50	122

The formula for converting °C to °F is:
°C x 9 ÷ 5 + 32 = °F

WEIGHTS AND MEASURES

Metric

Weight
1 Kilogram (Kg) = 2.205 pounds
1 metric ton = 1.102 short tons

Length
1 millimetre (mm)= 0.03937 inch
1 metre = 3.281 feet
1 kilometre (km) = 0.621 mile

Area
1 heactare = 2.471 acres
1 square km = 0.386 sq mile

Capacity
1 litre = 0.220 imperial gallon
= 0.264 US gallon

Volume
1 cubic metre (m^3) = 35.31 cubic feet
= 1.31 cubic yards

British and US

Weight
1 pound (lb) = 454 grams
1 short ton (2,000lbs) = 0.907 m ton
1 long ton (2,240lbs) = 1.016 m tons

Length
1 inch = 25.417 millimetres
1 foot (ft) = 0.305 metre
1 mile = 1.609 kilometres

Area
1 acre = 0.405 hectare
1 sq mile = 2.590 sq kilometre

Capacity
1 imperial gallon = 4.546 litres
1 US gallon = 3.785 litres

Volume
1 cubic foot (cu ft) = 0.028 m^3
1 cubic yard (cu yd) = 0.765 m^3

NB 5 imperial gallons are approximately equal to 6 US gallons

Tinted boxes

Illustrations

Index

Q

R

U

V

W

Z

Maps

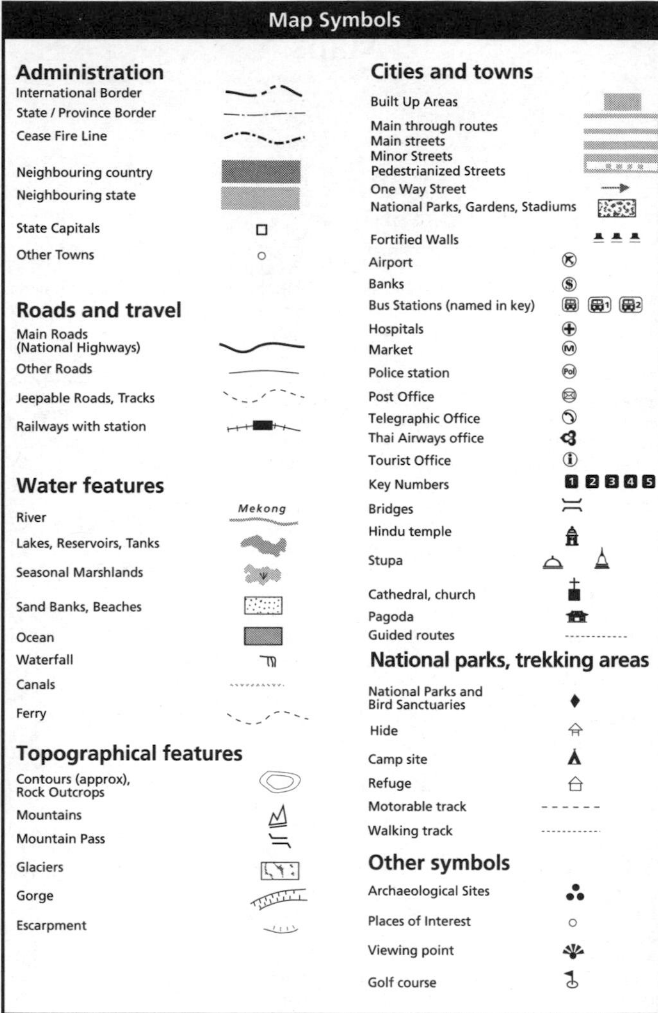
Map Symbols
Administration
International Border
State / Province Border
Cease Fire Line
Neighbouring country
Neighbouring state
State Capitals
Other Towns
Roads and travel
Main Roads
(National Highways)
Other Roads
Jeepable Roads, Tracks
Railways with station
Water features
River
Mekong
Lakes, Reservoirs, Tanks
Seasonal Marshlands
Sand Banks, Beaches
Ocean
Waterfall
Canals
Ferry
Topographical features
Contours (approx),
Rock Outcrops
Mountains
Mountain Pass
Glaciers
Gorge
Escarpment
Cities and towns
Built Up Areas
Main through routes
Main streets
Minor Streets
Pedestrianized Streets
One Way Street
National Parks, Gardens, Stadiums
Fortified Walls
Airport
Banks
Bus Stations (named in key)
Hospitals
Market
Police station
Post Office
Telegraphic Office
Thai Airways office
Tourist Office
Key Numbers
1 2 3 4 5
Bridges
Hindu temple
Stupa
Cathedral, church
Pagoda
Guided routes
National parks, trekking areas
National Parks and
Bird Sanctuaries
Hide
Camp site
Refuge
Motorable track
Walking track
Other symbols
Archaeological Sites
Places of Interest
Viewing point
Golf course

Footprint Handbooks

All of us at Footprint Handbooks hope you have enjoyed reading and travelling with this Handbook, one of the first published in the new Footprint series. Many of you will be familiar with us as Trade & Travel, a name that has served us well for years. For you and for those who have only just discovered the Handbooks, we thought it would be interesting to chronicle the story of our development from the early 1920's.

It all started 75 years ago in 1921, with the publication of the Anglo South American Handbook. In 1924 the South American Handbook was created. This has been published each year for the last 73 years and is the longest running guidebook in the English language, immortalised by Graham Greene as "the best travel guide in existence".

One of the key strengths of the South American Handbook over the years, has been the extraordinary contact we have had with our readers through their hundreds of letters to us in Bath. From these letters we learnt that you wanted more Handbooks of the same quality to other parts of the world.

In 1989 my brother Patrick and I set about developing a series modelled on the South American Handbook. Our aim was to create the ultimate practical guidebook series for all travellers, providing expert knowledge of far flung places, explaining culture, places and people in a balanced, lively and clear way. The whole idea hinged, of course, on finding writers who were in tune with our thinking. Serendipity stepped in at exactly the right moment: we were able to bring together a talented group of people who know the countries we cover inside out and whose enthusiasm for travelling in them needed to be communicated.

The series started to grow. We felt that the time was right to look again at the identity that had brought us all this way. After much searching we commissioned London designers Newell & Sorrell to look at all the issues. Their solution was a new identity for the Handbooks representing the books in all their aspects, looking after all the good things already achieved and taking us into the new millennium.

The result is Footprint Handbooks: a new name and mark, simple yet assertive, bold, stylish and instantly recognisable. The images we use conjure up the essence of real travel and communicate the qualities of the Handbooks in a straightforward and evocative way.

For us here in Bath, it has been an exciting exercise working through this dramatic change. Already the 'new us' fits like our favourite travelling clothes and we cannot wait to get more and more Footprint Handbooks onto the book shelves and out onto the road.

James Dawson

The Footprint list

Andalucía Handbook
Cambodia Handbook
Caribbean Islands Handbook
Chile Handbook
East Africa Handbook
Ecuador Handbook
with the Galápagos
Egypt Handbook
India Handbook
Indonesia Handbook
Laos Handbook
Malaysia & Singapore Handbook
Mexico & Central America Handbook
Morocco Handbook
with Mauritania
Myanmar (Burma) Handbook
Namibia Handbook
Pakistan Handbook
Peru Handbook
South Africa Handbook
South American Handbook
Sri Lanka Handbook
Thailand Handbook
Tibet Handbook
Tunisia Handbook with Libya
Vietnam Handbook
Zimbabwe & Malawi Handbook
with Botswana, Moçambique & Zambia

New in Autumn 1997
Israel Handbook
Nepal Handbook

In the pipeline
Argentina Handbook
Brazil Handbook
Colombia Handbook
Cuba Handbook
Jordan, Syria & Lebanon Handbook
Venezuela Handbook

Footprint T-shirt

The Footprint T-shirt is available in 100% cotton in various colours.

Mail Order

Footprint Handbooks are available worldwide in good bookstores. They can also be ordered directly from us in Bath (see below for address). Please contact us if you have difficulty finding a title.

The Footprint Handbook website will be coming to keep you up to date with all the latest news from us (http://www.footprint-handbooks.co.uk). For the most up-to-date information and to join our mailing list please contact us at:

Footprint Handbooks
6 Riverside Court
Lower Bristol Road
Bath BA2 3DZ, England
T +44(0)1225 469141
F +44(0)1225 469461
E Mail handbooks@footprint.cix.co.uk